ENCYCLOPEDIA OF COMPUTER SCIENCE AND TECHNOLOGY

VOLUME 3

INTERNATIONAL EDITORIAL ADVISORY BOARD

SHUHEI AIDA, Tokyo, Japan

J. M. BENNETT, Sydney, Australia

DOV CHEVION, Jerusalem, Israel

LUIGI DADDA, Milan, Italy

RUTH M. DAVIS, Washington, D.C.

A. S. DOUGLAS, London, England

LESLIE C. EDIE, New York, New York

S. E. ELMAGHRABY,
   Raleigh, North Carolina

A. P. ERSHOV, Novosibirsk, U.S.S.R.

HAROLD FLEISHER,
   Poughkeepsie, New York

BRUCE GILCHRIST,
   New York, New York

V. M. GLUSHKOV, Kiev, U.S.S.R.

C. C. GOTLIEB, Toronto, Canada

EDWIN L. HARDER,
   Pittsburgh, Pennsylvania

GRACE HOPPER, Washington, D.C.

A. S. HOUSEHOLDER,
   Knoxville, Tennessee

MANFRED KOCHEN,
   Ann Arbor, Michigan

E. P. MILES, JR., Tallahassee, Florida

JACK MINKER, College Park, Maryland

DON MITTLEMAN, Oberlin, Ohio

W. J. POPPELBAUM, Urbana, Illinois

A. ALAN B. PRITSKER,
   Lafayette, Indiana

P. RABINOWITZ, Rehovot, Israel

JEAN E. SAMMET,
   Cambridge, Massachusetts

SVERRE SEM-SANDBERG,
   Stockholm, Sweden

J. C. SIMON, Paris, France

WILLIAM A. SMITH, JR.,
   Raleigh, North Carolina

T. W. SZE, Pittsburgh, Pennsylvania

RICHARD I. TANAKA,
   Anaheim, California

DANIEL TEICHROEW,
   Ann Arbor, Michigan

ISMAIL B. TURKSEN, Toronto, Canada

MURRAY TUROFF, Newark, New Jersey

MICHAEL S. WATANABE,
   Honolulu, Hawaii

ENCYCLOPEDIA OF COMPUTER SCIENCE AND TECHNOLOGY

EXECUTIVE EDITORS

Jack Belzer   Albert G. Holzman   Allen Kent

UNIVERSITY OF PITTSBURGH
PITTSBURGH, PENNSYLVANIA

VOLUME 3
Ball to Box

MARCEL DEKKER, INC. • NEW YORK and BASEL

COPYRIGHT © 1976 by MARCEL DEKKER, INC.
ALL RIGHTS RESERVED

Neither this book nor any part may be reproduced or transmitted in any form or by any means, electronic or mechanical, including photocopying, microfilming, and recording, or by any information storage and retrieval system, without permission in writing from the publisher.

MARCEL DEKKER, INC.
270 Madison Avenue, New York, New York 10016

LIBRARY OF CONGRESS CATALOG CARD NUMBER: 74-29436
ISBN: 0-8247-2253-1

Current printing (last digit):
10 9 8 7 6 5 4 3 2 1

PRINTED IN THE UNITED STATES OF AMERICA

CONTENTS OF VOLUME 3

Contributors to Volume 3		v
BALLISTICS CALCULATIONS	John H. Giese	1
BAND LIMITED FUNCTIONS	R. W. Hamming	23
BANKING	Joseph E. Michini	26
BARGAINING THEORY	Guillermo Owen	43
BARRIER METHODS FOR NONLINEAR PROGRAMMING	Anthony V. Fiacco	52
"BASIC" COMPUTER LANGUAGE	Thomas W. Hall, Jr.	114
BASIC FEASIBLE SOLUTIONS	Gerald E. Bennington	122
BAYESIAN STATISTICS	Melvin R. Novick	126
BEAM EQUATIONS	Gerald M. Smith	133
BEHAVIOR AND COMPUTERS	Anthony Debons	170
BELGIUM, COMPUTERS IN	D. Ribbens and P. de Marneffe	191
BELL LABORATORIES	Bell Laboratories Staff	196
BELLMAN'S PRINCIPLE OF OPTIMALITY	Michael J. Magazine	230
BENCHMARK	Stanley J. Walljasper	235
BENDERS' PARTITIONING METHOD	Robert Richardson	250
BENDIX COMPUTERS CDC	Manuel Langtry	255
BERNOULLI PROCESS	Raymond H. Burros	261
BERNOULLI'S METHOD	A. S. Householder	269
BETA SYSTEM	A. P. Ershov	272
BIHARMONIC EQUATIONS, SOLUTION METHODS	V. Vemuri	274
BINARY SEARCH	Peter Dorato	298
BINOMIAL DISTRIBUTION	Raymond H. Burros	300
BIOMEDICAL SCIENCES	Patricia M. Britt	307

CONTENTS OF VOLUME 3

BIRTH AND DEATH PROCESSES *Joseph A. Panico*		348
BIVARIATE: THE PROBABILITY DISTRIBUTION OF THE LOGARITHM OF THE SUM OF TWO LOG-NORMALLY DISTRIBUTED RANDOM VARIABLES *Chris P. Tsokos*		405
BLENDING PROBLEM *Ben T. Bernacchi and T. J. Usher*		442
BOLT BERANEK AND NEWMAN INC. *Phil Bertoni and Paul A. Castleman*		454
BOLZANO SEARCH *Ralph G. Stanton and W. D. Hoskins*		478
BOREL FIELD (BOREL SET) *B. B. Bhattacharyya*		486
BOX-JENKINS APPROACH TO TIME SERIES ANALYSIS AND FORECASTING *David W. Bacon*		488

CONTRIBUTORS TO VOLUME 3

DAVID W. BACON, Department of Chemical Engineering, Queens University, Kingston, Ontario, Canada: *Box-Jenkins Approach to Time Series Analysis and Forecasting*

BELL LABORATORIES STAFF, Bell Laboratories, Inc., Murray Hill, New Jersey: *Bell Laboratories*

GERALD E. BENNINGTON, The MIREW Corporation, McLean, Virginia: *Basic Feasible Solutions*

BEN T. BERNACCHI, Manager, Commercial Analysis and Information Systems, United States Steel Corporation, Pittsburgh, Pennsylvania: *Blending Problems*

PHIL BERTONI, Computer Systems Division, Bolt Beranek and Newman Inc., Cambridge, Massachusetts: *Bolt Beranek and Newman Inc.*

B. B. BHATTACHARYYA, Department of Statistics, North Carolina State University, Raleigh, North Carolina: *Borel Field (Borel Set)*

PATRICIA M. BRITT, Department of Biomathematics, School of Medicine, UCLA, Los Angeles, California: *Biomedical Sciences*

RAYMOND H. BURROS, Ph.D., Research and Development Division, Engineering Division, The Port Authority of New York and New Jersey, Jersey City, New Jersey: *Bernoulli Process* and *Binomial Distribution*

PAUL A. CASTLEMAN, Bolt Beranek and Newman Inc., Cambridge, Massachusetts: *Bolt Beranek and Newman Inc.*

ANTHONY DEBONS, University of Pittsburgh, Pittsburgh, Pennsylvania: *Behavior and Computers*

P. DE MARNEFFE, Université de Liege, Computer Science Department, Liege, Belgium: *Belgium, Computers In*

PETER DORATO, Professor, Department of Electrical Engineering, University of Colorado at Colorado Springs, Colorado Springs, Colorado: *Binary Search*

A. P. ERSHOV, Siberian Division of the Academy of Sciences, Novosibirsk, USSR: *Beta System*

ANTHONY V. FIACCO, The George Washington University School of Engineering and Applied Science, Institute for Management Science and Engineering, Washington, D.C.: *Barrier Methods for Nonlinear Programming*

JOHN H. GIESE, Department of Statistics and Computer Science, University of Delaware, Newark, Delaware: *Ballistics Calculations*

CONTRIBUTORS TO VOLUME 3

THOMAS W. HALL, Jr., Language and Systems Development, Inc., Silver Spring, Maryland: *"BASIC" Computer Language*

R. W. HAMMING, Bell Laboratories, Murray Hill, New Jersey: *Band Limited Functions*

W. D. HOSKINS, Department of Computer Science, University of Manitoba, Winnepeg, Canada: *Bolzano Search*

A. S. HOUSEHOLDER, Malibu, California: *Bernoulli's Method*

MANUEL LANGTRY, Langtry Associates, Palo Alto, California: *Bendix Computers CDC*

MICHAEL J. MAGAZINE, Department of Industrial Engineering, North Carolina State University, Raleigh, North Carolina: *Bellman's Principle of Optimality*

JOSEPH E. MICHINI, Central National Bank of Cleveland, Cleveland, Ohio: *Banking*

MELVIN R. NOVICK, College of Education, Division of Educational Psychology, Measurement and Statistics, The University of Iowa, Iowa City, Iowa: *Bayesian Statistics*

GUILLERMO OWEN, Mathematical Sciences, Rice University, Houston, Texas: *Bargaining Theory*

JOSEPH A. PANICO, Chairman, Division of Management Sciences, Franklin University; President, APIS, Maynard Training Center, Columbus, Ohio: *Birth and Death Processes*

D. RIBBENS, Universite de Liege, Chaire d'Informatique, Liege, Belgium; *Belgium, Computers In*

ROBERT RICHARDSON, Pfizer, Inc., New York, New York: *Benders' Partitioning Method*

GERALD M. SMITH, Professor and Chairman, Engineering Mechanics Department, University of Nebraska, Lincoln, Nebraska: *Beam Equations*

RALPH G. STANTON, Department of Computer Science, University of Manitoba, Winnipeg, Manitoba, Canada: *Bolzano Search*

CHRIS P. TSOKOS, Professor of Mathematics and Statistics, Department of Mathematics, University of South Florida, Tampa, Florida: *Bivariate: The Probability Distribution of the Logarithm of the Sum of Two Log-Normally Distributed Random Variables*

T. J. USHER, MS.I.E., Ph.D., Operations Research, Assistant to the General Superintendent, Southworks, U.S. Steel, Chicago: *Blending Problem*

V. VEMURI, School of Advanced Technology, State University of New York at Binghamton, Binghamton, New York: *Biharmonic Equations, Solution Methods*

STANLEY J. WALLJASPER, Computer Science Department, University of Pittsburgh, Pittsburgh, Pennsylvania: *Benchmark*

BALLISTICS CALCULATIONS

INTRODUCTION

Ballistics has been defined [1] as "The science or art of hurling missile weapons by the use of an engine; the science of the motion of projectiles." Without amplification, this definition may create an impression of narrowly exclusive concern with the dynamics of rigid bodies. In modern practice "ballistics" has actually been much more broadly construed to deal with almost all aspects of conventional weaponry as well as the effects of nuclear weapons, extending from research for development of the technological base for design to evaluation of predicted or observed performance, product improvement, doctrine for use, and quality control for manufacturing tolerances or for monitoring of deterioration in storage. The action involved in the definition is intended to destroy, defeat, damage, or even merely to threaten a remote target. Targets may include various kinds of structures (e.g., buildings, dams, bridges, docks), vehicles (tanks, trucks, trains, ships, aircraft), equipment, industrial plants, storage or supply dumps, transportation facilities, communications systems, information-gathering ability, personnel, or morale. The damage-producing mechanism may be impact of the projectile on the target; blast wave loading from the detonation of chemical explosives; impact of fragments of shell casings, bombs, mines, or grenades; penetration by high-speed metal jets; fire produced by impact with pyrophoric materials; smoke for concealment; illumination for exposure; noise; or even the psychological effect of propaganda leaflets.

Delivery of the warhead to the target can be accomplished by use of rockets, which are self-propelled; by firing nonself-propelled projectiles from guns, howitzers, or mortars; by dropping bombs from aircraft or depth charges from ships; by launching torpedoes or missiles from submarines; by soldiers throwing grenades; or mobile targets may pass unintentionally over land or sea mines. If we disregard grenades, bombs, mines, depth charges, and torpedoes, the motion is generated by the direct interaction with the projectiles of gases formed by the combustion of chemical propellants. After launching there follows a period of flight subject to gravity, aerodynamic forces generated by the interaction of the shell with the atmosphere, and possibly continued thrust for rockets or tracer ammunition. Eventually, by the use of a fuse actuated, e.g., by impact or by a timer, the warhead will be triggered close to the target if the target's location relative to the launching site is accurately known; if the weapon is accurate; if it has been correctly calibrated, aimed, or adjusted; and if it has performed properly. The damage inflicted is a complicated function of the nature of the target and of the forces applied thereto. Since damage is the ultimate purpose of all of the preceding actions, estimation of the vulnerability of targets becomes one of the principal objectives of ballistics, from the point of view of the attackers. Conversely, determination of measures for reduction of vulnerability is a primary concern of the defenders.

Intended to deal systematically with a great variety of targets, possible forms of damage, and agents to accomplish this, ballistics must clearly be based on a tremendous interdisciplinary body of engineering science and technology. No individual can hope to master all aspects of the subject in total relevant detail. Thus, as detailed development and expansion of the field has occurred, ballistics has been split into progressively narrower subdivisions, but with correspondingly increased well-grounded specialized content. During the past 20 years, a generally acceptable productive subdivision into major technical specialties would be:

Interior ballistics
Exterior ballistics
Terminal ballistics
Vulnerability/vulnerability reduction
Weapons systems analysis

The problems to be considered have to be solved by a mixture of intuition, empiricism, tests or experiments, and theory.

The theories originate in physics (largely but not exclusively mechanics), geophysics, and chemistry. Generally they are phrased in mathematical or statistical terms. The equations and constraints are usually nonlinear. To solve problems, at least approximately, or to gain insight into the general behavior of their solutions, three approaches are generally attempted:

Seek special solutions, particularly similarity solutions and principles.
Linearize, especially if this leads to classical equations with extensive accumulations of theory, of simple representations of solutions, or of transformations to reformulate problems in more tractable forms.
Resort to numerical methods.

In general, if nonlinear problems include realistic details, the only general widely effective method available to determine approximate solutions is computation. Until the emergence of the electronic computer the principal deterrent to the computational approach was the prodigious amount of calculation required, of course. Nevertheless, for some of the simpler kinds of nonlinear problems, of which we shall discuss two types, the need very long ago for results was desperate enough to warrant the enormous effort required to compute with inadequate equipment. Accordingly, hand computations had to be undertaken for them with whatever resources were available.

The first type included calculation of orbits in astronomy; the preparation of nautical almanacs and ephemerides; and later on the closely related calculation of trajectories to construct firing tables for artillery. Much of this work involves the numerical solution of small systems of ordinary differential equations. In the context of construction of firing tables, the equations of motion contain aerodynamic forces and moments as well as physical parameters that depend on the particular shell. The initial conditions depend on the angle of elevation of the gun barrel and on the powder charge (which determines the initial velocity). A common practical problem is to determine combinations of elevations and charges that produce sets of equally spaced horizontal ranges, between which the gunner can easily interpolate, if necessary. If table preparation is to be attacked numerically without any kind of computer more elaborate than an abacus, the most likely approach would be to calculate a few trajectories for each charge and then to fill in the desired table by a mixture of direct and inverse interpolation, probably with some reservations or misgivings about the accuracy of the results. In slightly less austere circumstances, with an electromechanical desk calculator of vintage 1940, it took an average of about 20 hours to compute a trajectory. To obtain smooth enough results for accurate interpolation, as many as 50 elevations and seven charges might have had to be used. At this preelectronic speed it would have taken about 2.8 man-years to produce the table for a particular shell. It should also be mentioned that there may be several types of shell for each of a great variety of weapons. Furthermore, recomputations may be required if dynamically significant changes are made in existing types of shell. All of this implies a large computing load that obviously calls for much faster and more efficient means for computation.

As a second kind of early exploration of numerical methods important for ballistics even prior to the appearance of electronic computers, various calculations for problems in continuum mechanics should be mentioned. In general, these would require the approximate solution of nonlinear partial differential equations. However, the numerical treatment of even linear equations was quickly found to require great volumes of computation. To make it clear that awareness of such ideas and difficulties was widespread, it should suffice to recall some of the early publications on this subject. Theoretical foundations for the validity of various algorithms for the numerical solution of typical classical linear partial differential equations were established by Phillips and Wiener [2], and Courant, Friedrichs, and Lewy [3]. Extensive applications which were heuristically plausible methods at the time and computational short cuts to specific problems were made, e.g., by Southwell [4] and Shortley [5] and their associates. Preliminary studies of the numerical solution of nonlinear partial differential equations were made at about the same time by Friedrichs and Lewy [6] and Frankl and Aleksjeva [7]. It may even be worth mentioning, as an indication of its possible origin in a problem in ballistics, that the latter paper refers to earlier publications on the same problem in Soviet technical military journals.

We have briefly suggested the need in ballistics to be able to perform, rapidly and easily, massive amounts of calculation. Obviously this was just a reflection of the even more extensively perceived and acknowledged needs of all kinds of engineering and of the physical sciences, as a whole, for computation on a grand scale. Perusal of the early volumes of one of the first exclusively applied mathematics journals, the *Zeitschrift fuer angewandte*

Mathematik und Mechanik, reveals that astonishing numbers of papers on numerical methods were published in the 1920s and 1930s. The times cried out for efficient automatic aids to computation. The first responses to this growing need were various kinds of electromechanical desk calculators, more elaborate commercial accounting machines, differential analyzers, and relay computers. Eventually these were followed by an all-electronic computer, its appearance hastened by military needs. An accident of history brought about very productive close professional associations of talented ballisticians, engineers, chemists, physicists, mathematicians, and statisticians at the military and civilian research laboratories of the major warring nations during World War II. One such group at the Ballistic Research Laboratories (BRL) at Aberdeen Proving Ground, Maryland used a Vannevar Bush differential analyzer for part of their mission, the preparation of firing tables. There was a life and death urgency for preparing many new firing tables for new weapons or new ammunition more rapidly than ever. In this connection, the Moore School of Electrical Engineering of the University of Pennsylvania, comparatively nearby in Philadelphia, also had a Bush differential analyzer. As an obvious measure to double the BRL's computing facilities, an additional group of computers was established to prepare firing tables on the Moore School's machine. Association with or awareness of this important task inspired some of the faculty of the Moore School to speculate about designing, with modern high-speed electronic counting techniques, a digital computer that would perform arithmetic at millisecond rates. Eventually support of their proposal by the U.S. Army Ordinance Department to produce a device that would radically speed up the preparation of firing tables led to the construction of the world's first all-electronic digital computer, the ENIAC. In operation it actually achieved computing speeds in the desired range, viz. 0.2 msec for addition and 3.4 msec for multiplication. Detailed accounts of the development and technical background of this machine are contained in Goldstine's recently published authoritative history of digital computers [8].

For histories of ballistics the reader should consult the works of Charbonnier [9], Mandryka [10], Szabo [11], and Barnes [12]. The published lectures of Cranz [13, 14], also available in English translations, provide definitive texts that have exerted international influence on the development of ballistics. A testimonial to their widely acknowledged importance is the compilation of modern advances published in the Cranz Centennial volume, edited by Nelson [15]. Specialized accounts of exterior ballistics, some of which contain more modern material, are presented in the books of Bliss [16]; Garnier [17]; McShane, Kelley, and Reno [18]; lectures by Green [19]; and reports by Murphy [20a, 20b]. References for interior ballistics are books by Corner [21] and Tranter [22]; a more recent (popular) account has been written by Lowry [23]. The reader cannot have failed to notice the preponderance of exterior ballistics in these references. This can be explained partly by the fact that as a subject ultimately based on particle or rigid body dynamics, exterior ballistics had its theoretical beginnings in late seventeenth century science, partly because of the apparently much greater complexity of the subject matter of the other subdivisions of ballistics. By contrast with the relative antiquity of exterior ballistics, Corner has remarked that, with one exception, modern interior ballistics began in about 1840. The remaining subdivisions of modern ballistics, listed earlier, have been established since World War II. To the extent that their subject matter is of widespread importance outside of ballistics, general reference works can easily be found in large technical libraries. Specialized accounts of terminal ballistics and vulnerability estimation tend to have rather limited circulation.

A SHORT SURVEY OF PROBLEMS IN BALLISTICS

As a preliminary to discussing selected ballistic computations in the next section, we mention some general types of scientific and engineering problems of ballistics. To be sure, many of these problems also occur in nonmilitary contexts and have been studied at great length. If they have been treated numerically, the computational algorithms and computed results have very likely been published in technical journals or in series of laboratory reports that are readily accessible to the general professional public. Many references to such material can be found by looking under index headings such as blast waves, boundary layers, detonation, explosions, impact, jets, nozzle flow, reacting flow, shells (structural), shock waves, and systems identification in the author's bibliography for the numerical solution of partial differential equations [24]. Hence there is no need for extended consideration of such universal calculations (see the section entitled Selected Examples of Computation in Ballistics for a discussion of computations that have some features peculiar to ballistics).

We shall organize our survey in accordance with the specialized subdivision presented in the Introduction.

Interior Ballistics is dedicated primarily to the events that culminate in the launching of a projectile or a rocket. First, there are problems in chemistry. Combustion [25, 26] of a chemical propellant in a gun produces gas at high pressures which sets the projectile in motion at high speed. In a rocket motor it produces a flux of momentum across the exit plane of the nozzle that thrusts the rocket forward. Searches for new or better propellants and igniters begin from chemistry or chemical engineering considerations. To try to determine the necessary chemical and physical properties of potential or proposed propellants completely by theoretical means leads to problems in quantum mechanics. For reactions that involve more than about five atoms, the calculations are beyond the capabilities of present-day computers. Semiempirical approaches to more complicated reactions have greater prospects for success. For the most immediate response to the needs of interior ballistics technology, chemical reaction rates have to be determined experimentally. Interpretation of the data comes down to a problem of parameter identification. The reaction rates in the systems of ordinary differential equations of chemical kinetics must be adjusted to fit observed results. Unfortunately, such systems are the archetypal *stiff differential equations,* notoriously difficult to handle numerically.

Second, there are problems in fluid mechanics of various degrees of complexity associated with the behavior of the propellant gases. In the pre-computer era a similarity solution was often used to approximate the gas velocity, pressure, etc., but experience has shown this to be inadequate. Consequently, more elaborate computations of the development of the gas flow-field have been undertaken. In this connection, one of the simplest classical problems is a one-dimensional nonsteady idealization of the motion of a projectile in a gun barrel, the so-called problem of Lagrange [21, 27–29]. Another commonly encountered simple example is the approximation of a steady plane or a symmetric flow through a nozzle. Both problems can be characterized mathematically by hyperbolic systems of partial differential equations, subject to appropriate boundary and initial conditions. One of the principal problems in undertaking computations for such problems is general uncertainty about the choice of initial conditions. Success of the calculations may depend on the fact that the flow is so extensive and of such long duration that the influence of the initial conditions decays comparatively rapidly, giving the boundary conditions the predominant effect in determining the solution. Speculation about these matters could lead to the following inverse form of Lagrange's problem. Supplement the gasdynamics equations by experimental observations of the motion of the projectile in the gun tube to try to determine the initial conditions for the propellant gas. Variants of all of these fluid dynamics problems result from adding more realistic features, e.g., chemical reactions, more elaborate geometry, asymmetry, which will increase the number of independent variables; additional physical properties of the gases or fluids, such as viscosity and heat conduction; variations in the cross-sectional area of the bore; and bore friction.

Third, there are problems of rigid body dynamics. One arises in the in-bore motion of projectiles. In general, it would simplify the analysis if the axis of symmetry of the shell moved along the axis of symmetry of the barrel. In reality, the paths of points of the projectile's axis will resemble spirals. This can happen because there can be some "play" in the way the projectile's driving band engages and its bourrelet rides on the rifling. Another source of problems is the functioning of mechanical fuses which may depend on the constrained rigid body motion of some of their components.

Fourth, there are many kinds of mechanical engineering problems. Continuum mechanics problems will appear in the design of gun barrels to resist the high-pressure loading produced by the propellant gases. For most kinds of gun mounts it will be necessary to provide spring or hydraulic cylinder recoil mechanisms. Various problems of vibration or wave motion are associated with automatic weapons. Tracking and aiming at moving targets involve problems in the dynamics of combinations of rigid and elastic bodies, to say nothing of the associated control or optimal control problems. For both artillery shell and rockets the period when the projectile begins free flight involves phenomena, such as muzzle blast or launcher interaction, that limit the accuracy of the presumed initial conditions of the trajectory and hence the accuracy of the location of the predicted impact point. Also associated with this phase of projectile and gun dynamics are problems of muzzle brakes, flash suppressors, and silencers. In addition to everything else that has been mentioned, there are numerous mechanical problems involved in the design of shell and fuses to withstand high g-loadings inside the gun barrel.

Fifth, there obviously must be many problems associated with the analysis of test and experimental data or the correction of malfunctions. These will involve probability theory, statistics, design of experiments, reliability studies, and many matters related to quality control. As a curiosity we mention, in this connection, that the manufacturing lot to lot variations of propellant behavior have to be taken into account in preparing and using firing tables.

Exterior Ballistics deals with the phenomenon of flight from launch site to burst or impact point. In this realm, first there are problems in the dynamics of rigid bodies related to trajectory calculation or flight performance. These are associated with the equations of motion, a system of six second-order differential equations which contain parameters and functions that have to be specified to deal with a particular projectile. The parameters include the mass and principal moments of inertia. The functions are components of forces and moments. In ballistics these are (1) the force due to gravity, and (2) the aerodynamic force and moment expressed in terms of the shape, location, orientation, and state of motion of the projectile. These can be approximated by appeal to a mixture of theory and experiment, to be discussed later. If the motor of a rocket operates during flight, then the mass will vary with time, and the resultant thrust will have to be added somehow to the forces acting on the projectile. To complete the specification of a particular trajectory for shell or rockets, in the generality we have been contemplating, requires initial data for the projectile: (1) location of its center of mass, (2) its orientation, (3) its velocity, and (4) its angular velocity. In addition, generalized meteorological information concerning atmospheric density and wind distribution will be required, since these affect the forces and ultimately the burst or impact point.

An example of motion of several rigid bodies arises, e.g., when it has been found desirable to use subcaliber ammunition. To support the projectile in the gun and to seal in the propellant gases, a sabot is attached to or fitted around the projectile. By this means a finned projectile can be launched from a rifled gun. After emergence, centrifugal force can be used to cause a well-designed sabot to separate and fly away from the projectile. Concern for the safety of gun crews and friendly troops dictates the need to analyze such motion thoroughly.

Second, there are modeling problems associated with simplification of the equations of motion. It should be mentioned that accurate computation of the complete six-degrees-of-freedom equations of motion must be carried out with very small time increments. This implies a very long time to compute a trajectory and a high computing cost per trajectory. But such calculations also yield details about the fine structure of a trajectory which are unnecessary for most applications. For problems that involve great volumes of trajectory calculation, the need to reduce costs or time provides an incentive to try to simplify the equations of motion without unacceptable losses of accuracy. We have already mentioned that the preparation of firing tables is a classical example of this type. Another is the determination of aerodynamic forces and moment functions from photographic records of projectiles in free flight in elaborately instrumented firing ranges. Suppose that the aerodynamic functions have known plausible approximate functional forms that contain several parameters. Then an attempt can be made, e.g., to adjust the parameters to make the corresponding calculated trajectory fit the observed data as well as possible. Simplicity of the equations or approximate solutions is also imperative if small programs stored in a small field computer are to be used as substitutes for firing tables. Speed is an incentive for real time (or faster) tracking and control for automatic weapons, e.g., antiaircraft guns. On-board computers for large missiles also have similar needs for speed, which can be partly achieved by use of simplified models.

Third, there are problems of accuracy and stability. To be employed effectively against a remote target, a weapon with an ordinary high-explosive warhead, which has a limited lethal volume, must be sufficiently accurate. Accuracy depends on the extent to which the weapon's performance is reproducible within tolerances accepted partly on grounds of experience. In general, the solutions of the equations of rigid body motion depend continuously on the projectile parameters, aerodynamic force and moment functions, initial conditions, and meteorological conditions. Loosely speaking, this means that we would expect, with an exception to be discussed later, that small enough variations from standard tabulated conditions should have small enough effects, i.e., the artillerist's problems, insofar as they concern trajectories, should be well posed. To determine what perturbations are actually permissible for a given tolerance is a matter best decided by computation. Many errors originate in manufacturing ammunition, e.g., variations in mass, in location of the center of mass, in moments of inertia, unintentional geometrical asymmetries, or variations of composition and loading of propellants and explosive. All of these perturbations, plus wear or erosion of the gun barrel, produce variations in initial conditions that, in turn, produce changes in range. That there are inevitable variations in meteorological conditions need scarcely be mentioned.

A more serious and difficult problem, with important implications for accuracy, arises as follows. To design projectiles that will fly farther (by virtue of reduced aerodynamic drag) and carry a large payload of explosive, shell shapes that are elongated in the direction of motion and have somewhat streamlined noses must be used. In general, in flight the axis of symmetry of the shell should form a small angle (which in the nature of things cannot be zero) with the tangent to the trajectory of the center of mass. To develop a qualitative description of the motion of the shell, temporarily consider a rather specialized case of motion. Suppose that the center of mass moves on a plane trajectory, and that the instantaneous axis of rotation is normal to this plane. Then a classical theorem in hydrodynamics [30] states that the axis of symmetry will tend to turn to a position athwart the trajectory or to tumble end-over-end. Such a motion would radically increase the aerodynamic drag and disastrously decrease the range. Of course, such behavior would render a projectile useless for close support of friendly troops. If such dangerous behavior is to be prevented, the instantaneous axis of rotation cannot be normal to the plane of the trajectory. A substantial component of angular velocity must be introduced in this plane. This can be accomplished by spinning the projectile by firing it from a rifled gun barrel. Now the angular part of the motion of the shell will become comparable to the well-documented and thoroughly understood oscillatory behavior of a top or gyroscope. Stability criteria involving shell rigid-body parameters and aerodynamic (or ballistic) coefficients, state of motion, and atmospheric properties have been developed [18] but will not be discussed here. For calculations to discuss in-flight observations of misbehavior of unstable projectiles, or to interpret or reduce flight data for satisfactory projectiles, or to determine the effects of design changes on stability, it may be necessary to use the full six-degrees-of-freedom equations of motion, or simplified versions that contain terms not ordinarily used for firing tables calculations.

Fourth, there are problems in fluid mechanics. These may include matters of universal interest, such as similarity principles, e.g., for transonic flow. More frequently, there are efforts to devise analytical approximations for force and moment coefficients for projectiles. If such formulas can be derived by truncating some kind of series expansions, e.g., in terms of relevant parameters, this would be a fertile field for use of symbol-manipulating programs. To validate such mathematical models, one option would be first to determine the flow field about the projectile by solving numerically, for various levels of physical and geometrical complexity and realism, the fundamental equations of hydro- or gas-dynamics. From such information further straightforward computation would yield some of the forces and moments. Another kind of problem, which introduces an internal flow field, occurs for shells that contain liquids or thixotropic substances liquefied by the tremendous setback pressures created at the instant of firing. Motion of the liquid cargo may alter the projectile's stability characteristics and dynamic behavior radically enough to cause unacceptable deterioration in accuracy. Analysis of the basic viscous flow leads to difficult high-order eigenvalue problems, so far satisfactorily solved for only the simplest cavity shapes.

Fifth, there are numerous requirements for quantitative interpretation of test and experimental data, i.e., systems or parameter identification problems. For each production lot of propellant, full-scale proof tests of production or prototype ammunition from an actual gun are performed to obtain values of ballistic coefficients or empirical correction factors, primarily from observations of dispersions of range and lateral deflection. Rocket or bomb flight data can be recorded by photogrammetric or cinetheodolite methods. Radar tracking or on-board radio transmitters can also be used to acquire appropriate forms of trajectory data. Models can be fired in carefully and elaborately instrumented spark ranges to produce numerous crossed photographs from which the location and orientation of the projectile can be seen at many points of a flat trajectory. Similarly, high-speed motion pictures can be made of unsupported models launched for brief periods of flight upstream in a supersonic wind tunnel's test section. For strut-mounted, possibly spinning models, more straightforward and direct measurements of forces and moments can be made in wind tunnels, although these results require correction to eliminate the effects of strut interference on the flow at the base of the model. To turn to flow data less immediately related to forces and moments, in addition to ordinary spark photography, which reveals discontinuities or rapid changes of second partial derivatives of air density in the flow field, schlieren or interferometric techniques [31], respectively, produce photographic records of first derivatives or of the density itself. In particular, the unscrambling of interferometric records of axisymmetric flows (traversed by an interferometer beam perpendicular to the axis of symmetry) reduces to the numerical solution of an Abel integral equation [32].

Terminal Ballistics is concerned with the basic phenomena in the infliction of damage on a great diversity of targets, matched by great diversity of weapons to inflict the damage. Small arms perforate weak targets, generally by impact of a solid metal slug. Grenades, land mines, and some larger projectiles damage unarmored or lightly armored targets with a spray of metal fragments produced by detonation of an explosive charge. Shaped charges perforate heavy armor with an explosively produced hypervelocity metal jet. Bombs, depth charges, torpedoes, and naval mines produce blast waves in air or water which impulsively overload a target, in order to rupture, permanently deform, or weaken it. If the target contains fuel or other combustible material, an attempt may be made to ignite it. In general, the logical scope of terminal ballistics ranges over explosives, explosions, transmission of their energy through some intermediary (air, water, or fragments) to a target, and the mechanical response of the target to the energy it has absorbed.

With regard to computation, first there are problems in chemistry. Searches for new or improved explosives start from chemical, chemical engineering, or physical considerations. In principle, the properties of energetic materials should be derivable from applications of quantum and statistical mechanical concepts. The difficulties involved in doing this in practice and the need to resort to semiempirical methods have been alluded to already in connection with similar theoretical studies of propellants and igniters in interior ballistics.

Second, there are problems in fluid mechanics associated with the behavior of gaseous explosion products (in which chemical reactions may be occurring) and the transmission of blast waves into the surrounding air or water (or even metal!). Even after radical simplification is achieved by ignoring chemical reactions, viscosity, heat conduction, and temperature dependencies of various physical parameters, so that the type of partial differential equations will be hyperbolic, the problems that arise, at least with realistic geometry, can be discouragingly complex and can consume enormous amounts of computer time. To give some idea of the nature of the problems to be solved, let us start with the simplest example of transmission of energy from one gas to another as it occurs in a shock-tube [27]. Consider a closed rigid tube which contains at one end a uniform stagnant "driver"-gas at high pressure, separated by a plastic film membrane from another uniform stagnant "driven"-gas at lower pressure at the other end. When the membrane is ruptured, the driver-gas expands to compress the driven-gas. This generates a complex but qualitatively easily comprehended system of expansion-, compression-, and shock-waves, eventually jumbled by many reflections at the ends of the tube and at the interface between the driver- and driven-gas. The motion of the two gases can be described as a nonsteady one-dimensional inviscid readily computable flow. By rough analogy, we can now idealize an explosion, as follows, as a "spherical shock-tube." Suppose that at time zero a uniform spherical mass of stagnant gaseous "explosion products" is surrounded by an infinite uniform stagnant "atmosphere" at very much lower pressure. The subsequent expansion of the explosion products against the atmospheric resistance, which among other things produces a spherical shock wave advancing into the atmosphere, is a more difficult but still comparatively readily computable spherically symmetrical nonsteady flow. By introducing a rigid immovable wall, which does not intersect the original sphere of stagnant explosion products, we have a crude model of an airburst near the surface of the earth. After the originally spherical atmospheric shock wave touches the plane, the flow becomes axisymmetric rather than spherically symmetric. The corresponding required increase in the number of independent variables, from two to three, makes the computation of the gas motion much more complicated and much slower than for the previous example. If on the same side of the plane as the explosion products we rigidly attach a rigid rectangular block, the flow will eventually become three–dimensional and, of course, still much harder to compute. Problems with more realistic geometry, physics, and chemistry obviously rapidly become even more difficult to compute, to the point of surpassing the limitations of known techniques and existing or planned computers. It should also be mentioned that the physical processes involved in problems similar to the examples just considered may be unstable. Thus experimental flows intended to be describable with only one geometrical independent variable may in reality require two or three. In fact, such a superficially simple matter as the detonation, initiated at one end, of an explosive mixture of gases in a closed tube does not proceed as a plane or rapidly decay to plane flow, but manifests the phenomenon of "spinning detonation," which has to be treated as three-, rather than one-dimensional [26]. Whatever the sufficiently correct system of partial differential equations of motion may be, it seems that the initial-boundary value problems for the tube or more complicated geometries are probably not very well posed. Another important type of flow problem is concerned with the formation of a jet by detonation of an explosive that contains a cavity with a thin metal lining. A rough qualitative steady-state explanation of the phenomenon is implicit in the well-known plane steady incompressible potential flow in two equal impinging inward-flowing jets from which two additional outward-flowing jets result [30, 33]. More realistic treatments of time-dependent axisymmetric jet flow have to be determined by computation, the task being rendered more difficult by the fact that the linear material undergoes extreme changes of shape. Attempts to study by computation alone conditions that lead to break-up of jets are close to if not beyond the limitations of existing computational techniques.

Third, there is a wide variety of problems in solid continuum mechanics. For example, when a shaped charge jet strikes a slab of armor plate, it digs a hole and forms a crater out of some of the excavated material. The depth of penetration of a finite jet is a function of its length and its inclination to the plate. A jet that perforates the plate may, in conjunction with material spalled off of the back surface of the armor, seriously damage the hitherto protected target. Considering the time, labor, and cost of testing cratering and perforation, there is a strong incentive to develop computer programs to calculate such processes, since materials and parameters can be more readily changed in computation. Impact of a metal jet on armor has been simulated with a hydrodynamic model, viz., by hypervelocity impact of a cylinder of some material on a slab of the same material. The results are qualitatively satisfactory. Efforts have been made to modify the computation to incorporate material strength and to permit the "jet" and slab to be composed of different materials. Another very common problem is to determine the dynamic response of shell structures, e.g., aircraft, missiles, or fuel storage tanks, attacked with various kinds of overloads. Elaborate computer programs have been developed to predict the response by use of finite difference methods [34–36]. One of the difficulties encountered in this approach results from the very large numbers of values of dependent variables that have to be stored from one time level to the next. One cause for concern about this point is the fact that in order to validate a finite-difference method, it would generate confidence if it could be shown that the approximate solutions will converge to the exact solutions of the partial differential equations as the increments of the geometrical independent variables vanish. If this is attempted by repeated halvings of increments, then at the nth halving for a k-dimensional motion the amount of memory required for temporary storage will be 2^{nk} times that used for the original choices of increments. At present the value of n attainable in customary direct access memories is very small.

Fourth, there are also the invariable requirements for quantitative interpretation of test and experimental data. The variety is so extensive that we shall mention only three types. First, solid materials in continuum mechanics are described by constitutive equations (e.g., Hooke's law), insight about or the validity of which have to be determined by experiments which may at least be compared with the computed dynamic behavior of the test solid. Second, there are numerous explosion experiments in which pressure histories are recorded at numerous nearby points, at which various kinds of targets may also be located. Finally, fundamental data on detonation, explosions, and on shock-wave propagation in metals can be obtained for explosive charges and metal slabs of simple shapes by flash radiography.

Vulnerability/Vulnerability Reduction deals with the sensitivity of targets to combat damage mechanisms and, conversely, with the application of design techniques to reduce or eliminate the effects of such mechanisms. By contrast with the more general basic scientific and technological concerns of Interior, Exterior, and Terminal Ballistics, vulnerability analysis is concerned with much more specific matters, e.g., if a projectile traveling in a specified direction strikes a specified point on the skin of an aircraft, will it subsequently hit a fuel line, an oil line, control cables, stored ammunition, etc.? Or, how much damage must be inflicted on a radar antenna to render it inoperative?

We have already remarked that the damage mechanisms include blast, bullets, fragments, shaped charges, and flame and incendiary devices. Assessment of damage that may be inflicted will require target descriptions, damage or "kill" criteria, conditional kill-probabilities, and methodology with which to convert this information into the desired assessment. Target descriptions consist of basic information about dimensions; external configuration; functional or operational data; locations of critical components; thickness of skin, armor, or outer covering; locations of items that may serve as shielding; and composition of all materials used to construct the target. Kill criteria are levels of damage to or degradation of performance of the target which will give the attackers a significant advantage. Furthermore, a kill criterion should also have assigned to it a "cost" to the enemy and a cost to the attackers. Next, for each target component conditional kill probabilities, given that a hit has occurred, must be determined, frequently by experiments. Finally, a methodology must be developed to exploit this information. Of course, this should include algorithms needed to estimate the final vulnerability or vulnerability reduction. When such algorithms have been validated, computer programs are prepared, the outputs of which serve as inputs of vulnerability information for follow-on systems analyses and cost-effectiveness studies. In addition, methodology includes generation of mathematical relationships of the loading or damaging parameters of a munition to the target response, or the generation of mathematical models or computer programs that yield parametric response data from complex boundary value problems. Also included is the development of scaling techniques and similarity principles.

Systems Analysis, in the context of ballistics, deals with such specific matters that, except for the following vaguely phrased problem, we shall merely refer the reader interested to articles related to systems analysis in this encyclopedia. The design of tanks, as well as that of all other complicated and extremely expensive equipment, is subject to many conflicting requirements and constraints. To suggest a kind of abstract problem that arises early in the design process, let us suppose that the most important functions to be performed by the vehicle have been decided. Suppose, further, that a gross weight has been specified. Then, to name only a few of the competing features, how shall this weight be apportioned to engine, fuel, armor, armament, and ammunition?

SELECTED EXAMPLES OF COMPUTATION IN BALLISTICS

Interpretation of Microwave Interferometric Time-Travel Data[1]

In the section on Interior Ballistics we referred to Lagrange's problem, to determine the motion of a projectile in a gun tube. Experimentally, the location

---

[1] Reprinted by permission of the publisher from *Applications of Digital Computers,* edited by Walter F. Freiburger and William Prager, copyright 1963 by Ginn and Company.

BALLISTICS CALCULATIONS

$x(t)$ of the projectile can be ascertained as a function of time, t, by microwave interferometer techniques. From these time-travel data we wish to find, among other things, the acceleration d^2x/dt^2. Early routine attempts to fit the curves by polynomials in t led to ridiculous results for the acceleration. We might conjecture that we could treat this problem as part of a one-dimensional nonsteady flow calculation, with appropriate modifications to adjust the values of several parameters. Since it would be difficult and uncertain to determine improvements in the fit so calculated for $x(t)$, since the computing time might be excessive, and since it seems absurd to have to calculate an entire flow to find the motion of one boundary, we would be led to consider the use of some simpler method. Interior ballistic phenomenological descriptions of the motion have been devised which exploit, among other things, some of the properties of certain approximate solutions of Lagrange's problem. By using one described by Corner [21], Leser and Lanahan [37] transformed our original numerical differentiation problem for that part of the motion which occurs during the burning of the propellant, to the problem of integrating

$$dx/dt = Q/1 - (bx + 1)^{-m} \tag{1}$$

where Q, b, and m are positive constants that depend on the physical and chemical parameters of the motion. The fitting is most conveniently accomplished with the series solution

$$t = T + Q^{-1} \sum_{j=0}^{\infty} (1 - mj)^{-1}(bx + 1)^{1-mj} \tag{2}$$

truncated at a point that depends on and varies with the data we are trying to fit, in accordance with an accuracy criterion built into the computer program. In particular, a least squares and differential corrections method was used to fit the successive partial sums of Eq. (2). The computation was terminated when the sums of the squares of the residuals for the currently considered partial sum became less than some preassigned tolerance. The period after the completion of burning was accounted for by a similar treatment of the equation

$$dx/dt = \{(2B/n)[1 - \alpha(x + l)^{-n}]\}^{\frac{1}{2}} \tag{3}$$

Once the seven parameters Q, b, T, B, n, α, and l have been chosen, d^2x/dt^2 can be found by differentiation. The fits of time-travel curves were phenomenally good, and the accelerations obtained were compatible with independently observed pressures at the bases of the projectiles. From the values of the seven parameters it was also possible to deduce, as an unexpected by-product, one of the physical parameters of the propellant gas.

Computation of Firing Tables [38]

For present purposes a firing table is primarily a listing of gun-barrel quadrant elevations and of times of flight as functions of horizontal range and of weight of propellant. In addition, it lists fuse settings and numerous corrections for various departures from standard conditions. To name only a few: corrections for wind, nonstandard atmospheric temperature and density, and nonstandard propellant temperatures. Input for the preparation of a table comes from range test firings of actual ammunition from actual guns, from wind tunnel tests of model projectiles, and from spark range test firings of actual or model projectiles. We shall not discuss the first two types of tests, and shall defer to the next section the consideration of the third. The most important feature of the calculation is the formulation of the equations of motion. Until comparatively recent years the firing tables prepared at the U.S. Army Ballistic Research Laboratories treated the projectile as a point-mass subject to gravity and air-drag, a choice originally dictated by the need to keep computation simple during the precomputer era. The calculated ranges could be adjusted to be fairly satisfactory by proper choice of a "ballistic coefficient" in the equations of motion. The times of flight, especially for high launch elevations, were inaccurate. The poor predictions for high-angle fire were attributed to the occurrences of large yaw angles near the summit of the trajectory, a phenomenon that the point-mass equations could not be expected to represent properly. An obvious remedy, once computation ceased to be an obstacle *per se,* would be to use the full six-degrees-of-freedom rigid-body equations of motion. Unfortunately, the time required to calculate a rigid-body trajectory is from one hundred to one thousand times that for a point-mass trajectory. In fact, on a second generation computer a rigid-body calculation for one table would have required about 4 seconds of machine time per second of real time of flight versus 0.006 for the point-mass. Calculation of a few hundred rigid-body trajectories could be undertaken without qualms about efficiency. But for a table based on about 25,000 trajectories, the computer time was estimated to be about 10,000 hours (over a year!) for the rigid body versus 20 hours for the point mass. With regard to this extremely unfavorable comparison, it should be mentioned that the longer calculation generates enormous volumes of superfluous detailed information. As a very crude analogy, the long calculation could be compared to responding to the request, "Is your top spinning? Please answer, 'Yes' or 'No'," by submitting a long strip chart record of its precession and nutation.

The preceding considerations raise the question whether by judicious simplification a good compromise between the rigid-body and the point-mass equations can be found. Lieske and Reiter [39] have developed such an intermediate system which yields radically improved results for only double the time required for a point-mass calculation. Their work can be summarized roughly as follows. Relative to ground-fixed rectangular coordinates, the equations of motion of a spin-stabilized body of revolution can be stated as

$$dX/dt = \mathbf{u} \tag{4}$$

$$d\mathbf{u}/dt = -\frac{\rho d^2}{m}(K_{D_0} + \alpha^2 K_{D_\alpha})v\mathbf{v} + \frac{\rho d^2}{m} K_L[\mathbf{v} \times (\mathbf{x} \times \mathbf{v})] \\ -\frac{\rho d^3}{m} K_S v \frac{d\mathbf{x}}{dt} + \frac{\rho d^3 K_F N}{m}(\mathbf{x} \times \mathbf{v}) + \mathbf{g} + \mathbf{\Lambda} \tag{5}$$

where the symbols are defined in Table 1. The total angular momentum of the

BALLISTICS CALCULATIONS

TABLE 1
Definitions of Symbols[a]

Roman

A	Axial moment of inertia
B	Transverse moment of inertia
C	Ballistic coefficient
d	Reference diameter of projectile
g	Acceleration due to gravity
H	Total angular momentum or
K	Force or moment coefficient specified by subscript
l	Lift factor
m	Mass of projectile
N	Axial spin
Q	Yaw drag factor
t	Time
u	Velocity of projectile with respect to ground
v	$= u - w$
w	Velocity of the wind
x	Unit vector along longitudinal axis of the projectile
X	Position of the projectile's center of mass relative to ground fixed coordinates

Greek

α	Angle of yaw of projectile, i.e., angle between x and v
Λ	Coriolis acceleration due to rotation of the earth
ρ	Air density as a function of altitude

Subscripts

α	Yaw angle
A	Spin damping moment
D	Drag force
e	Repose
F	Magnus force
H	Damping moment
L	Lift force
T	Magnus moment
0	Zero yaw; Surface value
s	Standard mass
S	Pitching force

[a] Boldface characters denote vectors. The corresponding lightface character denotes its scalar magnitude, e.g., $|g| = g$.

projectile is

$$H = ANx + B\left(x \times \frac{dx}{dt}\right) \qquad (6)$$

and the angular motion about the center of mass is governed by

$$dH/dt = \rho d^3 K_M v(v \times x) - \rho d^4 K_H v\left(x \times \frac{dx}{dt}\right) \qquad (7)$$
$$+ \rho d^4 K_T N[x \times (x \times v)] - \rho d^4 K_A Nvx$$

Let α denote the angle of yaw formed by the projectile's axis of symmetry and the relative velocity of the air, v (directed along the tangent to the trajectory in the absence of wind). Then α appears explicitly in Eq. (5) and implicitly in Eqs. (6) and (7), if we note that

$$|v \times x| = v \sin \alpha, \qquad v \cdot x = v \cos \alpha$$

It is known that for stable projectiles the value of α approaches a limit, α_e, the yaw of repose. In principle we could attempt to replace α by the yaw of repose in Eqs. (4) to (7). By making this substitution and other simplifications, Lieske and Reiter obtained from Eq. (7) the approximation

$$\alpha_e = (\alpha_b - \alpha_a)(v \times du/dt) - \alpha_b(v \times g) \tag{8}$$

where

$$\begin{aligned}\alpha_a &= AK_L N/(\rho d^3 K_L K_M v^4 + \rho d^5 K_F K_T N^2 v^2) \\ \alpha_b &= mK_T N/(\rho d K_L K_M v^4 + \rho d^3 K_F K_T N^2 v^2)\end{aligned} \tag{9}$$

Eventually Eq. (5) is simplified to

$$du/dt = -(\rho m_s/144 C_s m)\{K_{D_0} + K_{D_\alpha}[Q\alpha_e]^2\}vv + (\rho d^2/m)K_L v^2 l\alpha_e + g \tag{10}$$
$$+ \Lambda + (\rho d^3/m)K_F NQ(\alpha_e \times v)$$

That the System (10) is a plausible compromise of the type desired becomes evident if we note that for $Q = l = 0$, it reduces to the traditional point-mass equations of motion. To carry out an actual computation we would need additional equations to define N, g, and Λ. Since these are not essential for our discussion, we shall omit them.

To complete our account, it remains to choose a numerical method to integrate the System (10). Because there is a superabundance of methods, a systematic investigation of the more promising ones was undertaken by Breaux [40] to compare their performances in firing-table calculations. It was found that use of a Euler predictor and Heun corrector was accurate, simple, efficient, and fast. Other methods did not offer sufficient advantages over the Euler-Heun method to warrant adopting one of them. Finally, we should mention that an operations count for the numerical solution of Eq. (7) makes it credible that the case $Ql = 0$ will require about twice as much computation per point of the trajectory as for the point-mass case $Q = l = 0$.

Interpretation of Spark-Range Free-Flight Data

The complete rigid-body equations of motion of a spin-stabilized body of revolution, Eqs. (4) to (7), contain nine *a priori* unknown force and moment coefficients $K_{D0}, \ldots, K_A$. Let us consider how they could be determined experimentally. In this connection, note that every summand in these equations involves at least one of the six vectors $d^j X/dt^j$ or dx^j/dt^j for $j = 0, 1, 2$. Now suppose we can determine a table of components of $X = (X_1, X_2, X_3)$ and $x = (x_1, x_2, x_3)$ for some set of discrete times. In principle these tabulated functions could be used to approximate Eqs. (4) to (7) by a system of difference equations. This would yield an overdetermined system of linear equations for the nine force and moment coefficients K, which could then be approximated by least squares methods. In practice, since a great deal of thought has been lavished on the description of projectile motion, subtler methods have been devised to solve this systems-identification problem. Since the methods are very elaborate (one manual [20b] uses at least 125 symbols!), we shall have to confine our discussion to a few particular features. For complete accounts the reader should consult the reports by Murphy [20a, 20b, 20c] and some more recent developments [41–44].

The general experimental process can be described as follows. At numerous closely spaced points along a long horizontal baseline parallel to the X_3-axis, place instrumentation that includes two spark light sources at positions c_n, and place photographic plates in two nonparallel planes π_n (ordinarily orthogonal to each other and both parallel to the baseline), defined by

$$a_n \cdot X_n = b_n, \qquad n = 1, 2 \tag{11}$$

Then we intend to fire projectiles along a flat trajectory close to the base-line. If the projectile is electrostatically charged soon after emergence from the muzzle, and if the instrumentation is properly designed and adjusted, the sparks at any station will be triggered by nearby passage of the projectile. This will produce a photographic record of the projectile's shadows in the planes of the plates. In addition, the time at which the flash occurred should be recorded.

Now let X_n be the shadow of X on π_n, and let x_n be a unit vector on the shadow of the axis of symmetry. Then for perfect measurements of X_n, x_n, and c_n we can determine

$$X = c_n + s_n(X_n - c_n) \tag{12}$$
$$x = \pm(\nu_1 \times \nu_2)/|\nu_1 \times \nu_2| \tag{13}$$

where

$$\nu_n = x_n \times (X_n - c_n) \tag{14}$$
$$s_n = \nu_{3-n} \cdot (c_{3-n} - c_n)/\nu_{3-n} \cdot (X_n - c_n) \tag{15}$$

We shall touch briefly on only two phases of the unscrambling of the tabulated data X_n and x_n: Drag and yaw reductions [1, 20].

For the determination of the drag coefficient, first determine a least-squares fit of the tabulated values of X_3 vs t by

$$t = a_0 + a_1 p + a_2 p^2 + a_3 p^3 \tag{16}$$

where $p = X_3/d$. Then

$$u_3 = dX_3/dt = d/(a_1 + 2a_2 p + 3a_3 p^2)$$
$$d^3 K_D/m = (2a_2 + 6a_3 p)/(a_1 + 2a_2 p + 3a_3 p^2) \tag{17}$$

We shall not pursue the problem of determining the dependence of K_D on yaw angle and Mach number.

BALLISTICS CALCULATIONS

With regard to yaw data reduction, we begin by defining the complex yaw

$$\lambda = \lambda_H + i\lambda_V \tag{18}$$

where

$$\lambda_H = x_1 - dX_1/dX_3, \quad \lambda_V = x_2 - dX_2/dX_3 \tag{19}$$

define the horizontal and vertical yaws. Then the equations of motion imply, for flat fire,

$$\lambda'' + (\mathscr{H} - i\bar{\nu})\lambda' - (M + i\bar{\nu}T)\lambda = G \tag{20}$$
$$\bar{\nu}' = D\bar{\nu}$$

where ' denotes d/dp, and

$$\mathscr{H} = J(K_L - K_D + k_2^{-2}K_H)$$
$$\bar{\nu} = A\omega_3 d/u_3 B$$
$$M = JK_M$$
$$T = J(K_L - k_1^{-2}K_T)$$
$$G = igdu_3^{-2}[J(K_D + k_2^{-2}K_H) - i\bar{\nu}]$$

and where, in addition,

$$D = D + D_0/\nu$$
$$D = J(K_D + md^2K_A/A)$$
$$D_0 = D \text{ at Mach number } M_0$$
$$K_M = \text{overturning moment coefficient}$$
$$\omega = \text{angular velocity of the projectile}$$
$$k_1 \text{ or } k_2 = \text{axial or transverse radius of gyration}$$
$$J = \rho d^3/m$$

Then for slowly varying spin

$$\lambda = \lambda_R + \sum_1^2 K_n \exp[-\alpha_n p + i\varphi_n(p)] \tag{21}$$

where λ_R is the yaw of repose,

$$\varphi_n(p) = \varphi_{n1}p + \tfrac{1}{2}\varphi_{n2}p^2$$

and

$$-\alpha_n p + i\varphi_n(p) = \tfrac{1}{2}\int_0^p \{-\mathscr{H} + i\bar{\nu} - (-1)^n[-m + 2i\bar{\nu}(2T - \mathscr{H} - D)^{\frac{1}{2}}]\}dp \tag{22}$$

with

$$\bar{m} = \bar{\nu}^2 - 4M - \mathscr{H}^2$$

and

$$\lambda_R = -(gd/Mu_3^2)\bar{\nu}^{-i\sigma_3}(1 + \bar{\nu}^2T/M)^{-1} \tag{23}$$
$$\sigma_3 = -J(K_D - k_2^{-2}K_H) + \bar{\nu}^2T/M$$

Suppose the constants K_n, α_n, φ_{n1}, and φ_{n2} have been determined by fitting the

BALLISTICS CALCULATIONS

damped epicycloid (21) to the measured points $\lambda(p)$. Then the relations

$$\begin{aligned}
\bar{\nu} &= \varphi_1'(p) + \varphi_2'(p) \\
\mathscr{X} &= \alpha_1 + \alpha_2 \\
M &= \varphi_1'(p)\varphi_2'(p) - \alpha_1\alpha_2 \\
2T &= \mathscr{X} - (\alpha_1 - \alpha_2)[\varphi_1'(p) - \varphi_2'(p)]/[\varphi_1'(p) + \varphi_2'(p)]
\end{aligned} \qquad (24)$$

yield the spin and three linear combinations of five aerodynamic coefficients. If we can determine K_D and K_L independently from other parts of the overall data reduction process, we can then determine the three remaining coefficients. For more information the reader should consult Murphy's reports.

Another approach to the free-flight systems-identification problem has been developed by Chapman and Kirk [42, 43]. It can be described as follows in a general form which clearly includes (Eqs. (20). Consider the initial value problem

$$\begin{aligned}
\lambda''(x, C) + f(\lambda, C)\lambda'(x, C) + g(\lambda, C)\lambda(x, C) &= 0 \\
\lambda(0, C) &= h(C) \\
\lambda'(0, C) &= m(C)
\end{aligned} \qquad (25)$$

where the coefficients $f(\lambda, C)$ and $g(\lambda, C)$ and the initial values $h(C)$ and $m(C)$ are functions of p parameters C_j, $1 = j = p$. Suppose we know n measured values $\Lambda(x_i)$ of some phenomenon governed by Eqs. (25) for some initially unknown parameters C_j. Then we wish to determine sets of values C_j such that

$$F(C) = \sum_1^n [\Lambda(x_i) - \lambda(x_i, C)]^2 = \text{minimum} \qquad (26)$$

In an iterative method for solving Eq. (26), let us suppose we have determined a vector $C_j^{(n)}$ and want to determine an improved approximation

$$C_j^{(n+1)} = C_j^{(n)} + \Delta C_j^{(n)}$$

Then we have

$$\lambda(x, C^{(n+1)}) \simeq (x, C^{(n)}) + \sum_j P_j(x, C^{(n)})\Delta C_j^{(n)}$$

where we have set

$$P_j(x, C) = \partial\lambda(x, C)/\partial C_j \qquad (27)$$

The functions $P_j(x, C)$ satisfy the system of p ordinary differential equations and $2p$ initial values formed by partial differentiation of Eqs. (25) with respect to C_j, viz.:

$$\begin{aligned}
P_j''(x, C) + f(\lambda, C)P_j'(x, C) + [f_\lambda(\lambda, C)\lambda' + g(\lambda, C) \\
+ g_\lambda(\lambda, C)\lambda]P_j(x, C) + f_{C_j}(\lambda, C)\lambda' + g_{C_j}(\lambda, C)\lambda &= 0 \\
P_j(0, C) &= h_{C_j}(C) \\
P_j'(0, C) &= m_{C_j}(C)
\end{aligned} \qquad (28)$$

Systems (25) and (28) should be integrated simultaneously, of course.

Finally, we define ΔC_j by the usual normal equations

$$A \Delta C = B \tag{29}$$

where

$$A_{jk} = \sum_1^n P_j(x_i, C) P_k(x_i, C)$$

$$B_j = \sum_1^n [\Lambda(x_i) - \lambda(x_i, C)] P_j(x_i, C) \tag{30}$$

A more general formulation has been presented by Bradley in Ref. 45.

The Chapman-Kirk method has been adapted to the reduction of spark range data by Whyte, Jeung, and Bradley [44], and has been applied with good success to a number of test firings.

REFERENCES

1. *Webster's New International Dictionary*, 2nd unabridged ed., Merriam, Springfield, Massachusetts, 1951.
2. H. B. Phillips and N. Wiener, Nets and the Dirichlet problem, *J. Math. Phys.* **2**, 105–124 (1923).
3. R. Courant, K. O. Friedrichs, and H. Lewy, On the partial difference equations of mathematical physics, *Math. Ann.* **100**, 32–74 (1928). English translation in *IBM J. Res. Dev.* **11**, 215–234 (1967).
4. R. V. Southwell, *Relaxation Methods in Engineering Science. A Treatise on Approximate Computation*, Oxford University Press, New York, 1940.
5. G. Shortley and R. Weller, The numerical solution of Laplace's equation, *J. Appl. Phys.* **9**, 334–344 (1938).
6. K. O. Friedrichs and H. Lewy, The initial value problem for an arbitrary nonlinear hyperbolic differential equation, etc., *Math. Ann.* **99**, 200–221 (1928), in German.
7. F. I. Frankl and R. Aleksjeva, Two boundary value problems in the theory of second order hyperbolic partial differential equations, with applications to supersonic gas flow, *Rec. Math. Moscow* **41**, 483–502 (1934), in Russian.
8. H. H. Goldstine, *The Computer, from Pascal to von Neumann*, Princeton University Press, Princeton, New Jersey, 1972, xi + 378 pp.
9. P. Charbonnier, *Essais sur l'Histoire de la Balistique*, Paris, 1928.
10. A. P. Mandryka, *History of Ballistics (to the Middle of the Nineteenth Century)*, Izdat. Nauka, Moscow, 1964, 374 pp., in Russian.
11. I. Szabo, Die Anfaenge der aeusseren Ballistik, *Humanismus, Technik* **14**, 1–28 (1971).
12. G. M. Barnes, Research and development in the Ordnance Department, U.S. Army, *J. Appl. Phys.* **16**, 745–807 (1945).
13. C. Cranz, Ballistik, in *Encyklopaedie der Mathematische Wissenschaften*, Vol. IV.3, Teubner, Leipzig, 1901–1908, pp. 190–281.
14. C. Cranz, *Lehrbuch der Ballistik. I. Aeusere Ballistik. II. Innere Ballistik. III. Experimentelle Ballistik*, Springer, Berlin, 1925, 1926, 1927.

15. W. C. Nelson (ed.), *Selected Topics on Ballistics (Cranz Centenary Colloquium)*, Pergamon, New York, 1959, vii + 280 pp.
16. G. A. Bliss, *Mathematics for Exterior Ballistics*, Wiley, New York; Chapman and Hall, London, 1944, vii + 128 pp.
17. M. Garnier, La balistique exterieure moderne en France, *Mem. Artillerie Francaise* **28**, 117–234 (1954).
18. E. J. McShane, J. L. Kelley, and F. V. Reno, *Exterior Ballistics*, University of Denver Press, Denver, 1953.
19. J. W. Green, Exterior ballistics, in *Modern Mathematics for the Engineer* (E. F. Beckenbach, ed.), McGraw-Hill, New York, 1956, Chap. 3, pp. 36–58.
20a. C. H. Murphy, *Free Flight Motion of Symmetric Projectiles*, Ballistic Research Laboratories Report No. 1216, July 1963, 234 pp.
20b. C. H. Murphy, *Data Reduction for the Free Flight Spark Ranges*, Ballistic Research Laboratories Report No. 900, February 1954, 63 pp.
20c. C. H. Murphy, Comments on "A method for extraction of aerodynamic coefficients from free-flight data," *AIAA J.* **8**, 2109–2111 (1970).
21. J. Corner, *Theory of the Interior Ballistics of Guns*. Wiley, New York; Chapman and Hall, London, 1950.
22. C. J. Tranter, C. A. Clemmow, G. H. Hinds, and F. R. W. Hunt, *Internal Ballistics*, New York University Press, New York, 1951.
23. E. D. Lowry, *Interior Ballistics. How a Gun Converts Chemical Energy into Projectile Motion*, Doubleday, Garden City, New York, 1968.
24. J. H. Giese, *A Bibliography for the Numerical Solution of Partial Differential Equations*, Ballistic Research Laboratories, Memo Report No. 2114, July 1971, 516 pp. Available only from U.S. Department of Commerce, National Technical Information Service, Springfield, Va.
25. B. Lewis and G. von Elbe, *Combustion, Flames and Explosions*, Academic, New York, 1951.
26. R. A. Strehlow, *Fundamentals of Combustion*, International Textbook Co., Scranton, Pa., 1968, xiv + 465 pp.
27. R. Courant and K. O. Friedrichs, *Supersonic Flow and Shock Waves*, Interscience, New York, 1948, xvi + 464 pp.
28. A. E. H. Love and F. B. Pidduck, Lagrange's ballistic problem, *Phil. Trans. Roy. Soc.* (London) **222** 167–226 (1921–22).
29. M. C. Platrier, Analyse du probleme balistique de Lagrange, *Mem. Artillerie Francaise* **15**, 431–477 (1936).
30. L. M. Milne-Thomson, *Theoretical Hydrodynamics*, 3rd ed., Macmillan, New York, 1955.
31. R. Ladenburg, J. Winckler, and C. C. van Voorhis, Interferometric studies of faster than sound phenomena. I, II, *Phys. Rev.* **73**, 1359–1377 (1948); **76** 662–677 (1949).
32. F. D. Bennett, W. C. Carter, and V. E. Bergdolt, Interferometric analysis of airflow about projectiles in free flight, *J. Appl. Phys.* **23**, 453–569 (1952).
33. G. Birkhoff, D. P. MacDougall, E. M. Pugh, and G. I. Taylor, Explosives with lined cavities, *J. Appl. Phys.* **19**, 563–582 (1948).
34. J. W. Leech, E. A. Witmer, and T. H. H. Pian, Numerical calculation technique for large elastic-plastic transient deformations of thin shells, *AIAA J.* **6**, 2352–2359 (1968).
35. L. Morino, J. W. Leech, and E. A. Witmer, An improved numerical calculation technique for large elastic-plastic transient deformation of thin shells. 1. Background for large elastic-plastic formulas. 2. Evaluation and applications,

Trans. Amer. Soc. Mech. Engrs., Ser. E.-J. Appl. Mech. **38,** 423–428, 429–436 (1971).
36. J. M. Santiago, *Formulation of the Large Deflection Shell Equations for Use in Finite Difference Structural Response Computer Codes,* Ballistic Research Laboratories Report No. 1571, February 1972, 158 pp.
37. T. Leser and J. Lanahan, *New Method for Reducing Data on Interior Ballistic Trajectories,* Ballistic Research Laboratories Report No. 1024, 1957.
38. S. Gorn and M. L. Juncosa, *On the Computational Procedures for Firing and Bombing Tables,* Ballistic Research Laboratories Report No. R 889, 1954.
39. R. F. Lieske and M. L. Reiter, *Equations of Motion for a Modified Point Mass Trajectory,* Ballistic Research Laboratories Report No. 1314, March 1966, 26 pp.
40. H. J. Breaux, *An Efficiency Study of Several Techniques for the Numerical Integration of the Equations of Motion for Missiles and Shell,* Ballistic Research Laboratories Report No. 1358, February 1967.
41. T. M. Canning, A. Sieff, and C. S. James (eds.), Ballistic range technology, *AGARDograph* **138** (1970).
42. G. T. Chapman and D. B. Kirk, Obtaining accurate aerodynamic force and moment results from ballistics tests, *AGARD Conf. Proc.* **10,** *The Fluid Dynamic Aspects of Ballistics* (September 1966).
43. G. T. Chapman and D. B. Kirk, A method for extraction of aerodynamic coefficients from free-flight data, *AIAA J.* **8,** 753–758 (1970).
44. R. H. Whyte, A. Jeung, and J. W. Bradley, *Chapman-Kirk Reduction of Free-Flight Range Data to Obtain Nonlinear Aerodynamic Coefficients.* Ballistic Research Laboratories Memo Report No. 2298, May 1973, 67 pp.
45. J. W. Bradley, *CHLOE: A Fortran Subroutine for Fitting Ordinary Differential Equations to Observed Data,* Ballistic Research Laboratories Memo Report No. 2184, April 1972, 49 pp.

John H. Giese

BAND LIMITED FUNCTIONS

To motivate the theory of band limited functions, it is first necessary to digress and examine linear systems. For a mathematically linear system (time invariant), if the input x_1 produces output y_1 and input x_2 produces output y_2, then the input $c_1 x_1 + c_2 x_2$ produces output $c_1 y_1 + c_2 y_2$, where c_1 and c_2 are constants. We often find that over a reasonable range, physical systems are well approximated by this mathematical model.

If the input to a mathematical linear system is a sinusoid, say

$$x(t) = A_1 \cos \omega t$$

then the output will have the same frequency ω, but may have a different amplitude

[24]
BAND LIMITED FUNCTIONS

and relative phase; that is, the output will be of the form

$$y(t) = A_0 \cos(\omega t + \phi)$$

The coefficients A_0 and ϕ are functions of ω but not of t. Usually it is the ratio of the output to the input that is of importance, so we often study the *transfer function amplitude*

$$\left| A_0/A_1 \right|$$

as a function of frequency ω.

In physical systems it is quite common to find that this ratio is large for some interval in ω and small outside it. The interval is called a *band*. For example, a hi-fi system may have a transfer function amplitude that is large in a band, say from 16 to 18,000 Hz, and is small outside this band. Servo mechanisms and information transmission systems all tend to have fairly sharp bands of transmission.

A second basis for the importance of band limited functions arises in the mathematical approach to sampling at equally spaced intervals. If we sample at, say, $t = 0, 1, 2, \ldots$, we find that for a sinusoid $A \cos \omega t$, with ω so large that there are less than two samples in a complete cycle, we will seem to see a sinusoid of a lower frequency which has at least two samples in its cycle. This "aliasing" of high frequencies into lower frequencies can be understood as being a simple consequence of the trigonometric identity

$$\cos(\pi + a)t - \cos(\pi - a)t = -2 \sin \pi t \sin at = 0$$

for $t = 0, 1, 2, \ldots$. It is a familiar phenomenon to TV viewers of Westerns where the stage coach wheels appear to start turning, gradually come to a halt, and then appear to start turning backwards as the coach itself appears to gradually speed up. It is also seen when a stroboscope is used and the high frequency appears as a low frequency.

If the sampling interval is taken to be unity, then the band into which all higher frequencies are aliased is $-\pi \leq \omega \leq \pi$. This band, called the Nyquist interval, is thus a natural concept in any equally spaced sampling system.

The sampling theorem of information theory states that the formal expression

$$f(t) = \sum_{k=-\infty}^{\infty} f(k) \left[\frac{\sin \pi(t-k)}{\pi(t-k)} \right]$$

exactly reproduces the original band limited function $f(t)$ from its samples $f(k)$. Thus band limited functions have both a physical and a mathematical reality in sampling theory. Usually the physical realization is not sharply cut off at the ends of the band, but it does tend to fall off fairly rapidly.

In the theory of Fourier series the aliasing produces the following effect. Let the Fourier series expansion of the continuous function $f(t)$ be

$$f(t) = a_0/2 + \sum_{k=1}^{\infty} \left[a_k \cos\left(\frac{\pi k t}{N}\right) + b_k \sin\left(\frac{\pi k t}{N}\right) \right]$$

and let the finite Fourier series based on $2N$ equally spaced samples be

$$f(t) = A_0/2 + \sum_{k=1}^{N-1} \left[A_k \cos\left(\frac{\pi k t}{N}\right) + B_k \sin\left(\frac{\pi k t}{N}\right) \right] + (A_N/2) \cos(\pi t)$$

BAND LIMITED FUNCTIONS

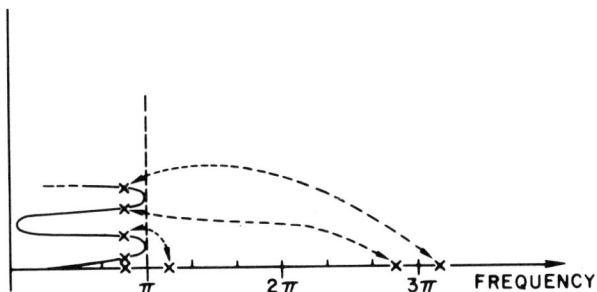

Fig. 1. Effect of aliasing.

($t = 0, 1, 2, \ldots, 2N - 1$). The coefficients of the two expansions are related by the equations

$$A_k = a_k + \sum_{j=1}^{\infty}\left[a_{2Nj-k} + a_{2Nj+k}\right]$$

$$B_k = b_k + \sum_{j=1}^{\infty}\left[-b_{2Nj-k} + b_{2Nj+k}\right]$$

From this we can see the general picture of the alias effect (Fig. 1).

Although we have discussed the aliasing effect based on the Fourier series representation of a periodic function, it also applies to the Fourier integral representation,

$$f(t) = \int_{-\infty}^{\infty} F(\sigma)e^{2\pi i\sigma t}\,d\sigma$$

$$F(\sigma) = \int_{-\infty}^{\infty} f(t)e^{-2\pi i\sigma t}\,dt$$

Since, as we have shown, there is a close parallelism between the physical and mathematical models, it follows that from one we can often accurately estimate the other. From the physics, or the engineering, we can often estimate the highest frequency present (to any great extent) and therefore know *before* we start a computation what sampling interval (rate) will be reasonable. Conversely, from the way the computation goes and what step sizes were necessary, we can thus know fairly accurately the highest frequencies present in the simulation.

In the Fourier integral approach we deal with the continuous distribution of functions

$$e^{2\pi i\sigma t} \equiv e^{i\omega t} \quad (\omega = 2\pi\sigma)$$

Given any linear formula, then to find what it does to various frequencies we have only to substitute $y(t) = e^{i\omega t}$ into the formula. For a linear formula it will always happen that the dependence on t (or on the variable sample point indexed by, say, n) will factor out and we get a form

$$H(\omega)e^{i\omega t}$$

**[26]
BAND LIMITED FUNCTIONS**

The term $H(\omega)$ describes what happens to a frequency ω. If

$$\left. \begin{array}{l} |H(\omega)| > 1 \text{ amplification} \\ |H(\omega)| < 1 \text{ attenuation} \end{array} \right\} \text{ at frequency } \omega$$

As an example, consider the difference operator

$$\Delta y_n = y_{n+1} - y_n = e^{i\omega(t+1)} - e^{i\omega t}$$
$$= ie^{i\omega/2}[2 \sin(\omega/2)]e^{i\omega t}$$

The first factor $ie^{i\omega/2}$ has size 1. The other factor $2 \sin(\omega/2)$ is less than 1 in size for $-\pi/3 < \omega < \pi/3$ (the Nyquist interval being $-\pi \leq \omega \leq \pi$). Thus the difference operator amplifies all frequencies in the original function $f(t)$ that are outside this band and attenuates those inside. Repeated differencing as in a difference table simply raises the factor $H(\omega)$ to higher and higher powers.

Linear formulas for differentiation, integration, and smoothing by least squares can similarly be analyzed.

BIBLIOGRAPHY

Hamming, R. W., *Numerical Methods for Scientists and Engineers*, 2nd ed., McGraw-Hill, New York, 1973.
Hamming, R. W., *Studies in Numerical Analysis: Papers Presented to Cornelius Lanczos*, Academic, London, 1974.
Lanczos, C., *Applied Analysis*, Prentice-Hall, Englewood Cliffs, N. J., 1956.
Lanczos, C., *Linear Differential Operators*, Van Nostrand, Princeton, N. J., 1961.

R. W. Hamming

BANKING

Computers in banking are used mainly as data processors capable of collecting, sorting, analyzing, storing, and transforming data into useful information. Electronic computers and their related technologies brought automation to banking in the form of electronic data processing (EDP).

The impact of computers on banking can best be examined by utilizing the concept of a computer "generation." This concept has been fostered as a means of describing the attributes of the kinds of computer systems in use during a specific time period.

BANKING

The "FIRST GENERATION" of business application computers relied on vacuum tubes and began with the delivery of a Remington Rand UNIVAC-1 in October 1954 and an IBM 650 in December of the same year. Computers entered the banking industry in 1955 with the delivery of an IBM 702 computer to the Bank of America in San Francisco. The computer was installed as an extension of the existing tabulating machine systems to perform general accounting and routine report listings. In September 1955, Stanford Research Institute publicly demonstrated the first electronic recording machine-accounting (ERMA) system that was capable of "reading" and processing paper checks. This pioneering work was sponsored by Bank of America and had taken 5 years to develop.

One of the most significant events during the first generation use of computers in banking was the July 21, 1956, report of the American Banking Association (ABA) committee recommending the adoption of magnetic ink character recognition (MICR) as a standard means of processing checks.

In 1958, the location, size, and type font (E-13B) to be used on MICR encoded checks was agreed upon, making possible a common machine language that would permit the automatic handling of checks throughout the banking system.

The use of MICR and the advent of second generation computers permitted a direct input from source documents (checks), thus removing one of the primary bottlenecks associated with check processing. The cost and clerical problems associated with transferring information from checks onto punch cards for use by first generation computers would have been prohibitive. To this day, check processing is one of the most labor intensive applications in a commercial bank.

SECOND GENERATION

The second generation of computers in banking began in 1958 with the delivery of a GE-100 to the Bank of America. The GE-100 was a transistorized computer and an integral part of the first full-scale ERMA system. Thirty ERMA systems using the GE-100 were placed in operation for the Bank of America and consisted of the following:

1. GE-100 computer.
2. A check reader-sorter that read magnetic ink encoded characters imprinted on the back of the check.
3. A high-speed printer.
4. Magnetic tape units.

With the advent of the second generation of computers (1958 through 1964) came the installation of computers in banks of all sizes, but mainly to banks with deposits of over $100 million. During this second generation there was a concentrated effort to convert as many of the manual procedures as possible to the computer. The justification for this approach was twofold:

1. The expected gain in efficiency and the increase in the volume processed brought about by the increased processing capabilities of the computer.

BANKING

    2. To offset the high rental cost of computer equipment by converting as many of the clerical tasks as possible, thereby decreasing the need for clerical-type employees.

As the manual procedures used in processing the different applications (checking accounts, savings accounts, installment loans, mortgage loans, etc.) were converted to second generation computerized systems, each was treated as a single application. Each application maintained its own data base, and cross referencing between data bases was difficult if not impossible. To determine if a customer had a checking account, a savings account, and a loan outstanding required a search of each of the different applications. Many banks created a central information file (CIF) to handle this problem. These CIFs were manual systems that could provide the type and number of accounts a customer had with the bank, but they could not provide timely information on the activity or the balances in those accounts.

THIRD GENERATION

With the announcement of the third generation microcircuitry computer and its orientation to direct access and communications processings, opportunities for the development of an automated central information system (CIS) seemed possible. The increasing demand for additional information that could be used by management (management information system—MIS) to evaluate the profitability of customer accounts and to define relationships between applications reinforced the need for a computer-controlled integrated data base.

In a CIS/MIS integrated system, there is a requirement for an inquiry-oriented information system with the ability to develop, maintain, and update a master account file that is organized in such a way that information processing and retrieval systems can both be accommodated, i.e., provisions for inquiry response and file interrelationships within a processing system. The immense difficulty involved in actually getting the highly complicated and interrelated bank MIS/CIS systems to operate within the multifile, multiprogramming (ability to process several jobs at the same time) capabilities brought about by third generation advances were not immediately apparent. For the purpose of efficiency, economy, and practicality, both a CIS and MIS should use the same data base, but the conflicting requirements of each system have limited their development to subsystems, e.g., customer information file (CIS subsystem) and financial information system (MIS subsystem).

The third generation hardware offered a tremendous increase in computing speed, massive internal and external storage capabilities at a greatly reduced cost from the second generation computer's capabilities, and the built-in hardware to adapt readily to the communications requirements for the checkless society contemplated by the banking industry.

From the theme of the 1967 American Bankers Association Automation Conference, "Stepping-Stones to the Checkless Society," one could infer that there was a consensus that sooner or later, in one form or another, there would evolve new systems for the transferring of money and that these systems would eventually lead to a plateauing and then a reduction in check usage. In all, five stepping-stones were thought to be necessary to realize a reduction in check usage. The first and second stepping-stones were the development of computer capacity and communications capabilities required to interface directly with the customer. The third stepping-stone was the customer terminal or, in more definitive terms, the point-of-sale terminal. A requirement of the point-of-sale terminal was the capability for customer identification and verification at the terminal itself. This requirement was referred to as stepping-stone 4. Following the development of the first four stepping-stones, banks would have to develop a host of new banking services that would utilize the systems of computers, communication links, terminals, and customer verification systems. This development of new services was referred to as the 5th stepping-stone.

FOURTH GENERATION

With the advent of fourth generation computers (1970–present) all five stepping-stones had been realized to a degree. The majority of the larger banks had converted their critical applications to third and/or fourth generation computers.

The trend has been to move from an operational philosophy of multiple smaller computers at different locations to a concept of a large, very powerful centralized computer system with communication capabilities for remote access computing. Two or more (multiprocessing) central computers with shared files and the capability of handling a multitude of jobs simultaneously (multiprogramming, time-sharing) would provide the bank with the centralized processing power and data base necessary for the creation and maintenance of an integrated CIS/MIS bank operating system. What is an integrated CIS/MIS? An objective and a utopia that is hard to describe or define, not to mention realize. Avoiding a definition, we will look at some of the requirements of a bank's total information system (CIS/MIS).

Genuine management information used in the administration of a bank consists of the quantitative (numerical) and the qualitative (relational) descriptions of how effectively the bank is matching its resources with the opportunities and realities of the market. An example of the quantitative aspect, of the management information requirement, would be the fact that income received from auto loans was $125,000 during the last quarter of 1972. The value $125,000 is a piece of purely numerical information which is of significance even if it is out of context with regard to the economic environment, service method (direct or indirect markets), bank marketing objectives, and any other factors which imply a relationship. In contrast, qualitative information defines relationships as structural causality. The same information in structural form would be the following:

$$\text{Auto loan income} = \text{direct market} + \text{indirect market}$$
$$= \text{auto loan-bank} + (\text{auto loan-dealer} + \text{auto loan-agency})$$

This, too, is information even though it contains not a single numerical value. It expresses the relationship that total auto loan income is received by providing loan services directly to customers and indirectly to the same class of customers through intermediaries. It is a piece of purely relational data without regard to numerical

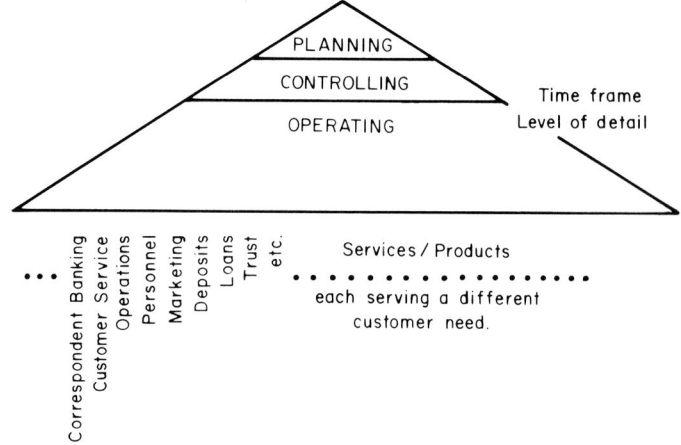

Fig. 1. Three levels of management information requirements.

content. The purpose of this example is to illustrate that there are different types of information—numerical and relational.

To be effective, a computerized information system must maintain two different and separate repositories—the first containing the numerical data and the second containing the relationships. The numerical data repository is called the data base and the relationship repository is called the model. The data base provides an on-going image of the (day-to-day) operations of the organization. The function of the model is to improve the information available to management and consequently improve management's ability to carry out its activities. An effective information system must filter and condense detailed information in order to yield what is relevant and useful. The rules for filtration, condensation, etc., are precisely what we mean by a model. The model reflects the information requirements of the different activities of managers.

For purpose of illustration, we can oversimplify the activities of managers into three basic categories—planning, controlling and operating. This is the traditional management pyramid model based on the assumption that the activities of managers are subordinate to their organizational position, or vice versa. Figure 1 is a representation of the three different levels of management's information needs.

The three levels of management activities are differentiated by the time horizon and level of information detail required. At an operating level, a manager would need to know the outstanding balance in an account on a day-to-day basis. At a control level the manager would be interested in only the average balance in an account for the month or quarter. At a planning level a manager would not be interested in the average balance in a specific account but rather the average balance in all accounts serving a specified market. The added relationships or dimensions may be visualized as the 3-dimensional cube shown in Fig. 2.

The information used in either strategic planning or management control requires periodic accumulation and analysis. The information that is accumulated and used by higher level management is mostly that which is collected and maintained at the operational level. One of the most common mistakes has been that of providing one level of management with information designed for use by another level. Many of the so-called customer information files (CIF), customer relation files (CRF), central information files (CIF), and automated central files (ACF) are designed to profile each customer and define a single customer's account relationships with the bank but cannot assist management in defining customer characteristics and/or needs. A bank's own customers provide one of the best sources for market research information, but its use is normally limited to operational requirements. Few, if any, of the present CIF, CRF, or ACF systems could produce a composite profile of, say, their customers to determine:

> How many of them use other bank services and what are the services most frequently used by mortgage borrowers with our bank.
> The average income of the borrower with relation to the size of the mortgage and to the number of other services desired.
> If the borrower has a checking account, what is the relationship of the number and average amount of debits to his account and to the number of other services.

A CIF, CRF, or ACF should be capable of measuring advertising or promotional effectiveness. This would include an information processing ability of assisting in the determination of the role of advertising and promotions in the customer's decision-making process, and of measuring the results of specific campaigns. If we add this customer information requirement as a fourth dimension (Fig. 3) to our 3-dimensional information cube, you can begin to see the difficulty of maintaining an integrated CIS/MIS.

If we return to our first assumption that to be effective a computerized information system must maintain two different and separate repositories—the first containing the numerical (alphameric) data base and the second containing the relationship—an integrated CIS/MIS would be an overlay of a relationship and alphameric data base. Its purpose would be to provide management with information about the internal (MIS) and external (CIS) environment in which the bank operates.

The data base problem can be solved by the advent of the high-speed monolithic memories, with storage cycle access speeds of less than 2 μsec to eight bytes of data,

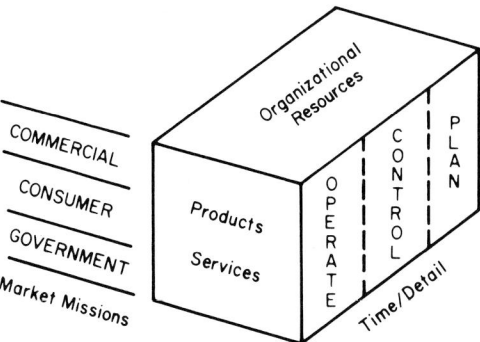

Fig. 2. Time horizon and level of detail required to support the management functions.

BANKING

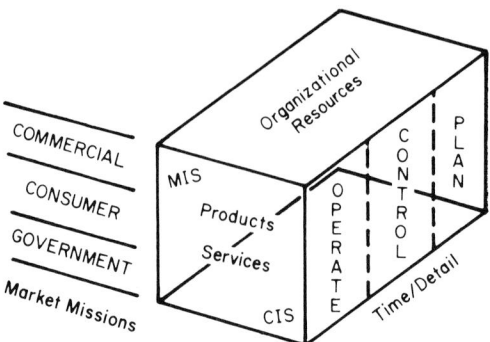

Fig. 3. Addition of the customer information requirement.

brought about by fourth generation equipment. The real unsolved problems are the definition and utilization of the relationships contained among the elements in the data base and the "integrated" CIS/MIS which combines the horizon of product–market strategy planning with the details of operations.

COMPUTER APPLICATIONS IN BANKING

Banking is a service industry providing a host of financial services (products) to the consumer and commercial markets. Computers have made possible the transformation of banks from a paper-shuffling, record-keeping operation to a manufacturer of financial and processing services. In 1968 the American Bankers Association's Department of Automation provided a list of services for banks to use when preparing an inventory of the services offered by the bank. Table 1 is a copy of that list. Even then, the list was thought to be incomplete, but was representative of the varied services offered by banks. Since that time many new services have been created. To explain all the services listed in Table 1 and to enumerate and explain all the new services presently available in banking is obviously beyond the scope of a broad definition of "computers in banking," but an explanation of a representative service is in order.

The most labor intensive service in banking today is the check processing operation—demand deposits. A recent survey by the Banking Administration Institute revealed that to process 10,000 items, the average bank will require approximately 7.4 hr of encoding, 5 hr for balancing and correction, 1.7 hr for reader-sorter operation, 3.7 hr for cash letter make-up and microfilming, 11.7 hr for processing on-us items, 2.6 hr for tracing and adjustments, and 9 hr of miscellaneous labor. This is a total of 41.1 hr to process 10,000 items.

The different operations within the check processing operation are described in detail in the following pages. The reason for giving an overview of the process at this time is to relate to the reader the magnitude of the workload created by check processing.

TABLE 1.
Preliminary Categorization of Bank Functions (and/or Services)

EXCHANGE FUNCTION
- Currency
  - United States
  - Foreign
- Official checks, money orders, etc.
- Tellers' checks
- Foreign drafts
- Travelers' letters of credit
- Travelers' checks
- Mail, wire, cable transfers

REVENUE-PRODUCING FUNCTION
- Bonds
- Stocks
- Trading
  - Bonds
  - Foreign exchange
- Business loans
  - Brokers
  - Demand
  - Time
  - Term
  - Revolving credits
  - Advances
    - Against letters of credit
    - Against collections
  - Commercial paper
  - Acceptances
    - Bankers
    - Customers
  - Chattel mortgage financing
  - Real estate loans
  - Ship loans
  - Lease financing
  - Railway equipment leasing
  - Floor plan financing
  - Warehouse receipt financing
  - Participations
  - Accounts receivable financing
  - Trust receipt financing
  - Commercial letters of credit
  - Guarantees and endorsements
  - Commitments
- Supplemental record keeping
  - Central liability
  - Collateral
  - Credit files
  - Accruals
- Consumer loans
  - Noninstallment

(continued)

BANKING

TABLE 1 (continued)

        Installment
        Revolving check credit
        Credit cards
        Passbook loans
        Guaranteed education loans
        Home improvement loans
        Insurance premium financing
        Dealer paper
    Mortgages
        Home mortgages
        Building loans
        "Single debit" serviced mortgages
        Mortgage servicing
        Mortgage warehousing
        Escrow records

DEPOSIT FUNCTION

    Demand
        Government
        Due to banks
        Checking accounts
        Customers foreign currency
        Federal funds
        Preauthorized transfers
        Account analysis
    Time
        Savings
        Club accounts
        Certificates of deposit
        Savings certificates
        Time open accounts

FIDUCIARY FUNCTION

    Corporate
        Registrar
        Transfer agent
        Dividend paying agent
        Bond trustee
        Stock and bondholder records
        Other agencies
    Personal
        History file
        Guardian
        Investment management
        Investment advisor
        Estate administration
        Trustee
        Committee
        Safekeeping
        Custody
    Pension trust
    Mutual funds

TABLE 1 (continued)

    Employee welfare funds
    Common trust funds

COLLECTION FUNCTION

    Inward
    Outward
    Clean drafts
    Documentary drafts
    Coupon
    Proof and transit
    Freight payments clearing
    Lockbox
    Night depository

ACCOUNTING FUNCTION

    Land
    Other real estate
    Banking premises
    Furniture and fixtures
    Forms and supplies
    Depreciation schedules
    Supervisory reports
    Taxes
    Personnel
        Payroll
        Profit sharing
    Auditing
    Correspondence files
    Stenography and typing
    Stockholder records and transfer
    Dividend accounting—stockholders
    Accounts receivable
    Accounts payable
    Budgets
    Cost accounting
    Computer log analysis
    General ledger
    Expense accounting
    Daily profit and loss

RESEARCH FUNCTION

    Marketing
    Economics

SERVICE FUNCTION

    Consumer
        Automatic insurance draft plan
        Safe deposit box rental
        Insurance policies
        Travel agency
        United States savings bonds

(continued)

BANKING

TABLE 1 (continued)

Business
Mathematical models
Correspondent portfolio review
Demand deposits for correspondents
Account reconcilements
Inventory
Payroll
Sales analysis
Graphs
Gold handicaps
Registration mailing
Accounts receivable billing
Franchise agency
Church pledges
Retail
Cable television
Country club
Medical
Professional
Sewer authority
Real estate
Rents
Water department
Municipal tax
Accounting for
Alumni fund
Agriculture
Auto lease
Brokerage houses
Clubs
Hospitals
Credit unions
Insurance company
Savings and loan associations

CHECK PROCESSING

Checks are received from a varied number of sources—the Federal Reserve banking system, the local clearing house, correspondent banks, and from the mail and counter depositories of the bank. The checks from other than internal sources are normally already coded with MICR. The checks that are not coded are sent through encoding machines where the amount of each check is MICR-encoded in the bottom right-hand corner of the check. Following encoding, the amount of the check is matched against the amount MICR-encoded on the check to insure that they have been encoded properly. Checks incorrectly encoded are reprocessed for correction. Checks are then batched and processed through computer-controlled MICR reader-sorters where the computer transfers the information on each check to a transaction tape and sorts them into two categories: those payable at the processing bank (on-us) and those payable at another bank.

Checks drawn on other banks are resorted by geographic location and either sent through the Federal Reserve Bank, the local clearing house, or a correspondent bank to the location of the paying bank. Accompanying the checks is a cash letter for the total amount of the checks. Cash letters are the means by which a bank bills another bank for paying checks drawn on their bank.

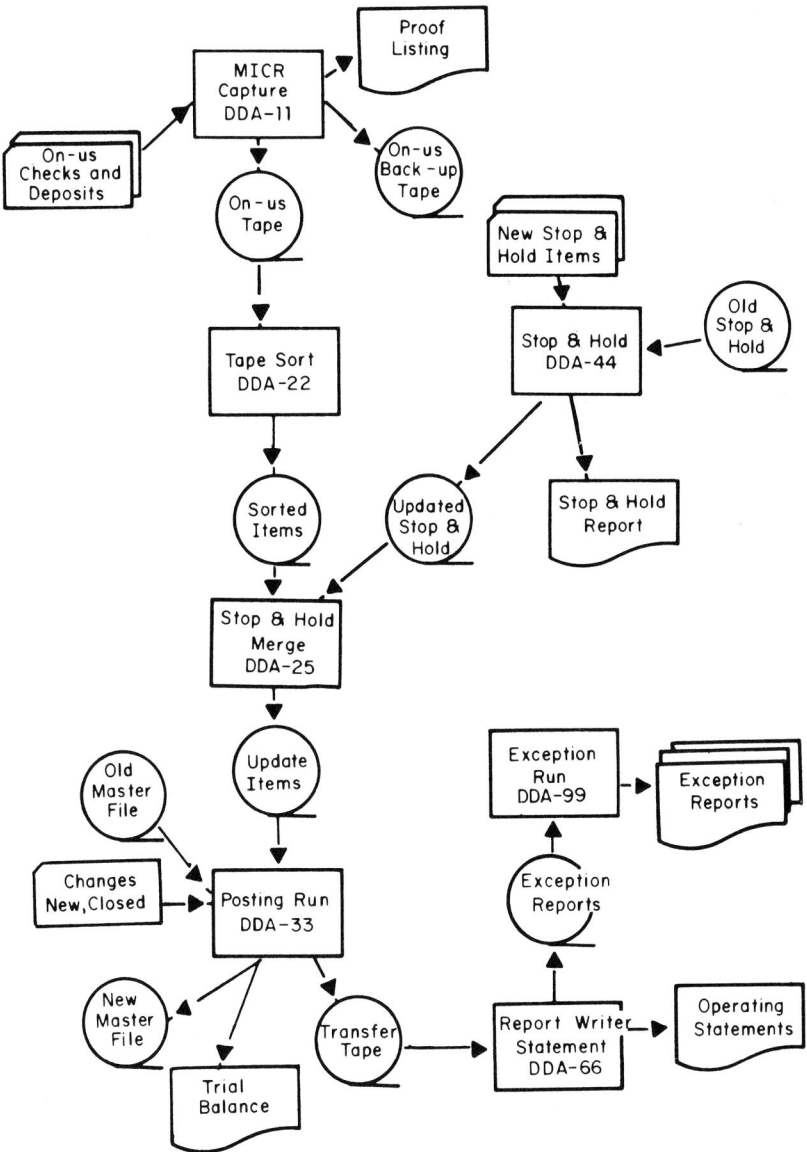

Fig. 4. Demand deposit accounting (DDA) systems flow chart.

BANKING

Checks drawn on the processing bank are resorted by account number and processed through the bank's demand deposit accounting (DDA) system. The DDA application handles all the bookkeeping associated with checking accounts. Figure 4 is a systems flow chart of a typical tape-oriented DDA system. An actual DDA system would require a greater degree of sophistication than illustrated to exemplify the flexibility contained in the DDA systems presently available.

A COMPUTER UTILITY

As mentioned earlier, the trend in banking has been to move from an operational philosophy of multiple smaller computers at different locations to a concept of a centralized computer utility with communications capabilities for remote access computing. A multiprocessor installation of two or more IBM System/370-165s with 2,000,000 characters of memory, each coupled with a "virtual memory" operating system, gives a bank an almost unlimited main memory capacity. It is not uncommon for a computer utility of this size to have an additional 4 or 5 billion characters of direct access disk storage. A computer utility of this size would provide the processing power, flexibility, and storage capacity necessary to control a wide range of communication terminals performing integrated on-line banking applications, as would be the mode of operations in a bank-wide teleprocessing network. The operation of a bank computer utility would not vary greatly from that of any other utility. The applications that are processed would be different but the operation would be similar. The real difference would be in the operations of the teleprocessing network and the type of terminals that would be employed.

TYPES OF TERMINALS

There are many types of terminals in a bank-wide teleprocessing network but all would fall under the following general categories of remote access terminals:

1. Intelligent terminals
   a. Satellite mode
2. Nonintelligent terminals
   a. Interactive mode
   b. Remote batch mode

The intelligent terminals are computers which have limited computing power and which can be programmed for certain bank functions. They employ a variety of the card, print, tape, disk, and reader/sorter peripherals required to serve as a satellite system for transaction or batch activities. The intelligent terminals are large enough to be used as stand-alone computers and alternatively used for either communications and local processing or, in some instances, with the communications load as a background function which runs concurrently with the normal processing operations. The nonintelligent terminal, which is not a computer *per se*, is linked to the central computer in an interactive or remote batch mode. The interactive mode is a back and forth communication link with the computer. For each request, there is an immediate reply. The interactive terminals range from simple CRT consoles used to enter or retrieve information from the central computer to elaborate teller or credit card point-of-sale terminals. The remote batch mode is a delayed communication link with the computer. Requests are not acted upon immediately. As requests are received by the computer, they are placed in a queue and the computer acts on the request as its work load permits. The remote batch terminals have 4 to $24K$ memory and the variety of card, print, tape, and disk peripherals required for remote job entry into and reply from the central computer.

COMMUNICATION LINKS

Remote terminals are connected to the central computer complex by various means with data transmission lines. The lines vary depending upon the line speed or the number of characters that can be transmitted, ranging from a low speed of 10 to 30 characters/sec for typewriter keyboard-type terminals using voice grade lines to speeds greater than 40,800 bits/sec, or 5100 characters/sec at 8-bits/character, utilizing microwave or wide-band telephone transmission techniques. (For comparison purposes, a 1000 line/min printer will print at about 2000 characters/sec maximum.) The communication link to the computer can be a simple dial-up arrangement on existing phone circuits or a dedicated leased line. Data sets (or modems) are required at both ends of the transmission lines to provide proper interfacing of the two systems using different signaling conventions, the computer system and the telephone network. The modem's basic function is to convert digital signals to analog signals and vice versa. The speed of transmission with modems or data sets is usually classified as follows:

Speed	Terminal mode
Low (up to 300 bits/sec)	Interactive
Medium (1200 to 2400 bits/sec)	Interactive/remote
High (3600 to 9600 bits/sec)	Remote/satellite
Very high (19,200 to 500,000 bits/sec)	Satellite

Presently, data sets have been marketed with capabilities above 2000 bits/sec for dial-up (2400, 3600 bits/sec) and at numerous speeds of transmissions for the leased lines (2400, 3600, 4800, 9600 bits/sec). This has made it possible to transmit to and from intelligent terminals and drive higher speed printers and card readers at reasonable rates of speed without resorting to wide-band or Telpac lines (19,200 and 40,800 bits/sec). Figure 5 is an illustration of a representative statewide bank teleprocessing network.

[40]
BANKING

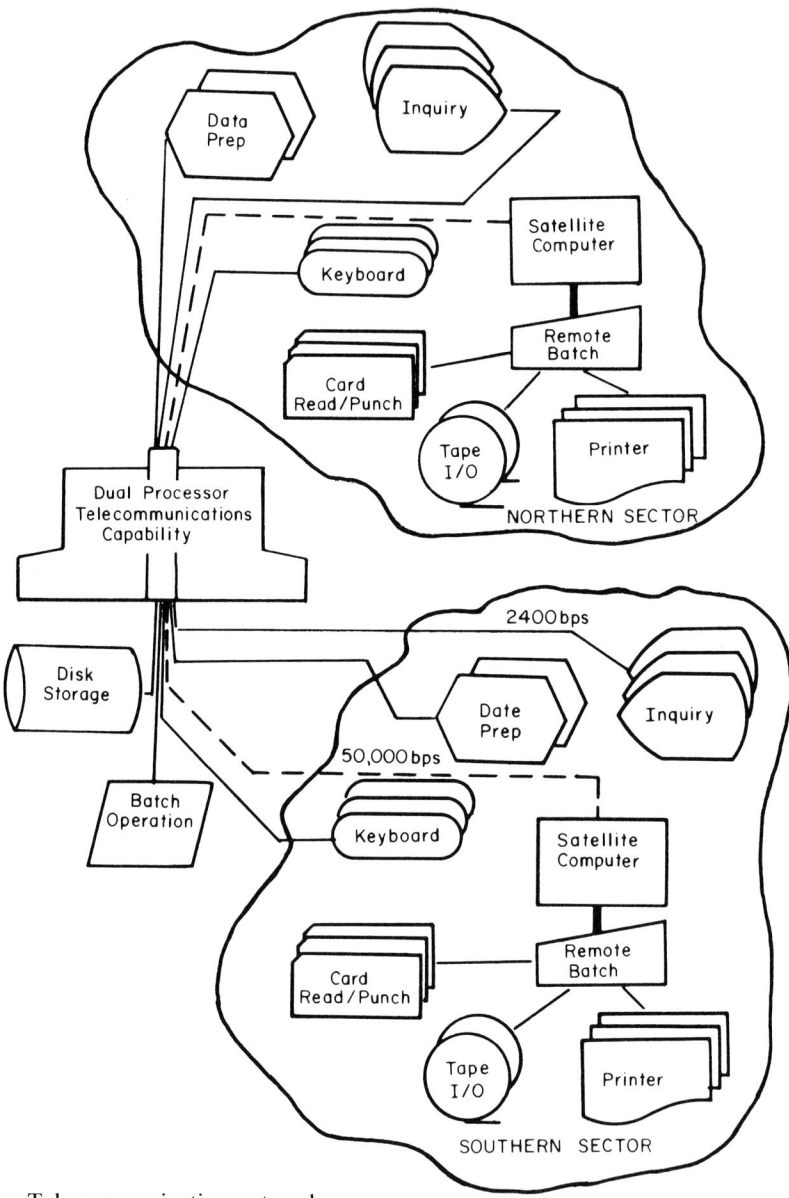

Fig. 5. Telecommunication network.

TELEPROCESSING SERVICES

Touch tone phones (or conventional phones with touch tone pads) may be connected to the computer and used as input-output devices. If the computer includes an audio response unit, a teller can key in an account number and an inquiry code, and the computer will "speak" in a pleasant feminine voice to the teller through the telephone, stating the customer's balances, a complete relationship, or whatever else the teller requests. The teller can also place stop-payment, record checks cashed, and the like. Using a two digit inquiry code, over 100 different options are possible. Inquiry terminals are used by tellers and bank officers for determining the status of an account, but they perform no actual posting. Savings teller terminals resemble savings window posting machines and post information to the computer record and to the customer's passbook. Savings terminals of this type are not only on-line but also real time—posting the bank's records while the transaction is being consummated. The cash-dispensing machine introduced by Docutel in 1969 and the total tellers introduced in August 1971 were not on-line real-time systems but rather intelligent terminals controlled by minicomputers. The newer cash-dispensing terminals have digital controllers (front end minicomputers) that dispense funds, continuously update, and maintain current balances on-line or off-line. Each cash-dispensing terminal has a slot to accept customers' magnetically encoded card (American Banking Association has standardized the magnetic tape stripe on the back of banking credit cards). Insertion of the card into the slot forms the first part of the authorization for withdrawal. The customer then keys in his own personal code, followed by the amount of cash he wishes to withdraw in prespecified increments (5, 10, 15, 25). His request for money is transmitted to the central computer via telephone lines. On receipt, the central computer system verifies that it is a valid request, that there are funds to cover the transaction, and the money is then issued by the machine. The total teller terminal permits withdrawal from savings accounts, checking accounts, transfer from a savings account to a checking account, etc. They provide a 24 hr/day completely unattended, totally automated, self-service banking facility.

The electronic fund transfer system links businesses and even individuals to banks. If a bank in Kansas City wishes to transfer $1 million to a bank in New York city, the Kansas City bank sends a message via its computer to the Federal Reserve Bank of Kansas. The Fed's computer checks the transmission for legitimacy and accuracy, then reformats the message and transmits it directly through the Federal Reserve communications facility at Culpeper, Va., and on through the Federal Reserve Bank of New York to the New York recipient bank. The methods of electronic funds transfer insures that data is properly routed and transmitted with electronic accuracy in a matter of minutes.

Another form of electronic funds transfer got underway on October 16, 1972, when California banks started a statewide program of paperless deposits and bill paying. Individual bank customers could authorize their employers to deposit their pay into their checking account automatically and/or arrange for automatic payments of some, or all, other recurring bills, such as mortgage and loan payments, insurance premiums, and utility bills. In January 1973, five banks in Atlanta, Ga. were in the process of implementing an automated clearing house and were gearing up a marketing strategy to sell a bill-payment and direct-deposit-of-payroll package similar to the one in California. These Atlanta banks were members of the Committee on Paperless Entries (COPE) and were contemplating a cooperatively owned citywide retail point-of-sale network including a check verification service, credit card authorization, credit data capture, and a cash card service. As proposed, the system would give the customer the option at the point of sale of paying for a purchase by check, or with a cash credit card that would be used to transfer the funds from the customer's checking account to the merchant's account instantly, or of paying with his bank credit card, thus deferring paying until a later date. If the system is accepted, Atlanta would move into the world of electronic money, beginning the evolutionary shift to on-line point of sale authorization, then to on-line point of sale entry capture, and perhaps transaction processing.

FUTURE

Future progress in the use of computers in banking could see credit card satellites orbiting earth, sending credit card data to a global credit card system of standardized computer processing and a guaranteed money exchange system tied to a magnetically encoded credit card—a true world of electronic money. In corporate banking, customers will be able to use a computer terminal to access the corporation's financial records (held by the bank for their corporate accounts) through the bank's computer. Corporate customers would dial a special number over normal telephone lines and, after identifying themselves through a security code, would be permitted to examine different levels of corporate financial information. Each level of information would be protected by a security procedure so that only authorized personnel could examine or alter information. Corporate treasurers could obtain real-time cash analysis, prearranged automatic extensions and repayment of credit, electronic fund transfers, receivable accounting, and just about any other kind of financial and information service he might want without any direct communication with anyone at the bank. Statements mailed to the corporate customer would show a current position summarized by type of deposit and withdrawals, plus comparisons to last month and last year in dollars, with percent changes indicated. Forecasts of projected cash requirements would also be provided for those customers who were willing to pay for the additional service. The bank will still have lending officers—men who can make deals and arrange for those computerized services that cannot be arranged in advance. He will be a financial consultant, but for the bank's standard products he will serve in more or less the fashion that other salesmen serve and simply act as a contact through which computer-based services will be sold.

Banking of the future *will* be different than banking as we know it today. The industry knows this and is involved in many and varied research projects to be prepared for the banking process of the future.

Joseph E. Michini

BARGAINING THEORY

In many situations of conflict it is found that participants can, through cooperation, obtain better results than those they can guarantee under independent action. On the other hand, there is generally no outcome which is best for all players simultaneously (there would then be no conflict of interest). It is therefore necessary—as a condition for cooperation—to determine which of the many possible outcomes will be pursued. In effect, each player must pay a price for the other players' cooperation, in the sense that he will accept an outcome less desirable than the very best he could hope to obtain. The process of determining the price of this cooperation is known as *bargaining*.

We distinguish two general types of problem: the dual problem, where only two parties are involved; and the plural problem, where three or more parties are involved, so that players have some choice as to their coalition partners. We discuss these two cases below.

TWO-PERSON BARGAINING

The Fixed-Threat Case

In the simplest case, two players can, through trading, cooperation, etc., obtain certain benefits (increments in utility). In case there is no cooperation, neither can affect the other in any way. As a trivial example, we may consider the case of a carpenter with a stack of lumber and a bricklayer with a pile of bricks. Neither one can accomplish anything by acting independently, but together they can build a shed which is worth much more than the original value of the bricks and the lumber. The problem, of course, is to determine how much each will obtain from the proceeds of selling the shed.

In an abstract setting it is assumed that each outcome can be represented by two numbers, u and v, the *utilities* to Players I and II, respectively, of the outcome. The set of all outcomes can then be represented by a set S in the (u, v) plane. The problem is then determined by the set S and by the two numbers, u_0 and v_0—the utility which I and II can obtain in the absence of cooperation. [Of course, it should be remembered that utility is defined only up to a linear transformation; thus a bargaining problem can be represented by many different triples (S, u_0, v_0).]

One further assumption concerns the form of the set S. Usually S is assumed compact (closed and bounded) or, at the very least, bounded above in the sense that the subset

$$S^+ = \{(u, v) \mid u \geq u_0, v \geq v_0\}$$

is compact. Moreover, S is nonempty, containing at least the point (u_0, v_0). Finally, S is convex (this convexity is obtained by means of joint randomizations).

BARGAINING THEORY

In this abstract setting it is impossible to predict the outcome of any bargaining. About all that can be said is that Player I should receive at least u_0, and II should receive at least v_0. "Reasonable" rules are given, however, which are suggested as "fair" outcomes to the bargaining situation and as rules for a possible arbitrator. We may define an arbitration rule as a function which assigns, to each triple (S, u_0, v_0), a pair $(\bar{u}, \bar{v})$, the *solution* (i.e., the suggested outcome) of the bargaining problem.

The most commonly accepted rule is based on a set of six axioms, due to Nash [1]. These axioms are usually known as: (1) feasibility (the point $(\bar{u}, \bar{v})$ should belong to S); (2) individual rationality (each player should get at least his minimal amount, u_0 or v_0); (3) Pareto optimality [there should be no feasible point which both players prefer to $(\bar{u}, \bar{v})$]; (4) invariance under linear transformations (if a problem is changed by a linear transformation, then the solution should be transformed in the same manner); (5) independence of irrelevant alternatives (if the set S is enlarged to a set T, then the solution of the new problem is either the solution of the old problem, or a point not in S); (6) symmetry [the outcome $(\bar{u}, \bar{v})$ must be as symmetric as the problem (S, u_0, v_0) itself].

It can be shown that there is a unique arbitration rule which satisfies these six axioms, and it is the rule which assigns, to the problem (S, u_0, v_0), that point in S^+ which maximizes the product

$$(u - u_0)(v - v_0)$$

Compactness and convexity guarantee that this point is unique.

Geometrically, the point $(\bar{u}, \bar{v})$ can be characterized as follows. It must lie on the Pareto-optimal (i.e., upper right-hand) boundary of the set S; moreover, the line joining (u_0, v_0) to $(\bar{u}, \bar{v})$ and the line which is tangent to S at $(\bar{u}, \bar{v})$ must have slopes which are negatives of each other. [This statement must be slightly modified if the boundary of S is not smooth at $(\bar{u}, \bar{v})$ so that no tangent exists there.] Figure 1 shows the situation here.

The same solution can be obtained by certain alternative arguments. For suppose that the point (u, v) on the Pareto-optimal boundary of S had been suggested as an outcome, and suppose that Player I is not satisfied with this. He may then suggest the point $(u + \Delta u, v + \Delta v)$, also on this boundary, with $\Delta u > 0$, $\Delta v < 0$. Under what conditions should II yield? Zeuthen [2] suggests that II, by yielding, will lose the amount $-\Delta v$; by not yielding, he stands to be reduced to v_0, so that he will lose $v - v_0$. In a similar way, I will lose Δu by yielding, but can lose as much as $u - u_0$ if he does not yield. It is then suggested that II should yield if his relative loss from not yielding is larger than I's loss, i.e., if

$$\frac{v - v_0}{-\Delta v} > \frac{u - u_0}{\Delta u}$$

or, equivalently, if

$$\frac{-\Delta v}{\Delta u} < \frac{v - v_0}{u - u_0}$$

Now, $\Delta v/\Delta u$ is approximately equal to the slope, dv/du, of the tangent line at (u, v).

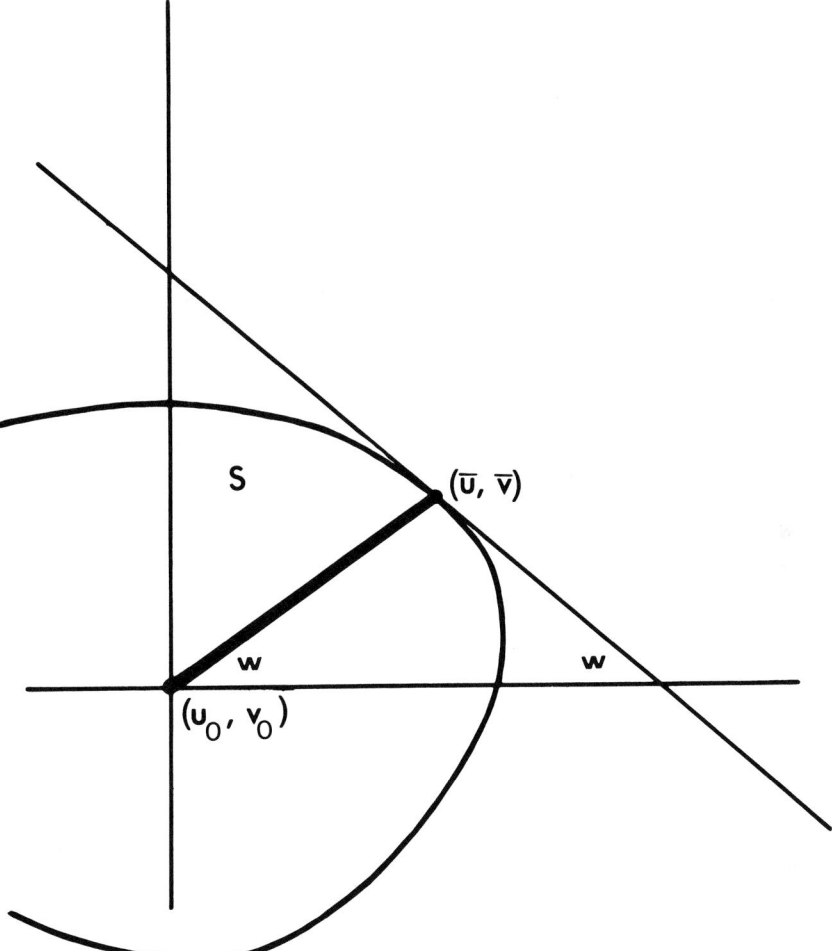

Fig. 1. The two angles w should be equal.

Thus II should yield if
$$-\frac{dv}{du} < \frac{v - v_0}{u - u_0}$$
and similarly, I should make a concession, from (u, v) to $(u - \Delta u, v - \Delta v)$, if
$$-\frac{dv}{du} > \frac{v - v_0}{u - u_0}$$
In this manner, it will follow that (u, v) is stable—in the sense that neither should make a concession if
$$-\frac{dv}{du} = \frac{v - v_0}{u - v_0}$$
This is precisely the characteristic condition given above for the Nash bargaining solution.

BARGAINING THEORY

One final argument can be given. Player I, in making an offer, runs the risk that his offer will not be accepted. It may be argued that II will accept I's offer of (u, v) with a probability that is roughly proportional to $v - v_0$. In this case, I would obtain an increment $u - u_0$ in his utility. His expected gain is therefore $(u - u_0)(v - v_0)$; this is, of course, maximized by the Nash solution.

THE VARIABLE-THREAT CASE

A considerably more complicated case arises when it is possible for the two players to affect each other even in the absence of agreement. The point is that in this case a player may have a wide range of threats, and that his bargaining position is directly affected by the threat which he chooses to employ (e.g., Player II is more likely to yield if Player I draws a gun and threatens to kill him). The situation is further complicated by the fact that the threats which hurt one player most also tend to hurt the other player; for example, I's threat to kill II will also hurt I in that it subjects him to a possible murder trial. Thus it is necessary to determine which player suffers more from a threat. Finally, there is a question of credibility: Will Player I actually pull the trigger? (There is even the problem that some people choose to leave their threats unspoken, being content to look fierce and let their opponent imagine the worst.)

However it may be, the most common model assumes that the threats are made explicit prior to the bargaining, and that there exists some mechanism to enforce the threats, i.e., the threats will definitely be carried out if no agreement is reached.

Suppose, then, that the players have announced their threat strategies, x and y, respectively. If no agreement can be reached, they will use these threats, and so they will receive payoffs which depend on x and y—say $A(x, y)$ and $B(x, y)$ respectively.

Under these circumstances, Players I and II are, in effect, entering a bargaining problem with conflict payoffs of $A(x, y)$ and $B(x, y)$. According to the previous model, they should agree on the point $(\bar{u}, \bar{v})$ which maximizes the product

$$[u - A(x, y)][v - B(x, y)]$$

in the set S^+.

In this model it is clear that the arbitration point $(\bar{u}, \bar{v})$ will depend on the threat strategies x, y. There is, of course, no way of guaranteeing $(\bar{u}, \bar{v})$, but apart from this we may think of the two parties as playing a game with strategies x and y and payoff functions $\bar{u}(x, y), \bar{v}(x, y)$. Figure 2 gives a geometric description of the situation. At each point on the Pareto-optimal boundary S^0 of the feasible set S, a line is drawn whose slope is negative to that of the tangent at that same point. At points such as C, where the tangent does not exist, two lines are drawn corresponding to the right and left tangents to the set.

Now, if the threat strategies, x and y, give a point such as P, on one of the lines, then the arbitrated solution will be the point Q at which this line cuts the curve S^0. If, on the other hand, the threat point is such as R (lying inside the angle between the two lines from C), then the arbitrated solution will be at C, the point at which the two lines meet S^0.

A question naturally arises as to the existence of equilibrium pairs, max-min strategies, values, and such. In fact, it turns out that the behavior of these games is

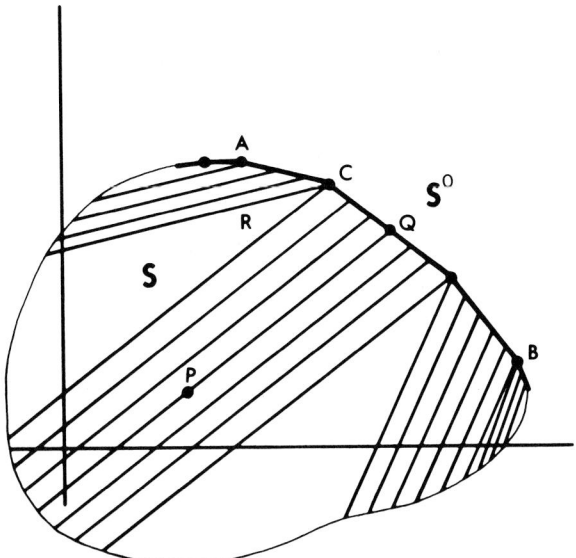

Fig. 2. The variable-threat case.

very similar to that of two-person zero-sum games. If each player has only a finite number of threat strategies, and if mixed strategies are allowed, then the game will have a saddlepoint and a value pair (u^*, v^*). This pair (u^*, v^*) is known as the *Nash solution* of the problem, while the threat strategies x^*, y^* which give rise to this are known as *optimal threat strategies*.

Computation of the optimal threats is quite complicated, since it must take into account both the threat payoff functions $A(x, y)$ and $B(x, y)$ and the shape of the set S (more precisely, its Pareto-optimal boundary S^0). In the finite case, the threat payoffs can be represented by two matrices, A and B; the payoffs for mixed strategies are then x^tAy and x^tBy. In this case the optimal threat strategies x^* and y^* are optimal strategies for a matrix game $C = mA - B$, where m is a positive number with the properties that: (1) the line through $(x^{*t}Ay^*, x^{*t}By^*)$ and (u^*, v^*) has slope m; (2) the line through (u^*, v^*) with slope $-m$ is a support to the set S (i.e., it lies entirely above the set). Solution can be obtained by iterative procedures which combine the simplex algorithm with the Newton-Raphson method.

TIME-PREFERENCE CONSIDERATIONS

The Nash-Zeuthen models described above, valuable as they are, suffer from one serious problem and that is the lack of an enforcing mechanism. Reasonable as the outcome may be, there is no way to force either party to accept it, and so each may hope, by being obstinate, to obtain his opponent's eventual acquiescence. There is much sense in this, since the model as given is static rather than dynamic; there is no consideration of time.

In many interesting cases, however, there is a definite time element; an agreement obtained now is usually worth more than an agreement in the future. (An obvious example is a strike.) Thus it may be worth a person's while to accept a lesser offer now than to hope for a larger one later (i.e., $100 per week for 2 weeks is better than $150 for 1 week).

Looked at in this manner, a bargaining problem can be represented as a game tree with offers and counter offers as moves. Ståhl [3] points out that such a game has perfect information (after all, each party is informed of the other's offers) and thus, in the finite case (i.e., when there is only time for a finite number of offers), it will have an equilibrium pair. Even in the infinite case it may have equilibrium pairs, especially if the parties' time preference is strong enough (i.e., if the discount rate is small enough). This equilibrium pair is generally unique and so can be considered a *solution* of the problem.

PROBLEMS OF INFORMATION

In the above models it is implicitly assumed that both players' capabilities and utility functions are known. Clearly, it may be in one player's interests to hide his true capacities, either bluffing to make them seem better or complaining to make them seem worse. For example, an employee may bargain for a raise by making believe that he has an offer from another firm—or, on the contrary, by claiming that he has abnormally high medical expenses. Either may serve to strengthen his bargaining situation.

It is difficult to see how one should proceed in the absence of such information. Harsanyi [4, 5] suggests that each player should work under the assumption that his opponent is telling the truth with a certain probability. Once these probabilities have been fixed, it becomes possible to decide the concessions that each player should make. The situation is similar to that in poker, where a player must decide whether to call an opponent's possible bluff.

There is one special case when it may be possible to obtain information as to the opponent's utility by observation. This occurs in situations where the value of an agreement decreases over time, e.g., in the case of a strike. In such cases the opponent's utility can at least be estimated by studying the rate at which concessions are made.

One model, which is essentially due to Cross [6], assumes that each player will expect the other to continue making concessions at the present rate, C. That being so, he can choose an "optimal" demand, $r(C)$—one which, given the opponent's present rate of concession, will maximize the present value of his payoff. This gives rise to a system of differential equations:

$$dr/dt = -c, \quad r = r(C)$$
$$dR/dt = -C, \quad R = R(c)$$

for the two players' demands, r and R, and their rates of concession, c and C. It is then possible to predict the eventual agreement to be reached, as well as the time of this agreement. Of course, it is still possible for either player to hide his true utility by modifying his rate of concession in some other manner; this will always be a difficult problem.

n-PERSON BARGAINING

Considerable problems arise when a third party enters into the bargaining. The point is that, in this case, each player has a choice of partners so that, in general, certain limitations are placed on the demands that one player may make of his partner: an excessive demand may cause the partner to break up the coalition. A trivial example is that of a seller in the presence of competition: if his prices are too high, customers will simply buy from other sellers. (Contrast this with a monopolist, whose customers have only the option of not buying.) Thus the bargaining must determine both the coalitions to be formed and the division of profits among the members of a coalition.

In the simplest case, we may assume that an *n*-person problem is adequately represented by a function, v, whose domain is the set of all subsets of $N = \{1, 2, \ldots, n\}$ (N being the set of all players for the game), and which takes values in the reals. This function, v, known as the *characteristic function* of the game, assigns to each coalition S (each subset of N) a number $v(S)$ which is the amount of utility, that the members of S can obtain by cooperation. (This done, they can then divide it among themselves in any way they wish.)

Several theories have been suggested for dealing with such problems. Best-known among these are the von Neumann-Morgenstern theory [7], based on *stable sets*; the Aumann-Maschler theory [8], based on *bargaining sets*; and the Shapley theory [9], based on a *power index*. We consider these in some detail below.

STABLE SETS

The von Neumann-Morgenstern theory begins with the concept of domination. Briefly speaking, an imputation is a way of dividing the profits which the set of all players, acting together, can obtain, i.e., it is a payoff vector $x = (x_1, \ldots, x_n)$ whose components add up to $v(N)$, and such that each player, i, receives at least $v(\{i\})$, the amount he could obtain without any other player's cooperation. Then an imputation x is said to dominate another imputation, y, if there exists some coalition, S (a non-empty subset of N), all of whose members prefer x to y, and with the power to enforce x (in the sense that they can guarantee their share of x). The notation for this is $x \succ y$.

It seems natural to look for the undominated imputations as the logical outcome of the bargaining process. In fact, the set of all such imputations, known as the *core*, corresponds (more or less) to the classical economic notion of a competitive equilibrium. Unfortunately, many interesting situations have empty cores. Thus it seems that one cannot require the very strong stability which is represented by the core.

This being so, von Neumann and Morgenstern looked for sets which would have a weaker kind of stability. By their definition, a set V (of imputations) is *stable* if (1) no imputation in V dominates another imputation in V; (2) any imputation *not* in V is dominated by at least one imputation in V.

The stable sets are interpreted as standards of behavior. Presumably, society chooses the particular stable set for a given situation; the participants then use their bargaining abilities to determine the particular imputation.

Difficulties obviously exist; there is generally no way to decide which imputation

BARGAINING THEORY

will be chosen from a particular stable set, nor (in case there is more than one stable set) for choosing a particular stable set. More serious is the fact that certain situations give rise to no stable sets; these can be characterized as inherently unstable, but still represent a serious defect in the theory.

THE BARGAINING SETS

The theory of the bargaining sets, due to Aumann and Maschler, attempts to reproduce the discussions which take part among members of a coalition to determine their division of profits.

As an example, let us suppose that an employee is not satisfied with his salary. If he has an offer from another firm, he might present this to his employer, who then has the option of raising the man's salary or letting him go. Presumably he will let the worker go if he feels that the man does not produce enough to cover his wages, or if he feels a replacement can be hired for the same (or less) money. He will raise the salary otherwise.

With this in mind, the theory defines a *coalition structure*, $\mathcal{T}$, as a collection of disjoint and exhaustive subsets of N. An individually rational payoff configuration (i.r.p.c.) is a pair $\langle \mathcal{T}; x \rangle$ where $\mathcal{T}$ is a coalition structure, and x a payoff vector such that, for each coalition $T \in \mathcal{T}$ (i.e., each coalition that actually forms) the members of T receive the amount $v(T)$, and each player receives at least the amount which he can guarantee himself.

Given an i.r.p.c., $\langle \mathcal{T}; x \rangle$, a player, i, can obtain his share x_i if none of his partners in $\mathcal{T}$ (those other players who are in the same coalition with i) object. The question is to determine when such objections will be made and upheld.

Given $\langle \mathcal{T}; x \rangle$, an objection of player j against his partner, i, is another i.r.p.c., $\langle \mathcal{U}; y \rangle$ such that (1) j receives more from y than from x; (2) all of j's partners in $\mathcal{U}$ receive at least as much from y as from x; (3) i is not a partner of j in $\mathcal{U}$.

Even if j objects, it may be possible for i to counter-object. A counter-objection for i is a third i.r.p.c., $\langle \mathcal{V}; z \rangle$ such that (1) i receives at least as much from z as from x (so that he protects his share of x); (2) all of i's partners in $\mathcal{V}$ receive at least as much from z as from x (or from y if they were among j's partners in $\mathcal{U}$); (3) j is not a partner of i in $\mathcal{V}$.

In this theory, an i.r.p.c. is stable if every objection has a counter-objection. It is important to note that, for any situation, and any coalition structure, $\mathcal{T}$, there is at least one payoff vector x such that $\langle \mathcal{T}, x \rangle$ is a stable i.r.p.c. The set of all stable i.r.p.c.'s is known as the *bargaining set*.

Different types of bargaining sets can be formed by modifying the definition, so that, say, objections can be made by sets of players rather than single players, by players who are not partners, etc.

THE POWER INDEX

A third theory, developed by Shapley, attempts to set an *a priori* expectation on the payoff to be obtained by each player. As such, it seems quite suitable for arbitration purposes. Essentially, Shapley develops his value from the axioms of (1) linearity (combining two situations by adding their characteristic functions should add their values); (2) symmetry (the value should be at least as symmetric as the situation); (3) efficiency (if a set of players control the situation entirely, then they should, all together, obtain as much as possible). Shapley shows that there is a unique value satisfying these axioms; this is the value $\phi[v]$ given by

$$\phi_i[v] = \sum_{\substack{T \subset N \\ i \notin T}} \frac{t! \, (n - t - 1)!}{n!} [V(T \cup \{i\}) - V(T)]$$

where t is the number of members of the coalition T.

For bargaining purposes, the power index suffers from the drawback of not taking any particular coalition into account (rather it seems to regard them all as, more or less, equally likely). Thus it does not pretend to tell us what will, or should, happen given a particular coalition structure. A modification due to Owen [10, 11] attempts to take this into account, giving a similar formula which depends, however, on the coalitions formed.

REFERENCES

1. J. Nash, The bargaining problem, *Econometrica* **18**, 155–162 (1950).
2. F. Zeuthen, *Problems of Monopoly and Economic Warfare*, Routledge, London, 1930.
3. Ingolf Ståhl, *Bargaining Theory*, Economic Research Institute, Stockholm, 1972.
4. J. C. Harsanyi, Approaches to the bargaining problem before and after the theory of games, *Econometrica* **24**, 144–157 (1956).
5. J. C. Harsanyi and R. Selten, A generalized Nash solution for two-person bargaining games with incomplete information, *Management Sci.* **18**, P80–P106. (1972).
6. J. Cross, A theory of the bargaining process, *Amer. Econ. Rev.* **55**, 67–94 (1965).
7. J. von Neumann and O. Morgenstern, *The Theory of Games and Economic Behavior*, Princeton University Press, Princeton, N. J., 1944, 1947, 1953.
8. R. J. Aumann and M. Maschler, The bargaining set for cooperative games, in *Advances in Game Theory* (Annals of Mathematics Studies No. 52), Princeton University Press, Princeton, N. J., 1964, pp. 443–476.
9. L. S. Shapley, A value for n-person games, in *Contributions of the Theory of Games, II* (Annals of Mathematics Studies No. 28), Princeton University Press, Princeton, N. J., 1953, pp. 307–318.
10. G. Owen, Political games, *Naval Res. Log. Quart.* **18**, 345–355 (1971).
11. G. Owen, Multilinear extensions of games, *Management Sci.* **18**, P64–P79 (1972).

Guillermo Owen

BARRIER METHODS FOR NONLINEAR PROGRAMMING

INTRODUCTION

An enormous variety of situations can be described as constrained "optimization processes," e.g., many "systems" appear to strive to maximize (optimize) their chances of survival subject to environmental restrictions and inherent limitations (constraints); numerous physical phenomena are concisely characterized in terms of minimization (optimization) of energy expenditure subject to certain universal laws (constraints) such as energy-mass balance equations; a corporation seeks to maximize profit subject to limitations on resources and legal restrictions; and a space vehicle is to be designed to maximize payload subject to requirements on velocity, acceleration, range reliability, economic and political restrictions, etc. The problem of determining how a mathematical model of any such process should be controlled to achieve its optimal objective has motivated intensive and fruitful research since the very beginning of scientific inquiry.

Aside from the unlimited possibilities regarding practical applications as suggested from the above general examples, the orientation toward optimization has been and continues to be extremely fertile in generating challenging theoretical problems. Answers to these problems have resulted in a "mathematics of optimization" encompassing extremal analysis, variational calculus, optimal control, and, more recently, "mathematical programming," drawing heavily from results in functional analysis, linear algebra, differential equations, numerical analysis, topology, and many other disciplines.

The mathematical programming problem may be defined as follows: Given a space X, a subset R of X, and a scalar-valued function $f(x)$ defined on R, find a vector x^* such that $f(x)$ attains its minimum over R at x^*. (We could, equivalently, address ourselves to maximization throughout.) Conditions guaranteeing the existence of a minimizing point have been known for some time. A detailed development of properties characterizing minimizing points (often referred to as "optimality conditions") and the development of algorithms (numerical procedures) and their computer implementation for solving such problems has been pursued vigorously, largely in the past three decades, the preponderance of the major results being forthcoming only within the past 15 years.

The tremendous variety of significant applications that can be formulated as mathematical programming problems is now well documented, and the list is still growing at an explosive rate. This fact, along with the great advances in computer technology and the accumulated experience of successful implementations, has precipitated and continues to stimulate considerable activity in developing iterative solution algorithms. Conceptual advances have stabilized somewhat, the most obvious strategies having been proposed and scrutinized rather thoroughly. Recent breakthroughs, such as the application of branch-

and-bound methods to solve nonconvex programming problems [1, 2], the development of algorithms for calculating fixed points [3–5], results for the complementarity problem [6–8], and the introduction of parallel processing computer systems [9], are stimulating promising new approaches.

The purpose of this article is to give a brief description of an algorithmic approach, the "auxiliary function" procedure, which has proven quite effective for a large class of mathematical programming problems. For greater clarity, attention is focused on important realizations of this approach, mainly on parametric "barrier" (interior) and "penalty" (exterior) methods, with major emphasis on the former. The auxiliary function idea has been especially useful for mathematical programming problems defined in terms of a set of nonlinear functional relationships, giving rise to a class of problems called "nonlinear programming problems." For a recent general survey of parametric and nonparametric auxiliary function methods applied to these problems, the reader is referred to Lootsma [10]. A chronological survey of developments up to 1968 in parametric auxiliary function methods is given in Fiacco and McCormick [11].

Although many of the results given can readily be extended, we shall for simplicity give most of our attention to the problem

$$\text{minimize } f(x) \quad s.t. \quad x \in R \subset X \qquad (P)$$

where the "objective function" $f(x)$ is continuous, the "feasible region" $R \equiv \{x \mid g(x) \geq 0, i = 1, \ldots, m\}$, where the $\{g_i(x)\}$ are continuous functions, and the space $X = E^n$ (Euclidean n-space). Additional assumptions will be invoked as needed for specific results.

It is probable that the reader has token familiarity with some of the better-known schemes for approximating a solution of (P). For convenience and perspective, we recall some of these at a general level and give references for further reading. (For a fairly comprehensive discussion of problem manipulations and solution strategies, the reader is referred to Geoffrion [12].) We categorize solution strategies as follows:

1. Ad hoc (i.e., techniques particularly tailored to the problem at hand, e.g., reduction and simplification by elimination, substitution and transformation of variables) [13–15].
2. Enumeration (e.g., exhaustive sampling, often involving systematic partitioning schemes such as those found in branch-and-bound methods) [16, 17].
3. Search (i.e., heuristic or random sampling to determine probable directions of improvement, often based on estimating gradients "in the large") [13, 14, 18].
4. Descent (e.g., steepest descent, minimization over one variable at a time, the simplex method, heuristic gradient methods, first- and second-order projected gradient methods, conjugate direction methods, Newton and quasi-Newton methods, the reduced gradient method) [15, 19, 20].
5. Feasible Direction (i.e., the generation of feasible directions of improve-

ment based on solving a succession of local subproblems, typically combined with linearization techniques) [15, 19, 21].
6. Reduction (i.e., the introduction of new constraints and conditions that progressively eliminate subsets of the feasible region that cannot contain a solution, such as cutting plane and branch-and-bound methods) [15, 16, 22].
7. Approximation (e.g., linearization, decomposition, relaxation, introduction of convex envelopes or other approximating functions, perturbation methods) [12, 23, 24].
8. Auxiliary Function (e.g., Lagrangian methods, methods-of-centers, barrier and penalty function methods) [11, 20, 23, 25, 26].

Thus we shall be concerned with one of numerous strategies that have proved fruitful, the auxiliary function procedure, and then only with certain variations of one important class of realizations of this basic approach. As indicated, auxiliary function methods have proved among the most powerful for estimating solutions of problems involving nonlinearities, particularly nonlinearities *in the constraint functions*. An extensive body of theory has been developed supporting the methodology. The level of theoretical development, computational experience, and utilization of auxiliary function methods in practical applications appears not to have been exceeded by any other known nonlinear programming approach.

The approach is introduced in the next section; basic convergence results are detailed in the Sections entitled Basic General Theoretical Results for Barrier Methods, Perturbation Analysis Based on Continuous Variation of the Barrier Function Parameter, Convex Programming by Barrier Methods, and connections with optimality conditions are shown in the section entitled Connections between Optimality Conditions and Convergence Properties of Barrier Methods. Algorithmic considerations are discussed in the section entitled A Basic Barrier Function Algorithm and Computational Considerations; the remaining sections deal with important extensions and applications.

EXAMPLES OF BARRIER AND PENALTY FUNCTIONS AND THE GENERAL AUXILIARY FUNCTION APPROACH

The barrier and penalty function methods to be considered are based on forming an "auxiliary function," usually involving the sum of the objective function and a perturbation term, the latter a function of the constraint functions and one or more parameters. When successful, minimizing points of the auxiliary function are "close" to a solution of Problem P for values of the parameters close to specified values. We can readily illustrate the idea and motivate the terminology by very simple examples.

Consider the problem in E^1, minimize x s.t. $x \geq 0$. Define the function $P(x, r_k) = x + r_k/x$, where $r_k > 0$ for all k. It is easily verified that this function is minimized in the region where $x > 0$ at $x(r_k) = r_k^{1/2}$. As $r_k \to 0$, $x(r_k) \to 0$, the solution of the problem.

BARRIER METHODS FOR NONLINEAR PROGRAMMING

Consider the problem in E^1, minimize x s.t. $x = 0$. Define the function $T(x, t_k) = x + t_k x^2$, where $t_k > 0$ for all k. It follows that $x(t_k) = -1/2t_k$ minimizes this function over E^1, and $x(t_k) \to 0$, the solution of the problem, as $t_k \to +\infty$.

The functions $P(x, r_k)$ and $T(x, t_k)$ are examples of barrier and penalty auxiliary functions, respectively, and the fact that their respective sequences of unconstrained minima (in certain designated domains) converge to solutions of constrained problems as the parameter values approach the indicated limits, as they do in these trivial examples, can be verified under very general conditions. As we shall see in the ensuing discussion, $P(x, r_k)$ is an example of an "interior" or barrier auxiliary function, a "minimizing sequence" of the function existing in the interior of the feasible region of the original problem. $T(x, t_k)$ is an example of an "exterior" or penalty auxiliary function, a minimizing trajectory converging to a solution of the original problem from the exterior of the feasible region of the given problem.

It is also possible to define mixed interior–exterior auxiliary functions, where some of the constraints are handled by an interior function approach and others by an exterior function approach. For example, consider the problem in E^2, minimize $x_1 + x_2$ s.t. $x_2 \geq 1$, $x_1 = x_2$. It is easy to see that the solution of the problem is $x^* = (x_1^*, x_2^*) = (1, 1)$. Defining the penalty function $W(x, r) = x_1 + x_2 + r/(x_2 - 1) + (1/r)(x_1 - x_2)^2$, it can be verified that this function is minimized over the region where $x_2 > 1$ (x_1 unrestricted) by $x(r) = (1 + r^{1/2}/2^{1/2} - r/2, 1 + r^{1/2}/2^{1/2})$. Observe that $x(r) \to (1, 1) = x^*$, the solution of the problem, as $r \to 0$.

Auxiliary function methods for Problem P are generally special cases of the following basic idea. Define a sequence of auxiliary functions $\{V_k(x)\}$ such that: (1) there exists at least one minimizing point x^k of $V_k(x)$, $k = 1, 2, \ldots$; (2) there exists at least one convergent subsequence of $\{x^k\}$; and (3) any convergent subsequence of $\{x^k\}$ converges to a solution of Problem P.

Thus Problem P is solved by solving a sequence of "auxiliary problems." Obviously, this approach has appeal providing suitable auxiliary functions for a given problem can readily be found and providing the effort to solve each auxiliary problem is appreciably less than the effort to solve Problem P.

The auxiliary functions used in the simple examples above give important realizations of this general approach. In fact, the two types of parametric auxiliary functions generally encountered are those giving rise to interior or exterior minimizing sequences, as exemplified by $P(x, r_k)$ and $T(x, t_k)$. We shall henceforward refer to these two basic types of auxiliary functions as "barrier" and "penalty" functions, respectively, for reasons that will presently be given. An understanding of why these particular functions work can give many useful insights in appreciating the validity and general applicability of auxiliary function methodology.

We are considering the problem of finding a vector in E^n that solves

$$\text{minimize } f(x) \text{ s.t. } g_i(x) \geq 0 \quad (i = 1, \ldots, m) \tag{P}$$

where $f(x)$ and the $g_i(x)$ are continuous and $R \equiv \{x \mid g_i(x) \geq 0 \ (i = 1, \ldots, m)\}$.

BARRIER METHODS FOR NONLINEAR PROGRAMMING

Define $R^\# \equiv \{x \mid g_i(x) > 0, i = 1, \ldots, m\}$. Define the associated auxiliary function

$$P(x, r) \equiv f(x) + r \sum_{i=1}^{m} \frac{1}{g_i(x)} \tag{1}$$

where r is a parameter to be specified. This function and the following approach were first proposed by C. W. Carroll [27, 28] and subsequently validated and developed by Fiacco and McCormick [11, 29–32]. Pomentale [33] provided an early generalization, and Lootsma [34, 35] contributed significantly to further extensions, as did Gould [36] and Roode [37].

Let us first indicate how sequential minimization of this auxiliary function for $r = r_k > 0$, $k = 1, 2, \ldots$, with $r_k \downarrow 0$, yields a feasible (interior) method and why such functions are appropriately called "barrier" functions.

Let r be any positive number. Suppose there exists a point x^0 such that $g_i(x^0) > 0$ for all i. Consider any continuous curve $x(\theta)$, $0 \le \theta \le 1$, such that $x(0) = x^0$ and such that $P[x(\theta), r]$ decreases monotonically as $\theta \to 1$. Then we must have $g_i[x(\theta)] > 0$ for all $0 \le \theta \le 1$, for otherwise $g_i[x(\theta)] \to 0$ for some i, and consequently $P[x(\theta), r] \to +\infty$, as $\theta \to \bar{\theta}$, where $0 < \bar{\theta} \le 1$, contradicting the assumption that $P[x(\theta), r]$ decreases monotonically as $\theta \to 1$. This means that any unconstrained minimization algorithm based on continuously decreasing $P(x, r)$ from a starting point in R will never generate a point outside $R^\#$ and, in this sense, feasibility is maintained with respect to any such algorithm, by definition of $P(x, r)$. It is seen that the term $r \sum_{i=1}^{m} 1/g_i(x)$ imposes a "barrier" that cannot be violated in the course of continuously reducing $P(x, r)$, starting from any point x such that $g_i(x) > 0$, all i. Thus, with $r > 0$, the P function enforces "interior feasibility" throughout any such minimization process and, hence, gives rise to an "interior" or "barrier" method.

In addition to imposing satisfaction of the constraints, which we are now able to realize through an appropriate P function unconstrained minimization process, Problem P simultaneously requires minimization of $f(x)$. It follows that reduction of $f(x)$ can be realized if the minimization of $P(x, r)$ in $R^\#$ is repeated with a reduced (positive) value of r; i.e., $f[x(r)]$ decreases as r decreases. This is expected since we are essentially minimizing the weighted sum of two functions. Reduction of r decreases the effect of the barrier terms while increasing the effect of $f(x)$ in $P(x, r)$. It is easily verified algebraically by noting that for any two values of r, say $r_k > r_{k+1} > 0$, it follows that

$$f[x(r_k)] + r_k \sum_{i=1}^{m} 1/g_i[x(r_k)] \le f[x(r_{k+1})] + r_k \sum_{i=1}^{m} 1/g_i[x(r_{k+1})] \tag{2}$$

and

$$f[x(r_{k+1})] + r_{k+1} \sum_{i=1}^{m} 1/g_i[x(r_{k+1})] \le f[x(r_k)] + r_{k+1} \sum_{i=1}^{m} 1/g_i[x(r_k)]$$

by definition of minimum. Adding the inequalities and rearranging gives

$$(r_k - r_{k+1}) \sum_{i=1}^{m} 1/g_i[x(r_k)] \le (r_k - r_{k+1}) \sum_{i=1}^{m} 1/g_i[x(r_{k+1})]$$

BARRIER METHODS FOR NONLINEAR PROGRAMMING

and since $r_k > r_{k+1} > 0$, we conclude that

$$\sum_{i=1}^{m} 1/g_i[x(r_{k+1})] \leq \sum_{i=1}^{m} 1/g_i[x(r_k)] \tag{3}$$

From (3) and the second inequality in (2), it follows that

$$f[x(r_{k+1})] \leq f[x(r_k)] \tag{4}$$

The combined effects of enforced feasibility and monotonic reduction of $f(x)$ suggests that $P(x, r)$ will yield a barrier method giving the desired results, as stipulated in the general definition of the auxiliary function approach at the beginning of this section. The suggestion is valid and fruitful. Of course, conditions must be given that guarantee the existence of a minimizing sequence $\{x(r_k)\}$ and a convergent subsequence, but these are not difficult to stipulate and will be further explored in the next section. Given their existence, convergence results are easily obtained, as we now indicate. The general argument given is a basic one in auxiliary function theory.

We assume that Problem P has a finite solution value $f(x^*)$ and that there are points in $R^\#$ that yield values of $f(x)$ as close to $f(x^*)$ as desired; i.e., there exists $x(\epsilon) \in R^\#$ such that $f[x(\epsilon)] \leq f(x^*) + \epsilon$, for any $\epsilon > 0$. (The latter assumption is indispensable if we hope to estimate a solution of Problem P by a method that generates points confined to $R^\#$.) Suppose $P(x, r_k)$ has a minimizing point $x^k \in R^\#$ for each k and that $\{x^k\}$ contains a convergent subsequence $\{x^{k_j}\}$ converging to y. Then we can prove that y is a solution of Problem P. This follows from the fact that, for any $\epsilon > 0$, we can first choose $x(\epsilon)$ and then r_ϵ such that $f(x^*) \leq f(x^k) \leq P(x^k, r_k) \leq P[x(\epsilon), r_\epsilon] \leq f(x^*) + 2\epsilon$ holds for all k such that $0 < r_k \leq r_\epsilon$. The first inequality holds because $f(x^*)$ is the optimal value of Problem P and x^k is a feasible point. The second holds by definition of $P(x, r_k)$ and the fact that $r_k > 0$ and $g_i(x^k) > 0$ for all i and each k. The third holds because reduction of r and minimization of P both result in reducing this function in $R^\#$, assuming $r > 0$. The last holds by our initial assumption and the fact that, having selected $x(\epsilon)$, we can choose r_ϵ to satisfy $r_\epsilon > 0$ and $r_\epsilon \sum_{i=1}^{m} 1/g_i[x(\epsilon)] \leq \epsilon$. (The inequalities are "logically" generated from right to left, choosing the indicated quantities in the following order: ϵ, $x(\epsilon)$, r_ϵ, r_k, and x^k.) Taking limits in this chain of inequalities evaluated over the convergent subsequence $\{x^{k_j}\}$ (and recalling that $f(x)$ is continuous) yields the conclusion that $f(y) = f(x^*)$. Since continuity of the g_i implies that y is feasible, it follows that y is a solution of Problem P.

The exterior penalty method idea may be conveyed by considering the problem

$$\text{minimize } f(x) \quad \text{s.t.} \quad h_j(x) = 0 \quad (j = 1, \ldots, p) \tag{T}$$

where the problem functions are all continuous, and the function

$$T(x, t) \equiv f(x) + t \sum_{j=1}^{p} h_j^2(x) \tag{5}$$

When $t = t_k$ for $k = 1, 2, \ldots$, $t_k \geq 0$ for all k and $t_k \uparrow +\infty$, then under general conditions it follows that sequential minimization of $T(x, t_k)$ defines a (feasible) exterior "penalty" method. This approach was first suggested by Courant [38] and was later developed and generalized by Rubin and Ungar [40], Kelley [41], Butler and Martin [42], Pietrzykowski [43], Zangwill [44], and Fiacco and McCormick [11, 45]. The basic idea may be rendered plausible by considering the following general argument.

Since $T(x, t_k)$ is defined over the entire space, we need not convince ourselves that minimization will or need be restricted to a smaller region to yield a "successful" minimization sequence, as with $P(x, r_k)$. Suppose $T(x, t_k)$ has a minimizing point x^k for each k and suppose $\{x^k\}$ contains a convergent subsequence $\{x^{k_j}\}$ converging to y. Then, if Problem T has a solution x^*, it follows that y is a solution of Problem T. To see this, observe that $T(x, t_k) \equiv f(x)$ for any x such that $h_j(x) = 0$ (all j). We may conclude that $f(x^k) \leq T(x^k, t_k) \leq T(x^*, t_k) = f(x^*)$ for all k, and hence evaluating this set of inequalities over $\{x^{k_j}\}$ and taking limits as $j \to +\infty$, we conclude that $h_j(y) = 0$ (all j) [since, otherwise, $T(x^{k_j}, t_{k_j}) \to +\infty$ as $t_{k_j} \to +\infty$, a contradiction] and $f(y) \leq f(x^*)$ [by continuity of $f(x)$]. The conclusion follows.

Another important fact concerning such exterior function methods should be mentioned. If there exists a feasible point x^* such that $f(x^*) \leq f(x)$ for all x, then *any* minimizing point of $T(x, t)$ for *any* $t \geq 0$ solves Problem T. This readily follows from the fact that, for any $t \geq 0$, $T(x^*, t) = f(x^*) \leq f(x) \leq T(x, t)$ for any x, and the fact that, if $\bar{x}$ is a nonfeasible point of Problem T or if $f(\bar{x}) > f(x^*)$, then $T(\bar{x}, t) > f(x^*)$ for all $t \geq 0$.

It may also be observed that inequalities precisely analogous to those obtained in (2) for $P(x, r_k)$ lead to the conclusion that

$$f(x^k) \leq f(x^{k+1}) \quad \text{and} \quad \sum_{j=1}^{p} h_j^2(x^{k+1}) \leq \sum_{j=1}^{p} h_j^2(x^k)$$

so that typically, the objective function monotonically increases and the penalty term monotonically decreases in the exterior penalty function approach.

The exterior penalty method is easily adapted to problems with inequality constraints, such as Problem P. For this problem, a suitable exterior function is

$$T(x, t_k) \equiv f(x) + t_k \sum_{i=1}^{m} g_i^2(x) H(g_i) \tag{6}$$

where $H(g_i) = 0$ if $g_i(x) \geq 0$ and 1 if $g_i(x) < 0$. The properties of the method based on this function are similar to those that hold for the equality-constrained technique above. Note that in both cases the terms added to the objective function have the effect of imposing a "penalty" (with respect to the goal of minimizing the auxiliary function) for constraint violation, whereas the added terms in the interior method imposed a penalty for approaching the infeasible region. Feasibility is enforced as the penalty for constraint violation becomes intolerable; hence the term "penalty methods" for such procedures.

BARRIER METHODS FOR NONLINEAR PROGRAMMING

Interior and exterior penalty terms such as those given above may be used in combination to define mixed barrier penalty functions that allow for different handling of various constraints. This was validated by Fiacco and McCormick [11, 32] and is illustrated by the third example given earlier. Also, the indicated penalty functions are special cases of a large class of functions that can be used to define barrier and penalty methods. In this article, however, we concentrate on particular realizations that have been used most extensively. For the general theory, the reader is referred to Fiacco and McCormick [11].

BASIC GENERAL THEORETICAL RESULTS FOR BARRIER METHODS

Convergence proofs for various types of barrier and penalty function methods follow the same pattern—so much so that a unified general theory comprehends most of the better known methods as special cases. We shall briefly survey some of the generalizations in the sections entitled Extensions and Ramifications and Future Research. Presently, we summarize key results for "basic" barrier methods. We begin with a general proof of convergence for the barrier function $P(x, r_k) \equiv f(x) + r_k \sum_{i=1}^{m} 1/g_i(x)$ used to solve Problem P: minimize $f(x)$ subject to $x \in R \equiv \{x \mid g_i(x) \geq 0, i = 1, \ldots, m\}$.

As before, define $R^{\#} \equiv \{x \mid g_i(x) > 0, i = 1, \ldots, m\}$. Define $v^* \equiv \inf_R f(x)$. The (scalar) parameter $r_k > 0$ for $k = 1, 2, \ldots$, and $\{r_k\}$ decreases to 0 as $k \to +\infty$.

Theorem 1. (Basic convergence theorem for barrier methods.) If
  (i) the functions defining Problem P are continuous,
  (ii) $\{x \in R \mid f(x) \leq \alpha\}$ is a bounded set for any finite α, and
  (iii) for any $\epsilon > 0$, there exists $x(\epsilon) \in R^{\#}$ such that $f[x(\epsilon)] \leq v^* + \epsilon$, then
  (a) there exists a point minimizing $P(x, r_k)$ in $R^{\#}$ for each k,
  (b) the set of minimizing points of $\{P(x, r_k)\}$ in $R^{\#}$ is bounded, hence any minimizing sequence $\{x^k\}$ of $\{P(x, r_k)\}$ has a limit point,
  (c) every limit point of $\{x^k\}$ solves Problem P,
  (d) $P(x^k, r_k) \to v^*$, $f(x^k) \to v^*$, and $r_k \sum_{i=1}^{m} 1/g_i(x^k) \to 0$ as $k \to +\infty$, and
  (e) $f(x^{k+1}) \leq f(x^k)$ and $\sum_{i=1}^{m} 1/g_i(x^{k+1}) \geq \sum_{i=1}^{m} 1/g_i(x^k)$ for each k.

Proof: We first note that the assumptions imply the existence of finite solution x^* of Problem P, so that $f(x^*) = \min_R f(x) \equiv v^*$, a finite number. (In fact, the set of solution points must be a nonempty compact set. The solution x^* may or may not be unique.)

Conclusion (a) may be proved as follows.
There exists $x^0 \in R^{\#}$ [since $R^{\#} \neq 0$, by (iii)]. Set $r = r_1 > 0$. If $x \in R^{\#}$ and $f(x) > P(x^0, r_1)$ or $r_1/g_i(x) > [P(x^0, r_1) - v^*]/m$ for each i, then $P(x, r_1) > P(x^0, r_1)$. Defining $S_1 \equiv \{x \in R^{\#} \mid P(x, r_1) \leq P(x^0, r_1)\}$, $S_1' \equiv \{x \in R^{\#} \mid f(x) \leq P(x^0, r_1), r_1/g_i(x) \leq [P(x^0, r_1) - v^*]/m$ for $i = 1, \ldots, m\}$ and $S_1'' \equiv \{x \in R \mid f(x) \leq P(x^0, r_1)\}$, it

follows that $S_1 \subseteq S_1' \subset S_1''$. S_1'' is a bounded set, by Assumption (ii), and since $f(x)$ and the $g_i(x)$ are continuous, S_1' is a compact set in $R^\#$. Therefore, S_1' is a compact set containing all candidate minimizing points of $P(x, r_1)$ in $R^\#$. Since $P(x, r_1)$ is continuous in S_1', we conclude that $P(x, r_1)$ attains a minimum value over $R^\#$ at some point $x' \in S_1'$. Repeating the argument for any $r_k > 0$ proves (a).

To prove (b), observe from above that $x^k \in \{x \in R \mid f(x) \leq P(x^0, r_k)\} \equiv S_k''$. Noting that $S_k'' \subset S_1''$ for $k = 2, 3, \ldots$, since $\{r_k\}$ is a positive decreasing sequence, we have that $\{x^k\} \subset S_1''$, a compact set. Since R is closed [by (i)], $\{x^k\}$ must have a limit point $y \in R$.

By Assumption (iii) we can satisfy $f[x(\epsilon)] \leq v^* + \epsilon$ for any $\epsilon > 0$ with $x(\epsilon) \in R^\#$. Select r_ϵ such that $r_\epsilon \sum_{i=1}^m 1/g_i[x(\epsilon)] \leq \epsilon$. Denoting by $x(r_\epsilon)$ a minimizing point of $P(x, r_\epsilon)$ in $R^\#$, the following chain of inequalities follows immediately for $0 < r_k \leq r_\epsilon$ from the definition of $P(x, r_k)$:

$$v^* \leq f(x^k) \leq P(x^k, r_k) \leq P[x(r_\epsilon), r_k] \leq P[x(r_\epsilon), r_\epsilon] \leq P[x(\epsilon), r_\epsilon] \leq v^* + 2\epsilon$$

Taking limits over the subsequence of $\{x^k\}$ converging to y yields $f(y) = v^*$. Since we showed that $y \in R$, y must be a solution of Problem P, and since the same argument applies to any limit point of $\{x^k\}$, (c) and (d) follow.

Conclusion (e) was shown under weaker assumptions in the section entitled Examples of Barrier and Penalty Functions and the General Auxiliary Function Approach, and the proof is complete.

The theorem demonstrates the wide applicability of the approach and the typical conclusions that follow when the method is successful, i.e., the barrier term vanishes in the limit along a minimizing sequence, resulting in the fact that both the penalty function values and the objective function values approach the optimal value of Problem P, and the objective function and barrier term change monotonically. Of course, the most important result is Conclusion (c).

The proof of the (exterior) penalty method for inequality and equality constraints proceeds in an analogous manner, under similar assumptions. An important difference is that Assumption (iii) is not required because the exterior functions are defined to be continuous over the entire space, so that points in a neighborhood of a candidate solution point are clearly in the domain of definition of the function. However, the barrier method is confined to $R^\#$ and it need not be true in general that points in $R^\#$ exist that are as close as desired to some solution point of Problem P. Without this property, the barrier method cannot succeed and hence a condition like Assumption (iii) is necessary.

In addition to $P(x, r_k)$ and $T(x, t_k)$, two of the best known auxiliary functions, another function that has been heavily utilized for Problem P is the "logarithmic" barrier function

$$L(x, r_k) \equiv f(x) - r_k \sum_{i=1}^m \ln g_i(x) \qquad (7)$$

where $r_k > 0$ and $\{r_k\} \downarrow 0$. It defines a barrier method under the same conditions required for the $P(x, r_k)$ barrier method. This function was first utilized by Frisch [46, 47] and subsequently developed as a barrier function by Lootsma [35, 48, 49], Parisot [50], and Fiacco and McCormick [11].

Mixed auxiliary function methods are readily defined (as previously indicated) by combining the handling of some constraints by a barrier approach and the rest by a penalty approach. For example the problem

$$\min f(x) \text{ s.t.} \quad g_i(x) \geq 0 \ (i = 1, \ldots, m) \quad h_j(x) = 0 \ (j = 1, \ldots, p) \quad (W)$$

may be solved by the mixed barrier-penalty function

$$W(x, r_k, t_k) \equiv f(x) + r_k \sum_{i=1}^{s} 1/g_i(x) + t_k \sum_{i=s+1}^{m} g_i^2(x) H(g_i) + t_k \sum_{j=1}^{p} h_j^2(x) \quad (8)$$

where $H(g_i) = 0$ or 1 in accordance with whether the constraint $g_i(x) \geq 0$ is satisfied or violated, respectively, and where $r_k > 0$, $t_k > 0$, $r_k \downarrow 0$, and $t_k \uparrow +\infty$. Conditions required to validate such mixed methods essentially require logically combining the "pure interior" and "pure exterior" conditions, applied to the relevant constraints, in a straightforward manner. A variety of mixed methods is thus available by utilizing the various combinations of the penalty terms that have been specified. The mixed approach was proposed and developed by Fiacco and McCormick [11, 32] and subsequently studied by Lootsma [34, 35].

Another class of penalty functions has been under recent development and should be mentioned: "exponential penalty" functions. For the Problem P, a typical example of such a function is

$$E(x, t) = f(x) + \sum_{i=1}^{m} \exp[-t_k g_i(x)] \quad (9)$$

where $t_k > 0$ and $\{t_k\} \uparrow +\infty$. If $R^\# \neq \emptyset$, this function (under appropriate conditions) defines a method such that any minimizing sequence is exterior (to the feasible region) until t_k reaches a certain magnitude, whereupon the minimizing sequence enters the feasible region and remains interior. If $R^\# = \emptyset$, the method (when successful) behaves like an exterior penalty method. Conditions for convergence are similar to those required for (exterior) penalty methods. Exponential penalty function methods may be traced back to an idea by Motzkin [51], and have been independently developed by Savir [52], Allran and Johnsen [53], Evans and Gould [54], and Murphy [55]. Recent interest has focused on using such functions to define "exact penalty functions" (see the section entitled Extensions and Ramifications).

Numerous other variations of barrier and penalty functions for Problem P have been proposed; e.g., the penalty function [56]

$$T(x, t) = f(x) - t \sum_{i=1}^{m} \min[g_i(x), 0] \quad (10)$$

BARRIER METHODS FOR NONLINEAR PROGRAMMING

and the barrier function [57–59]

$$P(x, r) = f(x) + r \sum_{i=1}^{m} 1/g_i^2(x) \tag{11}$$

The interested reader may consult the indicated references for more details, as well as the discussion in the sections entitled Extensions and Ramifications and Future Research, where a multitude of modifications and generalizations are indicated. Suffice it to say at this point that perturbation techniques, of which barrier and penalty functions may be viewed as particular examples, have been a standard device in analysis from the beginning, and it is now well known that the class of auxiliary functions that can be utilized is indeed large.

In the next three sections we shall state other significant theoretical results that have been developed in auxiliary function methodology. For simplicity, we shall confine our attention to barrier methods in general, and the barrier functions $P(x, r_k)$ and $L(x, r_k)$ for Problem P, in particular. However, we emphasize that all of the results we indicate have their analogy in exterior, mixed, exponential, and other auxiliary function approaches. Each result has numerous ramifications which we shall only touch upon here, depending on the great variety of conditions that can be assumed, and each has been or undoubtedly can be extended and generalized to larger classes of auxiliary functions, more general spaces, more complicated constraint-sets, etc. Inevitably, many interesting results will be omitted, though hopefully most of these are treated in the References and Bibliography following, or among the references contained in these works.

CONNECTIONS BETWEEN OPTIMALITY CONDITIONS AND CONVERGENCE PROPERTIES OF BARRIER METHODS

In a brief treatise such as this, it is not possible to stipulate all the necessary background material for the uninitiated. We shall only mention certain key facts and otherwise suggest appropriate references for further reading.

The problem we are considering is that of determining a solution of

$$\min f(x) \quad \text{s.t.} \quad g_i(x) \geq 0 \quad (i = 1, \ldots, m) \tag{P}$$

with the associated barrier functions

$$P(x, r_k) \equiv f(x) + r_k \sum_{i=1}^{m} 1/g_i(x)$$

and

$$L(x, r_k) \equiv f(x) - r_k \sum_{i=1}^{m} \ln g_i(x)$$

where, as usual, $r_k > 0$ and $\{r_k\} \downarrow 0$. The results given can readily be extended to accommodate equality constraints and other barrier and penalty methods.

BARRIER METHODS FOR NONLINEAR PROGRAMMING

There is a close connection between the optimality conditions that characterize a local solution of Problem P and the conditions characterizing a local minimizing sequence for $P(x, r_k)$ or $L(x, r_k)$. We first state some well-known first and second order optimality conditions for constrained and unconstrained minimization, the order referring to the degree of differentiability of the involved functions. A detailed treatment of first-order conditions may be found in Mangasarian [60] and a concise development of first- and second-order optimality conditions is given in Hestenes [61], Fiacco and McCormick [11, 26], and Luenberger [15].

Definition 1. The *Lagrangian* of Problem P is defined as

$$\mathscr{L}(x, u) \equiv f(x) - \sum_{i=1}^{m} u_i g_i(x) \qquad (12)$$

To avoid any ambiguity, we stipulate our meaning of local and global minimizing points.

Definition 2. A *local* minimizing point of Problem P is any feasible point $\bar{x}$ [i.e., such that $g_i(\bar{x}) \geq 0$ ($i = 1, \ldots, m$)] such that $f(\bar{x}) \leq f(x)$ for all feasible points in a neighborhood of $\bar{x}$. If $f(\bar{x}) \leq f(x)$ for *all x in a neighborhood* of $\bar{x}$, then $\bar{x}$ is an *unconstrained local* minimizing point of $f(x)$. If $f(\bar{x}) \leq f(x)$ for *all points in the domain* of $f(x)$, then $\bar{x}$ is an *unconstrained global* minimizing point of $f(x)$.

Lemma 1. (First order necessary conditions for a local solution of Problem P.) If $f(x)$ and $g_i(x)$ ($i = 1, \ldots, m$) are once continuously differentiable at a local minimum x^* of Problem P and if the gradients $\nabla g_i(x^*)$ ($i = 1, \ldots, m$), for i such that $g_i(x^*) = 0$, are linearly independent, then there exists a vector $u^* = (u_1^*, \ldots, u_m^*)$ such that (x^*, u^*) satisfies

$$g_i(x^*) \geq 0 \qquad (i = 1, \ldots, m) \qquad (13)$$
$$u_i^* g_i(x^*) = 0 \qquad (i = 1, \ldots, m) \qquad (14)$$
$$u_i^* \geq 0 \qquad (i = 1, \ldots, m) \qquad (15)$$

and

$$\nabla \mathscr{L}(x^*, u^*) = 0 \qquad (16)$$

The Conditions (13)–(16) were developed by Kuhn and Tucker [62] and are usually referred to as the "Kuhn-Tucker conditions." Condition (14) is called "complimentary slackness." These conditions are extremely useful in testing solution candidates for Problem P, but are not sufficient without further assumptions. They provide a basis for convergence criteria and have motivated the development of numerous algorithms.

A corollary of this result has been known for some time and may be recalled from elementary calculus.

Lemma 2. (First-order necessary conditions for a local unconstrained minimum.) If $f(x)$ is once continuously differentiable at a local unconstrained minimizing point x^*, then $\nabla f(x^*) = 0$.

First-order conditions have been indispensable in the development of mathematical programming methodology. However, they are based on a purely linear analysis and take no account of curvature. Hence, in the presence of nonlinearities, a higher order analysis is often essential and has given rise to a steadily increasing emphasis on the following second-order conditions. Although fragments of these results have been well–known for some time, only recently has the theory been unified and exploited in mathematical programming, and synthesized with the first-order results.

Lemma 3. (Second-order necessary conditions for a local solution of Problem P.) If $f(x)$ and $g_i(x)$ ($i = 1, \ldots, m$) are twice continuously differentiable at a local minimum x^* of Problem P and if the gradients $\nabla g_i(x^*)$, for i such that $g_i(x^*) = 0$, are linearly independent, then there exists a vector u^* such that (x^*, u^*) satisfies the Kuhn-Tucker first-order conditions (13)–(16) and such that $y^T \nabla^2 \mathscr{L}(x^*, u^*) \, y \geq 0$ for all y satisfying

$$y^T \nabla g_i(x^*) = 0 \quad \text{when } g_i(x^*) = 0 \text{ and } u_i^* > 0 \tag{17}$$
$$y^T \nabla g_i(x^*) \geq 0 \quad \text{when } g_i(x^*) = 0 \text{ and } u_i^* = 0 \tag{18}$$

Lemma 4. (Second-order sufficient conditions for a solution of Problem P.) If $f(x)$ and $g_i(x)$ ($i = 1, \ldots, m$) are twice continuously differentiable at x^*, if there exists u^* such that (x^*, u^*) satisfies the first-order conditions, and if, for $y \neq 0$, $y^T \nabla^2 \mathscr{L}(x^*, u^*) \, y > 0$ for all y satisfying (17) and (18), then x^* is an isolated (locally unique) local minimizing point of Problem P.

In the absence of constraints, the following well-known corollaries result.

Lemma 5. (Second-order necessary conditions for a local unconstrained minimum.) If $f(x)$ is twice continuously differentiable at a local unconstrained minimizing point x^*, then $\nabla f(x^*) = 0$ and $y^T \Delta^2 f(x^*) \, y \geq 0$ for all y.

Lemma 6. (Second-order sufficient conditions for a local unconstrained minimum.) If $f(x)$ is twice continuously differentiable at x^* and $\nabla f(x^*) = 0$ and $y^T \nabla f(x^*) \, y > 0$ for all $y \neq 0$, then x^* is an isolated local unconstrained minimizing point of $f(x)$.

The second-order conditions may be viewed as a quadratic analysis at the point x^*, since the terms up to the second degree in the Taylor's series expansion of the given functions are now involved. These conditions significantly increase the capability of discerning candidate local solution points. The second-order sufficient conditions have proved to be extremely useful in developing deeper results in nonlinear programming, e.g., in sensitivity analysis, the study of the rate of convergence of various algorithms, acceleration of convergence of penalty methods, and obtaining exact penalty

BARRIER METHODS FOR NONLINEAR PROGRAMMING

functions (i.e., penalty functions whose local minima coincide with the local minima of the given constrained problem for certain values of the parameter).

Returning to our line of discussion, let us briefly investigate the relationship of the convergence properties of $P(x, r_k)$ and $L(x, r_k)$ to these optimality conditions. Assume $f(x)$ and $g_i(x)$ ($i = 1, \ldots, m$) are once continuously differentiable. Then, at an unconstrained local minimizing point x^k of $P(x, r_k)$ in $R^\#$, we have from Lemma 2 that

$$\nabla P(x^k, r_k) = \nabla f(x^k) - r_k \sum_{i=1}^{m} [1/g_i^2(x^k)]\nabla g_i(x_k) = 0 \quad (19)$$

Comparing (19) to the gradient of the Lagrangian (12) of Problem P, given by

$$\nabla \mathscr{L}(x, u) = \nabla f(x) - \sum_{i=1}^{m} u_i \nabla g_i(x)$$

we find that if we define $u_i^k \equiv r_k/g_i^2(x^k)$, then

$$\nabla \mathscr{L}(x^k, u^k) = 0 \quad (20)$$

We also have the relations

$$g_i(x^k) > 0 \quad (i = 1, \ldots, m) \quad (21)$$
$$u_i^k g_i(x^k) = r_k/g_i(x^k) \quad (22)$$

and

$$u^k > 0 \quad (23)$$

Comparing the results (20)–(23) with the first-order Conditions (13)–(16) for Problem P stated in Lemma 1, the similarities are apparent. In fact, under the conditions of Theorem 1, we know that x^k exists for every k and we showed that limit points of $\{x^k\}$ solve Problem P, and, in particular, that $r_k \sum_{i=1}^{m} 1/g_i(x^k) \to 0$, or equivalently, that $u_i^k g_i(x^k) \to 0$ ($i = 1, \ldots, m$). Consequently, for k large, Conditions (20)–(23) may be viewed as a *perturbation* of the first-order necessary Conditions (13)–(16) holding at some local solution x^* of Problem P.

Note that we have not concluded that the sequence of multipliers $\{u^k\}$, as defined above, necessarily has a (finite) limit or a convergent subsequence, nor can we conclude without further assumptions (e.g., as in Lemma 1) that the Kuhn-Tucker conditions (13)–(16) are satisfied at x^*, even though a convergent subsequence of $\{x^k\}$ converges to x^*. It is possible that $x^k \to x^*$, but that components of $\{u^k\}$ are increasing without bound as $k \to +\infty$, so that there is no finite Kuhn-Tucker Lagrange multiplier u^* associated with x^*. This is not at all inconsistent with the fact that $u_i^k g_i(x^k) \to 0$, all i, nor with the fact that x^* is a solution of Problem P.

However, suppose that $x^k \to x^*$ and also that $u^k \to u^*$. (Conditions, such as those given in the section entitled Convex Programming by Barrier Methods for the convex problem, can be given such that (finite) limit points of u^k exist, and it follows from this discussion that these are optimal Lagrange multipliers associated with x^*.) Then we have that $g_i(x^k) \to g_i(x^*)$ ($i = 1, \ldots, m$), $\nabla \mathcal{L}(x^k, u^k) \to \nabla \mathcal{L}(x^*, u^*)$, and we can also conclude from (23) that $u^* \geq 0$. Thus the first-order necessary conditions are satisfied as the limit of the various conditions holding along the unconstrained minimizing sequence $\{x^k\}$ of $\{P(x, r_k)\}$.

Another way of viewing the Conditions (20)–(23) is based on the intimation that they appear to represent the first-order necessary conditions that x^k be a local solution of *a perturbation of Problem P*. This is, in fact, the case, and it is easy to verify from the fact that if $P(x^k, r_k) \leq P(x, r_k)$ for $x \in R^\# \cap N$, where N is a neighborhood of x^k, then x^k is a solution of

$$\min f(x) \quad \text{s.t.} \quad g_i(x) \geq g_i(x^k) \quad (i = 1, \ldots, m), x \in N \qquad (P^k)$$

This is of practical interest since it defines a feasible subproblem of Problem P that is solved with each minimization of the barrier function.

Relationships between barrier and penalty methods and the second-order conditions for a solution of Problem P have also been determined. Assume $f(x)$ and $g_i(x)$ ($i = 1, \ldots, m$) are twice continuously differentiable. Then, by Lemma 5, it follows that

$$\nabla^2 P(x^k, r_k) = \qquad (24)$$

$$\nabla^2 f(x^k) - r_k \sum_{i=1}^m [1/g_i^2(x^k)] \nabla^2 g_i(x^k) + 2r_k \sum_{i=1}^m [1/g_i^3(x^k)] \nabla g_i(x^k) \nabla g_i^T(x^k)$$

is a positive semidefinite matrix, i.e.,

$$y^T \nabla^2 P(x^k, r_k) y \geq 0 \text{ for all } y \qquad (25)$$

Noting that the Hessian of the Lagrangian (12) is given by

$$\nabla^2 \mathcal{L}(x, u) = \nabla^2 f(x) - \sum_{i=1}^m u_i \nabla^2 g_i(x) \qquad (26)$$

it is apparent from (24) and (25) that

$$y^T \nabla^2 \mathcal{L}(x^k, u^k) y \geq 0 \text{ for all } y \text{ such that } y^T \nabla g_i(x^k) = 0 \quad (i = 1, \ldots, m) \quad (27)$$

where u^k is defined as previously in (22). Observe that, using Lemma 3, (27) could also have been directly deduced from the fact that x^k solves Problem P^k. Comparing this with the second-order necessary conditions (Lemma 3) for a local minimizing point of Problem P, we again see a suggestive similarity. Suppose that for any z such that $z^T \nabla g_i(x^*) = 0$ where $g_i(x^*) = 0$ it follows that for the same indices: there exists $\{z_k\}$ such that $z_k^T \nabla g_i(x^k) = 0$ and $z_k \to z$. Then, assuming for simplicity that $x^k \to x^*$, $u^k \to u^*$, and $u_i^* > 0$, if $g_i(x^*) = 0$, it follows that

$$\lim_k z_k^T \nabla^2 P(x^k, r_k) z_k = z^T \nabla^2 \mathcal{L}(x^*, u^*) z \geq 0$$

for all z such that $z^T \nabla g_i(x^*) = 0$ when $g_i(x^*) = 0$. Combined with the previous observations, it follows that the second-order necessary optimality conditions for a solution of Problem P are satisfied in the limit. (It is emphasized that, unlike the first-order results, this requires something more than the fact that $x^k \to x^*$ and $u^k \to u^*$. We shall not pursue conditions under which there exists the stipulated sequence $\{z_k\}$. Some results related to this are indicated by Fiacco and McCormick [26], who explicitly derived the asymptotic analog of most of the best known first- and second-order optimality conditions.)

Connections with the second-order sufficient conditions (Lemma 4) have also been established and will be indicated in a subsequent result. A similar analysis can be done for any such auxiliary function method providing the function has the desired degree of differentiability. For example, the logarithmic barrier function yields analogous results with $u_i^k \equiv r_k/g_i(x^k)$.

PERTURBATION ANALYSIS BASED ON CONTINUOUS VARIATION OF THE BARRIER FUNCTION PARAMETER

It was indicated that optimality conditions can be used to *derive* algorithms—perhaps most (if not all) algorithms. An appropriate perturbation of the optimality conditions was observed above to be directly related to the conditions holding at an unconstrained minimizing point of the barrier function. This observation indicates a way of *deriving* large classes of auxiliary functions. For example, consider the perturbation of the first-order conditions (14)–(16) given by

$$u_i g_i(x) = r > 0 \quad (i = 1, \ldots, m)$$
$$u_i \geq 0 \quad (i = 1, \ldots, m)$$

and

$$\nabla f(x) - \sum_{i=1}^{m} u_i \nabla g_i(x) = 0$$

Suppose we assume there exists $[x(r), u(r)]$ satisfying this system. Then we conclude that $x(r) \in R^\#$ and that

$$\nabla f[x(r)] - \sum_{i=1}^{m} \{r/g_i[x(r)]\} \nabla g_i[x(r)] = 0$$

which says that the gradient of the logarithmic barrier function (7) vanishes, i.e., $\nabla L[x(r), r] = 0$. We might thus have been led to study the method based on $L(x, r)$. In principle, we could investigate any parametric perturbation of the optimality conditions such that the conditions are precisely satisfied for a given value (or limiting value) of the parameter and attempt to reconstruct the function from the specified conditions. The $P(x, r)$ barrier function and the $T(x, t)$ exterior penalty function can also be readily derived in this manner [11] and it is likely that most auxiliary functions can as well.

When the functions defining Problem P are twice differentiable, the next result gives an important application of the second-order sufficient conditions that a point be a local solution. It involves the perturbation analysis we have just been discussing, providing a deeper analysis of the behavior of the auxiliary function minima in a neighborhood of a local solution, when the parameter is allowed to vary *continuously*. We give the result in terms of the logarithmic barrier function $L(x, r)$, but it is clearly applicable to any *twice differentiable* auxiliary function. The requirement of twice differentiability is not satisfied *everywhere* in the domain of definition of the quadratic loss exterior penalty function (6) for *inequality* constraints, because the presence of the step function generally makes the second derivatives discontinuous wherever an inequality constraint is binding. However, the differentiability requirement is met *in a neighborhood* of a local solution, under the given conditions. The results are also readily adapted to the quadratic loss function $T(x, t)$ (5) applied to *equality* constraints, the exponential interior-exterior function $E(x, t)$ (9) applied to equalities or inequalities, the inverse-penalty barrier function $P(x, r)$ (1), and any mixed auxiliary function that has the property of carrying over the order of differentiability of the problem functions in a neighborhood of a local solution.

Theorem 2. [Existence of a once continuously differentiable trajectory $x(r)$ of minima of $L(x, r)$.] If
(i) f and $g_i(x)$ ($i = 1, \ldots, m$) are twice continuously differentiable,
(ii) the second-order sufficiency conditions (Lemma 4) hold at (x^*, u^*),
(iii) the gradients $\nabla g_i(x^*)$ of those $g_i(x^*) = 0$ are linearly independent, and
(iv) $u_i^* > 0$ for those $g_i(x^*) = 0$ (called "strict complementary slackness"),
then, in a neighborhood of $r = 0$,
(a) there exists a unique once continuously differentiable vector function $[x(r), u(r)]$ satisfying

$$u_i g_i(x) = r \quad (i = 1, \ldots, m)$$
$$\nabla \mathscr{L}(x, u) = 0 \text{ such that}$$

(b) $[x(r), u(r)] = [x(0), u(0)] = (x^*, u^*)$, where x^* is an isolated local solution of Problem P with associated unique Lagrange multiplier u^*,
(c) for $r > 0$, $x(r)$ is a (unique once continuously differentiable) trajectory of unconstrained local minima of $L(x, r)$ in $R^\#$,
(d) for $r > 0$, $\nabla^2 L[x(r), r]$ is a positive definite matrix, and
(e) if the problem functions are k ($k \geq 2$) times continuously differentiable, then the vector function $[x(r), u(r)]$ is $(k - 1)$ times continuously differentiable.

These results were given in the Fiacco-McCormick book [11]. They establish a basis for extrapolating along $x(r)$ to a solution estimate, e.g., by fitting a polynomial in r to each component of $x(r)$ through several points $\{x(r_1), x(r_2), \ldots, x(r_p)\}$ that minimize $L(x, r)$ for the indicated values of r. In particular, the theorem gives general conditions such that any minimizing sequence $\{x^k\}$ of $L(x, r_k)$ and the associated Lagrange multipliers $\{u^k\}$ [where $u_i^k = r^k/g_i(x^k)$] are unique and converge to unique locally optimal limits. Also, it shows that the matrix of second partial derivatives $\nabla^2 L(x, r_k)$ is "well-behaved" in a neighborhood of a minimizing point x^k, in a sense that is crucial to the success of some of the more powerful numerical techniques for determining an unconstrained minimizing point.

If additional conditions are assumed about the functions defining Problem P, then stronger conclusions follow. A now well-known set of conditions gives rise to a particularly important class of problems called "convex programming problems."

CONVEX PROGRAMMING BY BARRIER METHODS

Definition 3. (The convex programming problem.) If $f(x)$ is a convex function and $g_i(x)$ ($i = 1, \ldots, m$) are concave functions, then Problem P

$$\min f(x) \quad s.t. \quad g_i(x) \geq 0 \quad (i = 1, \ldots, m) \tag{P}$$

is a convex programming problem.

Numerous results have been obtained for convex programs, some of the most significant being the following.

Lemma 7. (Local-global property.) If Problem P is a convex programming problem, then any local minimizing point x^* is a global minimizing point.

Lemma 8. (Sufficiency of Kuhn-Tucker first-order conditions.) If the functions of the convex Problem P are once continuously differentiable at x^* and the first-order Kuhn-Tucker conditions (13)–(16) hold at (x^*, u^*), then x^* is a solution of Problem P.

A well-known corollary of this result follows immediately.

Corollary 1. (First-order sufficient condition for an unconstrained minimum.) If $f(x)$ is a convex function, once continuously differentiable at x^*, and if $\nabla f(x^*) = 0$, then x^* is an unconstrained global minimizing point of $f(x)$.

Lemma 9. (Necessity of Kuhn-Tucker first-order conditions.) If Problem P is a convex programming problem, $f(x)$ and $g_i(x)$ ($i = 1, \ldots, m$) are once continuously differentiable at a solution x^*, and either (i) the constraints such that $g_i(x^*) = 0$ are linear or (ii) there exists a feasible point x^0 such that $g_i(x^0) > 0$ for all nonlinear $g_i(x)$, then there exists u^* such that (x^*, u^*) satisfies the first order Kuhn-Tucker conditions (13)–(16).

Recall that the Lagrangian of Problem P is defined as

$$\mathscr{L}(x, u) \equiv f(x) - \sum_{i=1}^{m} u_i g_i(x)$$

The following result, provable under various regularity conditions, clearly shows the close connection between a mathematical programming problem and its associated Lagrangian.

Lemma 10. (A version of the Kuhn-Tucker Equivalence theorem [62].) If Problem P is a convex programming problem and if (i) or (ii) of Lemma 9 holds, then x^* is a solution of Problem P if and only if there exists $u^* \geq 0$ such that, for all $u \geq 0$ and all x, (x^*, u^*) is a saddlepoint of the Lagrangian, i.e., $\mathscr{L}(x^*, u) \leq \mathscr{L}(x^*, u^*) \leq \mathscr{L}(x, u^*)$ for all $x \in E^n$ and all $u \geq 0$.

The following duality results were obtained by Wolfe [63] and have important applications to barrier and penalty function methods.

Definition 4. (The dual of the convex Problem P.) If Problem P is a convex programming problem and the problem functions are once continuously differentiable, then the problem

$$\max \mathscr{L}(x, u) \quad \text{s.t.} \quad \nabla_x \mathscr{L}(x, u) = 0, \, u_i \geq 0 \quad (i = 1, \ldots, m) \quad (D)$$

is called the dual of Problem P, where maximization is over both x and u. Dropping the differentiability assumption, the dual problem is

$$\max \mathscr{L}(x, u) \quad \text{s.t.} \quad \mathscr{L}(x, u) = \inf_z L(z, u), \, u_i \geq 0 \quad (i = 1, \ldots, m) \quad (D')$$

The problems are dual in the following sense (where we assume differentiability holds where needed).

Lemma 11. (Duality relationships.) If Problem P is a convex programming problem, if y is a feasible point of Problem P and (x^0, u^0) a feasible point of Problem D or D', then $f(y) \geq \mathscr{L}(x^0, u^0)$. If x^* is a solution of Problem P and a suitable "constraint qualification" holds at x^* [e.g., in the differentiable case, linear independence of the binding constraint gradients suffices, and in either case, assumption (i) or assumption (ii) of Lemma 3], then there exists a solution (x^*, u^*) of Problem D (with differentiability) and Problem D' (with or without differentiability), and $f(x^*) = L(x^*, u^*)$.

For the convex problem, many additional results hold for barrier and penalty function methods, as they do in most other valid procedures. We shall again avoid encumbering refinements and summarize several key results in terms of the $P(x, r)$ barrier function. Corresponding results have been validated for large classes of barrier, exterior and mixed methods, more general spaces, and other convexity-concavity assumptions. The following theorem is due to Fiacco and McCormick [11, 30, 31]. (As usual, $r_k > 0$ and $\{r_k\} \downarrow 0$.)

Theorem 3. (Convexity results utilizing the $P(x, r)$ barrier function.) If Problem P is a convex programming problem, if the set of minimizing points of Problem P is bounded, and if $R^\# \equiv \{x \mid g_i(x) > 0, i = 1, \ldots, m\} = 0$, then

(a) $P(x, r_k)$ has a finite local unconstrained minimizing point in $R^\#$ for each k,

BARRIER METHODS FOR NONLINEAR PROGRAMMING

(b) $P(x, r_k)$ is convex in $R^\#$ for each k, hence every local minimum of $P(x, r_k)$ in $R^\#$ is a global minimum of $P(x, r_k)$ in $R^\#$,

(c) the set of local minimizing points of $\{P(x, r_k)\}$ in $R^\#$ is bounded, hence any local minimizing sequence $\{x^k\}$ of $\{P(x, r_k)\}$ has a limit point,

(d) every limit point of $\{x^k\}$ is a solution of Problem P,

(e) $P(x^k, r_k) \to v^* \equiv \min_R f(x)$ and $f(x^k) \to v^*$, and $r_k \sum_{i=1}^{m} 1/g_i(x^k) \to 0$ as $k \to +\infty$,

(f) $\{f(x^k)\}$ monotonically decreases and $\{\sum_{i=1}^{m} 1/g_i(x^k)\}$ monotonically increases,

(g) if $u_i^k \equiv r_k/g_i^2(x^k)$ ($i = 1, \ldots, m$), then (x^k, u^k) satisfies the constraints of the dual problem D' (and the constraints of the dual problem D if the problem functions are once continuously differentiable), and

(h) the sequence $\{x^k, u^k\}$ is bounded, hence has a limit point, and any such limit point (x^*, u^*) is a solution of Problem D' (and of Problem D, with differentiability).

This is one of the sharpest results that have been provided for the convex programming problem. The conclusions are numerous and collectively give a concise summary of the principal properties usually associated with barrier functions in convex programming.

Conclusions (a), (c), (d), (e), and (f) were proved for *global* minimizing points in Theorem 1 under more general conditions, and this part of Theorem 3 may be viewed as a corollary of Theorem 1. To verify this, it can be shown [11] that the assumptions of Theorem 3 imply the satisfaction of the assumptions of Theorem 1. However, Conclusion (b) of Theorem 3 gives a dramatic improvement by guaranteeing global results in terms of a local minimizing sequence $\{x^k\}$. Convexity of the Problem P carries over to $P(x, r_k)$, so that *any local* minimizing point x^k, $k = 1, 2, \ldots$, yields a *global* minimizing sequence. In Theorem 1 we concentrated on characterizing a global minimizing sequence, but there may also be present many *local* minimizing sequences (whose limit points may or may not be *local* solutions of Problem P).

Conclusions (g) and (h) are an added bonus resulting from the convexity assumption. There does exist an extremely important partial correspondence with Conclusion (g) that holds under the conditions of Theorem 1, if we further assume that the functions of Problem P are once continuously differentiable. It follows, then, that $\nabla P(x^k, r_k) = 0$ for each k so that $\nabla \mathscr{L}(x^k, u^k) = 0$ (as observed previously), with u^k defined as in Conclusion (g) of Theorem 3. This shows that the constraints of the form given in the dual problem D are satisfied under much more general assumptions, but this is as far as we can carry the analogy.

The implications of Conclusion (g) are especially important. Because of Lemma 11 and the fact that (x^k, u^k) is dual-feasible for each k, it follows that

$$\mathscr{L}(x^k, u^k) = f(x^k) - r_k \sum_{i=1}^{m} 1/g_i(x^k) \leq \min_R f(x) \leq f(x^k) \tag{28}$$

(of course, using also the fact that x^k is a feasible point of Problem P).

BARRIER METHODS FOR NONLINEAR PROGRAMMING

Consequently, when Problem P is convex, every unconstrained minimization of $P(x, r_k)$ in $R^\#$ yields *computable upper and lower* bounds on the optimal value of Problem P. This fact is extremely important, since it provides a measure of the deviation of x^k from a solution point. By presetting an acceptable tolerance, it provides a valuable convergence criterion for a computational algorithm. Any finite tolerance can be satisfied, in theory, since [by Conclusions (e) and (h)] $\lim_k \mathcal{L}(x^k, u^k) = \lim_k f(x^k) = v^* \equiv \min_R f(x)$; i.e., both bounds converge to the optimal value of Problem P. Also, since (28) implies

$$0 \leq f(x^k) - v^* \leq r_k \sum_{i=1}^{m} 1/g_i(x^k) \equiv \sum_{i=1}^{m} u_i^k g_i(x^k) \qquad (29)$$

we see that the deviation of $f(x^k)$ from optimality is bounded above by the value of the penalty term in $P(x, r_k)$ evaluated at x^k and this positive quantity, in turn, is precisely the extent by which the complimentary slackness condition is not satisfied.

The theorem, as noted by Lootsma [48] and Fiacco and McCormick [11], is valid for the logarithmic barrier function $L(x, r_k)$, providing we replace the second sequence in Conclusion (f) by $\{-\sum_{i=1}^{m} \ln g_i(x^k)\}$ and define $u_i^k \equiv r_k/g_i(x^k)$ ($i = 1, \ldots, m$) in Conclusion (g). The bounds now become

$$L(x^k, u^k) \equiv f(x^k) - mr_k \leq \min_R f(x) \leq f(x^k) \qquad (30)$$

where m is the number of constraints in Problem P. From this, we conclude, analogous to (29), that

$$0 \leq f(x^k) - v^* \leq mr_k \equiv \sum_{i=1}^{m} u_i^k g_i(x^k) \qquad (31)$$

An important advantage here is the fact that the deviation is now independent of x^k, so that a specification of the tolerable error in estimating the optimal value of Problem P immediately yields the smallest value of r_k for which it is necessary to minimize $L(x, r_k)$. Conversely, for any choice of r_k, bounds on $f(x^k) - v^*$ are known *a priori*.

Before proceeding to a discussion of a general algorithm, several observations are warranted concerning the foregoing results. It should be noted in the general convergence theorem (Theorem 1) *and* in the convergence theorem for convex programming (Theorem 3) that *convergence of a minimizing sequence $\{x^k\}$ to a solution of Problem P is not proved*—merely that, in a specified set, a convergent subsequence $\{x^{k_j}\}$ of $\{x^k\}$ exists and the limit of any such convergent subsequence is a solution of Problem P. This is an important distinction. Only under additional assumptions can it be concluded that a minimizing sequence $\{x^k\}$ (or a local minimizing sequence in a specified neighborhood) itself converges to a solution (or a local solution) of the given problem. For example, if it is assumed that x^* is the unique global solution of Problem P, then the convergence of $\{x^k\}$ to x^* follows as an immediate corollary of Theorem 1 or Theorem 3. (*Convergence* of a *local* minimizing sequence to a local solution x^* follows likewise under certain conditions, for example, under the conditions of Theorem 2—a consequence of the assumed second-order sufficient conditions which in turn imply the uniqueness of the local solution in a neighborhood.) Relinquishing the uniqueness assumption, Sandblom [64] has provided an example of a convex programming problem (i.e., convex according to Definition 3 *for x restricted to feasible points*) such that $P(x, r_k)$ is strictly convex for all k [so that a local minimizing point x^k of $P(x, r_k)$ in $R^{\#}$ is unique for each k], but $\{x^k\}$ has an *infinite* number of distinct limit points, all of which solve Problem P. Also, for the convex problem with $P(x, r_k)$ strictly convex in $R^{\#}$, it is shown that if there exists a point $\bar{x} \in R^{\#} \equiv \{x \mid g_i(x) > 0, i = 1, \ldots, m\}$ solving Problem P, then (under the usual conditions) it follows that any minimizing sequence of $P(x, r_k)$ in $R^{\#}$, $k = 1, 2, \ldots$, *converges* to a solution $x^* \in R^{\#}$.

It must be emphasized, however, that a barrier or penalty function minimizing sequence (for convex or nonconvex problems) *may converge* to a local solution of the given problem *without* the stipulation that the local solution be *locally unique*. Sandblom's counterexample simply tells us that the (entire) sequence *will not converge for certain problems*. Examples are easily given that illustrate convergence to a (local) solution that is not (locally) unique, e.g., minimize $x_1 + x_2$ s.t. $x_1 + x_2 \geq 1$, $x_1 \geq 0$, $x_2 \geq 0$, $x \in E^2$. The problem is solved by any point (x_1, x_2) such that $x_1 + x_2 = 1$, $x_1 \geq 0$, and $x_2 \geq 0$. However, it is easily verified that both barrier functions $P(x, r)$ (1) and $L(x, r)$ (7) and the Courant quadratic loss penalty function $T(x, t)$ (6) have unique minimizing trajectories converging to the particular solution (1/2, 1/2). The author conjectures that convergence of the minimizing sequence will follow for linear problems and for a large class of "well-behaved" problems without the uniqueness assumption. In fact, the Sandblom example took some ingenuity to construct and, apart from such concocted exceptions that we must presently regard as rather academic, convergence of the minimizing sequence has always been observed in practice (to the author's knowledge) whenever the minimizing sequence is uniquely determined. It is intuitively clear that the class of problems for which convergence to a local solution (without uniqueness of the local solution) follows is large. However, surprisingly, the question of when *convergence* of a (local or global) minimizing sequence does or does not occur is elusive and has not been adequately resolved.

Another caution should be raised that is often ignored but is of extreme importance in understanding the behavior of barrier and penalty functions and in correctly interpreting the results of computer implementations of these algorithms. Although every convergent subsequence $\{x^{k_j}\}$ of a *global minimizing* sequence $\{x^k\}$ converges to a *global solution* of Problem P under certain conditions (Theorems 1 and 3), it does *not* follow that *any* convergent subsequence of any *local minimizing* sequence converges to a *local solution* of the problem. Obviously, this difficulty is not encountered in the convex problem (Definition 3) where a local minimizing sequence is global (Theorem 3). In the nonconvex case, consider the trivial one-dimensional example: minimize x s.t. $x^2 \geq 0$. The feasible region is the entire space E^1, and the

BARRIER METHODS FOR NONLINEAR PROGRAMMING

problem has no finite lower bound. However, it is easy to verify that the barrier functions $L(x, r)$ and $P(x, r)$ have local minimizing sequences in $E_+^1 \equiv \{x \mid x > 0\}$ for any $\{r_k > 0\}$, and any such sequence will converge to $x = 0$, which is obviously not a local minimum of the problem! A somewhat analogous example in E^2 is given by: minimize $x_1 + x_2$, $x_1 x_2 \geq 0$. The solution is again not attained since $x_1 + x_2$ attains values in the feasible region below any specified finite bound. However, $P(x, r)$ and $L(x, r)$ have local minimizing points in $E_+^2 \equiv \{x \mid x_1 > 0, x_2 > 0\}$, and their minimizing sequences in this set converge to (0, 0), which is *not* a local minimizing point of the given problem. In both examples, it is easy to see that the set $R^\#$ is the union of disjoint sets, and hence it is clear that barrier methods can be "trapped" in various subsets of such a set. Nonconvexities can offer various kinds of difficulties to penalty methods and any other method as well, and in their presence one must bring other considerations to bear other than the fact that an algorithm has satisfied certain necessary conditions.

Another observation, this on the positive side, is worth emphasizing and applies to both barrier and penalty methods. These methods generate minimizing sequences that have convergent subsequences converging to a local solution of the given problem under extremely general conditions (e.g., those of Theorem 1). For example, they do not require that a determined local solution be a Kuhn-Tucker point or satisfy any particularly rigid regularity conditions. This is an important fact attesting to the "robustness" of the approach and is not an advantage shared by all methods.

A BASIC BARRIER FUNCTION ALGORITHM AND COMPUTATIONAL CONSIDERATIONS

In this section we discuss the computational implementation of a method for solving

$$\text{minimize } f(x) \quad \text{s.t.} \quad g_i(x) \geq 0 \quad (i = 1, \ldots, m) \quad (P)$$

based (for definiteness) on the logarithmic barrier function

$$L(x, r) \equiv f(x) - r \sum_{i=1}^{m} \ln g_i(x)$$

Most of our observations readily extend to problems involving equalities and to other barrier and penalty methods [11]. A general procedure may be summarized as follows:

(1) Find a point x^0 in $R^\# \equiv \{x \mid g_i(x) > 0 \ (i = 1, \ldots, m)\}$.
(2) Set $r = r_1 > 0$.
(3) Starting from x^0 use some unconstrained minimization technique to calculate a minimizing point $x^1 = x(r_1)$ of $L(x, r_1)$ in $R^\#$.
(4) Extrapolate for an estimated solution $\hat{x}$ of Problem P.

(5) Stop if $\hat{x}$ satisfies the convergence criteria. Otherwise, set $r = r_2 > 0$, where $r_2 < r_1$.
(6) Extrapolate for $\hat{x}_2$, a minimizing point of $L(x, r_2)$ in $R^\#$.
(7) Return to (3), replacing x^0 by $\hat{x}_2$ and increasing the indices by one, and continue for $r = r_3, r_4, \ldots$, where $r_k > 0$ for all k and $r_k \to 0$.

Let us briefly consider and discuss each step.

(1) Find $x^0 \in R^\#$

It is often possible to readily determine a point in $R^\#$ by a simple analysis of the constraints or through an understanding of the application that motivated the problem. When this is not true, then *any method* that can find a *solution* of Problem P can make this determination. We indicate how this may be done using a barrier method. The following approach was suggested by the author [65].

Suppose we are given $\bar{x}$ such that $g_i(\bar{x}) > 0$ ($i = 1, \ldots, q$) and $g_i(\bar{x}) \le 0$ ($i = q + 1, \ldots, m$). Then apply the barrier method to the problem.

$$\text{minimize } [-g_{q+1}(x)] \quad \text{s.t.} \quad g_i(x) \ge 0 \quad (i = 1, \ldots, q) \quad (P_{q+1})$$

using $\bar{x}$ to replace x^0 as the starting point in the procedure given above. Note that the constraints of Problem P_{q+1} will be strictly enforced by definition of the barrier method. If the optimal value of Problem P_q is positive, then $-g_{q+1}(x) > 0$ or, equivalently, $g_{q+1}(x) < 0$ for all x satisfying the constraints of (P_{q+1}). This means that the feasible region of Problem P is empty. If this value is zero, then $R^\# = \emptyset$ and the usual barrier method is not applicable, though the exterior method and other approaches not contingent on $R^\# = \emptyset$ can be applied. Assuming $R^\# \ne \emptyset$, the optimal solution value of Problem P_{q+1} will be negative, and consequently (since we are assuming continuity of the problem functions) a near-optimal solution point x' will yield $g_i(x') > 0$ ($i = 1, \ldots, q + 1$). We can now use x' as a starting point for Problem P_{q+2} and repeat the procedure until a desired point $x^0 \in R^\#$ is determined. (The above approach could provide some insights in isolating both "troublesome" and easily satisfied constraints, and yield much information concerning the structure of the problem.)

Numerous variations of the above idea are possible, e.g., we can satisfy the most violated constraint first, etc. Also, in the course of solving Problem P_{q+1}, we are well advised to monitor the sequence of unconstrained minimizing points of the barrier function and to redefine the problem and the associated barrier function accordingly to enforce those constraints that are fortuitously well satisfied in the process. A modification of the above approach that apparently has proved more effective computationally is to apply the method at hand to the problem

$$\text{minimize } \left[-\sum_{j=q+1}^{m} g_j(x) \right] \quad \text{s.t.} \quad g_i(x) \ge 0 \quad (i = 1, \ldots, q) \quad (\tilde{P})$$

the idea here being to work on the satisfaction of all violated constraints simultaneously. It is also advisable, and may be essential in using $(\tilde{P})$, to transfer "well-satisfied" functions g_j immediately to the constraint set of $(\tilde{P})$, since reductions in the objective function might otherwise be possible by unnecessarily increasing the value of functions defining constraints that are already satisfied. Alternatively, a weighted sum of the violated constraints might be more efficient, e.g., the respective weights being selected proportionate to a measure of the constraint violation. If upper and lower bounds on the variables are available, it is advisable to select the starting point $\bar{x}$ to satisfy these, and to insist on their satisfaction throughout the solution process.

Several observations on the foregoing feasibility search are important to keep in mind. The determination of an initial feasible point is not required by the (exterior) penalty methods, since the penalty functions are defined and minimized over the entire space. (This is a distinct advantage of exterior methods, though somewhat offset by the fact that, unlike barrier methods, all points in a minimizing sequence are generally nonfeasible.) Following Lootsma [34], we could (in some sense) make the best of initial conditions by defining a *mixed* barrier-penalty function such that a constraint is handled by a barrier or penalty term, depending, respectively, on whether or not the constraint is strictly satisfied at the starting point. An improved strategy might involve the application of the $\tilde{P}$ approach for several iterations, attempting to determine a point satisfying as many constraints as possible with token effort, and then proceeding to define a mixed auxiliary function as suggested. But assuming we wish to apply a barrier method, it is further noted that when $R^\# \neq 0$ the "feasibility phase" described above need not require *solving any* auxiliary problem completely. Whenever a point is determined that yields a positive value of *any* constraint of Problem P, this function may be transferred from the objective function to become a new constraint in another auxiliary problem. Also, assuming we can generate a minimizing sequence converging to a global solution of the auxiliary problems and the constraint functions of Problem P are continuous, the objective function of any auxiliary function as defined will eventually be negative in a *neighborhood* of an optimizing point. Third, it should be emphasized that if the constraints of Problem P are concave, then Problems P_{q+1} and $\tilde{P}$ are convex. Not only do the usual advantages of convexity apply in this instance, but additionally the dual lower bounds (on the optimal value of the auxiliary problems), that can be determined at any minimizing point of the barrier function (the preceding section) give important information. If a dual bound, say M, of P_{q+1} or $\tilde{P}$ is positive, then we can conclude that $-g_{q+1}(x) > M > 0$, or $-\sum_{j=q+1}^{m} g_j(x) > M > 0$ for all x satisfying the constraints of these problems, respectively. In either case, the implication is that the constraints of Problem P are inconsistent and calculations may be terminated. Fourth, if it is difficult to determine a feasible point, then indications are that the feasible region is "small" or "thin." In either case, determination of a feasible point may itself represent substantial progress towards determining a solution. Finally, it should be clear that the feasibility phase may yield much valuable diagnostic information concerning the problem structure, e.g., pin-pointing constraint subsets that are "easy" or "difficult" to satisfy and possible inconsistencies and deficiencies in the mathematical model. It is conceivable that such information may be more valuable to a user than a solution.

One word of caution: If the auxiliary Problems P_{q+1} or $\tilde{P}$ are not convex, then barrier methods or other techniques applied to these problems may yield only *local* solutions. The objective functions of either problem may very well be positive at a *local* solution, but unless this solution is also *global,* it cannot be concluded from this fact alone that the constraints of Problem P are inconsistent (i.e., inconsistent everywhere, though they would be inconsistent in a neighborhood of the determined local solution).

(2) Set $r = r_1 > 0$

The selection of r_1 is somewhat arbitrary, although guidelines can be given. Before suggesting some of these, it should first be indicated why it is not standard procedure to simply select $r_1 > 0$ and extremely small, since we know for the general problem that limit points of $\{x(r_k)\}$ solve the problem as $r_k \to 0^+$, when the method is successful. For the convex problem why not choose r_1 so that the computable lower bound on the optimal objective function value as given in (30) will be within a specified tolerance? This might lead to an acceptable estimate of a solution of Problem P by a *single* unconstrained minimization of $L(x, r)$, as the theory suggests.

One difficulty with this is the fact that the computational effort to minimize $L(x, r)$ is dependent, assuming that an iterative scheme must be utilized, on the location of the starting point x^0 relative to a minimizing point $x(r)$. Another factor on which this effort depends is the "eccentricity" of the isovalue surfaces defined by the barrier function, and on the curvature of these surfaces in the vicinity of x^0. A third factor is the proximity of $x(r)$ to the boundary of R. All these factors may be significantly affected by the choice of r and generally conspire to make calculations increasingly difficult as $r \to 0^+$. This is further complicated by the fact that the minimizing trajectory $x(r)$ exhibits smoothness properties that can be exploited by various extrapolation techniques, so that motion along this trajectory can generally be accelerated. Thus, an alternative and possibly better strategy than setting $r = r_1 > 0$ and very small, is to select that value of $r_1 > 0$ such that $x(r_1)$ is "easiest" to calculate, starting from x^0, so that extrapolation along $x(r)$ can commence as soon as possible. Note that such a value of r would also be as large a value as we would wish to select—any larger value $\bar{r}_1$ would determine $x(\bar{r}^1)$ that would be more difficult to compute (by assumption) than $x(r_1)$ and furthermore, we would have to do additional computations to work our way from $x(\bar{r}^1)$ back to a minimizing point for $r = r_1 < \bar{r}_1$. Selecting r_1 too large might also result in calculating $x(r_1)$ that yields $f[x(r_1)]$ substantially larger than $f(x^0)$, i.e., $x(r_1)$ would be much "worse" than x^0 in terms of our objective of reducing $f(x)$.

The above observations lead to the conclusion that there exists an upper and lower bound on the initial value of r, given a specified starting point x^0, and that an optimal value of r (in terms of overall computational efficiency) exists somewhere in this range. The precise determination of an optimal value of r has not been resolved. However, various rules can be given that have often proved adequate.

We indicate some heuristic rules that were given in Fiacco and McCormick [11]. If we accept the goal of proceeding from the starting point x^0 to a minimizing point $x(r_1)$ as quickly as possible, then, since $\nabla L[x, r] = 0$ for any x on a minimizing trajectory $x(r)$, a strategy motivated by this point of view is to select $r \geq 0$ such that $|\nabla L(x^0, r)|$ is minimized. This is a one–variable minimization problem that can readily be solved analytically. More generally, $\nabla^T L(x^0, r) H \nabla L(x^0, r)$ may be minimized, where H is a matrix that may be calculated from other considerations {e.g., H may be an estimate of the inverse of the Hessian matrix of $L(x, r)$ at x^0, in which case minimization of the indicated quantity over r tends to minimize $L(x^0, r) - L[x(r), r]$}. Another possibility is to associate a "weight" r_i with each constraint term of the penalty function, and minimize one of the indicated quantities above (appropriately modified) over $(r_1, \ldots, r_m)$, where each component is required to be nonnegative. This requires the solution of a structured quadratic programming problem [11].

Another idea for selecting r_1 is the following. It is based on a correspondence observed by the author [66] between parametric auxiliary methods and the method of centers [67]. Given $x^0 \in R^\#$, define the function

$$\tilde{L}(x, x^0) \equiv -\ln[f(x^0) - f(x)] - \sum_{i=1}^{m} \ln g_i(x) \tag{32}$$

Under the *same* conditions required for the $L(x, r)$ barrier method (e.g., the conditions given in Theorem 1), this function will have an unconstrained minimizing point x^1 in

$$\tilde{R} \equiv \{x \mid g_i(x) > 0 \ (i = 1, \ldots, m), f(x) < f(x^0)\}$$

Assuming the function is differentiable in $\tilde{R}$, it follows that $\nabla \tilde{L}(x^1, x^0) = 0$. Comparing this with the gradient of the logarithmic barrier function $L(x, r)$, it follows that $\nabla L(x^1, r_1) = 0$, providing $r_1 = f(x^0) - f(x^1)$. Thus we have essentially *derived* an initial value of r, or perhaps more accurately, we have calculated a point x^1 on a trajectory $x(r)$ of stationary points of $L(x, r)$ and have then selected the corresponding r_1 such that $|\nabla L(x^1, r)|$ is minimized (in this case, to zero). The advantage of this strategy is that the first stationary point x^1 calculated in the barrier method process will give $f(x)^1 < f(x^0)$. The fact that r_1 is calculated "automatically" and not "arbitrarily" is somewhat misleading and not necessarily an advantage. We might have introduced positive weights in the terms of (32) without vitiating the argument, but significantly affecting the location of a minimizing point, and setting all weights to unity is, in fact, an arbitrary choice. Also, the difficulty of minimizing $\tilde{L}(x, x^0)$ in $\tilde{R}$ starting from x^0 cannot be predicted and depends on factors quite difficult to analyze in general, like those affecting the difficulty of minimizing $L(x, r_1)$ from x^0 for a given choice of r_1. It is also quite conceivable that the starting point x^0 might be near a set of optimal points of a given problem, but the minimizing point x^1 of $\tilde{L}(x, x^0)$ in $\tilde{R}$ may be far removed from this set. This could happen even if the problem were convex. {Detailed treatment of a function, analogous to (32) but involving inverse-function barrier terms, and its relationship to the $P(x, r)$ barrier function, was given by Fiacco and McCormick [68]}.

Other choices of r_1 and techniques for selecting weights in the barrier function terms are given in Fiacco and McCormick [11], Box, Davies and Swann [58], and Davies [69]. Among these are techniques for individually selecting weights as the constraint boundary is approached from $R^\#$ in the course of minimizing $f(x)$, the idea being to systematically add barrier terms as needed to enforce feasibility. This could lead to considerable efficiencies in a problem having many redundant constraints, since many of these might never enter into the barrier function so constructed.

(3) Minimize $L(x, r)$ in $R^\#$

It is important to note that this step of the algorithm requires the solution of an "unconstrained minimization problem," i.e., the determination of a "free" minimum, although the search for a minimum of $L(x, r)$ is *confined to* $R^\#$. Though the constraints $g_i(x) > 0$ ($i = 1, \ldots, m$) define $R^\#$ and obviously significantly *influence the location* of a minimizing point $x(r)$ in $R^\#$, the function $L(x, r)$ is minimized at $x(r)$ in an open set containing $x(r)$ and [although this open set happens to be contained in $R^\#$ by the way $L(x, r)$ is defined] $x(r)$ therefore satisfies the usual definition of an unconstrained local minimizing point (Definition 2). Any suitable unconstrained minimization technique may be utilized to minimize $L(x, r)$ in $R^\#$.

The tremendous importance of unconstrained minimization methodology *per se*, and its obvious relevance to the successful implementation of auxiliary function methods, would seem to warrant some perspective.

When the author jointly validated the barrier approach [29], the thoroughly tested techniques for determining an unconstrained minimum of a function were surprisingly limited, primarily to variations of first-order gradient methods [70–72]. The Newton-Raphson (second-order gradient) method for several variables was certainly well understood in theory [73–75], but apparently computational experience was lacking. A then somewhat obscure paper on a "variable metric algorithm" by Davidon [76] was not yet widely nor fully appreciated, nor were all of the implications of a paper by Hestenes and Steiffel [77] on a "conjugate direction method" for solving linear simultaneous equations.

Our first efforts to implement barrier methods using first-order gradient techniques were unsuccessful, even on small linear problems [29]. Several algorithms were completely thwarted, until we utilized a variant of the Newton-Raphson method. Our success with the method contributed both to the recognition of the power of the method and the computational efficacy of barrier methods and other auxiliary function methods. Conversely, the successful implementations of both barrier and penalty methods helped to focus attention on the importance of unconstrained minimization, since these methods are based on explicitly converting a constrained problem into a sequence of unconstrained problems. (Later, it also became clear that auxiliary function minimization provided a severe test for unconstrained minimization techniques.) Aside from this, it was clear that the unconstrained minimization problem was nothing more than a special case of a constrained minimization problem, and generally a simpler special case at that, so that the successful resolution of this problem was a prerequisite to dealing adequately with the constrained problem. Further, constrained methods were viewed more and more as adaptations of unconstrained methods.

Given such motivation and the computer technology to implement and test various iterative approaches, the last decade has seen enormous strides in the art of unconstrained minimization. Newton's method, Davidon's variable metric method, and the Hestenes-Steiffel conjugate direction method provided a nucleus for the new generation of techniques now available. Most of these techniques can be readily adapted to the unconstrained minimization problems encountered in auxiliary function algorithms. We shall give a brief indication of some of the methods that have proved most effective.

As already implied, we have had considerable success with variants of the Newton-Raphson method in minimizing barrier functions. Once a (one-dimensional) search direction is determined, we prefer to make an "optimum" move (i.e., to a point minimizing the function on the direction vector) rather than move to a point minimizing the quadratic function that estimates the given function (as prescribed in the original approach). Like all methods, the approach has limitations and should not be applied without some prior assessment as to whether these limitations are acceptable in a given situation. In particular, the Hessian matrix (of second partial derivatives) of the function must be calculated and "well-behaved," i.e., positive definite and such that the ratio of the maximum eigenvalue to the minimum eigenvalue is "not too large." (The indicated ratio is a measure of the "condition number" of the matrix and is positively correlated with the computational difficulty of minimizing the given function, a problem identified and analyzed by Murray [78–81] for barrier functions, and also studied by Lootsma [35, 82], Fletcher and McCann [59], and others.) The method is one of the best currently available for twice differentiable auxiliary functions applied to "intermediate sized" problems (say, up to 100 variables), assuming the second derivatives are easy to calculate. It is particularly effective when a near-optimal point is available as a starting point and when the Hessian matrix is well-behaved.

The Fiacco-McCormick book [11] gives several variations of Newton's method, a modified variable metric method, and a method requiring only function values. The motivation for these second-order methods is to approach the performance exhibited by the Newton method (under the indicated ideal conditions) although one or more of the desired conditions may not be met in the problem at hand. (An important motivation is to relieve the user of the task of calculating second derivatives.) Promising results are indicated for those methods, as well as for variable metric methods, particularly the revision by Fletcher and Powell [83] of a method due to Davidon [76], and conjugate direction methods proposed by Fletcher-Reeves [84], Powell [85], Zangwill [44, 56], and others. Further evidence is given of the inadequacy of the (first-order) gradient descent method to minimize barrier functions. Numerous suggestions for exploiting problem structure by way of barrier and penalty methods are given that lead to significant numerical efficiencies in utilizing the various unconstrained minimization techniques.

Lootsma [86] has recently conducted extensive computational experiments with various proposed methods for unconstrained minimization and concludes in favor of a first derivative variable metric method independently developed by Broyden [87], Fletcher [88], Goldfarb [89], and Shanno [90], and a modified Newton second derivative method described in the Fiacco-McCormick book [11]. Lootsma concludes that the (very popular and well-known) Davidon-Fletcher-Powell [83] is superseded by the Broyden-Fletcher-Goldfarb-Shanno method. The conjugate direction method by Powell [85] not requiring derivatives (generally conceded to be one of the best for a large class of functions) is adjudged insufficiently robust for minimizing barrier and penalty functions.

Kowalik and Osborne [91] report somewhat uniform results using unconstrained minimization conjugate direction methods devised by Davidon [76] and Powell [85], and a descent method (based on a modified version of Powell's technique) by Davies, Swann, and Campey [69, 92] to minimize the $P(x, r)$ (1) barrier function. Other proposals for efficiently minimizing barrier functions have been given by Box, Davies, and Swann [58], Davies [69], and Lasdon [93].

More recently, Bensasson [94] has conducted numerous computational comparisons and indicates very satisfactory results using a modification of Powell's method [85] if derivatives are not defined or readily available, the Broyden-Fletcher-Goldfarb-Shanno method if first derivatives are at hand, and the modified version of Newton's method devised by McCormick [11] if second derivatives are not difficult to evaluate.

It should be emphasized that unconstrained minimization algorithms are iterative procedures, typically generating a sequence of "search directions" $\{s^j\}$ along which the given function $F(x)$ is systematically reduced according to some prescribed rule. When successful, these procedures determine a corresponding "minimizing sequence" $\{x^j\}$ having accumulation points where certain necessary conditions for unconstrained minimization of $F(x)$ are satisfied (see the section entitled Connections between Optimality Conditions and Convergence Properties of Barrier Methods). Typically, if $F(x)$ is differentiable, a procedure is considered successful if any accumulation point $\hat{x}$ is a stationary point of $F(x)$, i.e., $\nabla F(\hat{x}) = 0$. Further, since a stationary point cannot generally be precisely determined, calculations are typically terminated at a "solution estimate" $\bar{x}$ satisfying $|\nabla F(\bar{x})| \leq \epsilon$ for some specified $\epsilon > 0$. In the absence of further information (such as conditions stated in the section entitled Connections between Optimality Conditions and Convergence Properties of Barrier Methods), an accumulation point may or may not be a local minimizing point. Further, the proximity of a solution estimate (satisfying the indicated convergence criterion) to a solution may be completely undetermined.

The importance of these facts in interpreting the results of the practical computational implementation of unconstrained minimization algorithms cannot be overemphasized. The same caution applies to constrained minimization as further indicated in the next steps of the present algorithm.

Before proceeding, it should be noted that many unconstrained minimization algorithms, having determined a point x^j and a direction vector s^j, determine $x^{j+1} = x^j + \bar{t}s^j$, where $\bar{t}$ is a local minimum of $F(x^j + ts^j)$ for $t \geq 0$. This one-dimensional problem, or "line search," is generally accomplished iteratively by a systematic sampling procedure or by fitting a sequence of curves to observed data using various interpolation devices. The most popular sampling procedures appear to be variants of Fibonacci search, requiring only function evaluations and known to be optimal (in a certain sense) when it is known only that the given function is unimodal (i.e., has one relative minimum in the interval of search). The most widely used curves are quadratic or cubic polynomials, which may be fit by using only function values or various combinations of function values and derivative information. Newton's method and the method of false position are widely used quadratic interpolation devices, the former requiring first and second derivative information at a point, the second requiring first derivative information at two points. These procedures are well-known and widely documented, and details may be found in Wilde [95], Wilde and Beightler [13], Kowalik and Osborne [91], Box, Davies, and Swann [58], Jacoby, Kowalik, and Pizzo [14], Luenberger [15], and most recent texts on nonlinear programming. For barrier function minimization, Fletcher and McCann [59], Lasdon, Fox, and Ratner [96], and others have suggested fitting (nonpolynomial) functions that more closely simulate the behavior of the barrier function, particularly near the constraint boundary. The Lasdon-Fox-Ratner method has reportedly recently yielded some of the best results to date for efficiently accomplishing the line searches for barrier functions, and is briefly described in the section entitled Future Research.

(4) Extrapolate for an Estimated Solution

Since $x(r_k)$ converges to a set of local minimizing points when the method is successful, the idea of extrapolating along a minimizing trajectory $x(r)$ to a solution estimate suggests itself as a possible device for accelerating convergence. We are thus led to studying the behavior of x as a function of r when the auxiliary function is minimized over x and r is varied. Theoretically, it is convenient and fruitful to allow r to vary continuously. Under various conditions, it develops that a locally unique minimizing trajectory $x(r)$ exists and has certain smoothness properties that establish extrapolation as both theoretically sound and computationally attractive. A basic result in this direction was given in Theorem 2.

BARRIER METHODS FOR NONLINEAR PROGRAMMING

Details and ramifications of extrapolation are somewhat involved, the interested reader being referred to Fiacco-McCormick [11], but the general idea may be readily conveyed. To be specific, suppose the conditions of Theorem 2 are satisfied. Then, there exists a once differentiable vector function $x(r)$ such that $x(0)$ is an isolated local solution of Problem P, $x(r)$ uniquely minimizes $L(x, r)$ in R near $x(0)$, and $\nabla^2 L[x(r), r]$ is positive definite for $r > 0$ and small. A necessary condition for unconstrained minimization (Lemma 2) is that $\nabla L[x(r), r] \equiv 0$ for r near 0, so application of the chain rule for differentiation is valid and yields

$$\nabla^2 L[x(r), r] \frac{dx(r)}{dr} + \frac{\partial}{\partial r} (\nabla L[x(r), r]) = 0 \tag{33}$$

The conditions allow us to conclude that

$$\frac{dx(r)}{dr} = -(\nabla^2 L)^{-1} \frac{\partial}{\partial r} (\nabla L) = \frac{1}{r} (\nabla^2 L)^{-1} \nabla f \tag{34}$$

all functions being evaluated at $x(r)$, and hence this can be used in Taylor's series to give the approximation

$$x(\bar{r}) \doteq x(r) + (\bar{r} - r) \frac{dx(r)}{dr} \tag{35}$$

for any $\bar{r}$ in a neighborhood of r. We can use (35) to estimate a new minimizing point $x(\bar{r})$ of $L(x, \bar{r})$ for $0 < \bar{r} < r$, as well as a solution of Problem P, by taking $\bar{r} = 0$.

When additional minima of $L(x, r_k)$ have been calculated, we can repeat the above procedure and, further, we can fit a vector function $x(r)$ through these points using various interpolation procedures. For example, we can fit a p-th degree polynomial to each component of the last $p + 1$ determined minima, $x(r_k)$ ($k = 1, \ldots, p + 1$), and use this to estimate $x(r_{p+2})$ and $x(0)$. To illustrate, when $p = 2$ we assume $x(r) \doteq a_0 + a_1 r + a_2 r^2$ and calculate the i-th components of the coefficient vectors a_0, a_1, a_2 from

$$\begin{aligned} x_i(r_1) &= a_{0i} + a_{1i} r_1 + a_{2i} r_1^2 \\ x_i(r_2) &= a_{0i} + a_{1i} r_2 + a_{2i} r_2^2 \\ x_i(r_3) &= a_{0i} + a_{1i} r_3 + a_{2i} r_3^2 \end{aligned} \tag{36}$$

given r_1, r_2, r_3, and the i-th components of the respective minimizing points, $x(r_1)$, $x(r_2)$, and $x(r_3)$. We can then obtain both the i-th component of the solution estimate $x(0)$ and the i-th component of the estimate of $x(r_4)$, for the minimizing point of $L(x, r_4)$, where r_4 is stipulated such that $0 < r_4 < r_3$. The particular structure of these equations allows for extremely efficient computation of the estimates by recursion formulas [11].

It is clear that we could utilize more general estimating functions and various approximation procedures based on both the sequence of determined minimizing points $\{x^k\}$ and the associated derivatives dx^k/dr to fit a function $\hat{x}(r)$ to $x(r)$. The use of second-order polynomial estimates (36) based on the last three successive minimizing points has proven quite powerful as an acceleration device, generally yielding substantial savings of computational effort [11, 59]. It has therefore become a standard option in some of the most heavily utilized computer programs of barrier function algorithms [97, 98]. (In fact, first-order extrapolation is often adequate.) The next estimating minimizing point becomes the new starting point for the next unconstrained minimization of the penalty function. Calculations are terminated, of course, if $x(0)$ satisfies the convergence criteria prescribed for the original problem. Other ideas for accelerating convergence have been given by Fletcher and McCann [59] and Osborne and Ryan [99, 100].

(5a) Stop if $\hat{x}$ Satisfies the Convergence Criteria

In applying any iterative algorithmic procedure, a stopping rule is essential. We are naturally led to criteria based on the various conditions for optimality, and ideally, it would be desirable to satisfy conditions that guarantee optimality, i.e., sufficient conditions for a global solution. Unfortunately, it is generally not even possible to guarantee local optimality and we encounter a law that pervades the theory of extrema: it is generally possible only to calculate a *local candidate* extremum that satisfies certain *necessary* conditions. Having done so, it is *sometimes* possible to invoke additional properties of the problem functions to conclude that the determined candidate is indeed a *local* extremum. In very particular circumstances, it can be argued that the *local* extremum must be *global*.

This law applies to general-purpose nonlinear programming algorithms in the following sense: in the absence of detailed prior knowledge concerning particular properties of a problem, it often cannot be asserted whether a given algorithm is applicable nor whether the algorithm will determine a local or global solution of a problem to which it is applicable. For example, unimodality or convexity, and other required regulatory conditions, may be too difficult to verify in a complex problem. A recurrent example is the fact that algorithms applied to problems involving differentiable functions are conventionally deemed theoretically successful if they generate minimizing sequences whose accumulation points are first order Kuhn-Tucker points, i.e., if x^* is an accumulation point, then there exists $u^* \geq 0$ such that (13)–(16) are satisfied. An *ad hoc* analysis is then required to determine the status of x^*. This analysis is often prohibitive in practice and the status remains conjectural. In fact, virtually all general nonlinear programming algorithms can guarantee *only* this type of convergence. The author knows of only one partial exception for differentiable functions in several variables, where accumulation points are guaranteed to satisfy the *second* order necessary conditions (Lemma 3): an algorithm for minimizing a nonlinear function subject to linear constraints due to McCormick [101]. This state of affairs is certainly not due to a lack of imagination on the part of those who devise algorithms, but is indicative rather of the elusiveness of the general problem in the absence of rather severe restrictions.

BARRIER METHODS FOR NONLINEAR PROGRAMMING

The above observations apply to nonlinear programming methods in general, and to auxiliary function methods in particular. Results like Theorem 1 may lead us to believe that accumulation points of these procedures will yield local minima (and not just first-order Kuhn-Tucker points, assuming differentiability). However, these results are *contingent on solving* mathematical programming subproblems—in the present algorithm, on the unconstrained *minimizations* of $\{L(x, r_k)\}$ in $R^\#$ for $\{r_k\} \downarrow 0$. In view of the discussion in Step (3) of the algorithm, we find we are generally only able (in practice) to determine an approximation of a stationary point $x(r)$ of $L(x, r)$ in $R^\#$ for specified $r > 0$.

Hence, when the computational algorithm is successfully implemented, we can at the k-th iteration only expect to determine $x(r_k)$ such that $\nabla L[x(r_k), r_k] \doteq 0$ for $r_k > 0$. Furthermore, even if the stationary points $\{x(r_k)\}$ were *precise minimizing points* of $\{L(x, r_k)\}$ in $R^\#$, although the theory may guarantee that these exist for all $r_k > 0$ and that accumulation points of $\{x(r_k)\}$ are local solutions of the given problem, we cannot in practice calculate $x(r_k)$ for r_k arbitrarily small, for reasons indicated in Step (2) of the algorithm. The required accuracy in estimating a candidate solution $\hat{x}$ would then hopefully be attained by extrapolation. (Analogous difficulties are encountered by virtually all algorithms.)

With this perspective, we return to the determination of stopping rules for the present algorithm. Having calculated $x(r_k)$, we have, then, presumably satisfied the criterion $|\nabla L[x(r_k), r_k]| \leq \delta$ for some prespecified value of $\delta > 0$, as indicated in Step (3). Recalling the connections between the stationarity of $L(x, r)$ and the first-order Kuhn-Tucker conditions that were indicated in the section entitled Connections between Optimality Conditions and Convergence Properties of Barrier Methods, it follows that $|\nabla \mathscr{L}[x(r_k), u(r_k)]| \leq \delta$ if we define the i-th component of $u(r_k)$ as $u_i(r_k) \equiv r_k/g_i[x(r_k)]$, $i = 1, \ldots, m$. Since $x(r_k) \in R^\#$, $g_i[x(r_k)] > 0$ and $r_k > 0$, we have that $u(r_k) > 0$. Also, since $u_i(r_k)g_i[x(r_k)] = r_k$, $i = 1, \ldots, m$, we observe that the first-order Kuhn-Tucker necessary conditions for local optimality are approximately satisfied by $[x(r_k), u(r_k)]$, with the indicated tolerances. Thus, as already noted in the section entitled Connections between Optimality Conditions and Convergence Properties of Barrier Methods, the connection between the barrier function minimization (or better, stationarity) conditions and first-order necessary conditions for a constrained local minimizing point of the associated problem are direct and immediate.

An obvious procedure, then, for this algorithm and any general purpose nonlinear programming algorithm involving differentiable functions is to stipulate acceptable tolerances on the Kuhn-Tucker conditions, and terminate the process when these are achieved. For unconstrained barrier and penalty methods, at an unconstrained stationary point of the auxiliary function, the required check on the stationarity of the Lagrangian coincides with the check on the stationarity of the auxiliary function, once $u(r_k)$ is properly defined. The complementary slackness condition involves very little additional calculation.

Whenever extrapolation along $\{x(r_k)\}$ is used to determine an estimated solution $\hat{x}$, we can also extrapolate for the associated Lagrange multipliers $\hat{u}$ by using the relations $u_i(r_k) = r_k/g_i[x(r_k)]$ ($i = 1, \ldots, m$). We can then test $(\hat{x}, \hat{u})$ in the Kuhn-Tucker first-order relations, and terminate the process if the required thresholds are satisfied.

If Problem P is convex, the above criteria can be applied as well, and, in addition, as observed in the section entitled Convex Programming by Barrier Methods, we have the very significant additional information that can be calculated at any stationary point $x(r)$ of $L(x, r)$: a lower bound, $f[x(r)] - mr$, on the optimal value of Problem P, resulting from the application of duality theory. Thus an additional criterion may be imposed, i.e., a threshold on the allowable error in calculating the *optimum value* of Problem P. For the logarithmic barrier function, this is tantamount to selecting the smallest value of $r > 0$ such that a stationary point of $L(x, r)$ is required. Also, it follows that stationarity at $x(r)$ and convexity of $L(x, r)$ in $R^\#$ imply that $x(r)$ is a *global minimum* of $L(x, r)$ in $R^\#$. Any accumulation point x^* of the global minimizing sequence $\{x(r_k)\}$ is known to satisfy the first-order Kuhn-Tucker conditions for the convex problem. Consequently, since the Kuhn-Tucker conditions and convexity are sufficient for optimality, x^* would be a global minimizing point of Problem P (the latter conclusion also being a direct result of Theorem 3).

(5b) If an Acceptable Solution Estimate Has Not Been Determined, Reduce r and Continue

Like the initial selection of r, the reduction of r is also essentially arbitrary, and rigorous techniques for calculating an "optimal" rate of reduction have not been determined. Guidelines and heuristic arguments can be given, however.

Suppose we have calculated $x(r_k)$. If r_{k+1} is chosen too small, then the next stationary point $x(r)$ of $L(x, r_{k+1})$ may be far removed from $x(r_k)$ and extremely difficult to calculate, using any available unconstrained minimization technique, with $x(r_k)$ as a point of departure. If r_{k+1} is too close to r_k, then the effort to calculate $x(r_{k+1})$ may be nominal, but $x(r_{k+1})$ may be computationally indistinguishable from $x(r_k)$. It seems clear that, in general, there exist $\bar{r}$ and $\bar{\bar{r}}$ such that an "acceptable" r_{k+1} is any such that $0 < \bar{r} \leq r_{k+1} \leq \bar{\bar{r}} < r_k$. (These bounds undoubtedly depend on the iteration k, on the accuracy with which the stationary point has been calculated, on round-off error, etc., if we press the issue.)

Suppose $\bar{r}$ and $\bar{\bar{r}}$ were known. One might argue that it would be desirable to select $r_{k+1} = \bar{r}$, assuming the resulting unconstrained minimization problem is "not difficult," since the maximum reduction of r_k would then be realized in the "acceptable" range. On the other hand, since $\bar{\bar{r}}$ is closest to r_k in the given range (assuming $\bar{r} < \bar{\bar{r}}$), the effort to calculate $x(\bar{\bar{r}})$, starting from $x(r_k)$ would generally be expected to be less than that required to calculate $x(r)$ for any $0 < r < \bar{\bar{r}}$. Further, it would then be possible to extrapolate through $x(\bar{\bar{r}})$ to an estimate of a candidate solution and, if the estimate did not satisfy the convergence criteria, to an estimate of a stationary point of $L(x, r)$ for a reduced value of r. Thus both strategies are appealing and it is not clear which would be more efficient, or whether some intermediate value of r would be preferred.

Computational experience would appear to indicate that the overall effort to calculate an estimated solution of a problem using barrier or penalty methods is rather insensitive to the reduction factor of the parameter, within very wide tolerances [11, 29]. This tends to corroborate the above intuitive argument, which suggests compensating advantages to utilizing either bound in the indicated range. In practice, a given problem may be solved, or its solution initiated, using various reduction rates, as well as various initial values of the parameter. The initial value of the parameter and the reduction rate giving the best results are then utilized on future calculations involving similar problems. That is, diagnostic experiments are conducted, essentially providing a sensitivity analysis on these factors, to home in on these otherwise arbitrary and intractable "control variables."

A relevant consideration may be offered as regards the way the parameter is reduced. When each component of a trajectory $x(r)$ of minimizing points is developed in terms of polynomials in the parameter r, as is typically done and briefly indicated in Step (4), it turns out that the calculations required to obtain the coefficients of the resulting system of equations [of the type given in (36)] is greatly simplified if the parameter r is reduced by multiplication by a constant factor. For example, if $r = r_1$ is the initial value, choose $r_2 = r_1/c$, $r_3 = r_2/c = r_1/c^2$, etc., where $c > 1$. Details are given in Fiacco and McCormick [11].

A technique for calculating a value of c may be proposed as follows. Using the method-of-centers idea given in Step (2), calculate $r_1 = f(x^0) - f(x^1) > 0$ as indicated there, where x^0 is a given starting point in $R^\#$. Now replace x^0 by x^1 and repeat the process, minimizing the Function (32) modified accordingly to obtain a new minimum x^2 and yielding $\nabla L(x^2, r_2) = 0$, with $r_2 = f(x^1) - f(x^2) > 0$. We may then set $c = r_2/r_1 = [f(x^1) - f(x^2)]/[f(x^0) - f(x^1)]$, as long as $c > 1$ (which it is if the problem is convex). This calculation would completely eliminate the arbitrariness in choosing r_1 and c, setting these in correspondence with the values that corresponding quantities take on in the first two iterations of a "parameterless" related method-of-centers approach. In view of the possibility of introducing weights and scaling, however, the "elimination" of arbitrariness is somewhat misleading, as discussed in Step (2). Nonetheless, this possibility is intriguing and has not been tried to date to the author's knowledge.

Another possible approach should be mentioned. Once a minimizing trajectory $x(r)$ of $L(x, r)$ in $R^\#$ has been estimated by another vector function $\hat{x}(r)$ [e.g., by way of polynomials in r as in Step (4)], it is possible to evaluate $L[\hat{x}(r), r]$ in $R^\#$ for any value of $r > 0$. Since $L[x(r), r]$ converges to a locally optimal value of Problem P as $r \to 0$ when the method is successful, one could endeavor to estimate that value of $r > 0$ that yields $\min_{r>0} L[\hat{x}(r), r]$ in $R^\#$, using the last calculated stationary point $x(r_k)$ as a point of departure. In general, this should yield $\bar{r}$ such that $0 < \bar{r} < r_k$, which could then yield the next value of r, i.e., $r_{k+1} = \bar{r}$. Thus the reduction factor would be implicitly *determined* at each iteration, depending on this "joint variation" approach, allowing x and r to vary simultaneously. Numerous experiments involving related ideas have been conducted by various users but the author is unaware of whether this particular approach has ever been attempted. It would seem promising and not difficult to implement, depending simply on a one-dimensional minimization subproblem after each iteration of the process. Note that the solution of any such subproblem could yield a solution of P. Other ideas for reducing r may be found in Box, Davies, and Swann [58] and Davies [69].

(6) Estimate the Next Minimizing Point of $L(x, r_k)$ in $R^{\#}$

This step has already been described as a possibility for accelerating convergence, particularly in discussing extrapolation in Step (4). Once we have calculated $\{x(r_1), \ldots, x(r_k)\}$ and fit a vector function of r through these points, we can (if extrapolation does not solve the problem) extrapolate to estimate $x(r_{k+1})$ and use the estimate as a point of departure for minimizing $L(x, r_{k+1})$ in $R^{\#}$. This procedure has met with some success in computational implementations and is widely used.

EXTENSIONS AND RAMIFICATIONS

In this section we shall indicate a number of extensions and variants of the barrier and penalty function methods that we have summarized in the previous part of this article and briefly attempt to motivate each. We cannot include all the important results, but we shall endeavor to cover the principal direction of significant developments and suggest the numerous implications and ramifications. The interested reader may also wish to consult the surveys given by Fiacco and McCormick [11] and Lootsma [10] and the literature referenced in this article for additional results and details.

Conditions holding at an unconstrained minimizing point of the auxiliary function are directly related to optimality conditions of the constrained problem, as we indicated in the section entitled Connections between Optimality Conditions and Convergence Properties of Barrier Methods. As the auxiliary function parameter goes to its limiting value, the associated optimality conditions correspond more and more closely. This observation, aside from being of intrinsic interest in verifying and characterizing auxiliary function convergence properties, can also be exploited in the converse direction: to validate and derive optimality conditions for the constrained problem. This was suggested by Courant [38,102] in his early papers proposing a penalty method, and has been exploited using both barrier and penalty methods. For example, as indicated previously, Fiacco and McCormick [11] obtained the asymptotic analog of most of the better-known optimality conditions, making use of barrier and penalty function convergence results to simplify several of the proofs. Beltrami [103, 104] exploited penalty function properties to give constructive proofs of certain necessary conditions. Osborne and Ryan [99] have shown, under fairly general conditions, that if the sequence of Lagrange multipliers $\{u^k\}$ obtained as a usual byproduct of the sequence of barrier function minimizations (see the section entitled Connections between Optimality Conditions and Convergence Properties of Barrier Methods) has no finite limit points, then, assuming the associated minimizing sequence $\{x^k\}$ converges to a local solution x^* of Problem P, the Kuhn-Tucker conditions (13)–(16) do not hold at x^*. (Remark: Barrier and penalty functions do not require the existence of finite Kuhn-Tucker Lagrange multipliers for convergence, e.g., finite multipliers need not exist under the assumptions of Theorem 1.) The idea of deriving conditions for an extremum of a given problem by a perturbation analysis is well known in classical analysis, the above results essentially representing applications of this principle.

The basic auxiliary function approach has been validated in various general topological spaces by Rubin and Ungar [40], Butler and Martin [42], Stong [105], Fiacco and Jones [106], and others. In this connection, it has been demonstrated that the usual convergence results (somewhat analogous to Theorem 1) are essentially valid for problems in optimal control, given the appropriate generalization of the assumptions, by Russell [107], Okamura [108], Lasdon, Warren, and Rice [109], Balakrishnan [110], Cullum [111], Jones and McCormick [112], Tabak [113], and others. The author [114] has shown the validity of the approach for general constraint sets (not necessarily defined through functional inequalities or equalities), which includes programming over discrete sets (in which case the penalty function is "exact," i.e., requires a single unconstrained minimization to solve the given problem, when the parameter is sufficiently close to its limiting value).

Several general classes of barrier and penalty functions have been delineated by various authors, e.g., Russell [107], Okamura [108], and Pomentale [33] define general barrier functions and the author [66, 114] has given a few simple defining properties that describe a huge class of nonparametric and parametric interior and exterior auxiliary functions (including most of those mentioned in this article). Zangwill [44, 56] defines a large class of penalty functions and the Fiacco-McCormick book [11] is largely devoted to synthesizing numerous realizations of both barrier and penalty methods in one unified general treatment. For example, under general conditions (e.g., those given in Theorem 1) the function $U(x, r) \equiv f(x) + rI(x)$ defines a barrier function for Problem P if $I(x)$ is continuous in $R^\#$ and if $I(x^k) \to +\infty$ whenever $\{x^k\} \subset R^\#$ and $g_i(x^k) \to 0$, for any i. Considerably more generality is possible [11]. Lootsma [35] further categorizes various subclasses of penalty and barrier functions in accordance with their behavior at the boundary of the feasible region.

Roode [115] and Gould [116] provided a synthesis of this methodology with Lagrangian theory by subsuming the usual penalty functions in the concept of a "generalized Lagrangian." This orientation has been particularly fruitful in generating various extensions of results that were originally based on the usual Lagrangian. For example, Roode [37] and Gould [36] used the approach to define a large class of barrier function algorithms, Gould [116] and Gould and

BARRIER METHODS FOR NONLINEAR PROGRAMMING

Howe [117] applied the idea to provide saddle-point equivalence results under weaker assumptions, and Evans and Gould [54] applied the approach to define a class of exponential penalty functions and investigate certain questions regarding stability in nonlinear programming. Murphy [55] utilized exponential penalty functions in lieu of the usual Lagrangian to devise new column generation algorithms based on the Dantzig-Wolfe decomposition method for nonlinear programming. Widhelm and O'Neill [118] have also investigated this approach, which computational experiments suggest may converge more rapidly then the usual approach utilizing the conventional Lagrangian, for certain classes of problems. Fromovitz, Kim, and Morton [119] have also investigated column generation methods in conjunction with penalty functions. The Lagrangian interpretation leads to the use of penalty functions in eliminating "gaps" associated with Lagrange multipliers, as well as suggesting a host of new algorithms, as shown by Gould [116], Bellmore, Greenberg, and Jarvis [120], Greenberg and Pierskalla [121], and Greenberg [122]. These papers, along with the work of Roode [115], give numerous interesting connections between auxiliary function and Lagrangian theory. Besides being of theoretical interest, such results give immediate extensions of Everett's generalized Lagrange multiplier method [123], Falk's Lagrangian approach [124, 125], and other techniques involving minimization of the Lagrangian.

As mentioned in discussing Step (3) of the algorithm in the section entitled A Basic Barrier Function Algorithm and Computational Considerations, the Hessian matrix of twice differentiable barrier and penalty functions (e.g., $\nabla^2 L(x, r)$) has been the subject of considerable attention, since the "degree of difficulty" in finding an unconstrained minimizing point of any function is related to various properties of its Hessian matrix. We indicated that the difficulty in minimization appears to vary directly with the ratio of the maximum eigenvalue to the minimum eigenvalue of the associated Hessian, this ratio being conventionally referred to as the "condition number" of the matrix. For barrier and penalty methods, it is now well known that the condition number generally increases without bound along a minimizing trajectory as the parameter goes to its limiting value. Under usual conditions, for the logarithmic barrier function it increases in the order $1/r$. As noted earlier, this was observed by Murray who provided a detailed asymptotic analysis [79, 81] and suggested a different approach [80, 126] to avoid some of the associated disadvantages. Lootsma has also analyzed the conditioning problem [82], showing additionally that methods-of-centers types of approaches experience the same difficulty [35].

This has given impetus to a search for modified and hybrid penalty and barrier methods that are well-conditioned, motivating the development of "exact auxiliary functions" (briefly mentioned in the section entitled Basic General Theoretical Results for Barrier Methods), i.e., functions that have well-conditioned unconstrained minimizing points coinciding (or nearly coinciding) with local constrained minimizing points of the given problem for certain parameter values. This is typically done at the expense of adding additional parameters or terms, usually associated with estimates of the Lagrange multipliers, and hence these functions might more descriptively be called generalized or "augmented" Lagrangians (following Fletcher [127]), respectively. Powell [128] suggested an exact variant of the Courant quadratic loss function (5) and a simple iterative technique for adjusting the parameters for the nonlinear problem with nonlinear equality constraints. Hestenes [129] and Haarhoff and Buys [130] independently proposed a mixed Lagrangian-penalty function method as well—observed subsequently by Osborne (Lootsma [10]) to be coincident with the method proposed by Powell. Fletcher [127] presented a class of continuously differentiable augmented Lagrangian exact penalty functions for equality constrained problems, subsequently extended to inequalities by Lill [131] and Fletcher [132]. Gould and Howe [117] and Evans, Gould, and Tolle [133] proposed a family of piecewise differentiable exact exponential (interior-exterior) penalty functions and Gould [134, 188] proposed a new exact interior-exterior differentiable class of auxiliary functions for solving problems subject to stipulated tolerances.

Aside from the usual Lagrangian which may itself be viewed as a penalty function, and which may be exact under certain conditions, the first exact penalty function for convex programming was apparently proposed by Zangwill [44, 56] and recently extended to nonconvex programs by Pietrzykowski [135]. Although shedding additional insights on the more subtle convergence properties of penalty functions, significant improvements in computational efficiency for the general unstructured problem, beyond the basic algorithm with extrapolation described in the section entitled A Basic Barrier Function Algorithm and Computational Considerations, appear not to have been definitively realized as yet by these methods. Tentative exceptions to this based on limited computational experiments have been reported, however. For example, Conn [136] has devised a gradient technique for implementing the "exact potential method" of Pietrzykowski [135] and reports extremely favorable results on a number of test problems, compared against several of the better known barrier and penalty methods. Also, Fletcher and Lill [137] report very promising computational results in applying Fletcher's augmented Lagrangian approach to equality constrained problems, as does Lill [131] in extending this approach to inequalities. Similarly, encouraging results are beginning to be reported utilizing some of the other techniques mentioned above. Improved techniques for adjusting the parameters and for minimizing the resulting nondifferentiable penalty functions may yield computational breakthroughs.

Osborne [138] gave a brief summary of the most promising acceleration devices for barrier and penalty methods and indicated another possible approach. This is an adaptation of the strategy for equality constraints suggested by Powell [128], who accelerates and conditions Courant's penalty function approach for equality constraints by adding iteratively modified "slack" variables (to the constraints) and weights (to the penalty terms). The suggestion is that this idea can be adapted to the barrier function to define a well-conditioned pure barrier method. The estimates of the Lagrange multipliers that are provided with each unconstrained minimization of the barrier function are used explicitly in the indicated procedure. The idea appears intriguing and could yield an "exact barrier method" of some promise, if the convergence to an optimal set of parameters is sufficiently fast.

Osborne and Ryan [100] define a hybrid barrier-penalty for the general inequality-equality constrained problem, combining Powell's modification of Courant's penalty function to efficiently handle constraints identified as active, with barrier function terms to handle inequality constraints that may or may not be active. Constraints identified as inactive are ignored. Classification of constraints is updated as new information is accumulated at each minimization of the auxiliary function, there being made important use of the Lagrange multiplier estimates that are obtained as the usual byproduct of barrier and penalty function minimizations. Encouraging results are indicated and a substantial improvement over the conventional barrier-penalty method with extrapolation for the problems tested is reported.

A modified version of the logarithmic barrier function where the barrier terms are modified recursively at each iteration was proposed by Osborne and Ryan [99, 100]. Though exhibiting an improved convergence rate in a particular sense, the function does not appear to circumvent the conditioning problem and does not lend itself easily to extrapolation.

Another approach to resolving the conditioning problem is the *avoidance* of minimizing the auxiliary function for values of the parameter near its limiting value. This reinforces the importance of extrapolation devices such as those briefly summarized in Steps (4) and (6) of the general algorithmic procedure. Obviously, the more accurate the extrapolation, the fewer the number of auxiliary function minimizations required to estimate a solution, and the fewer the number of calculations required to determine a subsequent auxiliary function minimum. In view of the conditioning problem, extrapolation may be *essential* to achieving a desired degree of accuracy, rather than simply a device for accelerating convergence, if no other measures are taken to counter ill-conditioning. To the author's knowledge, second-order extrapolation methods have generally yielded satisfactory practical implementations of barrier methods. Because of the potentially significant additional advantages, Fletcher and McCann [59] have experimented with techniques for *extrapolation* of estimates of *the Hessian matrix* of the $P(x, r)$ barrier function along a minimizing trajectory. They reported substantial savings in computational effort (beyond that realized using only second order "point" extrapolation) and solidly corroborated the enormous savings that have generally been realized when using second-order methods to estimate the solution and the next minimizing point (as opposed to using no acceleration devices), as suggested by Fiacco and McCormick [11].

Numerous additional modifications of penalty and barrier function methods have been developed to make the approach more versatile and efficient and to accomplish various stipulated objectives more effectively. The author [139] has shown the validity of the barrier method modified to accommodate constraint perturbations that are gradually eliminated as the barrier function parameter approaches its limiting value. This allows barrier methods to be applied to problems with equality constraints, for example, by initially relaxing the

BARRIER METHODS FOR NONLINEAR PROGRAMMING

equalities and gradually removing the slack as iterations proceed. This modified barrier function approach, though applicable under the *same* conditions as the exterior penalty approach, remains to be tested computationally. In principle, any penalty method can solve a given problem by applying it to a *sequence of problems* that appropriately "converge" to the original problem as the penalty parameter approaches its limit. Falk [189] proposed a one-parameter class of barrier functions based on utilizing a method-of-centers type function to define the barrier term. A feasible minimizing sequence is shown to exist and conditions (similar to those usually required) are given such that accumulation points of the minimizing sequence solve the (convex) problem. A distinct feature of this barrier method is the fact that the limiting (barrier) parameter value is not known in advance, but can only be approached based on information generated at previous iterations. Except for some preliminary experiments by Falk, this method also remains untested. It should be remarked that Falk's barrier functions qualify as exact auxiliary functions, as described earlier. In fact, the *ad hoc* determination of an "optimal" parameter value seems to characterize the exact auxiliary function approach.

In the context of the latter technique, it is important to emphasize the great similarity between methods of center and auxiliary function methods, as already indicated in the discussion of Steps (2) and (5) of the general algorithmic approach. This was delineated in some detail by the author [66], who in fact was led by the correspondences to defining a large new class of "exterior" methods of centers, most previously determined classes apparently being only interior methods. (In fact, the only exception known to the author is a method based on the Courant quadratic loss function [57].) Under appropriate conditions (e.g., when the problem is convex), any method of center and the appropriate penalty method can be placed in precise correspondence. Fiacco and McCormick detailed this equivalence for the $P(x, r)$ barrier function and the natural centers-function analog of this function [68]. Lootsma [35] has made detailed comparisons, also involving conditioning and rates of convergence. Not only are such results useful in synthesizing the theory of the basic algorithms, but they allow computational advantages of either approach to be exploited by the other, e.g., primal-dual bounds, extrapolation, and adjustment of penalty parameters [as specifically suggested in Steps (2) and (5) of the logarithmic barrier function algorithm].

Auxiliary function methods are easily used together with other algorithms to define hybrid or "composite" algorithms, often allowing a user to introduce computational advantages by exploiting problem structure. We have already indicated (see the sections entitled Examples of Barrier and Penalty Functions and the General Auxiliary Function Approach, and Basic General Theoretical Results for Barrier Methods) that barrier and exterior penalty terms may be used simultaneously in a mixed auxiliary function approach. It is also possible to handle various parts of the problem by different methods altogether, perhaps the most important and obvious example of this being the incorporation of nonlinear constraints into the penalty function, leaving the linear constraints to be handled separately by specified techniques. The resulting sequence of linearly constrained nonlinear minimization problems may then be accomplished by *any* algorithm that is known to be effective for this class of problems. Some work in this direction has been initiated. For example, Ryan [140] discusses *projection methods* for handling linear constraints that are particularly suited to minimizing a barrier or penalty function subject to linear constraints. He uses a modified combination of the Davidon-Fletcher-Powell method [83] and a projection method due to Murtagh and Sargent [141], the technique utilizing partial linear searches with cubic extrapolation and interpolation. We find arguments supporting the conclusion that it is advantageous to handle *active* linear constraints by projection methods. (It should be remarked that the problem of identifying the active constraints is generally by no means trivial, thus somewhat complicating the issue for linear inequality constraints. Also, in a recent paper, Sargent and Murtagh [142] have extended their work and report on several projection algorithms for solving nonlinear programming problems, including various hybrid algorithms involving penalty functions.) Separate handling of linear constraints by projection methods, for maximum computational efficiency, is also suggested by Osborne and Ryan [100].

Another natural composition arises from the application of barrier methods to solve constrained subproblems that may be generated by any iterative procedure. For example, to solve a nonlinear convex separable highly structured problem which arises in large-scale economic planning problems, Wong [143] used a decomposition method due to Kronsjö [144], in conjunction with a barrier method [30, 31], and a penalty method [45] to solve the resulting nonlinear convex master and subproblems. This approach was compared against the use of one of the indicated barrier or penalty methods to solve the original problem directly (i.e., without exploiting structure, as by decomposition). The overall result was markedly in favor of the combined decomposition-barrier-penalty approach for those test problems involving a large number of variables. {As a matter of interest, this analysis was pursued by Sandblom [145], who addressed the question of whether there might exist an "optimal" decomposition (using the above method) that need not involve decomposing the entire problem. For the test problem considered, "total" decomposition and reduction of the size of the master problem proved to be most effective.}

For convex subproblems, the primal-dual bounds obtained at each barrier function minimization apply and may eventually be used to eliminate such subproblems from further consideration in seeking a global solution. This idea was indicated in conjunction with techniques described in Step (1) of the general algorithmic procedure for calculating a suitable feasible starting point. It has also been apparently successfully exploited by McCann and Soland [146] in a branch-and-bound procedure for *globally* solving a class of nonconvex problems that are defined by functions that are the sum of concave separable functions and general convex functions. The nonlinear subproblems generated are convex and are solved by a barrier method.

The indicated use of a barrier or penalty function as a generalized Lagrangian in lieu of the usual Lagrangian, e.g., in decomposition [55, 118] is another example. Mathematical programming procedures often can be freely

BARRIER METHODS FOR NONLINEAR PROGRAMMING

mixed, depending largely on problem structure and the ingenuity of the user to effectively utilize the output of information at each interface. As some final examples of the great variety of possibilities, we mention that Weisman [147] devised a method combining direct search, random search, and penalty methods. In this approach the Courant quadratic loss function with weighted penalty terms is minimized by Kooke and Jeeves [148] direct search method whereupon a random search for a "better" point is performed in a large neighborhood of the determined minimizing point, the process then being repeated. Luenberger [15] provides still other interesting and potentially promising hybrid algorithms, indicating how to combine modified versions of Newton's method, conjugate gradient methods, and gradient projection methods with penalty methods to obtain valid composite algorithms with good rates of convergence. He also suggests techniques for initially "normalizing" a penalty function to reduce the condition number of the associated Hessian matrix.

The theoretical "rate of convergence" of barrier and penalty methods is implicit in results such as those given by Fiacco and McCormick [11, 29] and, for the logarithmic barrier function, by Lootsma [49, 82]. A typical indicator of this is the ratio $|x^{k+1} - x^*|/|x^k - x^*|$: the smaller the limiting value of the fraction, the better the asymptotic convergence rate. Under conditions such as those given in Theorem 2, $|x^k - x^*|$ is of the order r_k and hence this ratio for k large is of the order r_{k+1}/r_k for the logarithmic barrier function. With respect to computational effort, this fact is rather academic, however. First, it does not account for the rate of convergence of the unconstrained minimization method used to calculate *each* minimizing point x^k of the penalty function. Second, even if we knew the latter, we would still not generally be able to estimate computational effort since we could not determine in advance the *number* of iterations required to calculate an unconstrained minimizing point, nor the number of unconstrained penalty function minimizations required to satisfy the stipulated convergence criteria. Third, the effect of extrapolation is not reflected. These facts dramatize the loose correlation between computational effort and theoretical convergence rate. In fact, since we know that the condition number (a measure of the computational effort) increases as $r_k \to 0^+$, we observe the following *negative* correlation: Without loss of generality, suppose $r_{k+1} = r_k/c$, where $c > 1$. Then as c is selected larger and larger, the theoretical convergence rate improves monotonically while the condition number associated with a minimizing point $x(r_{k+1})$ generally increases without bound!

Lootsma [35, 149] explored whether certain members of a family of parametric penalty and barrier functions might yield better convergence properties than others and compares these properties to analogous method-of-centers type procedures. It is concluded that there is no reason for preferring method-of-centers type functions (where the involved parameter sequence is determined automatically by the method itself) over parametric penalty and barrier methods, and that there are certain reasons to conclude (among parametric methods) in favor of the logarithmic barrier and Courant quadratic loss exterior penalty terms, both conclusions deriving from arguments involving conditioning of the Hessian and rate of convergence.

Mifflin [150] explicitly obtained convergence rates for the logarithmic barrier function applied to the convex problem. Under usual nondegeneracy assumptions he establishes that the convergence of a minimizing sequence $\{x^k\}$ and a corresponding sequence of Lagrange multipliers $\{u^k\}$ is linear in the barrier function parameter r_k. An interesting part of the analysis is that fact that *precise minimization* of the barrier function at each parameter value is *not assumed*, and minimization is required only in a limiting sense.

PRACTICAL APPLICATIONS

Auxiliary function methods are particularly well suited to applications, being easy to implement and requiring little finesse to provide rough estimates of solutions to a large class of nonlinear programming problems. They enable a user to solve constrained problems if he has computational capability to solve unconstrained problems. Another advantage of these methods is that calculations are generally never entirely wasted if the procedure must be terminated before convergence is achieved. The subproblem (unconstrained minimization) solution estimates are also estimates of readily identified perturbations of the original problem. This is useful sensitivity information, as is the generation of estimates of the Lagrange multipliers that are provided at no significant additional expense.

The development of auxiliary function methodology for mathematical programming was actually motivated by practical applications. We find that extensive use of this approach was being made well before the rich theoretical groundwork of the resulting methodology was cultivated, and in fact before the appearance of the better-known convergence results. For example, the Courant quadratic loss penalty method was first established theoretically as a mathematical programming method by Butler and Martin [42]. They were apparently *motivated* by successful applications of this procedure, notably by Kelley [41] who had made extensive use of the technique in problems of optimal control. Rubin and Ungar [40] had also previously used the procedure and provided a detailed analysis and convergence proofs for a class of variational problems, and undoubtedly there are many other early applications. In the context of solving large econometric models, Frisch [46] had made early use of the logarithmic barrier function as a computational device to accelerate convergence in a hybrid algorithm for large-scale programing. Carroll [27] subsequently proposed the inverse function barrier method, applying the approach to estimate solutions of problems arising in a paper-pulp manufacturing process. However, barrier methods were not established theoretically or computationally until a later date by Fiacco and McCormick [29]. Numerous additional examples of early applications surely exist, pre–dating the emergence of a

BARRIER METHODS FOR NONLINEAR PROGRAMMING

unified theory, since the basic idea of solving a problem by solving an appropriate perturbation of the problem was well known.

More recently, auxiliary functions algorithms have been applied to virtually all areas where nonlinear programming is applicable, e.g., engineering design, resource management, pollution control, statistical sampling and regression analysis, budget allocation, and problems in the physical sciences.

A collection of examples of the above applications and a discussion of their solution by the logarithmic barrier method may be found in the Bracken-McCormick book [151]. Numerous recent practical applications of barrier penalty methods have been made. Some representative current applications of barrier methods are the following, given by: (1) Tillman *et al.* [152], to find the optimal parameters of a life support system for a two-man space capsule which maximizes the system's reliability; (2) Soland [153], to find the optimal number of each of several variates to sample from a general population to determine the minimum cost sample satisfying certain variance constraints; (3) Schrady and Choe [154], to determine the optimal inventory policy for a multi-item stochastic inventory system constrained by investment capital available and reorder workload constraints; (4) Tabak [155], to determine the optimal shutdown procedure of a nuclear reactor during conditions of xenon poisoning; (5) Brusch [156], to find the control parameters that optimize the trajectory of a space shuttle subject to constraints on acceleration load, dynamic pressure, and angle of attack; (6) Anderson [157], to find the design parameters of an asphalt plant to satisfy certain air pollution criteria at minimum cost; (7) Kavlie, Kowalik, Lund, and Moe [158], to design optimal ship structures; and (8) Thornton and Schmit [159], to optimize the structural synthesis of an ablating thermostructural panel.

Numerous additional applications of auxiliary functions may be found in the published literature, primarily in the professional journals devoted to a particular area of application. The interested reader is referred to the Bracken-McCormick book [151] for preliminary reading, and to the books by Fox [160], Kowalik and Osborne [91] and Jacoby, Kowalik and Pizzo [14] for a fairly comprehensive introduction to the basic methodology somewhat from the practitioner's point of view.

FUTURE RESEARCH

All the numerous variations of the auxiliary function procedure mentioned in the section entitled Extensions and Ramifications are obvious potential topics for future research and are subject to considerable refinement and development. We shall single out several additional topics here that are felt to be of particular importance and warrant further analysis.

The iterative composition of a barrier function, based on initially applying an effective unconstrained minimization algorithm to the objective function and thereafter systematically incorporating constraints as they are encountered to systematically construct the barrier term, could possibly lead to substantial computational efficiencies. This idea, proposed and somewhat elaborated on in the Fiacco-McCormick book [11], was described briefly in the section entitled A Basic Barrier Function Algorithm and Computational Considerations, and probably merits further development. In a problem involving numerous constraints, the majority of which are nonbinding at a solution, the technique could result in significant computational savings. (Note that penalty methods applied to inequality constraints automatically "eliminate" nonbinding constraints eventually, by definition.) In conjunction with this idea, the development of additional criteria and techniques for "weighting" the terms of a barrier or penalty function and scaling the variables could lead to improvements in stability, accuracy, and efficiency of these methods. (It should be noted that Carroll [27] suggested using weights when he proposed the barrier method idea.) This could be updated iteratively, based on previously generated information, and systematically so as to allow the incorporation of convergence acceleration devices such as extrapolation.

The exploitation of problem structure and auxiliary function structure in barrier and penalty function methodology has been somewhat neglected and could lead to enormous computational savings. One reason for the neglect was an initial emphasis on providing a general purpose methodology that was reasonably robust, easy to apply, and readily accessible. The basic barrier and penalty function approach without refinements has all these attributes, and consequently has been and continues to be heavily utilized by practitioners— most successfully on moderately sized problems where efficiency is not at a premium. However, as larger problems are attempted, or as a given type problem must be solved repeatedly, or as speed and accuracy become more critical, it becomes increasingly important to take advantage of structure.

A number of ways of exploiting structure are given in the Fiacco-McCormick book [11], e.g., techniques for efficiently inverting the Hessian matrix of the auxiliary functions, taking advantage of the particular form of the Hessian matrix, separability, factorability, and other special structures that are invariably present in practical problems. Another important way to tailor the method more closely to the problem was mentioned in the section entitled Extensions and Ramifications, i.e., using the auxiliary function to absorb only certain constraints, leaving others (e.g., linear constraints) to be handled by other methods known to be more efficient. Extrapolation techniques, such as those indicated in the section entitled A Basic Barrier Function Algorithm and Computational Considerations and developed in Fiacco and McCormick [11], exploit barrier and penalty function structure to introduce efficiencies. Extrapolation of the Hessian matrix of these functions along ideas such as those suggested by Fletcher and McCann [59] for barrier functions could further significantly accelerate convergence for certain classes of problems, as might their proposal to accomplish the one-dimensional searches (needed by many of the more effective unconstrained minimization techniques) by fitting functions that are specifically tailored to the auxiliary function being minimized. Lasdon, Fox, and Ratner [96] have also proposed the latter idea, consisting essentially of fitting linear or quadratic functions to the *problem* functions along the search direction. The one variable estimating functions is then substituted back into the barrier function, and the resulting function defines the desired approximation of the barrier function. Based on experiments with the $P(x, r)$ (1) function, and using Newton's method to minimize the estimating function, the results excel even those obtained using the interpolation proposed by Fletcher and McCann [59] and appear to represent some of the best results obtained to date for one-dimensional minimization of barrier functions.

Lasdon [93] extensively developed and generalized the latter idea to produce an entirely new algorithmic approach: fit linear functions to the problem functions at a given starting point, then apply a barrier (or penalty) method to the linearized problem in a suitable neighborhood to determine a locally optimal search direction and extrapolate along this direction to reduce the auxiliary function as much as possible (i.e., apply a "feasible-direction" type iteration), up-date the linearization, and proceed. The algorithm converges under the usual conditions. The approach could prove extremely effective on certain types of problems, particularly if combined with extrapolation. It assuredly warrants further development and testing, as do the other possibilities for exploiting structure. To date, the computational experience on these refined approaches, though promising, is extremely limited. (An idea for combining successive linearizations with a novel penalty function that is modified with each iteration was proposed by Goldstein and Kripke [161]. Developments of this approach, briefly described in Fiacco and McCormick [11], are unknown to the author).

Parameter initialization and adjustment in barrier and penalty methods remains somewhat enigmatic and arbitrary and we have only been able to give heuristic guidelines. Every method for iteratively solving mathematical programming problems involves a degree of arbitrariness, and this is generally impossible to eliminate. It is conceivable, however, that more can be done for particular classes of problems, e.g., for linear and quadratic programming problems, "optimal control" of the auxiliary function parameters may be realizable or "nearly" realizable, in which case we could build on this for more general classes of problems.

In addition to the possible parameter controls that we have indicated, some others can be suggested that may warrant future investigation. The first is obvious: if a given problem is to be solved repeatedly with small changes in the data, then the parameter values can be altered systematically to yield information on the sensitivity of computational effort to variations in the parameter values, and hence, subsequent adjustments that are likely to be favorable. Second, it is possible to change the parameter value *before* a corresponding unconstrained minimization of the auxiliary function is accomplished, e.g., after a single iteration of the unconstrained minimization algorithm being utilized. Theoretically, this is a valid procedure providing we succeed at least in minimizing the auxiliary function *in the limit* as the parameter goes to its limiting value [11, 162]. Computational efficacy would be primarily a function of controlling the rate of change of the parameter, and should have much less dependence on initial parameter values than does the usual procedure. Since the change in the parameter value could be made proportionate to the reduction of the auxiliary function in the previous iteration, this could lead to an automated and hopefully self-correcting procedure. Disadvantages are that dual feasible points and the resulting lower bounds on the optimal value (for the convex problem) would not generally be available (since the unconstrained minimizations must be completed to obtain these) and that extrapolation would probably be somewhat erratic.

Realizations of the above idea have been proposed for penalty methods, and preliminary results indicate a significant economy in computations. Biggs [163] proposed a technique for approximating a minimizing trajectory of the Courant quadratic-loss penalty function method, as developed by Fiacco and McCormick [11, 26, 45], by solving an appropriate sequence of equality-constrained quadratic programming problems. The approach does not depend on sequential unconstrained minimization of the penalty function, but only on systematic reduction of the penalty function along the search directions determined by the quadratic subproblems. The penalty function parameter is then adjusted using current information. The idea is similar to one proposed by Murray [126], who utilized inequality constrained quadratic programming subproblems. {These techniques are suggestive of the joint variation approach mentioned in the section entitled A Basic Barrier Function Algorithm and Computational Considerations under Step (5) of the algorithm; e.g., for the logarithmic barrier method, obtain x as a function of r and proceed to minimize $L[\hat{x}(r), r]$ in $R^\#$.} Substantial economies in both function evaluations and computer time are reported over both the usual inverse barrier and quadratic loss penalty methods that rely on extrapolation (through previously obtained minimizing points) for acceleration of convergence. Indications are that the method also represents some improvement over Murray's technique, which itself appears more efficient than the usual extrapolation method. In terms of computational efficiency, these are among the best results reported for penalty methods, to the author's knowledge. Biggs utilized a variable metric method which he developed [164] to minimize the barrier and penalty functions in his comparisons.

Bigg's experiments include the application of a projection method due to Davies [165], which performed more effectively than the barrier or penalty approach on test problems having *only linear constraints*. This somewhat supports the conjecture that the separate handling of linear constraints (in a problem that also involves nonlinear constraints), by methods that can exploit the linear structure, is generally more efficient than incorporating these in a barrier or penalty function. This agrees with the findings of Osborne and Ryan [100] and Ryan [140] mentioned earlier. However, this conclusion is at variance with that reported by Lootsma [35], who appropriately observes that the effort to solve a sequence of *linearly constrained* barrier functions may be appreciable and competitive with absorbing all the constraints in the barrier function at the outset. Certainly, an *a priori* judgment cannot be made and the issue remains to be clarified by many more computational experiments.

Suggestions for replacing the sequential minimization of barrier or penalty functions by a sequence of univariate searches, in the spirit of the methods proposed by Biggs and Murray, have also been proposed by Zoutendijk [166] using barrier functions and by Butz [167] using penalty functions.

If the preceding strategies are taken to their extreme, we are led to *continuous alteration of the auxiliary function parameter* as we *simultaneously change the "state" variable x* to reduce the auxiliary function in a continuous manner. This leads to a continuous or, perhaps more accurately, *differential* analog of the usual ("large step") auxiliary function procedure. Some results for this have been obtained by Fiacco and McCormick [11] for the inverse barrier function $P(x, r)$ (1). Essentially, under usual conditions for the problem involving differentiable functions, it follows that a well-defined trajectory (i.e., a vector function, the "state" variables, and the Lagrange multipliers defined as functions of the penalty parameter) exists from *any* point in a suitable neighborhood of a solution set and all limit points of the trajectory satisfy the first-order necessary Kuhn-Tucker optimality conditions (13)–(16). The trajectory is characterized *uniquely,* for given initial conditions, as the solution of a specified nonautonomous differential equation gradient system. For the convex problem, the initial state variable may be *any* point in the interior of the feasible region and any limit point of the trajectory is a *global solution* of the problem. In this context, a *minimizing* trajectory of the barrier function is simply *a particular realization* of this large family of curves. This result is intriguing, since it gives additional theoretical motivation and justification for eliminating the unconstrained minimizations entirely and perhaps bypassing some of the difficulties associated with parameter adjustments. Other than token experimentation with some small problems on the analog computer by Bombart and Hipp [168], also reported in Fiacco and McCormick [11], the idea has not been computationally developed, to the author's knowledge.

Another approach is based on the natural idea of attempting to minimize an unconstrained function by following its precise negative gradient trajectory from a specified starting point. This also gives rise to a differential gradient approach, but one distinctly different from the procedure mentioned in the last paragraph. Having defined an appropriate auxiliary function (e.g., the usual Lagrangian, a penalty or barrier function, or a method-of-centers function), fix the initial conditions and define an *autonomous* differential gradient system for (unconstrained) reduction of the given function. This is the spirit of the Arrow, Hurwicz, and Uzawa [25] differential gradient saddle-point approach, the auxiliary function being the usual Lagrangian, the problem variables and Lagrange multipliers being treated as independent variables, and the gradient system being adapted to the saddle-point (min-max) and Lagrange multiplier nonnegativity requirements. One of the earliest penalty function examples of this approach was given by Ablow and Brigham [169], who devised analog computer techniques based on continuous descent of the gradients of the Courant (6) and Zangwill (10) penalty functions. Motivation for such methods is, of course, the fact that, under appropriate conditions, such as have been indicated previously, the unconstrained minimization of the auxiliary function

BARRIER METHODS FOR NONLINEAR PROGRAMMING

yields an approximate solution of the associated constrained problem when the auxiliary function parameter is sufficiently large.

The above approaches and their analog computer implementations have apparently met with some success and have often been quoted in the foreign literature, though references in the American literature are scattered and virtually absent in modern texts on nonlinear programming. For this reason, and since experimentation involving barrier functions, exponential penalty functions, and exact penalty functions appears to be nil and well worth trying, we shall briefly indicate some past results.

Motivated by analog computer implementation requirements, Rybashov [170] developed the theoretical basis for a differential equation approach based on the continuous descent of the gradient trajectory of a general class of convex penalty functions. Conditions are obtained that guarantee convergence of the solution of the autonomous gradient system to a minimizing point of any penalty function in this class for any *fixed* value of the penalty function parameter. This provides the basis for an approximation technique for convex programming, by using an appropriate penalty function [e.g., the Courant quadratic loss function (6)], by setting the penalty function parameter at a sufficiently large value.

Dudnikov and Rybashov [171] gave a survey of methods for solving many different types of mathematical programming problems on the analog computer. They consider gradient systems of differential equations based on Lagrange saddle-point methods, methods based on the Courant (6) and Zangwill (10) penalty functions, and simplex methods. Included are techniques for linear programming, convex programming, quadratic programming, parametric programming (with emphasis on applications to fractional programming), and solutions of systems of equations and inequalities. It is interesting to note that the barrier function $P(x, r)$ (1) is mentioned but dismissed as being too cumbersome for analog computation. Emphasis is placed on deriving the appropriate differential equations for the methods considered, and on implementing a solution technique on the analog computer. Several practical examples are given and their solution processes detailed, including detailed circuit diagrams for the analog computer. Numerous references (about 50) are cited of methods that have been devised and implemented, and it is apparent that this approach is effective for solving certain types of problems (particularly where the number of variables is not excessive). It assuredly has not been ignored, nor should it be in future applications.

Finally, it is observed that *any* problem involving constraints, other than the mathematical programming problem (and whether or not the problem involves optimization, for that matter) is probably susceptible to transformation to an unconstrained problem by way of a barrier or penalty function approach, or other auxiliary function technique. As an example of an application of this principle, Savir [52] showed that a class of two-person concave nonzero sum constrained games can be solved by means of exponential functions that convert any such game to a sequence of unconstrained games. He gave detailed theoretical results and provided a computational algorithm. Thus it seems reasonable to infer that the auxiliary function strategy has enormous potential applicability to other problem areas that remain to be exploited.

A recent development is the theoretical validation by the author of a technique, applicable to any twice differentiable barrier or penalty function approach, to estimate the sensitivity of a solution point of a parametric nonlinear programming problem to perturbations of the problem parameters. A first-order sensitivity analysis of a solution point was given in the Fiacco-McCormick book [11] for a certain class of parametric perturbations. These results have been generalized by Robinson [172] and the author [173]. Additionally, it is shown in Fiacco [173] that the sensitivity of a solution to changes in the problem parameters may be approximated by the sensitivity of an unconstrained minimizing point of the auxiliary function as the function parameter approaches its limiting value. Computational experiments have been successfully conducted on several sample problems by Armacost and Fiacco [174], and a computer program has been completed by Mylander and Armacost [175]. This provides a mixed barrier (for inequality constraints) penalty (for equality constraints) computational technique that automatically provides a postoptimality first-order sensitivity analysis as a user option.

CONCLUDING REMARKS

Barrier and penalty function methodology will undoubtedly always be an important and useful part of the methodology for nonlinear programming. These methods are easy to understand and implement, since they are based on transforming a constrained problem to the more tractable and better-known unconstrained problem. They are robust, requiring little finesse to obtain useful approximations to difficult nonlinear problems, and the auxiliary function minimizing point solves a readily identifiable subproblem of the given problem. The connection between the optimality conditions of the given problem and the conditions associated with minimization of the auxiliary function is direct and clear, since the Lagrange multiplier estimates are explicitly generated. The approach easily allows for exploitation of problem structure, e.g., it is readily combined with other techniques.

In applying any given auxiliary function method, obviously any appropriate unconstrained minimization technique can be utilized and parameter adjustments are likewise somewhat arbitrary, as are the procedures for extrapolation. This arbitrariness is undoubtedly a mixed blessing, but it points up the following fact. The auxiliary function approach, like the method of feasible directions and the branch-and-bound method, for example, is essentially a *strategy* rather than a well-defined technique. Consequently, it has virtually unlimited versatility and flexibility.

For a practitioner's point of view, we briefly summarize several observations given by Fox in his book, *Optimization Methods for Engineering Design* [160]. Regarding a choice of an automated procedure for nonlinear programming, he considers the following criteria for assessing the expected required effort and resulting use associated with a computer program implementing the procedure: (1) development costs, (2) calendar time to develop, (3) running-time costs, (4) reliability, (5) flexibility, (6) generality, and (7) ease of use and interpretation of results. Factors (6) and (7) are adjudged to be contingent on the way any particular procedure is coded, while barrier and penalty function methods are generally conceded to be unexcelled in the other categories, with barrier methods being largely favored.

Recent comparisons between algorithms proposed in Fiacco and McCormick [29] (a barrier method), Kowalik, Osborne, and Ryan [176] (a mixed interior-exterior Courant-type method-of-centers approach, combining methods due to Schmit and Fox [177] and Morrison [178]), and Powell [128] (a modified Courant-type method), the last two modified in a straightforward manner to handle inequality constraints, were conducted by Asaadi [179] on several test problems having nonlinearities in both the objective function and the constraints. The methods were coded in the same computer language and tested on the same computer, using the Davidon algorithm as revised by Fletcher and Powell [83] to perform the unconstrained minimizations required by each algorithm. It is concluded that Powell's method performed best in terms of the number of function evaluations, while the Fiacco-McCormick method proved best in terms of computer running time.

One of the earliest efforts to compare the performance of several nonlinear programming codes was conducted in 1968 by Colville [180]. More recently, Himmelblau has conducted a number of comparisons of several methods of unconstrained and constrained minimization. His evaluations and reports of additional evaluations obtained by others may be found in Himmelblau [18] and Lootsma [20].

For a concise and incisive introduction to the pros and cons of using barrier and penalty methods in lieu of other methods, and indications of the relative efficacy of various approaches, the reader is referred to a paper by McCormick [181]. A subjective analysis of when to use what type of algorithm has been offered by Fletcher [182]. Although there are general guidelines that can be suggested for problems having special structure, there is not enough reliable comparative data concerning the respective merits of the numerous general purpose programming algorithms that have been proposed to substantiate well-delineated preferences for general classes of problems.

Extensive and compelling experiments regarding the relative efficacy of various nonlinear programming algorithms remain to be accomplished and documented. The interested user is generally advised to peruse the scattered evaluations that are available, such as those referenced in this paper, and to form his own conclusions regarding the most accessible methods that best suit his needs.

For a comprehensive introduction to current unconstrained and constrained optimization techniques, the reader is advised to consult the various surveys and expository material that have been published, e.g., Refs. 13, 16, 20, 22, 58, 69, 91, 183–187.

BARRIER METHODS FOR NONLINEAR PROGRAMMING

REFERENCES

1. J. E. Falk and R. M. Soland, An algorithm for separable nonconvex programming problems, *Management Sci.* **15** 550–569 (1969).
2. R. M. Soland, An algorithm for separable nonconvex programming problems II: Nonconvex constraints, *Management Sci.* **17** 759–773 (1971).
3. H. Scarf, The approximation of fixed points of a continuous mapping, *SIAM J. Appl. Math.* **15**(5), (1967).
4. B. C. Eaves, Computing Kakutani fixed points, *SIAM J. Appl. Math.* **21**(2), (1971).
5. O. H. Merrill, Applications and Extensions of an Algorithm That Computes Fixed Points of Certain Upper Semi-Continuous Point to Set Mappings, Ph.D. Thesis, University of Michigan, 1972.
6. C. E. Lemke, Recent results on complementarity problems, in *Nonlinear Programming* (J. B. Rosen, O. L. Mangasarian, and K. Ritter, eds.), Academic, New York, 1970.
7. R. W. Cottle and G. B. Dantzig, A generalization of the linear complementarity problem, *J. Combinatorial Theory* **8**(1), (1970).
8. F. J. Gould and J. W. Tolle, *A Unified Approach to Complementarity in Optimization,* Report 7312, Center for Mathematical Studies in Business and Economics, University of Chicago, Chicago, 1973.
9. T. A. Straeter, *A Parallel Metric Optimization Algorithm,* NASA, Langley Research Center, Hampton, Virginia, paper presented at the Symposium on Nonlinear Programming, The George Washington University, Washington, D.C., March 14–16, 1973.
10. F. A. Lootsma, A survey of methods for solving constrained minimization problems via unconstrained minimization, in *Numerical Methods for Non-Linear Optimization* (F. A. Lootsma, ed.), Academic, New York, 1972.
11. A. V. Fiacco and G. P. McCormick, *Nonlinear Programming: Sequential Unconstrained Minimization Techniques,* Wiley, New York, 1968.
12. A. M. Geoffrion, *Elements of Large-Scale Mathematical Programming,* Working Paper No. 144, Western Management Science Institute, University of California, Los Angeles, 1968.
13. D. J. Wilde and C. S. Beightler, *Foundations of Optimization,* Prentice-Hall, Englewood Cliffs, New Jersey, 1967.
14. S. L. S. Jacoby, J. S. Kowalik, and J. T. Pizzo, *Iterative Methods for Nonlinear Optimization Problems,* Prentice-Hall, Englewood Cliffs, New Jersey, 1972.
15. D. G. Luenberger, *Introduction to Linear and Nonlinear Programming.* Addison-Wesley, Reading, Massachusetts, 1973.
16. E. M. L. Beale, *Mathematical Programming in Practice,* Pitmans, London, 1968.
17. J. Abadie (ed.), *Integer and Nonlinear Programming,* North Holland, Amsterdam, 1970.
18. D. M. Himmelblau, *Applied Nonlinear Programming,* McGraw-Hill, New York, 1972.
19. E. Polak, *Computational Methods in Optimization: A Unified Approach,* Academic, New York, 1971.
20. F. A. Lootsma (ed.), *Numerical Methods for Non-Linear Optimization* (Papers from the Conference Sponsored by the Science Research Council, University of Dundee, Scotland, 1971), Academic, New York, 1972.

21. G. Zoutendijk, *Methods of Feasible Directions.* Elsevier, Amsterdam, 1960.
22. J. Abadie (ed.), *Nonlinear Programming,* Wiley, New York, 1967.
23. W. I. Zangwill, *Nonlinear Programming: A Unified Approach,* Prentice-Hall, Englewood Cliffs, New Jersey, 1969.
24. L. S. Lasdon, *Optimization Theory for Large Systems,* Macmillan, New York, 1970.
25. K. J. Arrow, L. Hurwicz, and H. Uzawa, *Studies in Linear and Nonlinear Programming,* Stanford University Press, Palo Alto, California, 1958.
26. A. V. Fiacco and G. P. McCormick, *Asymptotic Conditions for Constrained Minimization,* Technical Paper RAC-TP-340, Research Analysis Corporation, McLean, Virginia, 1968.
27. C. W. Carroll, An Operations Research Approach to the Economic Optimization of a Kraft Pulping Process, Ph.D. Dissertation, Institute of Paper Chemistry, Appleton, Wisconsin, 1959.
28. C. W. Carroll, The created response surface technique for optimizing nonlinear restrained systems, *Operations Res.* 9(2), 169–184 (1961).
29. A. V. Fiacco and G. P. McCormick, *Programming Under Nonlinear Constraints by Unconstrained Minimization: A Primal-Dual Method,* Technical Paper RAC-TP-96, Research Analysis Corporation, McLean, Virginia, 1963.
30. A. V. Fiacco and G. P. McCormick, The sequential unconstrained minimization technique for nonlinear programming: A primal-dual method, *Management Sci.* 10(2), 360–366 (1964).
31. A. V. Fiacco and G. P. McCormick, Computational algorithm for the sequential unconstrained minimization technique for nonlinear programming, *Management Sci.* 10(2), 601–617 (1964).
32. A. V. Fiacco and G. P. McCormick, Extensions of SUMT for nonlinear programming: Equality constraints and extrapolation, *Management Sci.* 12(11), 816–829 (1966).
33. T. Pomentale, A new method for solving conditioned maxima problems, *J. Math. Anal. Appl.* 10, 216–220 (1965).
34. F. A. Lootsma, Constrained optimization via penalty functions, *Philips Res. Rept.* 23, 408–423 (1968).
35. F. A. Lootsma, *Boundary Properties of Penalty Functions for Constrained Minimization,* Philips Research Reports Supplements, Eindhoven, 1970.
36. F. J. Gould, A class of inside-out algorithms for general programs, *Management Sci.* 16(5), (1970).
37. J. D. Roode, *Interior Point Methods for the Solution of Mathematical Programming Problems,* paper presented at the Symposium on Mathematical Programming, Princeton, August 14–18, 1967.
38. R. Courant, Variational methods for the solution of problems of equilibrium and vibrations, *Bull. Amer. Math. Soc.* 49, 1–23 (1943).
40. H. Rubin and P. Ungar, Motion under a strong constraining force, *Comm. Pure Appl. Math.* 10, 65–87 (1957).
41. H. J. Kelley, Method of gradients, in *Optimization Techniques: With Applications to Aerospace Systems* (G. Leitmann, ed.), Academic, New York, 1962, pp. 206–254.
42. T. Butler and A. V. Martin, On a method of Courant for minimizing functionals, *J. Math. Phys.* 41, 291–299 (1962).
43. T. Pietrzykowski, Application of the steepest descent method to concave

programming, in *Proceedings of the International Federation for Information Processing Symposium, Munich, 1962,* North Holland, Amsterdam, 1962, pp. 185–189.
44. W. I. Zangwill, Non-linear programming via penalty functions, *Management Sci.* **13**(5), 344–358 (1967).
45. A. V. Fiacco and G. P. McCormick, The slacked unconstrained minimization technique for convex programming, *SIAM J. Appl. Math.* **15**(3), 505–515 (1967).
46. K. R. Frisch, Principles of linear programming—with particular reference to the double gradient form of the logarithmic potential method, memorandum of October 18, 1954, University Institute of Economics, Oslo.
47. K. R. Frisch, The logarithmic potential method of convex programming, memorandum of May 13, 1955, University Institute of Economics, Oslo.
48. F. A. Lootsma, Logarithmic programming: A method of solving nonlinear-programming problems, *Philips Res. Rept.* **22**, 329–344 (1967).
49. F. A. Lootsma, Extrapolation in logarithmic programming, *Philips Res. Rept.* **23**, 108–116 (1968).
50. G. R. Parisot, Résolution numérique approchée du problème de programmation linéaire par application de la programmation logarithmique, *Rev. Fr. Recherche Operationelle* **20**, 227–259 (1961).
51. T. S. Motzkin, New techniques for linear inequalities and optimization, in *Project SCOOP, Symposium on Linear Inequalities and Programming,* Planning Research Division, Director of Management Analysis Service, U.S. Air Force, Washington D.C., No. 10, 1952.
52. D. Savir, *Two-Person Concave Games,* paper presented at the Third Annual Conference on Operations Research, Technion, Israel, 1969.
53. R. R. Allran and S. E. V. Johnsen, An algorithm for solving nonlinear programming problems subject to nonlinear inequality constraints, *Comput. J.* **13**, 171–177 (1970).
54. J. P. Evans and F. J. Gould, *Stability and Exponential Penalty Function Techniques in Nonlinear Programming,* Institute of Statistics Mimeo Series No. 723, University of North Carolina, 1970.
55. F. H. Murphy, *Topics in Nonlinear Programming: Penalty Functions and Column Generation Algorithms,* Technical Report No. 34, Department of Administrative Sciences, Yale University, New Haven, 1971.
56. W. I. Zangwill, *On Minimizing a Function without Calculating Derivatives,* Working Paper 210, Center for Research in Management Science, University of California, Berkeley, 1967.
57. J. Kowalik, Nonlinear programming procedures and design optimization, *Acta Polytech. Scand. Math. Comput. Mach. Ser.* **13**, (1966).
58. M. J. Box, and W. H. Swann, *Nonlinear Optimization Techniques* (ICI Monograph of Mathematics and Statistics No. 5), Oliver and Boyd, London, 1969.
59. R. Fletcher and A. P. McCann, Acceleration techniques for nonlinear programming, in *Optimization* (R. Fletcher, ed.), Academic, New York, 1969, pp. 203–214.
60. O. L. Mangasarian, *Nonlinear Programming.* McGraw-Hill, New York, 1969.
61. M. R. Hestenes, *Calculus of Variations and Optimal Control Theory,* Wiley, New York, 1966.
62. H. W. Kuhn and A. W. Tucker, Non-linear programming, in *Proceedings of the*

BARRIER METHODS FOR NONLINEAR PROGRAMMING

Second Berkeley Symposium on Mathematical Statistics and Probability (J. Neyman, ed.), University of California Press, Berkeley, 1951.
63. P. Wolfe, A duality theorem for nonlinear programming, *Quart. Appl. Math.* **19**(3), 239–244 (1961).
64. C. L. Sandblom, *On the Convergence of SUMT*, National Economic Planning Research Paper No. 64, University of Birmingham, Great Britain, 1972.
65. A. V. Fiacco, Comments on the paper of C. W. Carroll, *Operations Res.* **9**, 184–185 (1961).
66. A. V. Fiacco, Sequential Unconstrained Minimization Methods for Nonlinear Programming, Ph.D. Dissertation, Northwestern University, 1967.
67. P. Huard, Résolution des P. M. a constraintes non-linéaires par la méthode des centres, *Electricité de France,* Note No. HR 5.690, 1964.
68. A. V. Fiacco and G. P. McCormick, The sequential unconstrained minimization technique without parameters, *Operations Res.* **15**, 820–827 (1967).
69. D. Davies, Some practical methods of optimization, in *Integer and Nonlinear Programming* (J. Abadie, ed.), North Holland, Amsterdam, 1970.
70. A. Cauchy, Méthode générale pour la resolution des systèmes d'équations simultanées, *Compt. Rend.* **25**, 536–538 (1847).
71. H. B. Curry, The method of steepest descent for non-linear minimization problems, *Quart. Appl. Math.* **2**(3), 250–261 (1944).
72. A. A. Goldstein, Cauchy's method of minimization, *Numer. Math.* **4**, 146–150 (1962).
73. J. B. Crockett and H. Chernoff, Gradient methods of maximization, *Pacific J. Math.* **5**, 33–50 (1955).
74. E. W. Cheney and A. A. Goldstein, (1959). Newton's method for convex programming and Tchebycheff approximation, *Numer. Math.* **1**, 253–268 (1959).
75. A. A. Goldstein, On Newton's method, *Numer. Math.* **7**, 391–393 (1965).
76. W. C. Davidon, *Variable Metric Method for Minimization,* Research and Development Report ANL-5990 (Revised), Argonne National Laboratory, U.S. Atomic Energy Commission, 1959.
77. M. R. Hestenes and E. Stiefel, Method of conjugate gradients for solving linear systems, *J. Res. Nat. Bur. Stand.* **49**, 409–436 (1952).
78. W. Murray, *Ill-conditioning in Barrier and Penalty Functions Arising in Constrained Non-Linear Programming,* paper presented at the Symposium on Mathematical Programming, Princeton, August, 14–18, 1967.
79. W. Murray, *Behavior of Hessian Matrices of Barrier and Penalty Functions Arising in Optimization,* Report No. NA 77, National Physics Laboratory, Teddington, England, 1969.
80. W. Murray, *Constrained Optimization,* Report Ma79, National Physical Laboratory, Teddington, England, 1969.
81. W. Murray, Analytical expressions for the eigenvalues and eigenvectors of the Hessian matrices of barrier and penalty functions. *J. Optimization Theory Appl.* **7**(3), (1971).
82. F. A. Lootsma, Hessian matrices of penalty functions for solving constrained-optimization problems, *Philips Res. Rept.* **24**, 322–331 (1969).
83. R. Fletcher and M. J. D. Powell, A rapidly convergent descent method for minimization, *Comput. J.* **6**, 163–168 (1963).
84. R. Fletcher and C. M. Reeves, Function minimization by conjugate gradients, *Comput. J.* **7**, 149–154 (1964).

85. M. J. D. Powell, An efficient method for finding the minimum of a function of several variables without calculating derivatives, *Comput. J.* **7**(2), 155–162 (1964).
86. F. A. Lootsma, Penalty-function performance of several unconstrained-minimization techniques, *Philips Res. Rept.* **27**, (1972).
87. C. G. Broyden, The convergence of a class of double-rank minimization algorithms, *J. Math. Appl.* **6**, 76–90, 222–231 (1970).
88. R. Fletcher, A new approach to variable metric algorithms, *Comput. J.* **13**, 317–322 (1970).
89. D. Goldfarb, A family of variable-metric methods derived by variational means, *Math. Comp.* **24**, (1970).
90. D. F. Shanno, Conditioning of quasi-Newton methods for function minimization, *Math. Comp.* **24**, 647–656 (1970).
91. J. Kowalik and M. R. Osborne, *Methods for Unconstrained Optimization Problems*, Elsevier, New York, 1968.
92. W. H. Swann, *Report on the Development of a New Direct Search Method of Optimization*, Central Instrument Laboratory Research Note 64/3, Imperial Chemical Industries, 1964.
93. L. S. Lasdon, An efficient algorithm for minimizing barrier and penalty functions, *Math. Programming* **2**, 65–106 (1972).
94. A. Bensasson, *Etude comparative des performances de differents algorithmes et de differentes fonctions penalités dans la minimisation avec contraintes*, Reference 72318, La Radiotechnique, Division Télévision, Suresnes, France, 1973.
95. D. J. Wilde, *Optimum Seeking Methods*, Prenctice-Hall, Englewood Cliffs, New Jersey, 1964.
96. L. S. Lasdon, R. L. Fox, and M. W. Ratner, An efficient one-dimensional search procedure for barrier functions, *Math. Programming* **4**(3), (1973).
97. G. P. McCormick, W. C. Mylander, III, and A. V. Fiacco, *Computer Program Implementing the Sequential Unconstrained Minimization Technique for Nonlinear Programming*, Technical Paper RAC-TP-151, Research Analysis Corporation, McLean, Virginia, 1965.
98. C. W. Mylander, R. Holmes, and G. P. McCormick, *A Guide to SUMT-Version 4: The Computer Program Implementing the Sequential Unconstrained Minimization Technique for Nonlinear Programming*, Technical Paper RAC-P-63, Research Analysis Corporation, McLean, Virginia, 1971.
99. M. R. Osborne and D. M. Ryan, On penalty function methods for nonlinear programming problems, *J. Math. Anal. Appl.* **31**(3), (1970).
100. M. R. Osborne and D. M. Ryan, A hybrid algorithm for non-linear programming, in *Numerical Methods for Non-Linear Optimization* (F. A. Lootsma, ed.), Academic, New York, 1972.
101. G. P. McCormick, *An Arc Method for Nonlinearly Constrained Programming Problems*, MRC Technical Summary Report 1073, Mathematics Research Center, The University of Wisconsin, 1970.
102. R. Courant, *Calculus of Variations and Supplementary Notes and Exercises* (mimeographed notes), Supplementary Notes by M. Kruskal and H. Rubin, revised and amended by J. Moser, New York University, 1956–1957.
103. E. J. Beltrami, A computational approach to necessary conditions in mathematical programming. *ICC Bull.* **6** 265–273 (1967).
104. E. J. Beltrami, A constructive proof of the Kuhn-Tucker multiplier rule, *J. Math. Anal. Appl.* **26**, 297–306 (1969).

105. R. E. Stong, A note on the sequential unconstrained minimization technique for non-linear programming, *Management Sci.* **12**(1), 142–144 (1965).
106. A. V. Fiacco and A. P. Jones, Generalized penalty methods in topological spaces, *SIAM J. Appl. Math.* **17**(5), (1969).
107. D. L. Russell, Penalty functions and bounded phase coordinate control, *SIAM J. Control, Ser. A* **2**, 409–422 (1965).
108. K. Okamura, Some mathematical theory of the penalty method for solving optimum control problems. *SIAM J. Control, Ser. A* **2**, 317–331 (1965).
109. L. S. Lasdon, A. D. Warren, and K. K. Rice, An interior penalty function method for inequality constrained optimal control problem, *IEEE Trans. Automatic Control* **AC-12**, 388–395 (1967).
110. A. V. Balakrishnan, (1968). On a new computing technique in optimal control, *SIAM J. Control* **6**, 149–173 (1968).
111. J. Cullum, Penalty functions and nonconvex continuous optimal control problems, in *Computing Methods in Optimization Problems—2* (L. A. Zadeh, L. W. Neustadt and A. V. Balakrishnan, eds.), Academic, New York, 1969, pp. 55–67.
112. A. P. Jones and G. P. McCormick, A generalization of the method of Balakrishnan: Inequality constraints and initial conditions, *SIAM J. Control* **8**, 218–225 (1970).
113. D. Tabak and B. C. Kuo, *Optimal Control by Mathematical Programming*, Prentice-Hall, Englewood Cliffs, New Jersey, 1971.
114. A. V. Fiacco, Penalty methods for mathematical programming in E^n with general constraint sets, *J. Optimization Theory Appl.* **6**(3), (1970).
115. J. D. Roode, Generalized Lagrangian Functions in Mathematical Programming, Ph.D. Thesis, University of Leiden, The Netherlands, 1968.
116. F. J. Gould, Extensions of Lagrange multipliers in nonlinear programming, *SIAM J. Appl. Math.* **17**, 1280–1297 (1969).
117. F. J. Gould and S. Howe, *A New Result on Interpreting Lagrange Multipliers as Dual Variables,* Institute of Statistics Mimeo Series No. 738, University of North Carolina, 1971.
118. W. B. Widhelm and R. P. O'Neill, *Penalty Functions in Decomposition Techniques,* paper presented at the Symposium on Nonlinear Programming, The George Washington University, Washington, D.C., March 14–16 1973.
119. S. Fromovitz, C. Kim, and R. L. Morton, *A Decomposition Algorithm for Nonconvex Mathematical Programming Problems,* paper presented at the ORSA-TIMS-AIIE Joint National Meeting in Atlantic City, New Jersey, November 8, 1972.
120. M. Bellmore, H. J. Greenberg, and J. J. Jarvis, Generalized penalty-function concepts in mathematical optimization, *Operations Res.* **18**(2), (1970).
121. H. J. Greenberg and W. P. Pierskalla. Surrogate mathematical programming. *Operations Res.* **18**(5), (1970).
122. H. J. Greenberg, *The Generalized Penalty Function—Surrogate Model*, Technical Report CP 70005, Computer Science Center, Southern Methodist University, 1970.
123. H. Everett, Generalized Lagrange multiplier method for solving problems of optimum allocation of resources, *Operations Res.* **11**, 399–417 (1963).
124. J. E. Falk, A Constrained Lagrangian Approach to Nonlinear Programming, Ph.D. Dissertation, University of Michigan, 1965.
125. J. E. Falk, Lagrange multipliers and nonlinear programming, *J. Math. Anal. Appl.* **19**(1), (1967).

BARRIER METHODS FOR NONLINEAR PROGRAMMING

126. W. Murray, An algorithm for constrained minimization, in *Optimization* (R. Fletcher, ed.), Academic, New York, 1969.
127. R. Fletcher, A class of methods for nonlinear programming with termination and convergence properties, in *Integer and Nonlinear Programming* (J. Abadie, ed.), North Holland, Amsterdam, 1970.
128. M. J. D. Powell, A method for nonlinear constraints in minimization problems, in *Optimization* (R. Fletcher, ed.), Academic, New York, 1969.
129. M. R. Hestenes, Multiplier and gradient methods, *J. Optimization Theory Appl.* **4,** (1969).
130. P. C. Haarhoff and J. D. Buys, A new method for the optimization of a nonlinear function subject to nonlinear constraints, *Comput. J.* **13,** (1970).
131. S. A. Lill, Generalization of an exact method for solving constrained problems to deal with inequality constraints, in *Numerical Methods for Non-Linear Optimization* (F. A. Lootsma, ed.), Academic, New York, 1972.
132. R. Fletcher, *An Exact Penalty Function for Nonlinear Programming with inequalities,* Technical Paper 478, Atomic Energy Research Establishment, Harwell, England, 1972.
133. J. P. Evans, F. J. Gould, and J. W. Tolle, Exact penalty functions in nonlinear programming, *Math. Programming* **4**(1), (1973).
134. F. J. Gould, Non-linear tolerance programming, in *Numerical Methods for Non-Linear Optimization* (F. A. Lootsma, ed.), Academic, New York, 1972.
135. T. Pietrzykowski, An exact potential method for constrained maxima, *SIAM J. Numer. Anal.* **6**(2), (1969).
136. A. R. Conn, *A Gradient Type Method of Locating Constrained Minima,* Department of Applied Science and Computer Science Research Report CSRR 2032, University of Waterloo, Ontario, Canada, 1971.
137. R. Fletcher and S. A. Lill, A class of methods for nonlinear programming: II. Computational experience, in *Nonlinear Programming* (J. B. Rosen, O. L. Mangasarian and K. Ritter, eds.), Academic, New York, 1970.
138. M. R. Osborne, On penalty and barrier function methods for mathematical programming, in *Optimization* (R. S. Anderssen, L. S. Jennings, and D. M. Ryan, eds.), University of Queensland Press, St. Lucia, Queensland, 1972.
139. A. V. Fiacco, A general regularized sequential unconstrained minimization technique, *SIAM J. Appl. Math.* **17**(6), (1969).
140. D. M. Ryan, Projection methods for linearly constrained problems, in *Optimization* (R. S. Anderssen, L. S. Jennings, and D. M. Ryan, eds.), University of Queensland Press, St. Lucia, Queensland, 1972.
141. B. A. Murtagh and R. W. H. Sargent, A constrained minimization method with quadratic convergence, in *Optimization* (R. Fletcher, ed.), Academic, New York, 1969.
142. R. W. H. Sargent and B. A. Murtagh, (1973). Projection methods for nonlinear programming, *Math. Programming* **4**(3), (1973).
143. K. P. Wong, *Computer Implementation of the Decomposition of Nonlinear Convex Separable Programmes,* National Economic Planning Research Paper No. 40, University of Birmingham, Great Britain, 1971.
144. T. O. M. Kronsjö, Decomposition of a large nonlinear convex separable economic system in the dual direction (varii auctores), in *Optimation et Simulation de Macro-décisions, Recherches théoriques et appliquées,* Collection "Economie mathématique at econométrie," No. 3, Facultés Notre-Dame de la Paix, Namur—Editions Duculot, Gembloux, 1970.

145. C. L. Sandblom, *A Computational Investigation into Nonlinear Decomposition,* National Economic Planning Research Paper No. 67, University of Birmingham, Great Britain, 1972.
146. R. B. McCann and R. M. Soland, *Preliminary Experience with a Computer Code for Nonconvex Programming,* paper presented at the Symposium on Nonlinear Programming, The George Washington University, Washington, D.C., March 14–16, 1973.
147. J. Weisman, Engineering Design Optimization under Conditions of Risk, Ph.D. Dissertation, University of Pittsburgh, 1968.
148. R. Hooke and T. A. Jeeves, "Direct search" solution of numerical and statistical problems, *J. Assoc. Comput. Mach.* **8,** (1961).
149. F. A. Lootsma, Constrained optimization via parameter-free penalty functions, *Philips Res. Rept.* **23,** 424–437 (1968).
150. R. Mifflin, *Convergence Rates for a Method of Centers Algorithm,* Rept. ORC-71-10, Operations Research Center, University of California, Berkeley, 1971.
151. J. Bracken and G. P. McCormick, *Selected Applications of Nonlinear Programming,* Wiley, New York, 1968.
152. F. A. Tillman *et al.,* Optimal reliability of a complex system, *IEEE Transactions on Reliability* **r-19**(3), (1970).
153. R. M. Soland, Optimal multivariate stratified sampling with prior information, *Skand. Aktuarietidskr.* **39,** 1–6 (1956).
154. D. A. Schrady and U. C. Choe, Models for multi-item continuous review inventory policies subject to constraints, *Naval Res. Logist. Quart.* **18**(4), (1971).
155. D. Tabak, *Application of Linear and Nonlinear Programming in Optimal Control of Nuclear Reactors,* paper presented at the Symposium on Mathematical Programming, Princeton, August 14–18, 1967.
156. R. G. Brusch, *A Nonlinear Programming Approach to Space Shuttle Trajectory Optimization,* paper presented to the XXII Congress of the International Astronautical Federation, Brussels, Belgium, September 20–26, 1971.
157. R. J. Anderson, Ph.D. Thesis, Purdue University, 1969.
158. D. Kavlie, J. Kowalik, S. Lund, and J. Moe, Design optimization using a general nonlinear programming method, *European Shipbuilding* **4,** (1966).
159. W. A. Thornton and L. A. Schmit, Structural synthesis of an ablating thermostructural panel, *AIAA/ASME 9th Annual Structures, Structural Dynamics and Materials Conference,* Palm Springs, California, Preprint No. 68-332, 1968.
160. R. L. Fox, *Optimization Methods for Engineering Design,* Addison-Wesley, Reading, Massachusetts, 1971.
161. A. A. Goldstein and B. R. Kripke, Mathematical programming by minimizing differentiable functions, *Numer. Math.* **6,** 47–48 (1964).
162. R. Mifflin, On the convergence of the logarithmic barrier function method, in *Numerical Methods for Non-Linear Optimization* (F. A. Lootsma, ed.), Academic, New York, 1972.
163. M. C. Biggs, Constrained minimization using recursive equality quadratic programming, in *Numerical Methods for Non-Linear Optimization* (F. A. Lootsma, ed.), Academic, New York, 1972.
164. M. C. Biggs, Minimization algorithms making use of non-quadratic properties of the objective function, *J. Inst. Math. Appl.* (1971).
165. D. Davies, *The use of Davidon's Method in Non-linear Programming,* Imperial Chemical Industries Report MSDH/68/110, 1968.

166. G. Zoutendijk, Nonlinear programming: A numerical survey, *SIAM J. Control* **4**, 194–210 (1966).
167. A. R. Butz, Iterative saddle-point techniques, *SIAM J. Appl. Math.* **15**, 719–725 (1967).
168. J. Bombart and F. C. Hipp, *Analogue Computer Solution of Programming Problems*, memorandum, Research Analysis Corporation, McLean, Virginia, 1963.
169. C. M. Ablow and G. Brigham, An analog solution of programming problems, *Operations Res.* **3**, 388–394 (1955).
170. M. V. Rybashov, The gradient method of solving convex programming problems on electronic analog computers, *Automat. i Telemeh.* **26**(11), 1955–1967 (1965).
171. E. E. Dudnikov and M. V. Rybashov, Methods for the solution of mathematical programming problems on general purpose analog computers (survey), *Automat. i Telemeh.* **5**, 109–152 (1967).
172. S. M. Robinson, *Perturbed Kuhn-Tucker Points and Rates of Convergence for a Class of Nonlinear-Programming Algorithms*, MRC Technical Summary Report 1298, Mathematics Research Center, University of Wisconsin—Madison, Madison, Wisconsin, 1973.
173. A. V. Fiacco, *Sensitivity Analysis for Nonlinear Programming Using Penalty Methods*, Technical Paper Serial T-275, Program in Logistics, The George Washington University, Washington, D.C., 1973.
174. R. L. Armacost and A. V. Fiacco, *Computational Experience in Sensitivity Analysis for Nonlinear Programming*, Technical Paper, Serial T-276, Program in Logistics, The George Washington University, Washington, D.C., 1973.
175. W. C. Mylander and R. L. Armacost, *A Guide to a SUMT-Version 4 Computer Subroutine for Implementing Sensitivity Analysis in Nonlinear Programming*, Technical Paper Serial T-287, Program in Logistics, The George Washington University, Washington, D.C., 1973.
176. J. Kowalik, M. R. Osborne, and D. M. Ryan, A new method for constrained optimization problems, *Operations Res.* **17**(6), (1969).
177. L. A. Schmit and R. L. Fox, *Advances in the Integrated Approach to Structural Synthesis*, A.I.A.A. Sixth Annual Structures and Materials Conference, Palm Springs, California, 1965.
178. D. D. Morrison, Optimization by least squares, *SIAM J. Numer. Anal.* **5**, 83–88 (1968).
179. J. Asaadi, A computational comparison of some nonlinear programs, *Math. Programming* **4**,(2), (1973).
180. A. R. Colville, *Nonlinear Programming Study Results as of November 1968*, IBM New York Scientific Center, New York Technical Report No. 320–2949, 1968.
181. G. P. McCormick, Penalty function versus non-penalty function methods for constrained nonlinear programming problems, *Math. Programming* **1**(2), (1971).
182. R. Fletcher, *Methods for the Solution of Optimization Problems*, report prepared at the Atomic Energy Research Establishment, Harwell, England, 1970.
183. H. A. Spang, A review of minimization techniques for nonlinear functions, *SIAM Rev.* **4**(4), 343–365 (1962).
184. H. P. Kunzi, W. Krelle, and W. Oettli, *Nonlinear Programming*, Blaisdell, Waltham, Massachusetts, 1966.

BARRIER METHODS FOR NONLINEAR PROGRAMMING

185. P. Wolfe, Methods of nonlinear programming, in *Nonlinear Programming* (J. Abadie, ed.), North Holland, Amsterdam, 1967.
186. R. Fletcher (ed.), *Optimization, Proceedings of the 1968 Keele University Conference on Nonlinear Programming,* Academic, New York, 1969.
187. A. M. Geoffrion, *Perspectives on Optimization: A Collection of Expository Articles,* Addison-Wesley, Reading, Massachusetts, 1972.
188. F. J. Gould, *Continuously Differentiable Exact Penalty Functions for Nonlinear Programs with Tolerances,* Institute of Statistics Mimeo Series No. 744, University of North Carolina, 1971.
189. J. E. Falk, A relaxed interior approach to nonlinear programming, *Z. Wahrscheinlichkeitstheorie Verw. Gebiete* **11**, 327–337 (1969).

Anthony V. Fiacco

"BASIC" COMPUTER LANGUAGE

BASIC is an acronym for "Beginners' All-purpose Symbolic Instruction Code," an artificial language designed for computer programming. BASIC is perhaps the simplest commonly used programming language. Normally found in a time-sharing environment, BASIC is primarily used by persons at remote teletypewriter terminals. However, it is also used on a one-user-at-a-time basis for programming minicomputers and even some of the larger programmable calculators. The simplicity and wide availability of BASIC often make it the language of choice, especially for those computer users who are not extensively trained or experienced as programmers.

HISTORY

BASIC was originated as part of the Dartmouth Time-Sharing System, which was conceived, designed, and implemented by a small group of professors and student programmers at Dartmouth College with the effort concentrated in the first half of 1964. In particular, two men were responsible for both the design and implementation of BASIC—Thomas E. Kurtz and John G. Kemeny. Dr. Kurtz has since become director of the Kiewit Computation Center at Dartmouth while Dr. Kemeny has risen to the post of president of Dartmouth College. The objectives of these men in designing BASIC should be carefully noted. The goal of Dartmouth College in acquiring and utilizing its computers was to make the power of the computer directly available to a majority of its students and faculty. It was necessary that even the liberal arts students, who would not always be willing to enroll in a complete computer programming course, could learn to write a simple program, run it, correct errors if necessary, and get their answers. To achieve this goal, the people at Dartmouth decided on two primary tactics. First, they would provide the computer's services on a conversational time-sharing basis. In this fashion, each user would essentially appear to be talking to the computer on a one-to-one basis in which the user could tell the computer what to do next based on previous results. The conveniences and pedagogical benefits accruing from such a system were felt, and are still felt, by Dartmouth to be tremendous. Second, the Dartmouth group would provide the users with a simple language in which to "speak to" or program the computer. At that time the higher level languages FORTRAN and ALGOL were already well established, as were the individual assembly languages (machine level languages) of each computer. However, it was felt that the existing higher level languages had some avoidable complexities which made them powerful and efficient but harder to learn for beginners. The assembly languages were unsuitable for even more compelling reasons. It was decided to develop a new, simpler language for use by beginners. Since the new language was still to be flexible and general enough to be used for almost any programming purpose, and since it was a symbolic language for coding instructions to a computer, the name "Beginner's All-purpose Symbolic Instructions Code" was aptly applied. That the acronym BASIC is so obviously appropriate is, of course, not entirely accidental.

In line with these ideas, the Dartmouth group went about realizing its goals. The project was backed by National Science Foundation grants and later by a contribution for new computer facilities from an alumnus, Mr. Peter Kiewit, whose name was given to the computer center he helped build. With advice from General Electric Corp. Dartmouth settled on a GE-235 central computer with a GE Datanet 30 computer to handle communication with the users. By the fall of 1963, students and professors both were starting to learn about the new machinery in advance of its delivery. When the equipment actually arrived in February 1964 and achieved operational status in mid-March, development of what was to become the Dartmouth Time-Sharing System (DTSS) began in earnest in parallel with the design and implementation of BASIC. By May 1, 1964, enough of the system was working to run a BASIC program typed in from a teletypewriter. In June the system was stable enough to increase the number of teletypewriters able to access the computer. As early as the fall of 1964, BASIC was being taught to Dartmouth students and had become a well-established entity.

With Dartmouth working in close association with General Electric, the Dartmouth system, including BASIC, began to spread. In 1965, GE established a commercial time-sharing service using the Dartmouth system under the name Mark I. GE and Dartmouth continued to work together to upgrade both the hardware and software of their time-sharing systems, but by this time BASIC was unleashed on the world. As the success of both time-sharing as a whole and BASIC in particular became obvious at Dartmouth and GE, other suppliers of computers and computer time were not slow in developing systems of their own. By 1967, at the latest, several independent efforts had resulted in time-sharing systems offering BASIC. The proliferation of BASIC continued until it was available, in some form, on every major manufacturer's computer equipment, with no notable exceptions.

The advent in recent years of the minicomputer industry has added a new dimension

[116]
"BASIC" COMPUTER LANGUAGE

for the expansion of BASIC. The small memory size, limited instruction repertoire, and lack of mass storage of the minimum-level minicomputers combine to hamper the implementation of such complex languages as FORTRAN, ALGOL, and COBOL. However, the simplicity of BASIC has made it possible for many minicomputer suppliers to offer BASIC as a programming language on even the smallest computers. In some cases the bare minimum configuration for a minicomputer may make it programmable only in its assembly language or BASIC, even if FORTRAN and ALGOL are offered for larger configurations. On an even smaller scale, some of the newest programmable calculators use BASIC as a basis for their operating and programming methods. Although the programming language offered by the calculators may be implemented in hardware and may be used in a noticeably different way from that of a time-sharing system, they both show the common characteristics inherited from the original Dartmouth BASIC.

CHARACTERISTICS

With a large number of computer types offering the BASIC language in some form, it is necessary to specify what characteristics of a programming language identify it as truly being BASIC. Although it is not feasible to give a complete definition of the BASIC language at this time, there are some characteristics of BASIC which make it readily recognizable. These characteristics were the product of the guidelines behind the design of the language at Dartmouth. In fact, the guidelines for the design of BASIC, taken as a whole, almost completely characterize the finished product. In addition to the over-all goal of simplicity, more specific criteria were established. It was decided BASIC should interpret arithmetic formulas and obvious grammatical constructions in a normal fashion—giving the results a novice would expect. The language had to have a simple, easily learned level; but it also had to permit extension to allow more expert programmers to perform more complex tasks. However, it was important that the more complex features of the language never be introduced in such a way as to disturb the elementary level and make it harder to learn. Further, the learner of BASIC should be able to go on to learn other computer languages, principally ALGOL and FORTRAN at the time, without undue effort. To this end it was desirable to avoid radical departure from the English-like and mathematical construction of statements and expressions in these languages.

In addition to conforming to these requirements, BASIC was also designed with consideration given to its eventual implementation and use. The compiler for the language was required to produce understandable diagnostics to help the novice user correct his program without recourse to a technical manual. Also, the user had to be able to change his program easily and rerun it. The compiler had to be both fast and small in order to provide good service to a large number of users. Indeed, several of the simplicities built into BASIC were designed not only to be easy to learn but also to be easily compiled and executed by the computer. For example, the limited number of very

"BASIC" COMPUTER LANGUAGE

short variable names allowed in BASIC was an aid in simplifying compilation of the language.

The influence of all these design criteria can be seen in BASIC as it finally emerged. The final structure of BASIC can best be illustrated by explaining a very simple example. The following is the text of a complete BASIC program.

```
10  REMARK DEFINE FNS FUNCTION TO GIVE SQUARES
20  DEF FNS(X)=X*X
30  DATA 6,1.24,−4.1,921,−2,0
40  DIM A(100)
50  GOSUB 100
60  FOR J=I TO 1 STEP −1
70  PRINT FNS(A(J)),ABS(A(J))
80  NEXT J
90  GOTO 200
100 REMARK READ LIST FROM DATA
110 REMARK LOOK FOR 0 AT END OF LIST
120 FOR I=1 TO 100
130 READ (A(I)
140 IF A(I)=0 THEN 160
150 NEXT I
160 RETURN
200 END
```

The above program is written more to illustrate the features of BASIC than to do useful work. The task it would perform when executed by a computer would be to read a list of numbers given in the statement beginning "30 DATA" and find a value of zero. It would then print out the square and absolute value of each number in the list in reverse order starting with the zero. To complete this task, the program deliberately uses almost every feature of the elementary level of BASIC. Before explaining the program further, some overall observations about it are necessary.

First, every line is preceded by a number. This number labels each line, identifying its position in the program and supplying a way to refer to that line. This numbering of statements usually plays a large role in writing and correcting BASIC programs and avoids some complications present in other programming languages which label only some statements.

Second, each line begins with a pronounceable "keyword" which is either an English word or a straightforward abbreviation of one. This keyword makes the general intent of the statement clear from the beginning, which is a boon for the computer programs (compilers or interpreters) responsible for getting the BASIC program executed.

Third, the data elements handled by the program are numbers, and only one type of number is considered, real numbers. There is no distinction made between integer and noninteger numbers. This convention was one of the simplifications departing from FORTRAN and ALGOL, avoiding some pedagogical difficulties in explaining the

"BASIC" COMPUTER LANGUAGE

distinctions between integer and floating point arithmetic. For example, there is no distinction between the constants written as 1 and 1.0; and the value of the expression "1/2" is .5, not zero as it would be in FORTRAN.

Fourth, the variables in the program—I, J, A, and X—have minimally short names. A letter followed by a single digit is the longest a variable name can be. This restriction also contrasts sharply with other programming languages, but it serves several purposes. Principally, it avoids confusion between the variables and the keywords and standard mathematical function names built into the language. It is possible for the compiler (or interpreter) for BASIC to recognize variable names unambiguously, even without resort to looking through any list.

Fifth, the program reports its results, via the PRINT statement numbered 70, without reference to any sort of "format." The lack of detailed formats is characteristic of at least the elementary level of BASIC. All data that goes into or comes out of the program does so in loosely formatted or "free-formatted" representations. In addition, the statements in the language are not strictly formatted—the number and position of blanks (spaces) in the illustrated statements are of no concern. The absence of formats contributes to making the language both easier to teach and easier to implement on a computer.

The individual statements in the illustrated program are probably self-explanatory if the reader has any programming experience in any computer language. However, a short description of each statement may be of interest. The REMARK (or just REM) statements, numbers 10, 100, and 110, give no instructions to the computer. They are included solely to carry commentary information for the readers of the program. The DEF statement (20) defines an arithmetic function which can then be used inside the program to avoid rewriting the expression defining the function. The letters FN followed by one letter are used to name such user defined functions to avoid conflict with the usual arithmetic functions already inherent in BASIC, normally including ABS (absolute value), SQR (square root), LOG (natural logarithm), EXP (natural exponential), trigonometric functions, and some others. Statement 30 supplies a list of numbers which the program can use as the data from which it is to compute its answers. The READ statement (130) is used to get the next number out of the list given by the DATA statement. In the DIM statement (40) an array A is declared to have a dimension of 100 possible elements. If an array need have fewer than eleven elements, no DIM statement is required. The GOSUB statement (50) temporarily interrupts the sequence in which the statements of the program are executed. The execution of statements will jump after statement 50 to statement 100. The statements from 100 through 160 form a subprogram or subroutine which the GOSUB statement causes to be executed. In this particular program, there was no real need to make these statements a subroutine since they are only used once. In the subroutine, the IF statement (140) tests for a value of zero and if the test succeeds, program execution skips to statement 160.

The RETURN statement (160) ends the subroutine and returns to the execution of statements after the GOSUB statement. Statements 60 through 80 and 120 through 150 form loops—sections of the program that are to be repeated a specified number of times. The combination of the FOR and NEXT statements delimit the loop and provide a variable whose value changes after each iteration of the loop. A PRINT statement (70)

"BASIC" COMPUTER LANGUAGE

causes the value of the expressions given in the statement to be displayed for the user to read. After the loop finishes, the GOTO statement (90) is reached and it transfers execution to statement 200, an END statement which marks both the physical and logical end of the program.

EXTENSIONS

Although the illustrated BASIC program does demonstrate essentially all of the various statement types contained in the elementary level of the language, more advanced features do exist in BASIC. However, while there is general agreement on the features of BASIC already described, there is considerably less agreement as to what constitutes more advanced levels of BASIC. The major extensions to BASIC can be divided into several areas. A particular implementation of BASIC may be lacking in capabilities in any of these areas, or different implementations may have tackled the extensions in noticeably different ways.

One area of extension is the handling of character string data, or "strings." Strings appear in even the elementary level of BASIC, at least in output statements, so that a program can "say" words to the user rather than just numbers. In all but the most primitive BASIC, string data can be stored in a special class of variables (whose names contain a dollar sign at the end), read as data, compared to other strings, and printed. Common extensions in this area include the existence of arrays of strings and functions or operators to manipulate strings in detail. Functions to take strings apart, put them together, convert them to numbers and vice versa are fairly standard.

Another common addition to BASIC is a set of statements to deal with matrices. These statements begin with the keyword MAT and specify one of several basic operations on the matrices given. The matrix functions normally consist of inversion, transposition, both scalar and matrix multiplication, addition and subtraction plus the mechanisms for copying one matrix into another, setting a matrix to all zeroes or all ones, or filling a square matrix to make it the identity matrix used in matrix arithmetic. Statements to read and print matrices are also included.

A third area of extension adds to BASIC abilities to read and write mass storage data files. Statements to declare which data files are to be referenced as well as statements to read, write, and reposition these files are incorporated into the language. Sequentially accessed files are the first target of the extensions, but random access files appear also in several implementations. The capacity for manipulating data files, especially when used in conjunction with the string features, considerably widens BASIC's scope of application in nonmathematical fields. A virtually unlimited variety of true data processing applications becomes possible, complementing BASIC's traditional problem-solving role.

One other set of enhancements also increases the applicability of BASIC by providing mechanisms for linking together programs and subprograms into flexible systems. The advantages associated with modular programming become available to the BASIC user. The power to create and use separate subroutines and separate program modules means that the user is not hindered by his desire for a reasonable size limit for a single program, or by the computer's need for such a limit. Means of linking to subroutines in languages other than BASIC are occasionally provided in this area, but this is strictly a part of the particular implementations of BASIC and not the language itself.

STANDARDIZATION

As noted in the discussion of the characteristics and extensions of the language, there are differences between independent implementations of all but the lowest level of BASIC. As of this writing, no official standard exists for BASIC. Possibilities for at least a standardized subset of BASIC seem good since there is already considerable agreement between implementations in the elementary level of the language. This agreement is due to the existence of Dartmouth BASIC as a model. When several independent versions of BASIC had been put into operation, divergent evolution began. Shaped by the desires of different groups of users, requirements for extensions varied. Moreover, the independent implementors' varying philosophies about programming languages and their alternate designs for BASIC compilers sometimes resulted in the same basic idea for an extension appearing in syntactically different ways in the extended languages. Although Dartmouth was contemporarily extending its own BASIC, the work on extended BASIC's for other computer systems was too nearly concurrent to allow the Dartmouth version to become established as an obligatory standard. Also, a certain number of the disagreements in the implementation of BASIC's can be traced to imprecision in the manuals various implementors chose to use for their definitions of BASIC.

Some effort has been made recently to move toward standardization of BASIC. The American National Standards Institute (ANSI) could eventually approve a standard, although one should not be expected for a few years yet. To date (summer 1973) only the preliminary actions have been taken. The responsible committee (X3) of ANSI has received a recommendation from its SPARC subcommittee that at least a subset of BASIC be standardized. The X3 committee still must decide whether or not to undertake the project. When it does so decide, considerable machinery must be put in motion to organize groups to draw up tentative standards, debate them, and revise them until they are suitable for adoption. To aid the standardization process, Dartmouth has recently published a rather precise specification of their current implementation. This might provide the basis for a standard, possibly one prescribing the minimum required standards for a BASIC together with optional modules of regulated extensions. It is, however, too soon to say for sure how the standardization effort will end.

BIBLIOGRAPHY

There is a natural shortage of scholarly literature on BASIC since it is not intended as a very formal or deep language. Every manufacturer supplying BASIC for his computer systems has his own BASIC manual. In addition, several major suppliers of computer

"BASIC" COMPUTER LANGUAGE

services offer their own unique implementations of BASIC and manuals relating thereto. Some of these manuals are designed for accurate technical reference while others are simplified guides for novice BASIC users. Apart from manuals, there are many active or potential textbooks available on BASIC. Since these may be available in institutional libraries, a sample list is included from major publishers. Of major interest are the publications from Dartmouth, the specifications manual, and any available edition of their BASIC manual. An article by the originator of BASIC on its history is included as is an interesting article on the proliferation of unstandardized extensions to BASIC.

Barnett, Eugene H., *Programming Time-Shared Computers in BASIC*, Wiley-Interscience, New York, 1972.

Farina, Mario V., *Programming in BASIC*, Prentice-Hall, Englewood Cliffs, N.J., 1968.

Garland, Stephen J., *Dartmouth BASIC: A Specification,* Kiewit Computation Center, Dartmouth College, Hanover, N.H., 1973.

Gateley, Wilson Y., and Gary G. Bitter, *BASIC for Beginners,* McGraw-Hill, New York, 1970.

Gruenberger, Fred J., *Computing with the BASIC Language,* Canfield, San Francisco, 1972.

Hare, Jr., Van Court, *BASIC Programming,* Harcourt, Brace and World, New York, 1970.

Hare, Jr., Van Court, *Introduction to Programming: A BASIC Approach,* Harcourt, Brace and World, New York, 1970.

Kemeny, John G., and Thomas E. Kurtz, Dartmouth time-sharing, *Science* (October 11, 1968).

Kurtz, Thomas E., and John G. Kemeny, *BASIC Programming,* Wiley, New York, 1971.

Murrill, Paul W., and Cecil L. Smith, *BASIC Programming,* Intext Educational Publishers, Scranton, Pa., 1971.

Nolan, Richard L., *Introduction to Computing Through the BASIC Language.* Holt, Rinehart and Winston, New York, 1969.

Ogdin, Jerry L., The case against . . . BASIC, *Datamation* (September 1, 1971).

Pavlovich, Joseph P., and Thomas E. Tahan, *Computer Programming in BASIC,* Holden-Day, San Francisco, 1971.

Pegels, C. Carl, *BASIC. A Computer Programming Language with Business and Management Applications,* Holden-Day, San Francisco, 1973.

Sharpe, William F., and Nancy L. Jacob, *BASIC: An Introduction to Computer Programming Using the BASIC Language,* Free Press, New York, 1971.

Spencer, Donald D., *A Guide to BASIC Programming—A Time-Sharing Language,* Addison-Wesley, Reading, Mass., 1970.

Waite, Stephen V. F., and Diane G. Mather (eds.), *BASIC.* 6th ed., University Press of New England, Hanover, N.H. 1971. Earlier editions by Thomas E. Kurtz and John G. Kemeny.

Thomas W. Hall, Jr.

BASIC FEASIBLE SOLUTIONS

The term "basic feasible solution" arises in the solution of a set of simultaneous linear equations with nonnegative variables. This situation is usually related to operations research or management science applications of optimizing a linear objective function subject to a set of linear inequalities and nonnegative variables. This type of problem is called linear programming and has been very successful for many applications.

To develop the idea of a basic feasible solution, first consider the set of m equations with n variables

$$a_{11}x_1 + a_{12}x_2 + \ldots + a_{1,n-1}x_{n-1} + a_{1n}x_n = b_1$$
$$a_{21}x_1 + a_{22}x_2 + \ldots + a_{2,n-1}x_{n-1} + a_{2n}x_n = b_2$$
$$\ldots\ldots\ldots\ldots\ldots\ldots\ldots\ldots\ldots\ldots\ldots\ldots\ldots$$
$$a_{m,1}x_1 + a_{m,2}x_2 + \ldots + a_{m,n-1}x_{n-1} + a_{m,n}x_n = b_m$$

If this set of equations has a solution, there is a set of row operations that transforms the equations into the form below. Gaussian elimination is a common procedure for performing these row operations. [Permissible row operations are (1) multiplying a row by a nonzero constant; (2) adding a row to another.] The columns are assumed to have been renumbered if necessary. In some cases this procedure will result in rows for which all the coefficients are zero. We will assume that these rows have been eliminated. This representation is called the *explicit form*.

$$x_1 \qquad\qquad + a'_{1,m+1}x_m + \ldots + a'_{1,n}x_n = b'_1$$
$$\quad x_2 \qquad + a'_{2,m+1}x_m + \ldots + a'_{2,n}x_n = b'_2$$
$$\ldots\ldots\ldots\ldots\ldots\ldots\ldots\ldots\ldots\ldots\ldots\ldots$$
$$x_m + a'_{m,m+1}x_m + \ldots + a'_{m,n}x_n = b'_m$$

To illustrate this procedure, consider the set of equations

$$-4x_1 + 3x_2 + 2x_3 = -2 \qquad (1)$$
$$5x_1 - 4x_2 + x_2 = 3 \qquad (2)$$

The row operations yield the set of equivalent equations.

$$x_1 \qquad - 11x_3 = -1 \qquad (3)$$
$$\quad x_2 - 14x_3 = -2 \qquad (4)$$

From this form it is apparent that there are an infinite number of solutions that are determined by selecting arbitrary values for x_3, e.g., $x_3 = 1.2$ implies that $x_1 = 0.2$ and $x_2 = 14.8$.

A *basic solution* is a solution where $x_{m+1}, \ldots, x_n$ are all zero and $x_1 = b'_1, \ldots, x_m = b'_m$. The first m variables are called *basic variables*, and the remaining $n-m$ variables are referred to as *nonbasic variables*. A set of equations may be represented in terms of several different sets of basic variables.

BASIC FEASIBLE SOLUTIONS

A different set of row operations will yield the equations below in terms of x_1 and x_3:

$$x_1 - \frac{11}{14}x_2 = 8/14 \tag{5}$$

$$x_3 - \frac{1}{14}x_2 = 2/14 \tag{6}$$

To determine which sets of variables may constitute a basic solution, the concept of linear independence must be introduced. A column $\bar{a}_j$ will be referred to as the vector of coefficients $(a_{1j}, a_{2j}, \ldots, a_{m-1,j}, a_{m,j})$.

A set of columns is said to be linearly independent if no nontrivial linear combination of the columns equals the zero vector, i.e.,

$$\sum_j \lambda_j \bar{a}_j = 0 \text{ implies } \lambda_j = 0 \text{ for all } j$$

In our preceding example the columns $\bar{a}_1$ and $\bar{a}_2$ are independent, since Eqs. (3) and (4) make it evident that the only way to obtain linear combination of $\bar{a}_1$ and $\bar{a}_2$ equal to the zero vector is with $\lambda_1 = \lambda_2 = 0$. In a similar manner a column $\bar{a}_0$ is said to be linearly-dependent on some set of columns if it can be represented as a linear combination of these columns, i.e.,

$$\bar{a}_0 = \sum_j \lambda_j \bar{a}_j \text{ and } \lambda_j \neq 0 \text{ for some } j$$

The column $\bar{a}_3$ is linearly dependent on a_1 and a_2 since $-\frac{11}{14}\bar{a}_1 - \frac{1}{14}\bar{a}_2 = \bar{a}_3$.

In a similar manner, linear independence and dependence of the rows can be defined. If the m rows are not linearly independent, then at least one row can be eliminated or the problem is infeasible. For the remainder of this discussion, assume that the rows are linearly independent and that $n > m$. With these definitions a *basis* is any set of m linearly independent columns, and a *basic solution* is the solution resulting from setting the nonbasic variables equal to zero and solving the $m \times m$ set of simultaneous equations for the values of the basic variables. Although each basis yields an infinite number of solutions, there can be at most $\binom{m}{n}$ basis and basic solutions.

The preceding discussion sketched some concepts and procedures for solving m simultaneous equations with n variables. Many problems in operations research and management science require that the variables be nonnegative, i.e., $x_j \geq 0$. The variable may represent the water level of a reservoir, a time parameter, or the amount of wheat in a cereal recipe. In addition, the inclusion of nonnegative variables permits inequalities to be converted to equations.

The inequality

$$x_1 + x_2 \leq 6$$

is equivalent to the equation

$$x_1 + x_2 + x_3 = 6 \text{ and } x_3 \geq 0$$

In a similar manner the inequality $2x_1 - x_2 \geq 6$ is converted to $2x_1 - x_2 - x_3 = 6$

BASIC FEASIBLE SOLUTIONS

and $x_3 \geq 0$. So the use of nonnegative variables not only permits the modeling of many new problems but it also permits sets of inequalities to be treated as equations with nonnegative variables.

A *basic feasible solution* is a basic solution for which the values of the basic variables are all nonnegative. In the previous example

$$-4x_1 + 3x_2 + 2x_3 = -2$$

$$5x_1 - 4x_2 + x_3 = 3$$

the solution corresponding to a basis of x_1 and x_2 given by Eqs. (3) and (4) would not have been a basic feasible solution since $x_1 = -1$ and $x_2 = -2$ are negative. The basis x_1 and x_3 given by Eqs. (5) and (6) would be a basic feasible solution because setting $x_2 = 0$ yields nonnegative values for x_1 and x_3, i.e., $x_1 = 8/14$ and $x_3 = 2/14$.

The basic feasible solutions corresponding to a set of inequalities and nonnegative variables have a helpful geometric interpretation. Consider the system of inequalities

$$x_1 + x_2 \leq 2 \tag{7}$$

$$x_1 \leq 1 \tag{8}$$

and

$$x_1 \geq 0, \quad x_2 \geq 0$$

The region satisfying Eqs. (7) and (8) and the nonnegativity restrictions is shaded in Fig. 1. The shaded region forms a convex set. A *convex set* is defined as a set for which the line joining any two points in the set lies entirely in the set. The four points labeled I, II, III, and IV are of special interest, and are called *extreme points*. An extreme point has the property that it is not contained in any line segment joining two other distinct points. Extreme points are of special interest because if there is a finite optimum to the *linear programming problem*

$$\max c_1 x_1 + c_2 x_2 + \ldots + c_n x_n$$

subject to

$$a_{11} x_1 + a_{12} x_2 + \ldots + a_{1n} x_n \leq b_1$$

$$a_{21} x_1 + a_{22} x_2 + \ldots + a_{2n} x_n \leq b_2$$

$$\ldots \ldots \ldots \ldots \ldots \ldots \ldots \ldots \ldots \ldots$$

$$a_{m1} x_1 + a_{m2} x_2 + \ldots + a_{mn} x_n \leq b_m$$

$$x_1, x_2, \ldots, x_n \geq 0$$

it will always occur at an extreme point of the convex set defined by the above inequalities.

The inequalities (7) and (8) are equivalent to the following equations with nonnegative variables:

$$x_1 + x_2 + x_3 \qquad = 2 \tag{9}$$

$$x_1 \qquad\qquad + x_4 = 1 \tag{10}$$

BASIC FEASIBLE SOLUTIONS

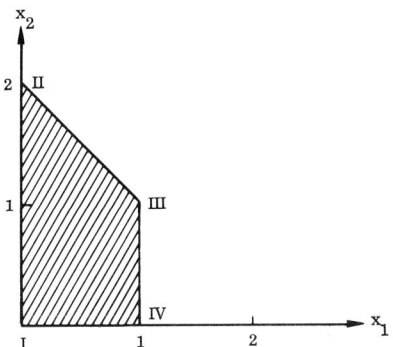

Figure 1

and
$$x_1 > 0, x_2 \geq 0, x_3 \geq 0, x_4 \geq 0$$

The four extreme points correspond to the four basic feasible solutions to Eqs. (9) and (10):

$$\begin{aligned}
\text{I:} \quad & x_3 = 2, x_4 = 1, x_1 = 0, x_2 = 0 \\
\text{II:} \quad & x_2 = 2, x_4 = 1, x_1 = 0, x_3 = 0 \\
\text{III:} \quad & x_1 = 1, x_2 = 1, x_3 = 0, x_4 = 0 \\
\text{IV:} \quad & x_1 = 1, x_3 = 1, x_2 = 0, x_4 = 0
\end{aligned}$$

Thus, in solving linear programming problems, the optimization is restricted to searching for the best basic feasible solution. This reduces the problem to considering a finite number of alternatives rather than dealing with the infinite set of solutions to the inequalities. The simplex method for linear programming extends this result to develop an efficient procedure for finding the best basic feasible solution. The simplex method starts by selecting an arbitrary basic feasible solution and determines if increasing the value of any nonbasic variable (currently equal to zero) will increase the function being maximized.

To determine which nonbasic variables may increase the objective function, represent the objective function in terms of the nonbasic variable through the *explicit form*.

The new objective function is

$$\sum_{j=1}^{m} c_j b'_j + \sum_{j=m+1}^{n} (c_j - \sum_{i=1}^{m} a'_{ij} c_j) x_j$$

The first summation is a constant and the second summation gives the change in the objective function if the nonbasic variable $x_{m+1}, \ldots, x_n$ are changed from their current zero value. If one of the terms

$$c'_k = c_k - \sum_{i=1}^{m} a'_{ik} c_k > 0$$

then increasing x_k will increase the objective function at a rate c'_k.

BASIC FEASIBLE SOLUTIONS

If one or more of the basic variables has $b'_i = 0$, the solution is called *degenerate*. In this case it may happen that the new basic feasible solution formed will have $x_k = 0$ and the objective function will not actually increase.

If no variable will improve the solution, the current basic feasible solution is optimal. If some nonbasic variable has the potential for improvement, some row operations are performed to form a new basic feasible solution and the procedure is repeated until all $c'_j \leq 0$.

There are some special cases where the basic feasible solutions have a structure worthy of note. If the matrix of coefficients $A = (a_{ij})$ is totally unimodular, then every basic feasible solution will be integral valued for *every* set of integer constants $b_1, b_2, \ldots, b_m$. The matrix A is said to be totally unimodular if every square submatrix of A has a determinant of 0, $+1$, or -1. Network flow problems, including the transportation and shortest route problem, all possess this property and have yielded highly efficient special purpose algorithms.

BIBLIOGRAPHY

Dantzig, George B., *Linear Programming and Extensions,* Princeton University Press, Princeton, N.J., 1963.

Gass, Saul I., *An Illustrated Guide to Linear Programming,* Prentice-Hall, Englewood Cliffs, N.J., 1970.

Simmonard, Michel, *Linear Programming,* Prentice-Hall, Englewood Cliffs, N.J., 1966.

Wagner, Harvey M., *Principles of Operations Research,* Prentice-Hall, Englewood Cliffs, N.J., 1969.

G. Bennington

BAYESIAN STATISTICS

The Bayesian approach to statistical inference provides a formal mechanism for coherently combining observational information with prior information or beliefs to provide posterior, or after the experiment, probability distributions for parameters of interest. Such parameters in education might be student abilities, institutional mean values, or regression coefficients relating performance criteria to test scores. In the biological/medical fields such parameters might be postoperative recovery rates. In business these parameters might be mean rates of investment return and in engineering mean service lifetimes of machine components.

The posterior probability distribution is a formal numerical representation of the state of knowledge about the parameter of interest. Certain characteristics of this posterior Bayes distribution are of particular interest. For example, such measures of central tendency as the mean, the median, and the mode are useful as general descriptors, the mode being the most probable value of the parameter. The reciprocal of the variance of the posterior distribution is frequently interpreted as a measure of the precision of available information, and the standard deviation as a measure of dispersion. The Bayesian system permits direct probability statements about parameters. For example, following a unit of individually prescribed instruction, posttest results can be combined with prior information to yield a statement of the form, "The probability is .80 that the examinee's proficiency level is greater than the required criterion level," which is the level of functioning considered desirable before a student is moved to the next level of instruction. In individually prescribed instruction, proficiency levels of .70 to .85 are typically required, indicating a desire to have a student attain this level of proficiency, and a 75% or more certainty (probability) of this attainment is usually deemed necessary.

The heart of the Bayesian method is Bayes theorem which says that, given the data, the posterior distribution of the parameter is proportional to the product of the distribution of the data, given the parameter, and the prior (or before the sample) distribution of the parameter. In effect, Bayes theorem combines sample information with prior information to provide a formal representation of posterior information. This posterior representation is in the form of a probability density function from which probabilities of events in the parameter space can be calculated. The price one pays for the elegance of the Bayesian analysis is the need for specifying a prior Bayes distribution summarizing prior information or beliefs.

Characteristically, a researcher will wish to be completely free of restraints in specifying his prior distribution. Realistically, however, the probability of the sample data given the parameter is of a particular form, and if its prior distribution is not of a "conjugate" form, it will not be possible to express the exact form of the posterior distribution except through numerical procedures. For situations in which a single parameter is involved, this will typically not involve difficult computational work. However, when many parameters are involved, the numerical work can be complex.

Raiffa and Schlaifer [1] point out that in selecting a family of prior distributions, several characteristics are desired.

    1. It should be reasonably easy to determine the posterior distribution given the prior distribution and the sample information.
    2. It should be possible to express in convenient form the expectation of some utility function with respect to any member of the family.
    3. If the prior is a member of the family, then the posterior should also be a member of the family.
    4. The family should be diverse enough to adequately describe the probability assessor's beliefs in most situations.
    5. The family should be well known (i.e., tabulated) and, hence, readily usable.

They go on to demonstrate that these criteria can be met for many common statistical models. That is, for many models there exists a particular family of distributions called a natural conjugate family. If a distribution from this family is used, properties 1–5 will hold. For example, with a binomial model, if the prior distribution is one from the Beta class, then the posterior distribution will also be in the Beta class. In most inferential situations where a natural conjugate family exists, prior knowledge can be adequately described by a member of that family or by a linear combination of members of that family. If the prior distribution is a linear combination of distributions from the conjugate family, then properties 1–4 will hold, and percentiles and moments can easily be obtained numerically.

Because of the necessity of specifying prior distributions and because Bayesian methods are most advantageously applied when some decision-theoretic considerations are included, Bayesian methods are inevitably more complex than simple classical methods of confidence intervals and tests of point hypotheses. Thus substantive researchers have found it difficult to attain or maintain the necessary skills for doing Bayesian analysis. However, work in computer-assisted instruction (CAI) has shown that a computer can be used interactively with people to break a complex task down into simple components, and that the computer can be used in a conversational mode to lead a person step-by-step through a complex operation. Thus it seemed logical to attempt an interactive computerized monitoring of Bayesian analysis.

Schlaifer [2] developed a very elaborate, sophisticated, and attractive interactive computerized system, MANECON. The MANECON collection of computer programs was written to facilitate the analysis of problems of decision under uncertainty. Thus the collection consists of a number of self-contained programs for interactive assessment of probability distributions and of preference (utility) functions. Another set of self-contained programs provides solutions for typical Bayesian statistical problems such as computation of posterior probability distributions, evaluation of the net gain to be expected as a result of sampling or experimentation, and determination of optimal sample size. The remainder of the collection consists of a set of subroutines and functions intended to facilitate the writing of special programs for analysis of decision problems too complex to be conveniently analyzed by use of a general-purpose interactive program.

The MANECON collection is written in standard FORTRAN IV. It is currently available in two versions, one for the IBM 360/67 operating under CP/CMS and the other operating on the PDP-10 with standard DEC software. At present, MANECON is directly transportable only to IBM 360/67 computers operating under CP/CMS or DEC PDP-10 computers operating under standard DEC level C monitor. MANECON is not immediately transportable to IBM 360 or 370 computers that do not use the CP/CMS operating system. If INTERACTIVE FORTRAN is available, it is possible to modify MANECON; but strictly speaking the original program is not transportable.

A second approach to interactive computing for Bayesian analysis has been developed by Novick [3] and his associates Isaacs [4] and Christ [5] and called *computer-assisted data analysis* (CADA). This system is designed to facilitate persons relatively inexpert in Bayesian statistical methods to analyze data more expertly. The CADA program is designed to lead the researcher step-by-step through a data analysis in much the same way as a CAI program leads a student through an instructional sequence. The CADA programs are intended to be instructive in nature, and thus of pedagogical value; however, they are equally meant to be used "on the job" by persons concerned with the substance rather than the methodology of a science.

With CADA, a greater effort has been made to be relatively detailed and directive in the scripts so that a person can "get started" with very little background and proceed with the analysis even if he has little understanding of the "why" of each question he is being asked by the computer. Also, in the development of the CADA programs, considerable attention is given to the pedagogical value of the programmed interaction.

Since CADA was meant as a research tool for general application, a search was made to find the most effective means of facilitating wide distribution of the monitor for use on many computing systems. Due to limitations in time, manpower, and money, reprogramming on a system-by-system basis was rejected as a viable method of implementing CADA. Since no entirely transportable language for all interactive systems existed, a strategy was pursued which involved interdialect translation rather than actual programming. Examination of available hardware and software pointed toward the BASIC programming language as the only possibility for translatability across several manufacturers. A study was then made by Isaacs [4] which showed that programs written in one dialect of BASIC could easily be translated into that of many other manufacturers' dialects provided certain specified constraints on the initial programs were observed.

Four programming capabilities are required if a project of any magnitude or complexity is to be undertaken. The first of these is computational ability and precision. A second necessary capability of any dialect is that it has the ability to execute a program of the desired size. The third capability that a dialect should have is the means for accessing and creating external data files. A fourth important capability for a dialect is its conduciveness to generating formatted output.

The translation of most statements into a new BASIC dialect is trivial or no translation is necessary. Operands, relations, names, string, arrays, functions, input, and branching can be translated with little effort or time. The three difficulties that are encountered are file handling, chaining or subroutine calling, and output formatting. Since there is no exact standard for these areas, a knowledge of the statement formats in these areas can help to minimize the expenditure of time and energy. Isaacs gives 21 specific rules for BASIC transportability. These ideas were used in the translation of the CADA monitor into various other BASIC systems. In the CADA project, programs were initially developed in the HP 2000C and the DEC PDP/11 RSTS dialects of the BASIC programming language with immediate applications provided in the behavioral sciences; however, the programs are applicable in any science that uses Bayesian methods.

In this review we shall not be giving a formal technical presentation of Bayesian statistics. Such a presentation is contained in a recent monograph by Lindley [6]. Extensive bibliographies pertaining to Bayesian statistics can be found in the monograph by Lindley and in an article by L. J. Savage [7]. Relatively nontechnical introductions to Bayesian statistics with stress on decision aspects have been supplied by Raiffa [8] and by Lindley [9]. An early history of Bayesian statistics was written by Barnard [10].

A completely contemporary history cannot be supplied here because of the rapid pace of development in the field. However, the dominant feature of the evolution over the past two decades can be noted. The publication of Savage's work [11] resulted in a reawakening of interest in Bayesian methods, and there then ensued a continuing debate between Bayesian and classical statisticians. The debate began to move from philosophy and rhetoric to data analysis with the publication of Schlaifer's texts [12,

13]. A more mathematically oriented text by Raiffa and Schlaifer [1] serves until this day as an encyclopedic repository of Bayesian distribution theory. Pratt, Raiffa, and Schlaifer [14] provide a clear exposition of the foundations of decision under uncertainty. Papers by Edwards, Lindman, and Savage [15] and Meyer [16] forcefully demonstrated the practical advantages of the Bayesian methods of statistical inference. Some applications-oriented discussions are contained in Meyer and Collier [17]. In particular, the paper by Cornfield in the book is a clear exposition of the contrast between classical and Bayesian methods of inference. Also, the paper by Geisser on discrimination is of interest. The philosophical and mathematical basis for Bayesian statistics are the result of fusing two lines of thought. The first deals with rational approaches to decision making under uncertainty and can be found in the work of Borel [18], von Neumann and Morgenstern [19], and Wald [20]. The second is the development of a rigorous personalistic view of probability. This development may be traced in Borel [21], Ramsey [22], De Finetti [23, 24], Jeffreys [25], Koopman [26–28], and Good [29, 30]. Bayes' original work [31] has been reprinted in *Biometrika* (1958). Prior to 1959, the only text in Bayesian statistics was that of Jeffreys [32].

Edwards, Lindman, and Savage [15] give examples illustrating that often evidence which, for a Bayesian statistician, supports the null hypothesis leads to rejection of that hypothesis by standard classical procedures. They also point out that the likelihood principle emphasized in Bayesian statistics implies, among other things, that the rules governing when data collection stops are irrelevant to data interpretation. It is entirely appropriate to collect data until a point has been confirmed or discredited, or until the data collector runs out of time, money, or patience.

Meyer [16] examines the use of Bayesian statistics in an educational setting. He emphasizes that an investigator's decisions should depend on the relative losses or regrets for making an incorrect decision. He also points out that scientific objectivity cannot seriously be claimed since the design of a study, the equipment, etc., are all used at the personal discretion of the investigator. Even the problem to be studied is itself chosen through personal decision. Certain areas of research are or are not studied partly because of certain *a priori* probabilities accepted by the research worker.

In 1964 the monumental work by Mosteller and Wallace [33] decided the authorship of the disputed Federalist papers and, much more importantly, clearly established the usefulness of Bayesian methods. Another important paper on the applications of Bayesian methods is by Cornfield [34].

In 1965, Lindley's two-volume work on probability and inference appeared and provided useful material for Bayesian data analysis [35]. Two useful essays on Bayesian methods have been provided by Good [29, 30]. In 1969, Schmitt's *Measuring Uncertainty: An Elementary Introduction to Bayesian Methods* provided a relatively introductory treatment of Bayesian methods [36]; and in 1968, I. R. Savage's *Statistics: Uncertainty and Behavior* provided an interesting general orientation to Bayesian methods for nonstatisticians [37]. Recent useful books for Bayesian statisticians have been provided by Box and Tiao [38], De Groot [39], Press [40], and Zellner [41]. These texts contain references that document the recent development of Bayesian methodology. Each of these is definitive in a particular aspect of Bayesian statistics. The Box-Tiao text is the first experimental design book from a Bayesian point of view. The Zellner book is currently the standard reference in Bayesian econometrics. The De

BAYESIAN STATISTICS

Groot work provides a definitive mathematical-theoretical treatment stressing the decision theory aspects of the subject. The Press book provides a coverage of both experimental design and multivariate analysis methods. A book by Novick and Jackson [42] provides a relatively elementary treatment of some of the topics covered in these books.

A promising new development in Bayesian statistics is in the area of the simultaneous estimation of many parameters. While the ideas have their origins in classical statistics [43], and the models have been treated by others [44–46], the general theoretical-mathematical development of the Bayesian theory required for application is due to Lindley [47] and to Lindley and Smith [48]. Some specialization of this theory to the simultaneous estimation of proportions is available [49, 50]. The first of these references also provides an outline of applications to computer-based, instructional technology and other educational applications.

The theoretical foundations of Bayesian inference were given important new clarity and refinement for English readers by the publication of the translation (by A. Muchi and A. Smith) of De Finetti's *Theory of Probability* [51]. This, together with the translation of earlier writings of De Finetti [52], should define the field of discourse on Bayesian theory for a decade.

REFERENCES

1. H. Raiffa and R. Schlaifer, *Applied Statistical Decision Theory*. Division of Research, Harvard Business School, Boston, 1961.
2. R. Schlaifer, *Computer Programs for Elementary Decision Analysis*. Division of Research, Graduate School of Business Administration, Harvard University, Boston, 1971.
3. M. R. Novick, High school attainment: An example of a computer-assisted Bayesian approach to data analysis, *Int. Stat. Rev.* **41**, 264–271 (1973).
4. G. L. Isaacs, *Interdialect Translatability of the BASIC Programming Language*, ACT Technical Bulletin No. 11, The American College Testing Program, Iowa City, Iowa, 1973.
5. D. E. Christ, *The CADA Monitor*, ACT Technical Bulletin No. 12, The American College Testing Program, Iowa City, Iowa, 1973.
6. D. V. Lindley, *Bayesian Statistics, A Review*, CMBS, Regional Conference Series in Applied Mathematics No. 2, 1972.
7. L. J. Savage, Reading suggestions for the foundations of statistics, *Amer. Stat.* **24**(4), 23–27 (1970).
8. H. Raiffa, *Decision Analysis: Introductory Lectures on Choices Under Uncertainty*, Addison-Wesley, Reading, Mass., 1968.
9. D. V. Lindley, *Making Decisions*, Wiley-Interscience, London, 1971.
10. G. A. Barnard, Thomas Bayes—A biographical note, *Biometrika* **45**, 293–295 (1958).
11. L. J. Savage, *The Foundations of Statistics*, Wiley, New York, 1954.
12. R. Schlaifer, *Probability and Statistics for Business Decisions: An Introduction to Managerial Economics Under Uncertainty*, McGraw-Hill, New York, 1961.
13. R. Schlaifer, *Introduction to Statistics for Business Decisions*, McGraw-Hill, New York, 1959.

BAYESIAN STATISTICS

14. J. W. Pratt, H. Raiffa, and R. Schlaifer, The foundations of decision making under certainty: An elementary exposition, *J. Amer. Stat. Assoc.* **59**, 353–375 (1964).
15. W. Edwards, H. Lindman, and L. J. Savage, Bayesian statistical inference for psychological research, *Psychol. Rev.* **70**(3), 193–242 (1963).
16. D. L. Meyer, A Bayesian school superintendent, *Amer. Educ. Res. J.* **1**(4), 219–228 (1964).
17. D. L. Meyer and R. O. Collier, Jr. (eds.), *Bayesian Statistics*, Peacock, Itasca, Ill., 1970.
18. E. Borel, La théorie du jeu et les équations intégrales à noyau symétrique, *C. R. Acad. Sci., Paris,* **173**, 1304–1308 (1921); Translated by L. J. Savage, *Econometrica* **21**, 97–124 (1953).
19. J. von Neumann and O. Morgenstern, *Theory of Games and Economic Behavior*, Princeton University Press, Princeton, N.J., 1947, 3rd ed., 1953.
20. A. Wald, On the principles of statistical inference, *Notre Dame Mathematical Lectures, No. 1.*, Edwards, Ann Arbor, Mich., 1942, litho.
21. E. Borel, A propos d'un traité de probabilités, *Rev. Phil.* **98**, 321–336 (1924); Reprinted in *Valeur pratique et philosophie des probabilités*, Gauthier-Villars, Paris, 1939, pp. 134–136.
22. F. P. Ramsey, Truth and probability (1926), and Further considerations (1928), in *The Foundations of Mathematics and Other Essays*, Harcourt, Brace, New York, 1931.
23. B. De Finetti, Fondamenti logici del ragionamento probabilistico, *Boll. Un. mat. Ital. (Ser. A)* **9**, 558–261 (1930).
24. B. De Finetti, La prévision: Ses Lois Logiques, ses sources subjectives, *Ann. Inst. Henri Poincaré* **7**, 1–68 (1937).
25. H. Jeffreys, *Scientific Inference*, Cambridge University Press, Cambridge, 1931; 3rd ed., 1957.
26. B. O. Koopman, The axioms and algebra of intuitive probability, *Ann. Math.* [2] **41**, 269–292 (1940).
27. B. O. Koopman, The bases of probability, *Bull. Amer. Math. Soc.* **46**, 763–774 (1940).
28. B. O. Koopman, Intuitive probabilities and sequences, *Ann. Math.* [2] **42**, 169–187 (1941).
29. I. J. Good, *Probability and the Weighing of Evidence*, Griffin, London, 1950.
30. I. J. Good, *The Estimation of Probabilities*, M.I.T. Press, Cambridge, Mass. 1965.
31. T. Bayes, Essay towards solving a problem in the doctrine of chances, *Phil. Trans. Roy. Soc.* **53**, 370–418 (1763); Reprinted in *Biometrika* **45**, 292–315, (1958).
32. H. Jeffreys, *Theory of Probability*, Clarendon, Oxford, 1939; 3rd ed., 1961.
33. F. Mosteller and D. L. Wallace, *Inference and Disputed Authorship: The Federalist*, Addison-Wesley, Reading, Mass., 1964.
34. J. Cornfield, Sequential trials, sequential analysis, and the likelihood principle, *Amer. Stat.* **20**(2), 18–23 (1966).
35. D. V. Lindley, *Introduction to Probability and Statistics from a Bayesian Viewpoint*, 2 vols., University Press, Cambridge, 1965.
36. S. A. Schmitt, *Measuring Uncertainty: An Elementary Introduction to Bayesian Statistics*, Addison-Wesley, Reading, Mass., 1969.
37. I. R. Savage, *Statistics: Uncertainty and Behavior*, Houghton-Mifflin, Boston, 1968.
38. G. E. P. Box and G. C. Tiao, *Bayesian Inference in Statistical Analysis*, Addison-Wesley, Reading, Mass., 1973.

39. M. H. De Groot, *Optimal Statistical Decisions*, McGraw-Hill, New York, 1970.
40. S. J. Press, *Applied Multivariate Analysis*, Holt, Rinehart, and Winston, New York, 1972.
41. A. Zellner, *An Introduction to Bayesian Inference in Econometrics*, Wiley, New York, 1971.
42. M. R. Novick and P. H. Jackson, *Statistical Methods for Educational and Psychological Research*, McGraw-Hill, New York, 1974.
43. C. Stein, Confidence sets for the mean of a multivariate normal distribution, *J. Roy. Stat. Soc. Ser. B* **24**, 265–296 (1962).
44. G. E. P. Box and G. C. Tiao, Bayesian estimation of means for the random effect model, *J. Amer. Stat. Assoc.* **63**, 174 (1968).
45. G. C. Tiao and W. Y. Tan, Bayesian analysis of random effect models in the analysis of variance: Posterior distribution of variance components, *Biometrika* **52**, 37 (1965).
46. B. M. Hill, Inference about variance components in the one-way model, *J. Amer. Stat. Assoc.* **60**, 806–825 (1965).
47. D. V. Lindley, The estimation of many parameters, in *Foundations of Statistical Inference* (V. P. Godambe and D. A. Sprott, eds.), Holt, Rinehart, and Winston, Toronto, 1971.
48. D. V. Lindley and A. F. M. Smith, Bayes estimates for the linear model, *J. Roy. Stat. Soc., Ser. B* **34**, 1–41 (1972).
49. M. R. Novick, C. Lewis, and P. H. Jackson, The estimation of proportions in *m* groups, *Psychometrika* **38**(1), 19–46 (1973).
50. T. Leonard, Bayesian methods for multinomial data, *Biometrika* **59**(3), 581–589 (1972).
51. B. De Finetti, *Theory of Probability*, Vol. I, Wiley, New York, 1974.
52. B. De Finetti, *Probability, Induction, and Statistics*, Wiley, New York, 1972.

Melvin Novick

BEAM EQUATIONS

INTRODUCTION

Elongated-shaped bodies that bend due to forces applied transverse to the long dimension of the body are referred to as beams. Because the beam element is so frequently encountered in so many different ways in our physical world, the behavior of members subjected to bending has been of great interest to the scientific world for many years. Beams are, of course, one of the most common elements in all types of structures and machines. For example, the wing and fuselage of aircraft are in themselves complex beam systems that contain many smaller beams, or flexural members, as components. Small beams are also used in a variety of ways as important elements in instruments and control devices. An interesting application of the beam element is that of a very small transducer used to measure the tongue and cheek forces acting on a human tooth [1]. The tongue and cheek forces cause the small beam element to bend and the output of SR-4 electric strain gauges, attached to the beam element, indicates the magnitude of the forces.

The basic, or fundamental, considerations in the study of beam behavior comprise the analysis of stresses and deflections due to bending. Before proceeding to the discussion of stresses in beams, it is desirable to clarify some of the terminology associated with the classification of beams.

Classification of Beams

Beams are frequently classified according to the type of supports, or reactions. A *simply supported* beam (Fig. 1a) is supported at the ends by pins or rollers which offer no resistance to rotation. If the beam has more than two supports (Fig. 1b), it is referred to as a *continuous beam*. A support which prevents rotation of the end of a beam is referred to as a fixed support. A beam with one fixed end and one free end is called a *cantilever beam* (Fig. 1c).

The beam deflections, $y = f(x)$, for the various beams shown in Fig. 1 have been exaggerated in order to illustrate the general shape of the bent beams and the corresponding geometric conditions at the ends. In the solution of beam equations, consideration must be given to the end conditions, or boundary conditions, which are established by the type of end supports. Therefore, beams are frequently described in terms of their end supports. For example, the zero deflection at both ends of a *simply supported* beam (Fig. 1a) follows from the designation *pinned-pinned* beam. In addition, the designation *pinned-pinned* also signifies zero moments at the ends, or supports, since a pin connection can offer no resistance to a rotation. The *fixed-fixed* beam (Fig. 1d) implies that the deflections and slopes are zero at $x = 0$ and $x = l$. That is,

$$y(0) = y(l) = y'(0) = y'(l) = 0$$

Similarly, the known boundary conditions for a *fixed-pinned* beam are

$$y(0) = y(l) = y'(0) = 0$$

When the number of reactions (forces or moments) at the supports is no more than two, the beam is said to be *statically determinate* since the unknown reactions can be determined from a free-body diagram and the equations of equilibrium. Referring to the free-body diagrams shown in Fig. 2, it is apparent that the simply supported beam (pinned-pinned) and the cantilever beam (fixed-free) are statically determinate.

Types of Loads

Beams may be subjected to *static* or *dynamic* type loads, or forces. When the rate of loading is gradual so that the acceleration of the beam is essentially

BEAM EQUATIONS

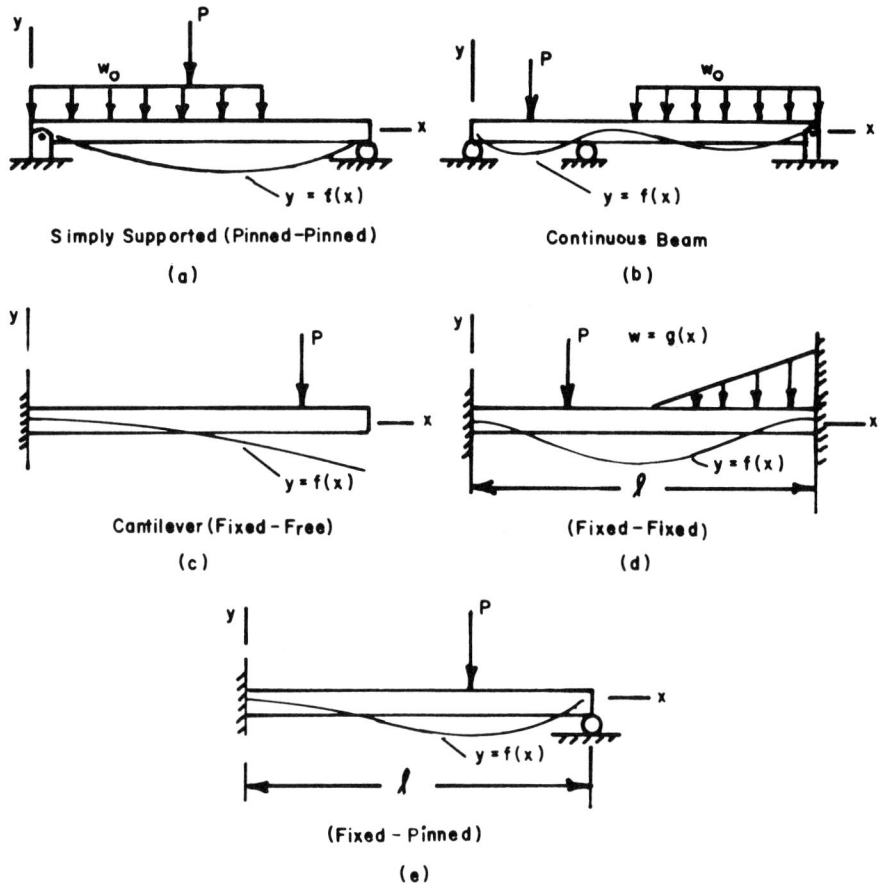

Fig. 1.

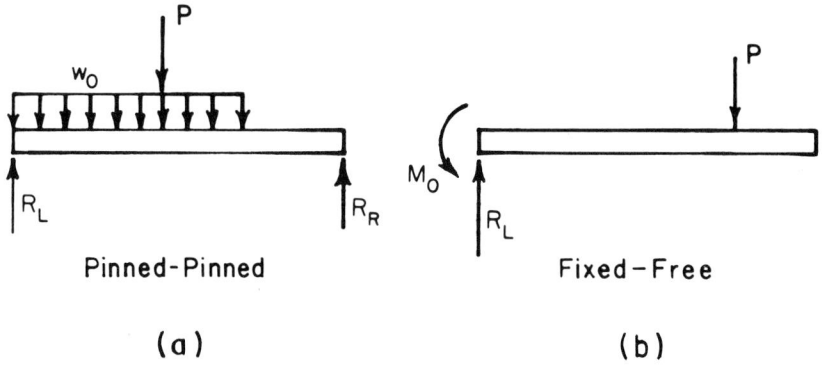

Fig. 2.

BEAM EQUATIONS

zero, the applied loads are called static loads. However, when the rate of loading is fairly rapid, the beam will experience accelerations of varying magnitude along its length and the applied loads are called *dynamic loads*. Dynamic loads which are applied very suddenly are referred to as *impact loads*.

A load which is distributed over a distance that is small, in comparison to the length of the beam, is usually considered to be concentrated at a point for all practical purposes and is called a *concentrated load*. Concentrated loads are denoted as P in Fig. 1. When a load is distributed over a considerable portion of the beam, the load is said to be a *distributed load*. Loads may be uniformily distributed as shown in Figs. 1(a) and 1(b) or they may vary according to some function, $w = g(x)$, of x as shown in Fig. 1(d).

STRESSES IN BEAMS

When beams bend due to lateral loads, *flexural stresses* and *shear stresses* develop within the beam. Herein, the term "stress" denotes force per unit area and is abbreviated as psi (pounds per square inch). The flexural stresses at a cross section include both tensile and compressive stresses which act normal to a plane transverse to the longitudinal beam axis, whereas the shear stresses act parallel to the transverse section. In general, the flexural stresses and shear stresses vary in magnitude from top to bottom of a beam at a given cross section.

The free-body diagram, Fig. 3(b), of the portion of the beam, Fig. 3(a), between the left reaction R_L and the section a–a shows an internal transverse shear force V and an internal moment M necessary for equilibrium of the beam segment. Above the *neutral axis* (N.A.) the beam fibers shorten due to compressive stresses σ_c acting normal to the cross section a–a as shown in Fig. 3(c). Below the neutral axis the beam fibers lengthen due to tensile stresses which are also normal to the cross section. It will be shown later that the flexural stresses (tensile or compressive) vary linearly from the neutral axis to maximum values in the outer beam fibers. The resultant of the compressive stresses, σ_c, is equal to the force F_c which is equal and opposite to the resultant force F_t of the tensile stresses. This force system constitutes a couple which is equal to the resultant internal resisting moment M. That is, $F_c d = M$.

The resultant of the shear stresses, τ, is equal to the transverse shear force V.

Flexure Stress Formula

In the derivation of the elementary flexural formula for calculating normal stresses (tensile or compressive), it is assumed that plane sections remain plane during bending. Although this assumption is not strictly true when a cross shear force V is acting on the plane, the warping of a cross section during bending is very slight due to the shear stresses associated with V. Therefore,

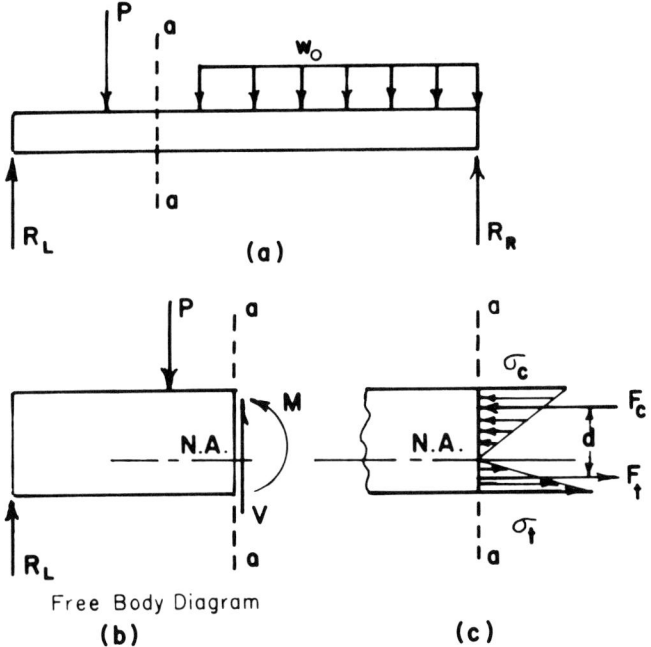

Fig. 3.

the assumption that a plane section remains plane during bending is made in the derivation [2] of the flexural stress formula.

The elementary flexural stress formula is

$$\sigma = Mz/I \tag{1}$$

where σ is the normal stress in a beam fiber z distance from the N.A.; M is the internal moment which is equal to the moment, with respect to the N.A., of all external loads and reactions acting to the right, or left of the cross section in question; and

$$I = \int_A z^2 \, dA$$

is the second moment of the cross-sectional area A with respect to the N.A.

It is easy to show from

$$\int_A \sigma \, dA = \frac{M}{I} \int_A z \, dA = \frac{M}{I} \bar{z} A = 0 \tag{2}$$

that the *N.A. coincides with the centroidal axis of the beam's cross-sectional area*. Equation (2) follows from the fact that the summation of forces in the x-direction must equal zero to satisfy equilibrium conditions. Equation (1) shows that the maximum normal flexural stress, σ, in a beam occurs in the outer fibers at a cross section where M is a maximum.

BEAM EQUATIONS

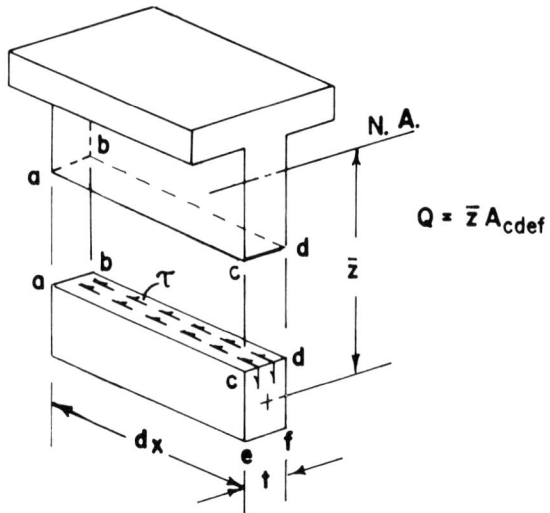

Fig. 4.

Shear Stress Formula

The shear stress formula found in any elementary mechanics of materials text [2] is

$$\tau = VQ/It \tag{3}$$

where τ is the horizontal (and vertical) shear stress at a given point of a given cross section of the beam, V is the shear force at the cross section in question, Q is the moment with respect to the N.A. of the part of the cross-sectional area between the horizontal plane where the shear stress is wanted and the top (or bottom) of the cross section, t is the width of the cross section at the horizontal plane where τ is being computed, and I is the second moment (moment of inertia) of the entire cross-sectional area with respect to the N.A.

To aid in the interpretation of Eq. (3), a beam segment of length dx having a T-shaped cross section is shown in Fig. 4. The shear stresses, τ, are uniformly distributed over the internal horizontal plane $abcd$ and are equal to the shear stresses on the vertical plane at cd. From the shear stress distribution over the entire vertical cross-sectional area A, it follows that

$$V = \int_A \tau \, dA \tag{4}$$

From Eq. (3) it should be apparent that the maximum longitudinal and transverse shear stress occurs at a given cross section where Q/t is a maximum. For cross sections having rectangular shapes, such as the T-section in Fig. 4, the maximum shear stress occurs at the neutral surface, or N.A. However, for triangular and circular cross sections, the maximum shear stress

BEAM EQUATIONS

does not occur in the neutral surface since Q/t is not a maximum at the neutral surface.

Relation between Load Intensity, Shear, and Bending Moment

The mathematical relations between the load intensity w, transverse shear V, and bending moment M may be determined by considering the equilibrium conditions of a beam segment of dx length shown in Fig. 5. The load intensity w (lb/in.) is considered to be constant in the length dx. The load intensity w is also considered to be positive when acting in the direction of the positive y axis. The shear V and moment M are also considered as being positive as shown.

Since the element is in equilibrium, the $\Sigma F_y = 0$ gives

$$\Sigma F_y = V + w\,dx - V - dV = 0$$

which reduces to

$$dV/dx = w \tag{5}$$

Equation (5) shows that the rate of change of the shear V at a given cross section is equal to the load intensity at the cross section. When w is a known function of x, it also follows from Eq. (5) that

$$\int_{V_1}^{V_2} dV = V_2 - V_1 = \int_{x_1}^{x_2} w\,dx \tag{6}$$

which states that the change in shear between the sections at x_1 and x_2 is equal to the area under the load intensity diagram between the two sections.

From Fig. 5, the $\Sigma M_0 = 0$ gives

$$\Sigma M_0 = 0 = M - M - dM + V\,dx + w\,dx\left(\frac{dx}{2}\right)$$

Neglecting the second-order differential, the $\Sigma M_0 = 0$ reduces to

$$dM/dx = V \tag{7}$$

which states that the rate of change of the moment M at a cross section is

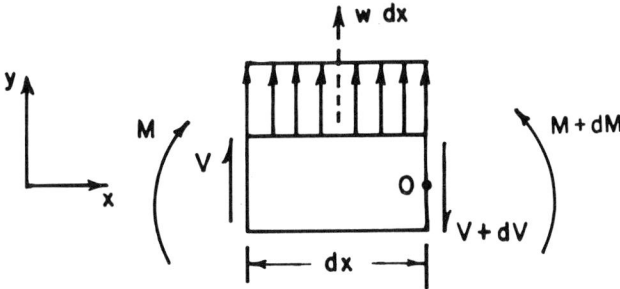

Fig. 5.

BEAM EQUATIONS

equal to the shear V at the cross section. It also follows from Eq. (7) that

$$\int_{M_1}^{M_2} dM = M_2 - M_1 = \int_{x_1}^{x_2} V\, dx \tag{8}$$

which states that the change in moment between sections at x_1 and x_2 is equal to the area under the shear diagram between the two sections.

The mathematical relations expressed in Eqs. (5), (6), (7), and (8) are fundamental to the graphical construction of *shear* and *moment diagrams* which facilitate the location of critical cross sections with regard to V_{max} and M_{max}. In general, V_{max} and M_{max} may or may not occur at the same cross section.

BEAM DEFLECTIONS—STATIC LOADS

The lateral displacement y of a point on the neutral surface is called the *deflection* of the beam at that point, and the curve $y = f(x)$, describing the beam deflections, is defined as the *elastic curve* (see Fig. 1). Frequently the deflection of beam elements in machines and structures must be kept below certain allowable limits in order to function properly. For example, it is frequently specified that the deflection of any beam in the support structure for a turbogenerator unit shall not exceed 1/2000 of the beam's length.

Relation between Moment and Radius of Curvature

The radius curvature $\rho(OA)$ for the elastic curve of a beam segment of length dx is as shown in Fig. 6. The planes of the beam segment remain plane during

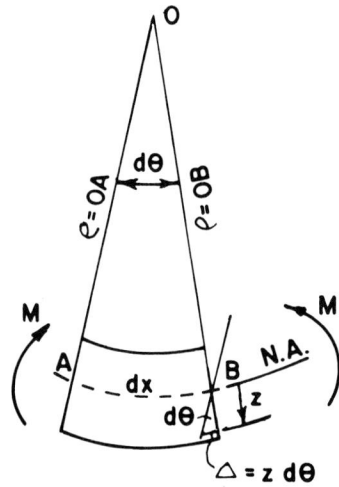

Fig. 6.

bending under the action of the internal moment M, and the total deformation Δ of a fiber z distance from the N.A. is $z\,d\theta$. The strain (in./in.) of this fiber is

$$\epsilon = \frac{z\,d\theta}{dx} \tag{9}$$

Noting that dx is equal to $\rho\,d\theta$ and that the strain ϵ is equal to the stress σ divided by the modulus of elasticity E, Eq. (9) gives

$$\epsilon = \sigma/E = z/\rho \tag{10}$$

It is well known from the calculus that

$$\frac{1}{\rho} = \frac{d^2y/dx^2}{\left[1 + \left(\frac{dy}{dx}\right)^2\right]^{3/2}} \tag{11}$$

Combining Eqs. (1), (10), and (11) gives

$$\frac{d^2y/dx^2}{\left[1 + \left(\frac{dy}{dx}\right)^2\right]^{3/2}} = \frac{M}{EI} \tag{12}$$

which is the differential equation for the elastic curve in which M/EI is, in general, a function of x. Beam deflections are usually very small in comparison to the beam length, l, and in such cases the slope dy/dx is very small and its squared quantity in Eq. (12) can be neglected in comparison to unity. Thus, for small deflection theory, Eq. (12) reduces to

$$EI\frac{d^2y}{dx^2} = M \tag{13}$$

It now follows from Eqs. (5), (7), and (13) that the beam equations, in terms of y and its derivatives, for small deflection theory are

$$y = \text{deflection} \tag{14a}$$

$$\frac{dy}{dx} = y' = \text{slope} \tag{14b}$$

$$EI\frac{d^2y}{dx^2} = M \text{ (moment)} \tag{14c}$$

$$\frac{d}{dx}\left(EI\frac{d^2y}{dx^2}\right) = \frac{dM}{dx} = V \text{ (shear)} \tag{14d}$$

$$\frac{d^2}{dx^2}\left(EI\frac{d^2y}{dx^2}\right) = \frac{dV}{dx} = w \text{ (load intensity)} \tag{14e}$$

Beams of Two Materials

Frequently two different materials with different moduli of elasticity are used to fabricate a beam. If two materials are bonded together (Fig. 7) so as to act

BEAM EQUATIONS

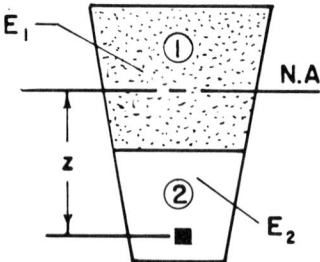

Fig. 7.

as a unit, the strain in either material is proportional to the distance z from the N.A. When the modulus of elasticity E_1 for Material 1 is different from the modulus of elasticity E_2 for Material 2, there is an abrupt change in the flexural stress at the junction of the two materials. The flexural stresses and shear stresses can be analyzed from an *equivalent cross section* for a beam of one of the two materials. The procedure for locating the N.A. and analyzing the stresses in beams of two materials, by the equivalent cross-sectional method, may be found in most elementary books on the mechanics of materials [2].

For a beam of two materials, the EI values in Eq. (14) must be replaced by $E_1 I_1 + E_2 I_2$ in which I_1 and I_2 are the cross-sectional area moments of inertia with respect to the N.A. of Materials 1 and 2, respectively.

Beam Deflections by Successive Integration

There are a variety of methods suitable for the determination of beam deflections. One of the most widely used methods is simply the successive integration of the expressions of Eq. (14). Analytical solutions are easily obtained if the beam EI value is constant throughout the interval of integration. Four successive integrations are required to obtain $y = f(x)$ when starting with the load intensity function w [see Eq. (14e)]. However, only two successive integrations are required when starting with Eq. (14c) in which the moment M must be expressed as a function of x. In general, the functions of M, V, or w usually take on abrupt changes throughout the interval of integration. To circumvent this problem, singularity functions are used.

Example. The beam shown in Fig. 8 will be used to illustrate the successive integration method. The beam is simply supported at $x = 0$ and $x = a$ and, for specified values of w_0 and P, the support reactions R_1 and R_2 are easily calculated from equilibrium conditions. In the region $0 < x < l$, R_2 may be considered as a concentrated force with an infinite intensity (lb/in.). With this concept, the load intensity function $w = f(x)$, within the interval $0 < x < l$, is simply

$$w = -w_0 + w_0 u(x - a) + R_2 \delta(x - a) \tag{15}$$

BEAM EQUATIONS

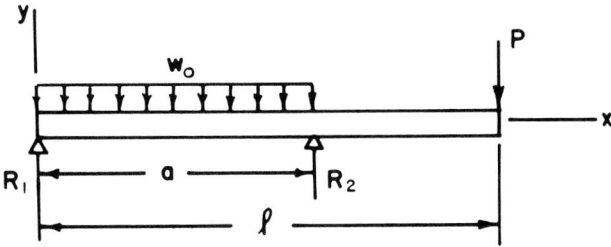

Fig. 8.

where

$$u(x - a) = \begin{cases} 0 & x < a \\ 1 & x > a \end{cases} \quad \text{Unit step function}$$

$$\delta(x - a) = \begin{cases} 0 & x < a \\ \infty & x = a \\ 0 & x > a \end{cases} \quad \text{Dirac delta function}$$

Thus, from Eq. (14e):

$$EI \frac{d^4 y}{dx^4} = -w_0 + w_0 u(x - a) + R_2 \delta(x - a)$$

Successive integrations result in

$$EI \frac{d^3 y}{dx^3} = V = -w_0 x + w_0 (x - a) u(x - a) + R_2 u(x - a) + C_1$$

$$EI \frac{d^2 y}{dx^2} = M = -\frac{w_0 x^2}{2} + \frac{w_0}{2} (x - a)^2 u(x - a) + R_2 (x - a) u(x - a) + C_1 x + C_2$$

$$EI \frac{dy}{dx} = -\frac{w_0 x^3}{6} + \frac{w_0}{6} (x - a)^3 u(x - a) + \frac{R_2}{2} (x - a)^2 u(x - a) + \frac{C_1 x^2}{2} + C_2 x + C_3$$

$$EI y = -\frac{w_0 x^4}{24} + \frac{w_0}{24} (x - a)^4 u(x - a) + \frac{R_2}{6} (x - a)^3 u(x - a) + \frac{C_1 x^3}{6} + \frac{C_2 x^2}{2} + C_3 x + C_4$$

The constants of integration (C_1, C_2, C_3, and C_4) are readily determined from the following boundary conditions:

$$V|_{x=0} = R_1 = C_1$$
$$M|_{x=0} = 0 = C_2$$
$$y|_{x=l} = 0 \text{ (determines } C_3\text{)}$$
$$y|_{x=0} = 0 = C_4$$

Numerical Integration of Beam Equations

When the quantity EI is a function of x, or when large deflections are involved, analytical solutions to the beam equations may be difficult or tedious. In such cases it is desirable to resort to a numerical integration process

BEAM EQUATIONS

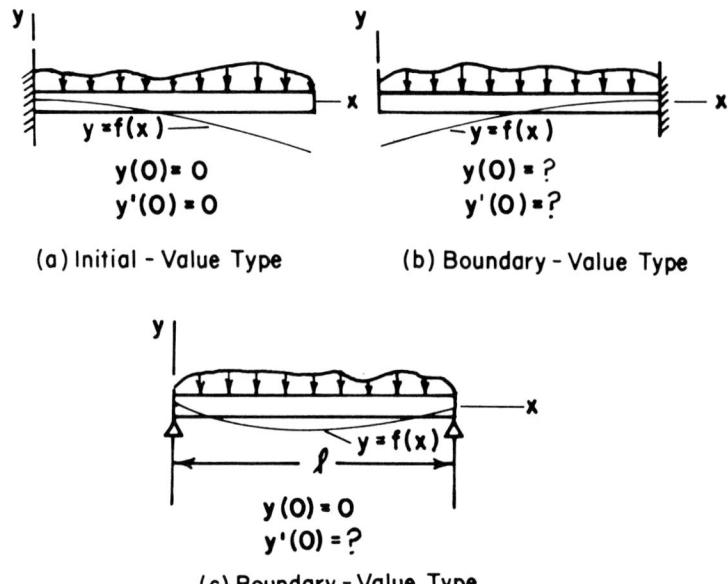

Fig. 9.

programmed to the digital computer. For numerical integration, it is usually desirable to start with the moment equation [see Eqs. (12) and (14c)], i.e.,

$$\frac{d^2y}{dx^2} = \frac{M}{EI}\left[1 + \left(\frac{dy}{dx}\right)^2\right]^{3/2} \quad \text{(large deflection theory)}$$

or

$$\frac{d^2y}{dx^2} = \frac{M}{EI} \quad \text{(small deflection theory)}$$

The approach, or method, for a numerical integration of these equations depends to some extent upon the boundary conditions involved. When the beam deflection y and slope dy/dx are known at the point in which integration begins, it is an *initial-value* type problem. On the other hand, when either y or dy/dx is unknown at the beginning of the integration, the problem is of the *boundary-value* type. The cantilever beam of Fig. 9(a) is of the initial-value type whereas the beams in Figs. 9(b) and 9(c) are of the boundary-value type.

Initial-Value-Type Problem

If small deflection theory is applicable, the deflection for the cantilever beam, Fig. 9(a), can be obtained simply by a direct integration method such as the trapezoid rule or Simpson's rule. The solution of the equation $d^2y/dx^2 = M/EI$ involves the determination of y for a series of equally spaced x values.

From a known M/EI diagram, Fig. 10(a), the curve of y' vs x, Fig. 10(b), may be easily obtained, since the value of y' is known at $x = 0$, and the change in y' from x_i to x_{i+1} is equal to the area under the M/EI diagram between stations i and $i + 1$. In a similar manner, the y vs x curve, Fig. 10(c), is obtained from the y' curve since y is known at $x = 0$ and the change in y between two stations is equal to the corresponding area under the y' curve.

For large deflections, Eq. (12) must be used and the direct integration approach is not possible since the d^2y/dx^2 is not only a function of the independent variable x but also the derivative dy/dx. There are numerous methods (Euler's methods, Runge-Kutta methods, Milne's method, etc.) suitable for numerical integration of differential equations of the general form [3]

$$y^n = \frac{d^n y}{dx^n} = f(x, y, y', \ldots, y^{n-1}) \tag{16}$$

It is noted that Eq. (12) is of the form $d^2y/dx^2 = f(x, y')$.

Since the Runge-Kutta methods are relatively easy to program for digital computer computation, these methods are widely used for numerical integra-

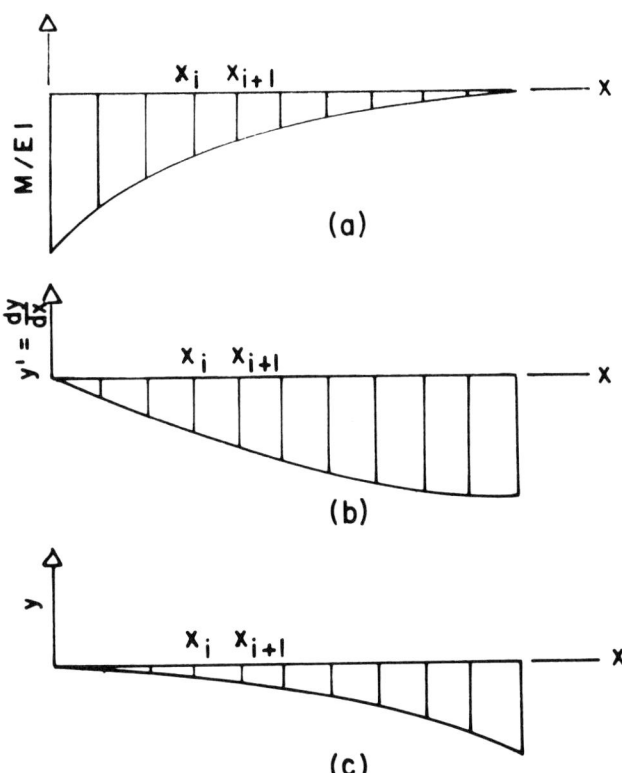

Fig. 10.

BEAM EQUATIONS

tion of differential equations. The beam equation for large deflections, Eq. (12), is a second-order differential equation which can be transformed to a set of two simultaneous first-order differential equations for solution by the application of two Runge-Kutta formulas. Letting $v = dy/dx$, Eq. (12) can be transformed to the two first-order differential equations

$$\frac{dv}{dx} = f(x, v) = \frac{M}{EI}\left[1 + \left(\frac{dy}{dx}\right)^2\right]^{3/2} \quad (17)$$

$$dy/dx = v \quad (18)$$

For example, considering fourth-order Runge-Kutta formulas [3], Eqs. (17) and (18) can be solved by programming the following equations:

$$v_{i+1} = v_i + \frac{1}{6}(k_1 + 2k_2 + 2k_3 + k_4) \quad (19)$$

where

$$\begin{aligned}
k_1 &= (\Delta x)f(x_i, v_i) \\
k_2 &= (\Delta x)f\left(x_i + \frac{\Delta x}{2}, v_i + \frac{k_1}{2}\right) \\
k_3 &= (\Delta x)f\left(x_i + \frac{\Delta x}{2}, v_i + \frac{k_2}{2}\right) \\
k_4 &= (\Delta x)f(x_i + \Delta x, v_i + k_3)
\end{aligned} \quad (20)$$

and

$$y_{i+1} = y_i + \frac{1}{6}(q_1 + 2q_2 + 2q_3 + q_4) \quad (21)$$

where

$$\begin{aligned}
q_1 &= (\Delta x)F(v_i) = \Delta x(v_i) \\
q_2 &= (\Delta x)F\left(v_i + \frac{k_1}{2}\right) = \Delta x\left(v_i + \frac{k_1}{2}\right) \\
q_3 &= (\Delta x)F\left(v_i + \frac{k_2}{2}\right) = \Delta x\left(v_i + \frac{k_2}{2}\right) \\
q_4 &= (\Delta x)F(v_i + k_3) = \Delta x(v_i + k_3)
\end{aligned} \quad (22)$$

Boundary-Value Problems

There are two elementary methods used for solving boundary-value type problems: one method consists of a trial-and-error procedure frequently referred to as the *shooting method*; the other method involves the solution of simultaneous algebraic equations resulting from the use of finite-difference expressions. The solution of the beam equation (Eq. 12 or 14c) by the trial-and-error method is not practical when the initial values of both y and dy/dx are

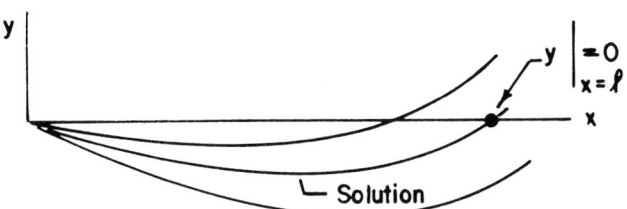

Fig. 11.

unknown, due to the large number of trial solutions required. However, if only one initial condition (y or dy/dx) is unknown, this method, in conjunction with a linear interpolation formula [3], is an effective and efficient method for the numerical integration of the beam equation. The trial-and-error method involves assuming an initial value for the unknown deflection y or slope dy/dx. This, in effect, reduces the problem to an initial-value problem. After a trial solution is made, a known boundary value (deflection or slope) at the end of the integration is compared with the corresponding value obtained by the trial solution. For example, a trial solution with an assumed value for the unknown slope $y'(0)$ of the simply supported beam, Fig. 9(c), would be compared with the required zero deflection y at $x = l$. If the value of y at $x = l$, from the trial solution, is greater than zero, a new initial value of y' is chosen which is smaller than the original approximate value used, and another trial solution is made. Conversely, if the resulting value of y at $x = l$ is less than zero, a larger initial value for $y'(0)$ is chosen for another trial solution. This procedure continues until the value of y is approximately equal to zero at $x = l$, within some prescribed limit of accuracy. The trial-and-error procedure is shown graphically in Fig. 11.

The *simultaneous-equation* method for the solution of boundary-value problems is usually reserved for the solution of ordinary linear differential equations, since the resulting algebraic equations are also linear and are more easily solved than those evolving from nonlinear differential equations. Therefore, the discussion of this method will be limited to that of small deflection theory as described by Eq. (14c).

The simultaneous-equation method consists of expressing Eq. (14c) in the finite difference form

$$y_{i+1} - 2y_i + y_{i-1} = \frac{M_i(\Delta x)^2}{(EI)_i} \tag{23}$$

where the d^2y/dx^2 is approximated by the central-difference equation. The application of Eq. (23) to n equally spaced stations along a beam yields a set of $n - 2$ algebraic equations which can be solved simultaneously to obtain the desired deflection values. Numerous methods are available for programming to the digital computer for the simultaneous solution of algebraic equations. The Gaussian elimination, the Gauss-Jordon elimination, and the matrix-inversion

BEAM EQUATIONS

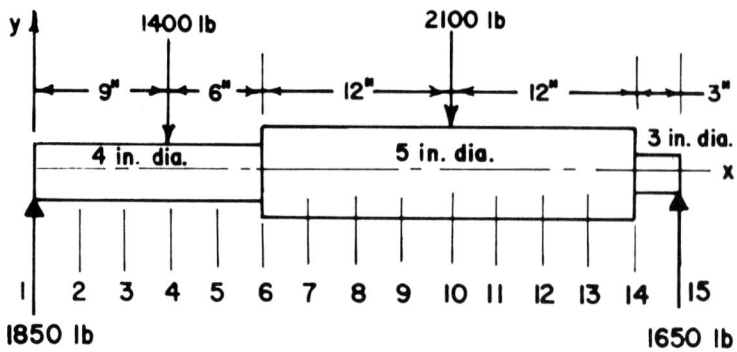

Fig. 12.

are several of the more commonly used methods for the simultaneous solution of algebraic equations.

Example. The simultaneous-equation method will be illustrated with the simply supported beam shown in Fig. 12. The application of Eq. (23) at stations 2 through 14 results in the following set of algebraic equations:

$$y_1 - 2y_2 + y_3 + (0)y_4 + \cdots + (0)y_{15} = \frac{M_2}{(EI)_2} (\Delta x)^2$$

$$(0)y_1 + y_2 - 2y_3 + y_4 + (0)y_5 + \cdots + (0)y_{15} = \frac{M_3}{(EI)_3} (\Delta x)^2$$

$$(0)y_1 + (0)y_2 + y_3 - 2y_4 + y_5 + (0)y_6 + \cdots + (0)y_{15} = \frac{M_4}{(EI)_4} (\Delta x)^2$$

$$\vdots$$

$$(0)y_1 + (0)y_2 + \cdots + (0)y_{12} + y_{13} - 2y_{14} + y_{15} = \frac{M_{14}}{(EI)_{14}} (\Delta x)^2$$

Since $y_1 = y_{15} = 0$, the above set of equations consist of 13 independent algebraic equations containing 13 unknowns. The required values of M and I at each station can either be computed as a part of the computer program or they can be determined manually beforehand and introduced into the computer program as input data. For a steel beam having a modulus of elasticity, E, equal to 30×10^6 lb/in.^{2}, the required values for input data are shown in Table 1. At stations where abrupt changes occur in the cross section, an average value of I is obtained by averaging the I values from the adjacent sections.

The solution of the 13 simultaneous equations by the *Gauss-Jordon elimination method* resulted in a displacement at Station 10 of $y_{10} = 5117 \times 10^{-6}$ in. as compared to the value of 5196×10^{-6} in. determined by Castigliano's method [4]. This shows, in general, that reasonable and practical engineering accuracy can be obtained by the finite difference method without resorting to a large number of stations. Increasing the

TABLE 1

Station	M_i (lb-in.)	I_i (in.^{4})	$\dfrac{M_i}{(EI)_i}(\Delta x)^2$ (in.)
1	0	12.57	0.0
2	5,550	12.57	132.5×10^{-6}
3	11,100	12.57	264.9×10^{-6}
4	16,650	12.57	397.4×10^{-6}
5	18,000	12.57	429.6×10^{-6}
6	19,350	21.63	268.4×10^{-6}
7	20,700	30.68	202.4×10^{-6}
8	22,050	30.68	215.6×10^{-6}
9	23,400	30.68	228.8×10^{-6}
10	24,750	30.68	242.0×10^{-6}
11	19,800	30.68	193.6×10^{-6}
12	14,850	30.68	145.2×10^{-6}
13	9,900	30.68	96.8×10^{-6}
14	4,950	17.33	85.7×10^{-6}
15	0	3.98	0.0

number of stations will, of course, improve the accuracy of the solution. However, an excessive number of stations may lead to a loss in accuracy due to the large number of calculations required in the solution of a large set of algebraic equations.

Analog Computer Simulation of Beam Equations

The electronic analog computer (EAC) is a powerful tool for solving beam-deflection problems which involve nonuniform cross sections or complicated loadings [5]. Basically, an EAC consists of high-gain dc, negative-feedback amplifiers which are used in conjunction with resistor-capacitor (R-C) circuits. In addition, present-day EACs are equipped with a variety of special devices such as function multipliers, function generators, diodes, and relays of various types for the simulation of a variety of operations and logic required for the solution of complex engineering systems. Problem solution by the EAC is accomplished by analogy in which the computer is programmed so that the circuit equations have the same mathematical form as the problem equations. In the solution of problems with an EAC, voltages represent various physical quantities such as temperature, velocity, deflection, and force. *Scale factors* relate the voltages to the physical quantities. Most commercially available EACs are limited to ±100 or ±10 V. Unlike the digital computer, the EAC performs its operations as a *continuous process* and the computing time required may be varied at the discretion of the operator. Making the computing time different from that of the real problem time is known as *time scaling*.

Three basic amplifier operations are shown symbolically in Fig. 13. The

BEAM EQUATIONS

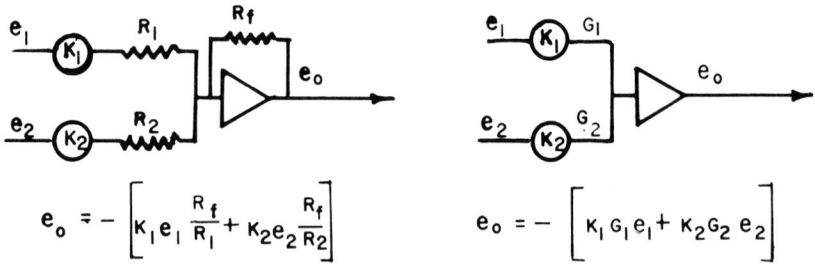

a) Summing Amplifier

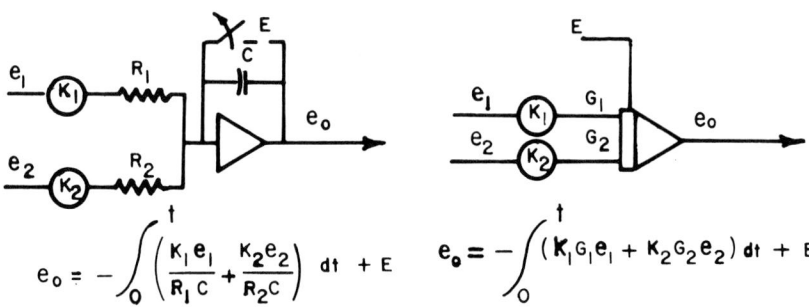

b) Summing Integrator

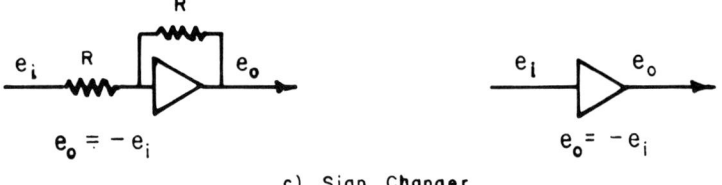

c) Sign Changer

Fig. 13.

notation in the left column is frequently used for plug-in type resistors, R, and capacitors, C. The notation in the right column is usually used with computers having internally fixed resistors and capacitors that provide for several input gains, G_n, to an amplifier—usually 0.1, 1, and 10. The potentiometer settings, K_n, and the gain values are determined from the analogies existing between the EAC circuit equations and the problem equations.

For the *summing amplifier*, Fig. 13(a), the circuit equation relating the amplifier output voltage e_0 to the input voltages e_1 and e_2, is

$$e_0 = -[K_1 G_1 e_1 + K_2 G_2 e_2] \tag{24}$$

where $G_1 = R_f/R_1$ and $G_2 = R_f/R_2$. Although only two inputs (e_1 and e_2) are shown, input jacks are normally provided for four or five inputs into an amplifier.

The circuit equation for a *summing integrator* is

$$e_0 = -\int_0^t (K_1 G_1 e_1 + K_2 G_2 e_2)\, dt + E \tag{25}$$

where $G_1 = 1/R_1 C$ and $G_2 = 1/R_2 C$. The initial voltage E across the capacitor corresponds to an *initial condition,* or boundary value, of the problem being solved. The EAC integrates with respect to time in seconds due to the units of R (megohms) and C (microfarads). In the integration of the beam equations, the independent variable x along the beam corresponds to time and if x is in inches, then 1 in. = 1 sec. However, if the units of E, I, and y are such that the units of x are in feet, then 1 ft = 1 sec.

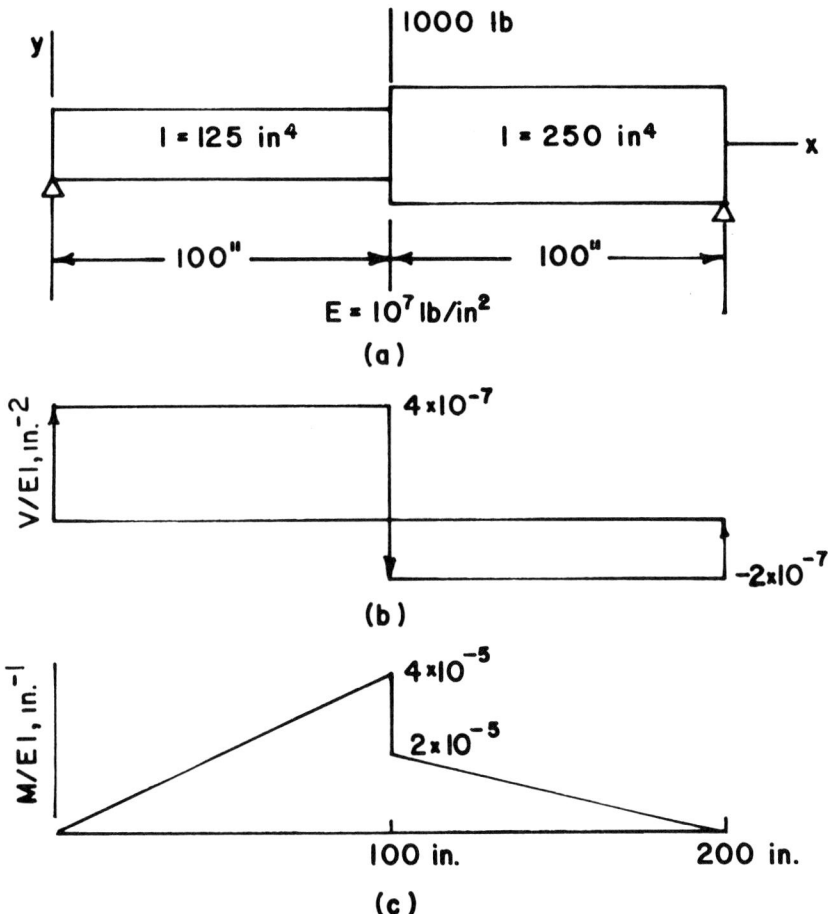

Fig. 14.

BEAM EQUATIONS

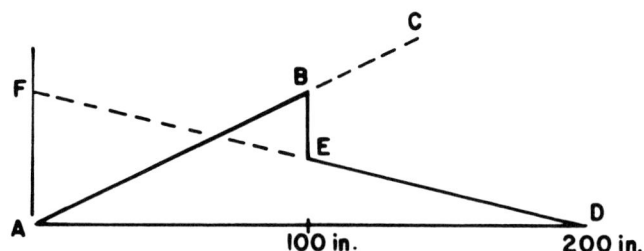

Fig. 15.

Example. The simply supported beam shown in Fig. 14(a) will be used to illustrate the general programming procedure for the analog computer simulation of the beam equations. The *V/EI* diagram, Fig. 14(b), is easily obtained from statics, and the *M/EI* diagram, Fig. 14(c), readily follows from Eqs. (7) and (8). The *M/EI* diagram may be generated by two straight-line segments *ABC* and *FED* as shown in Fig. 15. The straight lines, *ABC* and *FED*, are generated simultaneously, but are switched in and out of the

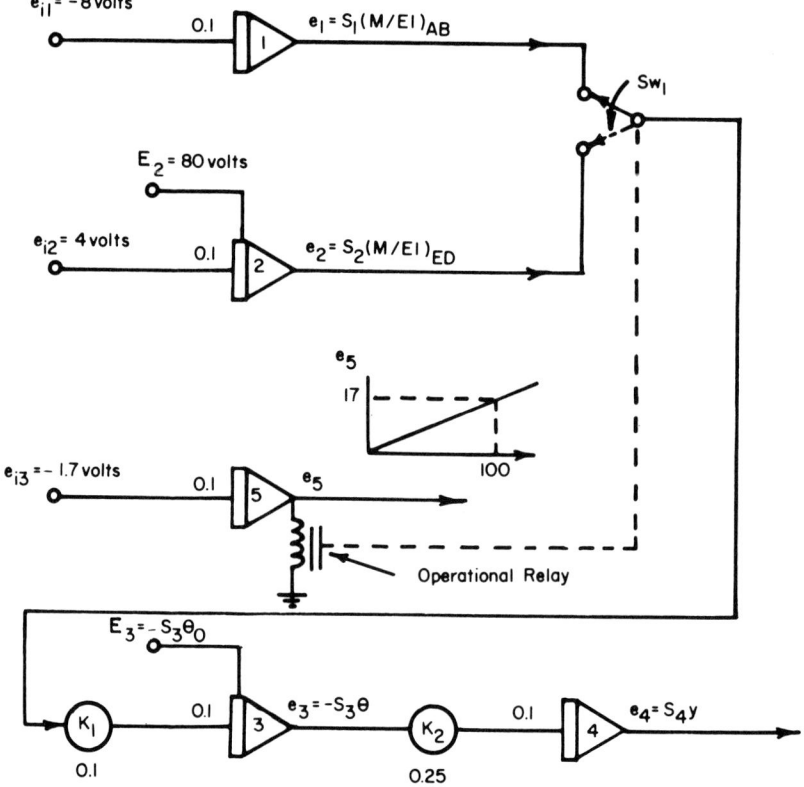

Fig. 16.

main computer circuit by energizing an operational relay at a time corresponding to $x = 100$ in. That is, when the time corresponding to $x = 100$ in. is reached, the ramp function ABC is switched out of the main computer circuit and the function FED is switched in. Thus the two segments AB and ED define the M/EI function, and two successive integrations will result in the beam-deflection curve. The straight lines are generated on the EAC by considering the slope-intercept form of the equations:

$$(M/EI)_{AB} = 4 \times 10^{-7} x \qquad 0 \leq x \leq 100 \text{ in.} \qquad (26)$$
$$(M/EI)_{ED} = -2 \times 10^{-7} x + 4 \times 10^{-5} \qquad 100 \leq x \leq 200 \text{ in.} \qquad (27)$$

Equations (26) and (27) are simulated by two integrating amplifiers (see Fig. 16).
The beam equations to be simulated are

$$d^2 y/dx^2 = M/EI \qquad (28a)$$

$$\theta = dy/dx = \int_0^l (M/EI) \, dx \qquad (28b)$$

$$y = \int_0^l \theta \, dx \qquad (28c)$$

Equations (28b) and (28c) are simulated by two summing integrators. Thus the EAC circuit shown in Fig. 16 is readily formulated by reference to Eqs. (26), (27), (28b), and (28c). Amplifiers 1 and 2 generate the straight-line segments for the M/EI function. The coil of the relay, for activating Switch sw_1, is energized by the output of Amplifier 5 which generates a ramp function by integrating a constant input voltage e_{i3}. The input voltage e_{i3} is set so that the relay is activated when $x = 100$ in. (sec), at which time the Switch sw_1 connects the output of Amplifier 2 to the input of Amplifier 3.

Referring to Eqs. (26), (27), (28b), and (28c), the problem equations in voltage form are

$$e_1 = S_1 (M/EI)_{AB} = -\int (-S_1 4 \times 10^{-7}) \, dx + S_1 (M/EI)^0$$
$$e_2 = S_2 (M/EI)_{ED} = -\int (S_2 2 \times 10^{-7}) \, dx + S_2 4 \times 10^{-5}$$
$$e_3 = -S_3 \theta = -\int S_3 (M/EI) \, dx - S_3 \theta_0 \qquad (29)$$
$$e_4 = S_4 y = -\int (-S_4 \theta) \, dx + S_4 y_0^0$$

where S_1, S_2, S_3, and S_4 are scale factors.

From Eq. (25) and the computer circuit, Fig. 16, the circuit equations are

$$e_1 = S_1 (M/EI)_{AB} = -\int_0^t e_{i1} G_1 \, dt$$

$$e_2 = S_2 (M/EI)_{ED} = -\int_0^t e_{i2} G_2 \, dt + E_2$$

$$e_3 = -S_3 \theta = -\int_0^t K_1 G_3 S_1 (M/EI)_{AB} \, dt + E_3 \qquad (30)$$

BEAM EQUATIONS

or

$$e_3 = -S_3\theta = -\int_0^t K_1 G_3 S_2 (M/EI)_{ED}\, dt + E_3$$

$$e_4 = S_4 y = -\int_0^t -K_2 G_4 (S_3\theta)\, dt + \cancel{E_4}^{\,0}$$

By selecting suitable scale factors, the gains, pot settings, initial condition voltages, and input voltages are obtained from the analogies existing between Eqs. (29) and (30). For example, K_2 and G_4 follow from the analogy

$$S_4\theta = K_2 G_4 (S_3\theta)$$

so that

$$K_2 G_4 = S_4/S_3$$

The gains, pot settings, etc., shown in Fig. 16 were obtained for the scale factors

$$S_1 = S_2 = 2(10)^6 \text{ V}/(M/EI)$$
$$S_3 = 2(10)^4 \text{ V/rad}$$
$$S_4 = 5(10)^2 \text{ V/in.}$$

In general, scale factors are determined from a consideration of maximum allowable amplifier output (± 100 V for the circuit shown in Fig. 16) and maximum values anticipated for the variables which the voltages are to represent. That is,

$$S = \frac{100}{|\text{estimated maximum variable value}|}$$

A trial-and-error procedure must be used to obtain a solution to the simply supported beam since the slope θ_0 is unknown. Thus the initial voltage E_3, Fig. 16, which corresponds to the initial negative slope θ_0, must be varied until the deflection y at the right end of the beam is zero at the time corresponding to $x = 200$ in.

The M/EI diagram, slope θ, and deflection y are easily plotted on an XY plotter by monitoring the various amplifier outputs.

The EAC has certain advantages over the digital computer in the solution of differential equations involving trial-and-error solutions such as that of the simply supported beam. Analog computers equipped with the REPETITIVE OPERATION MODE permit the display of an entire solution at a given instant on an oscilloscope. In this mode the computer can be automatically time scaled so that the computing time is only 1/1000 of the problem time. For the 200-in. beam, the computing time would only be 0.2 sec, and by repeating the solution over and over, the entire solution would appear as one continuous plot on the oscilloscope screen. It should be apparent that by varying a voltage or pot setting that a trial-and-error solution can be made in a matter of seconds by observing the entire solution displayed as the parameters are varied.

VIBRATION OF BEAMS

Partial differential equations describing the vibration of beams take a variety of forms depending upon the kind of damping considered and whether rotary inertia and shear effects are included. In general, the motion of a vibrating beam is described by the solution of a partial differential equation in which the lateral displacement y is a function of the distance x along the beam and the time t. That is,

$$y = f(x, t)$$

Euler-Beam Equation

The Euler-beam equation is the simplest equation for the vibration of beams and is easily formulated from Eq. (14e). If the beam is subjected to an external load intensity $w(x, t)$, then the total load intensity w is equal to the algebraic sum of $w(x, t)$ and the inertia force $\gamma \partial^2 y/\partial t^2$ in which γ is the mass per unit length. It must be emphasized that y is measured from the static equilibrium position so that the weight of the beam per unit length is not included in the load intensity function w. Observing that the inertia force acts in the opposite sense to the positive y upward, the Euler-beam equation for a uniform beam is

$$EI \frac{\partial^4 y}{\partial x^4} = w(x, t) - \gamma \frac{\partial^2 y}{\partial t^2}$$

or

$$EI \frac{\partial^4 y}{\partial x^4} + \gamma \frac{\partial^2 y}{\partial t^2} = w(x, t) \tag{31}$$

In this equation the effects of damping, shear, and rotary inertia have been neglected. In general, the dynamic behavior of a beam is characterized by its natural frequencies and normal mode shapes which depend upon the boundary conditions. Since the natural frequencies and mode shapes evolve from a free vibration analysis, a general solution to the equation

$$\frac{EI}{\gamma} \frac{\partial^4 y}{\partial x^4} + \frac{\partial^2 y}{\partial t^2} = 0 \tag{32}$$

is first obtained before considering specific boundary conditions.

A general solution to Eq. (32) is obtained by the separation of variables by assuming a solution of the form

$$y = XT \tag{33}$$

where X and T are functions of x and t, respectively. The substitution of Eq. (33) and its derivatives into Eq. (32) result in the following two ordinary linear differential equations:

$$X'''' - k^4 X = 0 \tag{34}$$

$$T'' + p^2 T = 0 \tag{35}$$

BEAM EQUATIONS

where $p^2/a^2 = k^4$ and $a^2 = EI/\gamma$. By assuming solutions of the form $X = e^{rx}$ for Eq. (34) and $T = e^{mt}$ for Eq. (35), the general solutions to Eqs. (34) and (35) are found to be

$$X = A \cosh kx + B \sinh kx + C \cos kx + D \sin kx \tag{36}$$
$$T = E \cos pt + F \sin pt \tag{37}$$

The parameter p in Eq. (37) is the natural circular frequency (rad/sec) which depends on the parameter k in Eq. (36). However, the value of k depends upon the manner in which the beam is supported at the ends. Since there are actually an infinite number of k values corresponding to the eigenvalues, the natural frequencies p_i are determined from the relation

$$p_i = a k_i^2 = \sqrt{\frac{EI}{\gamma l^4}} (k_i l)^2 \tag{38}$$

where $i = 1, 2, 3, \ldots$ for the first mode, second mode, etc. The lowest frequency p_i corresponds to the first or fundamental mode of vibration. The frequency f_i in cycles per second (Hz) is simply

$$f_i = p_i/2\pi \tag{39}$$

The four boundary conditions applicable to the various end conditions (see Eq. 14) are shown in Fig. 17. The function X_i corresponding to a $k_i l$ value for a specific set of boundary conditions is the shape function for the ith *normal mode* of vibration.

Example. The general procedure for obtaining the eigenvalues, $k_i l$, and eigenvectors, X_i, will be illustrated with reference to the fixed-free beam, Fig. 17(e).

Applying the conditions $y(0, t) = 0$ and $\partial y/\partial x(0, t) = 0$ to Eq. (36) gives $A = -C$ and $B = -D$.

The conditions

$$\frac{\partial^2 y}{\partial x^2}(l, t) = 0$$

and

$$\frac{\partial^3 y}{\partial x^3}(l, t) = 0$$

result in the following set of homogeneous equations:

$$A(\cosh kl + \cos kl) + B(\sinh kl + \sin kl) = 0 \tag{40}$$
$$A(\sinh kl - \sin kl) + B(\cosh kl + \cos kl) = 0 \tag{41}$$

Setting $|D| = 0$ and simplifying, the frequency equation is found to be

$$\cosh kl \cos kl + 1 = 0 \tag{42}$$

The positive roots to the transcendental equation, Eq. (42), determine the natural frequencies (see Eq. 38) and configurations for the cantilever beam. The first four roots (eigenvalues) to Eq. (42) are $k_1 l = 1.875$, $k_2 l = 4.694$, $k_3 l = 7.855$, and $k_4 l = 10.996$. To obtain the shape function X_i for a normal mode, B may be obtained in terms of A from

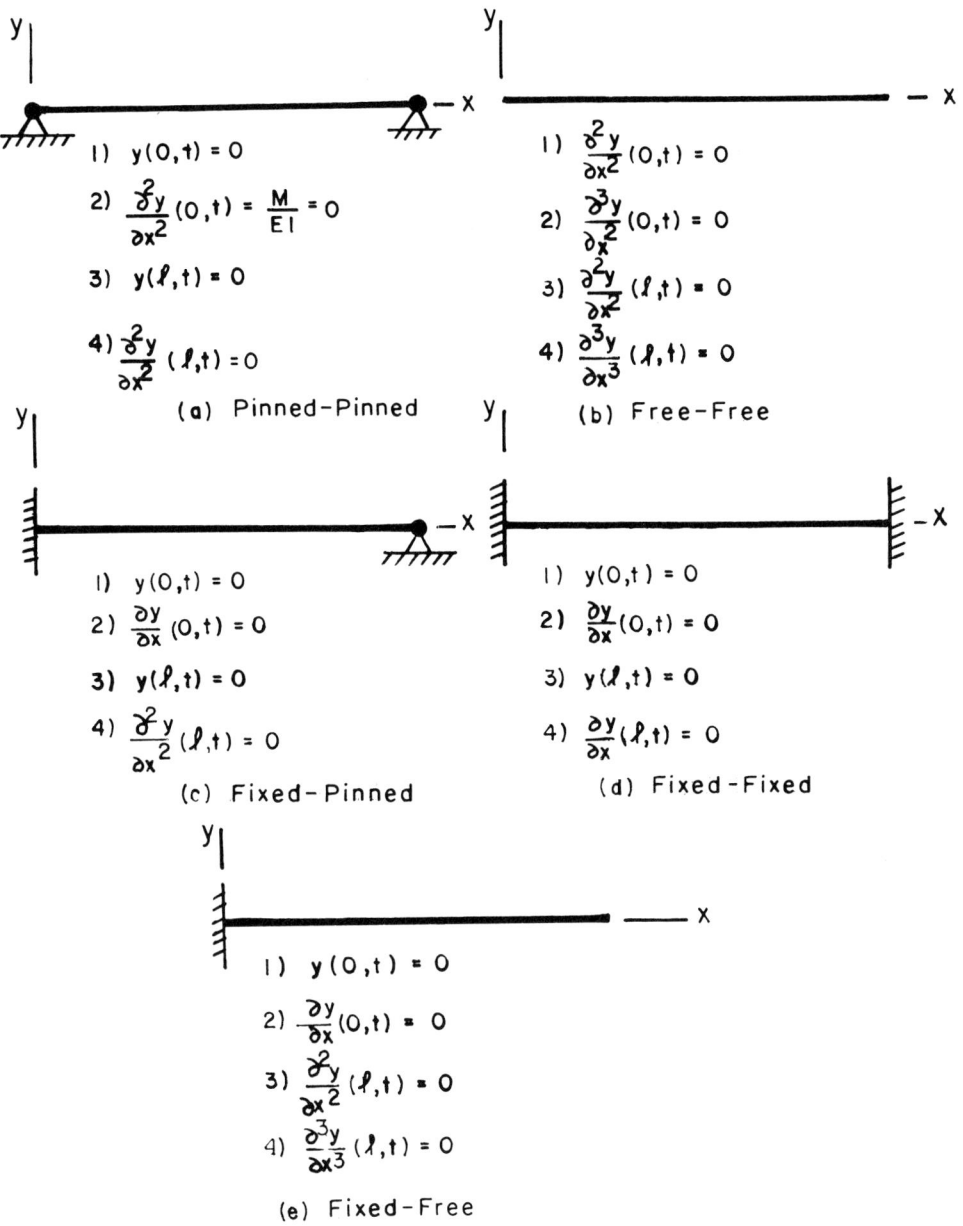

Fig. 17.

either Eq. (40) or (41). Using Eq. (40) gives

$$B_i = -\frac{(\cosh k_i l + \cos k_i l)}{\sinh k_i l + \sin k_i l} A_i$$

The shape function may be normalized by letting $A_i = 1$. Recalling that $C = -A$ and

BEAM EQUATIONS

that $D = -B$, the shape function for the ith mode is found to be

$$X_i = \cosh k_i x - \cos k_i x - \alpha_i(\sinh k_i x - \sin k_i x) \tag{43}$$

where

$$\alpha_i = \frac{\cosh k_i l + \cos k_i l}{\sinh k_i l + \sin k_i l}$$

A general characteristic of the eigenvalues associated with the Euler-beam equation is that the difference between successive eigenvalues for the higher modes approaches π. For example, the difference between $k_2 l = 4.694$ and $k_3 l = 7.855$, for the cantilever beam, is 3.161, and the difference between $k_4 l = 10.996$ and $k_3 l = 7.855$ is 3.141, which is very close to π. Therefore, it is only necessary to determine a sufficient number of eigenvalues so that the difference between successive values is equal to π within the desired accuracy.

Properties of Normal Mode Functions

The normal mode functions X_i evolving from the Euler-beam equation are orthogonal functions. Thus

$$\int_0^l X_i X_j \, dx = \begin{Bmatrix} 0 & i \neq j \\ \lambda_i & i = j \end{Bmatrix} \tag{44}$$

where $\int_0^l X_i^2 \, dx$ equals a constant λ_i when $i = j$. In addition to Eq. (44), the following relationships [6] facilitate the numerical integration of complicated integrals encountered in the analysis of free and forced vibrations of beams:

$$\int_0^l X_i^2 \, dx = \frac{l}{4} [X_i^2 - 2X_i' X_i''' + (X_i'')^2]\Big|_{x=l} \tag{45}$$

where

$$X_i' = \frac{1}{k_i} \frac{dX_i}{dx}, \qquad X_i'' = \frac{1}{k_i^2} \frac{d^2 X_i}{dx^2}, \qquad X_i''' = \frac{1}{k_i^3} \frac{d^3 X_i}{dx^3}$$

$$\int_0^l \left(\frac{d^2 X_i}{dx^2}\right)^2 dx = \frac{p_i^2}{a^2} \int_0^l X_i^2 \, dx \tag{46}$$

To illustrate the use of Eq. (45), consider the evaluation of the integral $\int_0^l X_i^2 \, dx$ for the fixed-free beam in which X_i is defined by Eq. (43). For the fixed-free beam, the shear and moment are zero at $x = l$, so that X_i'' and X_i''' are also zero at $x = l$. Evaluating X_i at $x = l$, Eq. (45) gives

$$\int_0^l X_i^2 \, dx = \frac{l}{4} [X_i(l)]^2$$

for the evaluation of the integral.

Free Undamped Vibrations

If a beam is given an initial velocity and/or displacement at time $t = 0$, the motion of the beam at any instant of time thereafter will, in general, include

BEAM EQUATIONS

participation of all the normal modes. The motion can be described by the series

$$y = \sum_{i=1}^{\infty} X_i (E_i \cos p_i t + F_i \sin p_i t) \tag{47}$$

where E_i and F_i for each mode participation depend upon the initial conditions. For example, if $y(x, 0) = f(x)$ and $\dfrac{\partial y}{\partial t}(x, 0) = 0$, then $F_i = 0$ and

$$f(x) = \sum X_i E_i \tag{48}$$

Multiplying both sides of Eq. (48) by X_j and integrating over the length l of the beam, gives

$$\int_0^l f(x) X_j \, dx = \int_0^l (\sum X_i E_i) X_j \, dx$$

It now follows from the orthogonality property (see Eq. 44) that

$$E_i = \frac{\displaystyle\int_0^l f(x) X_i \, dx}{\displaystyle\int_0^l X_i^2 \, dx} \tag{49}$$

It should be evident from Eq. (49) that all the modes will be present unless $f(x)$ happens to correspond to one of the normal mode functions.

In general, the series, Eq. (47), converges quite rapidly and a satisfactory solution can usually be obtained by considering the first few modes.

In some cases it may be necessary to resort to a numerical integration process for the evaluation of the numerator of Eq. (49). As previously mentioned, Eq. (45) may be used to facilitate the evaluation of the denominator of Eq. (49).

Forced Vibrations—Modal Summation Method

Forced vibrations of beams with damping may be taken in the form

$$y = \sum q_i X_i \tag{50}$$

where q_i is the generalized coordinate which is a function of time, and X_i is the function for a normal mode.

By using the principles of energy and Lagrange's equation, a second-order linear differential equation in terms of q_i is obtained. The solution to this differential equation provides the time functions necessary for the modal summation, Eq. (50).

Lagrange's equation [4] is

$$\frac{d}{dt}\left(\frac{\partial T}{\partial \dot{q}_i}\right) - \frac{\partial T}{\partial q_i} + \frac{\partial V}{\partial q_i} = Q_i \tag{51}$$

BEAM EQUATIONS

where T is the kinetic energy of the beam, V is the potential or strain energy, and Q_i is the generalized nonpotential force (damping and excitation).

The kinetic energy T for a uniform beam of mass γ per unit length is

$$T = \frac{\gamma}{2}\int_0^l \left(\frac{\partial y}{\partial t}\right)^2 dx = \frac{\gamma}{2}\int_0^l (\sum \dot{q}_i X_i)^2 \, dx \qquad (52)$$

and the strain energy V due to bending is

$$V = \frac{EI}{2}\int_0^l \left(\frac{\partial^2 y}{\partial x^2}\right)^2 dx = \frac{EI}{2}\int_0^l \left(\sum q_i \frac{d^2 X_i}{dx^2}\right)^2 dx \qquad (53)$$

Performing the operations indicated in Lagrange's equation and noting the orthogonality properties, Eqs. (52) and (53) give

$$\frac{d}{dt}\left(\frac{\partial T}{\partial \dot{q}_i}\right) = \gamma \ddot{q}_i \int_0^l X_i^2 \, dx \qquad (54)$$

$$\partial T/\partial q_i = 0 \qquad (55)$$

$$\frac{\partial V}{\partial q_i} = EI q_i \int_0^l \left(\frac{d^2 X_i}{dx^2}\right)^2 dx \qquad (56)$$

The generalized nonpotential force Q_i is obtained by considering the differential work dW done by all nonpotential forces due to the variation dq_i of a *particular* coordinate. That is,

$$dW = Q_i \, dq_i \qquad (57)$$

For an exciting force per unit length of $w(x, t) = \psi(t) f(x)$,

$$dW = \psi(t) \int_0^l [f(x) \, dy] \, dx \qquad (58)$$

Since $dy = dq_i X_i$ for the variation dq_i of a particular coordinate, Eq. (58) yields

$$dW = \psi(t) \, dq_i \int_0^l [f(x) X_i] \, dx$$

so that

$$Q_i = \psi(t) \int_0^l [f(x) X_i] \, dx \qquad (59)$$

In the case of a viscous damping force per unit length of $c(\partial y/\partial t)$,

$$dW = -c\int_0^l \left[\frac{\partial y}{\partial t} \, dy\right] dx = -c \, dq_j \int_0^l (\sum \dot{q}_i X_i) X_j \, dx$$

Noting the orthogonality property

$$dW = -c(dq_i)\dot{q}_i \int_0^l X_i^2 \, dx$$

BEAM EQUATIONS

Thus

$$Q_i = -c\dot{q}_i \int_0^l X_i^2 \, dx \tag{60}$$

Substituting Eqs. (54), (55), (56), (59), and (60) into Lagrange's equation gives

$$\ddot{q}_i + \frac{c}{\gamma} \dot{q}_i + p_i^2 q_i = \frac{\psi(t) \int_0^l [f(x) X_i] \, dx}{\gamma \int_0^l X_i^2 \, dx} \tag{61}$$

where

$$p_i^2 = \frac{EI}{\gamma} \frac{\int_0^l \left(\frac{d^2 X_i}{dx^2}\right)^2 dx}{\int_0^l X_i^2 \, dx}$$

The solution to Eq. (61) consists of a homogeneous solution $q_i)_h$ plus a particular solution $q_i)_p$ which must satisfy the right-hand side. Very seldom is there any difficulty in obtaining an analytical solution to Eq. (61). However, the summation of the series, Eq. (50), to obtain numerical answers usually requires the use of a computer because of the large number of computations involved.

Example. It is desired to determine the steady-state response for the displacement y and the flexural stress σ for the simply supported beam shown in Fig. 18. The beam is subjected to a sinusoidal force of intensity w_0 over the region $0 \leq x \leq l/2$. The damping is viscous (proportional to the velocity).

From the boundary conditions of Fig. 17(a) and Eq. (36), the normal mode functions are found to be simply

$$X_i = \sin k_i x = \sin \frac{i \pi x}{l} \quad (i = 1, 2, 3, \ldots) \tag{62}$$

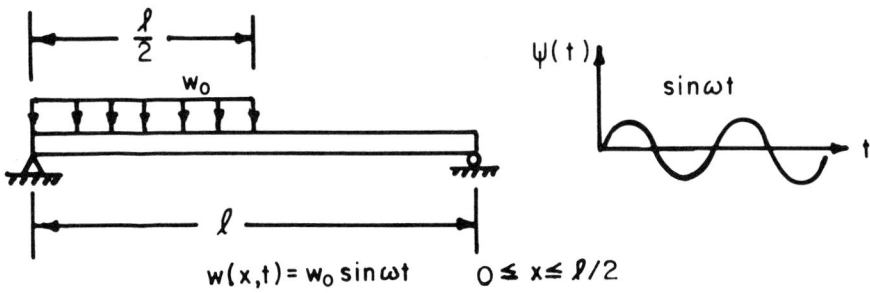

Fig. 18.

BEAM EQUATIONS

Since $k_i = i\pi/l$, then

$$p_i = \sqrt{\frac{EI}{\gamma} \frac{i^2\pi^2}{l^2}}$$

Thus the right-hand side of Eq. (61) gives

$$\frac{w_0}{\gamma} \sin \omega t \; \frac{\int_0^{l/2} \sin \frac{i\pi x}{l} \, dx}{\int_0^l \sin^2 \frac{i\pi x}{l} \, dx} = \frac{2w_0}{i\gamma\pi}\left[1 - \cos \frac{i\pi}{2}\right] \sin \omega t$$

Denoting c/γ as $2\xi_i p_i$, where ξ_i is a damping parameter in which $\xi_i = 1$ for critical damping, Eq. (61) becomes

$$\ddot{q}_i + 2\xi_i p_i \dot{q}_i + p_i^2 q_i = \frac{2w_0}{i\gamma\pi}\left[1 - \cos \frac{i\pi}{2}\right] \sin \omega t$$

The steady-state solution (particular) to this equation is readily found to be

$$q_i = \frac{2w_0}{i\gamma\pi p_i^2} \frac{\left[1 - \cos \frac{i\pi}{2}\right]}{\sqrt{\left[1 - \left(\frac{\omega}{p_i}\right)^2\right]^2 + \left(2\xi_i \frac{\omega}{p_i}\right)^2}} \sin(\omega t - \phi_i) \qquad (63)$$

where

$$\phi_i = \tan^{-1}\left[\frac{2\xi_i \frac{\omega}{p_i}}{1 - \left(\frac{\omega}{p_i}\right)^2}\right] \qquad (i = 1, 2, 3, \ldots)$$

The steady-state response for y follows from the summation of Eq. (50) in which X_i and q_i are as defined by Eqs. (62) and (63).

From Eqs. (1), (14c), and (50), the steady-state flexural stress is found to be

$$\sigma = Ez \frac{\partial^2 y}{\partial x^2}$$

or

$$\sigma = Ez \sum q_i \frac{d^2 X_i}{dx^2}$$

where q_i is defined by Eq. (63) and $d^2X_i/dx^2 = -(i^2\pi^2/l^2) \sin i\pi x/l$.

Since $p_i^2 = EIi^4\pi^4/\gamma l^4$ in Eq. (63), it would appear that Eq. (50) converges very rapidly. However, it is well known from elementary vibration theory that the response peaks sharply for low damping when the exciting frequency ω is close to the natural frequency. In view of this, the radical term in the denominator of Eq. (63) may be very small when ω is close to one of the natural frequencies p_i with the result that a higher mode term will have a strong influence on the response. Therefore, the numerical evaluation of Eq. (50) must be carried out with caution so as to include the dominate terms. In fact, if ω equals some particular p_i, then only the one term for that particular mode is required for fairly accurate results since all the other terms are negligible. For example, if $\omega = p_3$ and $\xi_3 = 0.01$, the response for all practical purposes is simply

$$y = \frac{100 w_0 l^4}{(3\pi)^5 EI} \sin(\omega t - \phi_3) \sin \frac{3\pi x}{l}$$

For computation purposes, the ratio ω/p_i in Eq. (63) may be expressed in terms of the fundamental frequency p_1 by noting that $p_i = i^2 p_1$.

Synthesis of Damping Models—Sinusoidal Varying Boundary Conditions

Frequently beam elements of machines and structures are subjected to sinusoidal motion at the ends due to motion of the beam's support structure. With sinusoidal time varying boundary conditions, the steady-state response of beams can be described by closed form solutions. When some form of damping is included in the Euler-beam equation, the closed form solutions involve functions with complex arguments. This, however, presents no problem for computation of the steady-state response since functions with complex arguments and complex algebra are easily programmed for machine computation in the FORTRAN IV language.

The partial differential equations with the inclusion of damping in the form of a complex modulus, a viscoelastic material, and a viscous type damping are as follows [7]:

Complex modulus damping

$$\frac{E^* I}{\gamma} \frac{\partial^4 y}{\partial x^4} + \frac{\partial^2 y}{\partial t^2} = 0 \tag{64}$$

where $E^* = E(1 + j\delta)$
  E = Young's modulus
  $j = \sqrt{-1}$
  δ = loss factor
  γ = mass of beam/unit length

Viscoelastic damping (Kelvin model) [8]

$$\frac{EI}{\gamma} \frac{\partial^4 y}{\partial x^4} + \frac{FI}{\gamma} \frac{\partial^5 y}{\partial x^4 \partial t} + \frac{\partial^2 y}{\partial t^2} = 0 \tag{65}$$

where F is a viscoelastic constant for the Kelvin model in which the stress σ depends upon the strain ϵ and the strain rate $\dot{\epsilon}$ according to the equation

$$\sigma = E\epsilon + F\dot{\epsilon}$$

Viscous damping (proportional to velocity)

$$\frac{EI}{\gamma} \frac{\partial^4 y}{\partial x^4} + \frac{c}{\gamma} \frac{\partial y}{\partial t} + \frac{\partial^2 y}{\partial t^2} = 0 \tag{66}$$

where c is a viscous damping constant.

If the ends (one or both) of a beam are subjected to sinusoidal motion of frequency ω, the steady-state solution may be taken in the form

$$y = X e^{j\omega t} \tag{67}$$

[164]
BEAM EQUATIONS

TABLE 2

Damping model	k^*	Remarks
Complex modulus	$\left(\dfrac{\gamma\omega^2}{EI}\right)^{1/4}(1 + j\delta)^{-1/4}$	For a constant loss factor, δ, the damping is independent of frequency
Viscoelastic	$\left(\dfrac{\gamma\omega^2}{EI}\right)^{1/4}\left(1 + \dfrac{j\omega F}{E}\right)^{-1/4}$	For constant values of E and F, the damping parameter, $\omega F/E$, increases with frequency
Viscous	$\left(\dfrac{\gamma\omega^2}{EI}\right)^{1/4}\left(1 - \dfrac{jc}{\gamma\omega}\right)^{1/4}$	For constant values of c and γ, the damping parameter, $c/\gamma\omega$, decreases with ω

Substituting Eq. (67) and its derivatives into either Eq. (64), (65), or (66) gives

$$X'''' - (k^*)^4 X = 0 \tag{68}$$

where k^* is a complex quantity in which the imaginary part describes the system damping. The general solution to Eq. (68) is

$$X = A \cosh k^*x + B \sinh k^*x + C \cos k^*x + D \sin k^*x \tag{69}$$

where A, B, C, and D are complex constants that depend upon the boundary conditions which include the support excitation at the ends. The complex quantity k^* for the different damping models is shown in Table 2.

Example Determine the equations for machine computation of the steady-state strain ϵ at $x = 0$ for the beam shown in Fig. 19. Assume that the damping is viscous.

The strain (Eq. 10) in a fiber z distance from the N.A. is $\epsilon = z(\partial^2 y/\partial x^2)$. It now follows from Eqs. (67) and (69) that the complex strain at $x = 0$ for all time is

$$\epsilon(0, t) = z(k^*)^2(A - C)e^{j\omega t} \tag{70}$$

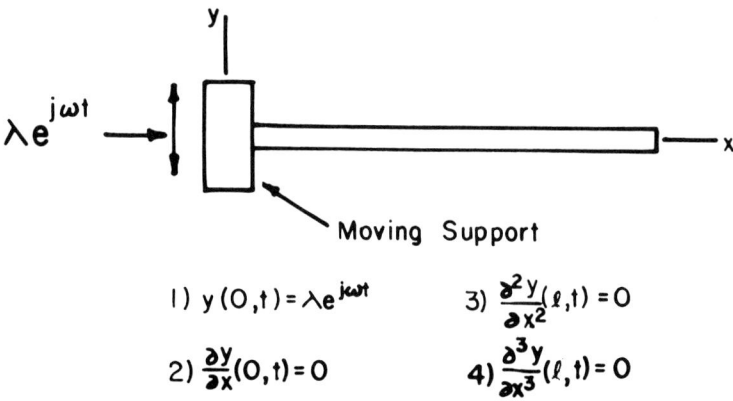

1) $y(0,t) = \lambda e^{j\omega t}$
2) $\dfrac{\partial y}{\partial x}(0,t) = 0$
3) $\dfrac{\partial^2 y}{\partial x^2}(\ell,t) = 0$
4) $\dfrac{\partial^3 y}{\partial x^3}(\ell,t) = 0$

Fig. 19.

BEAM EQUATIONS

From the first two boundary conditions shown in Fig. 19, we find

$$A + C = \lambda \tag{71}$$

$$B + D = 0 \tag{72}$$

The third and fourth boundary conditions, in combination with Eqs. (71) and (72), result in two algebraic equations which give

$$A = \lambda \frac{(\cosh k^*l \cos k^*l + \sinh k^*l \sin k^*l + 1)}{2(\cosh k^*l \cos k^*l + 1)} \tag{73}$$

From Eq. (71) we find $A - C = 2A - \lambda$. Hence the *magnitude* of the steady-state response can be formulated in the dimensionless form

$$\left| \frac{\epsilon(0, t)l^2}{z\lambda} \right| = |(k^*l)^2(2A' - 1)| \tag{74}$$

where

$$A' = \frac{\cosh k^*l \cos k^*l + \sinh k^*l \sin k^*l + 1}{2(\cosh k^*l \cos k^*l + 1)} \tag{75}$$

For computation purposes, k^*l of Eq. (74) may be expressed in terms of a frequency ratio ω/ω_1, where ω_1 is the natural frequency (rad/sec) of the first mode. By defining a damping parameter α as $c/\gamma = \alpha\omega$, and noting that $\omega_1^2 = (EI/\gamma)k_1^4$, the quantity k^*l for viscous damping may be written as

$$k^*l = (k_1 l)\left(\frac{\omega}{\omega_1}\right)^{1/2}\left(1 - j\alpha \frac{\omega_1}{\omega}\right)^{1/4}$$

Since $k_1 l = 1.875$ (eigenvalue for first mode),

$$k^*l = (1.875)\left(\frac{\omega}{\omega_1}\right)^{1/2}\left(1 - j\alpha \frac{\omega_1}{\omega}\right)^{1/4} \tag{76}$$

Thus the magnitude of the steady-state response, $|\epsilon(0, t)l^2/z\lambda|$, may be obtained by a programmed computation of Eqs. (74), (75), and (76). By specifying different values for the damping parameter α, a family of response curves as shown in Fig. 20 can be obtained as a function of the frequency ratio ω/ω_1. The machine computation involves functions with complex arguments which are easily handled by FORTRAN IV [3]. For each value of ω/ω_1 and a specified α value, the computed quantity includes a real and an imaginary part in which the magnitude of the response is simply the square root of the sum of the squares of the real and imaginary parts.

Experimental response data, from support excited beams, can be correlated with closed form solutions of the different damping models to determine an appropriate model for describing the damping behavior of a material or a beam system. Knudson and Smith [7] used such an approach in the study of the dynamic response of slender tubes in coaxial fluid flow.

Additional Equations for Beam Vibrations

Axially Loaded Beams

Frequently beams are subjected to axial forces (tension or compression) which may have an effect on the lateral vibrations. In general, tensile forces

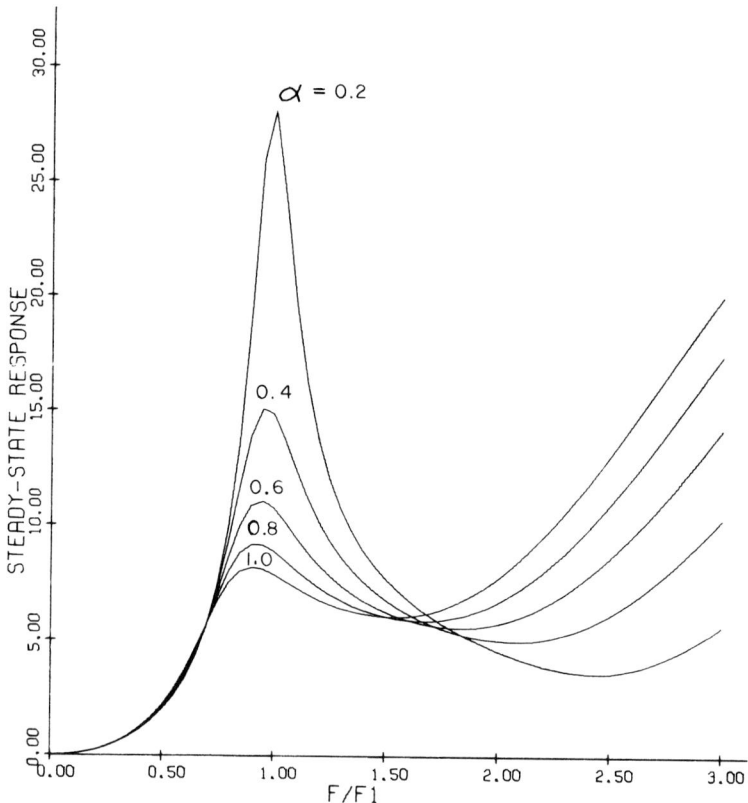

Fig. 20. Fixed-free beam (viscous damping).

tend to increase the natural frequencies whereas compressive forces tend to decrease the frequencies. In the case of a compressive load equal to the buckling load, the natural frequency goes to zero and the beam will not vibrate.

Tightly stretched fiber glass cables are being used a great deal today to support tall towers. Since tightly stretched cables may be excited by Karman vortex shedding, such cables are susceptible to fatigue failures if the frequency of vortex shedding corresponds to one of the natural frequencies. Usually long cables are analyzed by the one-dimensional wave equation which does not include bending stiffness. However, in the case of stiff cables and high wind velocities, the bending stiffness may be significant due to the tendency to vibrate in a relatively high mode configuration.

The equation of motion [6] for an axially loaded beam excited by vortex shedding of frequency f is

$$\frac{EI}{\gamma}\frac{\partial^4 y}{\partial x^4} + \frac{\partial^2 y}{\partial t^2} - \frac{P}{\gamma}\frac{\partial^2 y}{\partial x^2} = \frac{C_k v^2 A}{\rho}\sin(2\pi f)t \qquad (77)$$

where P = axial tensile force
C_k = aerodynamic constant (C_k = 1 for a cylinder)
v = wind velocity
A = projected area of beam perpendicular to flow velocity v
ρ = mass density of flowing fluid
EI = beam stiffness factor
γ = mass of beam per unit length

It is noted that the second and third terms in the left-hand side of Eq. (77) are the simple one-dimensional wave equation.

The frequency f of vortex shedding, Fig. 21, on alternate sides of a cylinder [9] is

$$f = Sv/d \tag{78}$$

where S = Strouhal number
d = cylinder diameter
v = velocity of fluid flow

For Reynolds number $R < 200{,}000$, the value of the Strouhal number S is usually taken as 0.2. For large amplitudes A_0, the effective diameter is $d + 2A_0$, which means that the excitation frequency f can be a function of the vibration amplitude as well as of the fluid velocity v.

The effects of the various parameters on the natural frequencies f_i are of primary importance in the study of Eq. (77). By taking the right-hand side of Eq. (77) equal to zero, the separation of variables approach gives

$$X'''' - \frac{P}{EI} X'' - \frac{p^2}{(EI/\gamma)} X = 0 \tag{79}$$

and

$$T'' + p^2 T = 0 \tag{80}$$

The solutions to Eqs. (79) and (80) are found to be

$$X = A \cosh r_1 x + B \sinh r_1 x + C \cos r_2 x + D \sin r_2 x \tag{81}$$
$$T = E \cos pt + F \sin pt \tag{82}$$

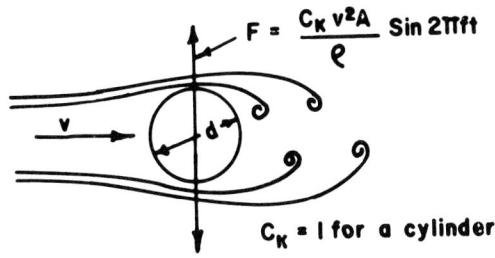

Fig. 21.

BEAM EQUATIONS

where

$$r_1 = \left[\frac{P}{2EI} + \sqrt{\left(\frac{P}{2EI}\right)^2 + \left(\frac{p^2}{EI/\gamma}\right)}\right]^{1/2} \quad (83)$$

$$r_2 = \left[\sqrt{\left(\frac{P}{2EI}\right)^2 + \frac{p^2}{(EI/\gamma)}} - \frac{P}{2EI}\right]^{1/2} \quad (84)$$

Considering the boundary conditions for a pinned-pinned beam, Eq. (81) yields

$$r_2 = i\pi/l \quad (i = 1, 2, 3, \ldots) \quad (85)$$

and

$$X_i = \sin\frac{i\pi x}{l} \quad (86)$$

It now follows from Eqs. (84) and (85) that

$$f_i = \frac{p_i}{2\pi} = \frac{i^2\pi}{2l^2}\left[\frac{EI}{\gamma}\left(1 + \frac{Pl^2}{EIi^2\pi^2}\right)\right]^{1/2} \quad (87)$$

It is evident from Eq. (87) that the axial force P becomes less and less important as the mode number i increases. Thus a long cable of length l may be fairly flexible for low values of i but will be relatively stiff when it vibrates in a high mode with i sinusoidal half waves as shown in Fig. 22.

If P is a compressive force, then all the signs for the P terms are opposite to those shown in Eqs. (77) through (87).

Timoshenko's Beam Equation [6]

The Timoshenko beam equation, which includes the effects of shear and rotary inertia, is

$$\frac{EI}{\gamma}\frac{\partial^4 y}{\partial x^4} + \frac{\partial^2 y}{\partial t^2} - r^2\left(1 + \frac{E}{k'G}\right)\frac{\partial^4 y}{\partial x^2 \partial t^2} + r^2\frac{\gamma}{Ak'G}\frac{\partial^4 y}{\partial t^4} = 0 \quad (88)$$

where γ = mass of beam per unit length
A = cross-sectional area
$r = \sqrt{I/A}$ = radius of gyration
E = modulus of elasticity
G = modulus of elasticity in shear
k' = numerical factor depending on the shape of the cross section

In general, the effects of rotary inertia and shear on the lower mode natural frequencies are negligible for slender beams in which the ratio of the depth d to the length l is fairly small. In the case of a rectangular cross section with $d/l < 0.1$, the shear and rotary inertia effects may be neglected in the computation of the lower modes. However, these effects should be considered

Fig. 22.

in the case of short, or stubby, beams or in the case of high modes for slender beams.

In the case of a pinned-pinned beam, it is easily shown that

$$y = C \sin \frac{i\pi x}{l} \sin p_i t \qquad (i = 1, 2, 3, \ldots) \tag{89}$$

satisfies Eq. (88) and the end conditions. Timoshenko [6] shows that the substitution of Eq. (89) into Eq. (88) gives

$$p_i = \frac{\pi^2 i^2}{l^2} \left(1 - \frac{\pi^2 r^2 i^2}{2l^2}\right) \sqrt{\frac{EI}{\gamma}} \tag{90}$$

when the effect of rotary inertia is taken into account. He further shows that

$$p_i = \frac{\pi^2 i^2}{l^2} \left[1 - \frac{\pi^2 r^2 i^2}{2l^2}\left(1 + \frac{E}{k'G}\right)\right] \sqrt{\frac{EI}{\gamma}} \tag{91}$$

when the effect of shear is taken into account.

Equations (90) and (91) show that the effects of rotary inertia and shear depend on the wave length $\lambda = l/i$. By taking $E = 8G/3$, $k' = 0.833$ for a rectangular cross section, and λ equal to ten times the beam's depth, the combined correction for both rotary inertia and shear is only 2%.

In the case of beams having end conditions other than pinned-pinned or with nonuniform cross sections, it is usually necessary to resort to some sort of a computer solution of Eq. (88). Thomson [10] describes a digital computer technique which involves the solution of four first-order equations which are formulated in the derivation of Eq. (88). Howe and Howe [11] show that the analog computer is a fast and accurate method for studying the Timoshenko beam equation. In general, the procedure involves the analog simulation of three ordinary coupled equations which evolve naturally in the derivation of Eq. (88). Due to the ease of making trial-and-error solutions to satisfy boundary conditions, the analog computer is a very powerful tool for the analysis of beams having nonuniform cross sections.

REFERENCES

1. D. C. Haack, L. Y. Morris, B. B. Snyder, H. E. Attaway, and S. Weinstein, On an equilibrium theory of tooth position, *Angle Orthodontist* **33**(1), 1–26 (1963).

BEAM EQUATIONS

2. A. Higdon, E. H. Ohlsen, W. B. Stiles, and J. A. Weese, *Mechanics of Materials,* 2nd ed., Wiley, New York, 1960.
3. M. L. James, G. M. Smith, and J. C. Wolford, *Applied Numerical Methods for Digital Computation,* International Textbook Co., Scranton, Pa., 1967.
4. G. M. Smith and G. L. Downey, *Advanced Engineering Dynamics,* 2nd ed., International Textbook Co., Scranton, Pa., 1968.
5. M. L. James, G. M. Smith, and J. C. Wolford, *Analog Computer Simulation of Engineering Systems,* 2nd ed., Intext Educational Publishers, Scranton, Pa., 1971.
6. S. Timoshenko and D. H. Young, *Vibration Problems in Engineering,* 3rd ed., Van Nostrand, New York, 1955.
7. G. M. Smith and S. A. Knudson, Dynamic response of sender tubes in parallel flow when subjected to time varying boundary conditions, in *Proceedings of the Conference on Flow-Induced Vibrations in Reactor System Components,* May 15–16, 1970, Argonne National Laboratory, pp. 67–90 (ANL-7685).
8. G. L. Rogers, *Dynamics of Framed Structures,* Wiley, New York, 1959.
9. G. B. Warburton, *The Dynamical Behaviour of Structures,* Macmillan, New York, 1964.
10. W. T. Thomson, *Vibration Theory and Applications,* Prentice-Hall, Englewood Cliffs, N.J., 1965.
11. C. E. Howe and R. M. Howe, Application of the electronic differential analyzer to the oscillation of beams, including shear and rotary inertia, *J. Appl. Mech.* **22**(1), (March 1955).

Gerald M. Smith

BEARINGS; *see* Lubrication

BEHAVIOR AND COMPUTERS

Because of the breadth of the area, it is important to clarify the context in which behavior and computers are discussed in this article. Behavior refers to organismic functioning. This includes both the physiological and psychological counterparts of organismic activity. Behavior is not intended here to be relegated entirely to homo sapiens because other species have enjoyed similar attention in the linkage of computers to behavior. The interaction will be considered to be with digital computers, although analog computers have played a distinct role in the study of behavior.

Behavior and computers enjoy an unprecedented alliance, perhaps une-

BEHAVIOR AND COMPUTERS

qualed since the matching of the horse to the carriage experienced earlier in history. The alliance refers to the incorporation of the computer as an extension of human functioning, often referred to as "man–machine symbiosis" [1]. The meaning of this alliance is not entirely clear. At best it is shaky and speculative.

The alliance has come about through several ways. The large studies in computer technology, particularly the development of large memories, fast pressers, and excellent symbol manipulation created the possibility that such advances could supplement human capabilities and thus enhance his behavior. For example, these advances were seen as providing the possibility of improving decision making and problem solving. Second, there have been several publications which pioneered in fostering the alliance (Borko, Green, Sackman, and others). Third, the complexities largely intrinsic to the study of social behavior veiwed the computer as a breakthrough in methodology [49–51].

In the understanding of the alliance of behavior to computers, it would be best to outline what could be considered to be the substance of the relationship that is implied. In each case it should be stressed that computers in no way are considered as capable of doing any more than executing the instructions constructed by the programmer.

1. Computers can serve as machines that can be made to initiate an act or behave as humans.
2. The understanding of behavior is seen as facilitated through machines like computers that are capable of rapid data manipulation.
3. The understanding of behavior can be facilitated through machines like computers capable of conceptual shaping of organismic performance, thus enabling hypothesis generation and theory formulation of behavior.
4. Computers aid action, individual and collective, by serving as estimators of the future as well as reporters of the past.
5. Computers serve as experimental apparatus for the conduct of behavioral research. Computers as experimental apparatus range from generating stimuli that are presented to subjects that are used as study objects; recording and assessing their responses to the generation of conditions wherein large segments of the population are subject to test, such as the social experiment.
6. Computers serve as devices for the elicitation of behavior.

As such, the linkage existing between behavior and computers will be pursued by an exposition of the theoretical base relevant to the linkage. Specifically, automata theory and themes related to human information processing will be discussed first. This will be followed by an exposition of those factors that facilitate the analysis and measurement of behavior through computers. Application of computers to social behavior will then be discussed, and finally the impact that computers have assumed on behavior.

BEHAVIOR AND COMPUTERS

THEORETICAL REFERENCE

Behavior and computers are linked by theory as well as by practice. There are numerous theories from a variety of disciplines (biology, psychology, sociology, etc.) that are directly applicable to the correlation of behavior to computers. Those selected for this statement are considered to underlie most of the references when behavior and computers are discussed. Although each theory is identified separately, there is no intent to consider them as such. Each of the theories relates to each of the others in an interwoven interdisciplinary mesh.

Automata Theory

An automation is conceived as a black box characterized by a finite number of states (its excitation variables) and they produce outputs (their response variables). The intermediate variables are imbedded in the black box which define its state. Every system represented by an automation defines that system completely.

The correspondence of automata theory to computers is not difficult for it is sufficient to say that the development of the computer is basically correlated to the development of automata theory. Consequently, automata theory underlies the discussions of all the other theories relating computers to behavior. Several scholars, such as Goldstine [2], Licklider [1], and Tou [3], have shown the richness of the applications of this theory to behavior, when behavior is considered in its broadest application. For the present purpose, it is sufficient, therefore, to highlight two specific applications that merit individual reference at this point.

Neurological Functioning

The classical work of McCulloch and Pitts [4] on neural networks is an attempt to develop a mathematical model of the human nervous system. The research led to the conclusion that anything that can be described completely can be designed to operate as a neural network. This work led to Von Neumann's interest in the design of a self-reproductive automata—and particularly a model of the function of the biological cell.

Artificial Intelligence

Artificial intelligence refers to the capacity of a machine to perform functions which could be considered analogous to human functions. Basically, automata theory provides the basis for generating logical functions—both inductive and deductive—that approximate procedures undertaken by humans in intellectual operations. Artificial intelligence implies simulation of intellectual operations but does not restrict such simulation to those aspects that are limited by human capacities.

Human Information Processing and Related Theories

Human information processing can perhaps be considered generic to behavior. Life could not proceed without the capacity of an organism to take the raw input from the event (external) world and transform these to "significations," meanings—information, if you will—that enables the organism's survival. Sensory reception, neural transmission, memory, cognitive organization, perception, thinking, and learning are all involved. In psychological parlance, however, human information processing theory is expressed within certain frames of reference. These frames of reference are briefly outlined as they specifically relate to computers. In each instance, the computer is seen as offering the possibility of simulating the functions involved [52].

Brain or Neural Function

Human information processing theory as brain or neural function finds its expression in bionics. Bionics is the study of human functions as these functions can be represented in the design and engineering of technology to achieve such functions. Much of the research conducted by individuals engaged in bionics concerns the mapping of neural operations as represented in the central nervous system to determine the *mechanisms* central to these operations. Human information processing is conceived as an aggregate of such operations.

Another expression of human information processing utilizes the nature of brain processes to describe the reception of the signal, its retention in storage (visual icon), and its subsequent use in purposeful action [5]. The theory attempts to postulate the relation between visual imagery and cognitive functioning (perception, thinking, learning, etc.). Models of such functioning have been advanced in attempts to computer simulate such models [6–8].

Learning

Psychologists view learning as a process through which the organism initiates a change in the response to a particular state of his environment. The change cannot be considered to be the result of his natural endowment (maturation) or specific states such as fatigue and drugs [9]. The development of concepts of learning have a long historical background. Learning theory has its basis in education and was given emphasis by the work of Pavlov on the conditioning of dogs to salivate at the response of a bell. Classical conditioning was followed by Skinner's instrumental conditioning of a rat to a bar-pressing operation with the subsequent reinforcement of the subject by a food pellet. These theories of how learning manifests itself were accompanied by other theories encouraged or prompted by pedagogical issues [10, 11]. The distinctions among the theories can be summarized by indicating what major questions facing the process remain, namely, is there one or more kinds of learning? What is the importance of reward or punishment in learning, and a third question which centers around the nature of the stimulus that mitigates against learning; for example, what function does the entire environment of stimuli play on the learning process? Learning theory has benefited considerably from computers. Research on the learning process could proceed through mathematical formalization of the important variables. This formalization, or model, would represent a theoretical statement of the underlying processes of learning which would be subsequently simulated through the computers as a test of the theory.

Problem Solving

A problem may be defined as a situation where the individual wishes to attain a goal or objective but does not know at the time what he should do to obtain it [12]. Problem-solving theory attempts to detail the manner in which humans proceed to solve problems. In general, two theories exist. One theory claims that humans solve problems sequentially, step by step. Another theory purports parallel processing of input data.

The work of Newell, Shaw, and Simon [13] is classical in this area. The research was prompted by the availability of a computer by means of which they were able to demonstrate the underlying theory of simulating the processes. The initial work by Newell, Shaw, and Simon [13] concerned proving theorems in symbolic logic. The logic theorist (LT) was a computer program which simulated the processes through which an individual would solve a problem through the application of symbolic logic. The problem-solving task was to select a path that leads to a given theorem. Applying heuristics, the program develops the sequence toward solution backwards—working each step and establishing a rule for the successes or failures as encountered. Such heuristics could then be represented in a computer program wherein the process is simulated. In this way, Newell, Shaw, and Simon derived ideas about how humans attempt to solve problems.

The work by Newell and his colleagues has been extended. For example, application of the principles to geometry [14] and to calculus [15] have also been attempted. In general, the studies on problem solving point out the revolutionary effect the computer has had and is continuing to have on the methods used in the behavioral sciences. The level or detail and initial analysis of the phenomena required to elicit the greatest effectiveness from the computer in the study of behavioral phenomena is quite explicit.

Related to problem solving is *game theory*. It is based largely on the mathematical work of Von Neumann [16]. The theory of games applies statistical logic to the choice of strategies (*Columbia Encyclopedia*, p. 792). In games there is some measure of conflict; an adversary. The objective is to engage in moves leading to a particular goal according to specifically established rules. The chess game has been used by Simon [12] and others to demonstrate the behavior of a game player and subsequently simulating such behavior on the computer to validate the underlying logic for each of the moves in question. A number of computer programs of this kind have been developed. To date, no computer program, however, has been devised which can successfully match behavior as indicated by a human player.

The application of the computer directly to the behavior of the human in problem solving has been attempted Newell and Simon [17]. The General Problem Solver (1959) is a program which systematically, through a set of routines, analyzes the differences between a set of stimulus presentations (usually alphanumeric forms or symbols). Each step in a series of steps to a specific behavioral goal involves the analysis of features of such presentations. The individual's response to the presentation indicates whether or not the response was correct to the ultimate goal. Subgoals within subgoals to goals are generated in the process. The steps and procedures are then formulated into a computer program for the validation of the logic underlying the action taken.

Perception

Perceptual theory concerns the organization of sensory data for cognitive functioning. Perceptual theory covers the broad range of sensory operations, namely, the various sensory mechanisms and processes; and attempts to link these to learning, thinking, and concept formation; and in a broader scope to human cognitive and intellectual development. Of direct interest is pattern and form recognition, which computer scientists find of direct interest whether in connection with artificial intelligence or recognition of form by whatever means (e.g., photoprints and facsimiles).

Theories of perception come in many forms, and the focus of the theory depends essentially on the interest as to the nature of the stimulus and response, respectively. The organization of sensory input has been the major emphasis of gestaltists who propose that the perceptual response is a function of all of the elements in the environment impinging on the sensory mechanisms. Other perceptual theorists assume a more structuralist position by emphasizing the importance of specific characteristics of the stimulus (form) in deriving the perception [53, 54].

Theories of perception find comfortable expression in both computer and behavioral circles in the interest centering around machine pattern recognition. The question is how to build a machine that could display some of the capabilities that man does in identifying forms or patterns. One theory applies *statistics* to pattern recognition, assuming that each spatial element of a form or pattern has a certain probability for scanning. Each of the responses to the respective elements or segments would culminate to the final response which would be the identification of the form. The statistical expression would account for the differences among the different segments of the total form. Another theory concentrates on feature *analysis*. This is generally applied to the differences found in alphanumeric characters or handwriting profiles. The concept is to apply a template matching operation where the features of any form are assessed for correspondence. Of course, the cardinal problem is the range of variance with which the matching system can contend. There are alternate means, of course, which can be applied, such as serial as well as parallel processing of form detail and feature counting upon which ultimate decisions can be made. Computer programs have been successfully developed. To date, machines have not been able to tell us much about man's perceptual behavior—particularly about pattern or form recognition. What has been achieved is the capability of some computer programs to do some things man can successfully do with his visual sense.

Decision Theory

Computers have been seen as aids to management, particularly in respect to planning and control of operations. Central to this relationship of computers to management is decision theory. Decision theory attempts to relate the manner in which individuals apply past experiences and available information to situations where alternative actions are possible. Decision theory encompasses many of the aspects of the other theories included in human information processing (e.g., learning and perception).

Because of the breadth of the subject matter, it is only possible to include those highlights which relate decision theory to specific reference to the computer. Excellent reviews of the entire scope of the decision theory literature are available [18, 19, 55].

The dimensions of decision theory that deal essentially with behavior and to which the computer has been used as a modeling, simulation tool are the following:

1. The selection of alternatives that minimize loads and maximize gain; namely, utility [20–22].
2. The influence of past experiences in the individual's judgment, the probability of occurrences, and the selection of courses of actions according to this estimate.
3. The application of strategies in games involving moves (as in chess) where minimal strategies can be applied [12, 23, 24].
4. "Real life" situations where the decision maker is faced with making risk-oriented actions, such as the selection of stock, or where the selection of a course of action is dependent on an assessment of highly interrelated riskful alternatives as found in military command-control situations.

Information Retrieval

The term "information retrieval" may possess different connotations depending on what one considers "information" to be, or what one intends information to be. Psychologists would likely consider information retrieval to be a subject of learning theory as discussed in short-term or long-term memory. In this case what is retrieved is presumably some form of the stimulus generated by the environment, transmitted by the sensory apparatus, and stored in some part of the brain (metaphorically). For some information professionals, particularly librarians and/or documentalists, information may represent a document, a record, or a book, in which case information retrieval is the logistics engaged in "ordering" (placement) the books in some physical space and providing some identity (classification code) for its location to insure its quick retrieval upon demand of a user of such a commodity. Similarly, librarians and/or documentalists may consider "information" retrieval to be "fact," "data" retrieval. In "data retrieval" some specific fact or statement contained in the media (book, record, etc.) is searched and delivered upon demand of a user.

Information retrieval theory can be considered as essentially classification theory inasmuch as the main ingredients of the position attempt to relate the *means* and the *methods* for search of data or information to the nature of the ordering algorithm. The theory proposes to align the classification algorithm with retrieval effectiveness based on some criterion of relevancy of the document pursued and delivered based on the needs of the user.

Information retrieval theory has had its widest application to computers in the generation of computer programs which attempt to study the processes underlying question formulation behavior for document retrieval. These programs establish the possibility of assessing the behavior of the user of information on-line [25].

Another aspect of information retrieval theory which ties behavior to computers is data base structure.

Inasmuch as the computer can provide the possibility of numerous arrangements of data within it, some theory of the optimization of such data so as to maximize human behavior would seem desirable. In this connection, information retrieval theory finds its expression in file structure optimization. Distinctions are made between time-sharing and batch processing systems, and evaluations concerning the retrieval effectiveness of each in relation to the file structure involved are advanced [26].

Data Organization

Data organization refers to the manner in which different alphanumeric codes or lines are placed spatially, temporally arranged, and presented. To the best of the author's knowledge, no theory presently exists which directly deals with principles of data organization optimization other than that which is inherent in mathematical theory. But data organization is of direct interest to behavioral science as well as to computer science because of its pertinence to the man–machine interaction. Of relevance is the effort by the M.I.T. group [27] who pioneered in computer graphics and particularly in the development of the "sketch pad" technique, where the computer permits the user to sketch alternate geometric configurations as likely to be encountered in a number of engineering enterprises (e.g., airflow profiles, architectural configurations, and mechanical designs).

There is one aspect of data organization in which a "theory" may be considered to exist, namely, in perception. Gestalt theory had its birth at the turn of the century and asserted that stimuli operate interactively with each other—each influencing each, but that the sum was not really the sum of its part, but greater than its parts. Gestalt theory is advanced through experiments on human visual processes, particularly in relation to form and pattern-recognition behavior. Computer simulation of varying shifts in pattern movement and configuration presented on electronic displays permits the study of numerous behavioral variables which would not ordinarily be possible with static displays.

Man–Machine Symbiosis

Although not so considered, man–machine symbiosis may be deemed a theory if indeed the basic formulation of such a theory is the proposition that laws exist that govern the extension of human functioning through machine, and that the ultimate state is man and machine in synchrony. Man–machine symbiosis finds clear expression in *human factors engineering,* where optimization of human functioning via machine design and operation is the ultimate goal. Simulation of environmental states through the computer to determine the character of human performance under various conditions of stress have been extensively applied (as in aircraft piloting) [28, 29]. The original concept of man–machine symbiosis [1] was an attempt to realize the means wherein the computer could augment man's motion and cognitive capabilities. The researchers representing the Stanford group have applied the concept to the augmentation of human intellect [30], and others concerned with other aspects of human behavior (learning, training) have similarly applied the concept of man–machine symbiosis as found in the University of Illinois extensive work in computer-aided instruction.

COMPUTER AND MEASUREMENT OF BEHAVIOR

Data Facilitation

Organismic behavior yields data at the macro- as well as at the microlevel. The collection of data is a limiting factor in most attempts to understand behavior because of the variance incurred in the recording of response and the time delays that are experienced in the accumulation of the data. Computers enable the programming of collection and recording mechanisms, thus reducing possible human error both in the recording of responses and the way the responses are presented for study. Because in experimentation on organisms the sensitivity of the measure used in the experiment is often vital in eliciting a meaningful response, computers provide access to the recording of the response at the microlevel often not available by other means. Of particular importance, computers provide the possibility of real time manipulation of data, thus enabling the experimenter to test and validate different dimensions of one hypothesis or to alter the hypothesis for theoretical formulation.

Statistical Analysis of Behavior

The normative nature of behavior often requires large sampling procedures. The volume of data is often prohibitive for the quick analysis of results. Computers facilitate statistical analysis of the results from such samples. Yet, computers are valuable in other matters pertaining to sample structure. In many instances the dimensions of the variables under study as well as the sample composition do not lend themselves to satisfy the usual assumptions of normative statistics. In the latter case, statistical analysis require nonparametric analysis. Computers provide a greater capability to deal with nonparametric analysis. Similarly, factor analysis, a statistical method for eliciting the relative influence of organismic variables among a wide range of variables, has achieved greater use and sophistication in its application to the study of behavior through the computer.

Scaling Techniques

The nature of behavior is such that measurement techniques as well as the philosophy underlying measurement play a very important part in the disciplines that deal with behavior. Stevens [31] defines measurement: "Measurement is the assignment of numerals to events or objects according to rule." Scaling is a type of measurement that assigns numbers to objects or events (e.g., ordinal, nominal, interval, and ratio). Scaling techniques are part of statistical analytical operations. Scaling is fundamental in the study of behavior because of the difficulty of obtaining absolute values of the variables that influence behavior either directly or indirectly. Consequently, the use of a scale may be the only recourse available to the scholar in understanding the position of the event or function in the phenomena he is attempting to understand. Scaling operations may vary from simple arithmetic treatment of data to rather sophisticated manipulations involving higher mathematics. In either case, the computer has been exceedingly beneficial in expediting experimental results which require scaling operations, as well as providing new approaches to scaling problems [56].

BEHAVIOR AND COMPUTERS

Stimulus Generation

Computers serve as mechanisms for the generation of stimuli used in the study of behavior. The stimulus may assume any physical form capable of inciting the organism's sensory mechanism (e.g., visual, tactual, auditory, olfactory, and kinesthetic). The computer is programmed to generate the required excitation based on study or experimental requirements. For example, in studies conducted by B. F. Skinner [32] the subject is provided a reinforcement (a pellet of food) to a response (bar pressing). The episode of the bar press may be recorded by the computer; the delivery of the pellet to the subject may similarly be regulated and governed by the computer which functions in accordance with the wishes of the investigator.

Stimulus generation has a wider connation to behavior than the delivery of some external physical event capable of inducing a response in the organism. The computer has been discussed as capable of generating complex reactions (e.g., chess playing where the computer serves the role of an opponent) for which the reaction in such cases serves as stimulus requiring a response or counter response [17].

Response Data Representation

When a subject responds to a physical stimulus or event (e.g., shock, food, light, and sound), the reaction of the subject to the stimulus or event is recorded. The way that the reaction is recorded may be in many forms (e.g., hard copy and digital readout on CRT). The computer serves to extend the many ways that the response data may be represented for the study of behavioral phenomena (e.g., computer graphics, color, and alphanumerics).

Pattern Analysis

Patterns in data can be discerned, of course, through statistical analysis. Computers can considerably facilitate the process through programs directed at orthogonally rotating variables in rapid sequence, or by applying mathematical formulations to the data which would otherwise be prohibitive through the application of manual techniques.

Model Construction

Previously it was indicated that personality could be studied through the computer by simulating personality dimensions and related variables. Much of this simulation, of course, is dependent on the establishment of conceptual models. Such models have been generated to deal with learning and cognition [12, 57]. Many models of perception have been attempted [33–35]. Brain functioning models have also been discussed [6, 7], and models have been developed to study the nature and behavior of organizations [36]. The literature is rich in the description of the research in these areas.

Conferencing

A recent development in the application of computers to human behavior is computer conferencing [37]. Computer conferencing permits the expression of human response to human issues to be systematically detailed. The expression occurs in a dialog between the individual and the computer approximating a dialectic encounter. The end point of the encounter is the surfacing of a concurrence or lack of concurrence on issues of importance. The conference technique is highly provocative in encouraging arrangements among individuals of varying professional inclinations located both in distance and time apart from each other.

Analysis and Diagnosis

Simulation

Computer technology enables the creation of situations varying in complexities in which specific environmental and behavioral variables can be interjected systematically to determine their functional relation and their influence on other variables. Investigators like Newell and Simon have used the computer to study systematically the manner in which man processes and uses information and making decisions. Other investigators have developed programs which focus on replicating both affective as well as effective human behavior. Some have attempted to develop models of the brain [58] which would then shed light on the functional relationship of the various parts of the brain to human behavior.

Gaming

A game is "an organized play having definite rules and different roles for participants, and usually competitive" [59, p. 220]. Computers permit the generation of programs which attempt to create environmental states wherein individuals can be asked to execute roles which may be in conflict with the roles of others as well as their own. The computer in this case can be delegated the role of the other, interacting with the main player who is guided by the investigator.

War gaming is an essential ingredient in military science, where data are collected on exercises involving opposing forces. The behavior of the participants involved in a simulated or real (field) game can be evaluated quickly by the computer. In this case the computer can act as the generator of the game, the evaluator of the game, or the player(s).

BEHAVIOR AND COMPUTERS

Intelligence Testing

Despite the fact that there is no general agreement as to what constitutes intelligence, there have been a number of advances in the technology of intelligence measurement. These advances have largely enabled a quick assessment of test results through at times ingenious means for the recording and compilation of responses by the computer. Moreover, the computer has played a more decisive role in intelligence testing by its ability to analyze patterns of intelligence behavior that may be highly influenced by geographical-regional, genetic, social, and other variables [38, 60].

Physiological/Psychophysical Experimentation

In the early days of space exploration, the requirement for predicting the relationship between environmental factors and human performance became paramount. Experiments by the military on g forces on aircraft pilot behavior and, later, NASA's studies using monkeys and chimpanzees to determine the influence of high acceleration and nongravity on internal as well as external organismic functioning required sophisticated telemetry to elicit responses from such organisms in space. Where man–space experiments were conducted following these earlier studies, telemetry was used to guide human activity in space as well as to record psychological effects. In all of these instances the computer was an essential tool in the collection of behavioral data as well as an analytical tool that provided quick response data regarding physiological-psychological malfunction.

Computers and behavior have also been linked to the study of the influence of drugs on behavior. Digital computers have studied resting and sleep patterns under various drug (alcohol, molindone) induced conditions. Such studies often use electronic devices (e.g., EEG) to record changes in both physiological and psychological functioning [39, 40, 61].

Exploration of Personality Traits

The use of computers directly to the study of personality has intrigued psychiatrists, clinical psychologists, sociologists, and others. Basically, the general direction of such studies has centered around the simulation of personality—particularly the cognitive (memory, thinking, emotion) aspects [41]. The thrust has been to develop programs that enable the simulation of personality variables: variables that are generally agreed in the field to reflect personalistic dimensions (e.g., inferiority–superiority, anxiety, and motivation). The programs so developed enable the generation of simulation studies based on concepts underlying specific theoretical constructs [56].

Predicting Voter Behavior

Throughout recent years, voter behavior has gained increasing importance to the interests of social and behavioral scientists. Voter behavior is used in the development of theories that bind political–economic and social factors related to changes in the culture and its institutions [42].

Although somewhat biased because of the skewed distribution of the population who actually vote, data from voters represent a rich source for analysis. Because of the large numbers in sample size and the possible behavioral parameters that may be involved, the computer plays an important role in the quick assessment of voter variables. The established polls (Gallup, Roper, Harris, and others) have been quite effective in using the computer in this respect. Consequently, the prediction of voter behavior has almost approached the position of a science. Whether it has achieved this laudable status or not, the prediction success (or failure) has certainly changed in the past decade to the extent that political scientists are more sensitive to the products of such activities.

Content Analysis

Studies of behavior often lead to protocols that consist mainly of verbal reactions of either the subject who is responding to the experimenter or the assessment of the experiments to the subject. The analysis of the content of these reports is difficult and unwieldy. Because the experimenter is often influenced by the analysis procedure, there may be sequential effects that cannot be overcome. Computer analysis of the content of the protocols can be undertaken through the design of specially established programs. In behavioral studies the establishment of computer programs to accomplish the content analysis is more formidable than the behavioral study itself. The reason for this difficulty is that often the hypothetical concepts underlying the functions studied are not understood to the extent that they enable the generation of specific requirements upon which the analytical program will be based.

Language Processing

Language is the technology for the transfer of information communication. The symbols of language as well as their arrangement are part of the technology. Language is often the only means for the behavioral scientist to study behavior. The way that language is used is often critical. Computer analysis of language or computer processing of language has been discussed in regard to the capability of the computer to translate one language to another. For example, considerable work has been done in translating the Russian language to English, with moderate success [62].

BEHAVIOR AND COMPUTERS

APPLICATIONS

Social Functions

Dissemination of Job Information

When shifts in job markets occur, the impact on individuals who are responsible to counsel on job opportunities becomes exceedingly complex and sensitive. Large differences exist in the administrative practices regarding the reporting of occupational vacancies and the educational requirements to meet these vacancies. Consequently, counselors are often misinformed about these positions. Recently, the computer has come to the rescue in facilitating the dissemination of such information to the school counselor [43]. Such dissemination will have an impact in guiding the behavior of high school students in the selection of the appropriate education or training for the vocation most suitable to the individual's interests.

Collective Human Arrangement

Increasing social complexity makes manifest the need for resource sharing. The resource in this sense can be the physical aspects of the environment as well as the capacity and character of the organism that relates to this environment. Physical and organismic (human) resources can be capitalized (extended, formed) as well as depleted. In either case, the behavior of the organism is central to the control of resources. With shrinking resources there are needs for identifying ways that these resources can be shared most effectively. For example, with the energy crisis the need for the conservation of fuel has mandated the establishment of arrangements where individuals with large cars can extend their transportation resource to others who also may possess automobiles but who would be able to relinquish using them by riding with others who may be proceeding to similar destinations. The change in behavior is central to such arrangements. Because the computer can assemble data regarding routes and available vehicles readily, the computer can be seen as facilitating the acceptance of such arrangements. Recently, the computer has also emerged as a mechanism for facilitating human arrangements of a more emotional nature, namely, dating. When linked effectively, computer dating can be a source of human comfort. The computer can be programmed to be sensitive to realistic personality dimensions. When properly applied, a match between the behavioral predispositions of two individuals can be achieved. Psychologists and sociologists are currently attempting to understand the power of such arrangements [44].

Promotion of Social Theories

By and large, the development of social theories have been conceived in "static" dimensions inasmuch as they result in perceptions about social phenomena either completed (historical) or frozen under conditions mandated by the investigator. The computer as a tool for the study of social phenomena first found its expression in the study of large social activities mainly military in character [36]. The computer enables the artificial generation of a large organizational complex wherein social processes established to follow certain set rules could be studied experimentally. Such operations involve highly intricate communicative, procedural arrangements. These arrangements are abstracted to conform to specific study requirements. In other areas the computer has been used as a tool in the study of behavior underlying conflict resolution, and in the simulation of factors that govern international relations and diplomacy.

Training, Planning and Management

Computer-Assisted Instruction

Perhaps in no area has the computer been more directly linked to behavior than in the area of training. Training has reaped great benefits from the computer because of the fortunate circumstance of the emergence of related theory. B. F. Skinner's learning theory, heavily behavioristic in character, provided the impetus for the application of computers to training. Behaviorism as a general system regards behavior as mandated by a linkage between stimulus and response. Behaviorists are concerned with the relation of the stimulus and response and are only marginally interested in the physiological and cognitive underpinnings (emotion, motivation). The later are generally considered as intervening variables. The so-called "Skinner Box" was designed to systematically provide a reinforcement to the subject (initially mice) when the subject pressed a bar. Data were collected which indicated the rate of response was dependent on the experimental variables under study. These data supported the learning theory which predominantly stressed the importance of environmental control (reinforcement). The "Skinner Box" was eventually to be used as the paradigm for the construction of arrangements where the computer and man interfaced in reinforcing sets. The decade from the early sixties to the present is replete with efforts to bring such arrangements (computer-assisted instruction, computer-aided instruction) to formal educational establishments. The movement has achieved a modicum of success, but considerable resistance has been experienced in the acceptance of the conclusion that such instruction is a substitute for the teacher in the formal class situation. Rather, the tendency has been to move in the direction of accepting computer-related instruction as a supplement to formal instruction, with the supplemental form being relegated to relatively routine, well delineable dimensions of instruction which ordinarily would consume some time of the instructor without providing the opportunity for the expression of more personalistic, experiential aspects of teaching [63].

There are other aspects, however, to the computer-assisted instruction movement that have been widely accepted and in which much research is being conducted. Reference is made to the use of computers linked to Braille as an aid to the teaching of the blind and others who may be handicapped in sensory functions. Prosthetics have been linked to computers in enabling individuals to achieve motor-sensory efficiency not possible through other training procedures.

Command-Control

Command-control refers to the arrangement (system) of man and machines, the primary function of which is to enable the direction, regulation, and surveillance of events and resources necessary to man's functioning and survival. Originally, the command and control of events and resources largely depended on man's native sensory capabilities (voice, sight, etc.). On the battlefield, Alexander had a personal view of the battle occurring and directed his troops accordingly. In the early days of the industrial revolution, the owner of a business enterprise had an intimate understanding and knowledge of his operations. Today, most of the military events occur great distances away from individuals responsible for the direction of these events. Similarly, industrial complexes involve operations that are distributed in location. This aspect of remoteness influences decision making, particularly when time considerations such as those experienced in crisis are pertinent. In the latter situations, communications and the processing of data from communication sensors is quite critical. In this regard the computer has been a highly important tool in the development of command and control, and management information systems. The computer facilitates the computation of the likely occurrence of events, and the probable consequence of such events. The data presented on electronic display serve as the basic input to the decision behavior of the general or the business executive. A vast array of literature is now available in addressing this aspect of command and control [64].

Crisis Management

When crisis emerges, the recipient(s) involved in the crisis are expected to respond quickly. The response to crisis is highly dependent on effective communicative devices and a technology that can process the incoming data quickly. For example, alerting population of impending weather conditions (tornadoes, hurricanes, floods) very often involves highly sensitive decisions concerning dislocations of populations, establishment of expensive countermeasures, etc. Information concerning impending strikes may influence many industrial operations. The occurrence of viral epidemics in one part of the world is of vital concern to those responsible for generating research to counter the onslaughts of the epidemic. In all these instances the behavior of man is quite vulnerable to the amount of data he receives, when he receives it, and how quickly he can process the data that will enable him to make a decision.

In several military crises (Cuban, Gulf of Tonkin, etc.), the outcomes (in terms of the behavior of those responsible) were very much dependent on the data processing (computer) capabilities of the military establishment.

Computer-Assisted Diagnosis

Several systems are now available for the diagnosis of several organic (cancer, heart) and functional (psychological) maladies. These systems enable the collection of symptoms directly from the patient, and their transmittance to a centralized, data processing center. The report is quickly transmitted (through communication links) to the physician or investigator. The physician or investigator may benefit from the state of the patient previously recorded or processed. The system may also provide the capability of comparing the results to other patients with similar physical or psychiatric symptoms. The latter systems are now in early development. The need for such systems is not questioned although reservations exist as to their possible effectiveness in altering the behavioral habits of physicians who have been trained to depend on classical approaches to diagnosis. As in command and control, the computer is often regarded as assuming the perogatives of the decision maker.

Retrieval of Knowledge

The significant increase in publications experienced in the last three decades has created a dilemma to man. Knowledge is highly desirable to man's purpose and survival. Man's behavior is directly linked to how much he knows and how he applies it. Yet, an increase in the amount of knowledge available to him may represent a debilitating effect. In order for knowledge to be useful to man, it should be readily accessible to him. The knowledge he receives, through whatever access system, needs to be relevant to his purpose. Present indications are that retrieval systems are not commensurate to the demands that are placed on them [45]. There are many unsolvable problems that deal with the ability to predict what knowledge should be acquired for ready accessibility, to determine the behavioral ingredients that are the basis for judging whether the retrieval of a document is indeed relevant to the users needs, etc. In all these matters, the computer has played a decisive role in altering the way we classify and access knowledge. Vast stores of knowledge can be placed in the computer for ready accessability. Such data bases are now available to scientists to be used in the course of their investigations. National computerized networks of data bases are now being considered for the storage of technical information. These developments will undoubtedly influence the behavior of the user of the library and, in general, the user of knowledge.

IMPACT OF COMPUTERS ON BEHAVIOR

The literature is rich in the discussion of the possible influence that computers may extend on the individual, the culture, and society at large [46,

47]. The importance of the role of the computer has been the subject of wide interest and investigation by the Conference Board [48] of New York, an organization consisting of leading industrialists, governmental representatives, and scientists.

Where the impact of computers on behavior is discussed, what is generally inferred is the psychological effect that computers have on man's performance, and the impact of the computer on organizational behavior, namely, the influence of the computer on organizational management and operation. The impact of computers in both of these contexts has been studied by a number of investigators [65,66]. The psychological effects have been summarized as representing a strong reservation and even fear of the acceptance of the computer lest it interfere with the motivation and career goals of the individual [48]. The organizational effects relate to the decentralization and centralization of function with the resultant changes in the way that the individuals in the organization see themselves.

Of considerable import to the issue of computers and human behavior is the instigation of the violation to personal integrity that such machines imply. Matters such as individual privacy and confidentiality, that computers seem to invade, have surfaced as major issues of national concern. The proliferation of data banks on personal histories, easy access to such data banks with concomitant problems of computer security, and the elicitation by governmental agencies of highly clandestine data stored in computers (via census data, IRS records, etc.) have clearly pointed to the fact that computers may indeed influence the life of each member of society—perhaps not favorably.

But computers may relate to behavior indirectly (or perhaps directly, depending on how you perceive the matter). The possibility of a cash-less society promoted by sophisticated banking arrangements, the diagnosis of maladjustments both in mental or physical health, self-paced education through computer-generated programs available at residences, and computer community car pools all influence the action of individuals and dramatize emphatically the possible role of computers on the behavior of humans in future generations [66, 67].

REFERENCES

1. J. C. R. Licklider, Man machine symbiosis, *IRE Trans. Hum. Factors Electron.* **2**(1), 4–11 (March 1960).
2. H. H. Goldstein, *The Computer from Pascal to Von Neumann,* Princeton University Press, Princeton, New Jersey, 1972.
3. J. T. Tou (ed.), *Advances in Information System Science,* Plenum, New York, 1969.
4. W. S. McCulloch and W. Pitts, A logical calculus of the ideas in management in nervous activity, *Bull. Math. Biophy.* **5,** 115–137 (1943).
5. U. Neisser, *Cognitive Psychology,* Appleton-Century-Crofts, New York, 1967.
6. M. A. Arbib, *The Metaphonical Brain,* Wiley, New York, 1973.

7. M. Cunningham, *Intelligence: Its Organization and Development,* Academic, New York, 1972.
8. M. R. Quillian, *Semantic Memory,* Technical Report AFCRL66-189, Bolt Beranek and Newman, Cambridge, Massachusetts, 1966.
9. E. R. Hilgard and G. H. Bower, *Theories of Learning,* Appleton-Century-Crofts, New York, 1956.
10. E. Thorndike, *Human Learning,* M.I.T. Press, Cambridge, Massachusetts, 1931.
11. R. V. Guthrie (ed.), *Psychology in the World Today: An Interdisciplinary Approach,* Addison-Wesley, Reading, Massachusetts, 1968.
12. H. A. Simon, A note on mathematical models for learning. *Psychometrika* **27,** 417–418 (1962).
13. A. Newell, J. C. Shaw, and H. A. Simon, Elements of a theory of human problem solving, *Psychol. Rev.* **65,** 151–166 (1958).
14. H. Gelernter, Realization of a geometry theorem proving machine, in *1959 International Conference on Information Processing,* UNESCO, Paris, 1959, pp. 273–282.
15. J. Slagle, A Computer Program for Solving Freshman Calculus (Saint), Doctoral Dissertation, Massachusetts Institute of Technology, 1961.
16. J. Von Neumann, *The Computer and the Brain,* Yale University Press, New Haven, Connecticut, 1958.
17. A. Newell and H. A. Simon, *Human Problem Solving,* Prentice-Hall, Englewood Cliffs, New Jersey, 1972.
18. W. Edwards and A. Tuersky (eds.), *Decision Making,* Penguin, Hammondsworth, England, 1967.
19. R. D. Luce and P. Suppes, Pererence, utility and subjective probability, in *Handbook of Mathematical Psychology,* Vol. 3 (R. D. Luce, R. R. Baugh, and E. Galanter, eds.), Wiley, New York, 1965.
20. E. Kauder, Genesis of the marginal utility theory from Aristotle to the end of the eighteenth century, *Econ. J.* **63,** 638–650 (1953).
21. G. J. Stigler, The development of utility theory, *J. Polit. Econ.* **58,** 307–327, 373–396 (1950).
22. J. Viner, The utility concept in value theory and its critics, *J. Polit. Econ.* **33,** 369–387, 638–659 (1925).
23. I. Kister, P. Stein, S. Wain, W. Walden, and M. Wells, Experiments in chess, *J. Assoc. Comput. Mach.* **4,** 174–177 (1957).
24. A. M. Turing, On computable numbers, with an application to the entscheidung problem, *Proc. London Math. Soc. (Ser. Z)* **42,** 230–265 (1936).
25. F. W. Lancaster and E. G. Fazen, *Information Retrieval On Line,* Melville, Los Angeles, 1973.
26. K. L. Montgomery, *Document Retrieval Systems: Factors Affecting Search Time,* Dekker, New York, 1975.
27. I. E. Sutherland, Computer inputs and outputs, in *Information* (D. Flanagan, ed.), Freeman, San Francisco, 1966.
28. G. E. Briggs, *Brasuit and Compensory Models of Information Display: A Review,* USAF, AMRL, TBR 62-93, August 1962.
29. P. M. Fitts, Engineering psychology and equipment design, in *Handbook of Experimental Psychology* (S. S. Stevens, ed.), Wiley, New York, 1964.
30. S. L. Englebardt, *Computers,* Pyramid, New York, 1962.
31. S. S. Stevens, Mathematics, measurement and psychophysics, in *Handbook of Experimental Psychology* (S. S. Stevens, ed.), Wiley, New York, 1964.
32. B. F. Skinner, *Cumulative Record,* rev. ed., Appleton, New York, 1961.

33. O. Selfridge, Pandemonium: A paradigm for learning, in *Proceedings of the Symposium on the Mechanism of the Thought Processes* (D. V. Blake and A. M. Uttley, eds.), H.M.S.O., London, 1959, pp. 511–529.
34. M. Minsky, Artificial intelligence. *Sci. Amer.* **215**, 246–263 (1966).
35. L. Uhr, Pattern recognition computers as models for form perception, *Psychol. Bull.* **60**, 40–73 (1963).
36. B. K. Rome and S. C. Rome, Levianthan: A simulation of behavioral systems to operate pymairically on a common language for machine searching and translation, in *Symposium on Mechanization of Thorough Processes* (D. V. Blake and A. M. Utterly, eds.), National Physical Laboratory, Teddington, England, H.M.S.O., London, 1959.
37. M. Turoff, Introduction to Delphi, in *Information Science: Search for Identity* (A. Debons, ed.), Dekker, New York, 1974, pp. 221–224.
38. D. Paitich, Computers in behavioral science: A comprehensive automated psychological examination and report, *Behav. Sci.* **18**(2), 131–136 (March 1973).
39. T. Itil et al., Digital computer analyzed resting and sleep EEG investigations and clinical changes during molindone treatment, *J. Psychiat. Res.* **9**(1), 45–49 (December 1971).
40. K. L. H. Ting et al., Applications of artificial intelligence: Relationship between mass spectra and pharmacological activity of drugs, *Science* **180**(4084), 417–420 (April 1973).
41. S. S. Tomkins and S. Messick, *Computer Simulation of Personality*, Wiley, New York, 1962.
42. J. S. Lee and A. Kronberg, A computer simulation model of multi party parliametry recruitment, *Simulation and Games* **4**(1), 37–58 (March 1973).
43. P. Equi and H. Donnan, A system for computer dissemination of occupational information, *School Counselor* **19**(4), 271–274 (March 1972).
44. C. Byrne, C. R. Ervin, and J. Lamberith, Continuity between the experimental study of attraction and real-life computer dating. *J. Pers. Soc. Psychol.* **16**, 157–165 (1970).
45. A. Kent, Unsolvable problems, in *Information Science: Search for Identity* (A. Debons, ed.), Dekker, New York, 1974.
46. C. C. Gotlieb, *Social Issues in Computing*, Academic, New York, 1973.
47. A. Toffler, *Future Shock*, Random House, New York, 1970.
48. The Conference Board, *Information Technology: Some Critical Implications for Decision Makers*, New York, 1972.
49. H. Borko, *Computer Applications in the Behavioral Sciences*, Prentice-Hall, Englewood Cliffs, New Jersey, 1962.
50. B. F. Green, Jr., *Digital Computers in Research. An Introduction for Behavioral and Social Scientists*, McGraw-Hill, New York, 1963.
51. H. Sackman, *Computers, System Science, and Evolving Society: The Challenge of Man-Machine Digital Systems*, Wiley, New York, 1967.
52. E. A. Feigenbaum and J. Feldman, *Computers and Thought*, McGraw-Hill, New York, 1963.
53. D. H. Owen and D. R. Brown, Visual and tactual form complexity: A psychophysical approach to perceptual equivalence, *Percept. Psychophys.* **7**, 225–228 (1970).
54. I. Pollack, Methodological examination of the PEST (Parametric Estimation by Sequential Testing) procedure, *Percept. Psychophys.* **3**, 285–289 (1968).

55. A. Rapoport and T. J. Wallsten, Individual decision behavior, *Ann. Rev. Psychol.* **23,** 131–176 (1972).
56. J. C. Lingoes, A Fortran IV (G) program for Guttman-Lingoes conjoint measurement, *Behav. Sci.* **17,** 1333–1334 (1972).
57. B. W. White, Recognition of distorted melodies, *Am. J. Psychol.* **73,** 100–107 (1960).
58. W. R. Ashby, *Design for a Brain,* rev. ed., Wiley, New York, 1960.
59. H. B. English and A. C. English, *A Comprehensive Dictionary of Psychological and Psychoanalytical Terms,* Longmans, Green, London, 1958.
60. J. J. Hedc, H. F. O'Neil, and D. N. Hansen, Affective reactions toward computer-based intelligence testing, *J. Consult. Clin. Psychol.* **40**(2), 217–222 (April 1973).
61. S. D. Kalen and E. B. Swint, The present status of computer technology and its application areas among psycho physiologists with five year projections, *J. Psychophysiol.* **10**(2), 186–190 (March 1973).
62. R. F. Simmons, S. Klien, and K. McConologue, *Towards the Synthesis of Human Language Behavior,* SDC, SP-466, Santa Monica, California, 1961.
63. B. R. Gaines, The learning of perceptual materials by men and machines and its relationship to training, *Instruct. Sci.* **1**(3), 263–312 (October 1972).
64. A. Debons, Command and control: Technology and social impact, *Adv. Comput.* **11,** 319–390 (1971).
65. A. Debons, R. Mitchell, and W. Furdell, *The Effects of Automated Data Processing on Naval Command,* NRL, ONR Report N00014-66-C0283-A01, 1966.
66. C. A. Myers, (ed.), *The Impact of Computers in Management,* M.I.T. Press, Cambridge, Massachusetts, 1967.
67. J. Weizenbaum, On the impact of the computer on society, *Science* **176,** 609 (May 12, 1972).

Anthony Debons

BELGIUM, COMPUTERS IN

Commentators of the events of the last decade have often used the most lyrical terms to describe what they call "the computer revolution." It is also customary to evaluate the situation of computer science in a particular country by trying to evaluate the extent to which this country follows a development scheme used in the United States; such expressions as "from the point of view of technology, such a country is 3 or 4 years behind the United States" reflect of this evaluation method. Drawing up comparative tables of the number of computers per inhabitant or per corporation may lead to a series of quantitative ratios, but is this sufficient to give a full view of the computer scene in a country?

Our view is different. We think that the way a country introduces the production and the use of hardware and software into its economic system mainly depends on a series of characteristics peculiar to each country. We intend to determine the situation of computer science in Belgium from the point of view of production use and teaching.

PRODUCTION OF HARDWARE

Some United States firms (Burroughs, Memorex) have set up factories in Belgium for assembling central units and peripheral devices. However, there is no typically national production, except for input–output teletypewriters. This gap is not due to a lack of production capacity or to a lack of intellectual power, as is proved by the adoption by the European consortium UNIDATA (grouping Siemens, Philips, and the French company CII) of a system completely developed in Belgium by a Belgian company, the M.B.L.E. (Manufacture Belge de Lampes et Matériel Electronique); this system is commercialized under the name Unidata 7-720.

Belgium is a highly industrialized country; consumer goods and equipment represent 42% of its exports. Belgium is also an exporting country; the gross amount of its exports is nearly half the gross amount of Japanese exports (i.e., the total amount, not the amount per inhabitant[1]). However, Belgian firms have always preferred selling goods whose maintenance is the responsibility of the purchaser (individual weapons, for example) or whose after-sale maintenance involves only supervision and coordination by the seller.

This second category includes the supply of factories *clé sur porte*: in this market, the engineering and research department of "Traction et Electricité" (energy production), "Coppee-Rust" (chemical equipment) and "groupe Empain" (food industries) do particularly well. Actually, Belgian industry does not supply machines whose purchasing depends on the existence of a maintenance service *au jour le jour*.

Such industrial activity is condemned from the start because the narrowness of the national market (9 million inhabitants) would never enable a company whose major profit comes from foreign branches to resist a profit decrease due to any modification in exchange rates or too large an increase of import taxes. (For example, imagine what the plight of Volkswagen would be after the dollar devaluation if it did not have its home market of 50 million consumers).

On the other hand, Belgian law is relatively strict, so that the legalities of failures and bankruptcies is intricate enough to discourage any investor from planning an operation of the "météorite" type. The risk of having to answer for the recklessness that leads to bankruptcy deters the proliferation of enterprises whose chances of survival are low.

This explains the sales policy of M.B.L.E. which has tried to create its own

---

[1] The value of Belgium exports still reaches nearly half the value of the exports of Japan, and nearly reaches half the total exports of Great Britain. It represents 27% of United States exports (Federation des Industries Belges, June 1973).

production systems. Since the 1960s, through its fundamental research center (M.B.L.E. Research Laboratory), this company has been able to develop sufficient "know-how" to sustain the efforts of its development centers. The commercialization of its first system by Unidata, which uses both Siemens and Philips as its commercial organization, is the result of several years investment in research and development.

Belgium has no national military program ambitious enough to sustain fundamental and applied research work. Neighboring countries (Britain, France) have been able to help their national industries by their ambitions as nuclear powers. The only way the Belgian government helps in the production of hardware is by a "contrat de progrès," the beneficiaries of which are presently Siemens and Philips. In short, the government is required to acquire Siemens or Philips informational systems rather than those of other manufacturers if these companies set up their production unit in Belgian territory.

Other companies (A.C.E.C. and SAIT Electronics) supply control systems for industrial production by using central units purchased from other manufacturers.

Belgian companies have proved very cautious as far as national production of informational systems is concerned, and this cautiousness has often been interpreted as proof of obsolescence and a lack of initiative. The ups and downs of firms that, unlike the small Belgian market, may count on the vast market of important government contracts, may perhaps explain the attitude of Belgian industry.

Would a Belgian firm have been able to face a challenge that neither Bull, nor General Electric, nor RCA has been able to meet? The Danish firm Regentcentralen, which operates in circumstances rather similar to those a Belgian firm would have experienced, has been obliged to slow down its production of central units.

The only way out was to conceive and manufacture a product that others would be very happy to sell; the long goal of the M.B.L.E. is the carrying out of this strategy.

PRODUCTION OF SOFTWARE

Since 1973, Siemens and Burroughs have set up software development centers which develop the "operating systems" of their future equipment. For its part, M.B.L.E. produces various basic and applied softwares; it makes the best of the experiences of its research laboratory which finished an implementation of ALGOL 68 in 1973 and has carried out advanced studies on syntactic analyzers, on code optimization, and on the numerous problems brought by the operating systems (virtual memory, deadlock, synchronization of parallel processes, etc.).

A few firms develop general purpose programs for stock management, bookkeeping, and the management of industrial processes.

BELGIUM, COMPUTERS IN

USE OF COMPUTER SCIENCE

Manufacturers and heads of the Belgian governmental offices have not been enthusiastic about the introduction of computers into their management methods. The cost and rentability problem has always enabled them to reject the adoption (on the grounds that they were premature) of management systems which their promoters praised.

In fact, the computer made its way into business by quietly replacing punchcard equipment which was depreciated. The extension of its use into other fields (PERT planning, process control, etc.) was more complex and slower. Indeed, most companies had to resort to other firms (or to the manufacturers of the machines) for the study, the starting up, and the maintenance of these new applications, and this was a threat to their liberty of action and their independence. Since giving up their special applications was no solution, there was nothing left to do but to admit them (including the outside interference) and thus develop inside the company the possibility of regaining control.

The particular structure of the Belgian industrial world permitted this strategy because most companies depend on one of the two large holding companies: La Société Générale and La Compagnie Bruxelles-Lambert. Owing to the holding company structure, each was not compelled to develop a complete department devoted to computer science; it was enough for the group to possess a general department for the different partners. The Société Générale created the C.I.G., a company which gives employment to nearly 200 people and leases its service to the companies of the Générale group. Where the number or the peculiarity of the application made it necessary, some companies created their own research center for computer projects; e.g., the "department d'études de la SGB" which develops operational research banking applications.

On the governmental level, the most important achievements have been the setting up of a national card-index which groups administrative data (nonconfidential in principle, e.g., civil status and retirement number) of all the inhabitants of the country and the real time control of pollution and the flow of the Belgian hydrographical network. This application is meant to save water, a scarce commodity for 9 million inhabitants living on 35,000 square kilometers.

The use of computer science methods has reached the point where the man in the street can no longer ignore their existence; e.g., a "rationalization" of banking systems has replaced the five figures code of their bank accounts by a new system with twelve figures!

THE TEACHING OF COMPUTER SCIENCE

As everywhere else, some institutes thrive on the promise to teach all the mysteries of programming and give access to the highest paying jobs. A few technical schools also grant programmer certificates.

As far as computer companies are concerned, one example is IBM's European System Research Institute whose aim is to train personnel for the European branches of IBM and possibly their customers.

Universities have moved very cautiously, and computer science was admitted only after it had proved it could be a science. The organization of computer science courses is quite recent in most universities. The existence of a computing center did not necessarily involve the creation of a computer science curriculum.

In general, computer science courses must (or may) be taken by students in certain fields (mathematics, applied science, physics, economics, etc.). Most universities list the courses together, and they lead to a postgraduate certificate in computer science. There is the possibility of following a special curriculum in computer science in some universities, and the result is a "licencié en informatique" degree.

CONCLUSION

There was no computer science revolution in Belgium. Computers are there, but their appearance was noiseless, without foolish hope, but also without flourish! People have learned to live with them smoothly but also ungrudgingly.

Students cautiously follow some computer science courses if they have an opportunity; middle aged executives do likewise; everywhere people felt "that it might be useful."

The setting up was slow and hushed, and it caused no social problems. Any lyrical description of the "new industrial revolution" of computer science is a meaningless piece of rhetoric for the Belgian ear. Banks and insurance companies have long since given up putting computers in the windows of their branches; the halting movement of tape drives and the old washing machine shuddering of the disk storage units no longer catch the attention of passersby.

Thus, no revolution, but a hardly noticed change. And owing to this unobtrusiveness, a lasting change.

D. Ribbens and P. de Marneffe

BELL LABORATORIES

INTRODUCTION

Bell Laboratories, with headquarters in Murray Hill, New Jersey, has been the research and development branch of the Bell System of telephone companies since Bell Labs was organized in 1925. The company has made many contributions to data processors, hardware techniques, software systems, and computer applications. Bell Labs uses data-processing techniques extensively in its research and development programs, and in the telecommunications and business information systems it designs for the Bell System.

At the beginning of the modern computer age, Bell Laboratories' long experience in the technology of telephone switching systems, digital encoders, and transmission equipment put the company in a unique position for pioneer work in data handling. Telephone switching systems are digital devices; telephone transmission systems were, and still mostly are, analog. Bell Labs was thus specially fitted to contribute to the evolution of both digital and analog data processors.

THE DEVELOPMENT OF COMPUTERS

Relay Switching Systems

In the early 1900s Bell System engineers started the development of switching equipment that could process telephone calls automatically. An important part of the panel switching system [1] developed in the 1920s was its network of electromechanical relays. Relays are binary devices—they are either "off" or "on"—and in the panel system relays were used to form common-control equipment that set up and disconnected telephone calls. Two common-control units, the register-sender and the decoder, were relay circuits based on ideas advanced by E. C. Molina and his associates. The circuits accepted dialed telephone numbers, translated them to another numbering system, and stored the digits temporarily while the switching system set up the phone connection. A rudimentary form of error checking was used in this common-control equipment.

In the 1930s Bell Labs continued the evolution of telephone switching by designing the first of several systems based on the crossbar switch. Crossbar systems [2] have an efficient common-control subsystem built around relay circuits called "markers." Each switching system had several markers; each marker had as many as 2000 relays and probably represented the most complex relay circuits of the era.

Designing telephone relay circuits was at first a highly subjective art, successfully practiced by engineers who had a knack for it. But in 1937, Claude E. Shannon showed that Boolean algebra, described in 1847 by the English mathematician George Boole, could be used in the design of these circuits [3]. Shannon's work started a process that eventually changed relay-circuit design from an art to a science [4]. Originally applied to logic circuits in telephone switching, Boolean algebra has become a working tool for people who design computer circuits. A. W. Horton and W. H. T. Holden followed up Shannon's work with patents for two basic logic circuits. Horton's OR circuit (1941) and Holden's AND circuit (1942) were patented as part of Bell Labs' development of switching equipment.

The Complex Number Calculator

George R. Stibitz, another mathematician at Bell Laboratories, depended on desk calculators to solve complicated mathematical problems. As a way to save labor and time, Stibitz, in 1937, designed a unit called the Complex Number Calculator, subsequently built by Samuel B. Williams, an experienced switching engineer. The machine had 450 relays and 10 crossbar switches to perform mathematical operations in binary form, and it could find the quotient of two eight-place complex numbers in about 30 sec [5]. The calculator could be reached through three teletypewriter keyboards, and both calculator and keyboards (Fig. 1) were in the Bell Labs building at 463 West Street, New York City. This system, which went into operation on January 8, 1940, formed the first computing system with remote, multiple access.

On September 11, 1940, Bell Labs introduced the Complex Number Calculator to a meeting of the American Mathematical Society at Dartmouth College. To demonstrate the capabilities of the machine, a teletypewriter was set up in the lecture hall and connected to the calculator in New York. After Stibitz had described the computer, members of the audience were invited to try it out by typing problems through the teletypewriter keyboard. The demonstration equipment formed a system in which the computer was accessed over a long-distance data link.

World War II Digital Computers

World War II speeded Bell Labs' developments in computing technology [6]. The Complex Number Calculator, which remained in operation until 1949, eventually became known as the Model I Relay Computer. Model II, originally called the Relay Interpolator, was designed by Stibitz for the National Defense Research Council (NDRC). This relay computer produced punched paper tapes which antiaircraft artillerymen used as input to run dynamic tests on their fire-control equipment. Model II received its input on loops of punched paper tape and had seven registers on which numbers were stored. Its control system recognized 31 instructions, including the addresses of the registers. The machine also had an error-checking capability, designed by Stibitz and based on error-checking used in switching systems, that stopped the computer and sounded an alarm as soon as an error occurred. Model II was

BELL LABORATORIES

Fig. 1. Early digital computer. Bell Laboratories' Model 1 relay digital computer, built in 1939, had two main elements. Computations were done in the racks of relays and switches (above), and problems were entered from remote teletypewriter keyboards (p. 199). Model 1 was an early example of a remote-accessed data-processor.

built under the direction of E. G. Andrews and went into operation in September 1943. It was the first of several special-purpose digital computers designed by Bell Labs for military use during World War II, and was kept in service until 1961.

Models III and IV were also special-purpose machines. Bell Labs designed and built them to solve fire-control problems for land- and ship-mounted guns, but they had 10 registers and could handle many types of problems creditably. Model III, also called the Ballistic Computer, was built for NDRC and was put into operation in June, 1944; NDRC used it until 1958. Tables of numbers were punched onto paper tapes, with each block of table data given an address on the tape. By running the tape forward and backward through a tape reader, Model III could hunt through the tapes for the address of a block of data. Its designers gave it several teletypewriter outputs, several punched-paper inputs, 100% error checking, and a rudimentary form of indexing. By supplying it with problems and instructions, operators could leave it to run by itself at night and on weekends.

Model IV, completed for the Naval Research Laboratory in March 1945, was called the Mark 22 Error Detector by its Navy owners. It was much like the Model III but could calculate trigonometric functions—an important capability when solving ballistic problems for guns mounted on a rolling, pitching warship. The Model IV was taken out of service in 1961.

Bell Labs engineers produced three more digital relay machines. Unlike the special-purpose Models III and IV, the two units designated Model V were general-purpose types designed for the armed forces and used to solve complicated mathematical problems. One machine went into operation at the offices of the National Advisory Committee on Aeronautics in 1946; the other was delivered to the Ballistic Research Laboratory at Aberdeen Proving Ground in 1947. Each Model V had two processors, with access to the system at three or four positions where operators could load problems punched on paper tape. Each position had a tape reader for the input data, as many as five readers for programs of instructions, and up to six readers for loading tables of data into the machine. Permanently wired into the Model Vs were tables of logarithms, exponentials, sines, cosines, and arctangents. Operators of the two machines also had a library of subroutines punched onto loops of paper tape. The Model V computers operated with a floating decimal point—another Stibitz innovation—and performed multiplication by short-cut addition. They could perform automatic roundoff and recognize indeterminate mathematical operations. They also had a conditional transfer capability—made necessary by the frequent use of subroutines from the library of paper-tape loops.

The last of the line of Bell Labs' relay digital computers was the Model VI, put into service in 1950. Like Model I it was built for solving telephone research and development problems. While it was more compact than the two Model V machines, Model VI had several improvements. It had three storage tapes and several hundred semihard-wired subroutines, each of which could be used for problems of the same type with differing numbers of variables. There were also an end-of-numbers check signal and an automatic second-trial feature, which was particularly useful when the machine ran unattended after working hours.

Starting in the mid-1940s, Bell Labs switching engineers developed an Automatic Message Accounting (AMA) system for computing charges on local and long-distance telephone calls [7]. The first AMA equipment was driven by punched paper tape generated by switching system common-control circuits while the calls were in progress. AMA systems used relay computers to extract information about individual calls from the paper tape, compute the duration of the calls, apply billing information, and prepare a bill for each customer. First installed in Media, Pennsylvania, in 1948, AMA and its successor, CAMA (Centralized Automatic Message Accounting), made possible direct-distance dialing (DDD) in which telephone users can dial long distance without the help of an operator.

Analog Computers

Bell Labs' work on analog computers started about the same time Stibitz and Williams began to build the Model I digital machine. Analog and digital computer developments followed much the same pattern. After building a first machine by drawing freely on telephone technology, Bell Laboratories scientists and engineers found that the next stages of computer evolution proceeded under the pressure of special needs imposed by World War II. Postwar developments then returned to general purpose computers built to handle a variety of problems encountered during the continuing evolution of telephone systems.

T. C. Fry, another Bell Labs mathematician, about 1936 designed an early special-purpose analog machine called the Isograph [8]. It was a mechanical system designed to find the complex roots of polynomials—an essential job in the course of designing telephone circuits but also an excessively time-consuming job for people to do manually. Since it was difficult to program for particular problems, the Isograph was used mainly for demonstrations.

The Isograph and other early analog computers used both electrical and mechanical components, but in June 1940 C. A. Lovell and D. B. Parkinson of Bell Labs began the design of an all-electronic analog machine that would use vacuum tubes as the processing elements. Their computer was a special-purpose device for aiming antiaircraft guns [9]. Accepted by the U.S. Army in November 1940, by 1942 the analog machine was in production. It was designated the M9 Gun Director, and its development was based on telephone expertise in filter design, in smoothing and equalization techniques, in making shaped potentiometer cards, resistors, and capacitors with great accuracy, and especially in feedback amplifiers. (H. S. Black had invented feedback amplifiers at Bell Labs in 1927, and techniques for precise amplifier design were devised by H. W. Bode and his associates in the early 1930s.)

The M9 aimed and gave firing signals to antiaircraft batteries after gun crews supplied it with information including target position and range, projectile characteristics, and wind speed and direction (Fig. 2). By 1944 enough M9s were in service in England that the artillery they controlled brought down 76% of the V-1 buzzbombs the Germans fired across the English Channel at London.

Other analog computers designed by Bell Labs for the U.S. Army were the M8 Gun Director and the computers used to aim the Nike-Ajax and Nike-Hercules missiles [10]. The M8, designed to control the fire of coast defense artillery pieces, had to be even more accurate than the M9. Although it was never put into production, the M8 was a useful experimental device. The Nike computers were the "brains" of the antiaircraft systems deployed around American cities in the 1950s.

Fig. 2. M9 Gun Director. Antiaircraft gunners man the controls of the M9 Gun Director's analog computer, which during World War II controlled the firing of 90-mm antiaircraft artillery on battlefronts all over the world. The computer was developed at Bell Labs starting in 1940.

After World War II, Bell Labs engineers used leftover M8 parts to build Gypsy, a general-purpose analog computer that worked on telephone research problems [11]. Designed mainly by Bell Labs mathematician Emory Lakatos in 1946, Gypsy could handle a variety of mathematical operations: addition, subtraction, multiplication, division, differentiation, integration, and the generation of sine, cosine, and exponential functions [12]. Its computing units, each built around a three-stage negative-feedback amplifier, could in a few minutes trace out the solutions of certain kinds of problems that would have taken several days to do manually.

Under the Mark 65 program, a series of postwar U.S. Navy contracts, Bell Labs engineers designed a number of analog-computer controlled weapon-direction systems for Navy ships. These systems accepted target-position data from several radar and optical sensors mounted on the ship, analyzed and correlated the information, established target tracks, designated targets by threat priority, and assigned the ship's defensive weapons to the targets. The computers interacted with operators in the ship's combat command center through visual displays and manual controls. Among the systems developed during the Mark 65 program were the Weapon-Direction Equipment Mark 1 for destroyers and the Target Designation System Mark 3, Designation Equipment Mark 7, and Designation Equipment Mark 9 for cruisers.

BELL LABORATORIES

Transistorized Computers

In 1947 John Bardeen, Walter Brattain, and William Shockley invented the transistor at Bell Labs [13]. The transistor dramatically changed the future course of computing technology. Transistors are cheaper and more reliable, and they require less power, than the relays used in relay digital computers and the vacuum tubes used in early electric digital and analog machines. They have very long life and rarely require adjustment. Through use of transistor circuits, computers became smaller, faster, more reliable, cheaper to operate, and

Fig. 3. Transistorized digital computer (TRADIC). In 1955, Bell Labs engineers worked on the experimental model of TRADIC, the first completely transistorized general-purpose computer built at Bell Labs. TRADIC's programs were wired onto removable plug-in units like the one in the engineer's hands.

cheaper to build. They overcame the heating problems encountered with tubes, and the problems caused by dirt, dust, and wear in relays.

At Bell Labs, transistors were first used in computer circuits in 1949, when W. H. MacWilliams constructed a transistorized gating matrix for a simulated warfare computer furnished to the Bureau of Ordnance Mark 65 program. A few years later, in 1952, A. W. Horton designed a digital computer that used transistors throughout. Horton's machine was a special-purpose device that performed the real-time "track-while-scan" function for U.S. Navy antiaircraft guns. Then, in 1954, a group of Bell Labs engineers headed by Jean H. Felker designed a completely transistorized general-purpose computer called TRADIC, for TRansistorized Airborne DIgital Computer [14]. TRADIC, built for the U.S. Air Force, solved real-time bombing and navigation problems and used 700 point-contact transistors and 11,000 diodes (Fig. 3). Its programs were built into removable plugboards. TRADIC operated at a megacycle pulse rate and could multiply two 15-bit numbers in less than 300 μsec. It used only 60 W of dc power. The experimental model of TRADIC was followed by an airborne version which operated successfully in aircraft—an environment hostile to earlier types of computers.

Another experimental wcomputer built during the TRADIC project, Leprechaun, allowed Bell Labs engineers to study the application of the more stable junction transistors in data-processing machines [15]. Leprechaun incorporated circuits that used transistors alone instead of the transistor-diode combinations used in TRADIC. It had 5500 transistors and 18,000 memory cores and needed only 15 cubic feet of space (Fig. 4). It ran on 160 W of power. In 1959 Bell Labs turned Leprechaun over to the U.S. Air Force, where it was used to evaluate various weapon systems.

Another early development at Bell Labs which helped advance computer hardware technology was the air-cushioned magnetic-recording head. This grew out of work done in 1933 by A. C. Keller and I. S. Rafuse as part of the development of phonograph recordings. Seventeen years later Keller and J. R. Anderson used the technique for accurately positioning the read/write heads of off-line magnetic recording devices. The technique has been widely applied in commercial drum and disk storage systems.

COMPUTER SYSTEMS AND SOFTWARE

Although Bell Labs does not design commercial computer systems, the company has worked on many improvements and found many new uses for data processors. Since the early 1950s the company has relied on commercial general-purpose data processors to carry the bulk of its computing load. The principal Bell Labs contributions to computer technology since then have been in software, operating systems, problem-oriented languages, special hardware applications where very high reliability is a prime requirement, and computer-to-computer communications. Some of these projects took place while similar

Fig. 4. Leprechaun, a digital computer built at Bell Laboratories in 1957, was used by the Air Force as a test model for research on digital computers for military systems.

work was going on independently in other organizations, and are not unique contributions of Bell Labs.

Software Techniques

The relay computers that followed the Model I machine had a form of self-checking that caused the computers to stop processing and sound an alarm when an error was detected. The later machines in this relay-computer family also had a built-in second-trial feature that kept most transient errors from halting computer processing. As computer processing speeded up, however, the need for an error-correcting capability became evident. To meet this need, R. W. Hamming in 1950 developed at Bell Labs the theory for several error-correcting schemes in which the check and information bits that make up binary words are formed into patterns [16]. When a simple error occurs during transmission from one part of the machine to another, the pattern of the word changes and becomes invalid. The error circuitry recognizes the invalid pattern, and the word is retransmitted until it satisfies the checking procedure. Error-correction schemes featuring applications or variations of the techniques developed by Hamming were used in later digital data processors.

An important software contribution was the development in 1959 by M. Douglas McIlroy and D. E. Eastwood of techniques for extending computer languages. These techniques, known as macro instructions, allow programmers to add terms not included in the original programming language [17]. Macro instructions have became widely used tools that allow compilers to accept very general extensions of a source language. The original work, done at Bell Labs with assemblers for IBM 700-class machines, involved innovations that are now in general use throughout the industry.

In another software development, starting in 1965, Marshall E. Barton and his associates designed the Switching Assembler Program (SWAP) during work on the Electronic Switching Systems (ESS) at Bell Laboratories [18]. SWAP is novel and powerful as an assembler because it contains many features that previously existed only in separate programs. Like other assemblers, it converts a user's source program from symbolic language to machine language, and it allows the programmer to assign a symbolic representation to a memory location and then refer to the location symbolically in other instructions. Other SWAP features include macro instructions and the SNOBOL string-processing features described later. SWAP is a universal assembler that makes it possible for users to define and run programs written in languages as far removed from assembly language as FORTRAN and other higher-level languages. At Bell Labs SWAP is used to produce programs for the Safeguard antiballistic missile data processor, the IBM 360, and the control units of the No. 1, 2, 3, and 4 Electronic Switching Systems.

The Fourier transform—the famous mathematical tool developed over 100 years ago by the French mathematician Jean Baptiste Joseph Fourier—serves as a bridge from the time domain to the frequency domain. It allows engineers and scientists to go back and forth from signal waveforms to the associated frequency spectrum. The transform is a useful way to characterize linear systems and to identify the frequency components that make up a continuous waveform, such as that produced by human speech. The Fourier transform can be applied to digital computers by using a sampled version known as a discrete Fourier transform. In 1965 J. W. Cooley of IBM and J. W. Tukey of Bell Labs and Princeton University developed the Fast Fourier Transform (FFT) algorithm, an efficient way of computing discrete Fourier transforms on digital machines. By reducing from minutes to seconds the machine time it takes to perform Fourier operations, FFT has revolutionized digital processing of waveforms [19]. The algorithm can be used to compute spectrograms (displays of power spectrum vs time), perform digital filtering, and correlate two waveforms. It is especially useful for solving signal-processing problems in real time at the rate the signal is received. It has been used to process sonar, radar, and speech signals. It has also been used for off-line analysis of large amounts of data in radio astronomy and in crystallography.

In the area of computer graphics, work started in 1960 at Bell Labs by J. F. Kaiser and C. F. Pease resulted in a set of computer programs, called TPLOT, which gave users versatility in producing complete computer-generated plots and graphs on microfilm [20]. This package of microfilm subroutines serves as a link between a user and the plotter. By greatly augmenting the low-level language of commercial microfilm plotters, it gives the user a wide choice of graphs and plots, with a selection of plot sizes, scales, lettering and character sizes, and format features (Fig. 5). Originally written in FORTRAN for an IBM 7000-class machine and now available for many different computers, the routines produce magnetic tape in the language used by the plotter. The tape is then used to guide the plotter in producing the desired graphic displays on microfilm, which can be enlarged and printed as hard copy.

In late 1963 the graphics work for microfilm plotters was extended by W. H. Ninke's development of GRAPHIC 1, a Bell Labs-designed experimental input-output console [21]. The console, which allowed the user to communicate with the computer through a graphic display, contained a small general-purpose computer and display connected to a central data processor. Graphs, block diagrams, and other pictorial forms of data were displayed on the console's CRT. By operating a light pen and a keyboard (Fig. 6), the user could modify the display, enter data for computation of a new display, or control the sequencing of a set of calculations. The console computer held the simpler and most frequently used programs, while the main computer held the data base, programs used less often, and programs for solving problems involving extensive computation. A larger, more flexible, and more readily accessible system was provided by GRAPHIC 2, which went into use during 1968 [22]. It was part of a system that included a commercial microfilm recorder, a commercial plotter, a unit for producing paper copies of the displays, a system of Bell Labs-designed CRT consoles, the GRAPHIC 2 interactive console, and several commercial keyboard units. GRAPHIC 2 gives circuit designers, draftsmen, and engineers a powerful, convenient tool for solving many types of technical problems. Now used at Bell Labs to produce hundreds of drawings each month, GRAPHIC 2 is also in use at several universities.

Monitors and Operating Systems

In the early 1950s Bell Labs began to acquire commercially built computers to replace the Bell Labs relay and vacuum-tube digital and analog machines. In

[208]
BELL LABORATORIES

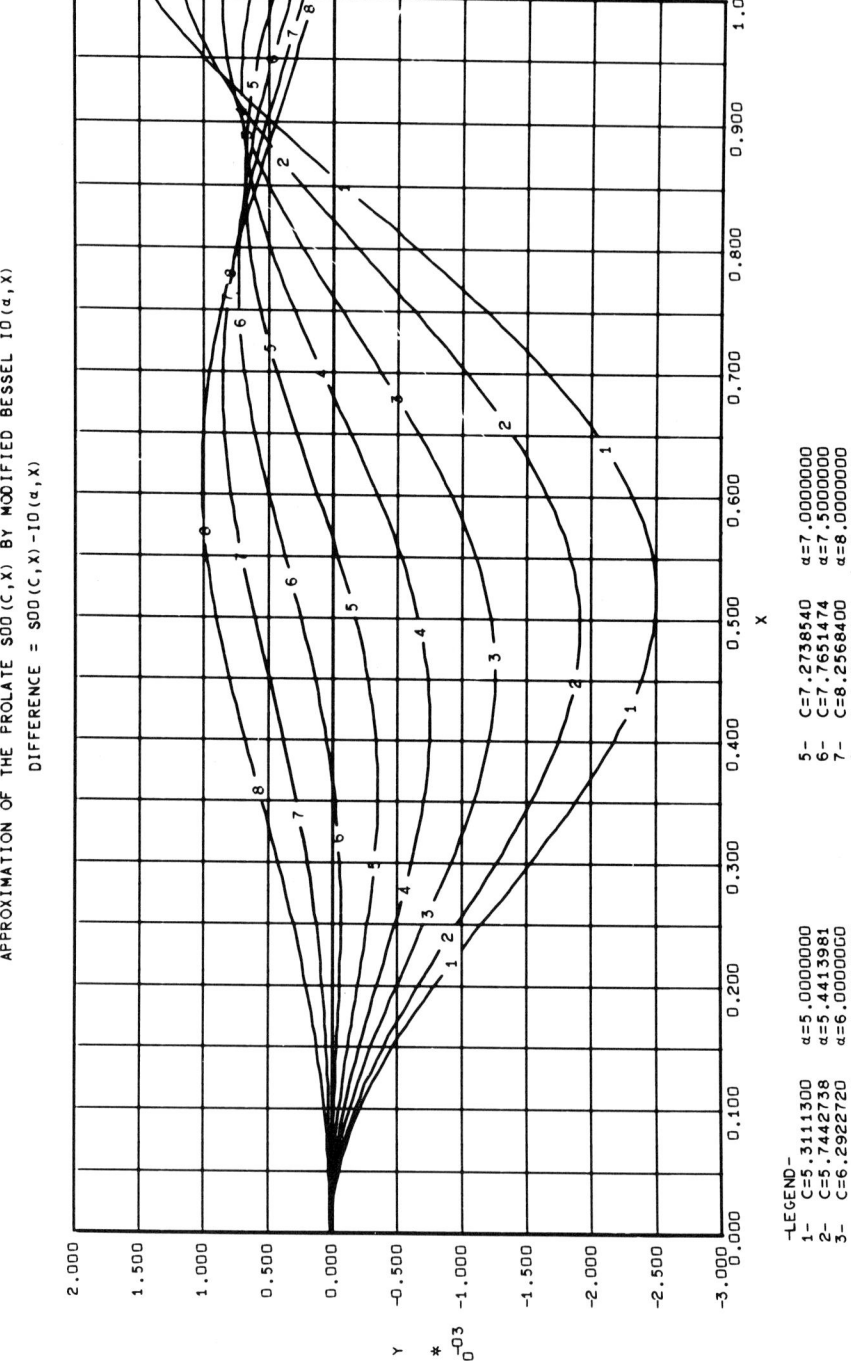

Fig. 5. Computer graphics. Sample of a graph produced under control of TPLOT, a program that provides Bell Labs scientists and engineers with a wide selection of features in pictorial presentation of data. TPLOT was developed at Bell Labs in the early 1960s.

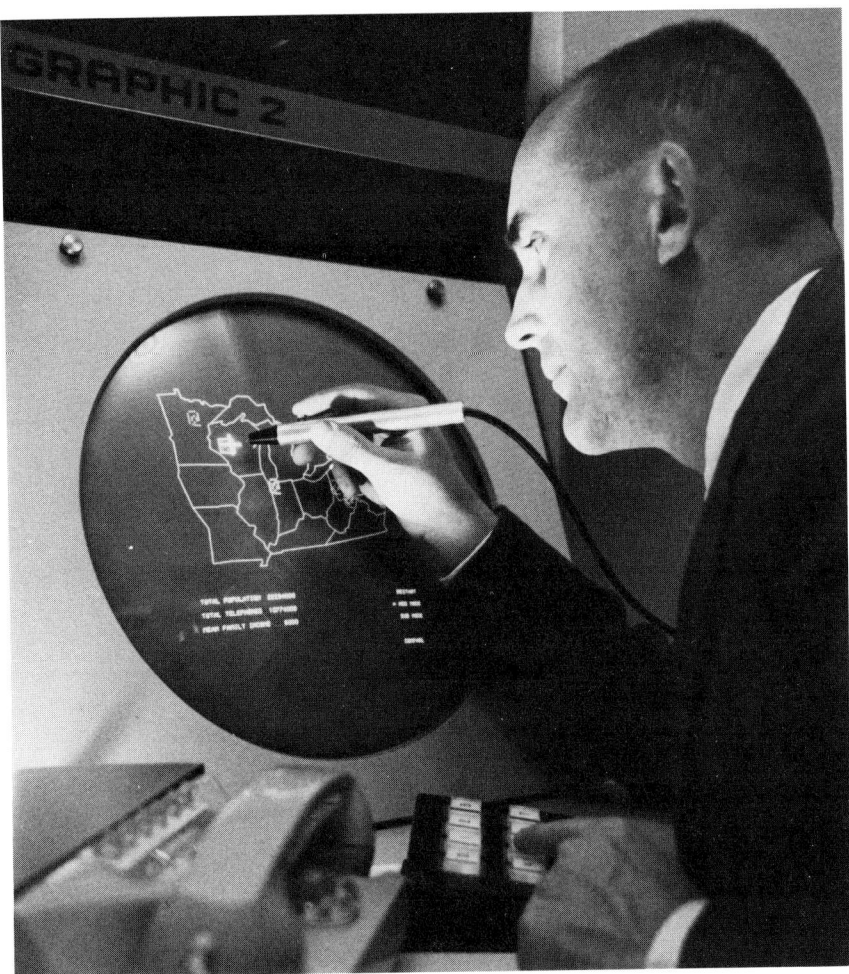

Fig. 6. Interactive graphics. A Bell Labs engineer uses a light pen and keyboard to control GRAPHIC 2, a system designed at Bell Labs in 1967. GRAPHIC 2 allows people to interact directly with information stored in a digital computer.

1955 the company put into operation two IBM 650s which had to be programmed in machine language. To make the data processors easier for engineers and scientists with little background in programming to use, and to encourage people with time-consuming mathematical calculations to bring them to the computation center, V. M. Wolontis and R. W. Hamming in 1956 devised the L1 and L2 automatic programming systems (known to 650 users outside Bell Labs as Bell 1 and Bell 2). L1 and L2 allowed users to communicate with computers in a language far simpler than the basic machine language; thus they made it easier for computation center customers to use the machines directly instead of going through programming specialists. L1 was a general-purpose, floating-decimal interpretive system [23]; L2 was similar except that it relieved programmers of having to specify detailed storage assignments for instructions. L1, in particular, was widely disseminated throughout the community of data-processor builders and users.

In another development, George H. Mealy in 1958 developed BESYS (for BEll SYStem), an operating monitor for the IBM 704 computers Bell Labs had acquired to augment its data-processing facilities. Since the 704 worked many times faster than the 650, an automatic monitor was needed to control the flow of operations in the system. BESYS was a complex software package that provided convenient input/output and integrated disk file storage facilities. Since it served as the operating system for the many IBM 7000 series computers used at Bell Labs, the evolution of BESYS continued into the late 1960s.

From 1965 to 1969 Bell Labs participated in the design and development of MULTICS (MULTiplexed Information and Computing System) [24]. The program was influenced by Bell Labs' experience with BESYS and by MIT's experience with Project MAC (Multiple Access Computing) and CTSS (the Compatible Time-Sharing System). MULTICS, which involved many innovations in both hardware and software, attempted to make available a variety of computing modes within a single system that would provide sophisticated time-sharing features. Among the features to be provided by MULTICS were an independent virtual memory work space for each user; controlled access by each user to other users' programs stored in memory; the ability to run large jobs easily; and the ability to handle interactive jobs, remote batch processing, and traditional batch processing simultaneously. MULTICS was the first large operating system to be itself implemented in a high-level language, rather than in machine language, so that changes could be made without directly writing new machine code. The system was easy to learn and use; it influenced the development of such time-sharing systems as GECOS (GEneral Comprehensive Operating Supervisor) and IBM's TSS (Time-Shared System). A MULTICS computing system is produced by Honeywell Information Systems, Inc.

From the MULTICS experience, Bell Labs' computer researcher Kenneth Thompson in 1969 developed UNIX, a time-shared operating system for minicomputers [25]. UNIX gives users a sophisticated file-management system and a wide range of software facilities. UNIX can run on a machine with as little as 12,000 16-bit words of storage. It provides effective text editing and formatting software as well as facilities for general-purpose computing. An assembler and compilers for FORTRAN, BASIC, and other languages are available. In addition, the UNIX system has access to a large number of applications programs.

First used at Bell Labs for research, editing text, and preparing documents, UNIX has also been adapted to the administration and testing of Bell System telephone switching systems. In document preparation, a manuscript, including mathematical formulas, can be typed on a keyboard and stored in the computer's file system, and editing changes can be made through the keyboard. The computer may then directly drive a typewriter, printer, or phototypesetting machine which produces pages ready for reproduction. In telephone offices, UNIX receives trouble reports directly from switching systems, processes the data, and notifies repair personnel about problems that need human attention.

Problem-Oriented Languages

In 1960, R. E. Griswold and his associates at Bell Labs produced SNOBOL (String Oriented Symbolic Language), a programming language that gave users considerable power and flexibility in manipulating strings of characters [26]. SNOBOL has two sets of functions, a basic set built into the program and a set used at the programmer's discretion. The basic set allows programmers to form, examine, and rearrange strings of characters; the other set lets them design their own functions for manipulating the program. SNOBOL made it convenient to design recursive features into programs. It has been used widely outside Bell Labs for developing compilers, assemblers, translation algorithms, and information retrieval systems.

Another problem-oriented language, L^6 (Laboratories Low Level Linked List Language), was developed by Kenneth C. Knowlton at Bell Labs in 1965 [27]. Like other "list-processing" languages, it permits programmers to manipulate complexly linked data. However, L^6 allows programmers to work closer to the machine language, so they can write faster-running programs, use computer storage more efficiently, and build a variety of linked data structures. L^6 has been applied to problems involving simulation, game-playing, information retrieval, and graphics manipulation. The language is also useful for quickly implementing higher-level list languages. Since its development, L^6 concepts have been built into other languages, notably PL/1, and implemented on a number of commercial computers. It is used at several universities, and an L^6 users' group has been formed in Tokyo.

Another early 1960s development that grew out of Bell Labs' efforts to make computers easier to use is BLODI (BLOck DIagram Compiler) [28]. Using BLODI, circuit designers can study the behavior of proposed electrical circuits without going to the trouble, time, and expense of actually building physical models. By giving the computer a block diagram of the circuit, a designer can study circuit response to changes in input and circuit configurations, and new designs and ideas can be evaluated within a few days instead of in a few weeks or months. The program was designed by John L. Kelly, Jr. and V. A. Vyssotsky. Its simple input language is especially useful for simulating the operation of pulsed digital circuits that handle speech and other signals.

Also in the area of problem-oriented languages, starting in 1961 W. S. Brown and his associates developed the ALTRAN language for performing symbolic computations on algebraic data [29]. The basic capability of the language is to perform rational operations on rational expressions in one or more indeterminates and on numerical data. Procedures are also provided for side relations, truncated power series, and systems of linear equations. Both at Bell Labs and at a number of universities, ALTRAN is used to deal with a variety of large algebraic problems.

BELL LABORATORIES

In 1960 Max V. Mathews and his associates at Bell Labs produced a computer program called MUSIC for synthesizing music and other acoustic signals on a digital computer [30]. MUSIC capitalizes on the ability of digital-to-analog converters to change numbers into a continuous signal, where signal amplitude is proportional to the number. The technique makes it possible to overcome some of the mechanical and acoustic limitations of conventional musical instruments and sound sources. In MUSIC, the user furnishes the computer with cards containing macro instructions specifying the instruments, then with a set of cards describing the notes—their pitch, amplitude, and duration. Guided by the MUSIC program, the computer operates on the notes and produces a digital magnetic tape, which can be played through a digital-to-analog converter, a filter, and a loudspeaker to reproduce the musical composition. The technique continues to be used at Bell Laboratories in studies of the nature of sound and human hearing.

High Reliability Systems

In the area of high reliability systems, Zeus, the first ABM defense system, used a digital computer developed through the joint efforts of Bell Labs and Univac. To meet the high reliability objectives of an ABM defense, a switching transistor that had a failures rate of 6 fits (six failures in 10^9 hr) was developed at Bell Labs for the Zeus computer. Bell Labs also devised a "twistor" variable memory and a magnetic wire fixed memory for this computer. During the early 1960s, a Zeus system with a number of these computers for acquisition, tracking, and guidance was installed on Kwajalein Island in the Pacific. It became the first defense system in the free world to successfully intercept ICBMs.

In 1963 Bell Labs started design of a large, highly reliable digital computer that could carry out detection, tracking, discrimination, and guidance tasks for the Army's Safeguard antiballistic missile defense system. An interactive, self-contained data processor, the Safeguard computer operates in real time and is capable of multiprogramming and multiprocessing. The computer was designed to withstand many faults, and still perform its mission, through use of back-up equipment and the concept of "graceful degradation," in which the machine as it loses capability abandons its least important tasks and concentrates on the most important. Reliability is augmented through fail-safe techniques, the use of back-up spares, a reconfiguration capability, and a special maintenance subsystem that detects faults, isolates them, and restarts the system as necessary.

Another significant development in the area of high-reliability systems involves computer architecture—the relationship among the various major subsystems within the machine. PEPE, for Parallel Element Processing Ensemble, was devised at Bell Labs in the late 1960s by J. A. Githens, B. A. Crane, and their associates [31]. Based in part on C. Y. Lee's earlier work on digital logic systems for data retrieval, PEPE performs simultaneous, parallel tracking computations on large numbers of radar targets. The system uses two digital computers—one general-purpose, the other special-purpose. The special-purpose computer has a common control and an indefinite number of parallel elements, each in effect a small digital computer with a correlation unit, an arithmetic unit, and a memory (Fig. 7). Each detected radar target is assigned to a separate element in the ensemble that makes up the special-purpose device. Once assigned a target, the element works with the general-purpose machine to process that target, independently of the other elements in the ensemble. The general-purpose machine has a large memory, which holds the programs and data, and performs sequential operations needed in solving the radar tracking problems. PEPE is being evaluated elsewhere as part of an advanced radar data-processing system.

In addition to the high-reliability defense hardware systems described above, Bell Labs has developed high-reliability software. One set of programs was built around equations worked out in the early 1960s by M. J. Evans and his associates for command guidance—the control of space shots from a ground

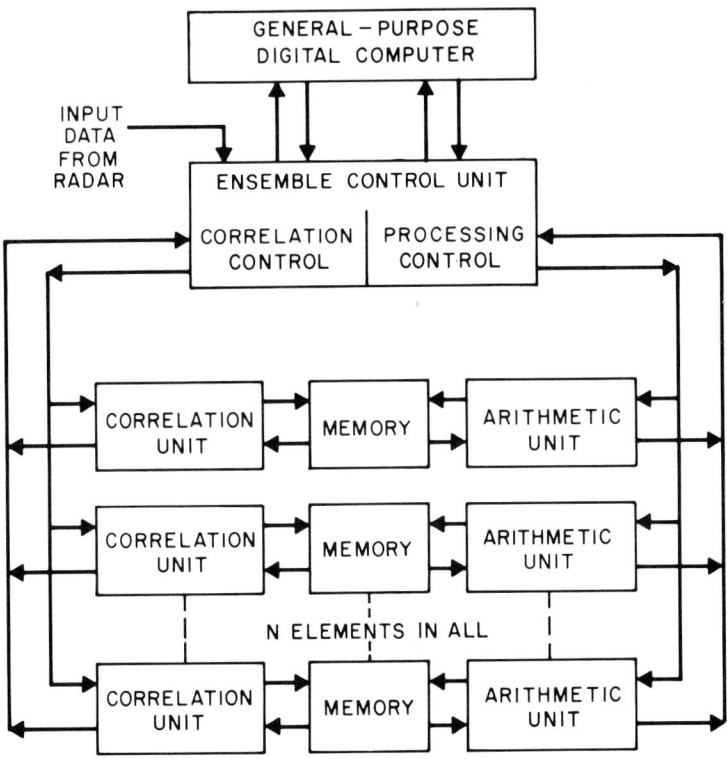

Fig. 7. PEPE. Block diagram of PEPE, the Parallel Element Processing Ensemble, devised by Bell Laboratories in the 1960s for defensive radar systems. PEPE uses two digital computers (one general, one special) to carry on simultaneous tracking computations on large numbers of radar targets.

station [32]. These command-guidance software systems have been used in a UNIVAC computer to control several hundred unmanned space shots, both ballistic and orbital. Using radar tracking data on missile position as input, the Bell Labs program calculated steering and engine-cutoff commands. Both the guidance equations and the computer have worked without failure throughout each mission.

Also in the area of high-reliability systems is the Bell Labs work on electronic switching systems. Although these telephone systems are not computers, parts of them—particularly the subsystems used in common for the control of all telephone connections within a switching office—use certain logic, memory, and programming techniques related to those of calculating machines but developed specifically for the particular characteristics, complexities, and reliability requirements of telephone. Thus the line of development which produced the early Bell Labs contributions to computers later bore on the design of modern switching systems.

After a period of research on experimental systems [33-35], the company began development of an Electronic Switching System (ESS) whose common-control unit used digital processing and stored programs [36]. The common control was a general-purpose machine with duplicated processing units and storage to provide high reliability, but it had the special purpose of managing telephone calls in the switching system. The first ESS common-control subsystem used diode-transistor logic, barrier grid data storage, and an optical program memory. ESS was used in a trial in Morris, Illinois, in 1960—the first public use of a telephone exchange controlled by a stored program system. In 1963 the first commercial electronic switching system—an automatic private branch exchange called No. 101 ESS [37]—went into service in Cape Kennedy, Florida.

In 1965 the first commercial telephone office design, No. 1 ESS [38], started service in Succasunna, New Jersey. The No. 1 ESS common-control unit uses low-level logic circuitry, temporary data storage in a ferrite sheet memory, and permanent program storage in a magnetic twistor memory. Included in the processor as advanced features are a high degree of automatic self-diagnosis and fault isolation, automatic recovery from mutilation of the system memory (see audits programs below in the section titled In Industry), and a very high system availability (Fig. 8). The processor is time-shared among many users, which allows real-time response to customer requests for service (i.e., dialed telephone calls). A multiprocessing capability was added to the ESS processor in 1968 [39].

Besides serving local telephone customers in urban exchanges, ESS-type switching systems are being used for suburban local switching, for rural switching systems [40], for long-distance switching systems, for Bell System operator services (the TSPS, Traffic Service Position System [41] operator's console), and for military communications (AUTOVON, for AUTOmatic VOice Network). As of 1972, ESS systems had logged more than five-million cumulative service hours and have demonstrated a 99.997% availability—which

Fig. 8. Electronic switching systems. Bell Labs engineers checking out the master control equipment of a No. 1 Electronic Switching System (ESS) installed in a telephone office in 1966. ESS systems are controlled by stored-program equipment and designed to operate continuously for 40 years with less than 2 hr of out-of-service time.

means a typical system is out of service for about a minute every 3 weeks. On the average, an ESS records one failure in each year of operation.

Remote Terminals and Networks

In 1956 Bell Labs demonstrated long-distance magnetic tape-to-tape transmission over dialed telephone lines. The company has also pioneered in use of data links for supervising widely separated computing centers and making the memories and computing abilities of large data processors accessible to small computers [42]. Starting in 1962, Bell Laboratories interconnected computers at its widely separated locations over broad-band data links, an arrangement that allows the machines to back up each other and balance computation loads [43].

The development of remote typewriter terminals is related to Bell Labs experiments for remotely connecting computer peripheral storage and input/output devices to central processors for exchange of data. While Stibitz' Model

BELL LABORATORIES

1 digital computer could be reached through three teletypewriters stationed some distance away, Model II and the later relay and early transistor machines communicated with users through punched cards, punched paper tapes, and magnetic tape fed directly into the machines. In 1964 Bell Labs set up two typewriter consoles at its Murray Hill, New Jersey, laboratory and connected them through specially designed hardware and voice-grade telephone circuits to an IBM 7094. Later in the year a similar experimental setup went into operation at Bell Labs in Holmdel, New Jersey. Linking the typewriters to the computer as remote input/output units required a considerable amount of software development as well as the specially built hardware interface. The typewriter terminals gave users access to large computers at stations remote from computation centers. Typewriter terminals for remote access to computers are now built by a number of companies.

APPLICATIONS OF COMPUTERS

In Research and Development

About 1960, computing science had matured enough that substantial numbers of Bell Labs scientists and engineers began to apply its powers as convenient tools in the company's research and development projects. Since then, most of Bell Labs' work on computer technology has been devoted to two main fields. One area includes sophisticated applications programs in support of communications research and development; the other consists of programs to meet the manufacturing and operating needs of the Bell System.

In the 1960s Bell Labs began to make substantial use of computer animation [44]. To analyze the motions of earth satellites during their prestabilization period after launch, Edward E. Zajac programmed the differential equations of motion that described the satellite's movements. The solutions derived by the computer were displayed as a series of pictures on a CRT face (Fig. 9). By using successive CRT photographs as the frames of a motion picture, Zajac produced a movie that showed the satellite tumbling until its gyros gradually stabilized it. This technique of graphics in motion has subsequently been applied to a number of problems in analytic mechanics, providing useful insight into nonlinear dynamic systems. Other problems studied involve moon landings, global telephony, and meteorology. J. B. Kruskal has used computer-generated motion pictures to display a complex iterative numerical procedure for solving a psychometric problem, F. W. Sinden has produced educational movies that explain geometrical and mathematical principles, and A. M. Noll has made a variety of hyperdimensional studies (involving more than three dimensions) [45]. K. C. Knowlton has designed several languages that simplify the specification of computer movies [46]. These languages have been used to produce several award-winning computer-made scientific and artistic films.

Analysis and simulation of human speech have been Bell System concerns since the invention of the telephone. In recent research, computers have been

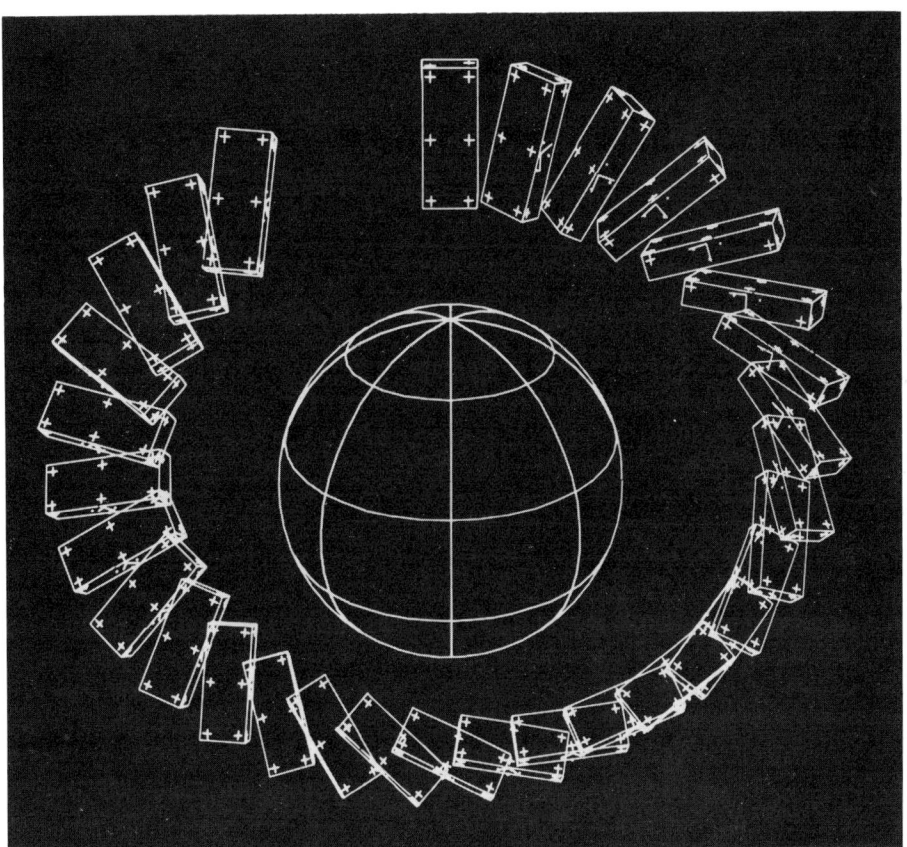

Fig. 9. Computer movies. A composite of many frames of a motion picture produced by a computer at Bell Labs during the 1960s. The motions of a satellite, tumbling in orbit before it stabilized, were analyzed by the computer, which then produced successive cathode-ray-tube pictures of the satellite position. The pictures form a movie that provides insight into satellite motions during the prestabilization phase.

programmed to synthesize human speech with the inflections, pauses, and other qualities of the human voice. The work involves study of human sounds to discover the rules that govern pitch, tone, stress, and other characteristics [47]. Through suitable computer programs, these essentially nonlinear rules must be converted to instructions for the computer to follow in synthesizing human speech. The ultimate objective is to program a computer to produce natural speech by giving it text and associated acoustic and linguistic data.

As a by-product of this research work, James L. Flanagan and his associates have used a computer-controlled synthesizer to produce tape cassettes of spoken instructions for assembly workers in Western Electric Company plants (Fig. 10) and installers in Bell System central offices [48]. A punched card deck carrying a list of interconnections is read into the computer, which converts

Fig. 10. Synthesized speech. An employee in a Western Electric Co. plant, following verbal instructions produced by a computer, has both hands and both eyes free to concentrate on wiring a telephone switching system assembly. Instructions produced and synthesized into human-like speech by a computer have been recorded on magnetic tape, which the employee plays back on the cassette.

them to spoken instructions. Wiring personnel do not have to cope visually and manually with sheets of printed instructions, and they have both hands free for the wiring job. This computing technique makes updating easier, and leads to fewer errors than if the wiring list were recorded by a human announcer.

Another Bell Labs research project—speaker verification—complements work on synthetic speech. A computer that could accept a telephone call would be useful when a caller wanted to order goods from a store, ask a bank to transfer funds, or obtain information from a business [49]. While direct control of a computer by voice instruction is now possible in only a limited experimental way, considerable progress has been made in the simpler task of having a computer verify for a human user that a given speaker is who he says he is. Each human voice is unique—a product of the speaker's vocal tract and how he uses it. To verify the caller's identity, the computer compares characteristics of the caller's voice, as he speaks a specific utterance, with a set of characteristics previously derived for that caller (Fig. 11). These characteristics include voice pitch and intensity and their variations with time during the utterance. The computer must also allow for the fact that people never repeat the same word exactly the same way and at the same speed.

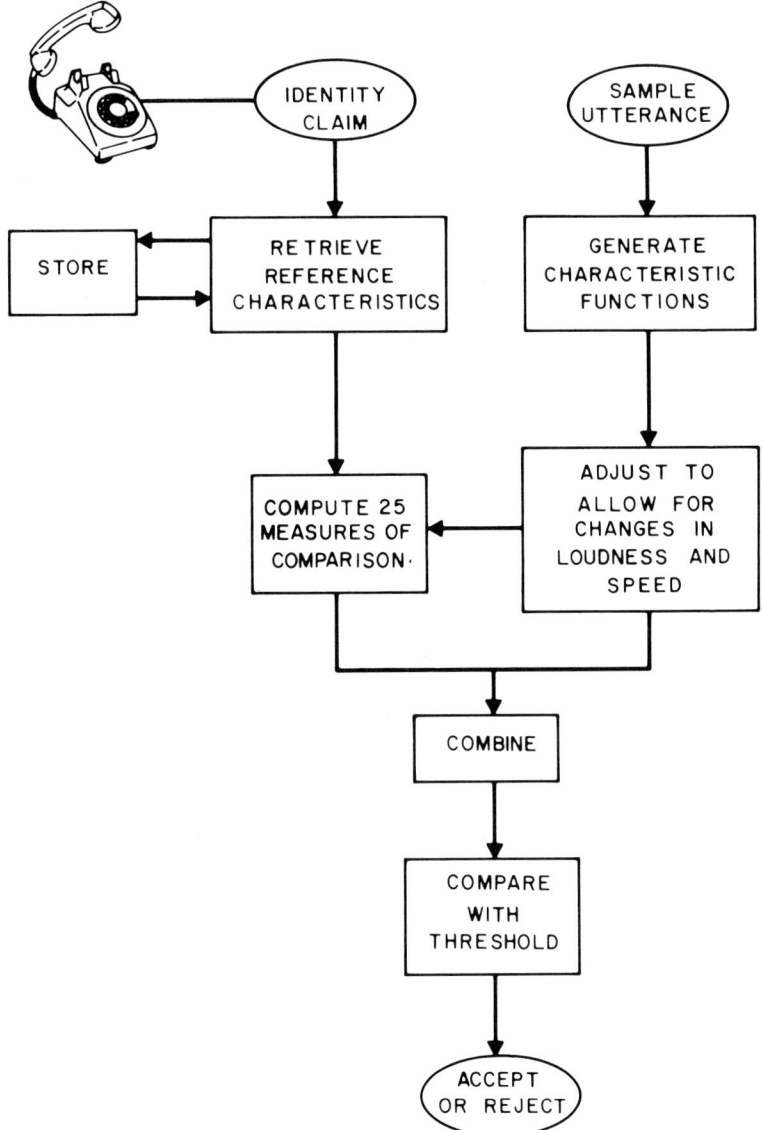

Fig. 11. Speaker verification. In speaker verification, a computer might be used to identify and verify a telephone caller's voice when he orders goods from a store, requests a transfer of bank funds, or asks for business information.

BELL LABORATORIES

VARIABLE	FORMULA
1. ALTITUDE	a
2. BASE AREA	b
3. CIRCUMFERENCE	$(2\sqrt{\pi})b^{1/2}$
4. SIDE AREA	$(2\sqrt{\pi})ab^{1/2}$
5. VOLUME	ab
6. MOMENT OF INERTIA	$(1/2\pi)ab^2$
7. SLENDERNESS RATIO	$(1/\sqrt{2\pi})ab^{-1/2}$
8. DIAGONAL-BASE ANGLE	$\tan^{-1}[(\sqrt{\pi}/2)ab^{-1/2}]$
9. DIAGONAL-SIDE ANGLE	$\cot^{-1}[(\sqrt{\pi}/2)ab^{-1/2}]$
10. ELECTRICAL RESISTANCE	ab^{-1}
11. CONDUCTANCE	$a^{-1}b$
12. TORSIONAL DEFORMABILITY	$(2\pi)ab^{-2}$

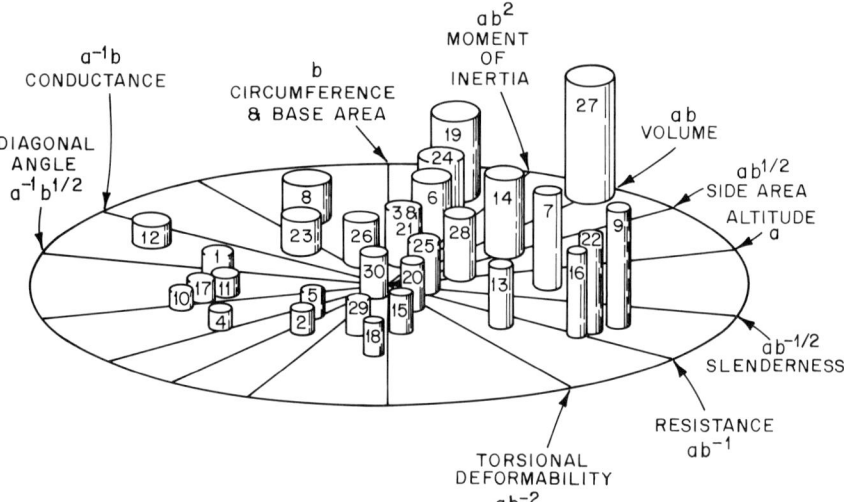

Fig. 12. Multidimensional scaling. Multidimensional scaling techniques developed at Bell Labs enable the computer to organize a profusion of data and display it so that the relationships between variables can be readily perceived. The sketch shows the relationship among 12 variable characteristics in a set of 30 cylinders. The ordering of some of the variables depends on the cylinders' positions relative to the circle and its radii. The proportionate volume *ab* of each cylinder, for instance, is shown by the relative distance of the cylinder from the point marked "*ab* volume" on the circle. The largest cylinder, 27, is closest to that point; the smallest two, 10 and 4, are the farthest away.

Work performed at Bell Laboratories by George Doddington, Robert C. Lummis, and Aaron E. Rosenberg shows that a computer programmed for speaker verification can perform more accurately than humans. However, more work needs to be done before this technique can be considered for commercial use.

Since 1959, Bela Julesz of Bell Labs has used digital computers as tools to extend understanding of stereopsis (the sensing of three dimensions from two-dimensional stimuli) and to study the human perception of form [50]. For this work a computer is used to generate dot patterns, called stereograms, with precisely controlled cues. Stereograms, when viewed monocularly, appear to be random, but when they are binocularly fused, predetermined areas appear to be at different depths. The technique permits bypassing many neural stages and displaying the stimulus on the "cyclopean retina," a group of cells in the brain's cortex, much closer to the central nervous system than the visual retina. Thus the researcher can tell whether perceptual phenomena—ranging from optical illusions to visual aftereffects—operate on cortical or retinal levels. A range of further neurophysiological experiments has been suggested from this research.

Other computer-related research at Bell Labs has been devoted to multidimensional scaling, a technique for graphically presenting data that contain a large number of variables [51]. R. N. Shepard, J. B. Kruskal, J. D. Carroll, and J. J. Chang developed programs that allow a computer to produce maplike displays on which several combinations of variables are isolated (Fig. 12). The relationships among the displayed combinations of variables can then be readily perceived. This method capitalizes on the fact that it often takes only a few "dimensions," or variables, to describe the differences among a set of fairly complicated subjective perceptions (such as the flavors of different foods). The problem is to find the right variables for making the necessary distinctions. The multidimensional scaling programs provide a way to extract the right variables from a list that compares the relative similarities of various items, and a way of telling how many variables are really needed to describe the data set accurately. Although the majority of applications are in the social sciences, the work has also been extended to the physical sciences.

In Industry

At Bell Labs, the design of very large electronic assemblies includes the preparation of manufacturing information. To save drafting personnel time and drudgery, to increase accuracy, and to speed up revision, Bell Labs early in the 1960s began to produce computer programs that generated wiring data [52]. Given a set of rules and formulas, the programs guided the machine in printing out lists of wiring interconnections and paths. Work was also done on methods for routing electrical interconnections automatically [53]. This work was later expanded by developing programs that aided equipment design, including the

BELL LABORATORIES

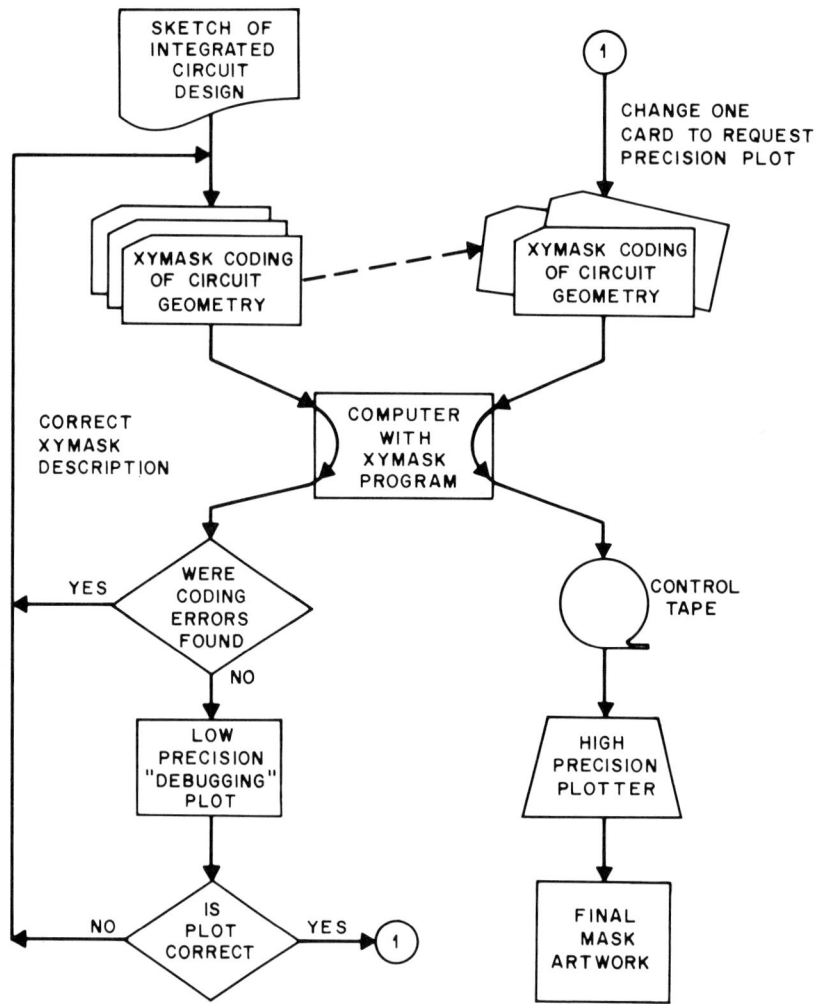

Fig. 13. Integrated circuit masks. A flow chart of the steps followed in using a computer to produce master artwork for integrated circuit masks. The XYMASK program was developed at Bell Labs.

design of new digital systems [54]. Supplied with equations, information on the number of connections, and the size and number of circuits, the computer simulated several possible design configurations for a new assembly or subassembly. The computer then evaluated the designs, selected the best one, and documented the selected design with manufacturing information [55]. In work on logic circuit testing, the performance of digital systems under normal and trouble modes was studied [56]. More recently, computers have been programmed for such tasks as guiding telephone craftspersons in interconnecting Electronic Switching System (ESS) equipment [57]. The programs allow data processors to specify the best of many thousand complex interconnection patterns and to furnish information for changing them as traffic flow changes within the telephone office.

Computer systems also help to solve problems associated with the increasing use of semiconductor integrated circuits in industry. Such increased use has multiplied the number of masks required for production. One integrated circuit may require as many as a dozen etchings and other treatments, each of which requires a mask. Since production of such masks by humans is tedious, time-consuming, and subject to error, a number of mask-producing machines have been developed in industry. Computer programs have been developed to produce magnetic tapes that drive the machines. Bell Labs has been a pioneer in this work. One of its most significant contributions is XYMASK (Fig. 13), a general program that produces tapes for any of a number of mask-producing machines [58]. XYMASK describes mask patterns in terms of basic geometric shapes and coordinates, which makes it particularly easy to program repetitive and multiple patterns.

Like all software programs, those developed for ESS require a flow chart that is a guide to and a record of the program steps. Work by P. M. Sherman in 1965 led to FLOWTRACE, a system that could produce flow charts of programs written in almost any programming language [59]. Bell Labs produces several thousand ESS flow charts each year, so in the late 1960s a system for producing them automatically was developed. The result was ESSFLO, a program that accepts a punched card input, prepares flow charts using L^6 and a macro instruction language, and drives a plotter that prints the sheets of flow charts [60]. Controlled by ESSFLO, the computer directs the plotter to draw

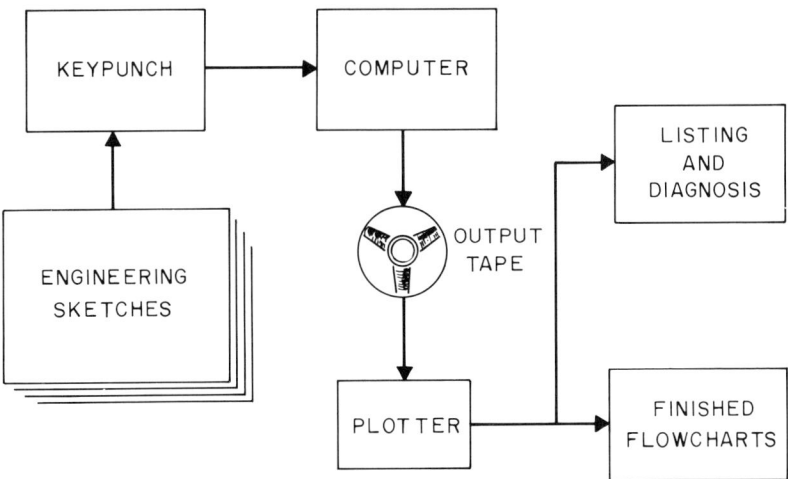

Fig. 14. Automatic flow charting. A block diagram of Bell Labs ESSFLO process for producing finished flow charts from programmer's sketches. ESSFLO saves time and drafting changes; makes it easy to change and update the flow charts required during large programming operations. It was developed in the late 1960s.

symbols and lettering, draw and label interconnecting lines, and position headings, titles, and page numbers (Fig. 14). The ESSFLO system can produce a flow chart in about 15 min, 16 times faster and 50% cheaper than manual methods.

In complex telephone switching equipment controlled by stored programs, continuous operation depends on reliable software as well as on reliable hardware. Systems such as ESS and the TSPS telephone operator's console are vulnerable to data mutilation—the introduction of erroneous information into system memory—from hardware faults, program faults that supply memory with erroneous data, and faulty input from humans. To prevent the system from losing "sanity" through destruction of its processing capability, Bell Labs engineers designed a system of programs that audit ESS and TSPS processing [61]. The programs monitor critical software processes, such as executive program sequencing, accuracy and timing of sequences, and crucial parts of memory. If errors are found, the auditing programs go through an ordered sequence of reconstruction phases, progressing to more drastic steps if earlier steps in the sequence fail to restore normal operation. Only the most severe reconstruction procedure involves disruption of telephone calls.

COMPUTING AND THE FUTURE

At Bell Labs, work continues on computer-oriented research and development and on novel applications for data processors. Computers are widely used in their traditional roles as calculators, problem-solvers, and simulators. Increasingly, they are employed for collecting and analyzing experimental data and for assimilating and presenting results in a variety of new forms that augment human perception and provide new insights. This expanding use of computers will inevitably require changes in computer programming practices and in the employment of computer hardware systems. Some of the trends that seem to be developing are discussed in the following paragraphs.

Software Portability

Since large amounts of time and money are spent on development of computer software, the resulting programs should be "portable," that is, able to run without change on a variety of different computers. Not only would portability make programs more widely available and hence more valuable, it would also make it unnecessary to rewrite them each time a computer is replaced. Because of the wide variety of computers at Bell Labs and throughout the Bell System, a number of Bell Labs workers have been attracted to the search for software portability.

Although higher level languages such as FORTRAN were originally expected to solve the portability problem, in general they have not done so. The reason is that each computer has its own independently developed compiler, which supports a particular "dialect" of the language. When they prepare software for that computer, programmers are tempted to use shortcuts that depend on special features of the language implemented on the particular machine. Such tricks make the programs unintelligible to every machine but the one they were originally written for. What is worse, two compilers may both accept the same instruction and interpret it differently because of omissions or ambiguities in the definition of the language that the compilers are supposed to represent.

A substantial amount of portability was achieved for the SNOBOL string-manipulation language. SNOBOL uses an implementation language based on carefully chosen macro instructions that are expanded into the assembly language of the particular computer.

Even more portability was achieved for the algebra-translation language ALTRAN by using American National Standard (ANS) FORTRAN supplemented by a very few macro instructions. These instructions are expanded into ANS FORTRAN tailored to the features of the computer that is to run the ALTRAN problems. This approach has been pioneered by A. D. Hall and his associates. To assure strict adherence to the rules of ANS FORTRAN, B. G. Ryder has written a "verifier" which checks both the subprograms and the interfaces between those subprograms that form a complete program [62].

Both of these approaches to portability, and probably others as well, will be pursued with increasing vigor.

Transaction-Oriented Computing Systems

Computers were first built to solve complicated, time-consuming mathematical problems, and their use as "number crunchers" will always be important. However, computers are being used increasingly in situations where computing power is secondary to the machine's ability to store masses of data and make it available to many users. To support this trend, Bell Labs since 1966 has been working on computer-based information systems for use by people unfamiliar with computer programming. The earliest of these systems, DATAPLUS [63], had a battery of English-like messages which allowed users to gain access to information stored in a computer. Messages were a sequence of phrases, each starting with a keyword that dictated the action the machine was to perform.

From DATAPLUS have evolved other systems that deal with a variety of situations where the primary purpose is to retrieve information stored in computers. One system, called Master Links, gives users the power to manage hierarchically organized data, and another system allows them to easily generate special languages for special applications. These techniques have been combined into an information-management package called the Off-the-Shelf System. This system gives users a complete capability for originating, storing, accessing, changing, and manipulating any hierarchically organized data, all without the need for any computer programming.

Another facet of transaction-oriented system studies is choice of the processing scheme. Is it better to centralize all data storage and processing in one large machine? Or should the processing be divided among a group of minicomputers, each shared by a small group of users? In the second scheme the minicomputers would access the central data base as necessary.

There are at least two advantages to decentralized processing. A small machine can easily be programmed to do a few simple tasks, but programming a large one to do many tasks simultaneously is difficult. A system of distributed processing would have better "fail soft" features than one in which all memory and processing were confined to one massive data processor. If the central processor malfunctions, the whole transaction-oriented system fails; but if one computer in a shared-processing network fails, its processing can be taken over by other machines until the failure is cleared. To furnish many users with simultaneous access to computing memory and processing units, optimum mixes of minicomputers and large data processors are under study at Bell Labs.

Computer Networks

Connecting two computers to exchange data has been practical for some time. To assemble a number of computers into a network is more challenging [64]. The best form for such a network is unknown; it probably depends on the size of the network, the kinds of machines involved, and the jobs the machines are performing. At Bell Labs the study of computer networks covers gradations between the extremes of distributed control and centralized control.

In distributed control [65], network switching would supply only the data links and a clocking mechanism. Computers in the net would be free to transmit data in any empty space on the data loop, and free to accept and use any data circulating in the loop. To exchange data with other computers, machines would be equipped to set up transmission times and arrange for error-checking and retransmission.

The centralized network would be switched by a sophisticated common control, which would itself be a minicomputer. The control unit would accept requests for service, set up connections, handle interface and error-checking arrangements, and store and forward data from a sender if a receiver were busy.

CONCLUSION

To laymen, computers sometimes appear to be either servants of the scientist or inscrutable bill-collectors that never admit to mistakes. But new generations of computer scientists will use computers in ways not yet thought of [66]. Computers are now used primarily as tools in business and in the physical sciences, but their power of massive computation and logical manipulation is also suitable for the social sciences. Large interacting computer systems can also be used to benefit industry and government, where the capabilities of the machine can be combined in ingenious ways. Far from being a threat to human dignity and individuality, computing science can provide ways to resolve the puzzles of the cosmos, of life, and of society.

REFERENCES

1. K. B. Miller, *Telephone Theory and Practice: Automatic Switching and Auxiliary Equipment,* McGraw-Hill, New York, 1933, pp. 183–248.
2. F. J. Scudder and J. N. Reynolds, Crossbar dial telephone switching system, *Bell Sys. Tech. J.* **18**(1), 76–118 (January 1939).
3. C. E. Shannon, A symbolic analysis of relay and switching circuits, *Trans. AIEE* **57,** 713–723 (1938).
4. W. Keister, A. E. Ritchie, and S. H. Washburn, *The Design of Switching Circuits,* Van Nostrand, New York, 1951.
5. G. R. Stibitz, The relay computers at Bell Labs, *Datamation* 39–44 (April 1967); 45–47 (May 1967).
6. E. G. Andrews, Telephone switching and the early Bell Laboratories computers, *Bell Sys. Tech. J.* **42**(2), 341–353 (1963).
7. G. V. King, Centralized automatic message accounting system, *Bell Sys. Tech. J.* **33**(6), 1331–1342 (November 1954).
8. R. L. Dietzold, The Isograph—A mechanical root-finder, and R. O. Mercner, The mechanism of the Isograph, *Bell Lab. Rec.,* **16**(4), 130–140 (December 1937).
9. Development of the electrical director, *Bell Lab. Rec.* **22**(5), 225–230 (January 1944).
10. W. E. Ingerson, The Nike Ajax computer, *Bell Lab. Rec.* **38**(1), 26–30 (January 1960); and J. L. Troe, Nike in the air defense of our country, *Bell Lab. Rec.,* **38**(4), 122–129 (April 1960).
11. A. A. Currie, The general purpose analog computer, *Bell Lab. Rec.* **29**(3), 101–108 (March 1951).
12. E. Lakatos, Problem solving with the analog computer, *Bell Lab. Rec.* **29**(3), 109–114 (March 1951).
13. J. Bardeen and W. H. Brattain, Physical principles involved in transistor action, *Phys. Rev.* **75,** 1208–1225 (April 15, 1949).
14. J. H. Felker, Performance of TRADIC transistor digital computer, in *Proceedings of the Eastern Joint Computer Conference, December 8–10, 1954,* pp. 46–49.
15. J. A. Githens, The TRADIC Leprechaun computer, in *Proceedings of the Eastern Joint Computer Conference, December 10–12, 1956,* pp. 29–33.
16. R. W. Hamming, Error detecting and error correcting codes, *Bell Sys. Tech. J.* **29**(2), 147–160 (April 1950).
17. M. D. McIlroy, Macro instruction extensions of compiler languages, *Commun. ACM* **3**(4), 214–220 (April 1960).
18. M. E. Barton, The macro assembler, SWAP—A general purpose interpretive processor, *AFIPS Conference Proceedings,* Vol. 37, 1970, pp. 1–8.
19. P. S. Fuss and J. C. Stuart, Jr., Making the fast Fourier transform really fast, *Bell Lab. Rec.* **51**(2), 49–54 (February 1973).
20. J. F. Kaiser, Graphs should be computer drawn, in *The Human Use of Computing Machines,* Bell Laboratories, Murray Hill, N. J., 1966, pp. 9–14.
21. W. H. Ninke, GRAPHIC 1—A remote graphical display console system, in *AFIPS Conference Proceedings,* Vol. 27, Part 1, 1965, pp. 839–846.

BELL LABORATORIES

22. C. Christensen and E. N. Pinson, Multi-function graphics for a large computer system, in *AFIPS Conference Proceedings,* Vol. 31, 1967, pp. 697–711.
23. V. M. Wolontis, A complete floating-decimal interpretive system for the IBM 650 magnetic drum calculator, *IBM Tech. Newsletter* **11** (March 1956).
24. F. J. Corbato and V. A. Vyssotsky, Introduction and overview of the MULTICS system, in *AFIPS Conference Proceedings,* Vol. 27, Part 1, 1965, pp. 185–196.
25. K. Thompson, *The UNIX Time-Sharing System,* presented at the ACM Fourth Symposium on Operating Principles, Yorktown Heights, N. Y., October 15–17, 1973.
26. D. J. Farber, R. E. Griswold, and I. P. Polonsky, SNOBOL: A string manipulation language, *J. Assoc. Comput. Mach.* **11**(1), 21–30 (January 1964).
27. K. C. Knowlton, A programmer's description of L^6, *Commun. ACM* **9**(8), 616–625 (August 1966).
28. J. L. Kelly, Jr., C. C. Lochbaum, and V. A. Vyssotsky, A block diagram compiler, *Bell Sys. Tech. J.* **40**(3), 669–676 (May 1961).
29. A. D. Hall, Jr., The ALTRAN system for rational function manipulation; A survey, *Commun. ACM* **14**(8), 517–521 (August 1971).
30. M. V. Mathews, *The Technology of Computer Music,* M.I.T. Press, Cambridge, Mass., 1969.
31. J. A. Githens, A fully parallel computer for radar data processing, in *1970 Proceedings of the National Aerospace Electronics Conference,* pp. 290–297.
32. M. J. Evans, G. H. Myers, and J. W. Timko, Command guidance of TELSTAR launch vehicle, *Bell Sys. Tech. J.* **42**(5), 2153–2168 (September 1963).
33. W. A. Malthaner and H. E. Vaughan, An automatic telephone system employing magnetic drum memory, *Proc. IRE* **41**(10), 1341–1347 (October 1953).
34. W. A. Malthaner and H. E. Vaughan, An experimental electronically controlled automatic switching system, *Bell Sys. Tech. J.* **31**(3), 443–468 (May 1952).
35. H. E. Vaughan, Research model for time-separation integrated communication, *Bell Sys. Tech. J.* **38**(4), 909–932 (1959).
36. A. E. Joel, Jr., An experimental switching system using new electronic techniques, *Bell Sys. Tech. J.* **37**(5), 1091–1124 (September 1958).
37. W. A. Depp and M. A. Townsend, An electronic-private-branch-exchange telephone switching system, *IEEE Trans. Commun. Electron.* **83**(73), 329–331 (July 1964).
38. No. 1 ESS, *Bell Sys. Tech. J.* **43**(5), Part 2, 1831–2609 (September 1964).
39. A. H. Doblmaier and S. M. Neville, The No. 1 ESS signal processor, *Bell Lab. Rec.* **47**(4), 120–124 (April 1969).
40. A. E. Spencer and F. S. Vigilante, No. 2 ESS: System organization and objectives, *Bell Sys. Tech. J.* **48**, 2607–2608 (October 1969).
41. R. J. Jaeger, Jr., and A. E. Joel, Jr., "TSPS No. 1: System organization and objectives, *Bell Sys. Tech. J.* **49**(10), 2417–2443 (December 1970).
42. R. C. Matlack, The role of communications networks in digital data systems, in *Proceedings of the Eastern Joint Computer Conference, November 7–9, 1955,* pp. 83–87.
43. G. L. Baldwin and N. E. Snow, Remote operation of a computer by high-speed data link, *AFIPS Conference Proceedings,* Vol. 22, 1962, pp. 170–176.
44. E. E. Zajac, Computer animation: A new scientific and educational tool, *J. SMPTE* **14**, 1006–1008 (November 1965).
45. A. M. Noll, Computer animation and the fourth dimension, in *AFIPS Conference Proceedings,* Vol. 33, Part 2, 1968, pp. 1279–1285.

46. K. C. Knowlton, A computer technique for producing animated movies, in *AFIPS Conference Proceedings,* Vol. 25, 1964, pp. 67–87.
47. J. L. Flanagan, Voices of men and machines, *J. Acoust. Soc. Amer.,* **51**(5), 1375–1387 (1972).
48. J. L. Flanagan, L. R. Rabiner, R. W. Schafer, and J. D. Denman, Wiring telephone apparatus from computer-generated speech, *Bell Sys. Tech. J.* **51**(2), 391–397 (February 1972).
49. R. C. Lummis, Speaker verification: A step toward the "checkless" society, *Bell Lab. Rec.* **50**(8), 254–259 (September 1972).
50. B. Julesz, *Foundations of Cyclopean Perception,* University of Chicago Press, Chicago, 1971.
51. J. B. Kruskal, in *Statistical Methods for Digital Computers* (A. J. Ralston, H. S. Wolf, and K. Enslein, eds.), Wiley, N. Y., to be published.
52. J. L. Kallas, Computer-aided wiring designs, *Bell Lab. Rec.* **42**(10), 343–349 (November 1964).
53. C. Y. Lee, An algorithm for path connections and its applications, *IRE Trans. Electron. Comput.* **EC-10**(3), 346–365 (September 1961).
54. R. T. Herbst, Designing equipment with computers, *Bell Lab. Rec.* **44**(4), 129–134 (April 1966).
55. C. W. Farlow, Machine aids to the design of ceramic substrates containing integrated circuit chips, in *Proceedings of the 1970 Design Automation Workshop, San Francisco.*
56. D. B. Armstrong, A deductive method for simulating faults in logic circuits, *IEEE Trans. Comput.* **C-21**(5), 464–471 (May 1972).
57. T. A. Gibson and R. F. Grantges, A computer program for No. 1 ESS junctor assignments, *Bell Lab. Rec.* **44**(6), 192–196 (June 1966).
58. B. R. Fowler, XYMASK, *Bell Lab. Rec.* **47**(6), 205–209 (July 1969).
59. P. M. Sherman, FLOWTRACE, A computer program for flowcharting programs, *Commun. ACM* **9**(12), 845–854 (December 1966).
60. R. M. Bilowos and F. E. Swiatek, Charting ESS programs . . . with ESSFLO, *Bell Lab. Rec.* **47**(2), 38–43 (February 1969).
61. J. S. Nowak, Emergency action for No. 1 ESS, *Bell Lab. Rec.* **49**(6), 176–179 (June/July 1971).
62. B. G. Ryder, The PFORT verifier, *Software Pract. Exper.* **4**(4), 359–377 (December 1974).
63. N. R. Sinowitz, DATAPLUS, A computer language for English-speaking people, *Bell Lab. Rec.* **46**(11), pp. 362–369 (December 1968).
64. A. G. Fraser, On the interface between computers and data communication systems, *Commun. ACM* **15**(7), 566–573 (July 1972).
65. J. R. Pierce, Network for block switching of data, *Bell Sys. Tech. J.* **51**(6), 1133–1145 (July–August 1972).
66. W. O. Baker, Computers as information-processing machines in modern science, *Daedalus* **99**(4), 1088–1120 (Fall 1970).

Bell Laboratories Staff

BELLMAN'S PRINCIPLE OF OPTIMALITY

Bellman's Principle of Optimality is a fundamental statement which is used as the basis for mathematically analyzing sequential decision processes. Bellman's statement (there are many variations) is

> An optimal policy has the property that whatever the initial state and decision are, the remaining decisions must constitute an optimal policy with regard to the state resulting from the first decision.

A sequential decision process can be thought of as following the behavior depicted in Fig. 1. Each of the boxes represents a stage in the N-stage decision process. The arrow coming into a stage indicates a particular state in which the system finds itself. From some admissible set of decisions, an alternative is chosen at each stage, from which two things occur. First, a return (reward, profit, cost) is derived. Second, a new state, the output state, represented by the arrow leaving the stage, is determined based on the input state and decision. A sequence of decisions, one for each stage, is called a policy. A policy is said to be optimal if it maximizes or minimizes a total reward function—a function (often sum) of the individual stage returns. A sequential decision process may be classified as finite or infinite, based on the number of stages; deterministic or stochastic; and discrete or continuous again based on the stage definition. The Principle of Optimality has been applied to each of these types of processes, with some modifications.

There are many ways to paraphrase the principle, each attesting to its apparent simplicity. For example,

> Once we arrive in a state it is of no consequence (for our future decisions) how we got there.

Or,

> If two policies are the same up to a point and one policy is better from that point to the end, then it is a better policy.

The proof of the principle, Bellman states, is immediate by contradiction. It might be stated as: If at some stage the remaining decisions were not optimal, then the whole policy cannot be optimal. This proof certainly seems true for deterministic and simple stochastic systems and, since it is independent of the structure of the problem, need not be repeated for each new problem. The Principle of Optimality should not be accepted axiomatically and may have to be justified for particular multistage decision processes. The essence of it, however, lies not in its validity but in its applicability to solving these problems. Here there are minor discrepancies of opinion.

The principle makes it possible to construct a computational procedure that maintains the structure of the problem while at the same time drastically

BELLMAN'S PRINCIPLE OF OPTIMALITY

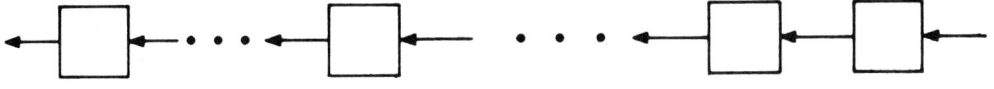

Fig. 1.

reducing computations. Bellman was the first to do this, but the problem is that his principle is not directly amenable to mathematical treatment. The principle can only be thought of as a necessary criterion for optimality. It is essential to mathematically require other conditions to hold so that the procedure is sufficient as well.

This mathematical procedure, called dynamic programming by Bellman, is based on the idea that all sequential decision processes can be decomposed into two parts: the first decision and the remaining ones. Dynamic programming takes a multistage decision process and decomposes it into a series of one-stage problems. In general, computations increase exponentially with the number of variables but only linearly with the number of subproblems. Hence the use of dynamic programming can make the difference as to whether a problem is solvable or not. Formulas that have been developed showing the computational savings due to dynamic programming should be examined carefully. They often do not show the extra optimizations which must be performed in these one-stage problems. These difficulties arise because the best decision must be found for each value the input state variable might achieve. This phenomenon, which sometimes makes solutions prohibitive, is often referred to as "the curse of dimensionality." Fortunately, there are many computation-saving schemes that have been developed permitting solution of otherwise insolvable problems.

When applied to a multistage system, the Principle of Optimality naturally gives rise to an iterative procedure. Dynamic programming, the name given to these iterative or recursive relationships, is thought of by many as a mathematical statement of the Principle of Optimality. The general procedure is to build up successively optimal policies for a 1-stage, 2-stage, ... , N-stage process, each time using the principle. These relationships and, hence, dynamic programming, arise naturally in many applications such as inventory theory, allocation, and control theory, and not so naturally in many others. To illustrate the procedure and an application of the principle, consider the following simple example.

Stagecoach Problem. Consider the network in Fig. 2 where each node represents a city and each directed arc a road between two cities. The number on each arc corresponds to the distance between cities. The problem is to find the path from City (1) to City (11) which can be traversed in the minimum distance.

In a sense this can be viewed as a problem of four stages, since four roads must be traveled to arrive at the destination. At each stage the state is the city (node) occupied and the decision is which road (arc) to take out of that city.

BELLMAN'S PRINCIPLE OF OPTIMALITY

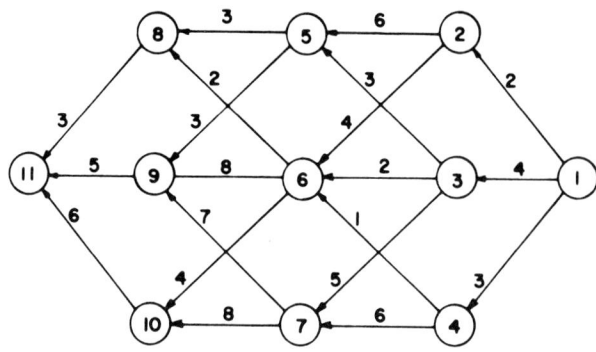

Fig. 2.

Notice that the number of available decisions might be different at each stage and state. The return from being in a state and making a decision is the distance that would be accumulated in moving on that arc. The sum of the individual returns is to be minimized.

One approach to solve this problem might be to determine the minimum path at each stage (Table 1). Unfortunately, this procedure does not generate a path from (1) to (11) and is not in general feasible.

A second method could be to determine the best initial decision, i.e., min (2, 4, 3) = 2; hence it is best to go from (1) to (2). Then given the state is (2), consider min (6, 4) = 4 yielding (6) as the next state. Continuing in this manner, a feasible path (1) → (2) → (6) → (8) → (11) will be generated with total distance 11, but alas it is not optimal. The problem stems from ignoring states, e.g., (3) and (4), which might lead to an optimal path once it is decided to go to (2).

The subtleties of the Principle of Optimality tell us, first, if some state is entered it is not necessary to consider how it is entered, and second, nonoptimal returns out of that state can be ignored. The analysis might proceed as follows: If our present state is (8), (9), or (10), there is no decision to be made and the return to the end is 3, 5, or 6, respectively. If the present state is (5), there are two possible paths with returns (3 + 3, 3 + 5); hence, if state (5) is entered, the optimal path must include the subpath (5) → (8) → (11) with distance 6 and similarly for nodes (6) and (7). If they are entered the optimal

TABLE 1

Stage	Return	Decision
1	min(2, 4, 3) = 2	Go from (1) to (2)
2	min(6, 4, 3, 2, 5, 1, 6) = 1	Go from (4) to (6)
3	min(3, 2, 3, 8, 4, 7, 8) = 2	Go from (5) to (8)
4	min(3, 5, 6) = 3	Go from (8) to (11)

BELLMAN'S PRINCIPLE OF OPTIMALITY

path must include (6) → (8) → (11) and (7) → (9) → (11) with returns 5 and 12. At the next stage the principle is most evident. At state (2) there are only 2 alternatives—either proceed to (5) and incur a return 6 + 6 or proceed to (6) and incur a return 4 + 5, which represent the immediate return out of the present state plus the best return from the ensuing node to the end (which has already been calculated). Continuing backwards in this manner until node (1) is reached, the optimal return is seen to be min [2 + 9, 4 + 7, 3 + 6] = 9 corresponding to the path (1) → (4) → (6) → (8) → (11).

The preceding analysis and calculations are depicted mathematically by the recursive equations of dynamic programming, i.e.,

$$f_n(s_n) = \min_{d_n \in D_n(s_n)} [r_n(s_n, d_n) + f_{n-1}(t_n(s_n, d_n))], \quad n = 1, 2, \ldots, N \quad (1)$$

where

s_n = state with n stages remaining (node)
d_n = decision when n stages are remaining (which arc to choose)
$D_n(s_n)$ = the set of available decisions with n stages remaining (the set of arcs available at node s_n)
$r_n(d_n, s_n)$ = the return (distance) incurred by choosing decision d_n when in state s_n
$f_n(s_n)$ = the optimal return when n stages are remaining when the present state is s_n
$t_n(s_n, d_n)$ = a transformation which produces an output state (new node) resulting from d_n and s_n. This output state becomes the input state at the next stage

Note that in this example $f_4(11)$ is the desired optimum and $f_0(\cdot)$ is defined as 0. By letting $n = 1, 2, 3, 4$ successively, the Principle of Optimality is used in this dynamic programming solution to the problem.

Many authors state that the equations of dynamic programming (1) are equivalent to the Principle of Optimality. This is where the problem surfaces. The applicability of Bellman's principle is general but not assured, and it is necessary to impose conditions on the problem that enable one to state this equivalence. In a sense the principle can be thought of as necessary and sufficient conditions for the validity of Eq. (1). The practicality of this statement is questionable, and many authors believe it is only of theoretical interest. In fact, the recursive equations can be developed and justified without using the Principle of Optimality. Often, only then can the principle be justified using these equations, i.e., Eq. (1) more easily proves the principle than vice versa. A natural question arises: If the principle does not hold for some multistage systems, what conditions must be imposed so that it is both useful and valid? Consider the objective function of a multistage decision process:

$$\max_{d_1, d_2, \ldots, d_N}(\min) [r_1(d_1, s_1) (+) r_2(d_2, s_2)(+) \cdots (+) r_N(d_N, s_N)] \quad (2)$$

$$s_{n-1} = t_n(d_n, s_n) \quad n = 1, 2, \ldots, N$$

BELLMAN'S PRINCIPLE OF OPTIMALITY

where (+) is a binary operator between the stages of the process, e.g., "+", "·", "min", which may differ from stage to stage. Essentially, dynamic programming interchanges the binary operator and the optimization yielding first,

$$\max_{d_N}[r_N(d_N, s_N) (+) \max_{d_1,\ldots,d_{N-1}} (r_1(d_1, s_1) (+) \cdots (+) r_{N-1}(d_{N-1}, s_{N-1}))] \quad (3)$$

$$s_{n-1} = t_n(d_n, s_n) \quad n = 1, 2, \ldots, N$$

and finally (1),

$$f_N(s_N) = \max_{d_N}[r_N(d_N, s_N) (+) f_{N-1}(s_{N-1})]$$

$$s_{N-1} = t_N(d_N, s_N)$$

Actually this interchange is performed $N - 1$ times, the last of which yields Eq. (1). There were two steps to this decomposition: the first was that the total objective function could be separated, i.e.,

$$r_N (+) r_{N-1} (+) \cdots (+) r_1 = r_N (+) (r_{N-1} (+) \cdots (+) r_1)$$

the second is that the maximization can be brought inside, i.e., that Eq. (2) is equal to Eq. (3). This is essentially the Principle of Optimality. However, either of these may fail to hold. Separability may not be possible. As an example, let Eq. (2) be

$$\max_{d_1,d_2,d_3} [r_1(d_1, s_1) + r_2(d_2, s_2) \cdot r_3(d_3, s_3)]$$

However, this is not

$$\max_{d_1,d_2,d_3} [\{r_1(d_1, s_1) + r_2(d_2, s_2)\} (+) r_3(d_3, s_3)]$$

for any (+) and decomposition cannot be performed. (It should be pointed out that a transformation of variables in this and many problems can alleviate the problem of separability.) Assume now that the total objective function is separable. Specifically, let it be

$$\max_{d_1,d_2} [r_1(d_1, s_1) \cdot r_2(d_2, s_2)]$$

with

$$r_1(d_1, s_1) = 3d_1$$
$$r_2(d_2, s_2) = d_2 s_2$$

with

$$-3 \leq d_2 \leq -1, \quad 1 \leq d_1 \leq 3, \quad s_2 > 0$$

The Principle of Optimality states first consider Stage 1, i.e.,

$$f_1(s_1) = \max_{1 \leq d_1 \leq 3} [r_1(d_1, s_1)] = \max_{1 \leq d_1 \leq 3} [3d_1] = 9$$

Then compose it with Stage 2,

$$f_2(s_2) = \max_{-3 \leq d_2 \leq -1} [r_2(d_2, s_2) \cdot f_1(s_1)] = \max_{-3 \leq d_2 \leq -1} [d_2 s_2 \cdot 9] = -9s_2$$

However,

$$\max_{d_1, d_2} [3d_1 \, d_2 \, s_2] = -3s_2$$

when $d_1 = 1$ and $d_2 = -1$, which is surely better than $f_2(s_2)$. Thus maximizing over d_1 first, fails to give the true optimum. To guarantee equality it is sufficient to require a monotonicity condition on the original objective function, i.e., for every feasible value of $r_n(d_n, s_n)$, the total objective function must be a nondecreasing function of the return from the first $n - 1$ stages. (Clearly in the example as r_1 increases, $r_2 \cdot r_1$ would decrease.) Therefore, to be able to decompose the N-stage decision problem into N 1-stage decision problems, both separability and this monotonicity condition are sufficient (but not necessary). In much of the literature of dynamic programming, "+" is the only binary operation considered. Both of these conditions hold in this case so no mention of problems in the use of the principle or decomposition for dynamic programming is ever mentioned.

BIBLIOGRAPHY

Bellman, R., *Dynamic Programming*, Princeton University Press, Princeton, N.J., 1957.
Gluss, B., *An Elementary Introduction to Dynamic Programming*, Allyn and Bacon, Boston, 1972.
Nemhauser, G., *Introduction to Dynamic Programming*, Wiley, New York, 1966.
Wagner, H., *Principles of Operations Research*, Prentice-Hall, Englewood Cliffs, N.J., 1969.

Michael J. Magazine

BENCHMARK

INTRODUCTION

In the early 1960s there was rapid growth in computer usage, which precipitated demands for larger, faster, and more powerful computer systems. The procurement of such a system became a major problem due to the large variety of computer systems that were constantly being improved. The problem was compounded by the keen competition and the fabulous claims of the

BENCHMARK

vendors. To handle these problems, a method of comparing systems was needed.

Originally, this was done by directly comparing the computer systems' hardware features, e.g., memory access time, execution time for the add instruction, and memory size. However, this simple comparison did not consider the biases or needs of a particular computer center. Eventually this was considered by weighting a collection of machine instructions (instruction mix).

The computer hardware improved with new sophisticated features such as interleaving of memory accesses and overlapped I/O. Unfortunately, instruction mixes did not measure these new and slightly unpredictable features. To measure and approximate the value of these features, certain simple skeleton routines, called kernal programs, were written and artificially timed. The emphasis was still on measuring hardware features.

Software systems and compilers were undergoing phenomenal growth and were having greater effects on the user community. Thus a simple measure of both hardware and software was needed. This led the computer center to take a sample of its programs, convert them, and test-run them on the proposed new systems. Such test-runs gave insights into the power of the computer system, potential conversion problems, and the system's reliability. This procedure has become known as benchmarking.

Benchmarking is still being used to study and compare computer systems. However, it can be used in other applications such as system/compiler testing and model validation. In the following sections, the steps of benchmarking, resulting problems, and applications are examined more closely.

OVERVIEW

A computer system or processor has a group of users who communicate their needs in the form of programs, data, and commands. This collection is called the workload. To represent this workload, benchmarks are usually collected. Formally, a benchmark may be defined as an ordered collection of routines that represent a particular workload on some computer system or processor.

In this definition of benchmark, "routine" is allowed to cover a broad spectrum ranging from source programs to simply program/problem specifications. The main purpose here is to specify the user's needs in the most simple and workable form. Thus, for example, data edits and sorts might be easier to describe as problem specifications, since the utility program packages may vary from system to system.

Now, the workload may have multiple entry points and a timing sequence for submittals. Thus routines in a benchmark are "ordered," i.e., partitioned into groups and then sequentially ordered within each group. This ordering allows a description of job mixes.

The most important aspect of a benchmark is that it resembles a particular workload. To do this, the workload must be well understood and characterized by certain variables.

An example of a benchmark is a random sample of FORTRAN programs collected to represent the workload on a FORTRAN compiler.

The benchmark can then be processed through some system and the resulting performance measures collected. For example, the sample of FORTRAN programs may be compiled by a new FORTRAN compiler; the resulting listings, diagnostic messages, time accounting, etc. are considered the performance measures. In this view, the processing system is essentially a simulator with the benchmark as the simulation data and the performance measures as the simulation output.

In order to define, limit, and document the simulation, a set of operational rules is needed. These rules should define the system configuration and parameters, state the performance measures to be collected, and give other controlling information. Thus a statement defining the number of tape drives to be attached to a system is an example of an operational rule.

A benchmark run can now be formally defined as the processing of a benchmark according to a set of operational rules, and the collection of resulting performance measures.

The results of a benchmark can be varied by either using different benchmarks or changing the operation rules or system. These results can then be studied and analyzed.

The combination of these steps, namely the selection of benchmarks, their runs, and subsequent analysis for some objectives, is called a benchmark experiment. In the following sections, these steps are examined more closely.

THE EXPERIMENTAL DESIGN

The benchmark experiment, like any scientific experiment, must be carefully planned in order to be successful. In the design stage, the objectives must be clearly stated, initial benchmark steps planned, and the feasibility of the design studied.

The benchmark steps are described in later sections. It suffices to note here that all steps, their purposes, and their interrelationships should be outlined. This allows basic questions to be raised and subgoals defined. The objectives and feasibility study are now examined.

Objectives

The objectives are the main questions which must be answered by the experiment. These objectives must be clearly stated and then broken down into detailed subgoals or questions. The importance here cannot be underestimated, since these statements help define experimental parameters such as workload descriptors, operational rules, and desired performance measures. As a result, the feasibility of the experiment can be defined, thereby avoiding excesses in size and number of benchmarks or runs, as well as effort in the analysis.

Some of the more common objectives are described below.

1. The Feasibility of a New Computer System. Some resulting subquestions would be—"Can it handle the current existing workload? Is there room for anticipated growth? Are there any unusual problems that might arise, such as translation difficulties?" (Normally, every computer center will run a minimal benchmark when purchasing a new computer system. This is usually done to substantiate claims, anticipate problems, and help alleviate fears of the user community.)

2. The Procurement of a New Computer System. Here the questions are similar in the feasibility study, but in addition, many different systems and configurations are examined. The purpose here is to decide which is best. Subquestions include—"What are the criteria for comparison? How are values ordered or weighted? What systems should be considered?"

3. The Tuning of an Existing System. A system can be varied by changing the location and organization of system files, modifying the schedulers, changing priority schemes, etc. These changes for the purpose of improving computer service are called system tuning. The questions here revolve around the effects of the different modifications on various characterizations of the workload.

4. The Validation of a New Processor. When a new compiler, system, or library program is about to be released, questions are often raised regarding its reliability, correctness, and performance. Some typical questions are—"Will it correct old processor problems? Are there any new side effects?"

Feasibility Study

Inquiries into the feasibility of the benchmark experiment should be raised immediately after defining the objectives. In particular, it should be asked whether a benchmark experiment can satisfy the goals [1]. An extreme case is the study of a new nonexistent system—here the benchmarks clearly have no value. However, if the objectives can possibly be accomplished by benchmarking, then the design stage may proceed.

Throughout the planning stage, more feasibility questions should be raised. These questions should try to resolve the following general issues:

1. Can the study be completed in the given time with the available resources?
2. Will the results be sufficiently reliable and accurate?
3. Is the expenditure of manpower, funds, and computer worth the resulting payoff?
4. Are there better alternatives?

BENCHMARK

The major point of this discussion is to think before doing any experiments. If possible, find the best method of satisfying the defined objectives and avoid wasted effort.

DEFINING BENCHMARKS

Benchmarks are a representation of the workload. Therefore, it is first necessary to understand and characterize the workload. After this, it is then possible to select and weight benchmarks. Finally, if possible, the benchmark should be measured for representativeness. For additional information, see Refs. 2–4.

Characterizing the Workload

Classification variables can be initially defined in terms of the experimental objectives. Some of the more common variables used in a computer systems procurement studies are

1. Processor and/or processor language
   a. FORTRAN
   b. COBOL
   c. Utility programs, etc.
2. Execution time
3. I/O time
4. Physical I/O resources used
5. Core requirements

These and other classification variables will normally produce a multidimensional classification of routines.

The investigator of the system can interrogate the job stream and tabulate the desired statistics (e.g., frequency) for each classification. An examination of the resulting tabulations will help determine the importance or weight of each category. Also the categories can be refined to eliminate small unimportant ones and also subdivide those which might be excessively large. The goal is to keep the classifications to a workable size and yet not eliminate any useful, discriminating classifications.

So far, the classification of routines has been static with no description of the interaction. In order to obtain a dynamic view, it is necessary to investigate additional variables such as the remote job entry station and time of job submittal. These parameters can give insights into the different nature of daytime, nighttime, and transitional workloads; the existance of job-submittal bursts; and loads on different remote job entry stations. These measurements are useful in characterizing different workloads, job mixes, and job queues.

Besides examining current workloads, some consideration ought to be given to potential growth and the influence a new system or processor might have on the user community. Growth factors or future workloads can be extrapolated from earlier descriptions of the workload and from investigations of new programming areas. However, the influence of a new system on the user community might be more unpredictable. For example, the introduction of time-sharing services might eliminate the importance of certain batch processors. Generally, it is advisable to find other computer centers that have made the proposed transition and enquire into the effects of the transition.

Representation of the Workload

There are two ways of representing the workload—natural and artificial. A natural benchmark is an actual sample of the existing workload. Artificial (synthetic) benchmarks are routines especially written to characterize each classification.

The natural routines are truly "representative" and often produce subtle side effects not completely described by the classification variables. An example is a program with a small syntax error that goes unnoticed during compilation and execution; yet on a new system, the program fails. It follows that natural benchmarks are useful in predicting subtle effects on the user community. Thus they are often used in validating system changes, testing compilers, and in feasibility studies. Also, they are the easiest to obtain.

The artifical routines are abstractions that epitomize the classification scheme. All frills are eliminated, as are the numerous and unpredictable side effects. Artificial routines can be used to simulate time-sharing users and other difficult categories. Artificial benchmarks are useful in studying difficult or hypothetical workloads. Artificial or synthetic benchmarks are becoming popular because they extend the usefulness of the benchmark experiment.

Benchmark Selection

For the natural benchmark, routines can be randomly or arbitrarily selected from each category of the real workload. Each selected routine should be "typical" of its classification and have potentially minimal side effects. Generally, it is important to thoroughly understand each benchmark routine in order to analyze any unusual result in the benchmark run.

Artificial benchmark routines for each category may be either selected from a library of such routines or written by the investigator. Even though these routines may be simply written, good abstractions are hard to define. Thus there is a great tendency to use natural routines or at least a combination of the two.

Weights for categories can be set by adjusting the number or duration of benchmark routines in each category. For artificial benchmarks this is done by the appropriate duplication of each representative routine. For natural benchmarks, this can also be done, or else the sample can be enlarged. The latter action will have a tendency to reduce the overall problems caused by a potential side effect.

Finally the routines should be partitioned and sequentially ordered to represent the multiple entries and job mix.

The size of the benchmark can affect the accuracy of the result. Also variances in the workload are best and most accurately represented by distinct benchmarks for each major variance.

A Measure of Representativeness

Once benchmarks have been defined, a question regarding their representativeness is often raised. If a benchmark is representative of a particular workload, then it ought to produce, in miniature, the same basic performance measures as the real workload. Thus the benchmark can be run on the current system and compared with the real workload. The similarities represent the degree of accuracy.

RUNNING BENCHMARKS

A benchmark run is the actual processing of a benchmark and the collection of the related performance measures. These runs are a critical data-collecting step and are controlled by sets of operational rules that govern the following categories.

1. Preparatory work on the benchmark
2. Processing configuration
3. Collection of performance measures
4. Exceptions

Preparatory Work

These rules govern the adaptation of a benchmark to a particular system, the benchmark set-up, and its initialization and termination procedures.

Typically, in the adaptation process, control cards are translated, some routines are coded, and programs are modified to work on the new system. All such changes and man-hour efforts should be documented. Rules should insure that no unexpected optimization takes place which could lead to unexpected or misleading results.

Also, set-up of the job queues and initialization of time-sharing jobs and peculiar problems should be carefully explained so as to minimize deviant actions.

BENCHMARK

Processing Configurations

The processing configuration is defined by the hardware and software configurations and certain system parameters, such as system priorities, schedulers, and the number of job initializers. The necessary elements of the processing configuration should be stated as a rule. The other elements can be optionally defined within given limits. The exercising of such options should be recorded.

Thus, for example, in studying computer systems for possible procurement, the vendor should meet a minimal hardware configuration. But then he might have options to add elements (within cost restraints), such as additional disk packs or drums, for the purpose of improving his systems performance.

These rules basically define or document the processing environment for a benchmark run, and in essence define the simulation model.

Collection of Performance Measures

Performance measures are the resulting output of the benchmark run and describe the processing of a routine and the total benchmark. Some typical examples are throughput time, I/O time, CPU time, system efficiency, man-hours for translation effort, and diagnostic messages. These measures will be used to form the basis of the benchmark analysis.

The rules should state the required performance measures and clear definitions of each. Often there are minor variations in the recording and definition of these measures. Again the variants should be recorded and an effort made to find some means to transform the measures into a standard form.

The inability to collect required measures or satisfactory substitutes weakens the value of a benchmark run. For many system studies the desired performance measures are simply not available. In such cases the investigator can try to modify the system so as to obtain the required measures or else he can simply complete the benchmark run with partial results.

Exceptions

An exception is any deviation from the standard operational rules or any unusual event occurring during the processing. The exception should be clearly described and the resulting course of action documented. Exceptions are unplanned events; thus little can be done except to try to salvage some partial results. The operator should try to maintain the flavor of the benchmark and complete as much as possible.

EVALUATION/ANALYSIS

After completing benchmark runs the resulting performance data are ready for analysis. These measures may be separated into two classes—analytic and descriptive measures.

Analytic measures are ordered, numerical data. For example, throughput time is a numerical measure such that the smaller the value, the faster the job is processed. If measures are taken for each routine, then these measures may be combined for all routines within a given set of classifications or even the entire benchmark. Thus, for example, an average compilation time may be computed for the small FORTRAN job classification. Finding averages like this can often allow the definition of a mix profile and the computation of load limits. Different analytic measures may be combined using weights or other subjective formulas. For example, (CPU time/throughput time) gives an indication of system efficiency while [throughput time—(throughput time/number of jobs) × number of job failures] is an adjusted throughput time. Analytic measures provide an easy basis for comparison.

Descriptive measures are logs of events that occurred during the processing. For example, diagnostic/error messages, memory maps, listings, and system logs are all descriptive measures. These measures provide useful insights into the system processing and related problems. These measures should be evaluated by a panel of experts who can place a subjective value on them. Thus, for example, system reliability and error handling might be determined by the number of system faults and the method used to handle them.

Whenever performance data are missing, they should be approximated as closely as possible. To a certain extent this can always be done with analytic measures; however, missing descriptive data might not be noticed. For example, unrecognized errors or lost jobs may produce a void. The absence of good descriptive data should be approached with caution.

Generally, each benchmark run has a minimal condition for the run to be acceptable for study. Some common minimal requirements are maximum cost and throughput time, minimal response time, and reliability conditions.

Once a run has been studied it can be used as the basis for defining another benchmark run. This is often the case in system tuning. Otherwise, the performance may be distinctly compared with other runs. The comparisons between widely varying benchmark runs are usually difficult and inaccurate due to many exceptions, missing or differing performance measures, and other variations. A noncomparable data base leads to a primarily subjective comparison.

However, if the systems have good performance measures and provide a common base for comparison, then primarily analytic comparisons can be made with a high degree of accuracy.

SUMMARY

Benchmark runs are real examples of processing; at most, only some routines of the benchmark may be artificial. Therefore the results are true to life and very convincing. The processing system needs no model validation or justification as do most simulation models.

Moreover, the concept of benchmarking is basically an extension of normal program testing with sample data. Thus the elements of benchmarking; namely, benchmarks (test data), benchmark run (test run), and analysis (debug or verify), are well understood by most programmers. Because of this, it is easy to find programming support for the design and implementation of the benchmark experiment.

The tools of benchmarking, namely, the benchmark and the processing system, are available, which leads to easily implemented and economical experiments.

On the other hand, there are many problems that may arise. A serious one is gaining access to the desired hardware and software configuration. This situation may be due to the nonexistence or unavailability of the system, or else to lack of funds to rent or purchase the hardware. Hence, for example, it is impossible to study the effects of a new system queue handler on the system throughput until the program is released.

Another common and major problem is the limited and often inadequate performance measures that are available. Normally, very little is recorded about system dynamics, such as page handling queue measures. Inadequate or limited measures can affect the ability to compare several benchmark runs. Also, the inability to obtain desired measures certainly negates a study.

As a result of these problems, benchmarking is not very suitable for investigating machines/systems under development, system mechanics, and many variations of the processor configuration. For these and similar studies, other discrete or continuous simulation models are recommended.

In spite of these problems, the simple merits of benchmarking stand out. Moreover, with constantly improving and newly available performance measures, the range of applications will increase. Also, the development of new ways of using synthetic routines to represent complex real situations is providing an additional impetus. An example of this is the use of benchmarks in a time-sharing system [5].

For additional information and references, see References 6 and 7.

AN EXAMPLE OF A BENCHMARK EXPERIMENT

This section describes a benchmark experiment which will illustrate many of the previously discussed ideas. Because of space, this description is sketchy and abbreviated. For a more detailed example, see Strauss [8].

Background

BM is a small research and development company that maintains its own computer center and uses it on an open shop basis. The current computer (System A) is nearing the saturation point and a replacement system (System B) is proposed. System B's hardware is approximately 75% faster than System A's. Moreover, System B provides additional time-sharing capabilities. The vendor presented a glowing picture of System B's software, implying that it could handle 75% more workload than System A and would present minimal conversion and retraining problems. The price of System B is satisfactory; however, numerous questions have been raised regarding conversion problems, reliability, and the actual increase in workload capacity. As a result, the computer center has been asked to investigate these and other related questions and to reply within a month. No extra funds are available for the investigation.

Objectives

After discussing the questions and related problems, it has been decided that the primary objectives of the study should be to determine the feasibility of System B as a replacement computer and to validate or discredit the vendor's claims. More specifically, the following secondary objectives have been defined.

1. Validate or estimate the workload capacity for System B in terms of current existing workload.
2. Estimate software conversion costs (time or money) and potential conversion problems.
3. Check the reliability and ease of use of System B.

These objectives could be partially achieved by converting a selected sample of the current workload and running it on System B. However, it has been noted that some conversions or reliability problems will probably go undetected due to the limited sample size and time involved. This does not seem a serious problem. The vendor has volunteered some computer time from a nearby computer facility and the assistance of a system programmer. Therefore, it is decided to use a short, benchmark experiment.

Defining the Benchmark

A log is kept of all batch jobs processed by System A. The following variable information is recorded for each job:

Processors or languages used
Execution (CPU) time in minutes
I/O (channel) time in minutes
Core size
Extra I/O devices used

The log is divided into two components for the day and night shifts. Then a cluster analysis is done to group the jobs and the summary statistics are in Tables 1a and 1b. The smallest isolated groups have been eliminated from the description.

BENCHMARK

TABLE 1a
Daytime Workload

Class	Processor	Core	I/O	CPU time	I/O time	% CPU	% I/O	% Jobs
	FORTRAN							
F1	Compile	16K	—	0 < 1	0 < 1	4	2	16
F2	Compile/go	32K	—	5 < 15	0 < 3	13	3	4
F3	Compile/go	48K	—	0 < 5	0 < 1	22	4	26
F4	Compile/go	16K	Tape	2 < 10	2 < 20	9	14	4
	COBOL							
C1	Compile	32K	—	0 < 2	0 < 2	4	3	11
C2	Compile/go	32K	Disk, tape	2 < 10	0 < 20	18	21	9
C3	Go	8K	Disk	0 < 3	0 < 15	6	25	14
U	Utility Program	8K	Disk	0 < 5	2 < 20	4	11	6
					Total	80	83	90

Table 1b
Nighttime Workload

Class	Processor	Core	I/O	CPU time	I/O time	% CPU	% I/O	% Jobs
	FORTRAN							
NF1	Compile/go	32K	—	0 < 5	0 < 5	4	3	25
NF2	Go	32K	Tape	5 < 15	5 < 30	11	16	13
NF3	Go	48K	Disk	15 < 30	0 < 5	49	1	11
	COBOL							
NC1	Compile/go	32K	Disk	0 < 5	0 < 5	3	5	17
NC2	Go	32K	3 Tapes	5 < 15	15 < 60	6	31	5
NC3	Go	16K	Disk, tape	5 < 10	5 < 30	8	21	12
					Total	81	77	83

Sample jobs are randomly collected for each category and placed in a representative order. The quantity of jobs selected is based on the frequency of the job category. The total set of jobs is to approximate about 1 hr of CPU time for each shift. Each job is quickly perused for potential conversion problems and representativeness of category.

The computer center has solicited additional sample programs and data files that might be indicative of conversion problems and not covered elsewhere. From this collection, a small and varied sample is selected for measuring conversion problems. This collection or queue represents the varied use of languages, processors, and data formatting.

BENCHMARK

These three queues form the benchmarks and are processed through System A separately. The processing statistical summary for the sample workloads is found in Tables 2a and 2b. The sample workloads are longer than desired, but seem very representative judging from their performance measures and a subjective review by the computer center staff.

TABLE 2a
Daytime Benchmark

Class	Jobs	System A		System B	Conversion	
		CPU	I/O	CPU	Team hr	Runs
F1	5	3.1	1.0	1.1	3	8
F2	2	12.7	1.3	7.4	2	3
F3	8	17.9	3.2	11.3	11	15
F4	3	8.1	8.6	5.9	10	9
C1	4	3.7	3.1	2.5	9	6
C2	3	13.5	11.5	9.4	12	7
C3	5	4.6	12.6	4.4	12	13
U	2	2.9	5.7	2.2	1	1
CB	1	11.1	0.1	15.2	1	2
Total	33	77.6	47.1	59.4	61	64
Throughput time		88 min		65 min		
Efficiency		.88		.91		

TABLE 2b
Nighttime Benchmark

Class	Jobs	System A		System B	Conversion	
		CPU	I/O	CPU	Team hr	Runs
NF1	4	6.1	3.1	3.8	2	6
NF2	2	12.3	18.7	8.7	6	5
NF3	2	31.6	1.5	21.6	2	4
NC1	3	6.4	7.2	4.4	6	7
NC2	1	7.5	35.7	6.1	10	4
NC3	2	11.2	23.2	9.1	5	4
CB	1	4.7	0.1	7.5	—	—
Total	15	79.8	89.5	61.2	31	30
Throughput time		85 min		66 min		
Efficiency		.93		.92		

BENCHMARK

Running the Benchmarks

The following operational rules have been defined for the processing of the benchmarks.

1. The processing hardware configuration should conform to the proposed System B.
2. The software system should be the latest, standard, supported version.
3. Conversion is to be done by a team of two (one from each staff). Each job is to be translated, *not rewritten,* for System B; this translation includes the job control statements, the program, and data if necessary. Records are to be kept of team hours, modifications made, number of test runs, exceptions, and other useful observations or comments. (For jobs in the conversion queue, this step is sufficient.)
4. Each workload queue is to be run separately on the system without any other programs executing. The operator is to terminate the job stream when all jobs except CB have been completed. CB is a background program of lowest priority and should be executed only when there is free CPU time.
5. All normal job and system accounting information is to be preserved. Any operating exception should be documented; any other useful comments would be appreciated.

Evaluations

After running the benchmarks, the performance measures are accumulated and are shown in Tables 2a and 2b. The I/O measures are not completely measurable and not comparable; hence they are omitted. In the course of running an F4 job, the program fails due to tape-related errors. No adjustments have been made since it was felt that, with respect to time, handling the error was equivalent to running the short program. Excluding the background job, CB, the increases in performance are $66.5/44.2 = 150\%$ and $75.1/54.7 = 137\%$ for the day and night queues, respectively. The improvement in elapsed (throughput) time is smaller. The efficiency of the system is defined as the ratio (total CPU time)/(throughput time). The increased capacities come from the faster hardware and compilers; but more poorly generated code and weak I/O routines hold the gains down. (This can especially be seen in the night queue.)

The FORTRAN conversions are relatively minor and easily accomplished. Diagnostic messages are initially confusing, but once understood, they are helpful. Accuracy differs due to the larger number of significant digits; this difference in answers can potentially cause some speculation as to the source. Tape-handling techniques are problematic because of differing tape formats and handling procedures. Non-FORTRAN tapes cause serious problems.

COBOL presents more difficult problems, particularly in the area of file handling. The differences are minor and can be circumvented by alternate techniques. Once the general problems are recognized and solved, the translation proceeds quickly.

The control language and utility programs are more restrictive than System A. For example, data formats are normally defined by the system and any exceptions have to be read/written by special I/O routines.

The biggest problems seem to be in the I/O area. The tapes have fairly numerous tape errors and the software cannot always eliminate or bypass them. Moreover, the I/O routines seem slow, error prone, and not generalized.

Conclusion

System B seems to offer an increased capacity of approximately 40% (30% or less if the job mix is not satisfactory). This performance should improve with better compilers, I/O routines, and system tuning.

Conversion for most programs and data is easy but time consuming. There are some program packages and languages that are not convertible. These account for less than 5% of the workload. To handle these problems, either locally alternate solutions must be found or else outside computer time should be purchased. In either case it does not seem to be a formidable problem.

Last, tapes were relatively unreliable and alternate models should be investigated. In addition, I/O routines should be improved and more inquiries made into this area.

REFERENCES

1. F. C. Ihrer, Benchmarking vs simulation, *Comput. Automation* **21**, 8–10 (November 1972).
2. D. Ferrari, Workload characterization and selection in computer performance measurement, *Computer* **5**, 18–24 (July 1972).
3. E. O. Joslin, Application benchmarks: The key to meaningful computer evaluations, in *Proceedings of the Association for Computing Machinery, 20th National Conference*, 1965, pp. 27–37.
4. E. O. Joslin, EDP equipment selection—Techniques of selection, *Data Processing* **14**, 115–119 (1970).
5. A. D. Karush, *Benchmark Analysis of Time-Sharing Systems*, System Development Corp., TM-4324, June 1969.
6. H. C. Lucas, Performance evaluation and monitoring, *Comput. Surveys* **3**, 79–91 (September 1971).
7. E. R. Miller, Jr., Bibliography on techniques of computer performance analysis, *Computer,* **5**, 39–47 (September 1972).
8. J. C. Strauss, A benchmark study, *Proc. Fall Joint Comput. Conf.*, **41**, 1225–1233 (1972).

S. J. Walljasper

BENDERS' PARTITIONING METHOD

INTRODUCTION

The development of efficient optimization techniques for large-scale mathematical programming problems is of major importance in economic planning, engineering, and management science. The distinguishing attribute of "large-scale programming" is not the size of the problem alone, but rather size in conjunction with structure beyond the usual convexity or linearity properties. The principal focus of large-scale programming is the exploitation of various special structures for theoretical and computational purposes [8].

In solving large-scale programs, partitioning methods enable a divide-and-conquer strategy. This technique separates a single large problem into two or more subproblems that are expected to be simpler to solve. Dantzig and Wolfe's decomposition principle [1] is the foundation for research in this area. Their method is designed to solve linear programs whose matrices have an independent block-diagonal structure linked by coupling constraints. The solution procedure transforms the original problem into an equivalent "master program" and uses the column generation technique to avoid storing the many columns of the master problem. An iterative process results between the set of independent subprograms and the master program. This partitioning method applies only to problems where all the variables are continuous and may assume any value on a given interval.

In 1962, Benders [2] presented a partitioning approach for solving programming problems that involve a mixture of either different types of variables or different types of functions. Two common applications are the solving of mixed integer linear programming problems and mixed linear and nonlinear problems. As applied to mixed integer problems, Benders' approach defined a pure integer problem that is equivalent to the original problem, and devised an iterative relaxation solution scheme for solving the pure integer problem. One drawback to this method is that it requires solving a pure integer problem at each iteration. Most of the references in the bibliography direct their attention to efficient methods for solving the pure integer problem.

BENDERS' PARTITIONING METHOD AND ALGORITHM

Benders' partitioning method is illustrated using a mixed integer problem where the model is separated into the pure integer problem and the continuous linear programming problem. The method requires that coupling constraints relate the continuous and integer variables. The general mixed integer problem is represented in matrix notation as

$$\begin{aligned}
\text{Min} \quad & z = f'y + c'x \\
\text{Subject to} \quad & Ay + Dx \geq b \\
& y, x \geq 0 \\
& x \text{ integer}
\end{aligned} \quad (1)$$

BENDERS' PARTITIONING METHOD

where y and x are solution vectors, f and c are given vectors, and A and D are given matrices with the appropriate dimension. Problem (1) is reformulated into the equivalent problem as

$$\begin{aligned}&\text{Min} \quad z \\ &\text{Subject to} \quad z - f'y - c'x \geq 0 \\ &\qquad\qquad\quad Ay + Dx \geq b \\ &\qquad\qquad\quad x, y \geq 0\end{aligned} \quad (2)$$

In this form, the Benders' procedure partitions the formulation into a continuous linear problem and an integer submodel which are solved by an iterative process.

If one lets the integer variables x assume some value, say $\bar{x}$, the dual of the remaining LP problem in (2) becomes

$$\begin{aligned}&\text{Max} \quad (b - D\bar{x})'u \\ &\text{Subject to} \quad A'u \leq f \\ &\qquad\qquad\quad u \geq o\end{aligned} \quad (3)$$

Note that the feasible region is now independent of the integer variable x. The solution of Problem (3) for each feasible combination of x solves the original Problem (1) by complete enumeration. Benders' iterative process develops a method that enumerates only a subset of the total in solving the problem.

The procedure advanced by Benders is:

Step 0: Initialization. Set k, the iteration counter, to 1. Select some $u^1 \geq 0$ such that $u^1 A \leq f$. If no feasible solution u^1 exists, then bound the original Problem (1) with a constraint $\Sigma x_i + \Sigma y_i \leq M$, where M is some large number. Now begin Step 0 over with the new problem created by the upper bound. If it is still infeasible, then there is no feasible solution to the original problem. If Problem (3) is now feasible, then the original problem is unbounded.

Step 1: Subprogram. Solve the pure integer problem. (Note that u^k is the vector of dual variables at the optimum of the master program solved in Step 2 at iteration k, for $k > 1$.)

$$\begin{aligned}&\text{Min} \quad z \\ &\text{Subject to} \quad z - c'x - \bar{u}^K D'x \geq b'\bar{u}^K \quad \text{for } K = 1, \ldots, k \\ &\qquad\qquad\quad x \geq 0 \quad x \text{ integer}\end{aligned}$$

If z is unbounded from below, take a z to be any small value $\bar{z}$. Designate the optimal solution $\bar{x}$.

Step 2: Master Program. Solve the linear programming problem for the fixed value of $\bar{x}$ obtained in Step 1.

$$\begin{aligned}&\text{Min} \quad f'y & &\text{or its dual} & &\text{Max} \quad (b - D\bar{x})'u \\ &\text{Subject to} \quad Ay \geq b - D\bar{x} & & & &\text{Subject to} \quad A'u \leq f \\ &\qquad\qquad\quad y \geq 0 & & & &\qquad\qquad\quad u \geq 0\end{aligned}$$

BENDERS' PARTITIONING METHOD

If u goes to infinity with $u(b - D\bar{x})$ finite, add the constraint $\Sigma u_i \leq M$, where M is a large positive constant, and resolve this problem. Set $k = k + 1$. Designate the optimal solution $\bar{u}^k$.

Step 3: Test. If $\underset{x}{\text{Min}}\, z = (b - D\bar{x})'u + c'\bar{x}$, this is the optimal solution, and the process terminates. Otherwise, go to Step 1.

This method provides the optimal solution in a finite number of iterations and indicates an upper and lower bound to the true optimum at each iteration. The solution value of Step 1 is the lower bound at each iteration. The upper bound from Step 2 is the minimum value of the problems examined through the current iteration. It is noted that each solution from Step 2 is adjusted by the constant term $c'\bar{x}$ for the fixed value of x. The convergence of these bounds in a finite number of iterations is obvious when one realizes that each new constraint reduces the solution space in Step 1. With each constraint further restricting the solution, the maximum number of iterations is the number of feasible integer combinations of x.

The basic features of the Benders' partitioning method are:

1. The algorithm divides the original problem into two submodels.
2. Upper and lower bounds are indicated at each iteration.
3. The algorithm generates new constraints or cuts as needed as opposed to enumerating the complete set.
4. Each constraint restricts the solution space in Step 1 until the optimal solution is found in a finite number of solutions.

APPLICATIONS

An aircraft routing problem [3] illustrates an interesting application of Benders' method. The "Port Linkage Problem" is a special routing problem encountered by airlines operating in extreme long-haul and low-density markets. It is concerned with the identification of a set of routes from one single origin over a selection of a few out of a large number of possible intermediate stops to a single destination. The objective of this model is to maximize the total profit (i.e., the difference between the revenue and costs). Details of the model and solution technique are presented in Richardson [3].

Computational experience with the "Port Linkage Problem" has been limited. Several models involving 12 cities have been solved in less than 8 min. Nine aircraft were routed over the 12 cities. A 17-city model required 12 min in determining the first aircraft routing.

In general, computational experience with 0-1 mixed integer models was reported on plant or facility location, project evaluation, and nonlinear multicommodity distribution problems. In each case the number of binary variables limited the size of problem that was solved. One model [4] involved

48 binary variables. Benders' method was also applied to a train-scheduling model with the solution terminated before optimality [5]. McDaniel and Devine [6] have reported several encouraging methods to reduce the time for solution. Further research is listed in the article by Geoffrion and Marsten [7], and others are listed in the Bibliography.

FUTURE RESEARCH

The direction of research in the future will be to improve the solution techniques for the submodels. The master problem, a linear programming model, is solved by any one of several available efficient codes. Current applications are restricted by the efficiency of the integer or nonlinear solution techniques. Better solution methods will combine schemes to solve efficiently the submodel within Benders' algorithm.

In research by Richardson [3], the algorithm was modified to replace the single initial constraint selected by the user to start Benders' method with a set of constraints. The set of constraints reduced the total solution time by solving fewer integer submodels. Another possible variation might be to generate two or more constraints at each iteration. Multiple cuts on the submodel may result in fewer iterations and also reduce solution time.

If the user employs a branch-and-bound technique in the submodel, several modifications are possible. The algorithm can be modified to terminate the branch-and-bound process with the first feasible solution whose value decreases the current upper bound. Tests indicated some promise in reducing solution time in over 50% of the cases [3]. Another modification of this concept is to generate a new constraint each time a potentially better solution is encountered, and the branching process continues from this point at the next iteration. The branch-and-bound process than becomes the guide in the search. This eliminates solving the complete integer submodel at each iteration for the current optimal solution. A third modification is to solve the integer model without the integer constraints. The linear model is easier and faster to solve.

As better solution techniques are developed for the linear, nonlinear, and integer models, the use of Benders' method will increase. Computational experience suggests that this approach may be competitive for mixed integer linear programs. The current implementations do not achieve the full potential inherent in the approach because they use only relatively rudimentary enumerative algorithms. Thus the computing time is excessive. Although there is inadequate computational experience to indicate the number of iterations required to solve a problem, the available evidence suggests some optimism. Often only a surprisingly small number of iterations has been necessary, and the number of iterations has usually not increased in proportion to the number of logical alternatives to be accounted for, or even in proportion to the number of integer variables [7]. As computer power increases and solution techniques improve, Benders' approach may become the chosen method for solving mixed integer models.

BENDERS' PARTITIONING METHOD

REFERENCES

1. G. B. Dantzig and P. Wolfe, The decomposition algorithm for linear programming, *Operations Res.* **8**(1), 76–92 (January–February 1960).
2. J. F. Benders, Partitioning in Mathematical Programming, Doctoral Dissertation, Utrecht, 1960.
3. R. J. Richardson, Benders' Decomposition Method Applied to an Airline Routing Problem, Ph.D. Dissertation, University of Pittsburgh, 1973.
4. J. P. Childress, *Five Petrochemical Industry Applications of Mixed Integer Programming,* Bonner and Moore Associates, Houston, March 1969.
5. M. Florian, G. Guerin, and G. Bushell, *The Engine Scheduling Problem in a Railway Network—Part I* (Publication No. 89), University of Montreal, Montreal, 1972.
6. D. McDaniel and M. Devine, *Alternative Benders-Based Partitioning Procedures for Mixed Integer Programming,* paper presented at ORSA Conference, Milwaukee, May 11, 1973.
7. A. M. Geoffrion and R. E. Marsten, Integer programming algorithms: A framework and state-of-the-art survey, *Management Sci.* **18**(9), 465–491 (May 1972).
8. A. M. Geoffrion, Elements of large-scale mathematical programming, *Management Sci.* **16**(11), 652–675 (July 1970).

BIBLIOGRAPHY

Aldrich, D. W., A Decomposition Approach to the Mixed Integer Problem, Doctoral Dissertation, School of Industrial Engineering, Purdue University, 1969.

Balas, E., Minimax and duality for linear and nonlinear mixed-integer programming, in *Integer and Nonlinear Programming* (J. Abadie, ed.), American Elsevier, New York, 1970, pp. 385–418.

Balinski, M. L., and K. Speilberg, Methods for integer programming: Algebraic, combinatoral and enumerative, in *Progress in Operations Research,* Vol. 3 (J. S. Aronofsky, ed.), Wiley, New York, 1969, pp. 195–292.

Balinski, M. L., and P. Wolfe, On Benders Decomposition and a Plant Location Problem, *Mathematica,* Working Paper ARO-27 (1963).

Benders, J. F., Partitioning Procédure for Solving Mixed-Variable Programming Problems, *Numerische Mathematik* **4,** 238–252 (1962).

Geoffrion, A. M., and G. W. Graves, *Multicommodity Distribution System Designed by Benders Decomposition,* Western Management Science Institute, UCLA, 1972.

Gray, P., Exact solution of the fixed-charge transportation problem, *Operations Res.* **19**(4), 1529–1538 (July-August, 1971).

Hue, T. C., *Integer Programming and Network Flows,* Addison-Wesley, London, 1969, pp. 259–277.

Inman, R., *User's Guide to IPE,* Memorandum 71-2, Development Research Center, International Bank for Reconstruction and Development, Washington, D.C., February 1971.

Lasdon, L. S., *Optimization Theory for Large Scale Systems,* Macmillan, New York, 1970.

Lemke, C. E., and K. Spielberg, Direct search algorithms for 0-1 and mixed integer programming, *Operations Res.* **15**(5), 892–914 (September-October 1967).

Manne, A. S., *A Mixed Integer Algorithm for Project Evaluation,* Memorandum 71-3, Development Research Center, International Bank for Reconstruction and Development, Washington, D.C., February 1971.

Robert Richardson

BENDIX COMPUTERS CDC[1]

HISTORICAL INFORMATION

Computers manufactured by the Computer Division of the Bendix Corporation are known today as either Bendix Computers or CDC G-15, CDC G-20 computers.

The history behind Bendix Computer Division is of interest today because it shows a pattern that was later to be often repeated in the computer field.

Northrop Aircraft, in the late 1940s, designed a family of incremental computers under the direction of Mr. Floyd Steal. These computers were primarily oriented to celestial navigation for SNARK missiles, and were called DIDA, MDDIDA22, DIDA44. Bendix bought the design of these computers, and marketed a digital differential analyzer that was quite successful.

Other offshoots of the Floyd Steal group were Computer Research Corp., founded by Floyd Steal, and later bought by NCR, and the ALWAC Company, which built a drum digital computer.

Branching of these original companies started most of the early southern California computer firms, excepting ELECTRODATA, which was an off-shoot from the University of California at Berkeley.

The Bendix Computer Division entered the general-purpose digital computer field with the G-15, based on a design from Dr. H. Huskey. In the early 1960s a new medium size computer, the G-20, appeared on the market.

The Bendix Corporation sold the computer division to Control Data Corporation in 1963.

---

[1] *Editors' Note*: It is of interest to note that most of the computer manufacturing companies formed in the early days (1940s), during the start of the development of the computer industry, were absorbed by larger companies that today represent the giants in the computer field. This article is offered as an example of how an early computer company participated in the development both of the technology and the formation of one of the giants.

BENDIX COMPUTERS CDC

At the time this machine was built, the only economical form of storage available was of a serial nature, either mercury delay lines or drums. The G-15 used a drum as the working memory; not only were programs and data in the drum, but all working registers as well.

The command structure of the machine is thus closely related to addressing operands and programs to minimize drum latency times. In fact, the important aspect of this type of computer was time: the time to pick up the operands, the time to pick up the next instruction.

A description of the drum memory is almost a description of the machine. The memory is made up of a number of recirculating lines in the drum. Each line has a read amplifier and a write amplifier in a track. All information flow is synchronized with a special clock track, which produces pulses at a 9.3 μsec rate. The physical distance between the write and the read amplifiers in a line dictates the memory capacity of that line. The memory consists of 21 long lines (108 words), 5 short lines of 4 words, 3 short lines of 2 words, and 2 short lines

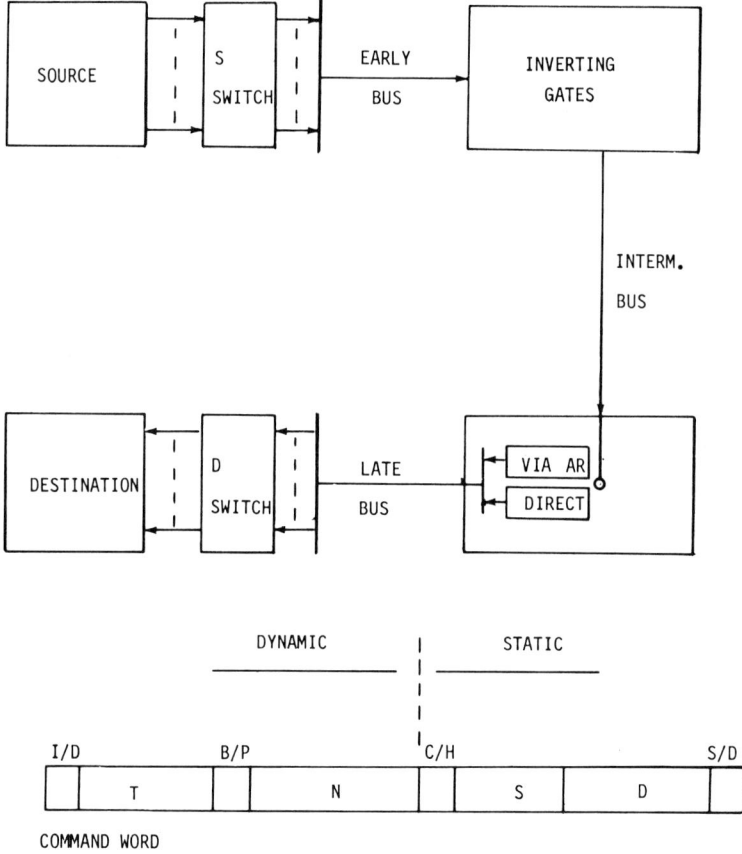

Fig. 1. Transfer of information transfer paths.

BENDIX COMPUTERS CDC

of 1 word, word size being 29 bits. In addition to the clock track, a timing track generates other specific timing signals required for the logic flow. The drum rotation time is 28.5 msec.

The G-15 is a two-address machine, with a third addressing dimension which specifies the (time) location of the next command. The command is structured as follows:

T29 T28		T21						T2 T1
I/D	T	BP	N	C H	S		D	S/D
29	28 27 26 25 24 23 22 21	20 19 18 17 16 15 14 13	12 11 10 9	8 7	6 5 4 3	2	1	
C_1	C_2	C_3	C_4	C_5	C_6	C_7		SIGN

where S and D are the source and destination line numbers, T is the time when the transfer (execution) takes place, and N is the location of the next command. BP allows the insertion of breakpoints in a program. I/D, which stands for immediate or deferred, and CH, which stands for characteristic, change the interpretation of T to set up certain modifications between S and the D at the transfer paths, respectively. Figure 1 shows the switching involved between sources and destinations . The only flip-flop type register in the machine is the one used to store and decode the command.

Figure 2 illustrates the timing aspects of the execution. Assume the following commands in the following locations in memory:

Location	Command	I/D	T	BP	N	S/D
0		1	2	0	4	0
	indicates a deferred transfer at word 2, and the next command at word 4.					
4		0	7	0	7	-
	indicates an immediate transfer of a block of words starting at LOC + 1 continuing but not including word 7. The transfer takes 2 words.					
15		0	17	0	18	-
	this is the only way for the machine to change the order of execution of instructions. Depending on the result of the test, the next instruction is either at N or at N + 1.					

Note the absence of any explicit operator in the format of the instruction. The reason is that some of the short lines, in addition to being used as regular working registers, are, in effect, function units that can perform serially arithmetic functions and logical functions. For example, line 28 is the AR

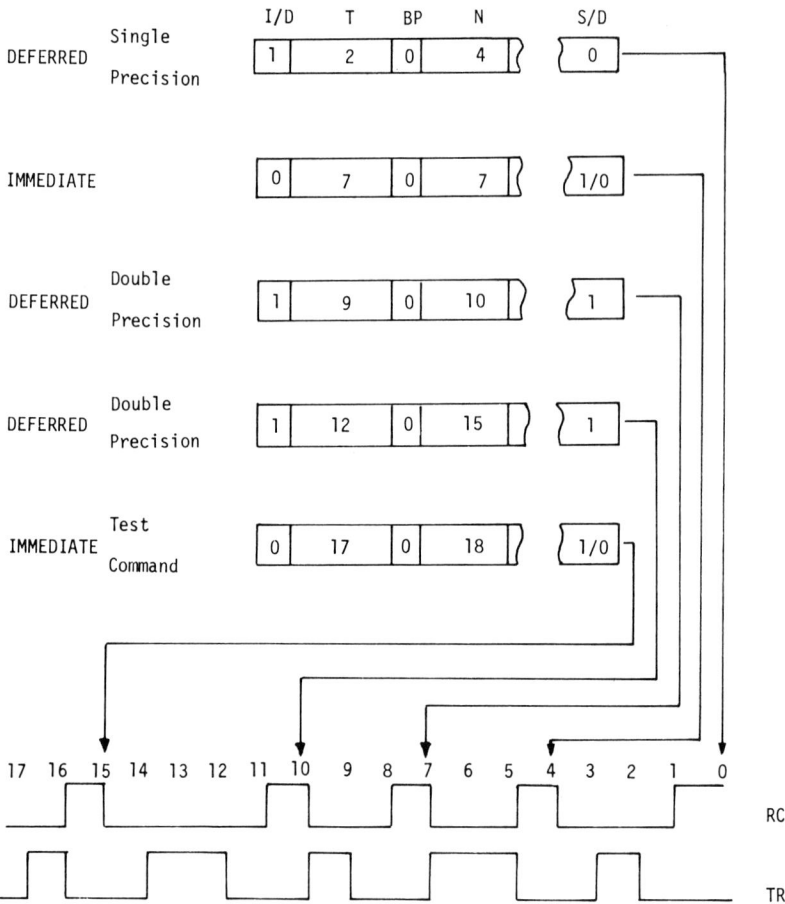

Fig. 2. Illustration of transfer times.

(accumulator register). An instruction with a destination of 29 will add to AR the source word or words, or perform a subtraction depending on the value of CH in the instruction field.

The functional lines are the following:

AR   accumulator register.   1 word
PN   product numerator register.   2 words
ID   multiplicand or denominator
MQ   multiplier or quotient

Logical operations are performed in three short lines; these lines when used as sources perform the following logic:

$$\text{line } 20 \wedge \text{line } 21;\ *\text{line } 20 \wedge \text{line } 21;\ 20.21 + *20.AR.$$

Thirty-two special operations are performed by using line 31 as a destination. For example, the G-15 executes in hardware built-in subroutines the following operations: MULTIPLY, DIVIDE, SHIFT, and NORMALIZE, which are invoked by using 31 as destination.

Numbers are stored as signed absolute values, either as single precision (@29 bits) or double precision fixed point. The accumulator, however, does arithmetic as twos complement numbers.

In multiply and divide operations, the value of T in the instruction field controls the precision of the result. For instance, a T = 114 causes double precision multiplication (which needs 57 two-word recirculation cycles), while T = 56 provides single precision. In divide, the precision of the value of the quotient is a function of the number of iterations, which is controlled by the value of T.

Subroutine jumps are interesting: A subroutine jump (called mark and transfer) specifies both the line and the first word of the subroutine; when this command is executed a timing mechanism essentially remembers the T field in the command. A return command in the subroutine specifies the location of the originating line (which makes it quite awkward) and the first command executed is at the occurrence of the timing pulse remembered.

Input–Output. An interesting feature of the G-15 was its buffered input–output through line 19 and 23. The G-15 was a paper tape oriented system; the tape was nicely packaged in a cartridge. Typical configurations involved in addition a typewriter and a plotter. The typewriter was originally numeric. With the introduction of the alphanumeric typewriter in 1959, the way was open for the use of symbolic languages. Cards and magnetic tape were also available.

Programming. Despite the time concerns of the programmer for optimizing the hardware, there existed an interpretive-floating point language, INTERCOM, which made it incredibly simple to use the machine. In 1960 a version of ALGOL 58 was introduced, which happened to be the first implementation of this algebraic language in a computer, although at this time the machine was already approaching the end of its commercial life.

The G-15 was properly human-engineered as a good, well-rounded package, which contributed notably to the success of the machine.

BENDIX G-20

The G-20 appeared in the marketplace in 1961. Mr. R. Kier designed the architecture of the machine and Drs. H. Huskey and D. C. Evans contributed certain important aspects of the system.

A machine should be studied within the perspective of the time of its conception. In the late 1950s the computer industry was preparing for take-off. In the scientific market, where the G-20 was primarily oriented, there was as yet no recognized leader. As such, the need for some degree of compatibility among manufacturers in terms of input-output media and of languages was not yet fully appreciated.

The G-20 was a 32-bit machine, with 8-bit oriented input–output, appearing at a time when 6-bit oriented machines were emerging as standard. The first algebraic compiler supplied with the machine was ALGOL, in a world that was becoming more FORTRAN oriented.

The G-20, a transistorized, single-address computer, with core storage and fast parallel arithmetic, contained features that were unique at that time, like the use of 63 Index Registers, powerful address preparation instructions, multilevel indirect addressing, interrupts, a simple input–output structure, and high-speed, high-density tapes.

The core memory contained a maximum of 32K words, with a 6-μsec cycle time. Machine timing was synchronous with a 1-μsec clock. In simple configurations, a system comprised a console, a 1000 or a 1500 line/min printer, card equipment, and 1-in., 120,000 character/sec magnetic tapes; all the I/O was programmed. In complex systems, special character-oriented processors (control buffers) controlled some of the I/O; in the latter part of the G-20 life, direct program channels were introduced.

Of special interest in the CP was arithmetic and addressing.

All arithmetic was done as double precision floating point. That is, there were no instructions for fixed point arithmetic. However, a number in the accumulator could be stored as a logic word, a single or double precision floating point, or as an integer (although a mode was used to prespecify the binary point; this mode, called pickapoint, was not a very fortunate approach and will not describe it).

Addressing was another interesting feature. A command word specifies a 15-bit base address field A and a 6-bit index field I. The effective address is, however, the result of those two vectors plus another vector which were the contents of a register called the Operand Assembly register OA. The various address modes were as follows:

Mode	Effective address
$\emptyset$	(OA) + A + (I) = X
1	(OA) + (A) + (I) = X
2	((OA) + A + (I)) = X
3	((OA) + (A) + (I)) = X

A set of address preparation instructions was used to calculate the contents of OA. These instructions added or subtracted to the accumulator the contents of the effective address and put the result in OA. Through these instructions an operand could be used as an address, or an arithmetic or logic result could be used as an address. This allowed for flexible addressing and indexing without disturbing the contents of the accumulator.

It was possible to execute a block of add/subtract operations, logic operations, arithmetic, or logic tests. A repeat command was a double word instruction, the second word specifying the length of the block. On repeated tests, the accumulator contained an address one greater than that for which the text failed.

The G-20 used the uppermost 2 bits of storage to mark words in a special way (this feature as well as the repeat instructions were probably a legacy of the G-15). A register, called the Control/Enable Register, served to enable internal interrupts upon encountering one of the two flags in a command word, a logic word, or a data word. Repeat test commands, for instance, were terminated upon encountering a flag enabled in the above register; any fetch from memory would cause an interrupt if the flag conditions were met. This feature, although expensive in terms of storage, was a very powerful program and hardware debug tool.

Input–output was either a single byte or a block of continuous bytes. Although I/O was 8-bit oriented, a 6-bit byte mode was incorporated for compact storage of 63 character alphabets; this mode packed one 8-bit and four 6-bit characters in one 32-bit word.

About 20 G-20 systems were installed. An interesting system in Carnegie Institute of Technology (now Carnegie Mellon University) was a dual G-20 processor (G-21) and remote access via phone lines from teletypes.

Manuel Langtry

BERNOULLI PROCESS

This article defines the Bernoulli process in terms of the satisfaction of the requirements for a particularly simple mathematical model to be presented. It shows that this model is the logical basis of the *binomial distribution,* which is discussed in its own article. Then, it shows briefly how this model is used to perform *statistical inference* about an uncertain parameter of the process. Finally, it suggests further reading about the application of such statistical inference to *statistical decision.*

To avoid unnecessary repetition, some concepts used in this article are explained and defined in the article *Binomial Distribution,* which should be read before this one.

BERNOULLI PROCESS

THE BINARY SEQUENCE

We are often interested in processes in the real world with two important properties. First, each process is *countable*: the process consists of a sequence of distinct trials that can be counted by pairing them with the elements of the set of positive integers: 1, 2, 3, 4, ... Second, there is a *phenomenon* that *may or may not occur* on each trial k, for all $k = 1, 2, 3, \ldots$. If the phenomenon successfully occurs on trial k, then there is a *success* on that trial, which is the event S_k. If, however, the phenomenon fails to occur on trial k, then there is a *failure* on that trial, which is the complementary event F_k. Since we are concerned with a sequence of trials, each of which has only two possible outcomes, we are discussing a *binary sequence*.

It is important to note that the terms *success* and *failure* are relevant only to the occurrence of the phenomenon. They say nothing about its desirability to you. Indeed, the phenomenon of interest is often undesirable; e.g., the malfunctioning of equipment or a human error in keypunching. In fact, its undesirability may be its major source of interest.

For any positive integer n, let us now consider the first n trials of a binary sequence. On each trial k, there are two possible outcomes: F_k or S_k. Let us call any possible pattern of outcomes of these n trials a *history*. Thus there are 2^n possible histories for the n trials.

To be specific, let $n = 4$. Suppose that S occurs on Trial 2, and F happens on Trials 1, 3, and 4. Then this particular history is $H = F_1 S_2 F_3 F_4$. It is only one of the $2^4 = 16$ possible histories.

There are three logically equivalent methods for representing any history of n trials of a binary sequence. The first method is to show the intersection, or joint occurrence, of the events on all n trials, as just shown. The second method is to specify the history as an n-tuplet. (Other names are n-dimensional vector or ordered list.) To do this, let us define

$$u_k = \begin{cases} 0 \text{ if } F_k \\ 1 \text{ if } S_k \end{cases} \text{ for all } k = 1, 2, \ldots$$

Then any history of n trials may be written as $(u_1, \ldots, u_n)$. Thus the previously mentioned history $F_1 S_2 F_3 F_4$ may be represented as the vector $(0, 1, 0, 0)$, which is a point in this four-dimensional finite discrete space. This space, of course, contains exactly 16 points.

The third equivalent method for writing any history is to delete the commas, to reverse the order of the components of the vector, and, finally, to treat the result as an n-place binary number. Thus deleting the commas and reversing the components of the vector $(u_1, \ldots, u_n)$ gives the n-place binary number

$$g = (u_n \ldots u_1)_2$$

For example, the previously mentioned history, $F_1 S_2 F_3 F_4$, gives the four-place binary number $g = (0010)_2 = 2$. Note that if F were then observed on a fifth trial, the history would become $F_1 S_2 F_3 F_4 F_5$, and the value of g would be unchanged for this larger sample size: $g = (00010)_2 = 2$. This simplicity justifies the reversal of the binary digits in writing the n-place binary number g.

Thus, corresponding to each of these 2^n possible histories, there is a unique number g with $0 \leq g \leq 2^n - 1$. We may identify History Number g, of a binary sequence of n trials, as H_{ng}. When this subscript g is written as an n-place binary number, it reproduces the complete details of this history in reverse order.

THE BERNOULLI PROCESS

A binary sequence is also *a Bernoulli process with known parameter p* if and only if the following additional relations hold for a known value of p such that $0 \leq p \leq 1$, and for every positive integer n:

$$P(S_{n+1} \mid H_{ng}) = P(S_{n+1}), \quad \text{for all } g = 0, 1, \ldots, 2^n - 1$$
$$P(S_n) = p$$

The vertical stroke is pronounced "given." Thus we say "P of S_{n+1}, given H_{ng}" for the conditional probability in the first equation above.

The first part of this definition says that the process is *a random sequence of trials*. The probability of S on Trial $n + 1$ is functionally independent of the history H_{ng} of the previous n trials. The event S_{n+1} is statistically independent of the joint event H_{ng}.

The second part of the previous definition says that the probability of success is a known constant over all the trials.

Thus we may summarize the previous discussion as follows: *A Bernoulli process is a binary sequence of independent trials with constant probability of success*. Until further notice, the constant p is assumed to be known.

Now let us consider the probability $P(H_{ng})$ of any history H_{ng} that might occur in these n trials of a Bernoulli process. Since the trials are statistically independent, $P(H_{ng})$ equals the product of the probabilities of all the events that occur in the history. To prove this, let X_k be the relevant event (either S_k or F_k) on trial k, for all $k = 1, 2, \ldots, n$, so that

$$H_{ng} = X_1 X_2 \ldots X_n$$

Even if the trials were not independent, the following equation, which depends upon no special assumptions, would hold for $n > 1$ by the definition of conditional probability:

$$P(H_{ng}) = P(X_1) \cdot P(X_2 \mid X_1) \ldots P(X_n \mid X_1 \ldots X_{n-1})$$
$$= P(X_1) \prod_{k=2}^{n} P(X_k \mid X_1 \ldots X_{k-1})$$

where the Greek capital pi means product. Since we do assume independence,

BERNOULLI PROCESS

however,

$$P(X_k \mid X_1 \ldots X_{k-1}) = P(X_k), \quad \text{for all } k = 2, \ldots, n, \text{ so that}$$

$$P(H_{ng}) = \prod_{k=1}^{n} P(X_k)$$

as stated.

Since the probability of success is constant over all the trials,

$$P(X_k) = \begin{cases} p, & \text{if } X_k = S_k \\ 1 - p, & \text{if } X_k = F_k \end{cases}$$

for all $k = 1, \ldots, n$.

This may be restated as

$$P(X_k) = (1 - p)^{(1-u_k)}(p)^{u_k}, \quad \text{for all } k = 1, \ldots, n$$

Therefore

$$P(H_{ng}) = \prod_{k=1}^{n} (1 - p)^{(1-u_k)}(p)^{u_k}$$

$$= (1 - p)^{\sum_{k=1}^{n}(1-u_k)}(p)^{\sum_{k=1}^{n} u_k}$$

Let us now define

$$r = \sum_{k=1}^{n} u_k$$

Thus r is the total number of successes in n trials. Also

$$\sum_{k=1}^{n} (1 - u_k) = n - r$$

which is the total number of failures in the n trials. Therefore

$$P(H_{ng}) = (1 - p)^{n-r} p^r$$

for all $g = (u_n \ldots u_1)_2$ such that $\sum_{k=1}^{n} u_k = r$. Thus *all histories of n trials with the same number r of successes have the same probability of occurrence, regardless of the order of successes and failures in the history.*

As long as you are willing to assume that you have a Bernoulli process with known parameter p, then you may apply this important formula to compute $P(H_{ng})$ for any history H_{ng} that could be generated by three different experimental designs. First, you may choose n in advance, for $n \geq 1$; then observe the sequence of n trials; and finally compute the randomly determined r by counting. Second, you may choose r in advance, for $r \geq 1$; and then continue to observe until you count r successes. The last S of these is, by definition, S_n. Therefore, n is determined at random, where $n \geq r$. Third, you may simply observe until you decide to stop observing for any reason.

Counting then gives r successes and s failures, so that the total number of trials is $n = r + s$. The same formula for $P(H_{ng})$ holds for all three designs.

The first experimental design, with known p and specified n, provides the logical basis for the binomial distribution. In the article with that title, we define the binomial coefficient $\binom{n}{r}$, and show that it gives *the number of combinations of n things taken r at a time*. Now, consider the history H_{ng} in which these n trials are found to have r successes and $n - r$ failures in the observed order specified by the n-place binary number g. How many different histories have the same value of r?

Each possible history may be defined by considering the n numbered trials to be the n things, and by considering the assignment of S to r particular trials as taking these n things r at a time. (Of course, the other $n - r$ trials receive F.) Thus the number of possible histories that have r successes, and $n - r$ failures, in n trials is clearly $\binom{n}{r}$.

All these histories having the same value of r are mutually exclusive. Also, as previously proved, they have the same probability. Thus it is easy to find the conditional probability (given n, p) that the random variable $\tilde{r}$ equals r, regardless of the order of successes and failures in the n trials. This equals the sum of all these equal probabilities. Therefore

$$P(\tilde{r} = r \mid n, p) = \binom{n}{r}(1 - p)^{n-r}p^r, \quad \text{for all } r = 0, 1, \ldots, n$$

This is the binomial distribution, which is discussed in its own article.

If, however, you consider the second situation with known p, chosen $r \geq 1$, and randomly determined n, then the probability that $\tilde{n} = n$, given r and p, is specified by the Pascal distribution. This is discussed in Section 5 of Chap. 9 of the book by Pratt, Raiffa, and Schlaifer [1].

NON-BERNOULLI PROCESSES

It is important to understand that the concept of a Bernoulli process is a mathematical idealization, and thus so is the binomial distribution. There are two important ways in which a real process may depart from the definition of a Bernoulli process and thus become a non-Bernoulli process. First, the trials may not be statistically independent. Second, the probability of success may not be constant over the trials.

Consider, for example, the process of generating errors during keypunching. The simplest mathematical model is that of a Bernoulli process. As previously stated, this assumes that on each trial k there is either S_k (an error) or F_k (a correct punching), that the trials are independent, and that the probability of S_k is the same constant for each trial k. Now suppose that the key-punch operator is inexperienced at first but, by hard practice, gradually learns to do the job correctly. Thus the probability of S_k (making an error) *decreases* over the trials. Clearly, for such an operator, the generation of errors is *not* a Bernoulli process at first.

BERNOULLI PROCESS

If the operator continues to practice hard, then the probability of error may become sufficiently small and essentially constant. Then the model will apply more adequately, as long as this probability does not increase temporarily because of boredom or other emotional distress. Presumably, sufficiently humane management can cope with this problem.

Whenever a process contains definite statistical dependencies, the model of a Bernoulli process does not apply. For example, if S_k = rain and F_k = lack of rain, and each trial k is 1 day of weather, then this is clearly not a Bernoulli process because weather tends to persist, day after day, until it changes. Similarly, if the key-punch operator makes an error, and then becomes anxious about it, the conditional probability of making another error may be considerably higher than the corresponding probability given a correct response. If so, then this keypunching behavior is no longer adequately represented by the model of a Bernoulli process. Again, humane management is required to cope with this problem. A trained psychologist may be indispensable.

Of course, this human factors problem, the statistical control of keypunching behavior, may be eliminated when character-reading machines become perfected. In this case a human Bernoulli process is replaced by a comparable machine process. Such replacement will solve the human factors problem by replacing it with the larger social and economic problem of unemployment, unless such workers can be retrained for other positions. Thus even such an abstract topic as the Bernoulli process has relevance to current social issues.

STATISTICAL INFERENCE

So far we have assumed that the parameter p is known. For example, if a well-balanced coin is to be tossed n times and S is defined as heads, then the binomial distribution (with $p = .5$) gives the probability of obtaining r successes in n trials (for all $r = 0, 1, \ldots, n$). If, instead, you plan to toss a well-balanced die n times, and you define S as one spot turning up, then the binomial distribution, with $p = 1/6$, provides the probability of r successes in n trials.

Suppose, however, that you judge that the generation of errors in keypunching by a newly hired but experienced key-punch operator is (at least approximately) a Bernoulli process. Although there are only two alternatives (S_k or F_k) on each trial k, you will be quite sure that $p < 1/2$ for that operator. At the same time, however, you are somewhat uncertain what the true proportion of S would be if you could observe an indefinitely large sample of trials from this human Bernoulli process. Thus you may want to gather a finite sample of data for statistical inference about the uncertain proportion $\tilde{p}$ in an infinite sample.

To keep matters simple, let us assume that there is a finite set $\{p_1, \ldots, p_c\}$ of possible values of $\tilde{p}$ that you are willing to consider for some integer $c > 1$. You must then represent your prior uncertainty about $\tilde{p}$ by a prior probability

distribution:
$$P(\tilde{p} = p_j) = h(p_j) > 0, \quad \text{for all } j = 1, \ldots, c$$
such that
$$\sum_{j=1}^{c} h(p_j) = 1$$

The assessment of prior distributions is discussed in the cited references.

Suppose that, after assessing your prior distribution, you observe n trials, and find a history H_{ng} containing r successes and $n - r$ failures in the observed order. You can now write the equation for the conditional probability of H_{ng}, given each possible value p_j that $\tilde{p}$ might take:
$$P(H_{ng} \mid \tilde{p} = p_j) = p_j^r(1 - p_j)^{n-r}, \quad \text{for all } j = 1, \ldots, c$$
Then multiplication of probabilities gives the joint probability:
$$P(\tilde{p} = p_j, H_{ng}) = h(p_j)p_j^r(1 - p_j)^{n-r}$$
so that, by summation,
$$P(H_{ng}) = \sum_{j=1}^{c} h(p_j)p_j^r(1 - p_j)^{n-r}$$

This is your probability of the history H_{ng} when the parameter of the process is uncertain. All histories with the same value of r clearly have the same probability.

By definition of conditional probability, the posterior distribution of $\tilde{p}$ is specified by
$$P(\tilde{p} = p_j \mid H_{ng}) = \frac{P(\tilde{p} = p_j, H_{ng})}{P(H_{ng})}$$
If we abbreviate this conditional probability as $h(p_j \mid r, n)$, then the posterior distribution may be written as
$$h(p_j \mid r, n) = \frac{h(p_j)p_j^r(1 - p_j)^{n-r}}{\sum_{j=1}^{c} h(p_j)p_j^r(1 - p_j)^{n-r}}$$

This is the famous Bayes' theorem.

Suppose, instead, that you wish to represent your prior uncertainty about $\tilde{p}$ by means of a probability density function h, such that $h(p) \geq 0$, and
$$\int_0^1 h(t)\, dt = 1$$

Then your posterior density will be given by the formula
$$h(p \mid r, n) = Kh(p)p^r(1 - p)^{n-r}$$

BERNOULLI PROCESS

where the constant K is determined so that

$$\int_0^1 h(t \mid r, n) \, dt = 1$$

This formula for the posterior density is another form of Bayes' theorem.

There are two possible uses for the posterior distribution of $\tilde{p}$. First, you can use it to make statistical inference about the uncertain proportion $\tilde{p}$. From the viewpoint of the four cited references, *statistical inference about a parameter means computation of a decision maker's posterior probability distribution, and its interpretation in terms of fair bets.*

When the sample size is small, then the posterior distribution is very sensitive to the postulated prior distribution. When, however, the sample size is large, then the posterior distribution is relatively less sensitive to the choice of the prior in the following sense: Rather different priors will combine with the likelihood $P(H_{ng} \mid \tilde{p} = p)$ to give essentially the same posterior. This important topic is well discussed in the cited references.

Although a complete specification of the posterior distribution is best, it is sometimes useful to abbreviate this by stating a Bayesian confidence interval. This has a specified high posterior probability that the uncertain parameter $\tilde{p}$ lies within the interval.

If the sample size n is large, then, as Lindley shows [2], the posterior probability density of $\tilde{p}$ is approximately normal, and the posterior mean of $\tilde{p}$ is the proportion

$$\hat{p} = r/n$$

of successes in the large sample, and the posterior standard deviation is

$$\hat{\sigma} = [\hat{p}(1 - \hat{p})/n]^{\frac{1}{2}}$$

If n is sufficiently large, then the Bayesian confidence interval about that mean $\hat{p}$ will be so small that every point in it will approximately equal the posterior mean $\hat{p}$ to (let us say) two decimal places. In this case the decision maker will be practically certain that his proportion $\hat{p}$, computed from the large sample, will approximately equal the proportion that could be computed from an indefinitely large sample if it were physically and economically possible to observe such. All this, of course, is based on the assumption that the sample is from a Bernoulli process.

STATISTICAL DECISION

When data can be obtained cheaply, as in the analysis of keypunching errors, then large samples are always taken. In some cases, however, observations are very expensive: for example, testing of rocket engines or operational testing of space vehicles. Moreover, in such cases the major interest is often not in statistical inference about uncertain parameters, but in *optimizing decisions under uncertainty*. In any decision problem the posterior probability distribution is an important quantitative input to a decision model. This is especially so when the posterior distribution is not tightly concentrated in a small interval.

Since it takes at least a small book to discuss statistical inference, and another to present decision theory, no attempt will be made here to show how inference about a Bernoulli process is used to compute an optimum decision. Instead, we shall give some hints for further reading.

First, Lindley [2] gives an excellent treatment of Bayesian statistical inference by means of posterior probability distributions, with only a limited discussion of decision theory. The major virtue of his book is that it shows how conventional statistical methods, developed without use of Bayes' theorem, can be reinterpreted in the newer context. This book helps to bridge the gap between the various philosophies of statistics. It requires a good knowledge of the calculus and some aquaintance with matrix algebra.

If you are mainly interested in a thorough analysis of decision problems in business, with a minimum of mathematics, then you should read Schlaifer [3]. If you want a little bit of mathematics and an elegant logical analysis of an artificial but relevant problem, then read Raiffa [4]. If you have a good command of the calculus, then read Pratt, Raiffa, and Schlaifer [1] for a rather complete discussion of theory and practice.

REFERENCES

1. J. W. Pratt, H. Raiffa, and R. Schlaifer, *Introduction to Statistical Decision Theory*, McGraw-Hill, New York, 1965.
2. D. V. Lindley, *Introduction to Probability and Statistics from a Bayesian Viewpoint. Part 1, Probability. Part 2, Inference*, Cambridge University Press, Cambridge, 1965.
3. R. Schlaifer, *Analysis of Decisions under Uncertainty*, McGraw-Hill, New York, 1969.
4. H. Raiffa, *Decision Analysis, Introductory Lectures on Choice and Uncertainty*, Addison-Wesley, Reading, Mass., 1968.

Raymond H. Burros

BERNOULLI'S METHOD

Given a polynomial

$$f(z) = a_0 z^n + a_1 z^{n-1} + \cdots + a_n = a_0(z - r_1)(z - r_2) \cdots (z - r_n), \tag{1}$$

this is the characteristic polynomial for the difference equation

$$a_0 \eta_{\nu+n} + a_1 \eta_{\nu+n-1} + \cdots + a_n \eta_\nu = 0. \tag{2}$$

It is known that a linear homogeneous difference equation has n linearly

BERNOULLI'S METHOD

independent solutions, and any solution is a linear combination of any fundamental set of linearly independent solutions. For any r_j, $\eta_\nu = r_j^\nu$ is a solution, and if the r_j are distinct, then these provide a fundamental set. Hence any solution has the form

$$\eta_\nu = \sum \gamma_j r_j^\nu. \tag{3}$$

Clearly, then, if

$$|r_1| > |r_2| \geq \cdots \geq |r_n|, \tag{4}$$

and if $r_1 \neq 0$, then

$$\lim_{\nu \to \infty} \eta_{\nu+1}/\eta_\nu = r_1. \tag{5}$$

This is the method of Bernoulli in its simplest form. It is easily verified that if r_j is a double zero of $f(z)$, then $\eta_\nu = \nu r_j^\nu$ is also a solution of the difference equation; if a triple zero, then $\eta_\nu = \nu^2 r_j^\nu$ is a solution; if of multiplicity m, then $\eta_\nu = \nu^{m-1} r_j^\nu$ is a solution. Hence, if (4) holds, then (5) does likewise, regardless of the multiplicities of the other zeros. The initial values $\eta_0, \eta_1, \ldots, \eta_{n-1}$ can be chosen arbitrarily provided only they yield a solution with $\gamma_1 \neq 0$, and with rounded computation this will always be the case.

Clearly we could as well form the difference equation

$$a_n \mu_{\nu+n} + a_{n-1} + \cdots + a_0 \mu_\nu = 0, \tag{6}$$

the solutions are linear combinations of $r_j^{-\nu}$, and, in the confluent case, $\nu r_j^{-\nu}$, $\nu^2 r_j^{-\nu}, \ldots$. Hence if

$$|r_n| < |r_{n-1}| \leq \cdots,$$

then

$$\lim_{\nu \to \infty} \mu_\nu/\mu_{\nu+1} = r_1. \tag{7}$$

In this form the method can be adapted to transcendental functions analytic within a circular disk within which the zeros are required, but the justification is less elementary. It is sufficient to consider a circular disk with center at the origin. The justification is based on *König's theorem*.

Let

$$h(z) = 1 + c_1 z + c_2 z^2 + \cdots$$

be analytic for $|z| < |r|$, *and in the circular disk* $|z| < R$ *let its only singularity be a simple pole at r. Then*

$$\lim_{\nu \to \infty} c_\nu / c_{\nu+1} = r.$$

Suppose, then, to change notation slightly, that

$$f(z) = 1 + a_1 z + a_2 z^2 + \cdots$$

is analytic for $|z| < R$ and let its zero of smallest modulus be r with $|r| < R$.

Let
$$g(z) = 1 + b_1 z + b_2 z^2 + \cdots$$
be analytic for $|z| < R$ with $g(r) \neq 0$. Form
$$h(z) = g(z)/f(z).$$
The coefficients c_ν can be formed by the simple algorithm
$$a_1 + c_1 = b_1,$$
$$a_2 + a_1 c_1 + c_2 = b_2,$$
$$a_3 + a_2 c_1 + a_1 c_2 + c_3 = b_3,$$

If $f(z)$ is a polynomial of degree n, one could choose $c_1, c_2, \ldots, c_{n-1}$ arbitrarily, which amounts to an implicit choice of $g(z)$ as a polynomial of degree $n - 1$, but this is not needed explicitly. The result, taking account of the slightly different notation for the coefficients of $f(z)$, reduces to Bernoulli's method in the form (6). But, as is seen, the method applies equally when $f(z)$ is transcendental with properties as stated, in which case one would normally take $g(z) \equiv 1$.

It is also possible to extend the method so as to obtain zeros of greater modulus within the domain of analyticity. The most extensive development is due to Aitken [1, 2; see also 3 and 4]. Form the Hankel determinants

$$H_{\nu,p} = \delta \begin{pmatrix} c_{\nu-p+1} & c_{\nu-p+2} & \cdots & c_\nu \\ c_{\nu-p+2} & c_{\nu-p+3} & \cdots & c_{\nu+1} \\ \cdots & \cdots & \cdots & \cdots \\ c_\nu & c_{\nu+1} & \cdots & c_{\nu+p-1} \end{pmatrix}$$

(here "δ" signifies the determinant). This determinant is of order p, and it is understood that
$$c_{-1} = c_{-2} = \cdots = 0.$$
Then if
$$|r_1| \leq |r_2| \leq \cdots \leq |r_p| < |r_{p+1}| \leq \cdots,$$
it can be shown that
$$\lim_{\nu \to \infty} H_{\nu,p}/H_{\nu+1,p} = r_1 r_2 \cdots r_p.$$

This is a corollary to Hadamard's extension of König's theorem [4].

The $H_{\nu,p}$ are related by an important identity
$$H_{\nu,p+1} H_{\nu,p-1} = H_{\nu-1,p} H_{\nu+1,p} - H_{\nu,p}^2.$$
Hence in the table

1	1	-1	-1	1	$\cdots$
1	a_1	H_{12}	H_{13}	H_{14}	$\cdots$
1	c_2	H_{22}	H_{23}	H_{24}	$\cdots$
1	c_3	H_{32}	H_{23}	H_{34}	$\cdots$

if the $H_{\nu,p}$ are all nonvanishing, they can be computed recursively to the right

BERNOULLI'S METHOD

and downward. But if $g(z) \equiv 1$, they can also be computed from the table

$$
\begin{array}{ccccccc}
1 & 1 & -J & -1 & 1 & 1 & \ldots \\
1 & -a_1 & -a_2 & a_3 & a_4 & -a_5 & \ldots \\
1 & H_{21} & H_{22} & H_{24} & H_{25} & H_{26} & \ldots \\
1 & H_{31} & H_{32} & H_{34} & H_{35} & H_{36} & \ldots
\end{array}
$$

and also more simply and more stably. This is the so-called progressive form.

But complications arise when there are multiple zeros, or even zeros that are merely equal in modulus, and in practice the Bernoulli method has largely been superseded by the more efficient qd algorithm due to Rutishauser. With this it is possible to obtain sequences of polynomials that converge to polynomials whose zeros are the zeros of $f(z)$ having equal moduli. By ingenious devices, Aitken was able to treat these cases, but only by robbing the method of its major appeal, which is its simplicity.

The Bernoulli method as such converges only linearly, but mention may be made of Bauer's form that gives quadratic convergence [5]. Also, Aitken accelerates convergence by making use of his δ^2 algorithm.

REFERENCES

1. A. C. Aitken, On Bernoulli's numerical solution of algebraic equations, *Proc. Roy. Soc. Edinburgh, Section A* **46**, 289–305 (1926).
2. A. C. Aitken, Further numerical studies in algebraic equations and matrices, *Proc. Roy. Soc. Edinburgh, Section A* **51**, 80–90 (1931).
3. A. S. Householder, *Principles of Numerical Analysis*, McGraw-Hill, New York, 1953.
4. A. S. Householder, *The Numerical Treatment of a Single Nonlinear Equation*, McGraw-Hill, New York, 1970.
5. Friedrich L. Bauer, Quadratische Konvergenz der Bernoullishchen Methode, *Angew. Math. Mech.* **34**, 287 (1954).

A. S. Householder

BETA SYSTEM

Beta is a programming system for a series of Soviet computers of the third generation "ES EVM," being developed at the Computer Center of the Siberian Division of the USSR Academy of Sciences (Novosibirsk) under the direction of Professor A. P. Ershov. The system is a universal programming processor of the translating type, which is common for any source language that can be described by means of the BETA system. Setting of the translator for some source language consists of constructing language tables and inserting them into the body of the translator. The first languages practicable in the BETA system were PASCAL PL/1, ALGOL 68, and SIMULA 67.

A multiphase series of optimizing translation is used in the BETA system in which, besides the source language and the target machine language, there are several levels of intermediate languages, namely Int L-1 and INTEL languages.

Int L-1 is the usual list structure language adapted to the BETA system. Translation of the source program into Int L-1 is a syntax-directed decomposition of the program into a treelike structure, the vertexes of which are notions of the source language, used in a semantic description of it, and the arcs recognize the relationship to be a constituent one. Furthermore, in the structure of the decomposed program there are "horizontal" arcs, combining concatenating concepts.

To translate into Int L-1, which includes lexical analysis, syntactical tables of a new type are used which permit analysis and decomposition of the text. These tables are the grammar of the language in the form of an annotated directed graph, the vertexes of which are terminal symbols of grammar. The memory elements (stacks or fifo lists) can be attached to certain vertexes, which make it possible to include into a grammatical rule a series of context conditions (pairing of brackets, coincidence of remote constructions of the language, etc.).

After translation into Int L-1, identification of declared variables is carried out by transferring information about the variable, taken from its declaration, into all occurrences of this variable pertaining to the declaration scope. After this, the process of semantic induction takes place consisting of inductive determination of the attributes of notions introduced into the program during its decomposition. Coercion is thus performed as a coordination of the semantic characteristic of the operand with the characteristic of the position occupied by it. These operations are all carried out by a certain subprocessor of the translator generated automatically according to language tables during the translator's setting for the given source language.

INTEL is the critical component of the translator. Methodologically, it is an attempt to combine the abstract concept of a program scheme with the practical problems of optimizing translation, controlled by the description of the language. The basic structures of INTEL are the control and information flow graph denoting the transfer of control and data from one statement of an INTEL program to another and mode graph, denoting the structure of compound variables being used in the problem. Finally, the parallel structures of the program are described as the task of INTEL. An interpretation of fundamental objects and operations of INTEL is selected so as to ensure adequate and uniform presentation of the semantics of the source languages in conjunction with its structural properties.

After completing the identification and semantic induction, total replacement of decomposed notions of the source program by corresponding INTEL constructions is carried out by a universal subprocessor, directed by a corresponding library of sematic subroutines.

The program being translated into INTEL is subjected to total analysis of its

BETA SYSTEM

logical and information connections in order to lay the groundwork for application of high-powered optimizing algorithms. Optimization consists of economization of common calculations, removals where possible, calculations from loops outside, the most economical means of organization of loops, and of the call for procedures.

The optimization phase is optional in the sense that after composing the INTEL representation of the compiled program, the latter can directly be translated into the object code.

The final part of the translator is the usual generator implementing the translation from INTEL into machine language, the connection of the program to the operational system, to the run-time library of the given language, and allocation of the program into the memory of the object computer.

During the development of the BETA system an attempt is being undertaken to use top-down design, implementation and verifying techniques based on structured programming ideas, and to organize the practical work according to the principle of the chief programmer supported by a technological team.

BIBLIOGRAPHY

Ershov, A. P., A multilanguage programming system oriented to language description and universal optimization algorithms, in *Proceedings of the IFIP Working Conference on Algol 68 Implementation,* Munich, July 20–24, 1970.

Ershov, A. P., *Problems in Many-Language Systems,* working materials for the lectures to the International Summer School on Language Hierarchies and Interfaces, Munich, July 23–August 2, 1975.

A. P. Ershov

BIHARMONIC EQUATIONS, SOLUTION METHODS

INTRODUCTION

The biharmonic partial differential equation has a peculiar, yet special, place among the class of partial differential equations (hereinafter referred to as PDEs) of applied interest. The elliptic, parabolic, and hyperbolic types of PDEs appear in almost all physical and engineering disciplines in which combinations of energy dissipators and energy reservoirs appear as distributed parameters. The biharmonic type apparently appears only in the study of elastic media.

Historically, the study of the behavior of vibrating elastic systems goes back to Jacob Bernoulli [1] who established the differential equation for the deflection curves of elastic bars, and to Leonhard Euler who investigated the vibration of a perfectly elastic membrane (Ref. 2, Chap. 2). The differential equations of vibrating thin plates can be traced to Kirchoff (Ref. 2, Chap. 8).

Mathematically, the biharmonic operator is elliptic. For this reason some of the biharmonic equations are sometimes referred to as fourth-order elliptic PDEs. The biharmonic PDE can also be looked upon as a fourth-order parabolic equation if it describes the transient nature of a problem. In spite of this proliferation of terminology, it is relatively easy to recognize a biharmonic equation merely by inspection as it is a fourth-order equation whereas the other three kinds of PDEs of practical interest are all of second order.

Although, in principle, problems governed by biharmonic equations may describe one, two, and three space-dimensional systems, only the first two of these are of practical interest at the present time. One-dimensional formulations serve well to describe the deflection and vibration of beams and other structural members which are long relative to their cross section. Vibration and deflection problems related to rockets and tall buildings, and some interesting problems in biomechanics can be approximated as one-dimensional problems. Two-dimensional problems are important in the analysis and design of elastic plates subject to deformation and warping.

MATHEMATICAL FORMULATIONS

In very general terms, an equation governing the deflection of elastic structures can be written as

$$\mathscr{L}\phi = k_1 \frac{\partial^2 \phi}{\partial t^2} + k_2 \frac{\partial \phi}{\partial t} + f(\phi, x, y, t) \qquad (1)$$

where $\mathscr{L}$ is a fourth-order Laplacian operator in two-space dimensions, ϕ is the deflection, and k_1 and k_2 are field parameters which may or may not depend upon x, y, t, and ϕ. Usually, however, only greatly simplified versions of Eq. (1) are of significant practical interest. For instance, the governing equation for the deflection of thin plates can be written, under very simplifying assumptions, as

$$\mathscr{L}\phi \triangleq \frac{\partial^4 \phi}{\partial x^4} + 2 \frac{\partial^4 \phi}{\partial x^2 \partial y^2} + \frac{\partial^4 \phi}{\partial y^4} = \frac{q}{D} \qquad (2)$$

where q is the load applied per unit area and D is flexural rigidity. Similarly, the equation for the transverse vibration of a structural member of nonuniform

BIHARMONIC EQUATIONS, SOLUTION METHODS

cross section and density can be written as

$$\frac{\partial^2}{\partial x^2}\left(E(x)I(x)\frac{\partial^2 \phi(x,t)}{\partial x^2}\right) = -\rho(x)A(x)\frac{\partial^2 \phi(x,t)}{\partial t^2} + f(x,t) \quad (3)$$

$$(-L/2 \le x \le +L/2); \quad t \ge 0$$

where $\rho(x)$ is material density, $A(x)$ is the cross-sectional area, $\phi(x,t)$ is the transverse displacement, $E(x)$ is the Young's modulus, $I(x)$ is the moment of inertia of the cross-sectional area about the neutral axis, and $f(x,t)$ is the applied load. For a uniform structural member with no external forcing function, Eq. (3) reduces to

$$EI\frac{\partial^4 \phi}{\partial x^4} = -\rho A \frac{\partial^2 \phi}{\partial t^2} \quad (4)$$

or

$$\frac{\partial^4 \phi}{\partial x^4} + k\frac{\partial^2 \phi}{\partial t^2} = 0$$

The biharmonic equation (3) or (4) may appear in several other disguises. In the analysis of bending phenomena, a number of other dependent variables, in addition to the deflection ϕ, are of interest. For instance, if the slope θ at any point is designated by

$$\theta = \partial \phi / \partial x \quad (5a)$$

the bending moment M is related to the slope by

$$M = E(x)I(x)\frac{\partial \theta}{\partial x} = E(x)I(x)\frac{\partial^2 \phi}{\partial x^2} \quad (5b)$$

and the shear stress S is related to M by

$$S = \frac{\partial M}{\partial x} = \frac{\partial}{\partial x}\left(EI\frac{\partial^2 \phi}{\partial x^2}\right) \quad (5c)$$

Thus, Eq. (3) can be rewritten, in another form, as

$$\frac{\partial S(x,t)}{\partial x} = -\rho(x)A(x)\frac{\partial^2 \phi(x,t)}{\partial t^2} + f(x,t) \quad (5d)$$

In the remainder of this article, discussion will be focused primarily on Eq. (2), (3), or (4). It is sometimes advantageous to reformulate these equations so that they reduce to a simpler form. For instance, by introducing a new variable,

$$u \overset{\Delta}{=} \frac{\partial^2 \phi}{\partial x^2} + \frac{\partial^2 \phi}{\partial y^2}$$

Eq. (2) reduces to

$$\frac{\partial^2 u}{\partial x^2} + \frac{\partial^2 u}{\partial y^2} = \frac{q}{D}$$

$$\frac{\partial^2 \phi}{\partial x^2} + \frac{\partial^2 \phi}{\partial y^2} = u$$

which are readily recognized as Poisson equations. Solution of Eq. (2) can therefore be obtained by solving these two equations in succession by using any of the methods that are available for solving PDEs of elliptic type.

Likewise, Eq. (3) or (4) can be reformulated in their *normal form* as two simultaneous second-order equations. For this purpose two auxiliary variables u and v are defined as

$$u \triangleq \frac{\partial \phi}{\partial t}; \quad v \triangleq EI \frac{\partial^2 \phi}{\partial x^2}$$

Now, Eq. (3) becomes

$$\frac{\partial u}{\partial t} = -\frac{1}{\rho(x)A(x)} \frac{\partial^2 v}{\partial x^2}$$

$$\frac{\partial v}{\partial t} = \frac{\partial^2}{\partial x^2}(E(x)I(x)u) \tag{6}$$

Similarly, Eq. (4) becomes

$$\frac{\partial u}{\partial t} = -\frac{1}{\rho A} \frac{\partial^2 v}{\partial x^2}$$

$$\frac{\partial v}{\partial t} = EI \frac{\partial^2 u}{\partial x^2} \tag{7}$$

Statement of the problem posed in Eq. (3) or (6), or equivalently in Eq. (4) or (7), is not complete without a specification of initial and boundary conditions. Since Eq. (3) is of fourth order in space, four boundary conditions are required. These can involve the specification of two quantities at each end of the beam, three quantities at one end and one quantity at the other, or even the specification of all four quantities at one end of the beam. The quantities that can be specified in this manner are any of (1) the deflection ϕ, (2) the slope θ, (3) the bending moment M, or (4) the shear stress S. There are therefore several combinations of end specifications which may arise in properly posed beam problems, and computer techniques must be available to handle each one of these. Fortunately, only a handful of these several combinations are of practical importance. In particular, the ends of a beam may be clamped in a way that prevents both deflection and bending at the end points; they may be pinned, preventing deflection but permitting rotation about the pin or they may be totally unconstrained. In terms of the variables defined above, these boundary conditions are:

(a) *Built-in or fixed or clamped end:*
$$\phi(\pm L/2, t) = 0$$
$$\frac{\partial \phi}{\partial x}(\pm L/2, t) = 0 \tag{8}$$

(b) *Hinged or pinned or freely supported end:*
$$\phi(\pm L/2, t) = 0$$
$$M \triangleq EI \frac{\partial^2 \phi}{\partial x^2}(\pm L/2, t) = 0 \tag{9}$$

(c) *Free or unconstrained end:*
$$M \triangleq EI \frac{\partial^2 \phi}{\partial x^2}(\pm L/2, t = 0$$
$$S \triangleq \frac{\partial}{\partial x}\left[EI \frac{\partial^2 \phi}{\partial x^2}(\pm L/2, t)\right] = 0 \tag{10}$$

Only rarely does one encounters a structural problem in which other than the above boundary conditions occur.

Now it is necessary to specify the initial conditions. As Eq. (3) is second order in time, two initial conditions are required. In particular the initial transverse deflection ϕ and the initial transverse velocity $\partial \phi/\partial t$ of the elastic structure must be specified at some prescribed time $t = 0$. That is,

$$\phi(x, 0) = f_1(x)$$
$$\frac{\partial \phi}{\partial x}(x, 0) = f_2(x) \tag{11}$$

Strictly speaking both ϕ and $\partial \phi/\partial x$ can be specified at two different time instances, t_1 and t_2, but this kind of specification leads to a problem that is not well posed and no solution may exist.

TYPES OF PROBLEMS AND FORMATS

In engineering studies of elastic systems, two kinds of problems are of general interest: the *direct* problem and the *inverse* problem. The direct or analysis problem is characterized by a specification of the system equation, such as Eq. (3) or (4), along with a specification of all boundary conditions and parameters such as E, I, ρ and A, together with a description of the forcing function $f(x, t)$, and one is required to find $\phi(x, t)$ and perhaps some of its derivatives. Thus solving the direct problem is tantamount to solving the biharmonic partial differential Eq. (3), (4), or (5) with one of the boundary conditions shown in Eq. (8), (9), or (10) and the initial conditions in Eq. (11) using one of the methods described in the following sections. The inverse problem is less direct and more difficult and may appear in many different disguises: In the *design* or *synthesis* problem one is required to find, for instance, $A(x)$ or $\rho(x)$ of a beam which, when subjected to a prescribed class of forces $f(x, t)$, results in a deflection $a \leq \phi(x, t) \leq b$ where a and b are some prescribed limits. In the *parameter identification* problem, one is required to find one or more of ρ, A, E, or I in Eq. (3) which would result in a deflection $\phi(x, t)$ that would resemble an observed deflection $\hat{\phi}(x_i, t_j)$ "as closely as possible" when a beam was experimentally subjected to a load $f(x, t)$. In *system identification,* one is required to determine the actual functional form of an equation whose solution $\phi(x, t)$ would resemble an experimentally observed deflection $\hat{\phi}(x_i, t_j)$ "as closely as possible" when a structural system was subjected to an external disturbance $f(x, t)$. Finally, the *control* problem is characterized by a specification of everything in Eq. (3), (4), or (5) except $f(x, t)$, and one is required to find an admissible $f(x, t)$ that produces the specified $\phi(x, t)$. In aircraft and spacecraft structures, vibration of the structural members may lead to failure due to fatigue. In this context, a control problem attempts to determine methods of controlling these vibrations.

All inverse problems are an order of magnitude more difficult to handle than direct problems. One reason for this difficulty stems from the fact that most methods of treating the inverse problem necessarily involve solving the direct problem, i.e., Eq. (3), (4), or (5), at least once or, in general, many many times. Therefore, the rest of this article is devoted to a description of methods for solving the direct problem.

The direct problem, though straightforward from a mathematical viewpoint, has many aspects of practical interest. If only the static or steady-state deflection or deformation of an elastic member is sought, then the governing equation contains no time dependence and Eq. (3) resembles Laplace's equation, except that fourth derivatives with respect to space variables arise in place of the usual second derivatives. The method of solution of such problems is not unlike that for solving elliptic PDEs. If the transient nature of the deflection of a beam is of interest and if damping can be neglected, the characteristic response is sinusoidal in nature and, under these circumstances, Eq. (3) resembles a wave equation except that fourth derivatives with respect to space appear instead of the usual second derivatives. Methods of handling this situation are analogous to those conventionally used for solving hyperbolic type PDEs. In many applications it is not necessary to determine the complete transient response. Instead it may be sufficient to determine the eigenvalues and eigenvectors of the structure. From a physical point of view eigenvalues, also termed characteristic values or normal modes, are those frequencies at which a structure, subject to specified boundary conditions, if excited would continue to vibrate indefinitely. Determination of eigenvalues or characteristic frequencies λ_i is therefore of practical interest and entails the solving of equations such as

$$\frac{\partial^2}{\partial x^2}\left[E(x)I(x)\frac{\partial^2 \phi(x, t)}{\partial x^2}\right] = -\rho(x)A(x)\lambda^2\phi(x, t) \qquad (12)$$

BIHARMONIC EQUATIONS, SOLUTION METHODS

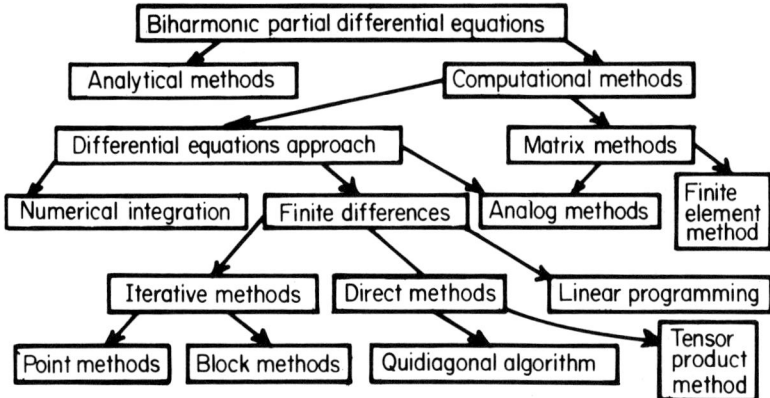

Fig. 1. Methods of solving the biharmonic equation.

DIGITAL COMPUTER METHODS

Figure 1 displays some of the more important methods of solving the biharmonic PDE. Among the computational methods there are two broad trends. In one approach, one writes a differential equation that is supposed to describe the required behavior of a vibrating system and then attention is focused on solving the differential equation model using one method or another. In the second approach a complete structural theory is developed *ab initio* in matrix algebra through all stages in the analysis. In this procedure the structure is first idealized into an assembly of discrete structural elements with

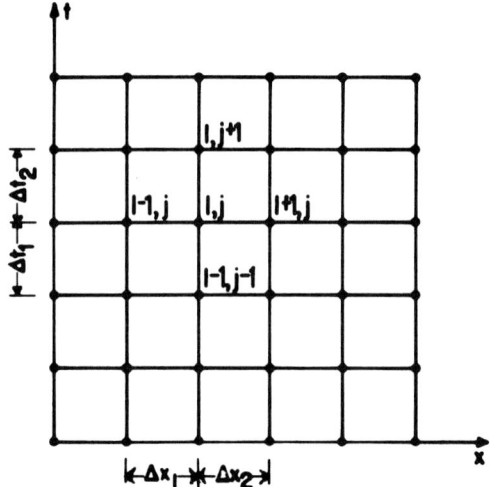

Fig. 2. A typical finite-difference grid in the x–t plane.

an assumed form of displacement or stress distribution, and a complete solution is then obtained by combining the individual stress or displacement distributions in some acceptable manner. Methods based on this philosophy, and in particular the *finite element method*, gained widespread popularity as they appear to be suitable for the analysis of structures with complex configurations. Although the end result is the same, it may be stated with some caution that the finite element method (which is really a version of the Raleigh-Ritz approximation technique) is not really solving the differential equation (which is merely a mathematical model of the system) but is seeking a solution by focusing on the system itself.

An alternative is to solve the matrix equations, obtained from the finite element method, on a special purpose analog computer called the *matric computer*. To this author's knowledge, no attempt has been made to implement this idea.

In the differential equation approach, once again, there are two broad trends: the digital computer approach and the analog computer approach.

The Finite Difference Grid

A first step in solving any PDE by digital computer methods is to define a *grid* or *mesh* over the region of interest (see Fig. 2). For simplicity only a uniform mesh with sides parallel to the coordinate axes will be used in the space domain. (If more than one space dimension is involved, one can use uniform mesh containing square, rectangular, triangular, hexagonal, or even irregularly shaped cells in the mesh.) The discretization is denoted by

$$R_x = \{x : x_l = l(\Delta x); \quad l = 0, \pm 1, \pm 2, \ldots\}$$
$$R_y = \{y : y_m = m(\Delta y); \quad m = 0, \pm 1, \pm 2, \ldots\}$$

The time domain is likewise discretized according to

$$R_t = \{t : t_j = j(\Delta t); \quad j = 0, 1, 2, \ldots\}$$

The *meshwidth* (Δx) and the *timestep* (Δt) are important discretization parameters; they not only determine the fineness of the discretization process but also govern such important computational characteristics as convergence and stability. After discretization, one will be essentially dealing with functions and solutions defined only on the mesh or node points.

Discretization Schemes

The next step is to replace all derivatives in the equation by properly chosen finite difference quotients and all integrals, if any, by properly chosen quadrature formulas. For instance, the first derivative, such as $\partial \phi(x, t)/\partial x$, can

BIHARMONIC EQUATIONS, SOLUTION METHODS

be approximated at a typical grid point (x_l, t_j) by

$$\left(\frac{\partial \phi}{\partial x}\right)_{l,j} \approx D_f \phi_{l,j} \triangleq \frac{1}{(\Delta x)}(\phi_{l+1,j} - \phi_{l,j}); \quad \text{forward difference} \tag{13}$$

$$\left(\frac{\partial \phi}{\partial x}\right)_{l,j} \approx D_b \phi_{l,j} \triangleq \frac{1}{(\Delta x)}(\phi_{l,j} - \phi_{l-1,j}); \quad \text{backward difference} \tag{14}$$

$$\left(\frac{\partial \phi}{\partial x}\right)_{l,j} \approx D_c \phi_{l,j} \triangleq \frac{1}{2}(D_f + D_b)\phi; \quad \text{central difference}$$
$$= \frac{1}{2(\Delta x)}(\phi_{l+1,j} - \phi_{l-1,j}) \tag{15}$$

Using the above equations as building blocks, any higher-order derivative can be approximated. For instance, $(\partial^2 \phi / \partial x^2)$ and $(\partial^4 \phi / \partial x^4)$ can be approximated at the grid point (x_l, t_j), or (l, j) for short, by say

$$\left(\frac{\partial^2 \phi}{\partial x^2}\right)\bigg|_{l,j} = \frac{\partial}{\partial x}\left(\frac{\partial \phi}{\partial x}\right) \approx \frac{\partial}{\partial x}(D_f \phi) = D_b D_f \phi$$
$$\approx \frac{1}{(\Delta x)^2}(\phi_{l+1,j} - 2\phi_{l,j} + \phi_{l-1,j}) \triangleq \delta_x^2 \phi_{l,j} \tag{16}$$

$$\left(\frac{\partial^4 \phi}{\partial x^4}\right)\bigg|_{l,j} = \frac{1}{(\Delta x)^4}(\phi_{l+2,j} - 4\phi_{l+1,j} + 6\phi_{l,j} - 4\phi_{l-1,j} + \phi_{l-2,j})$$
$$\triangleq \delta_{x^2} \phi_{l,j} \tag{17}$$

The symbols δ_x^2 and δ_x^4 are used above as a shorthand notation for the second- and fourth-central differences.

Approximating the first-time derivative is not as straightforward. For instance, $(\partial \phi / \partial t)$ can be approximated at (l, j) by a forward difference scheme in two different ways:

$$\left(\frac{\partial \phi}{\partial t}\right)\bigg|_{l,j} \approx \frac{\phi_{l,j+1} - \phi_{l,j}}{(\Delta t)}; \quad \text{single-step, forward} \tag{18}$$

$$\left(\frac{\partial \phi}{\partial t}\right)\bigg|_{l,j} \approx \frac{\phi_{l,j+1} - \phi_{l,j-1}}{2(\Delta t)}; \quad \text{multistep, forward} \tag{19}$$

The first scheme can immediately be used in successive calculations of the values of $\phi(x, t)$ for $t = \Delta t$, $2\Delta t$, etc. The second scheme requires the knowledge of at least the approximate values of $\phi(x, \Delta t)$ before marching in the time domain is possible. The former is an example of a single step scheme and the latter of a multistep scheme. Multistep schemes are physically more appealing, but it turns out that the particular scheme described by the second of the above equations is completely useless for digital computations.

The first time derivative $\partial \phi / \partial t$ can also be approximated by a backward difference scheme:

$$\left(\frac{\partial \phi}{\partial t}\right)_{l,j} \approx \frac{\phi_{l,j} - \phi_{l,j-1}}{(\Delta t)} \tag{20}$$

Use of backward schemes lead to problems which display superior stability characteristics.

Approximating $(\partial^2 \phi / \partial t^2)$ is more straightforward:

$$\left(\frac{\partial^2 \phi}{\partial t^2}\right)_{l,j} \approx \frac{\phi_{l,j+1} - 2\phi_{l,j} + \phi_{l,j-1}}{(\Delta t)^2} \tag{21}$$

Treatment of Boundaries

Approximating the various derivatives by finite difference expressions, such as those described above, is a straightforward operation for all the points l which are not in the vicinity of a boundary. Special care and attention are required for grid points lying either on the boundary or adjacent to a boundary. Consider, for instance, the one-dimensional elastic structure shown in Fig. 3. To approximate the fourth-space derivative at a grid point l, at least the values of ϕ at five consecutive values of l centered at l are required. For $l = 2, 3, \ldots, (N - 2)$, this requirement causes no special problem. However, for $l = 1$ and $(N - 1)$, a sufficient number of adjacent grid points is simply not available and values of ϕ lying outside the boundaries of the elastic structure are required. That is, values of ϕ at $l = -1$ and $(N + 1)$ must somehow be inferred. There are several methods available to handle this situation. For instance, if the deflection $\phi_0(t)$ is specified at $l = 0$, then one can write

$$\phi_{l,j} = \left(\frac{\partial \phi}{\partial x}\right)_{l,j} \quad \text{for all } l, j$$

For $l = 0$,

$$\phi_{0,j} \approx \frac{\phi_{0,j} - \phi_{-1,j}}{(\Delta x)}$$

which gives the "deflection" at $l = -1$ as

$$\phi_{-1,j} \approx \theta_{0,j} - (\Delta x)\theta_{0,j}$$

If, on the other hand, the deflection $\phi_0(t)$ and moment $M_0(t)$ are specified at $l = 0$, then

$$M_{0,j} \approx \frac{EI}{(\Delta x)^2}(\phi_{1,j} + \phi_{-1,j} - 2\phi_{0,j})$$

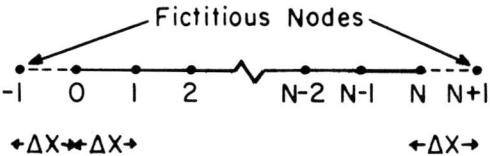

Fig. 3. Treatment of boundaries using fictitious nodes.

BIHARMONIC EQUATIONS, SOLUTION METHODS

which gives the "deflection" at $l = -1$ as

$$\phi_{-1,j} \approx 2\phi_{0,j} + \frac{(\Delta x)^2}{EI} M_{0,j} - \phi_{1,j}$$

Other Differencing Schemes

The three-point difference approximations used for second space derivatives and the five-point schemes used for fourth-order space derivatives are the simplest. A second derivative, such as $\partial^2\phi/\partial x^2$ can be approximated by using the values of ϕ at more than three grid points. Similarly, more than five points can be used to approximate the fourth derivative. However, it is convenient to restrict to the use of two-point and three-point formulas while approximating first- and second-time derivatives. It is customary to state the number of grid points that enter in the approximation of ϕ at any point. For instance, by an 11-point differencing scheme one means that the values of ϕ at 11 points are required in a finite difference expression (see last column of Table 1).

Explicit and Implicit Methods

The various difference schemes available to approximate space and time derivatives can be combined in a variety of ways. This leads to a large number of finite difference approximations to a given biharmonic PDE (see Table 1, for example). Some of these combinations may lead to completely useless finite difference schemes and some are superior, in some respects, to the others. For instance, approximation of Eq. (4) using Eqs. (17) and (21) leads to (see Entry 1 of Table 1).

$$\begin{aligned}\phi_{l,j+1} &= 2\phi_{l,j} - \phi_{l,j-1} + r^2\{\phi_{l+2,j} - 4\phi_{l+1,j} - 4\phi_{l-1,j} + \phi_{l-2,j} - 6\phi_{l,j}\} \\ &= 2\phi_{l,j} - \phi_{l,j-1} + r^2 \delta_{l,j}^2\end{aligned} \quad (22)$$

where

$$r \triangleq \frac{(\Delta t)}{\sqrt{k}(\Delta x)^2}$$

The above equation enables one to solve for $\phi_{l,j+1}$ (i.e., the value of ϕ_l at the next time step) explicitly (so the name *explicit method*) in terms of $\phi_{l,j}$ (i.e., the value of ϕ_l at the present time step) and $\phi_{l,j-1}$ (i.e., the value of ϕ_l at the previous time step). Thus marching forward in time is relatively straightforward. In spite of this simplicity, many explicit methods, including Eq. (22), are *computationally unstable* unless the condition

$$(\Delta t) \leq \frac{(\Delta x)^2}{2\sqrt{k}} \quad (23)$$

is satisfied. Stability, here, is essentially a requirement of uniformly continuous dependence of the discrete solution on its data. Indeed, Eq. (22) was useless because it is unconditionally unstable.

Explicit digital techniques can also be applied to solve the normal form shown in Eq. (6) or (7). For instance, combination of a central difference scheme for space derivatives and a forward difference scheme to the time derivative leads to

$$\frac{u_{l,j+1} - u_{l,j}}{(\Delta t)} = -a \frac{v_{l+1,j} - 2v_{l,j} + v_{l-1,j}}{(\Delta x)^2}$$

$$\frac{v_{l,j+1} - v_{l,j}}{(\Delta t)} = +a \frac{u_{l+1,j+1} - 2u_{l,j+1} - u_{l-1,j+1}}{(\Delta x)^2} \qquad (24)$$

where $a = (EI/A)^{1/2}$. Computational stability of Eq. (24) is also governed by Eq. (23).

Conditions such as Eq. (23) force one to make very many steps per unit time for small values of (Δx). If (Δx) is not small enough, the solution of the difference approximation may not be a faithful representation of the solution of the original PDE. Small values of (Δt) not only require more computer time to traverse a given time interval but also cause an accumulation of roundoff error.

Implicit approximations alleviate the situation by being unconditionally stable, which means that the solution of the difference equations varies continuously with data for any relation between (Δx) and (Δt). A widely used unconditionally stable implicit approximation to Eq. (4) at (x_l, t_j) is obtained by averaging the finite difference approximation for the fourth-derivative term at $(l, j + 1)$ and $(l, j - 1)$. The time derivative, as before, is approximated by a central difference scheme. Thus an implicit approximation to Eq. (4) may take the form (see the second formula in the table)

$$\frac{1}{2(\Delta x)^4} [\phi_{l+2,j+1} - 4\phi_{l+1,j+1} + 6\phi_{l,j+1} - 4\phi_{l-1,j+1} + \phi_{l-2,j+1}]$$

$$+ \frac{1}{2(\Delta x)^4} [\phi_{l+2,j-1} - 4\phi_{l+1,j-1} + 6\phi_{l,j-1} - 4\phi_{l-1,j-1} + \phi_{l-2,j-1}] \qquad (25)$$

$$+ \frac{k}{(\Delta t)^2} [\phi_{l,j+1} - 2\phi_{l,j} + \phi_{l,j-1}] = 0$$

or in δ-notation

$$\tfrac{1}{2}\delta_x^4 \phi_{l,j+1} + \tfrac{1}{2}\delta_x^4 \phi_{l,j-1} + k\delta_t^2 \phi_{l,j} = 0$$

The δ-notation is not only compact but is also extremely descriptive of how the differencing is done. Looking at the above equation, it is readily evident that the space derivative at (l, j) is approximated by taking the average of the approximations at $(l, j + 1)$ and $(l, j - 1)$.

The first part of Eq. (25) represents an approximation to $(\partial^4 \phi/\partial x^4)$ at (x_l, t_{j+1}); the second part at the point (x_l, t_{j-1}). At any time t_j the first part contains five unknown terms as they represent the solution at the next time step. Thus $\phi_{l,j+1}$ cannot be evaluated explicitly from Eq. (25). Indeed Eq. (25), when written out in full for all values of l, including boundary points, at any time t_j represents a

TABLE 1
Some Finite Difference Approximations to the Biharmonic Equation

Difference approximation to $\dfrac{\partial^4 \phi}{\partial x^4} + k\dfrac{\partial^2 \phi}{\partial t^2} = 0;\quad r \triangleq \dfrac{\Delta t}{\sqrt{k}(\Delta x)^2}$	Stability condition	Order of error	Type of method	Mnemonic of the difference scheme
(1) Collatz's explicit method $$\phi_{l,j+1} = 2\phi_{l,j} - \phi_{l,j-1} + r^2(\phi_{l-2,j} - 4\phi_{l-1,j} + 6\phi_{l,j} - 4\phi_{l+1,j} + \phi_{l+2,j})$$		$O(\Delta x)^2$	Explicit	$\quad\;*\quad\;\;j+1$ $*****\;\;j$ $\quad\;*\quad\;\;j-1$
(2) Crandall's 11-point implicit scheme (a quidiagonal matrix has to be solved) $$\phi_{l-2,j+1} - 4\phi_{l-1,j+1} + \left(6 + \frac{2}{r^2}\right)\phi_{l,j+1} + \phi_{l+2,j+1} - 4\phi_{l+1,j+1}$$ $$= \frac{4}{r^2}\phi_{l,j} - \left[\phi_{l-2,j-1} - 4\phi_{l-1,j-1} + \left(6 + \frac{2}{r^2}\right)\phi_{l,j-1}\right.$$ $$\left. - 4\phi_{l+1,j-1} + \phi_{l+2,j-1}\right]$$	$\Delta t < \infty$	$O(\Delta x)^2$	Implicit	$*****$ $\quad\;*$ $*****$

(3) Conte's 15-point implicit scheme (a quidiagonal matrix has to be solved) $\Delta t < \infty$ $0(\Delta x)^2$ Implicit   *****
***** *****

$$\phi_{l-2,j+1} - 4\phi_{l-1,j+1} + \left(6 + \frac{4}{r^2}\right)\phi_{l,j+1} - 4\phi_{l+1,j+1} + \phi_{l+2,j+1}$$

$$= -\left\{\phi_{l+2,j} - 4\phi_{l+1,j} + 2\left(3 - \frac{4}{r^2}\right)\phi_{l,j} - 4\phi_{l-1,j} - \phi_{l-2,j}\right.$$

$$\left. + \frac{1}{2}\left[\phi_{l+2,j-1} - 4\phi_{l+1,j-1} + \left(6 + \frac{4}{r^2}\right)\phi_{l,j-1} - 4\phi_{l-1,j-1} + \phi_{l-2,j-1}\right]\right\}$$

(4) Conte's 11-point implicit scheme (only a tridiagonal matrix is solved here) $\Delta t < \infty$ $0(\Delta x)^2$ Implicit   ***
***** ***

$$\phi_{l-1,j+1} - \left(2 + \frac{1}{r^2}\right)\phi_{l,j+1} + \phi_{l+1,j+1}$$

$$= \phi_{l-2,j} - 2(\phi_{l-1,j} + \phi_{l+1,j}) - (\phi_{l+1,j-1} + \phi_{l-1,j-1})$$

$$+ \left(2 + \frac{1}{r^2}\right)\phi_{l,j-1} + \left(2 - \frac{2}{r^2}\right)\phi_{l,j-1} + \left(2 - \frac{2}{r^2}\right)\phi_{l,j} + \phi_{l+2,j}$$

set of N simultaneous linear equations which can be compactly written in matrix notation as

$$A\phi_{j+1} = B\phi_{j-1} + C\phi_j \qquad (26)$$

where ϕ_j is an N-dimensional vector whose components are values of ϕ_j evaluated at the grid points $l = 1, 2, \ldots$, and A, B, and C are coefficient matrices. The right side of Eq. (26) contains terms evaluated at time levels j and $(j-1)$ and is therefore known at time level $(j+1)$. Therefore, Eq. (26) can also be written as

$$A\phi = b \qquad (27)$$

where the vector b is known at any time and ϕ is unknown. The above equation can be solved in a straightforward manner as

$$\phi = A^{-1}b \qquad (28)$$

as long as A^{-1} can be computed in some convenient fashion.

In practical problems, matrix A is generally of a large dimension and sparse. Inverting an $N \times N$ matrix by, say, Gaussian elimination requires of the order of $\frac{1}{3} N^3$ multiplications. If $N = 1000$ and if it takes 1 μsec to perform a multiplication, it will take approximately 5 min of central processing time to invert A once. Adding another 5 min to move data in and out of central memory (to tapes or disks), it takes 10 min to invert A once at a time level t_j. To advance 10 time steps it therefore requires about 1.5 hr. In simulation studies and while solving inverse problems, the above process has to be repeated again and again. Thus one pays a price by using implicit difference schemes in order to get unconditional stability.

It is pertinent at this juncture to note that some of the current research is directed at finding explicit differencing schemes that are unconditionally stable. Some such methods for solving parabolic type equations have been reported, but none to solve the biharmonic equation.

Direct Versus Iterative Methods

In practice, one does not always solve equations like Eq. (27) by Gaussian elimination. Typically, methods of solving equations like $A\phi = b$ fall into two broad categories: *direct* and *iterative* methods. At the time of this writing, the pendulum of conventional wisdom concerning the advantages of direct vs iterative methods is swinging too rapidly and one can make many claims and counterclaims for each approach. In general, direct methods, such as Gaussian elimination, are well suited in cases where A is small and dense. If A is sparse but exhibits a quidiagonal pattern in its nonzero entries, as in the case with Eq. (25), then the so-called quidiagonal algorithm can be applied to solve Eq. (27) directly (i.e., by direct inversion of A). Indeed, the quidiagonal algorithm is equivalent to Gaussian elimination. However, matrix A is not always quidiagonal; use of higher-order difference approximations or problems involving more than one-space dimension leads to equations where A is still sparse but no longer quidiagonal.

It is still possible to apply direct methods if A exhibits the so-called block quidiagonal structure; that is, if A has the form

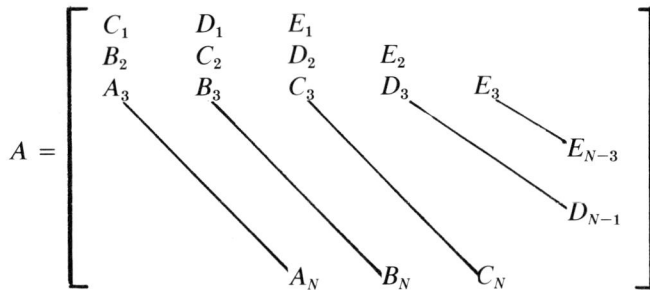

where the square diagonal submatrices are of order n_j, where n_j corresponds to the number of grid points on the jth horizontal line of the superimposed grid. The quidiagonal algorithm can be generalized to handle the above type of matrix if the vectors ϕ and b are suitably partitioned relative to A. In practice it was found that the advantage of the block quidiagonal algorithm quickly dwindles for large problems (say $N^2 \geq 500$). Furthermore, direct methods based on the block quidiagonal algorithm may prove quite costly in terms of computer storage requirements. The practical use of direct methods is that they have been successfully utilized in conjunction with iterative methods.

The central idea of iterative methods is splitting of matrix A into, say, two matrices as in

$$A = N - P \tag{29}$$

and rewrite Eq. (27), say, as

$$N\phi = P\phi + b \tag{30}$$

where N and P are some suitably chosen matrices satisfying Eq. (29). To generate an iterative method out of the above equation, it is rewritten as

$$N\phi^{(i+1)} = P\phi^{(i)} + b \tag{31}$$

where the superscript (i) indicates the iteration number. One starts with an initial guess or approximation $\phi^{(0)}$ and calculates $\phi^{(1)}$ using Eq. (31). The process is repeated until $|\phi^{(k+1)} - \phi^{(k)}|$ is less than a predetermined tolerance for some k, at which stage the iterative method is said to have converged. The rate at which this convergence occurs is of particular interest in iterative methods. Of the many available methods, the successive over relaxation method (or SOR) [3] and alternating direction iterative method (or ADIM) [4, 5] gained widespread popularity.

Central to the idea of the SOR method is the splitting of A as

$$A = D - E - F$$

where D is the diagonal portion of A, and E and F are strictly lower and upper

BIHARMONIC EQUATIONS, SOLUTION METHODS

triangular portions of A, respectively. Now Eq. (27) is written as

$$(D - \omega E)\phi^{(i+1)} = \{(1 - \omega)D + \omega F\}\phi^{(i)} + b \tag{32}$$

the rate at which the above process convergence depends, among other things, on the iteration parameter ω. If A is quidiagonal, then $(D - \omega E)$ would be tridiagonal and Eq. (32) can be solved for $\phi^{(i+1)}$ using a tridiagonal algorithm.

The ADIM is best explained in terms of a specific example. Consider

$$\frac{\partial^4 \phi}{\partial x^4} + 2\frac{\partial^4 \phi}{\partial x^2 \partial y^2} + \frac{\partial^4 \phi}{\partial y^4} = 0$$

A finite difference approximation to this can be written as

$$\delta_x^4 \phi_{l,m} + 2\delta_y^2 \delta_x^2 \phi_{l,m} + \delta_x^4 \phi_{l,m} = 0 \tag{33}$$

Inspection of the coefficient matrix A of Eq. (33) reveals that at least nine of the main diagonals contain nonzero entries and the quidiagonal algorithm is no longer applicable. To take advantage of the quidiagonal algorithm, Eq. (33) can be solved in a "hop, skip, and jump" fashion. First an initial guess $\phi^{(0)}_{l,m}$ is made at each of the grid points. Then the grid is scanned along the x-direction, first assuming that the values of ϕ at the grid points coming in the y-direction are known. Then the calculations are made by scanning the grid parallel to the y-direction. Thus during each scan only a quidiagonal matrix is inverted. The two scans are described by

$$\phi_{l,m}^{(i+1/2)} = \phi_{l,m}^{(i)} - \omega(\delta_x^4 \phi_{l,m}^{(i+1/2)} - 2\delta_y^2 \delta_x^2 \phi_{l,m}^{(i)} - \delta_y^4 \phi_{l,m}^{(i)}) \tag{34}$$

$$\phi_{l,m}^{(i+1)} = \phi_{l,m}^{(i+1/2)} - \omega(\delta_y^4 \phi_{l,m}^{(i+1)} + \delta_y^4 \phi_{l,m}^{(i)}) \tag{35}$$

Note that the iterative index $(i + 1/2)$ is only symbolic of splitting the iteration into two halves. Equations (34) and (35) are solved implicitly as usual. The rate of convergence in this case also depends upon the parameter ω (usually between 0 and 2).

Selection of iteration parameters is by no means simple because the optimal values of these parameters depend on a number of factors such as boundary conditions, shape of the boundaries, and on the equation itself. Both SOR- and ADIM-type methods work very well if the iteration parameters are chosen at their optimum values, otherwise their performance becomes questionable.

Indeed, the description of the iterative methods given above is deceptively brief. In devising iterative schemes it is important to see that the coefficient matrix A possesses properties such as diagonal dominance, consistent or σ-ordering, and "property A." Any standard book on numerical analysis can be referred to for an explanation of these concepts.

ANALOG AND HYBRID METHODS

Electrical networks can at times be used to solve biharmonic equations. These methods fall into two broad categories: methods using purely passive network elements and methods using both active and passive elements.

BIHARMONIC EQUATIONS, SOLUTION METHODS

Pure Passive Network Analogs

To illustrate the method of using passive networks for solving the biharmonic PDE the set of equations in Eq. (5) is considered once again with some simplifications.

$$\theta = \partial\phi/\partial x \tag{36}$$

$$M = EI\frac{\partial \theta}{\partial x} \tag{37}$$

$$S = \frac{\partial}{\partial x}\left(EI\frac{\partial \theta}{\partial x}\right) \tag{38}$$

$$\frac{\partial S}{\partial x} + m\frac{\partial^2 \phi}{\partial t^2} = 0 \tag{39}$$

These equations are now approximated by finite difference expressions as

$$\theta_{l+(\Delta x)/2} \approx \frac{\phi_{l+1} - \phi_l}{(\Delta x)} \tag{36a}$$

$$(\Delta x)S_{l+(\Delta x)/2} \approx \frac{EI_{l+1}}{(\Delta x)}(\theta_{l+(3\Delta x/2)} - \theta_{l+(\Delta x/2)}) + \frac{EI_l}{(\Delta x)}(\theta_{l-(\Delta x/2)} - \theta_{l+(\Delta x/2)}) \tag{38a}$$

$$S_{l+(\Delta x)/2} - S_{l-(\Delta x/2)} + (\Delta x)m_l\frac{\partial^2 \phi_l}{\partial t^2} = 0 \tag{39a}$$

In Eqs. (36a), (38a), and (39a) the subscript notation such as $l + (\Delta x/2)$ implies that the variable in question has been evaluated midway between two grid

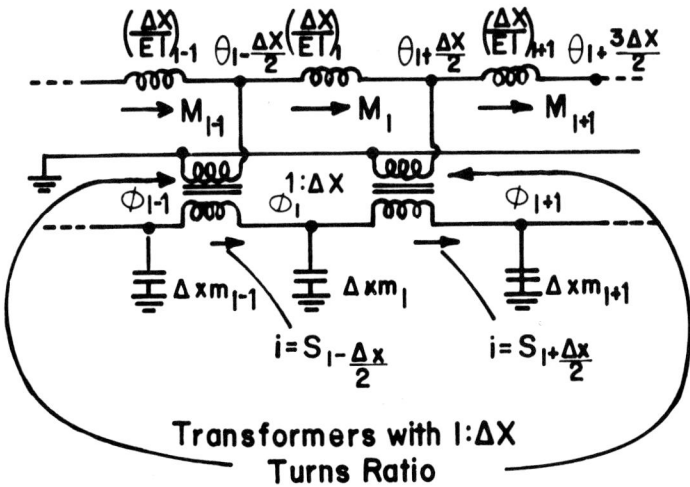

Fig. 4. A portion of typical passive-network mass-capacitance analog to implement Eqs. (36a), (38a), and (39a) using a dual-grid. Note the staggered nature of grid points in the Θ-grid and Φ-grid. The networks in both the grids are connected via transformers with turns ratio $1:\Delta x$.

points. Inspection of these equations reveals that they resemble Kirchoff's voltage law equations in a pair of electrical networks. In one network current and voltage simulate M and θ, respectively, while in the other network current and voltage represent S and ϕ. One realization, called the mass-capacitance analog, of such a circuit is shown in Fig. 4. In this network analog, capacitors are included in each section of the network to simulate the distributed mass of the beam. Numerous other modifications of this basic circuit are possible [6]. Network analogs of this type are particularly useful for the determination of normal modes, but can also be employed to find transient responses to specified transient initial and boundary conditions. In either case the network is excited by voltage and current sources. A major difficulty with network methods of this type is the specialized nature of the components required.

Active-Passive Network Analogs

The most commonly used active component in network analogs is a high gain dc amplifier called the operational amplifier. As operational amplifiers are standard building blocks in an analog computer, the methods described herein can be conveniently implemented on an analog or hybrid computer [7].

If an analog computer is used, the space derivatives in the biharmonic equation are approximated by finite-difference expressions while the time derivatives are kept in continuous form. This approach is particularly effective if both the moment M and the deflection ϕ are used as dependent variables. To illustrate this procedure, Eq. (3) is rewritten in a slightly modified form as

$$m(x) \frac{\partial^2 \phi}{\partial t^2} + \frac{\partial^2 M}{\partial x^2} = 0 \qquad (40)$$

where

$$M = EI(x) \frac{\partial^2 \phi}{\partial x^2} \quad \text{and} \quad m(x) = \rho(x) A(x)$$

Approximating the space derivative by the second central difference, Eq. (40) becomes

$$m_l \frac{d^2 \phi_l}{dt^2} + \frac{1}{(\Delta x)^2} (M_{l-1} - 2M_l + M_{l+1}) \approx 0 \qquad (41)$$

where

$$M_l = \frac{(EI)_l}{(\Delta x)^2} (\phi_{l-1} - 2\phi_l + \phi_{l+1})$$

The deflection ϕ at node point l is therefore obtained by integrating twice the sum of three terms which are proportional to the moments at node l and two adjacent nodes. An analog computer diagram for this process at one node point is shown in Fig. 5. To simulate a complete beam, it is necessary to

BIHARMONIC EQUATIONS, SOLUTION METHODS

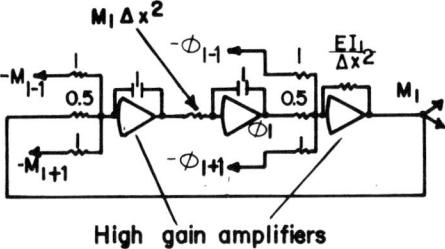

Fig. 5. A portion of an active-passive network analog to implement Eq. (41).

interconnect circuit modules of this type in cascade and by matching the specified boundary conditions at each end.

Equation (4) can also be solved on a hybrid computer. In the particular procedure presented here, Eq. (4) is rewritten as

$$\frac{\partial^4 \phi}{\partial x^4} + k \frac{\partial^2 \phi}{\partial t^2} = 0 \qquad (42)$$

A finite difference approximation to the fourth derivative is written in its usual form as

$$\left(\frac{\partial^4 \phi}{\partial x^4}\right)_{l,j} \approx \frac{1}{(\Delta x)^4} (\phi_{l+2,j} - 4\phi_{l+1,j} + 6\phi_{l,j} - 4\phi_{l-1,j} + \phi_{l-2,j})$$

Now the three middle terms are replaced by expressions involving values of ϕ at three time levels according to

$$4\phi_{l+1,j} = \phi_{l+1,j+1} + 2\phi_{l+1,j} + \phi_{l+1,j-1}$$
$$6\phi_{l,j} = 2\phi_{l,j+1} + 2\phi_{l,j} + 2\phi_{l,j-1}$$
$$4\phi_{l-1,j} = \phi_{l-1,j+1} + 2\phi_{l-1,j} + \phi_{l-1,j-1}$$

The time derivative is approximated in the usual manner using a central difference approximation centered at (l, j) as

$$\left(\frac{\partial^2 \phi}{\partial t^2}\right)_{l,j} \approx \frac{1}{(\Delta t)^2} (\phi_{l,j+1} - 2\phi_{l,j} + \phi_{l,j-1})$$

These approximations, when substituted in Eq. (42), yield after some rearrangement

$$\frac{2r+1}{r} \phi_{l,j+1} = \phi_{l+1,j+1} + \phi_{l-1,j+1} + f_{l,j} \qquad (43)$$

where $r = (\Delta t)^2/k(\Delta x)^4$ and $f_{l,j}$ represents a combination of known terms obtained from specified initial and boundary conditions or previous solution cycles. Now, Eq. (43) can be regarded as a specification of a summing circuit, in an analog computer, with three inputs (see Fig. 6). Two of these inputs can be obtained by "reading" the outputs from amplifiers representing two of the

BIHARMONIC EQUATIONS, SOLUTION METHODS

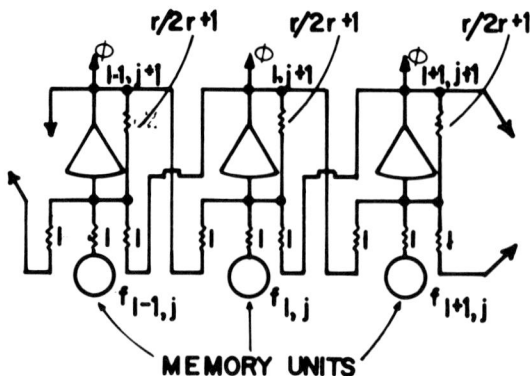

Fig. 6. A portion of a hybrid computer configuration to implement Eq. (43).

adjacent nodes in the space domain. The third input, representing $f(x, t)$, depends upon the previous solution cycle. That is, the solution obtained at the previous time step must somehow be stored so that it is available at the present calculation. This storage facility can be provided to the analog computer by hooking the analog computer to a digital computer—or equivalently using a hybrid computer.

It is not always necessary to use operational amplifiers as shown in Fig. 6. Equation (43) can also be simulated using a pure passive network analog and storage devices as shown in Fig. 7. All these networks have one major drawback. While solving nonhomogeneous equations, the network module can no longer be a standard module but should be tailor-made to suit the conditions at each node. If the equation is also nonlinear, the structure of any given module changes as the solution progresses—and this is a very difficult operation to mechanize. One method of avoiding this difficulty is to rearrange Eq. (43), after adding and subtracting $\phi_{l,j}$, as

$$-\phi_{l+1,j+1} + 3\phi_{l,j+1} - \phi_{l-1,j+1} = \left(1 - \frac{1}{r}\right)\phi_{l,j+1} + f_{l,j} \qquad (44)$$

As the unknown $\phi_{l,j+1}$ appears in both sides of the equation, the above

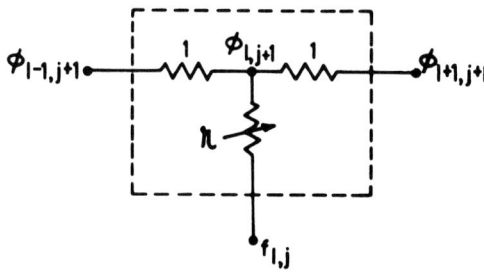

Fig. 7. A modification of Fig. 6 involving the use of fixed and variable resistors only.

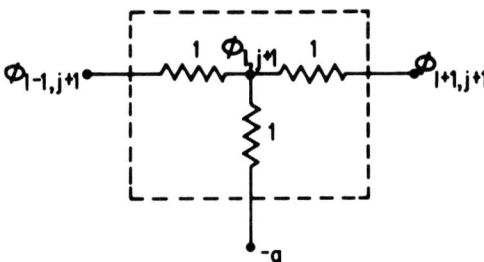

Fig. 8. Further modification of Fig. 6, involving the use of fixed resistors only.

equation has to be solved implicitly using an iterative procedure. Instead of doing this using pure digital procedures, one can use a resistance network to solve Eq. (44) at a typical node point (see Fig. 8).

METHODS IN THE MAKING

This section is intended to give an idea about some of the methods that have been and are being tried with claims of success. However, these methods have not attained widespread usage at the time of this writing. All the methods described hereunder do have merit and may attain popularity in the near future.

The Linear Programming Method

The biharmonic equation can also be solved using linear programming (or LP for short) methods. There are two possible approaches to the application of the LP method. One could possibly start with a PDE such as Eq. (2) and apply the LP method in conjunction with the method of particular solutions [8]. Alternatively, one could start with Eq. (27) and visualize the process of inverting the matrix A as an LP process. For instance, if one starts with an initial guess $\phi^{(0)}$, then in general the left side of Eq. (27) is either greater than or less than the right side. For concreteness, let

$$A\phi^{(0)} \leq b \qquad (45)$$

Defining the residual $\xi \triangleq b - A\phi^{(0)}$, Eq. (45) can be rewritten as

$$A\phi^{(0)} + r = b$$

Now the problem of solving Eq. (27) can be stated as

$$\text{Minimize } r$$
$$\text{subject to } A\phi^{(0)} + r = b \qquad (46)$$

which can be readily recognized as an LP problem in its standard format.

One of the advantages of this formulation is that one can readily take advantage of the sparsity of A using one of several decomposition algorithms

BIHARMONIC EQUATIONS, SOLUTION METHODS

available to solve LP problems. So far no conclusive work has been done to show the merits or demerits of the above two procedures.

The Tensor Product Method

Alternatively, a biharmonic PDE, such as Eq. (2), can also be solved using the tensor product (or TP) method. Central to the idea of the TP method is the assumption that the problem is separable. Then the solution can be expressed in terms of the tensor products (or direct products or Kronecker products) of solutions of lower-dimensional problems. A first step in applying this method is to write the difference equations of the given PDE and rearrange them as

$$(I \otimes A + A \otimes I)^2 \phi = g \tag{47}$$

where $\otimes$ stands for the tensor product. In Eq. (47), A and B are respectively $M \times M$ and $N \times N$ matrices where M and N are the number of grid points along the x- and y-directions, respectively. For sufficiently fine mesh size, A and B turn out to be diagonally dominant, nonsingular, and with distinct eigenvalues. Then there exist P and Q such that

$$Q^{-1}AQ = \Lambda(A)$$
$$P^{-1}BP = \Lambda(B)$$

where $\Lambda(A)$ and $\Lambda(B)$ are diagonal. It should be noted that the format shown in Eq. (47) can only be achieved if the finite difference equations to points near a boundary are treated in a special way.

The solution of Eq. (47) can be written as

$$\phi = [(I \otimes A + A \otimes I)^2]^{-1} g \tag{48}$$

The right side of Eq. (48) can be evaluated by using the following general relation for the inversion of a matrix. If

$$L = \prod_{i=1}^{k} (I \otimes A_i + B_i \otimes I)$$

then

$$L^{-1} = \prod_{i=k}^{1} (P_i \otimes Q_i)(I \otimes \Lambda(A_i) + \Lambda(B_i) \otimes I)(P_i^{-1} \otimes Q_i^{-1})$$

The TP method has been successfully applied [9] to elliptic, parabolic, and hyperbolic equations. Application of this method to a biharmonic PDE as outlined above has not yet been done.

The Dynamic Programming Method

This method takes Eq. (3) as a starting point. This method is derived by considering a discrete version of the variational problem corresponding to the given PDE as a multistage decision process. This method [10] is direct in nature and does not involve the determination of iteration parameters. The method has been applied to an elliptic equation, but its applicability to the biharmonic PDE has not been tested.

REFERENCES

1. J. Bernoulli, *Acta Eruditorum*, Leipzig, 1696, pp. 268–269.
2. S. P. Timoshenko, *History of Strength of Materials*, McGraw-Hill, New York, 1954.
3. G. J. Tee, A novel finite difference approximation to the biharmonic operator, *Comput. J.* **6,** 171–192 (1963).
4. S. D. Conte and R. T. Dames, An alternating direction method for solving the biharmonic equation, *Math. Tables Other Aids to Computation,* **12,** 198–205 (1958).
5. S. D. Conte and R. T. Dames, On an alternating direction method for solving the plate problem with mixed boundary conditions, *J. Assoc. Comput. Mach.* **7,** 264–273, 1960.
6. R. H. MacNeal, *Electric Circuit Analogies for Elastic Structures*, Wiley, New York, 1962.
7. W. J. Karplus, *Analog Simulation: Solution of Field Problems,* McGraw-Hill, New York, 1958.
8. O. L. Mangasarian, Numerical solution of the first biharmonic problem by linear programming, *Intern. J. Eng. Sci.* **1,** 231–240 (1963).
9. R. E. Lynch, Direct solution of partial differential equations by tensor product-methods, *Numer. Math.* **6,** 185–199 (1964).
10. E. Angel, Inverse boundary value problems, elliptic equations, *J. Math. Anal. Appl.* **30,** 86–98 (1970).

BIBLIOGRAPHY

Bekey, G. A., and W. J. Karplus, *Hybrid Computation,* Wiley, New York, 1970.

Bramble, J. H., A second order finite difference analog of the first biharmonic boundary value problems, *Numer. Math.* **9,** 236–249 (1966).

Conte, S. D., A stable implicit finite difference approximation to the fourth order parabolic equations, *J. Assoc. Comp. Mach.* **4,** 18–23 (1957).

Crandall, S. H., Numerical treatment of fourth order parabolic partial differential equations, *J. Assoc. Comput. Mach.* **1,** 111–118 (1954).

Fairweather, A., and A. R. Mitchell, A generalized alternating direction method of Douglas-Rachford type for solving the biharmonic equation, *Comput. J.* **7,** 242–245 (1964).

Keller, H. B., Special block-iterations with applications to Laplace and biharmonic difference equations, *Rev. SIAM* **2,** 277–287 (1960).

Komkov, V., *Optimal Control Theory for the Damping of Vibrations of Simple Elastic Systems,* Springer, Berlin, 1972.

Parter, S. V., On "two-line" iterative methods for the Laplace and biharmonic equations, *Numer. Math.* **1,** 240–252 (1959).

BIHARMONIC EQUATIONS, SOLUTION METHODS

Parter, S. V., Some computational results on "two-line" iterative methods for the biharmonic difference equations, *J. Assoc. Comput. Mach.* 359–365 (1961).
Smith, J., The coupled equation approach to the numerical solution of the biharmonic equation by finite differences I, *SIAM J. Num. Anal.* **5**(2), 323–339 (1968).
Zlamal, M., Asymptotic error estimates in solving elliptic equations of the fourth order by the method of finite differences, *SIAM J. Num. Anal.* **2**, 337–344 (1965).
Zlamal, M., Discretization and error estimates for elliptic boundary value problems of the fourth order, *SIAM J. Num. Anal.* **4**, 626–639 (1967).

V. Vemuri

BINARY ARITHMETIC
see Abstract Algebra

BINARY SEARCH

A binary search is a particular strategy for searching for an item in a file (list, table).

If the items of a file are arranged in a purely random fashion and one attempts to locate a given item by starting with the first entry, making a comparison and then continuing sequentially until the file is exhausted, it will require on the average $n/2$ (where n is the number of entries in the file) comparisons to locate the given item. This result follows from the fact that the average number of comparisons required is given by the sum

$$p(i = 1) + 2p(i = 2) + \ldots + np(i = n)$$

where $p(i = k)$ is the probability that the given item i is the kth item on the list. For a purely random distribution of items, each of the above probabilities is given by $1/(n + 1)$, and the above sum becomes equal to $n/2$.

If, however, the items are arranged in a suitable order, much more efficient methods can be used for searching, one of them being the so-called binary search. In particular, if the items are coded in a way that permits an ordering of items, e.g., lexicographic (alphabetic) coding, one can use the following (binary search) strategy to locate a given item. The list is entered at its midpoint, or a closest point to the midpoint if n is even, and a comparison is made with the given item. If the midpoint item is the same as the given item, the search is terminated. If it is not, one can eliminate, using the ordered

BINARY SEARCH

properties of the list, one of the halves of the list from further search. The above procedure is then repeated on the remaining half of the list and continued, if necessary, until the remaining list consists of a single item. After l comparisons the remaining list is reduced by a factor of 2^l. For a list with n items, l must be such as to satisfy the inequality $2^l \geq n$, or equivalently $l \geq \log_2 n$, in order to reduce the list to a single item. Thus the greatest number of comparisons required to locate a given item in a list of n items never exceeds the next integer value of $\log_2 n$. For this reason the binary search is sometimes referred to as the logarithmic search. As an example of the improvement possible with a binary search, for a list with 1024 entries ($\log_2 1024 = 10$), no more than 10 comparisons are required to locate any item, compared with 512 comparisons required, on the average, for a sequential search of a purely random list. The term *binary* in binary search relates to the fact that at each step the file length remaining to be searched is reduced by a factor of 2. The following simple example illustrates the binary search procedure.

Consider a file containing the following letters in alphabetical order; a, f, g, l, m, s, w, z. In the columns shown below, the numbers 1 through 8 are used to indicate the location of each file item (letter).

```
1    a
2    f
3    g
4    l
5    m
6    s
7    w
8    z
```

The problem is to search for the location (first column) of the letter w. In this example the midpoint of the file is 4.5. Either 4 or 5 may then be taken as a nearest item to the midpoint. Assume 4 is selected. The given item w is now compared to the item located at position 4, i.e., the letter l. Since w comes after l, the file items 1 through 4 (1/2 the initial file length) can be eliminated for further search. Next one can take 6 as a nearest point to the midpoint of the remaining file. The letter at this point is s. Since w comes after s one can now eliminate the items in locations 5 and 6 from further consideration. The remaining file now consists of two items, one at location 7 and one at location 8. If 7 is selected as a nearest midpoint, the search is completed since a comparison of the given item w with the item at location 7 will indicate a match.

A disadvantage of the binary search approach described above is that the file must be suitably ordered. This initial sorting problem can be rather involved. In practice a compromise must be reached between the complexity of the procedure for structuring (sorting) the file and the procedure for searching the file.

More details on the binary and other search procedures may be found in the items listed in the Bibliography.

BINARY SEARCH

BIBLIOGRAPHY

Brooks, Frederick P., Jr. and Kenneth E. Iverson, *Automatic Data Processing*, Wiley, New York, 1969, Sect. 7.2.

Gear, C. William, *Computer Organization and Programming*, McGraw-Hill, New York, 1969, Sect. 8.2.

Wegner, Peter, *Programming Languages, Information Structures, and Machine Organization*, McGraw-Hill, New York, 1968, Sect. 2.2.4.

Salton, Gerard, *Automatic Information Organization and Retrieval*, McGraw-Hill, New York, 1968, Sect. 3-3.

Peter Dorato

BINOMIAL DISTRIBUTION

The purpose of this article is to define *the binomial distribution*, and to deduce some of its mathematical properties. The derivation of the distribution itself from more fundamental concepts is discussed in the article *Bernoulli Process*, which should be read after this one.

PRELIMINARY INFORMATION

Before defining the binomial distribution, it is useful to present some preliminary definitions and proofs.

For any positive integer n, the quantity $n!$ (pronounced "*n factorial*") is defined as the product of the first n integers:

$$n! = \prod_{k=1}^{n} k = 1 \cdot 2 \cdots n$$

where the capital pi (Greek P) means product. Thus, $1! = 1$; $2! = 1 \cdot 2 = 2$; $3! = 1 \cdot 2 \cdot 3 = 6$; $4! = 1 \cdot 2 \cdot 3 \cdot 4 = 24$; and so forth. Since this definition does not tell us what zero factorial is, it is customary to define that quantity so that $0! = 1$. As we shall see, this definition is compatible with the one for positive n.

For any positive integer n, and for all $r = 0, 1, \ldots, n$, the *binomial coefficients* are defined by the formula

$$\binom{n}{r} = \frac{n!}{r!(n-r)!}$$

BINOMIAL DISTRIBUTION

Each coefficient may be pronounced "n over r." Thus, in particular,

$$\binom{n}{0} = \frac{n!}{0!n!} = 1$$

It is also easy to see that $\binom{n}{n} = 1$.

The binomial coefficient $\binom{n}{r}$ gives *the number of combinations of* n *things taken* r *at a time*. Since everything in this article rests upon this theorem, we shall prove it after giving some relevant definitions.

For any positive integer n, let us consider a finite set of n distinct things: $\{A_1, A_2, \ldots, A_n\}$. The things are commonly called elements. The braces containing the elements are commonly used to define a set. By definition, the order of the elements in the set is irrelevant. Rearranging the same things inside the braces in a different order does not change the set.

A more general discussion of set theory would not require that the things be distinct in a set. Thus $\{A, B\}$ and $\{A, B, A\}$ are the same set, since they contain the same two things: A and B, which we assume to be distinct. In this discussion, however, such freedom of duplication would only cause confusion. To retain clarity, therefore, each element of a set is henceforth considered to be distinct in this article. No duplication is allowed.

A combination of n *things taken* r *at a time* is any subset of r distinct things chosen from the original set of n distinct things. Again, the order of the chosen things is irrelevant. For example, given the set $\{A_1, A_2, A_3, A_4, A_5\}$ of five things, the apparently different subsets $\{A_2, A_5\}$ and $\{A_5, A_2\}$ are really the same subset, and thus are the same combination (of five things taken two at a time), while $\{A_3, A_5\}$ is a different combination.

A *permutation* is any ordered listing of the elements of a combination, and is here written inside parentheses. For example, (A_2, A_3, A_5) and (A_5, A_2, A_3) are two different permutations of the same combination $\{A_2, A_3, A_5\}$ of five things taken three at a time.

Let ^nC_r be *the number of combinations of* n *things taken* r *at a time*. Let ^nP_r be *the number of permutations of* n *things taken* r *at a time*. We wish to show that $^nC_r = \binom{n}{r}$, for all $r = 0, 1, \ldots, n$. To prove this, however, we shall count permutations.

There are two distinct methods for constructing and counting all possible permutations of n things taken r at a time: direct and indirect. The direct method is concerned from the very beginning with the order of the r things in the permutation. It picks them one at a time in their specified order. On the other hand, the indirect method ignores the order at first. It simply constructs all possible combinations of n things taken r at a time without regard to order. Then it makes all possible permutations of each combination. Since each method counts all possible permutations of n things taken r at a time, each gives the same value of ^nP_r.

Before applying these two methods for positive r, we must first dispose of the vacuous case where $r = 0$. Here we are not taking any of the n things. It is convenient to define $^nP_0 = {^nC_0} = 1$. The justification for doing this will be given soon.

BINOMIAL DISTRIBUTION

Now, let us apply the direct method for positive r. There are n ways of choosing Thing 1 of the permutation, since any of the n things can be chosen from the set. For each of these ways, there are $n-1$ ways of choosing Thing 2 if $r \geq 2$. Thus there are $n(n-1)$ ways of choosing the first two things. Then, if $r \geq 3$, there are $n-2$ ways of choosing Thing 3, and thus $n(n-1)(n-2)$ ways of choosing the first three things, and so on. The number of available things decreases at each step, and the number of ways requires multiplication. When Thing r is about to be chosen, $r-1$ things have already been removed from the set, so that the number remaining is $n-(r-1) = n-r+1$. Therefore,

$$^nP_r = n(n-1)\cdots(n-r+1) \quad \text{for all } r = 1, 2, \ldots, n$$

In this formula the factors of the product are written in decreasing order. They can also be written in increasing order:

$$^nP_r = (n-r+1)(n-r+2)\cdots n$$

The definition of the factorial shows that

$$(n-r)! = 1 \cdot 2 \cdots (n-r).$$

Thus by multiplication,

$$(n-r)!\,^nP_r = n!$$

so that, by division,

$$^nP_r = n!/(n-r)!$$

Although this formula is derived for positive r, it also holds for $r = 0$. This fact justifies our previous definition that $^nP_0 = 1$.

The formula for ^nP_r was just derived by the direct method. Now, let us consider the indirect method for positive r. Although we do not yet have the formula for ^nC_r, we can, in a conceptual sense, construct all the ^nC_r combinations of n things taken r at a time. Second, we can permute each of these combinations in all possible ways. Since the number of such permutations of each combination is $^rP_r = r!$, the indirect method gives

$$^nP_r = r!\,^nC_r$$

Therefore,

$$^nC_r = \frac{^nP_r}{r!} = \frac{n!}{r!(n-r)!} = \binom{n}{r}$$

Although this formula was derived for positive r, it also holds for $r = 0$. This is so because we previously defined $^nC_0 = 1$, and we proved that $\binom{n}{0} = 1$ after we defined $0! = 1$. Q.E.D.

The last important preliminary topic is *the binomial theorem,* which is based upon the previous theorem. For any positive integer n, and any real x and y,

$$(x+y)^n = \sum_{r=0}^{n} \binom{n}{r} x^{n-r} y^r$$

The simplest proof of this is combinatorial. Consider $(x + y)^n$ to be the product of n distinct factors, each of which happens to equal $x + y$. If you multiply them all out *without adding up equal terms,* you will have the sum of 2^n terms.

For example, the quantity

$$(x + y)^2 = x^2 + xy + xy + y^2$$

is the sum of $2^2 = 4$ terms. Multiplication of this by $x + y$ shows that $(x + y)^3$ is the sum of $2^3 = 8$ terms, and so forth.

In general, each of these 2^n terms can be rearranged to be of the form $x^{n-r}y^r$. This is the product of $n - r$ factors, each equal to x, and of r factors, each equal to y. When such equal products are to be added together, there are $\binom{n}{r}$ of them. This is the number of ways of choosing r of the y factors, and $n - r$ of the x factors, from the n distinct original factors, each of which equals $x + y$. Q.E.D.

THE BINOMIAL DISTRIBUTION

Now that the preliminaries have been presented, it is time to discuss the major topic of this article. *The binomial distribution* of the random variable $\tilde{r}$ states the probability that $\tilde{r} = r$, given the values of n and p, for all $r = 0, 1, \ldots, n$. It holds for any positive integer n, and for any p such that $0 \leq p \leq 1$. Its formula is here written as

$$f(r|n, p) = \binom{n}{r}(1 - p)^{n-r}p^r \quad \text{for all } r = 0, 1, \ldots, n$$

To apply this formula for the two extreme cases ($p = 0, 1$), we adopt the convention that $0^0 = 1$.

The left-hand member of this formula is pronounced "f of r, given n and p," to show that r varies for fixed n and p. Since n and p can also vary from one particular binomial distribution to another, this equation really defines *the binomial family of distributions.* The generic name "binomial distribution" is an abbreviation of this more precise name.

The previously derived binomial theorem shows immediately that the sum of all the $n + 1$ terms of the binomial distribution equals

$$\sum_{r=0}^{n} f(r|n, p) = [(1 - p) + p]^n = 1$$

Moreover, $f(r|n, p) > 0$ for all $r = 0, 1, \ldots, n$. Thus the two requirements for a *discrete probability distribution* (sometimes called a *probability mass function*) are satisfied.

It is useful now to introduce the concept of an *honest function.* The function q is honest if and only if $q(r)$ is finite at every point r in the domain $\{0, 1, \ldots, n\}$ of q. In particular, division by zero is never required. Thus, for example,

BINOMIAL DISTRIBUTION

we must exclude the function q_0, such that $q_0(r) = 1/r$, to avoid division by zero.

Suppose that q is an honest function. Then it transforms the random variable $\tilde{r}$ into the corresponding random variable $\tilde{q} = q(\tilde{r})$.

The *mathematical expectation* of the random variable $q(\tilde{r})$ is then defined as

$$E[q(\tilde{r})] = \sum_{r=0}^{n} q(r) f(r|n, p)$$

Three special cases of this definition are important to this discussion. First, consider $q_1(r) = r$. Then we have *the arithmetic mean* of the binomial distribution of $\tilde{r}$, which is commonly called μ:

$$\mu = E(\tilde{r}) = \sum_{r=0}^{n} r f(r|n, p)$$

It is well known that μ is a measure of the central tendency of the distribution.

The first term of this summation (for $r = 0$) clearly vanishes, and may be deleted from the equation. Thus, by simple algebra, using the previously given definitions,

$$\mu = np \sum_{r=1}^{n} \binom{n-1}{r-1}(1-p)^{(n-1)-(r-1)} p^{r-1}$$
$$= np[(1-p) + p]^{n-1}$$
$$= np$$

This is the specific formula for μ.

The second special case is $q_2(r) = (r - \mu)^2$. The expectation of this random variable $q_2(\tilde{r})$ is defined as the *variance*, and is commonly called σ^2:

$$\sigma^2 = E[(\tilde{r} - \mu)^2] = \sum_{r=0}^{n} (r - \mu)^2 f(r|n, p)$$

The positive square root of the variance, σ^2, is defined as the *standard deviation*, and is naturally called σ. This measures the extent to which the probability is dispersed about the mean, μ.

Another useful equation for σ^2 is easily derived from its definition:

$$\sigma^2 = E(\tilde{r}^2 - 2\mu\tilde{r} + \mu^2)$$
$$= E(\tilde{r}^2) - \mu^2$$

We have already shown that the specific formula for μ is $\mu = np$. Now we want to obtain the specific formula for $e(\tilde{r}^2)$, for derivation of the specific formula for σ^2; to get these, let us consider the third special case: $q_3(r) = r(r - 1)$. The expectation of this random variable $q_3(\tilde{r})$ is

$$E[\tilde{r}(\tilde{r} - 1)] = \sum_{r=0}^{n} r(r - 1) f(r|n, p)$$

The first two terms of this summation (for $r = 0, 1$) obviously vanish, and may be deleted from the equation. Thus, by simple algebra, using the previous definitions,

$$E[\tilde{r}(\tilde{r} - 1)] = n(n - 1)p^2 \sum_{r=2}^{n} \binom{n-2}{r-2}(1-p)^{(n-2)-(r-2)}p^{r-2}$$
$$= n(n - 1)p^2[(1 - p) + p]^{n-2}$$
$$= n(n - 1)p^2$$

But it is easy to see that

$$E[\tilde{r}(\tilde{r} - 1)] = E(\tilde{r}^2) - E(\tilde{r})$$

Thus

$$E(\tilde{r}^2) = E[\tilde{r}(\tilde{r} - 1)] + E(\tilde{r})$$
$$= n(n - 1)p^2 + np$$

It follows that

$$\sigma^2 = [n(n - 1)p^2 + np] - (np)^2$$

so that, by simple algebra, the specific formulas for σ^2 and σ are

$$\sigma^2 = np(1 - p)$$
$$\sigma = [np(1 - p)]^{1/2}$$

APPROXIMATIONS TO THE BINOMIAL DISTRIBUTION

Anyone with access to a time-sharing computer can compute almost any desired term, or sum of terms, of the binomial distribution with ease and accuracy. In the absence of both a computer and precomputed tables, however, computations based directly upon this distribution are extremely tedious. Some of the early mathematical research in the theory of probability was motivated by a search for practical approximations to the binomial distribution. Although such approximations are somewhat less important now, they are still useful for quick computations by hand. Perhaps much of their current interest lies in the insight that they give.

First, if p is small and n is large, then, for $\mu = np$,

$$f(r|n, p) \doteq e^{-\mu}\mu^r/r! \quad \text{for all } r = 0, 1, \ldots, n$$

where $\doteq$ means approximately equal. This is the *Poisson distribution*. In addition to its use as an approximation to the binomial distribution, the Poisson also arises as an exact distribution in its own right in the theory of stochastic processes. As an approximation to the binomial, the Poisson distribution has the advantage of having only one parameter (μ) instead of two (n, p). Therefore, instead of a table of triple entry (n, p, r), its table is only of double entry (μ, r).

BINOMIAL DISTRIBUTION

The second approximation is the *normal distribution*. The *normal probability density* is well known to be

$$\phi(z) = (2\pi)^{-1/2} \exp(-z^2/2)$$

for all real z. The *normal distribution function* is the integral

$$\Phi(z) = \int_{-\infty}^{z} \phi(t)\, dt$$

This is especially useful to approximate the sum of a large number of binomial terms when n is itself large. Suppose that we wish to compute Q_{12}, defined as

$$Q_{12} = P(r_1 \leq \tilde{r} \leq r_2 | n, p) = \sum_{r=r_1}^{r_2} f(r|n, p)$$

First, we express each bound r_i, for $i = 1, 2$, as a standardized variate:

$$z_i = (r_i - \mu)/\sigma$$

using previous formulas for μ and σ. Then we compute the approximate equality:

$$Q_{12} \doteq \Phi(z_2) - \Phi(z_1)$$

This approximation is usually improved by making a small correction for the discontinuity of $\tilde{r}$:

$$z'_1 = (r_1 - 0.5 - \mu)/\sigma$$
$$z'_2 = (r_2 + 0.5 - \mu)/\sigma$$
$$Q_{12} \doteq \Phi(z'_2) - \Phi(z'_1)$$

ADDITIONAL READING

It is hard to find a textbook on probability theory that does not discuss the binomial distribution and its approximations. Good treatments from the Bayesian viewpoint are given by Lindley [1] and by Pratt, Raiffa, and Schlaifer [2]. Parzen discusses it well from a frequentist viewpoint [3]. Both Parzen and Pratt, Raiffa, and Schlaefer give tables of the binomial and normal distributions. Parzen tabulates the Poisson distribution.

REFERENCES

1. D. V. Lindley, *Introduction to Probability and Statistics from a Bayesian Viewpoint. Part 1, Probability. Part 2, Inference*, Cambridge University Press, Cambridge, England, 1965.

2. J. W. Pratt, H. Raiffa, and R. Schlaifer, *Introduction to Statistical Decision Theory,* McGraw-Hill, New York, 1965.
3. E. Parzen, *Modern Probability Theory and Its Applications,* Wiley, New York, 1960.

Raymond H. Burros

BIOMEDICAL SCIENCES

No presentation short of several volumes can adequately cover the field of biomedical computing: the topic is too vast. Since computers have entered all areas of biomedicine, creating new techniques and subspecializations peculiar to each subject area, the topic is as broad as biomedicine itself. And, since a variety of special problems of data acquisition, handling, analysis, interpretation, and display are raised by the special requirements of biomedicine, discussion of hardware, software, and analytic methods is also required. There have been several books written on the subject. One of the most comprehensive is Stacy and Waxman, *Computers in Biomedical Research,* Academic, New York. It is in four volumes, published between 1965 and 1974, includes 60 articles covering a wide range of topics, and is written by approximately 90 different contributors. Nonetheless, it is only a sampling of the field.

Clearly a short article written from a single perspective can hardly touch this diversity. In order to avoid a featureless survey of projects which would still not be truly comprehensive, this review will present a very limited sample. An attempt has been made to convey the scope of the field, but no inference should be made that the general applications or specific projects described are the most important, most successful, or most promising. They have been selected to provide some sense of how computers are being used in biomedicine; nothing more is implied.

The presentation could be structured on any of a number of dimensions—e.g., *purpose* (research, clinical trials, clinical medicine, training); *tools* (statistics, modeling, pattern recognition, information systems, data acquisition systems); *hardware* (dedicated minicomputers, large shared systems, terminals, graphics devices, scanners, A/D conversion equipment); *subject matter* (neurophysiology, radiology, biochemistry, pharmacology). This could go on and on. Indeed, the multidimensional nature of the field makes it difficult to convey its breadth in all dimensions. In order to communicate several of these perspectives simultaneously, a structure was selected which crosses these dimensions and includes aspects of purpose, tools, and hardware. The general

BIOMEDICAL SCIENCES

topics presented are as follows:

> Statistical analysis
> Modeling
> Signal analysis
> Clinical applications
> Information systems
> Training
> Image processing
> Hardware and software

In each section, following a general introduction to the area, one or two specific applications are explored in more detail, giving the reader some idea of the nature of the problem, some of the approaches taken to a solution, and the current status of research in the area. While the topics covered overlap in a number of ways, the categories are not exhaustive. Several important areas of application of computers to biomedicine have been largely omitted. These include research in biochemistry and microbiology, psychology and mental health, and applications of artificial intelligence techniques to biomedicine. For example, computers are widely used for data acquisition and analysis in mass spectroscopy, amino acid analysis and sequencing, chromatography, enzyme kinetics, and crystallographic analysis. Some of the most effective patient information systems have been developed for the mental health field, and almost all research in psychology is heavily dependent on the computer. And exciting work is being done in applying the techniques of artificial intelligence to biochemistry and medical diagnosis. Thus the general topics covered are neither exclusive nor exhaustive. They do give some feeling for the diversity of the field and indicate directions for further reading. Some notes on publications in the field follow the subject matter presentations.

Ten years ago, computer-based projects in biomedicine were pioneering efforts; today, most research projects make at least some use of a computer. Nonetheless, it seems clear that biomedicine is still only on the threshold of discovering the full potential of the computer, and that the next decade will produce far greater changes than the last.

STATISTICAL ANALYSIS

Statistical analysis is ubiquitous in biomedical research. Most projects require at least some statistical support, while some are entirely projects in data gathering and statistical analysis. At the most elementary level, most data bases require screening techniques, including some method for looking at simple descriptors such as means and variances and identification of outliers. Studies which deal with direct entry of biological data (e.g., electroencephalograms or X-rays) require filtering techniques to obtain important information in the presence of noise. Many projects require statistical studies to validate nonstatistical techniques, while others require statistical methods for both analysis and validation. An example of the latter is the work of Dr. Hubert Pipberger, described below in the section entitled Physiological Signal Processing, where extensive statistical analysis has been used to validate a computer-based electrocardiogram interpretation program which is itself largely based on statistical methods. Many of the investigations of the electroencephalogram make heavy use of some of the more sophisticated statistical techniques—such as autocorrelation, cross-correlation, spectral analysis, and time series analysis—as well as filtering (see the section entitled Physiological Signal Processing). Work in medical diagnosis and definition of disease entities relies heavily on clustering and discriminant analysis, while statistical techniques, especially factor analysis, are basic to most studies in psychology and psychiatry. Finally, most clinical trials, retrospective studies of treatment methods, public health surveys, and studies in epidemiology, as well as specific studies in many other areas, are almost totally statistical.

The most widely reported statistical biomedical research projects are the large studies in which correlations are sought between diet, health practices, or environmental conditions on the one hand and disease on the other. Examples of such investigations are the studies linking smoking to cancer and heart disease, and of the relationship of cholesterol in the diet to heart disease. These studies require careful experimental design, design of a data base, data gathering and screening, selection of statistical methods, development or selection of computer programs for the analysis, the analysis itself, and its interpretation.

As the practice of medicine and the environmental factors affecting man become more complex, the problems which arise in biomedical research require increasingly sophisticated statistical procedures to disentangle the various essential factors and differentiate them from the nonsignificant. Key questions concern the effects of drugs on man; the possible hazards of antifertility compounds; the consequences of adulteration of air, food, land, and water; the stresses resulting from crowding and noise; the effects of dietary selectivity; etc.

Computers play a very significant role, both in handling the data base and in supporting the analysis. Indeed, significant advances in statistical methods have resulted largely from the availability of new and more powerful computational tools and from new challenges arising from attempts to apply accepted methods to specific research problems. To a considerable extent, the statistical problems attacked, the methods used to attack them, and even the way they are thought about have been affected by these factors. Thus in the 1930s the desk calculator provided an adequate tool for balanced analysis of variance designs and small regression analyses, which were applied to problems in agriculture and psychology. Later, the card sorter stimulated the development of contingency table analysis, especially applicable to research problems in medicine and the social sciences. Meanwhile, research problems in biology provided the stimulus and direction for a number of topics in mathematical statistics—such as multivariate analysis and decision theory—but the resulting methods remained largely untested. Theoretical problems were frequently proposed and solved, but only the most modest practical applications were possible because of the lack of computing power.

Thus the introduction of the modern computer into biological research put the familiar techniques of the statistician to a severe test—a test which frequently found them wanting. Many problems were a lot bigger than expected. Frequently, the basic problem was not how to look at a small set of data optimally, but how to look at a large set of data reasonably—or at all. Missing data became a fact of life, not a random accident. Bad data caused even greater problems. The thin tails of the normal distribution grew thick with real data outliers. Discrete and counted data were surprisingly common and frequently mixed with continuous data. And even continuous data often required transformation to make them acceptable for analysis.

The difficulty of analyzing biological data resides not only in their complexity, quantity, unavoidable and often conditional incompleteness, and large measurement errors, the basic interactions of variables often depart markedly from those assumed by classical statistical techniques. Indeed, much of the effort of biological research is addressed to characterizing these interactions. They often cannot be phrased explicitly, being couched in systems of differential equations or in simulation constructs. A vast new research area was opened by this need to develop new statistical and modeling techniques to guide efficient experimental planning and to develop validation criteria for hypothesis testing of realistic models.

The range of applications of computer-based statistics to biomedical research is really too great even to sample effectively. Instead of representative applications, a statistical system and one rather unusual example are presented here. Additional examples of the use of statistics abound in the remaining sections of this article.

The BMD Programs

While statistics is basic to much biomedical research, many scientists in the field are relatively uncomfortable with both statistics and computers. To make a computer usable for such an investigator is a major task, requiring demonstration of how his needs might be met, extensive consultation, and application-oriented software—all in terms natural to the user. The Health Sciences Computing Facility at UCLA, under the leadership of Dr. Wilfrid Dixon, has been funded since 1961 by the National Institutes of Health for developing computer-based support for biomedical research, with primary emphasis on statistical methods. This group has pioneered in providing a wide range of services to biomedical investigators and in developing a set of package programs—the BMD Statistical Programs—which have been distributed all over the world for use in nonbiological as well as biological research.

At the time this project was envisioned, computer manufacturers were supplying programming systems which permitted the user to work with useful programming languages, FORTRAN being the most notable of these for scientific computing. Such systems were a great improvement over what had been available in the early years, but did not make the computer readily usable for those who were obliged to hire expert programmers or spend a significant amount of their own time acquiring the necessary skills to do their own programming. The initial project was conceived in terms of "package programs" that would apply to a large but limited class of problems. The selection was of well-defined methods of statistical analysis. The objective was to construct programs such that only a few easily described control cards would be required in addition to the data. In this way a large amount of useful work could be carried out in a short time by personnel relatively unskilled with computers, and the efforts of the skillful could go into other programming projects. The resulting set of package programs has evolved over the years. While all of the programs are general purpose routines, each was originally developed to fill the needs of a real problem. The generalizations which followed were made in response to the demands of new problems. The programs are based on the data matrix concept and are written in FORTRAN for ease of export. A degree of standardization has been maintained throughout the collection.

With advances in system design, storage capabilities, and programming techniques, a new concept of package programs has evolved. The BMD programs are no longer independent, isolated tools to be used separately on a problem but are, rather, self-contained analytic procedures forming part of an integrated system of analytic procedures, consulting aids, file handling programs, etc., which are invoked as a sequence of operations on the data.

The "original" set of BMD programs now includes fifty-three programs, falling into the following categories:

>   Description and tabulation (13)
>   Multivariate analysis (8)
>   Regression (7)
>   Time series (4)
>   Analysis of variance (12)
>   Miscellaneous (9)

While many of these have presented already well-developed techniques in an easily used and easily exported form, some have represented important contributions to the application of computers to statistics.

Meanwhile, a new set of programs—the BMDP programs—is beginning to supplant the original set. The BMDP programs feature a more unified presentation, free form input, increased flexibility, and many additional new features; some new programs are also included in this series. Research in statistical methods continues, and a set of experimental programs is resulting from the application of new methods to newly raised specific problems. The Boolean factor analysis program described in the next example is typical of such new programs. Finally, the effective use of interactive techniques and graphical presentations is being explored. Such techniques, by providing assistance to the user on request, interactive consultation with a statistician when needed, and a natural presentation of results, promise finally to achieve the goal of making it possible for the unsophisticated user to specify and explore his analyses himself, although he will undoubtedly always require assistance with experimental design and interpretation of results.

The success of this effort to make computers readily usable through package programs is indicated by the fact that the BMD programs are available at computer centers throughout the world. Programmers typically prefer their own creations, so that their wide distribution indicates that it is generally far easier and less costly to use them than to construct tailored programs.

Tissue Typing for Organ Transplantation

A crucial problem in improving the success rate for organ transplants is finding methods for selecting donor organs that are sufficiently compatible with the recipient's immunological system that rejection is unlikely. The compatibility of a transplant is thought to be determined mainly by substances occurring in cell walls. These substances, referred to as antigens, are present in the cells of most types of tissue in the body, and are thought to be genetically determined. If the donor organ contains antigens not present in the recipient, the recipient's immune system manufacturers a defensive antibody that attacks the foreign antigen and leads to rejection of the transplanted tissue. At least some antigens important for transplantation occur on the lymphocyte, as well as other tissue, so that effort can be concentrated on these cells. Antibodies reactive with lymphocyte antigens occur in the blood serum of many individuals, particularly in women who have borne children. Thus, if lymphocyte cell suspensions from several subjects are allowed to react with sera from several sources, the pattern of outcomes of the two-way array of reactions can be used to study the variety of commonly occurring antigens and how these can be individually recognized. Using this approach, considerable progress has been made in identifying antigenlike specificities.

One of the leaders in this research is Dr. Paul Terasaki of UCLA. In a collaboration with statisticians at the UCLA Health Sciences Computing Facility, special statistical programs have been developed for determining the specificities detected in the analysis of sera. The problem can be formulated as a stimulus–response test in which a positive response is to be expected whenever the stimulus and the test preparation match up in a particular way— i.e., have one or more of a set of attributes in common. The stimuli are antibody-containing sera, the test materials are antigen-carrying cells, and the attributes are antigenic specificities. The objective is to define the specificities and to identify them in additional sera and subjects.

Linear methods of factor analysis are not applicable to this problem. The analytical difficulty is that the presence or absence of the different attributes, or even the number involved, is not independently assessable but must be inferred from experimental data. Since test techniques are being developed simultaneously, the analysis is further complicated by "false" negative and "false" positive reactions. The standard analytical methods do not apply to this problem. However, if the test results are represented by 0's and 1's (corresponding to negative and positive responses) arranged in the form of a matrix indexed by subjects and by test stimuli, the problem can be formulated in the above terms. A "Boolean factor analysis" program has been developed for this purpose. This formulation has been tested extensively in determining antigenic specificities of the HL-A system using lymphocytes as the test preparations. (HL-A is the name given to the system of *H*uman *L*eucocyte *A*ntigens.)

The use of computer analysis for the classification of sera and typing of subjects in terms of transplantation antigens provides a basis for several studies. For example, the Terasaki laboratory was the first to supply objective evidence that the lymphocyte antigens act as antigens in kidney transplants. In order to carry out these studies it is necessary to type prospective donors and recipients prior to transplantation; samples from many transplant centers throughout the country are received and typed by the laboratory.

A particularly important problem is whether adequate matches of cadaver organs can reasonably be expected. Consequently the typing of potential cadaver donors is of great research interest. In the typing of such donors, time is of basic importance, and it becomes necessary to be able to quickly select the best matching recipient. The larger the recipient pool, the more likely it is that a suitable match will be found. As the pool size increases, the search task becomes more demanding. Special files are maintained of potential recipients awaiting an appropriate donor organ. After the typing results are available for the prospective donor, the file can be searched for suitably matched recipients. As in many other studies, statistical methods are also applied to the follow-up data on transplant cases to evaluate the effectiveness of the selection criteria.

MODELING

Like data analysis, modeling is a tool, not an end in itself, and like data analysis, modeling encompasses a very wide spectrum of activities. There is a sense in which no one ever deals with anything but models of reality: our senses, our language, our culture, our personal perspectives all supply us with the constructs through which we view the world. At the other extreme, when we talk of modeling in biology, we often mean the specification of a set of differential equations with which we hope to adequately describe the functioning of some biological system: an ecology, the action of the hip joint, the respiratory control system, or whatever. Whereas the first definition is a bit broad for utility, the second is rather narrow. Modeling is a process through which we organize our knowledge, casting it in a form in which we can comprehend it comfortably, communicate it readily, and use it for prediction. The criteria by which we tend to judge a model are epistemological, not ontological. The primary constraint upon the model is that it not predict phenomena that conflict with reliable empirical data. Beyond this, models which are simple and comprehensive are preferred. Uniqueness is seldom ascribed to a model, and few scientists are seeking to reveal eternal verities through their theory formation. But it has been found possible to relate many phenomena to simple postulated underlying mechanisms, and such concepts have had great pragmatic value. The ability to relate different areas of scientific endeavor and to make sharply focused predictions goes beyond mere simplification, providing a potent stimulus for scientific enquiry.

Models in biology serve a number of purposes. A model may be used to summarize data in a convenient fashion. Much scientific investigation begins with a search for some structure in a set of data. Simple descriptors, such as the average values and the ranges of certain variables, facilitate the investigator's grasp of his data. Going a step further, a model may be used to explore processes for which no theory has been developed but which do exhibit established regularities. Next, given a proposed theory, a model may be used to test it. When a model has been devised which corresponds to the theory and accounts for all of the available data, it is used to predict the results of new experiments. Successful prediction tends to validate the model, and hence the theory it embodies, while failure discredits the theory. Similarly, a model may be used to test the consistency of a set of hypotheses and observations: can a model be developed which will fit them all? If not, something will have to be given up. Finally, given a well-accepted model of a process or system, it may be used to simplify the exploration of related or interacting entities of which less is known.

Mathematical, statistical, and conceptual modeling are by no means new in biology. What is new with the computer is the freedom to explore a model completely. The speed of the computer permits the investigator to test the model exhaustively against a very large volume of data and conditions, and, in the case of a probabilistic model, to explore it extensively enough to get beyond the chance occurrence to the essential operation of the model. Computer models also make an excellent instructional device. The student may probe the model at length to develop his intuitive understanding or he may construct his own models to test his comprehension of theory.

Much the same could be said for modeling in any discipline. However, there are some difficulties inherent in biological research which make the use of computer-based models particularly attractive. In the physical sciences, data bases are often simple enough for the investigator to grasp directly. In the biological sciences, this is seldom the case. A model can provide the unifying simplification needed. All modeling seeks to integrate knowledge. In a field as complex as biology, the required syntheses may involve systems of models. Integrative modeling may also expedite clinical implementation of research findings. Because of its potential medical significance, there is emphasis in biology on moving findings in basic sciences into the clinical domain. Insulin therapy did not await a full explanation of its action, and neutron therapy was used before it was fully understood. New integrated techniques for combining different treatment agents, for more strategic timing of doses, and the like, can be explored using models drawn from a number of separate sources. Finally, the difficulty of performing direct experiments makes the possible amplification of experiments through the use of simulation particularly attractive. Even where ethical considerations do not intervene, the very fragility of any living preparation limits the effective control the investigator has over an experiment. He must often design his experiments in such a way as to allow considerable latitude in the experimental conditions, or, indeed, he may have to wait for a suitable experiment to present itself. The theoretical experiment implicit in the use of a model is an attractive alternative. However, this very attraction has been the downfall of a number of promising projects. A mathematical model is not an end in itself, and it is useful only if it embodies and is in accord with the experimental evidence. Too many theoretical biologists have been concerned only with theory, and their models, while ingenious, have had little to do with biology. It is not the individual model which is important so much as the process of modeling.

Models have been used to investigate a variety of phenomena in biology. These include:

Physiological Control Systems. E.g., cardiorespiratory control, feedback in the endocrine system, temperature control. Early attempts were made to apply linear control theory directly to problems of this class, but most of the biological phenomena have proven too complex.

Physical Models of Organ Systems. E.g., fluid dynamics of the heart, filtration in the kidney, respiration; models often include the facility to study the effects of various abnormalities (atrial fibrillation, emphysema, etc.)

Compartment Models. Enzyme kinetics, membrane transport, electrolyte balance. A program for facilitating compartment analysis is discussed, as an example, below.

Pharmacokinetics. The activity of insulin and of digitalis have been widely modeled; simulation studies have been used in developing chemotherapeutic protocols, notably for leukemia.

Cellular Kinetics. Both deterministic and stochastic models have been used, particularly for studying possible etiologies of and treatments for cancer.

Neural Networks. There have been a number of efforts to build a theory of the functioning of the nervous system based on networks of neurons having specified properties and interactions. The goal of these modeling efforts is to start from physically realistic elements (i.e., consistent with what is known of the microanatomy of the nervous system) and to specify networks which function in a manner consistent with gross observations (EEG's and behavior).

Genetic Models. Developing pedigrees, the probabilities of the occurrence of various genetic anomalies, etc., is a very complex task (since the problem is essentially combinatorial), and is considerably aided by computer models.

Population Models. Genetic or epidemiological, of the diffusion of genetic traits or diseases through a population, in the presence of such inhibitors as bars to intermarriage or innoculation, and such enhancers as social groups, business and school relationships, etc.

Psychological Models. Belief systems, neurotic processes.

Ecological Models. Predator/prey competitions, etc.

Finally, models are being used increasingly to study health care needs, utilization of services, time spent in various activities, and the like, motivated by the urgency and complexity of the problems and the expense of making real trials of new methods.

It is difficult to select any specific models which exemplify the field. The model is part of the process of discovery, not an end in itself, so perhaps the most generally useful work in modeling is the development of tools which make it easy to develop specific models. Hence, the example chosen is a tool for compartment analysis, rather than a specific model.

General Purpose Program for Compartment Analysis

Dr. Mones Berman and his associates at NIH developed a program—Simulation, Analysis and Modeling (SAAM)—for fitting models to experimental data. This program permits the investigator to specify a model, using a set of mathematical equations (differential, integral, or algebraic) and experimental data. The program varies the parameters of the model to provide the best fit. The model can consist of any set of equations for which there is an analytic or numerical solution; subroutines for the solution of a number of equation types are provided as part of the program, and the user can add his own, as required.

Fitting the model to the data consists of solving the equations for the responses, matching the responses to the experimental data, and adjusting the parameters until a "best" fit is acquired. The latter is accomplished by using linear regression analysis to minimize the sum of the squares of the differences between experimental data and computed responses. This process is iterated until it converges.

This program has been widely used over a number of years and has been continually improved. It is mathematically good but still somewhat difficult for the uninitiated to use.

PHYSIOLOGICAL SIGNAL PROCESSING

Direct input of raw biological data was recognized early as a key requirement for effective use of the computer in biomedical research. Because of the complexity of biological phenomena, most studies of biological signals require large volumes of data. If the data must first be converted to a form which can be read by a human, next translated into an appropriate punched card format, and finally entered into the machine, much of the potential value of the computer will be lost, along with considerable accuracy. People are not very good at tedious recording tasks of this sort; computers can be excellent. Further, adaptive experiments where the course of the experiment depends upon intermediate results would be impossible, as would direct data entry.

The natural form for much biological data is either electrical (ECG's, EEG's, etc.) or visual (X-rays, blood smears, etc.). Much greater success has been achieved with computer acquisition of electrical data than visual data (see below in the section entitled Image Processing). Most physiological signals can be measured as electrical signals or can be converted to electrical signals using sensors or transducers. Examples of the latter include respiratory rates and volumes, phonocardiograms, intestinal wave phenomena, uterine contractions, and arterial and venous pressures. Most of these data are analog—i.e., appear as a continuous signal—and require an analog-to-digital converter to prepare them for processing on a digital computer. Indeed, some of the early ECG and EEG studies were done using analog computers, but a digital computer is really essential because of the variety of logical approaches required. Development of good techniques for input of such data was further motivated by the fact that the same kind of interface is needed for a wide range of experimental equipment—mass spectrometers, auto analyzers, and seismographs to name a few. These considerations led to the development of increasingly fast, accurate, and inexpensive analog-to-digital converters interfaced either to recorders which produce computer readable magnetic tape, or, increasingly, directly to small computers. Progress in the field of computer analysis of ECG and EEG signals only really began when reasonably good converters become available.

Most of the research effort has gone into analysis of the ECG and EEG. The ECG has received major attention from clinically oriented investigators, while much of the EEG work has been directed to gaining further insight into the functioning of the brain.

The EEG provides an indication of the electrical activity of the brain. In human subjects the EEG is usually obtained from electrodes on the scalp; implanted electrodes are used in animal experimentation. The EEG has been studied in a wide range of applications. Investigators have sought to establish the relationship between changes in the EEG on the one hand and thought, behavior, and learning on the other, and to correlate the activity of various portions of the brain with the EEG and with the control of specific cognitive and motor activities. Unlike the ECG, the physiological basis for the EEG is not understood; investigators have attempted to use the EEG in explorations of neuroanatomy and neurophysiology. Clinically oriented studies have sought to improve the effectiveness of the EEG in the diagnosis of epilepsy, tumors, and other pathological conditions. The EEG has been used to monitor sleep states in a wide variety of investigations ranging from studies of dreaming to attempts to gain insight into sudden infant death syndrome—a condition leading to the unexplained deaths of a large number of infants. The EEG has also been used to explore the physiology of meditation and other unusual states of consciousness, and to provide the data for biofeedback studies. Finally, the EEG is used

BIOMEDICAL SCIENCES

in studies of the activity of psychotropic drugs and as an indicator of whether treatment will be effective.

The specific phenomena studied include the on-going wave train activity, differences in potential between different locations, the immediate and long-range responses evoked by stimuli, and spike discharges from single neuron cells (detected using microelectrodes). Since EEG studies produce large volumes of data (at rates up to 100 Hz on a number of channels simultaneously), computer analysis of the resulting material offered the first opportunity for detailed analysis of these phenomena and required the development or adaptation of special techniques of analysis. Since the data are voluminous and noisy, sampling and filtering techniques are essential. Time series analysis (for both short and long epochs), spectral analysis, cross-correlation, and autocorrelation are commonly used in studying variations and time lags in patterns of activity within the same structures, between structures, and between hemispheres. Spectral analysis provides a more concise descriptor of on-going activity, as well as a measure of the relationship of spectral power to frequency. In studying evoked response, recordings from a number of similar experiments are averaged to eliminate the effects of irrelevant stimuli (including cognitive and motor activity of the subject). The resulting average evoked response has proven a useful indicator of the response to the stimulus alone.

All of these techniques are dependent on the availability of a computer—a rather powerful computer in some cases. We are still far short of a complete understanding of neurophysiology, but quantitative studies could only really begin with the advent of the laboratory computer.

ECG Analysis

The ECG provides data on the electrical activity of the heart. The sequence of events recorded in the ECG can be summarized as follows: first, the atrium of the heart discharges, producing the P-wave; next, the ventricles fire, producing the QRS complex—the major discharge; finally the heart repolarizes, producing the T-wave. If part of the conduction system is disrupted, there are changes in the timing and the shape of the curves produced in the ECG. The ECG is also an indirect indicator of changes in fluid dynamics.

The heart is actually active over its entire surface, but most computer analyses of ECG's have been based on the assumption of a dipole source (two sources at a distance from each other) which is moving in space as a function of time. Although this assumption is physically unrealistic, recent work seems to indicate that it is adequate, and use of higher order poles improves results only slightly but significantly increases the complexity of the model.

Attempts at computer interpretation of ECG's began in about 1961, but the early work was largely unsuccessful. Purposes of the research include improved understanding of the ECG and the electrical activity of the heart, epidemiological studies of heart disease, ECG screening, and consulting services for use where there are no expert electrocardiographers available.

There have been two general approaches to computerized ECG interpretation. Most investigators have attempted to reformulate the problem for the computer, using direct numerical criteria (usually statistical measures) of some kind to determine whether a reading is normal or abnormal, and, if abnormal, in what respects. The second approach, used by Dr. Ralph Smith at Mayo Clinic, is to model the behavior of the electrocardiographer—indeed, the computer scientist who produced the program modeled Ralph Smith. This led to a quite different program. Unfortunately, this is an IBM proprietary program not in the public domain.

One of the most successful analytic approaches to computerized ECG interpretation has been developed by Dr. Hubert Pipberger and his associates at George Washington University and the Veterans Administration Hospital in Washington, D.C. Using Veterans Administration data, Dr. Pipberger has developed a system, validated from independent data (surgery, autopsy, angiography) which competes well with expert cardiologists. This system uses input from an orthogonal Frank lead (3 lead) ECG. This lead system is based on the dipole assumption discussed above, recording the dipole's movement through space in the x, y, and z directions.

Following conversion of the analog data and filtering to minimize noise, the interpretation program performs the following steps: (a) recognition of the individual beats and the wave forms which comprise them; (b) measurement of waves and analysis of beat-to-heart rhythms; (c) diagnosis; and (d) report preparation. The recognition program locates spikes, identifies the beat cycle, and marks the beginning and end of the wave forms. The measurement program computes a large number of time intervals, wave magnitudes, and angles. The rhythm analysis determines whether the rhythm is regular or irregular and performs further classifications in each category. Diagnostic classification is based on the determination of the probability for each relevant diagnostic category. Each of these probabilities is calculated from the frequency with which the given set of measurements occurs for the diagnostic classification in question and the prior probability established for that classification. The diagnostic classification proceeds as follows:

1. If the QRS duration exceeds a specified limit, a conduction defect test is performed on the data and step (b) is bypassed. This test establishes probabilities for each conduction defect category (right ventricular conduction defect, right ventricular conduction defect with myocardial infarct, etc.).
2. Otherwise, a QRS diagnostic classification is performed, and probabilities are established for each of the diagnostic categories (pulmonary emphysema, anterior myocardial infarct, left ventricular hypertrophy, etc.).
3. Other tests are performed on the data as suggested by the measurements.

The output program selects the categories with reasonably high probabilities for the report.

This program has been in operation for several years and appears to yield good results for the VA population. Dr. Pipberger is currently extending it to other populations (for which the prior probabilities will presumably be different).

CLINICAL APPLICATIONS

Ten years ago it was commonly held among the relatively small group of people in the field that computers were on the brink of revolutionizing the delivery of health care. Vast and comprehensive medical record systems were being designed—first for hospital use, but ultimately for the complete medical histories of large populations. Hospital information systems were to direct the whole routine of the ward; nurses were to use a terminal to enter notes and receive instructions from the all-knowing computer. Image processing techniques were to be used for screening blood smears, chest X-rays, chromosome studies, etc. New advances in research were to result from the availability of the comprehensive diagnostic and treatment information coming from the new records systems. And computer-driven diagnosis was just around the corner.

Ten years later we find the whole apparatus of health care delivery in the country in increasing disarray, and the contribution of computers still relatively slight. Although it is a commonplace in the history of computing that new applications become practical realities long after they become technically feasible, nowhere has this halting progress been more frustrating than in clinical medicine. The most grandiose failures have been in hospital information systems (see section following), but disenchantment has pervaded the field. The major impact of computers in clinical medicine has been from research results, not from direct use of computers. After 10 years of intense and expensive effort in the field by a growing number of investigators, the real successes remain rather modest and affect a relatively small patient population. Almost all use of computers in clinical medicine has been associated with projects in teaching hospitals, and even there progress has been disappointing. Some of the most apparently promising projects have failed. In private practice outside of the hospital, computers have had almost no impact aside from accounting applications.

Basic biomedical research—supported by computers—has led to vastly improved treatment for specific diseases, and computers have had an important direct role in the diagnosis or treatment of a few (mainly catastrophic) conditions. However, it has become increasingly clear that the major health care problem of the country is effective delivery of the care we already know should be provided, rather than extension of knowledge. The basic stumbling blocks are such factors as high costs, insufficient manpower, inefficient allocation of resources, and limited access to the existing system. These are precisely the kinds of problems which computers once seemed likely to ameliorate. Instead, the problems are getting worse. What this suggests is not so much that there is something lacking in computers as that the problem is more fundamental than it once appeared. The computer is, after all, a tool which can assist in implementing well-specified objectives, not a panacea which leads magically to some broadly defined goal.

Indeed, the major problem clearly is not with the computer. On the contrary, in 1974 one finds that the American Red Cross is funding the development, by a university-based research medical computing group, of an inventory program for a blood bank. And the chairman of a department of medical information sciences can still point with some pride to a recent retrospective study derived from billing information which shows how the incidence of various categories of diagnoses in a university hospital differs from the usual experience in community hospitals. These examples epitomize the problem: in some respects, computing in clinical medicine is discouragingly far behind the most mundane industrial applications. It is hard to imagine a major industry which does not depend on computer programs more complex than the blood bank requires to manage inventories or which has not long been using computers to measure utilization of resources.

Thus the problems are not primarily technological; instead, they involve human factors, commitment, priorities, timing, and, in the end, the vast problem of the effective delivery of health care in this country. It is beyond the scope of this article to explore all of the reasons for the failure of computers to meet the original expectations for them in this field. Some of the reasons are fairly clear and differ from the experience in other fields only in the magnitude of the gap between hope and reality. First, the problem the computer is to solve is often poorly defined. Computers have been used to try to support an inadequate existing system. Few attempts have been made to define new modes of health care delivery which make appropriate use of computers (or anything else). Second, even more than in most fields, the users on whom the usefulness of the system depends (the physicians and nurses) are often not committed to the success of the system, understand it poorly, and sometimes actively oppose it. Physicians have been suspicious of computer systems, concerned about legal complications and questions of privacy, and reluctant to surrender any of their autonomy. On their side, the computer specialists—even those who are themselves physicians—have often been unrealistic in their expectations for both physician and computer. Systems were introduced prematurely—both technically and psychologically—leading to disenchantment, and the immediate benefits to the physician or nurse user were not sufficient to reinforce usage. In short, medical personnel have had unreasonable expectations for the computer: they have been overawed and afraid of it because they expect too much, and then unduly disappointed by the results, leading them ultimately to expect too little.

On the other hand, while progress has been disappointing, it is by no means wholly lacking. There have been many very successful projects, and bitter experience has led to more realistic approaches. Projects now being undertaken are generally well defined and well planned; they are also generally limited in scope. Two areas in which the use of computers has been quite successful are radiation treatment planning and patient monitoring. These topics are discussed in detail at the end of this section.

BIOMEDICAL SCIENCES

Some of the topics covered in other sections of this article also deal with possible direct applications of computers to clinical medicine. A project for matching donor and recipient in organ transplantations is discussed above in the section entitled Statistical Analysis. The techniques developed by this project are now coming into clinical use. Computer processing of physiological signals (primarily ECG's and EEG's) is described above in the section entitled Physiological Signal Processing; the ECG work is used in practice. Studies in pattern recognition for screening chromosome spreads, X-rays, blood smears, etc., are covered below in the section entitled Image Processing. Most of these techniques are still experimental, but it is notable that a new brain scanning device now in clinical use requires a computer for the interpretation of its output.

Much of the early effort in clinical application of computers was in hospital information systems, medical record systems, and the like. The current status of this field is covered below in the section entitled Information Systems. An important outgrowth of the early attempts at generalized information systems has been clinical laboratory automation. Originally, the laboratory was to be just one of many departments controlled by and feeding data into the central computer. However, the operation of the laboratory has long since been separated from the whole problem of an overall data flow, and relatively small computers have been assigned the sole task of running the laboratory. This does not make laboratory test results magically available on the ward via a terminal, but it has significantly improved the efficiency of the laboratory itself. Successful pilot systems for clinical chemistries were running several years ago, and reasonably effective systems are now available commercially. Some of these systems are complete machine control systems providing for control of the instruments, automatic reading of the results, etc., while others stop at managing the requests and data and performing some scheduling functions. Most large laboratories are automated to some degree, and there are a number of pilot projects in which the computer handles additional functions of the laboratory (e.g., hematology, bacteriology). For clinical chemistries, substantial cost savings have been demonstrated in automated laboratories running a large number of tests per day. In recent studies it was shown that, at a volume of 250 tests/day, the cost per test averaged 52¢ if done manually and 24¢ using an automated system, while it was reduced to 7¢ in automated laboratories with a daily volume of 2500 tests. Thus, this is an area in which automation would appear to be substantially improving the delivery of health care. Unfortunately, except in the very large laboratories, the cost saving does not reach the patient. Instead of performing only the requested tests, the automated systems typically perform standard sets of tests, so that more tests are performed per patient. This may or may not result in better care, shorter hospital stays, more rapid diagnoses, or more effective use of the physician's time. These issues require further investigation.

Finally, an important trend cutting across a wide variety of specific applications is to cast the computer in the role of expert consultant—on drug interactions, drug dosage optimization, dietary regulation, electrolyte balance,

ECG interpretation, or whatever. The goal is not to replace the physician as a diagnostician or therapist, but rather to provide him with a conveniently available consulting service which can supplement his own knowledge and experience and relieve him of routine calculations. There are an ever-increasing number of programs of this type designed for training, peer review, or explicitly for consultation—the lines between these purposes are rather fuzzy and most programs which will serve one will serve them all, at least to some degree. Certification of these programs is a key problem. A common procedure is to compare the operation of the computer with the decisions of a panel of experts in the field. This is unquestionably a useful standard to use in developing a program but it is not clear that programs which do somewhat less well than such a panel should be barred. There is an important question of audience. It is unlikely that members of a panel of expert electrocardiographers will use an ECG interpretation program: they will prefer their own interpretations. But what if this kind of program were available to a country doctor (via telephone), or possibly even to paramedical personnel? Indeed, in some cases the patient himself may be the most appropriate user—as in the case of programs to assist in diet planning, diabetes management, etc. Even if the program is not quite as good as the expert, it may be considerably better than the available human expertise. Testing against average clinical practice in the area to be served may be a more useful criterion. Since our most serious problem is one of making good medical care more widely available, this seems a more realistic goal. One example of such an approach is a neurological screening program for use in an outpatient department at Kings County Hospital in Brooklyn. This program replaces a screening clinic which has been held for 3 hr each week. The necessary history can be taken and entered on a terminal by a clerk. The program's performance is felt to be adequate (in deciding whether or not the patient should be referred to neurological testing).

In any case, the ethical and legal complexities of the practice of medicine by the computer will inevitably be explored. But expert consultation seems to be a more realistic mode of computerized diagnosis than the popular view of a computer which reads the history and laboratory results and spews out some pills. Like automation of laboratories, success in this field shows some promise of decreasing the cost of medical care and making good care more widely available. Applications in patient monitoring and radiation treatment planning, on the other hand, typify the use of the computer to improve highly specialized procedures. It is also worthy of note that computers have been most successfully applied to clinical practice where complex instruments other than computers are being introduced (e.g., automatic assay equipment, monitoring equipment, increasingly complex radiation treatment devices).

Patient Monitoring

Regular measures of key physiologic variables are kept on all critically ill hospital patients. When there is no automatic system available, the measures are taken approximately every 15 min. Automatic systems consisting of simple analog equipment with strip recorders are now fairly common in hospitals which have wards specifically designed to accommodate the critically ill (intensive care units, coronary care units, shock wards, etc.). Such systems typically record pulse, respiration, and ECG, and are equipped with alarm systems which are activated if any measure goes out of the specified range. A few systems also make periodic measures of blood gases, but this is usually still an entirely manual procedure.

Automatic systems have several advantages: they are less obtrusive; they tend to generate confidence, since the patient is always under observation; measurements can be made as frequently as necessary; and they are not dependent on human memory and priorities. However, the simple analog systems have no capacity to look for trends, to correlate and analyze several variables, to keep histories, or to provide more complex warnings. Introduction of a computer provides these capacities, permits various levels of warning signals, and presents the data in a more integrated, readily usable form. In short, the computer can perform the integrative function of the nurse who looks at several independent recordings, and can anticipate the need for further investigation or intervention. The computer can also be used to store treatment information, which can be used in analyzing the data and also can help the nurse schedule her activities.

In addition to monitoring intensive care unit and coronary care unit patients, several projects have been concerned with techniques for monitoring obstetrical patients during delivery. Oxygen deprivation during delivery often produces permanent brain damage in the child, which could be averted if detected in time. Although widespread monitoring of normal births would not be feasible, these projects variously aim to select high risk cases for whom monitoring would be desirable, to find simpler techniques for automatic detection and warning of impending complications, or to gain further insight into the mechanisms producing brain damage in the child.

One of the earlier computerized patient monitoring systems was developed by Dr. Homer Warner at the Latter Day Saints Hospital in Salt Lake City. This system is used in the catheterization and pulmonary function laboratories, for patients in the intensive care unit following open heart surgery, and for new-born infants.

Prior to open heart surgery, a special purpose catheter is placed in the patient's artery, and base values are established for the parameters to be measured. After surgery, output from pressure transducers connected to the catheter is continuously monitored by the computer. In addition to the continuous measurements, test results, treatment information, and other clinical data are entered into the system as required. For each heart beat cycle, values are recorded for stroke volume, heart rate, cardiac output, duration of systole, peripheral resistance, systolic pressure, diastolic pressure, mean central venous pressure, respiratory rate, and respiratory amplitude. These recorded values are compared over time to establish changes and trends: if a value more than three standard deviations from the expected value is sustained over a 16-beat cycle, a red light is turned on; a sustained deviation of more than one standard deviation activates a warning light. The system can be instructed to provide a warning when any prespecified set of conditions occurs, or to indicate when it is time for a scheduled treatment.

Dr. Warner's group continues to be innovative in exploring new techniques and applications. There is unusually good rapport among the physicians, nurses, and computer experts, which has led to unusually ready acceptance of the computer system as part of the hospital operation. The system uses a CDC 3200 computer and has been in operation since 1966. Most of the more recently developed systems use minicomputers.

Radiation Treatment Planning

Radiation kills the normal cells it encounters as well as the malignant cells; the objective in radiation therapy is to radiate the malignant cells as intensely as possible, while sparing enough normal cells to repopulate any essential area. Radiotherapists concentrate radiation in the tumor area in two general ways. With *external beam therapy,* two or more beams of radiation are directed into the body from the outside, intersecting in the tumor area. The intent is to limit damage to the normal tissue by passing only a fraction of the total dosage through it, while killing the tumor by giving it the full dose. One method of achieving this is to rotate the beam around an axis centered in the tumor. However, the difference between inadequate treatment of the tumor and killing all of the normal tissue is rather small, and the calculations are complicated by the differences in absorption of radiation by the various tissues the beams encounter in passing through the body (bone, skin, soft tissue, muscle, air spaces in lungs and esophagus, etc.). Thus penetration becomes irregular over the region. The second approach is *implantation therapy,* in which the radioactive source is implanted in the region of the tumor. This increases the accuracy of the delivery of the dose to the tumor, but, again, inhomogeneity of tissue can easily result in cold spots, allowing malignant cells to regrow. Dose distribution calculations are further complicated by the fact that the sources are typically complex 3-dimensional arrays and are often contained in hollow metal applicators which produce their own special absorption problem.

Given these difficulties, it is not surprising that radiation treatment planning was one of the early applications of computers to clinical medicine. By 1965 there were a number of programs in use for both types of therapy. These programs were awkward to use and their output was difficult to interpret, but in the hands of someone familiar with their use, they were a vast improvement over manual methods in both ease and accuracy. An important improvement was made with the Programmed Console, a graphical display supported by a very small computer. The PC was developed by Dr. Jerome Cox and his associates at Washington University in St. Louis. It permits the user to interact freely with the calculation, exploring the effects of changing beam positions, and provides for convenient input of parameters and display of

BIOMEDICAL SCIENCES

results. This system has been widely used and has been very popular because of its ease of use. Its main limitation is its lack of arithmetic power—it cannot perform the complex calculations required to take full account of tissue inhomogeneities and multiple radiation sources.

More recently, several systems have been developed which use a graphical station supported by a large computer, thus providing the best of both worlds. One such system is RADGRAF, developed by Dr. Carol Newton and her associates at UCLA. This system uses an IMLAC graphics terminal connected (by phone line) to a large IBM system. The IMLAC performs the graphical input and output, the large system the complex calculations. Both an external beam and an implantation program are available. The programs permit specification on an anatomical diagram of the location of the beams or sources. Calculation of the dosage distribution to the tumor and other affected areas is performed by the program.

INFORMATION SYSTEMS

A wide variety of information systems have been developed to support biomedical research. These range from hospital information systems and data handling systems for clinical studies to literature search systems and atlases of chemical formulas. Almost any large research project has a data base associated with it, and dealing with such a data base requires some kind of a retrieval system, albeit primitive. Handling biomedical data is complicated by the frequent occurrence of missing data and of multiple records of the same type. For example, in clinical studies, cases typically differ greatly in the number of observations made, not adapting themselves handily to a fixed rectangular format; and if all cases with any missing observations were eliminated, there would often be no data left. These special problems have made it difficult for biomedical investigators to use systems developed for business or the physical sciences, and have led to the proliferation of data manipulating systems designed to handle relatively limited classes of problems.

As in other fields, keeping up with the literature is a problem for the biomedical scientist, and a number of literature search systems have been developed. The most general is probably the MEDLARS system, developed under the auspices of the National Library of Medicine. MEDLARS contains abstracts of articles from a wide range of publications in biomedicine. In addition to serving as the basis for regular reports, the MEDLARS data base permits specification of a variety of search requests and can be used to generate special reports. A number of more specialized systems have also been developed. For example, the Brain Information Service at the University of California at Los Angeles maintains a similar service for studies relating to the brain, but provides much more complete coverage in this selected area. This group also provides special bibliographic services, based on this data base.

An information system less specific to biology is the Atlas of Protein Sequences and Structures, compiled and maintained by Dr. Margaret Dayhoff and her associates at George Washington University. This data base consists of a thoroughly investigated and up-to-date collection of all of the known protein sequences. The data base is used to produce the Atlas and is also available on tape. This service has been in existence for eight years, and the data base is growing rapidly. The Atlas is used by investigators in very diverse fields. A chemical information system with a quite different orientation is PROPHET, developed under NIH leadership. PROPHET provides the means for querying a large data base concerning the formula, activity, or structure of a drug. Great emphasis has been placed on making the system easy and natural to use.

But the area which has received the greatest attention has been automation of the medical record and the flow of information in the hospital. It was originally assumed that, given the technology, these tasks would be simple. Medical records are well known to be of widely varying quality and completeness, and to be difficult for any but the originator to interpret, while the flow of information in the hospital is typically slow and chaotic. The computer seemed to offer the ideal solution to these problems: vast quantities of data could be stored and retrieved, the central data files could be updated from terminals all over the hospital, the resulting data base could be used by all segments of the hospital staff from the business office to the teaching staff, and a standard file format would impose some structure on the medical record. Further, collections of comprehensive, well-structured records would be invaluable for research.

The model for most of the earlier systems was a central computer system, time shared among terminals and functions, but dedicated to the total information system, with terminals in admissions, the various laboratories and treatment units, housekeeping, the business office, and all of the wards. A comprehensive record would be kept for each patient. Data and requests for specific information would be entered from terminals. Regular reports would be prepared on patient flow, ward occupancy, utilization of treatment facilities, etc., and special reports—either scientific or administrative—could be prepared on request. At first, success seemed assured and its potential rewards great, so that a great many attempts were made to implement such systems. Unfortunately, there were few successes. Even less successful than the specific attempts to implement a centralized system were some commercial attempts—exemplified by IBM's Medical Information System—to provide a generalized central reporting system which would work anywhere.

The centralized systems have failed for several reasons. First, there has not been sufficient agreement concerning such key questions as what a medical record is for, how it is really used, what it should contain, what format it should have, what should be kept easily accessible, what placed in history files, and what deleted and when. All of the problems which have plagued medical record keeping were simply transferred to the computerized record; in a computer file, far from being solved, they became more obvious and more irritating. It is bad enough to attempt to scan a record which is poorly organized and mainly irrelevant; it is intolerable to grope around in one via a slow terminal. The computer cannot specify the goals for the investigator, it must be the other way around. In the case of the medical record, this truth was obscured by the implicit assumption that everyone knew what it was for and the hope that just collecting all of the information in the computer would somehow solve the problem. Second, most centralized information system projects have failed to get the willing cooperation of the physicians, nurses, and technicians upon whom they ultimately depend. The systems were generally installed prematurely, so that demands were placed on their users long before the users could derive any benefit from the system. The systems have also tended to be awkward and unreliable. Manual methods could not be discontinued because the automatic methods were not reliable enough, so the latter were nothing but an added nuisance. In short, the systems were dumped on their users as an additional burden. The key to successful development of any information system lies in tailoring it not only to the needs, but also to the desires, of those who will use it. The best system in the world can never be successful without the cooperation of the staff. It is remarkably easy for an antagonized staff to zero in on the weak points (which must exist in any new system) in such a way that it is doomed to failure. This was not sufficiently considered in most of the early medical information systems, and the only reasonably satisfied users were often the administrators. Not surprisingly, billing systems were often the only useful result. Perhaps this was inevitable: the administrators knew what they wanted from the beginning.

After several years of frustration with attempts at centralized systems, the trend has changed, and the predominant model is a set of information system modules, each designed to accomplish a relatively small task. Thus the systems are designed proceeding from the small to the large, not conversely. No attempt is made to design a single system which will satisfy all departments and functions; instead, specific functions are automated to the satisfaction of those responsible. These modular systems have been much more successful than the centralized ones. They don't provide a complete medical record for each patient or solve the problem of information flow through the hospital, but they do improve the functioning of individual departments and the interactions of those departments with others. Typical applications include systems for the intensive care units, the clinical laboratories, the pharmacy, radiology, etc. Examples of systems for intensive care units and clinical laboratories are included in the preceding section. A set of modular systems developed at the Massachusetts General Hospital is discussed below.

It is easy to see why a modular approach has been more successful. First, the information needs of a single department are usually well defined. Most of the modular systems have not attempted to deal with comprehensive medical records or to automate the ward (except for specialized wards like the intensive care unit). Since the problem is well defined, there is some hope of solving it. Second, when the system is developed in the unit where it is to be used, it is natural to involve the ultimate users in the design decisions. Thus cooperation is fostered from the beginning, and the system is tailored to its environment. Third, since the job is a more circumscribed one, the system can be brought into use and tested relatively early—before years of work go into it and while there is still enthusiasm. Accordingly, the system can evolve in use. Fourth, small machines are more reliable than large, and when the machine does fail, it affects a smaller portion of the hospital. It is also more practical to arrange for backup of systems of this scale. New systems can be developed without impacting those in regular operation, which is most emphatically not true of the centralized systems. And, finally, there is the psychological factor of commitment to the system. When the small computer in the unit goes down, everyone there knows about it and feels a part of the operation. When a large central system fails, the users feel powerless, isolated, and antagonistic.

On the other hand, the modular systems have not really solved the problems of information flow through the hospital, much less the maintenance of long-term medical histories. There are several current experiments with establishing communication among modules, and there are some attempts at partial centralization, with functions distributed but comprehensive records centralized. However, before much further progress is possible, a satisfactory format must be found for the medical record and a set of procedures established for handling it—all based on some agreement as to its purposes. One of two approaches is being used in most current systems: the encounter form or the problem oriented record. When the encounter form is used, the patient's record consists of a set of records of encounters: examinations, tests, treatments, consultations, etc. This format is closely analogous to the traditional medical record where entries are made in his chart each time the patient is seen or additional data are gathered on him. A medical record made up of encounter forms requires a fairly powerful search and editing system to make the data usable, but it may be most acceptable to physicians. The problem-oriented record has been developed by Dr. Lawrence Weed and used in his information system work at the University of Vermont. The patient's medical problems are categorized as primary, secondary, etc. or as temporary, and the file structure is based on the list of problems—i.e., all data relevant to a given problem are kept together. A file of this type is considerably easier to use; it is also argued that it may be valuable in imposing order on entry of information, and indeed, on the physician entering it. For exactly those reasons, it tends to meet with more resistance. Both the encounter and the problem-oriented formats are in common use. Indeed, both are used in (different) applications in the Massachusetts General Hospital system (see below). Obviously, even given an acceptable format, the questions of what must be easily assessible, what can be deleted when, etc., remain.

The systems developed at Massachusetts General Hospital exemplify the modular approach and are discussed below. Dr. Morris Collen and his associates at the Kaiser Foundation Research Institute in Oakland have also done extensive work in computer-based patient records systems. A computer system to support a "multiphasic health screening system" has been in operation for several years. Multiphasic screening is a service offered to its members by Kaiser-Permanente; the patient regularly receives a complete battery of standard tests, supplemented by further tests as indicated by his medical history. Most of the testing is carried out by paramedical personnel and it is semiautomated. The resulting data are stored in the computer as part of the permanent medical history. The computer also analyzes the data, provides a summary, and indicates suggestions for follow-up. The purpose of the screening system is to detect disease early and to provide a means for separating the well from the sick, preventing the former from swamping the physicians. There is considerable controversy about the effectiveness of this approach, but, given the goal, the computer system has been quite effective and generally well accepted. Dr. Collen's group has also done work in more general hospital information systems.

Modular Systems at Massachusetts General Hospital

The Laboratory of Computer Science at Massachusetts General Hospital, under the direction of Dr. Octo Barnett, was one of the leaders in the early attempts to implement a centralized hospital information system. As elsewhere, this effort was largely unsuccessful, but the group continued work on computerized information handling, evolving a set of modular systems. The current aims of the project include developing a computer-based medical record to supplant the conventional record, developing a common data base, and tying the modular systems together; meanwhile the modular systems are coming into regular use. In addition to improving patient care through these systems, there are plans to use the data for training, peer review, consultation, and long-range planning of health care facilities.

Having discovered the pitfalls of starting with a general all-encompassing scheme, the group is currently developing independent and relatively circumscribed systems to carry out functions which can be well defined and for which a computer-based information system seems to offer significant advantages. Specific applications have been selected on the basis of departmental needs. The systems currently in operation include:

- A computer-based medical record for the Harvard Community Health Plan (a prepaid group practice with approximately 35,000 members). This system is based on encounter forms (with a special form for each specialty) on which the physician or nurse makes appropriate check marks. A line of free text may also be entered. Laboratory test results, X-ray reports, etc. are also recorded in the patient's file. Various standard reports and summaries are produced by the system; it also indicates when specific patients are due for a visit, which patients should have special therapies (such as flu shots), and the like. Parts of this system are in routine use.
- A patient record system for nurse practitioners who provide primary care to patients with chronic medical problems requiring continuing supervision. This system is based on the problem-oriented medical record. The nurse uses a terminal to access the patient's record, which includes notes from

BIOMEDICAL SCIENCES

the last four visits, a list of current medications, laboratory results since the last visit, a history of laboratory results for selected tests, the patient's Master Problem List, and a "laboratory protocol" of tests which should be repeated at regular intervals. Progress notes are entered into the file from the terminal. This system is still experimental.

A record system for the intensive care unit.

A tumor registry.

A system for management of patients in respiratory failure. This system is a record keeping, consulting, and reminder system which has been used in teaching for some time and is now being considered for routine use in patient care.

A record system for use in the anticoagulant clinic, which stores records, indicates that it is time for an appointment, plans doses, etc.

A clinical laboratory reporting system (for chemistry and hematology) which has been in use for several years, has been widely copied, and is incorporated in a commercially available system.

A pulmonary function test reporting system (in routine use).

A medications system (discussed further below).

An intravenous additive system.

A radiology scheduling and reporting system.

The group is also working on general tools for storage, retrieval, analysis, and display of patient data, and on various training programs (discussed below in the section entitled Training).

The systems are implemented on Digital Equipment Corporation PDP-9's and PDP-15's, using MUMPS (*M*assachusetts *G*eneral *H*ospital *U*tility *M*ulti-*P*rogramming *S*ystem), a widely used interactive system developed by this group (see below in the section entitled Hardware and Software).

The Medications System provides a good example of both the advantages and shortcomings of the modular approach. Given a constant influx of new drugs and increasing knowledge concerning their potential adverse reactions and the interactions among them, the medications system in a hospital has become a critical and time-consuming activity. Physicians often write unclear orders, fail to recognize the nursing implications of a particular order, and fail to realize that the patient is taking other drugs which may interact with the new medication. Indeed, a physician in a large hospital may not know what other medications the patient is being given. The computer-based medications system at Massachusetts General is designed to perform the following functions:

Check the order to insure that it is complete and unambiguous.

Check whether the drug is available in the specified form and can be administered by the specified route (e.g., intramuscularly).

Check the formulary to provide information on the classification, indications, activity, adverse reactions, counterindications, and nursing implications of the drug.

BIOMEDICAL SCIENCES

Check whether the patient is known to be allergic or to have had adverse reactions to this drug or related drugs.

Check whether the patient is already receiving this drug or a related drug.

Check whether the specified dosage falls between the suggested minimum and maximum for the drug, based on the size of the patient.

In addition to warnings concerning adverse reactions, improper dosage, etc., the system makes suggestions concerning the patient's comfort and the nurse's convenience (e.g., it might suggest not giving a drug intramuscularly which is particularly painful if given that way). The system is designed to be used by the physician ordering the drug and the nurse in the ward in preparing the medications. The physician may call a technician in the pharmacy who will either assist him in entering the order or do it for him. The system is still in an experimental phase.

Obviously, such a system can offer a significant improvement in care and a saving in time for the physician. Adverse drug reactions constitute an important problem, but thorough researching of each order is both time consuming and redundant. Because of their obvious potential, such systems have been developed in a number of hospitals. The task has usually been grossly underestimated with the consequence that many have failed. This system seems to have overcome that initial obstacle. However, there is still the problem of the reluctance of the physician to accept such a system. Dr. Barnett's group is addressing this problem, but it is not yet clear whether they have succeeded. Finally, lacking a central medical record, it is difficult to coalesce all of the necessary data. The system requires information on the patient's size, his allergies, his history of adverse drug reactions, and at least part of his clinical record (e.g., renal function is very significant in determining the proper dosage of certain drugs). It would also be highly advantageous to have his laboratory test results and to be able to provide suggestions for follow-up tests. Laboratory tests are indicators of potential adverse reactions; on the other hand, some tests are invalidated by certain drugs. In other words, the patient is not just a receiver of medications; other aspects of his care are relevant as well. And once the computer is advising the physician, it must either provide complete advice or explicitly indicate its limitations. Still, this system, even as an independent entity, performs a very significant function. Further, it may be an important step toward definition of what really is important in a more complete record.

TRAINING

Computers have long had a role in training in biology. Where a computer has been readily available, students have been encouraged—or required—to develop or explore physiological models and to use package programs to study data. In departments with small dedicated computers, it has often been the graduate students who have become their most effective users; it is difficult to

BIOMEDICAL SCIENCES

decide where training stops and research support begins. However, as terminals have become increasingly available on both large and small computing systems, there has been a tremendous increase in the use of computers in training in biology, and, with the proliferation of interactive programs designed specifically for training purposes, such training has taken on a new dimension. The use of interactive programs in training has a number of advantages, including the following:

- The session can be tailored to the student's needs. Training programs are typically designed to proceed through the material in a manner determined by the student's responses, skipping quickly through material he knows well. Such personalized attention to the student is relatively rare in teaching today.
- A record of the encounter can be kept for evaluation of the student, and, since his answers are already recorded, the program can immediately explain his mistakes, instruct him further, or suggest reading material. Immediate feedback is much more valuable than the usual delayed feedback.
- The student can concentrate on the subject at hand, letting the computer take care of irrelevant calculations. On the other hand, if his ability to do the calculations is a point at issue, the program can evaluate his answer first, then give him the correct one if necessary, and allow him to proceed with the remainder of the problem.
- It is possible to separate the abilities to solve problems, to interpret data, and to recall facts, and to evaluate the student on each aspect of his work. Indeed, a variety of systems of evaluation can be explored since the program can test rate of learning and the like, as well as state of knowledge.
- If desired, the evaluation can be omitted and the session made entirely private. This can be useful in providing continuing education for physicians; the physician can avoid exposing his ignorance, working entirely with a nonjudgmental tutor he feels no need to impress.
- The computer is an attractive toy which often captures the student's interest. This may, of course, be a transitory phenomenon.
- The training program is available to the student whenever he can find time to use it; this is especially important for users who have clinical responsibilities.
- It is relatively easy to keep references and other such data current.

The increasing availability of terminals with graphical capabilities adds further dimensions to computer-based training in biomedicine. Most scientists lean heavily on graphical representations to communicate ideas. The blackboard, slides, and even motion pictures still lack the facility for modification to suit changing needs and lack the support of the computer to modify the graphs to reflect changing parameters and transformed variables. Certain scientific disciplines are particularly dependent on structural visualizations because of the complex interrelationships central to their study. For example, visualization of chemical processes can be greatly assisted by simulated experimentation, while a grasp of statistical concepts is greatly aided by multidimensional visualization. Indeed, most biomedical scientists find pictorial representations far more natural than mathematical formulations, and much of the relevant material is most naturally represented in pictorial form. Graphics terminals permit the use of all of these techniques in the training process. Since color is often an important aspect of biological data and an important cue to the investigator, color terminals will further enhance the use of graphics in both training and research.

A large number of programs have been developed which are specifically designed for training in clinical medicine. These are discussed below. Other areas of special emphasis include biochemistry, and mathematics and statistics for biologists. For example, Dr. Kent Wilson and his associates at the University of California at San Diego are using the computer to prepare some very original films used in presenting concepts of biochemistry to students. A number of investigators are working on the display of molecular structures using graphical terminals. The displayed molecules can be rotated, simplified (to look at substructures), and selected portions can be enlarged. These models are primarily designed for use in solving molecular structures, providing a much more flexible tool than the mechanical models traditionally used, but they also provide the student with an intuitive grasp of the structure of complex molecules.

Mathematical and statistical training programs for biologists can build upon the biologist's well-developed intuitive capabilities, moving him from the realm of intuitive description into that of mathematical description. For example, a teaching program on curve-fitting can help the student relate fits made by eye to those achieved using parameterization, explore the effects of removing or adding outliers, visualize the hazards of extrapolating polynomial fits, etc. Similarly, interactive modeling programs can provide valuable insights into the characteristics of both the modeled process and model building itself by permitting the student to monitor and interact with the model throughout its operation.

Interactive Programs for Training in Clinical Medicine

Training medical students to handle clinical problems effectively, providing continuing education for practicing physicians, developing methods for evaluating clinical judgment, and assessing professional competence in medicine are all crucial goals for our society. Computer-aided training has appeared to offer a valuable tool in these endeavors, and some of the specific advantages of interactive programs for training are especially applicable to clinical training.

Consequently, a large number of such systems have been developed. Many programs intended for consultation or direct clinical use are also valuable tools for training. Most of the systems described in the two preceding sections can either be used directly or easily modified for use in training. However, the most popular type of training program consists of an interactive interface with the student and a file of appropriately formatted case histories. The student is presented with a scenario concerning the presenting complaint of the patient, he can ask questions to obtain a medical history and a physical examination, and he can order various laboratory tests. He can also initiate treatment. The program typically indicates the progress of the patient and the passage of time (for tests, therapy, etc.). The student is graded on the relevance of his questions, the time taken to reach a diagnosis, the accuracy and logic of his diagnosis (he usually gets less credit for accurate wild guesses), and the appropriateness of his therapy. More specialized programs provide specific instruction in handling such problems as acid–base and electrolyte balance, hypercalcemia, and digitalis dosage adjustment. A number of these programs have been developed at Massachusetts General Hospital (see above in the section entitled Information Systems), the University of Illinois, Ohio State University, and elsewhere, and are available on a nationwide communications network under the auspices of the National Library of Medicine. The group at Massachusetts General Hospital is working on the problems of using such programs for board certification examinations and continuing peer review as well as in training medical and paramedical personnel.

The "coma program" is typical of training programs of this type. The user is presented with a short summary, including age and sex of patient, how he looks (e.g., grey, flushed), and the circumstances of his admission to the hospital. The user then asks for such data as blood pressure, respiration, and pulse, and is expected to initiate therapy early. He also typically asks for laboratory tests (and is charged time waiting for the results). Ultimately, he is expected to make a diagnosis and to treat the patient successfully. The program makes running comments on his treatment strategies and indicates the progress of the patient. If he gets stuck, he can ask for help. Assistance in running the program is free; medical assistance costs him points on his score. On request, he may receive a score and commentary on his performance. Programs in this series include gastrointestinal bleeding, pediatric cough and fever, jaundice, abdominal pain, cardiac arrest, respiratory failure, renal failure, cardiac arrhythmias, diabetic ketoacidosis, and use of anticoagulants.

These programs are in widespread use and appear to be quite popular. Questions of appropriate validation are yet to be resolved, and will be particularly crucial when the programs are used for evaluation or certification. Controlled studies of the effectiveness of these programs in training are also required. Similar techniques have been used elsewhere in developing training models of the psychiatric interview, but these systems have not been generally acceptable. This is probably a result of the greater complexity of the field and the lack of general agreement on how to proceed.

BIOMEDICAL SCIENCES

IMAGE PROCESSING

A significant fraction of biological data are most naturally presented as pictures or sequences of pictures; examples include X-rays, angiography, chromosome photomicrographs, electron micrographs of muscle fiber and nerve cells, and X-ray diffraction studies of molecules. Most commonly, such data are recorded on film and studied in that form. Such pictures often contain a very large amount of information which must be categorized, measured, and counted. When done manually by a technician, such processing can be extremely painstaking and time consuming; consequently, these studies are often expensive and their results unreliable. When such studies have clinical significance, facilities for processing them are often so taxed by handling abnormal samples that systematic study of normal variations is impractical. Thus it has seemed obvious that using a computer to automate the process would reduce costs, improve accuracy, and greatly increase output for studies of this type. However, progress toward these goals has been disappointingly slow.

The problem of automating the interpretation of images has two parts: first, the image must be converted to a form in which it can be handled by a computer; second, the computer must analyze the resulting data. One reason progress has been slow in this field is that major emphasis was placed on the first part of the problem, which requires expensive equipment, but is considerably easier to solve than the second part. Optical equipment which can convert an image into a matrix of density readings is well within the state of the art; computer programs which make sense of the result often are not. The recognition of a structure or a pattern in a picture is the kind of integrative perceptual activity that people perform well and computers do very poorly.

Images are prepared for the computer by a scanner of some type; a variety of different few-of-a-kind scanners have been developed. A common type is the so-called "flying spot" film scanner and its relatives. A spot of light from a cathode-ray tube is projected onto the film, the light transmitted through the film is detected using a photomultiplier, and a density is recorded. The beam is moved over a rectangular area on the film, producing the required density matrix. Such scanners commonly distinguish 64 grey levels and produce a matrix of approximately 16,000,000 points for each picture. A more versatile scanner, which can be attached directly to a microscope, uses a Vidicon. The face plate of the Vidicon is placed in the image plane of the microscope. The electron beam of the Vidicon reacts to the level of light at each point, and converts the image into a matrix of video signals. A similar technique can be used for X-ray equipment, and film can be projected and scanned if desired.

However constructed, most scanners ultimately produce a density reading for each of a very large number of points. The problem of obtaining this matrix of densities has been trivial compared to the problem of deciding what the computer should do with it. Various generalized schemes have been tried for edge detection and edge following, filtering to eliminate artifacts, and shape recognition by comparison with reference shapes. In dealing with specific problems, various numerical measures have been used in an attempt to characterize each of the objects to be recognized. These measures generally have little intuitive relationship to the characteristics of the images involved, but can be quite useful in finding the images. But, in spite of over 10 years of effort on these problems, progress has been mostly in areas where the images of interest are easily distinguished and well separated from other objects; in such cases the computer does an excellent job of making the necessary measurements, counts, etc.

There is a gestalt involved in the recognition process which we have been unable to transfer to the computer. Indeed, this problem has arisen not only in image processing but in most projects in the field of artificial intelligence. Many investigators have tried to start with something "simple" that a 5-year old child could handle. Such simple problems seem to fall inevitably into the domain of perceived structural relationships which the computer handles so poorly. Artificial intelligence is getting a tremendous boost from settling for "hard" problems, such as theory formation in chemistry. Part of the difficulty is probably that we handle the simple problems so naturally that we do not really know—in the sense of being able to give a step-by-step procedure for doing it—what it is we are doing when we recognize structures, or, even more important, when we generalize this recognition. There are children who cannot learn to generalize, who can only associate the word "dog" with a very limited set of animals or pictures, and who never get a feel for the inclusiveness of dogginess. Perhaps, if we could learn to instruct the computer in generalizing, we could instruct ourselves more effectively. Indeed, failure to communicate with the computer does usually lead to greater insight into what we are doing, although not at quite the needed level of generality. For example, radiologists who have attempted to serve as consultants for projects dealing with computer reading of X-rays have often discovered that they are not looking for what they thought they were in interpreting an X-ray; through instructing the very literal-minded computer, they are able to refine their understanding of their own diagnostic procedures. But such refinement is still not enough to enable us to tell the computer how to do some of the things we find easiest ourselves.

In any case, computers lag far behind most 5-year-old children in ability to recognize and generalize. On the other hand, once the limits of a structure are defined, the computer can measure and count very well indeed—and people do this poorly. Given a large field of small dots to count, the computer never loses its place or forgets its count. Nor does it become tired or bored or quit its job. Given the rules—which we are able to define—the computer is also able to do a remarkable job of three-dimensional reconstruction, integrating all of the information from many images into a whole which it can then present, in cross sections, as requested. Similarly, it can enhance a picture, bringing out the relevant features and suppressing the irrelevant, thus making the human a much more effective judge of the content.

Recently, there has been considerable progress in the field of image processing, resulting from recognition of the special limitations and advantages of the computer. For those problems where recognition of shapes is not required (e.g., grain counting) or where it is easily accomplished (e.g., many cineangiograms), progress would continue in any case. However, for those problems where shape recognition is crucial (e.g., chromosome studies), an approach is being taken which combines the best skills of both man and computer. This approach requires the addition of a versatile graphics terminal to the complement of scanning equipment; the terminal is used to display images for the human operator, who assists in resolving shapes, separating objects, indicating limits, and the like. Similarly, when the system is being used for three-dimensional reconstruction, the user may request displays of various cross sections of the object (which has been reconstructed from a series of views). When it is used for image enhancement, he may guide the enhancement process, indicating objects of interest. Thus the ideal of a completely automated process has been replaced, in many applications, by the goal of using the scanner to expedite the work of the technician. This approach requires a graphics terminal which can provide images of adequate quality for the application and which has sufficient interactive capacity to permit the user to guide the analysis.

There have been several specific applications of image processing in biology which have been explored by a number of investigators over a period of 10 years. Among the most popular are chromosome studies, X-ray studies of heart action, and microscopic analysis of blood cells. Since the chromosome work exemplifies many of the difficulties encountered in image processing, it is discussed in greater detail below. The blood cell work has also been enthusiastically pursued and involves many of the same kinds of problem. Unlike the chromosome studies, there is no dearth of data on blood cells; the tests are very commonly run. However, they are expensive to perform and results have been shown to be remarkably variable. Hence a good automatic method would be very desirable for routine use. Further, the frequency of occurrence of various types of abnormal cells in the "normal" population is unknown. Assuming that such cells occur in the blood of normal individuals in very small numbers, they could easily be missed using manual methods. Careful screening of all samples could settle such questions.

The first requirement for a system for blood cell analysis is identification of the various cell types found in the blood. These include red cells (erythrocytes), white cells (leukocytes, which can be further subdivided into monocytes, lymphocytes, and granulocytes, which last can again be further subdivided), and platelets. Second, the system must be able to provide additional information about the substructure of each cell type, recognizing various abnormalities in nucleation, size, and shape. Finally, counts must be provided for each distinguishable (normal and abnormal) type. Most work on the automation of blood cell analysis has been concerned primarily with white cells, and, in some studies, specifically with leukemic cells. There has been considerable progress, although these systems are still experimental. At least one specialized system for analysis of red cells is being developed for use as a production system.

In most applications of image processing to biology, the computer is a poor substitute for the human being. However, there is one new device, coming into use in clinical neurology, which could not exist without a computer. This is the EMI scanner (developed and marketed by EMI, Ltd., a British electronics company), which is used for X-ray studies of the brain. This device permits the physician to see cross-sectional representations of the patient's brain in the kind of detail and clarity presented in anatomy textbooks. It is used in diagnosing and evaluating tumors, cysts, stroke damage, and other structural abnormalities. An X-ray beam is sent through the head and received by a sodium iodide crystal detector on the other side. The computer calculates the difference between the beam emitted and the beam received by the detector. By moving the beam across the head, taking a large number of readings at different angles (28,000 readings are made for the complete study), sufficient information is obtained to reconstruct the three-dimensional brain in complete structural detail. This is a geometrical exercise of considerable complexity, but it is well within the powers of the computer since it requires only the manipulation and not the interpretation or recognition of images. The latter component is provided by the physician, who uses a cathode ray tube display to view images corresponding to requested cross-sectional views. These displays can be photographed for a permanent record. The system permits the physician to visualize the abnormality much more naturally and clearly than with the best conventional procedures, and, unlike the latter (which require injection of air or dye), it is noninvasive, presenting no danger to the patient and causing him no significant discomfort. The EMI scanner is being hailed as a major advance in radiology.

Chromosome Analysis

Chromosomes are examined and analyzed clinically in diagnosing radiation damage and certain congenital disorders, and in research studies of congenital disorders and of the effects of radiation and certain chemicals (e.g., LSD). Chromosomal abnormalities have also been reported in cancer patients. Chromosomal aberrations of two types are encountered: those involving an abnormal number of chromosomes (e.g., Down's syndrome), and those involving disturbances in the structure of individual chromosomes (e.g., radiation exposure). Cells of normal persons contain 22 pairs of autosomes and two sex chromosomes. The standard method for analyzing chromosomes is to make enlargements of chromosome photomicrographs, cut out the individual chromosomes, pair them, classify the pairs, and arrange them in a standard order called a karyotype. When the ordering is complete, an abnormal number of chromosomes will be obvious and other deviations can be observed. With increasing knowledge, it is hoped that an increasing amount of information can be obtained by studying the characteristics of the individual chromosomes.

Done manually, karyotyping is an extremely laborious task. It has been estimated that a team of investigators, consisting of a senior scientist and a

BIOMEDICAL SCIENCES

technician, can analyze only approximately 100 chromosome spreads per year. Consequently, relatively little could be discovered about normal variations within the general population. A large amount of normal data is required for an adequate perspective for any kind of population studies—either genetic or environmental. It is difficult to assess the significance of a chromosomal abnormality if the usual rate of occurrence of that abnormality is not known. Indeed, given the laboriousness of the process, the samples studied are inevitably primarily abnormal. Hence, as in similar instances, computer processing was hailed as a panacea.

Chromosome analysis has probably been attempted with every general purpose scanner to which biomedical investigators have had access, and a large number of different techniques have been explored for use in interpreting the resulting images. Indeed, this has tended to be the favorite problem of computer scientists working in image processing. The chromosomes are obtained from cells in the metaphase stage of mitosis, stained, and either photographed and scanned or scanned directly through the microscope. Preparation of the slides is, itself, a moderately complicated procedure. Once the image of a spread has been stored in the computer, the analysis has three parts: (1) recognizing each chromosome—which involves separating overlapping chromosomes, eliminating background junk, and delineating boundaries; (2) pairing and classifying the chromosomes—which requires measuring them; and (3) preparing a karyotype and indicating abnormalities. Most attempts to automate karyotyping have failed in step (1). It is difficult to recognize a chromosome, and it is particularly difficult to separate overlapping chromosomes and untwist distorted ones. Methods used to pick out chromosomes have included fitting "typical" curves to them, using edge-following programs which rule out shapes which are too long or too short in certain dimensions, preparing density histograms and comparing them to "typical" chromosome density histograms, etc. Most of these methods can be refined to be reasonably successful when applied to clean pictures of well-separated chromosomes, and are quite unsuccessful when these conditions are not met. The typical chromosome looks either like a rather thick letter X or half a letter X ("teleocentric" chromosome). The human eye can easily recognize variations on this theme, including cases where the X has its legs twisted or where two chromosomes overlap, but computer programs do not do this well. Thus the computer does well with (*a*) but not with (*b*) or (*c*):

(*a*) (*b*) (*c*)

The situation is further confounded by the fact that chromosomes tend to stain less darkly in the center, making it difficult to distinguish a single chromosome like (*a*) from two teleocentric chromosomes like (*d*):

(*d*)

In recent years, a staining technique has been used which produces easily recognized bands on the chromosomes. This helps determine whether a given blob is a chromosome or not and also assists in classifying them, since the banding patterns are different for different types. Most recent work has centered on banded chromosomes. However, the difficulties of separating and delineating chromosomes remain, and the only systems which seem to produce satisfactory results use a human operator to assist in selecting good spreads and in picking out the chromosomes.

HARDWARE AND SOFTWARE

The special requirements for computer support to biology arise from the characteristics of both the research and the researchers: the greater complexity of biological phenomena, the inevitable unduplicatability and incompleteness of data of most biological experiments, and the analog/pictorial nature of much of the original data impose one set of conditions, while the lesser training and interest in mathematical techniques and technology typical of the biological investigator result in less rapport with the computer and less facility in methods of analysis, thus imposing a further set of restrictions. Special equipment—analog-to-digital converters, film scanners, autoanalyzers, and the like—is required for direct input of the data. A small, inexpensive computer which is very reliable and can be dedicated to the task is needed for performing preliminary analysis on such data when feedback from the analysis is required to control the course of the on-going experiment. On the other hand, the complexity of the phenomena and the pitfalls in experimental design necessitate the application of sophisticated techniques of analysis, often to very large and ill-structured collections of data. This may require a system with significant computing power and storage capacity. Even more essential are easily used programs incorporating the required techniques, file processing capabilities, and extensive consulting support. Both the complexity of the problems and the special needs of the investigator call for the use of interactive terminals: timely interaction can facilitate insight and minimize the time spent exploring blind alleys in an analysis, while a friendly interactive system can remove much of the trauma from the submission of jobs, preparation of control cards, and correction of errors. Finally, graphical terminals are of particular value: they permit the use of more natural representations of data and results throughout the analysis, thus facilitating communication with users who find numerical representations artificial.

These complex special requirements can be seen as quite incompatible, and, indeed, support for biomedical computing has taken two generally diverging paths: the development of large general purpose central computing centers with software and consulting adapted to the needs of the biomedical investigator, and the dissemination of small dedicated computers. The latter have generally been acquired for data acquisition but found to be adequate for a fairly wide spectrum of other tasks as well. A schism arose between the small computer advocates and the large computer advocates which still persists in some groups. A more balanced position is, perhaps, that most biologists are best served by some combination of dedicated laboratory computer support and large systems support, and that the crucial questions concern how to provide the required types of access most effectively. Two general types of system may be distinguished: *minicomputers,* which are characterized by responsive interrupt systems, adaptable memory buses, flexible analog-to-digital conversion interfaces, relatively small memories, short word lengths, compact size, little site preparation, simple operating systems, dedicated use, little card/print input/output capability, and limited random access capacity; and *maxicomputers,* characterized by programmed interrupt systems, inflexible buses, large memories, longer word lengths, complex operating systems, time-shared or multiprogrammed operation, a hierarchy of peripheral storage devices including large random access files, and full card/print capabilities.

Optimality of a computer configuration cannot be meaningfully assessed apart from the job-mix it is to serve. It is difficult to think of an area of application where requirements differ more from location to location than in biomedical computing. What is good for control of on-line experiments in a physiological laboratory tends to be inefficient or altogether inadequate for processing the major statistical computations widely encountered in biology and medicine. Conversely, it is usually uneconomical to tie up a system well suited to statistical computations for continual monitoring of experiments. Not only is there a spectrum of biologists whose requirements range from control of experiments to complex modeling and statistical analysis, but the entire spectrum is often represented in the work of a single investigator. Thus, for example, after preliminary reduction by the laboratory computer, the neurophysiologist's data may require major statistical analysis. The spectrum of computing needs includes occasional use of a laboratory computer; dedicated use of a laboratory computer; further analysis, requiring considerable computing power, of data collected on a laboratory computer; complex analysis of such data, concurrent with the experiment; and problems requiring a large computer throughout.

Although a great many projects can afford a dedicated minicomputer, few can support a maxicomputer adequate to their most demanding tasks. Development of systems, applications programming, and consulting support is even more costly. Further, optimal hardware and software organizations differ for different areas of application, so that even large centers cannot afford to support all of the requirements of users in their immediate community. Hence development of large centers specializing in specific subject areas and supported by a reasonably inexpensive communications network appears to provide the most promising approach. Such centers would provide hardware, software, and consulting via terminals. A number of experiments in this kind of computing support are now in progress, using the existing networking facilities (ARPANET and commercial ventures principally).

To a large extent, these considerations apply to all research computing. However, the special requirements of biomedical research have often spurred developments which have affected the entire field. For example, the development of the LINC computer (described below) not only resulted in a good laboratory computer with reasonable facilities for A/D conversion, it also provided part of the impetus for the minicomputer revolution. The BMD statistical package programs (described above in the section entitled Statistical Analysis) were developed to support biomedical research, but have been widely used in applications ranging from petroleum exploration to economics, and have influenced the entire field. The MUMPS system (described below) is also in widespread use. The special requirements of biomedical research have also speeded developments in a number of other areas, including graphical terminals and scanning hardware.

In the mid-1960's, analog and hybrid (combined analog and digital) systems were commonly used in biology. The analog computer can handle analog data without conversion equipment and is very economical for the solution of systems of differential equations. Its principal disadvantage is lack of flexibility—it is suitable for only a relatively small set of tasks, and it is not easily adaptable even among those tasks. Hybrid systems are also somewhat inflexible because of the inflexibility of their analog component, and they require considerable skill for effective use. With the great increase in speed and decrease in cost of the digital computer over the past decade, analog and hybrid systems have largely disappeared, except where the analog part is a special purpose device always used for the same function. Analog computation remains more efficient for certain classes of problems, but the greater flexibility of the digital computer generally outweighs this advantage.

In the early 1960s there weren't any really effective laboratory computers. The available computers were either too large, costly, and inaccessible for use in the laboratory, or too slow, or both. All computers were designed more or less on the model of the maxicomputer described above, but exclusively for batch processing. In 1961, in a collaboration between computer groups at MIT and Lincoln Laboratories, the LINC (*L*aboratory *In*strument *C*omputer) was designed specifically for laboratory use. In an effort to provide a laboratory computer suitable for biologists, the National Institutes of Health set up a program for the evaluation, improvement, and dissemination of the LINC.

BIOMEDICAL SCIENCES

Investigators applied to NIH for the machines, which they received in kit form, with instructions for assembly. Classes were held at MIT for the prospective users, who learned to assemble, interface, maintain, and program their computers. The LINC consisted of four console modules cable-connected to a cabinet containing electronics and power supply. This construction made the system easy to set up in the laboratory. The console modules consisted of a control console, a tape console (incorporating two inexpensive digital tapes), a display console (providing an oscilloscope), and a terminal console through which other equipment could be interfaced. The terminal console provided connections for two plug-in units, permitting a wide variety of equipment to be attached easily without modifying the basic unit. The LINC had a 12-bit word; an 8-μsec memory cycle; a reasonably rich repertoire of arithmetic, logical, and control commands; and special commands for easy control of A/D conversion, the oscilloscope, the tapes, and transfer of information from one part of the machine to another. The LINC was acquired by the Digital Equipment Corp. which marketed it; it was the forerunner of the immensely popular PDP-12, and thus had an important impact on the entire minicomputer field.

When the group at Massachusetts General Hospital began to develop the information system modules described above in the section entitled Information Systems, software was required which provided (1) an operating system capable of handling several terminals concurrently; (2) a file system which would be easy to set up, alter, and search; and (3) a programming language suitable for string manipulation (processing subsequences of data) and text processing as well as the usual arithmetic operations. Minicomputers were to be used for the information systems, but minicomputers were generally supplied with little software beyond an assembler and a bad FORTRAN compiler. MUMPS (*M*assachusetts General Hospital *U*tility *M*ulti-*P*rogramming *S*ystem) was developed to meet that need. Emphasis was placed on making the programming chore as easy as possible so that people who knew the applications but were not professional programmers could take an active role in the development. MUMPS consists of a monitor which allocates time intervals to each user, an input/output handler, a tree-structured file system, and an interpretive language (also called MUMPS) with extensive string manipulating capabilities. MUMPS has been implemented on the DEC PDP-9, PDP-11, and PDP-15, and a number of different versions now exist. It is supplied by DEC and several commercial software companies provide it as part of applications software developments. MUMPS met a real need in the minicomputer field and has had considerable impact as a consequence.

BIBLIOGRAPHIC NOTES

A comprehensive bibliography would constitute a book in itself, and a suitably short version which pretended to be representative would be woefully incomplete. Instead, a few notes for further reading have been included;

specific references are given for all of the projects which have been described in detail.

There have been several annotated bibliographies prepared, each of book length. These include the following:

Allen, R., *Annotated Bibliography of Biomedical Computer Applications,* National Library of Medicine, Washington, D.C., 1970.
Olson, N., *Medical Information and Computers: A Bibliography,* State University of New York, Albany, 1972.

Unfortunately, such bibliographies also suffer from lack of completeness and become obsolete quickly. *Index Medicus* is a good source of further information, and, once a key article is found, the *Citation Index* can be used to track its descendents.

General works on computer applications in biomedicine include the following:

Ledley, R. S., *Use of Computers in Biology and Medicine,* McGraw-Hill, New York, 1965.
Siler, W., and T. Sterling, *Advances in Biomedical Computer Applications,* New York Academy of Science, New York, 1965.
Stacy, R. W., and B. Waxman, *Computers in Biomedical Research,* Academic, New York, 1965. This set of four volumes provides as comprehensive a review of the field as can be found. The first two volumes, which appeared in 1965, include contributions from many of the leaders in research use of computers in biomedicine, whose work has shaped the field. The third and fourth volumes, appearing in 1969 and 1974, respectively, place primary emphasis on the use of computers in clinical medicine. Specific references in these volumes covering projects described in detail in the foregoing article are given below. These volumes are referred to as "Stacy and Waxman" in the remainder of this section. It should be emphasized that, except for Vol. 4, these volumes do not present the latest work in the field.

An excellent source of papers covering a wide variety of topics is *Computers and Biomedical Research* (not to be confused with Stacy and Waxman), a journal which has been published bimonthly since 1967. Most of the investigators whose work has been cited have published key articles in this journal.

Some publications covering the fields described in this article are indicated below, by field.

Statistical Analysis

There are a great many books on the applications of statistics to biomedicine, but most of them are either attempts to explain statistical concepts to biologists or

BIOMEDICAL SCIENCES

explanations of specific techniques. One recent book which presents a number of examples of computer-based statistical analysis as applied to specific problems (not all of them biological) is W. J. Dixon and W. L. Nicholsen, *Exploring Data Analysis: The Computer Revolution in Statistics,* University of California Press, 1974. This volume is the proceedings of a conference to which the participants brought data for analysis and discussion.

Papers covering the specific examples presented in the section entitled Statistical Analysis include:

Dixon, W. J., *Biomedical Computer Programs,* University of California Press, Berkeley, 1974.

Dixon, W. J., Statistical packages in biomedical computation, in Stacy and Waxman, Vol. 1, 1965.

Opelz, G., and P. I. Terasaki, National utilization of cadaver kidneys for transplantation, *J. Amer. Med. Assoc.* **228,** 1260–1265 (1974).

Terasaki, P. I., and M. R. Mickey, Histocompatibility–transplant correlation, reproducibility, and new matching methods, *Transplantation Proc.* **3**(2), (1971).

Modeling

Volume 2, No. 1 of *Computers and Biomedical Research* is devoted to modeling, and other papers on models appear in most issues. Volumes 1 and 2 of Stacy and Waxman also include a number of papers describing various specific models. Publications covering the example include:

Berman, M., Compartment analysis in biology, in Stacy and Waxman, Vol. 2, 1965.

Jacquez, J. J., *Compartmental Analysis in Biology and Medicine,* Elsevier, New York, 1972.

Physiological Signal Processing

Section D of Vol. 1, Stacy and Waxman, includes three papers which give an overview of the early work in computer-based neurophysiology.

Caceres, C. A., *Clinical Electrocardiography and Computers,* Academic, New York, 1970.

Cornfield, J., R. A. Dunn, C. D. Batchlor, and H. V. Pipberger, Multigroup diagnosis of electrocardiograms, *Comput. and Biomed. Res.* **6,** 97 (1973).

Pipberger, H. V., Computer analysis of the electrocardiogram, in Stacy and Waxman, Vol. 2, 1965.

Schade, J. P., and J. Smith, *Computers and Brains,* Elsevier, New York, 1970.

Schmitt, O. H., and C. A. Caceres, *Electronic and Computer-Assisted Studies of Biomedical Problems,* Thomas, Springfield, Ill., 1964. This is a transcription of a meeting exploring effective computer usage, dealing primarily with the ECG. It is interesting as documentation of early efforts in the field.

Smith, R. E., and C. M. Hyde, Computer analysis of the electrocardiogram in clinical practice, in *Electrical Activity of the Heart* (G. W. Manning, ed.), Thomas, Springfield, Ill., 1969.

BIOMEDICAL SCIENCES

Clinical Medicine

As indicated earlier, Vols. 3 and 4 of Stacy and Waxman are primarily concerned with this topic. Chapters 8, 9, and 10 of Vol. 3 concern the use of computers in the intensive care unit. Chapters 1 and 2 of the same volume deal with automation of the clinical laboratory. The *Proceedings of the Third International Conference on Computers in Biology,* British Journal of Radiology Special Report No. 5, 1972, provides good background articles and a bibliography on this topic. Papers covering the specific examples include:

Cunningham, J. R., and J. Milan, Radiation treatment planning using a display-oriented small computer, in Stacy and Waxman, Vol. 3, 1969. This is a description of the Programmed Console system.

Newton, C. M., Planning radiotherapeutic strategy, in *Proceedings of the 1973 San Diego Biomedical Symposium.* This is a description of the RADGRAF system.

Warner, H. R., Computer based patient monitoring, in Stacy and Waxman, Vol. 3, 1969.

Information Processing

Baruch, J. J., Hospital automation via computer time-sharing, in Stacy and Waxman, Vol. 2, 1965. This is a description of the centralized system as originally envisioned at Massachusetts General Hospital, and is of interest as such.

Collen, M. F. (chairman), *Proceedings, Conference on Medical Information Systems,* National Institutes of Health, Washington, D.C., 1970.

DeLand, E. C., and B. D. Waxman, *Hospital Information Systems,* Rand Corp. Publication #P-4337, 1970.

Lindberg, D. A., *The Computer and Medical Care,* Thomas, Springfield, Ill., 1968.

Massachusetts General Hospital, Laboratory of Computer Sciences, *Computers in Patient Care and Education: Status Report,* Boston, 1974.

Weed, L. L., *Medical Records, Medical Education, and Patient Care,* Case Western Reserve University Press, Cleveland, 1969. This book includes a description and defense of the "problem-oriented medical record."

Training

Stacy and Waxman, Vol. 4, includes material on the use of computers in medical education, as do the Massachusetts General Hospital monographs and the book by Dr. Weed, cited in the previous section. Indeed, most publications on medical information processing also deal with training.

Image Processing

Caspersson, T., et al., TV based techniques for optical analysis of chromosome regions, *Exp. Cell Res.* **75,** 543–546 (1973).

The EMI-scanner: Computerized transverse axial tomography—A new technique, *Radiography,* **39,** 18–20 (1973).

BIOMEDICAL SCIENCES

Ledley, R. S., High speed automatic analysis of biomedical pictures, *Science* **146**, 216–223 (1964).

Lipkin, L., et al., The analysis, synthesis, and description of biological images, *Advances in Biomedical Computer Applications, Ann. N.Y. Acad. Sci.* **128**, 984–1011 (1966).

Ramsay, D. M., *Image Processing in Biological Sciences,* University of California Press, Berkeley, 1968.

Hardware/Software

Greenes, R. A., A. N. Pappalardo, C. W. Marble, and G. O. Burrell, Design and interpretation of a data management system, *Comput. Biomed. Res.* **2**, 409–415 (1969). Description of MUMPS.

Clark, W. A., and C. E. Molner, A description of the LINC, in Stacy and Waxman, Vol. 2, 1965.

P. M. Britt

BIRTH AND DEATH PROCESSES

INTRODUCTION

Whatever happened to the passenger pigeon? At one time their numbers darkened the skies. Hadn't conservationists stopped hunters from killing all of them? Yet, even these remaining numbers finally perished. At one time, after the killing of a very few, the pigeon flock would grow back—it sustained its population. It has been found that some species, through a natural phenomenon, can have their numbers reduced drastically and bounce back. Tamper with the population and they vanish. Buffaloes are one species that faced extinction and survived even though their numbers had been drastically reduced. Some fish populations are another. Every year we get reports on these species making progress and those being placed on the "endangered list."

Analytical studies have been made pertaining to the birth and death of species. One theory that prevailed was that of prey and predator. A complex mathematical theory suggests that as these relationships fluctuate, so do the species numbers. As one rises, the other diminishes. Could it be that as one species prevails a chain reaction occurs causing the numbers of other species to alter too? We find birth curves of owls react this way. When the owl feeds on rodents, their offsprings increase dramatically. But when they feed on other

BIRTH AND DEATH PROCESSES

birds, the birth rate decreases even more drastically. This theory of prey and predator has lost some prominence recently. In the northwestern United States we tried reducing the predator population of big cat species. According to our prevailing theory, the prey species would flourish once again. But to our amazement the prey population grew and diminished in size independent of the predator—just as though the predator was within their environment in what was considered previously as too large in number.

In some bacteria colonies the original growth rate is fantastic yet predictable. At a certain point this growth rate subsides and the bacteria colony remains in a stable state—a maintenance state. It stabilizes at a point wherein the population sustains itself comfortably. Cut this population in half and it grows again, reaching the same size stable state with respect to its present environment.

The human species is not without its studies and corresponding theories. Some environmentalists claim the Judeo-Christian doctrine gave man the right to ravage the earth, stripping away its raw materials without regard to its effect on our ecology and future generations. Other religions, they claim, cherish nature, offering forth the philosophy that man should work with nature in some harmonic revery.

In 1798 Thomas Robert Malthus published *An Essay on the Principle of Population as It Affects the Future Improvement of Society*. He offered that the world's population increased geometrically and foodstuffs increased arithmetically. Given the truth of this hypothesis, man would constantly face the problem of outstripping his food supplies. The factors of vice and misery were offered as the constraints to man's possible demise. Darwin's theories also hypothesized on population growth through a species' ability to adapt to its environment.

Today, as the world's population continues to grow, or as we control it, we must continue to ponder—where do we fit? Could our population be sliced in half, utilizing some magnificent randomizing device to assure homogeneity with respect to the world's previous population? If so, would the world bounce back? Take many years to recover? Not recover? Would we follow the passenger pigeon, the buffalo, or the maintenance state population growth patterns?

During the era when nuclear war seemed more probable than it does now, the government worked on studies relating to how long it would require mankind to return to its present population and standard of living. An alternate question obviously was: Would the species bounce back at all? If not, how long would the species survive? Mankind's birth rate reacts with respect to his environment and to nature.

There are many types of chemical reactions. Consider a batch chemical process where a number of chemicals remain at rest. There is no interaction between these chemicals and they will remain as they are—possibly forever. Now, let us add a catalyst and everything appears in turmoil. These chemicals react with one another and we attempt to control this reaction for our own advantage. We may seek a specific yield from this mass, or choose to continue it, or seek to stop this reaction at an exact point. We are successful at this in our chemical industries and will continue to get better. Yet, there are times when we lose control over our chemical reactions.

Turning to the case of human population, we think we have control—control of man's earthly destiny—much like the chemist who controls his chemical reaction. Controlling reactions requires precision. Ask the housewife, our first chemist, about making candy. She knows what happens if we miss this control point of "heat to stirring, ever so slightly." Obviously the product freezes! The action locks! We can be sure that this idea, so simple in format yet so catastrophic, plagues those who deal in population studies of man.

So we see how serious the studies of population growth and related studies of birth and death processes are with respect to living things. And, we may recognize the joys and tragedies that may confront us. We have undertaken many research studies pertaining to these problems and have attempted to quantify them for better understanding. This has brought forth the use of complex mathematical models, and these studies have been enhanced tremendously by the computer. Rather than work laboriously with complex mathematical models to explain the phenomenon of birth or death, or take years to observe what is happening, the scientist of today can describe analytically a model of his population, and through the use of a computer he may investigate many generations of growth in an extremely short interval of time.

More importantly, he can introduce new elements and take away others. In fact, he can drastically change the parameters and observe firsthand their effect on the population being studied. We all know the difficulty of writing life equations mathematically or even exploring them through the use of a computer. But there has been substantial progress in this area. At one time man could only philosophize how events took place. He still does, but with a broader spectrum of knowledge.

As a by-product of these further reaching studies of life, destiny, birth, and death came the studies of man's internal environment. The social reaction of man to his institutions is an example. Consider man's institutions as subsets of this total world. Would many of these subsets of the world, man's institutions, react in some way as did its population? Could man's government, economics, or work have similar interactions? Could they be measured in a way similar to that of his population—his birth and death processes? The concept of the universe as a whole has been an overriding one. Man and his social institutions are part of this system. For example: Are there ways to describe the birth and death of customers as a prey–predator model? Could a machine be designed from these studies? Do conveyorized assembly lines follow models investigated previously by population scientists? Can market saturation states be defined as biological maintenance states?

The scientific study of population and related birth-death models has helped us to quantify and assign distributions or series to the factors governing: inputs to the system (births), outputs to the system (deaths), and how they occur in concert with one another (input to output). Intuitively, and couched in

BIRTH AND DEATH PROCESSES

somewhat loose language, we may state that the relationships of births to deaths are in a decaying state with population size diminishing, an increasing state with population growing, or in a somewhat stable state—neither growing nor decreasing appreciably.

Let us assume that population growth for a particular birth and death model averages three births for every one death with the condition that the ratio of births to deaths occurs randomly. Given certain mathematical conditions and a fixed size population, this system will stabilize at an expected population level. We encounter these types of systems in the biological world where population size is fixed by the environment. Population size varies with the limitation that the environment cannot sustain more than a fixed number. This type of model also occurs in the business world. Consider a sales problem where two companies compete in a limited size market.[1] An example of this is found where state laws limit the types of products that may be sold in specific geographical areas. Dairy farms are a good example. The dairy herds are limited by the competitive market they service. At day's end, milk lines require cleaning. Other equipment also requires cleaning. The state regulatory agencies permit only two companies to compete in the sale of cleaning chemicals. Looking for a real world model, we find an example in the uses of chlorine or iodine sanitizing agents for dairy farm use. This model represents our condition where population is not growing or decreasing appreciably. It would be possible to assign probabilities to various population levels as they vary between a minimum and maximum. We must remember this is a fixed size universe. Thus in our marketing case let us assume that the market is bound to 16 farms. Now, we can assign probability levels to the various population states. Through methods of quantification to be examined later, we can find the probability of the size of the iodine market. What is the probability that the iodine market commands 10 farms, 11 farms, or 14 farms? These probabilities are 5, 10, and 22%, respectively. Through use of these techniques of quantification, we can make predictions about population sizes and use them advantageously.

What about those birth and death ratios when births increase at a rate faster than deaths? Inputs to the system are greater than the system's ability to dispose of them. Seemingly, population would increase without bound. As the world's human population increases, fears are raised as to the earth's ability to sustain life itself.

A few birth ratios are linear. The majority are exponential. Birth rates of fish when introduced to a new pond grow exponentially. With this rate of growth the physical size of the fish depends on the rate of growth versus the food to sustain it, and in some respects the boundaries of the environment itself. As numbers increase and food supplies become limited, the physical size of the fish changes. The bluegill population of farm ponds classically follow this growth rate to size ratio. After a few years the total population may be "stunted" and also be extremely cannibalistic.

---

[1] See Example 1 below in the section entitled Practical Examples for the solution of this problem.

BIRTH AND DEATH PROCESSES

In mankind's primitive societies where there is an absence of food, the babies suckle for 2 or more years. If a new baby is born during this time period, the mother disposes of the new offspring. These checks to population growth abound in our world of living things. Nature sees to it. It seems as though the number of living things is limited by numerous natural constraints, one being the ability of the environmental system to accept the new births. The rate of growth is important for predicting various population levels and the time span before saturation. Prediction can mean a greater degree of control, and with control we may achieve the harmony we seek.

In machine design we encounter the problem too. Oftentimes we must work with systems that supply too many parts in too short a time. Not being able to accept more than a given amount of items in one unit of time, this system, like that of the environment, is restrictive. In the biological world, according to Voterra's principle, the populations in a given area reach a natural equilibrium. The prey and predator survive in some harmony. But in the biological world there are numerous such relationships, all interacting. Change one at the expense of another, and you change another and change another. While we may conceive that the engineer can govern the input to the system and possibly cover a few successive events prior to or after the machine is designed, we must admit that in broad terms there is totality in his system too. We cannot in this broad sense divorce the machine from the economy, the society, or states of nature that constantly conflict with the environment. But we have a problem to solve, so we usually approach it without regard to far-reaching effects. Our ecological problems document this. And who can say that the amount of energy, in terms of fuel we use to farm an acre of ground, is regained by the products harvested? So the engineer designs his machine and controls only those few items directly affected.

Let us assume we are designing a nailing machine for use on our assembly lines.[2] This machine is constructed so that it has four separate driving heads and four separate supplying tubes. These tubes keep the head supplied with nails. With each stroke of the machine all heads are actuated and thus four nails are driven simultaneously. Nails are supplied to these tubes between strokes of the machine only. We design these nail storage tubes long enough so that each will hold an adequate supply of nails, thereby assuring the driving head of a nail for every stroke of the machine. Our tubes would have to be extremely long to guarantee this, and our space is limited. Also, we must remember that a nail cannot be admitted to the tube during a stroke. Thus the death of four nails—their use during a machine stroke—gives opportunity for four nails to enter the system—a birth between cycles. But nails enter the tubes on a probabilistic basis, even though they are in adequate supply. They may miss the opportunity to enter the tube because they are improperly oriented or could be in competition with others trying to enter this life cycle—the tube. If the tube held only one nail in reserve, the following sequence could occur: (1) machine strokes, (2) nail departs the tube, (3) feed mechanism opens

---

[2] See Example 2 below in the section entitled Practical Examples for the solution of this problem.

BIRTH AND DEATH PROCESSES

and awaits another nail to enter. But with conditions that could hinder a nail entering the tube, we can see that the machine could stroke the next time without a nail to drive. To design the tube with an infinite number of nails would require a tube of infinite length. So the size of the tube must be designed with respect to the environment surrounding the machine. How much space do we have? What are the consequences to our other systems if the machine does not make a quality product every time? These are important considerations. Thus we must look to those systems that immediately precede the machine and those that follow. It is hard not to draw an analogy to our life systems at this point. They are bound somewhat the same way as the machine.

Let us assume we choose a tube size that holds four nails. Let us further assume that five in 100 nails are properly aligned as they approach the feeding device. If the machine has a capacity of 100 strokes per minute but only 12 are used, then the probability of a birth is $5/100 = 0.05$ and the probability of a death is $12/100 = 0.12$. In this example births are less than deaths. Consider an alternative problem where birth probabilities are $20/100 = 0.20$ and death probabilities remain $12/100 = 0.12$. In this example births are greater than deaths. Using an integer step Markovian process, a mathematical technique particularly applicable to birth and death equations, we find a solution for both examples. In the case where births are less than deaths, the probabilities are:

$P_0 \doteq .584$ (the tube is empty)
$P_1 \doteq .256$ (the tube contains one nail)
$P_2 \doteq .099$ (the tube contains two nails)
$P_3 \doteq .038$ (the tube contains three nails)
$P_4 \doteq .001$ (the tube is filled)

And in the case where births exceed deaths:

$P_0 \doteq .041$ (the tube is empty)
$P_1 \doteq .086$ (the tube contains one nail)
$P_2 \doteq .158$ (the tube contains two nails)
$P_3 \doteq .290$ (the tube contains three nails)
$P_4 \doteq .425$ (the tube contains four nails)

Now we can compare the results of both systems. In the case where births are less than deaths the probability of the tube being empty is very high. This is not good for our design. More favorable probabilities are found in the second case where births are greater than deaths. Here the probability of a full tube is more favorable. Other birth and death ratios to a given space could prove even better. We control the design and by a change in our feed mechanism we can favorably alter our ratios. We act as the limiting force in this situation, but in the world of living things this control belongs to nature.

At this point we may ask how could a system, especially one where births are less than deaths, result in any probabilities whatsoever. Would not deaths finally kill off all births so no births could occur at all? In nature this happens. In terms of our own ecology this may occur too if we use our material resources faster than they can be recreated. Let us consider the physical

BIRTH AND DEATH PROCESSES

world. Suppose we are dealing with a system where births are infinite. Thus far man has not found limits to space or the atom. Predictions have been made as to the edge of the universe and also as to the amount of neutrons and protons available. These numbers are so large we may consider them infinite. Even if we could not consider them infinite, the removal of one item from such a vast storehouse would not appreciably change the probabilities of another being removed. Let us consider two urns. Urn 1 contains two red and two white balls. Urn 2 contains two million red and two million white. The proportions for urns are the same. If we wish to draw two white balls in two successive tries from these urns without replacing the ball drawn previously, the probability tree would be

Urn 1:

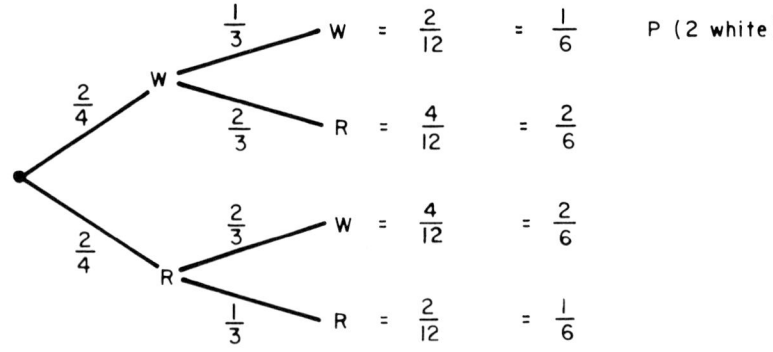

Drawing without replacement (finite),

Urn 2:

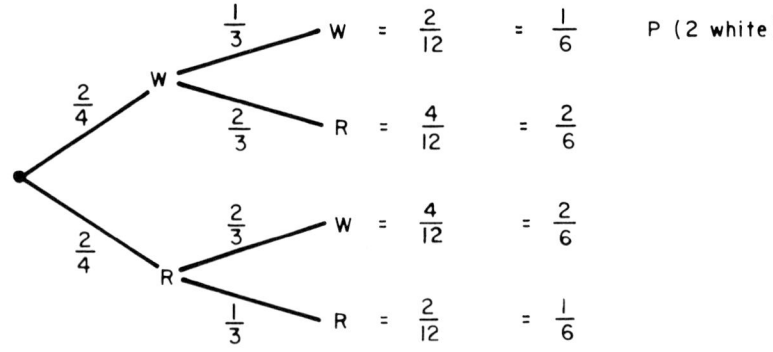

Had the ball drawn been returned to the universe from which it was drawn, the universe size would remain the same for each draw. Thus the probabilities for either urn would be the same.

BIRTH AND DEATH PROCESSES

Urn 1:

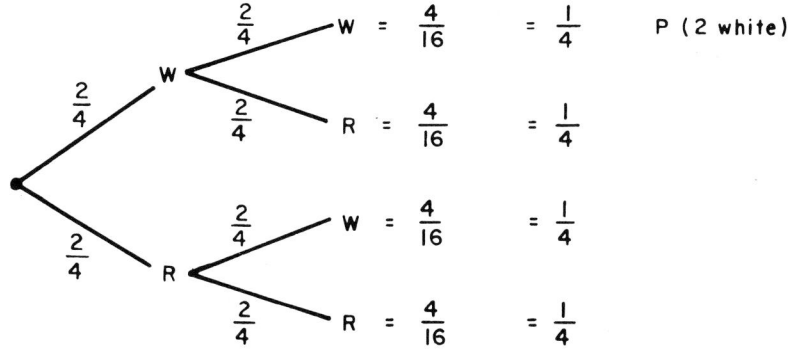

Drawing with replacement (infinite),

Urn 2:

Consider the finite universe trees. When the ball is not returned to Urn 1, the probabilities of two successive draws of a white ball are 1/6. Not replacing the ball drawn drastically alters the probability. The chance of getting a white ball on the second draw after drawing a white on the first goes from $P_1 = 1/2$ to $P_2 = 1/3$. The probability of both events together is $(1/2)(1/3) = 1/6$. Quite a change! In the case of the larger universe, Urn 2, the chance of getting a white ball on the second draw after drawing a white on the first goes from $P_1 = 2,000,000/4,000,000$ to $P_2 = 1,999,999/3,999,999$. The probability of both events together is

$$P\left(\frac{2,000,000}{4,000,000}\right)\left(\frac{1,999,999}{3,999,999}\right) = \frac{3,999,998}{15,999,996} \doteq \frac{1}{4}$$

Not a severe change at all. The probability of the second tree of the finite

BIRTH AND DEATH PROCESSES

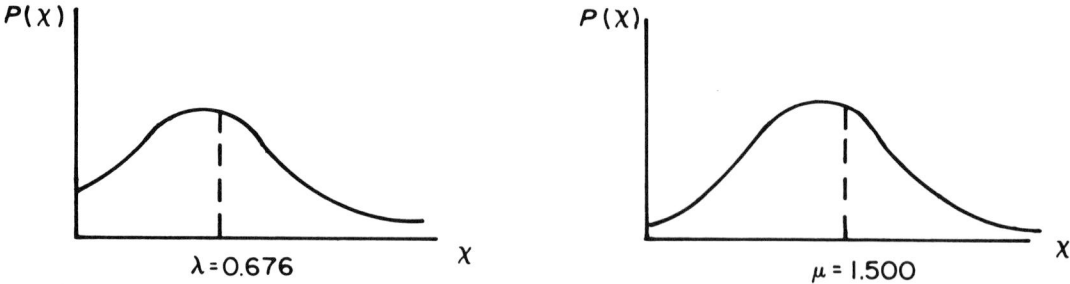

Fig. 1. A graph of the probabalistic distributions showing how births queue up before entering a system.

universe approximates that of the infinite universe. Using either tree of our second series, drawing with replacement, we note the probabilities of two successive draws from either tree is $P(2 \text{ white}) = 1/4$. In practice, depending on the number of draws and the fineness of our calculations, we consider drawing from Urn 2 of our first pair of trees as if they were drawn with replacement—a finite approximation of infinity.

Nature duplicates this tree by giving birth to an overabundance so that a few may survive. The predator, or other death-causing events, does not appreciably alter the number entering the life cycle. This remains true unless some external force causes changes to the interlocking chain of events either preceding or following this massive birth.

For conditions of this analysis let us consider these as births occurring randomly and emanating from an infinite universe. In the business world we encounter both finite and infinite birth models. Consider a river dam which can service an average of 1.5 boats per hour.[3] Also consider that boats arrive at the rate of 0.676 boats per hour. In this example, average births are approximately one-half that of average deaths. Yet a line of boats forms. We used the word "average" to describe births and deaths, and this implies a probabilistic distribution. A graph of these distributions can be used to show how births queue up before entering the system (Fig. 1).

A chronology of how births and deaths could occur illustrates how a queue forms even when births are less than deaths (Table 1).[4]

A distribution gives probabilities for a range of events. The arrival distribution has an average of 0.676. But there are numerous occasions where we have arrivals less than or greater than our average. Similarly, the service

---

[3] For a complete solution see J. A. Panico, *Queuing Theory—A Study of Waiting Lines for Business, Economics, and Science,* Prentice-Hall, Englewood Cliffs, New Jersey, 1969, pp. 53–58.
[4] Discrete variables involve counting such as we have listed in Table 1. They are properly depicted as line charts. Continuous variables involve measuring and are properly depicted as a continuous function. In advanced mathematics, we establish the specific conditions for which there is correspondence between discrete and continuous variables. For convenience, we show the discrete values of Table 1 as a continuous distribution. This is to help give clarity to our intuitive explanations.

BIRTH AND DEATH PROCESSES

TABLE 1

Hour	Number of boats arriving	Services per hour	Boats waiting service
1	0.676	1.5	0
2	0.676	1.5	0
3	1.500	1.5	0
4	0.250	2.0	0
5	1.000	1.0	0
6	1.500	2.5	0
7	1.750	1.0	0.75
8	1.250	0.75	$\{0.75 + 0.50\} = 1.25$
9	0.500	2.50	0

distribution has an average of 1.5. Here, too, there are times when services require either less than or greater than our average. We can see by Table 1 that as long as services (deaths) are greater than births for a given time period, the system clears. But service cannot be inventoried. In those cases where service is greater than arrivals, it cannot be inventoried for future use. Thus it represents lost opportunity. At Hour 2 we had average arrivals and average service. In Hour 4 our arrivals were less than average and services greater than average. In Hour 7 arrivals were greater than the ability to service, resulting in the arrivals (births) not being admitted to the system. In Hour 9 we cleared both the arrivals and those waiting because we had excess servicing capacity and could use it to clear those who were waiting. This is what happens when we try to combine two distributions in an act-event sequence. The birth rate may be over- or underaverage. The death rate may be over- or underaverage. When the act-event occurs where we have greater input to the system than the system's ability to output, then a line forms. In our illustration we saw a line form in the seventh hour and continue until the eighth hour. Had the life span of the birth been less than the time it had to wait prior to entering the system, then it would have died in line, never to enter the system at all. When we transport perishable products in the business world, it is to our advantage to know the waiting time at each station. Our product could degenerate and die too. News is probably one of our most perishable time-related products. Of what value is news if it arrives too late?

Just as we combine distributions for average arrivals less than average service, we can also combine distributions in an act-event sequence for average arrivals greater than average service. At first thought we might think the system would grow without bound—and it will, given certain conditions. We have already explored two conditions where this is not so: (1) the condition where the environment is capped, restrictive, and will not admit any additional elements to the system unless there is first a death; (2) the case where service cannot support the input and thus the product dies prior to entering the system.

BIRTH AND DEATH PROCESSES

Nature exacts heavy tolls in the case of imbalance. So does business in the way of competition. If we cannot service our customers, if they are dying waiting for our product, then the price rises according to supply and demand. But this invites competition which reduces our supplying universe appreciably. Nature is a competitive system too. We have previously established a correspondence between nature and business systems. This previous analogy dramatizes the relationship.

To conclude our intuitive introduction to birth and death models, let us consider the decaying state. We will example conditions where population grows rapidly at the beginning but later declines with greater rapidity almost to a dormant state. Virus populations are examples of this, requiring a host on which to live. Once infected, the host develops immunity characteristics. Thus the host becomes less susceptible to future contagion. A new generation of hosts may stimulate births of the virus once again. Also, variants to the original strain may by-pass previous immunities. Turning to business analogies once again, consider the hula hoop craze that swept the United States a few years ago. This had a rapid birth and death plus subsequent rebirth with some alterations to the original product. Men's and women's fashions follow the same cyclic patterns with the variant that old styles catch on once again.

Decay could be characterized by placing rats in a maze. If some paths lead to a breeding place and other paths lead to death, we could, in broad terms, consider this maze as a birth and death model. The rat makes unit steps through the maze. Some lead to a dead end, others to death, and others to life. Step-by-step the rat progresses. Some die, others survive. The rat has memory and can improve his chance of survival with each success. Each success brings multiple births, each failure brings death. If the death path is changed on a probabilistic basis, meaning the rat is absorbed (killed) on a probabilistic basis, then conversely multiple births will occur on a probabilistic basis. The ratio of successful paths to unsuccessful paths can be handled by mathematical techniques or computer simulation. If birth reproduction rates are so great they overwhelm deaths, then only a few need to be successful. If the ratio is unfavorable, the species could die or remain at some varying but closely predictable population size. If we close all death paths, births abound. If we do not alter the paths, births grow at a slower rate. In reality, as we change the paths, remove memory, or do other things to alter the experiment, births will vary according to the probabilities we introduce into the system. The population grows subject to the rats' successes or failures and reproducing rates. If we call a successful run of the path a contagion and a majority of paths lead to success, then population flourishes. But given the conditions that certain paths open or close probabilistically once a contact is made, or another condition that once a path closes it remains closed, then we can see how population will decay depending on the probabilities of a closing path. This model describes intuitively a special Markovian process called absorbing Markovian chains. Based on the probabilities of the experiment, it is possible to predict the mean number of times in each path before death, the mean number of paths used before death, and the probability of death once the initial path is chosen. Remember we try a path, change directions forward again and again, and either succeed or die.

If a rat were subjected to such a variety of things, it would roll up in a ball and lie there in utter confusion.

In marketing studies we know that too much variety deters sales. We could expand this concept to show death of a sale occurs here too—as with the rat. Virus growth patterns are curtailed by the immunity probabilities of the paths once traversed. The layout of customer flow patterns through a grocery store could be an analogy of our model. The greater number of paths a customer traverses, the higher the probabilities of an impulse sale, a death to the product. The longer in any area, the higher the probability of a death—another product purchased. We design our stores both to make the customer's route longer and slower. Necessary items are placed in positions to assure customer exposure to more shelf area for greater impulse buying. Immunity to the products occur as we traverse the same aisle again and again—the secret is exposure to all aisles for greater buying. This seems to be a converse model to our original rat-to-maze analogy, yet it ties together the analogy of immunity characteristics to the biological, bacterial, virus, and business worlds.

To summarize our intuitive introduction to birth and death processes, we have learned that life and death equations describe the critical ratios uniting our world. Nothing lives without killing something else. This is the reality of nature—the exchange of energy for energy.

From the study of how things are born, how they die, and how this occurs in relationship to one another, we are able to enhance our existence—the species of man—but we have also enhanced that of other species and organisms. Yet, we have pointed out the difficulty of predicting the chain reaction of events. We can predict influenza cycles, control insect populations, design production systems, and make market studies, and we can do many other things that have thus far made man's relationship to his environment more compatible.

Birth and death studies in relation to our economy could mean the birth of too many dollars (inflation) and the death of too many products (overconsumption). In fact, birth and death studies pervade so many relationships it would be easier to count those it did not involve in order to assess the magnitude of this far-reaching study. In the final analysis, nature plays the fiddle and all living things dance to the tune. We study birth and death models to broaden understanding and enrich our existence. Who can deny the benefits of birth and death studies of Louis Pasteur who saved the bacterial strains of French wine.

QUANTITATIVE ANALYSIS

Introduction

Thus far we have examined birth and death processes from a very loose intuitive approach. We have also examined how the birth and death models of our living and physical world are used in the analysis of events pertaining to

BIRTH AND DEATH PROCESSES

our society. Through the years we have become more definitive and also more quantitative with respect to births, deaths, and their interrelationships. As scientific inquiry increased, the topic area was given more worldwide attention. With this increased interest it becomes necessary to classify these topics, using symbols to represent certain events. As we progressed in our study we established λ as the symbol for birth and μ as the symbol for death. The study of birth and death models has been carefully classified so that scientists may readily communicate new ideas or extentions of old ideas. The mathematical techniques most commonly used in these studies are generally classified as stochastic processes. More specifically, they are probability studies involving various mathematical distributions and their interaction. Differential equations and Markovian processes predominate the mathematical derivations, but this should not discourage those nonmathematicians who wish to gain a general understanding.[5]

Mathematicians have given us useful formulas derived from the study of birth and death processes. These formulas have been reduced into forms usable

---

[5] Consider the birth–death equation

$$\frac{dP_n(t)}{dt} = pP_{n+1}(t) - [(m-n)\lambda + \mu]P_n(t) + (m-n+1)\lambda P_{n-1}$$

which, for conditions of equilibrium, reduces to the general equations

$$P_n = \frac{m!}{(m-n)!}\left(\frac{\lambda}{\mu}\right)^n P_0, \quad 1 \leq n \leq m$$

and

$$P_n = \binom{m}{n}\left(\frac{\lambda}{\mu}\right)^n P_0, \quad 0 \leq n \leq 1$$

from these we may refine our equations further to the expected values:

$$E_n = m - \frac{\mu}{\lambda}(1 - P_0)$$

$$E_w = m - \frac{\lambda + \mu}{\lambda}(1 - P_0)$$

These are a few of the general birth and death equations used in queuing theory to describe E_n, the expected number of elements in line plus those being serviced, and E_w, the expected number in queue in the awaiting line. In a production situation where $m = 4$ (there are a total of four machines in our system), $\lambda = 1$ (an average of one machine breaks down per hour, a birth to the service system), and $\mu = 8$ (a serviceman can repair an average of eight machines per hour, a death to the birth system). In the analysis of birth and death models, λ = births and μ = deaths. The ratio λ/μ is the rate at which the system is cleared. If λ is small in relation to μ, then the system clears easily. But if λ is large with respect to μ, the system has difficulty in clearing. In this model $\lambda/\mu < 1$. If $\lambda/\mu > 1$, then births would exceed deaths and the system would not clear. For example, if only one machine needs service in 1 hr and the repairman can service eight in 1 hr, then according to what we have studied previously, there will be times when a machine will have to wait for service because the repairman is working on another machine; but, in the majority of the cases, the machine will get instant attention. If $\lambda = 7$ the ratio $\lambda/\mu = 7/8$. We can see that now a large waiting line of machines will form, awaiting service. If $\lambda = 12$, the situation would be impossible for the one serviceman.

BIRTH AND DEATH PROCESSES

by a wide population of people. Thus managers may use these universal equations to gain a broader knowledge of how to set up a service system for a given size population of machines, or for other analyses.

For preciseness and clarity, birth and death processes have been classified as homogeneous and nonhomogeneous systems. Homogeneous models are derived with respect to population size, while nonhomogeneous models are derived with respect to time.

Homogeneous processes are basically classified as pure, general, and divergent birth processes. Conversely, we have pure and general death processes. When these are combined, we have birth and death relationships classified as pure birth and death and general birth and death processes.

We may ask, at this point, why be concerned with births and deaths as a function of popuation size or as a function of time. In examining births or deaths we wish to determine what can happen in one iteration of the population. In the case of births related to the total population, all could give birth, zero could give birth, or some other proportion of the total population could give birth. Any of these events may be described probabilistically. Let us restrict the analysis to one instantaneous event, exclusive of time. To make a determination of how the total reacts, we must determine how just one birth or death occurs. Once this is established, we may relate this finding to the whole.

The Pure Birth Process—Intuitive

To investigate this process, we establish the fact that these are one-way transactions. Population may increase, but not decrease. Only discrete, countable, births are considered. Births in process are voided. Births do not depend on time. If we could imagine starting our process by placing two organisms, both capable of giving birth, in a finite space, then over a given period of time we could have a huge population, still retain the two, or have some population size between these limits. But we are limited to only one observation. At this precise moment, what could be occurring? Let us return to the original beginning state. We had two organisms to begin with. What could happen in the next iteration? There would be two or three in the population. Why not four? We have made simultaneous births impossible by choosing the interval of our next observation so small that more than one birth cannot occur. Obviously, as the population size grows, it becomes more difficult to observe only one birth. In this case the time from the previously known

---

Originally, we had taken a complex mathematical equation and reduced it to a few basic algebraic formulas. By using these formulas and the data from our example:

$$E_n = 0.59704 \quad \text{and} \quad E_w = 0.17167$$

See J. A. Panico. *Queing Theory—A Study of Waiting Lines for Business, Economics, and Science*, Prentice-Hall, Englewood Cliffs, New Jersey, 1969, pp. 58–61.

BIRTH AND DEATH PROCESSES

population to the next observation is made smaller to assure only one birth. So we can see within these limitations that the probability of a population increase by one depends exclusively on the previous population size only, coupled with the probabilistic birth rate of the organism. If the population size were small and the probabilities of a birth small too, the chance of a birth during one iteration of the unit step life chain would be similarly very small. Change these conditions by increasing either the probability or population size, or change both, and the occurrence of one birth could increase enormously.

Pure Birth Processes—Mathematical[6]

Let

$x(t)$ = the population of our experiment at time t.
λ = probability of one birth.
$p_n(t)$ = probability of population size n during time interval t. In our case this means: $x(t) \to n$ [$x(t)$ goes to n] with probability $P_n(t)$.
Δt = a very small change in our time interval where the population increases by one or remains the same.

If λ equals the probability of a birth or, more specifically, if we let λ equal the probability of one change in a unit interval, then $\lambda \Delta t$ would be the probability of one change during interval Δt. The sum of all probabilities equals 1; therefore, $1 - \lambda \Delta t$ would be the probability of zero changes in the interval Δt. Symbolically, this reads:

The probability of n changes in interval t and zero changes in interval Δt.

Consider now the probability of $n - 1$ changes in interval t and one change in interval Δt. Again we are dealing with n changes in the interval $t + \Delta t$. $P_{n-1}(t)$ by definition represents the probability of $n - 1$ changes in the interval t, and $\lambda \Delta t$ is the probability of one change in the interval Δt. Therefore, we have:

The probability of $n - 1$ changes in the interval t and one change in the interval Δt.

$$= [P_{n-1}(t)][\lambda \Delta t]$$

According to our basic assumption, the probability of more than one change in the interval Δt is not admissable, based on Δt being very small. Thus the probability of n changes in the interval $t + \Delta t$ would be obtained by adding the two probabilities as previously derived:

$$P_n(t + \Delta t) = P_n(t)(1 - \lambda \Delta t) + P_{n-1}(t)(\lambda \Delta t)$$

[6] Adapted from J. A. Panico, *Queuing Theory—A Study of Waiting Lines for Business, Economics, and Science*, Prentice-Hall, Englewood Cliffs, New Jersey, 1969, pp. 73–88.

BIRTH AND DEATH PROCESSES

This is the probability of one birth by one member of the population universe. To convert this to the total population $X(t)$, we assign the probability that the whole population will produce a birth:[7]

$$\lambda X(t) \Delta t$$

Rewriting our previous equations with respect to population size and letting $n = X$, the equation is

$$P_n(t + \Delta t) = P_n(t)(1 - \lambda n \Delta t) + P_{n-1}(t)\lambda(n - 1)\Delta t$$

Returning to our assumption that Δt is very small, we will let Δt approach zero. In terms of the calculus, this has special meaning: when we let Δt approach zero, the result is the first derivative of $P_n(t)$ which we designate by $P_n'(t)$. Thus

$$P_n'(t) = \lambda(n - 1)P_{n-1}(t) - \lambda n P_n(t)$$

If $n = 0$, i.e., no change in the interval $t + \Delta t$, the term $\lambda(n - 1)P_{n-1}(t)$ cannot exist. Therefore

$$P_0'(t) = \lambda n P_0(t)$$

This equation shows that the first derivative is equal to a constant λn times the function itself $P_0(t)$. This is a unique functional derivative called the exponential function. Combining this with the fact that the probability of zero changes in the interval zero is equal to 1, and since we are assured of this correctness, we conclude that $P_0(t)$ is an exponential function:

$$P_0(t) = e^{-\lambda n t}$$

According to the graph of this function (Fig. 2), a negative exponential distribution, we assume the time between births diminishes as a function of population size. Empirical data show, however, that this distribution does not hold true in many special cases of population growth. We have explored population growth intuitively, presenting the idea that all births do not occur exponentially, nor do they occur deterministically.

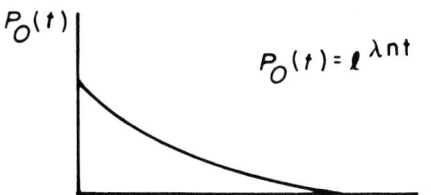

Fig. 2. A graph of the function $P_0(t) = e^{-\lambda n t}$.

---

[7] See N. T. J. Bailey, *The Elements of Stochastic Processes,* Wiley, New York, 1964; E. Parzen, *Stochastic Processes,* Holden-Day, San Francisco, 1962, for more comprehensive treatments of birth and death processes.

BIRTH AND DEATH PROCESSES

Thus far we have established methods for predicting the time elapsing between births as a function of the population size. It would also be of primary importance to our analysis to be able to assign probabilities of advancing by one to a new population size from a given population size at specific time t. Let us look into the chain of events building our population. Remember we are increasing by one or staying the same during each successive event. Thus, if we wish to determine $P_n(t)$, our present population size, we must analyze the previous population size and state of this unit integer step chain of events. The previous population could have been n or $n - 1$ when we view it from our present position $P_n(t)$. $P_n(t)$ could have occurred from the previous population n remaining stable, not growing by 1; or it could have resulted from the previous population $n - 1$, which grew by 1 to the new position $P_n(t)$. We had previously assigned probabilities to these events, writing these expressions of growth with respect to the present population size. This developed into the negative exponential distribution which gave the time elapsing between births with respect to population size. The expression could also be written without respect to total population size as:

$$P_0(t) = e^{-\lambda t}$$

This is the probability distribution for zero changes in the interval $t + \Delta t$. It follows that the probability of one change in the interval $t + \Delta t = (1 - e^{-\lambda t})$.

We wish to predict the population size n at time t. If the size of the universe had been n in the previous step, we could not determine how our population grew. Had the population size been $n - 1$, one less than the population size we seek, then a growth in population would have occurred. Thus we could develop formulas describing the characteristics of the distribution that grows step by step to any size population. To do this, we must look back at the previous step as though it had one unit less. We wish an expression allowing a population size of $n - 1$ to grow to a population size of n.

Consider our previous population of size $n - 1$. If $n = 11$, $n - 1 = 10$. This means the population grew, step by step, through various population sizes 1, 2, 3, 4, 5, 6, 7, 8, 9, and 10. Sometimes it grew one unit, sometimes it stayed the same; but it grew one at a time to 10. We start with one unit in the system capable of giving birth when dealing with population equations.

We have assigned the probability for a growth of 1 (a success) and the probability of remaining the same (a failure to grow). We have also described the present population size and have established that it grows step by step, discretely. This is characteristic of a binomial distribution $(p + q)^n$ which also grows step by step and lets us establish the probabilities for each step—depending on the value of p (a success) and n (the size of the population). To determine the values of any term of $(p + q)^n$, we use the formula $\binom{n}{x}p^x q^{n-x}$. In this formula x is the particular number for which we seek a probability. If the population size were $n = 11$ and we wished to assign probabilities for $x = 10$, then

$$P(x) = \frac{n!}{x!(n-x)!} p^x q^{n-x}$$

This equals

$$P(x = 10) = \frac{11!}{10!(11-10)!} p^x q^{n-x}$$

We could also find the probabilities for any number (0–11) by substitution into the formula. Increase n and we increase the number of events and also change the probability for each event. In our problem we wish to find the probability of $n = 11$, $P_n(t)$, from the previous binomial expression. Remembering that if we seek a new population size $n = 11$, the previous population was $n - 1 = 10$. Our previous expansion, step by step, was based on a successful growth probability $1 - e^{-\lambda t}$ versus a failure probability $e^{-\lambda t}$. The sum of a binomial probability distribution equals 1 and may be expressed as

$$\sum_{x=x'}^{n} \binom{n}{x} p^x q^{n-x} = 1$$

If we had summed our probability distribution when the population size was $n - 1 = 10$, the sum would have been 1. When our population size iterates in one step to $n = 11$, its sum will also be equal to 1. The total probability of 1 will be divided among an increasing number of discrete variables. Thus the probability for each variable will change proportionately and grow smaller.

In our problem we are looking backward at a population size $n - 1 = 10$. It is conceivable our population will never iterate to $n = 11$; will iterate to $n = 11$—the next step; or will require a number of iterations before changing to $n = 11$. In probability theory we can find the possibilities of a success by determining the number of failures and subtracting these failures from 1. Thus we obtain the probability of a success for a particular term we seek.

In our problem we wish to find the probability of growing from $n = 1 = 10$ to $n = 11$. Assume we determine the number of ways we can fail before proceeding to the next step. Now our problem of finding the probabilities of iterating to $n = 11$ is solved. The sum of all the failures preceding a successful move to the nth step, in our case $n = 11$, follows the Pascal distribution, more commonly referred to as the negative binomial distribution. The correspondence of the cumulative binomial distribution to the cumulative negative binomial distribution is given by[8]

$$1 - \sum_{x'=0}^{r-1} \binom{x+r}{x'} p^{x'} q^{x+r-x'} = \sum_{x'=0}^{x} \binom{x'+r-1}{r-1} p^r q^{x'}$$

or

$$\sum_{x'=r}^{x+r} \binom{x+r}{x'} p^{x'} q^{x+r-x'} = \sum_{x'=0}^{x} \binom{x'+r-1}{r-1} p^r q^{x'}$$

In our problem we wish to move from a population size of $n - 1 = 10$ to $n =$

---

[8] S. Selby, *Standard Mathematical Tables*, Chemical Rubber Publishing Co., Cleveland, 1971, p. 591.

BIRTH AND DEATH PROCESSES

11. Let us designate 0 as a failure to move and 1 as a successful move. One sequence of events through which we may have moved from $n - 1 = 10$ to $n = 11$ could be described as 0000100101010011001010100001001, where the final number is the nth step. There were thirty-one trials with $n = 11$ successful moves in this sequence of events. Prior to our moving to the nth step, our last success, we had:

$f = 20 =$ the number of failures to move one step from the preceding step

and

$n - 1 =$ the number of moves to a new population size—exclusive of the final population increase.

Our total number of trials preceding the move to our new population size may be described as

$$n - 1 + f = n + f - 1$$

If f equals the number of failures prior to a success, then

$$\binom{n + f - 1}{f}$$

equals the combination of failures f from a population size $n + f - 1$. Converting this to a binomial probability distribution, we have

$$\binom{n + f - 1}{f} q^f p^n$$

Returning to our previously derived formulas of success or failure $(1 - e^{-\lambda t})$ and $e^{-\lambda t}$, respectively, we can develop the equation for any $P_n(t)$ as[9]

$$P_n(t) = \binom{n - 1}{x - 1} e^{-x\lambda t}(1 - e^{-\lambda t})^{n-x}, \quad n \geq x$$

which is a negative binomial distribution.

Thus, from this analysis of a pure birth process, we find two useful formulas:

$$P_0(t) = e^{-\lambda t} \quad \text{(zero changes in the interval } t + \Delta t\text{)}$$

$$P_n(t) = \binom{n - 1}{x - 1} e^{-x\lambda t}(1 - e^{-\lambda t})^{n-x}$$

(probability of a population size n at time t)

The Pure Death Process—Homogeneous

A pure death process is the complement of the pure birth process. A birth is pure if $\mu_n = 0$ and a pure death process for all $\lambda_n = 0$. We had previously established the characteristics of a pure birth process, and knowing that the

---

[9] See R. B. Cooper, *Introduction to Queuing Theory*, Macmillan, New York, 1972.

BIRTH AND DEATH PROCESSES

pure death process is its converse, our death equation may be expressed as

$$P_0(t) = e^{-\mu t}$$

Here the time between deaths is expressed as a function of population size.[10]

Again we have the negative exponential distribution, this time written with respect to μ = death. If $P_0(t) = e^{-\mu t}$ is the probability for zero deaths in the interval $t + \Delta t$, then the probability for one death in the same interval is

$$(1 - e^{-\mu t})$$

A success and failure in our death equations are $(1 - e^{-\mu t})$ and $e^{-\mu t}$, respectively. These may be expressed once again by the binomial distribution. This time our set of deaths from a converse position is x and the subsets of x are n. If n is the population size and x the discrete number of births, then $\binom{n}{x}$ is the number of ways set n may be partitioned into subsets of x where x varies from zero through n. Intuitively and looking at the model conversely, the population set of deaths is x. Then $\binom{x}{n}$ where $0 \leq n \leq x$ represents the death population and the way n may be partitioned from set x.

We established previously that pure births iterate to a new population base on the negative binomial distribution. We also gave equations showing the correspondence of the binomial to the negative binomial. Based on this, we may write our converse birth equation as:

$$P_n(t) = \binom{x}{n} e^{-n\mu t}(1 - e^{-\mu t})^{x-n}$$

Pure Birth and Death Process—Homogeneous

Thus far we have examined pure birth processes and the corresponding pure death process. These both are unit step transition processes. When we place these two systems together in an input–output relationship, the population change will similarly expand by 1, decrease by 1, or stay the same. To increase population by one member during Δt was expressed as $\lambda \Delta t$, and the chance of dying during Δt is $\mu \Delta t$. If these equations are written with respect to current population size and we wish to assure their transition states,[11]

$P'_{i,i+1}(\Delta t)$ = the probability of starting in state i and ending in $i + 1$ in one step during Δt.

Birth Equation

$$P'_{i,i+1}(\Delta t) = \lambda_i x(t) \Delta t + 0(\Delta t)$$

---

[10] A complete treatment of birth–death processes may be found in E. Parzen, *Stochastic Processes*, Holden-Day, San Francisco, 1962, pp. 293–306.

[11] A concise treatment may be found in A. B. Clark and R. L. Disney, *Probability and Random Processes for Engineers and Scientists*, Wiley, New York, 1970.

BIRTH AND DEATH PROCESSES

Death Equation

$$P_{i,i-1}(\Delta t) = \mu_i x(t)\Delta t + 0(\Delta t)$$

$0(\Delta t)$ = the expression for more than one of these events.

Static Equation

$$P'_{i,i}(\Delta t) = 1 - (\lambda + \mu)x(t)\Delta t + 0(\Delta t)$$

Given we are in any population state, we may use these transition equations to determine:

The transition and state probabilities as functions of time.
Finding if the colony dies out—if not a regular chain.
The fixed vector listing the various probabilities as the matrix reaches a steady state—providing the chain is regular.
Mean death time.
The fraction of time there is no move from one state to another—zero birth.
The fraction of time that it grows by 1.
The fraction of time of zero deaths.
The mean birth time.

Let us consider the problem of the nailing machine described in the Introduction. Using the expression of λ and μ in a more convenient form, we can convert our previous expression to one usable in queuing theory—a special application of birth and death models. Later in our discussion we will use these same techniques to determine the chances of extinction. This will necessitate some change in our matrix of birth to deaths, still using this unit step process. If we were to change from this unit step rule and permit changes of 2 or more in the population during one step, then we would be dealing with the compound Poisson process. These conditions are explored in a later section.

General Birth Process—Intuitive and Mathematical

We previously established that the probability of a birth during Δt was $\lambda \Delta t$. This was written with respect to a given organism producing a new one. We further established that the whole population would produce a birth as $\lambda n \Delta t$. Thus the population size at $t + \Delta t$ was

$$P_n(t + \Delta t) = P_n(t)(1 - \lambda n \Delta t) + P_{n-1}(t)\lambda(n + 1)\Delta t$$

which leads to

$$P'_n(t) = \lambda(n - 1)P_{n-1}(t) - \lambda n P_n(t)$$

We can generalize this equation by assigning the probability of a birth during

BIRTH AND DEATH PROCESSES

Δt as $\lambda_n \Delta t$ where $\lambda_n = n\lambda$ and n is the population size at time t. In this pure birth process each population growth was $\lambda \Delta t$ and the probability that the whole population produced a birth was given as $\lambda n \Delta t$, with the restriction that population growth was in unit steps. From this special case we find the average rate of growth per individual is proportional to the population size. Going from the simple process to the general process, we let λ vary according to the previous population size. This is the average growth rate of a population size n. Thus we accelerate population growth. We still advance in unit steps, but with an increasing probabilistic birth rate. Thus, going from one population state to another in incremental steps changes from the pure state $\lambda \Delta t$ for each increment to $\lambda n \Delta t$. If we look at population growth according to the general theory, each population size would have its own λ_n and could be written as a functional equation.

Applying this to our unit step-growth processes, the transition from one state to another would enhance probabilistically as the previous population size expanded. Instead of a λ acting on a greater population, as we found in the pure linear process, the mean size λ_n is changing with each population change. With some modifications to our analogy, it would be similar to growth through a set rate of interest, with respect to a changing balance, versus growth through a changing rate of interest with each new balance. One changes at a constant rate, dependent on population size, while the other changes as a ratio to the entire population.

General Birth and Death Processes—Homogeneous

From our previous explanation of general birth processes, we may conclude that the chance of death during Δt is

$$\mu n \Delta t$$

In a birth and death model, the relationship of λ to μ determines the growth patterns. If $\lambda_n = 0$ as it iterates in unit steps to a new population n, it will have reached an absorbing state where any further growth was impossible, i.e., $P_n(t) = 0$. Let us set $\lambda_n < \mu_n$ with each λ and μ greater than zero. Now it is possible to determine the probability of each population size, $P_{n(t)}$, during the various growth steps of this birth and death model. As the ratio of λ_n to μ_n changes, the population could become boundless, without the restriction that $\lambda_n = 0$ for some $n \geq 1$.

Queuing theory is a special application of birth and death processes. When applied to business situations, we must be assured our waiting lines are stabilized and not boundless. A boundless situation would occur with an infinity of births over limited time. Also, the line size could become unmanageable with unfavorable birth to death ratios, i.e., $\lambda \doteq \mu$. With the limitation that deaths decay without birth input, we assume that our system

BIRTH AND DEATH PROCESSES

is now explosive and balanced by requiring that[12]

$$\lambda_n > 0; \quad n \geq a, \quad \text{when} \quad \sum_{n=a}^{\infty} \lambda_n^{-1} = \infty$$

and

$$\sum_{n=a}^{\infty} \frac{\mu_n \mu_{n-1} \cdots \mu_a}{\lambda_n \lambda_{n-1} \cdots \lambda_a} = \infty$$

Divergent Birth Processes—Homogeneous

Returning to our pure birth process, where the average rate of growth is proportional to the population size, consider the deterministic process. Here each unit increase equals $\lambda n \Delta t$ for each time Δt. Given that $P_n(t) \geq 0$, we would expect $\sum P_n(t) = 1$. But if we consider our population as a continuous variable, the whole population of size n would increase incrementally as $\lambda n(n) \Delta t$. This equals a condition where the rate of growth increases faster than the population size.[13]

Given

$$\lambda n(n) \Delta t = \lambda n^2 \Delta t$$

$$dn/dt = \lambda n^2$$

Initializing this process at $n(0) = i$:

$$n(t) = \frac{i}{1 - \lambda it} \ .$$

This implies an infinite growth in a finite time. We previously described this as a population explosion, therefore

$$\sum P_n(t) < 1$$

Introduction to Nonhomogeneous Processes

The nonhomogeneous birth and death processes are more complex in theory and usually demand a higher level mathematical treatment. We had studied previously that birth and death processes are homogeneous if n, $\lambda_n(t)$, and $\mu_n(t)$ do not depend on time t.

Thus we had considered birth and deaths as functions of population size only. But the nonhomogeneous processes are time dependent. To complete our

---

[12] Adapted from the complete study in N. T. J. Bailey, *The Elements of Stochastic Processes*, Wiley, New York, 1964.
[13] An excellent analysis is found in W. Feller, *An Introduction to Probability Theory and Its Applications*, Wiley, New York, 1968.

BIRTH AND DEATH PROCESSES

analysis, therefore, we examine birth and death rates as functions of time. By rewriting the pure birth and death equations in the sections entitled Pure Death Processes—Mathematical, The Pure Death Process—Homogeneous, and Pure Birth and Death Process—Homogeneous with respect to time, we can develop differential equations for the transition probability functions. The previous homogeneous equations for births

$$P_n(t) = \binom{n-1}{x-1} e^{-x\lambda t}(1 - e^{-\lambda t})^{n-x}, \qquad n \geq x,$$

is the probability of advancing from one state to another based on population size only. When we introduce the concept of time dependency, this formula develops somewhat differently.

Pure Birth Processes—Nonhomogeneous[14]

Using Kolmogorov differential equations, we can develop the transition probability function for nonhomogeneous birth and death processes. The partial differential equations for the transition generating function is expressed as

$$\Psi_{j,s}(z,t) = \sum_{k=0}^{\infty} z^k p_{j,k}(s,t), \qquad \text{for initial state } j \text{ times } s < t \text{ and } |z| \leq 1$$

and by interaction develops into the general form birth and death equation

$$\frac{\partial}{\partial t}\Psi_{j,s}(z,t) = \frac{\partial}{\partial z}\Psi_{j,s}(z,t)\{(z-1)[z\lambda(t) - \mu(t)]\}$$

Given $\mu = 0$, the general form equation becomes the birth equation

$$\frac{\partial}{\partial t}\Psi_{j,s}(z,t) = \frac{\partial}{\partial z}\Psi_{j,s}(z,t)\{(z-1)z\lambda(t)\}$$

which yields by successive steps the parameter p of the probability generating function of a geometric distribution

$$p = e^{-\{p(t) - p(s)\}}$$

which may be generalized further into the equation

$$P_n(s,t) = \binom{n-1}{x-1} p^x (1-p)^{n-x}, \qquad n \geq x.$$

This is the formula used to describe the process for going from the previous population $n - 1$ to state n from the earlier time s to the later time t. We now have established the formula to find any population size with respect to time based on births only.

---

[14] These sections are excerpts from the complete treatment of birth and death processes by N. T. J. Bailey, *The Elements of Stochastic Processes,* Wiley, New York, 1964, and E. Parzen, *Stochastic Processes,* Holden-Day, San Francisco, 1962.

BIRTH AND DEATH PROCESSES

Pure Birth and Death Processes—Nonhomogeneous

We had examined previously that populations may increase, decrease, or remain stable. The nonhomogeneous formulas for the pure birth and death process expressed in the preceding section will let us examine the population size for any given state. From this expression, mathematicians have established the transition generating function to be

$$\Psi_{1,0}(z,t) = 1 + \left\{ \frac{1}{z-1} e^{pt} - \int_0^t \lambda(\tau) e^{p(\tau)} d\tau \right\}^{-1}$$

When we set $z = 0$, this expresses the probability that the population has died out at time t.

By expanding these formulas we may write a general form equation to express the probabilities of any individual states.

$$P_n(t) = \sum_{j=0}^{\min(a,n)} \binom{a}{j} \binom{a+n-j-1}{a-1} \alpha^{a-j} \beta^{n-j} (1 - \alpha - \beta)^j$$

$$P_0(t) = \alpha^a$$

and may also write formulas yielding the probabilities of extinction:

$$\lim_{t \to \infty} \int_0^t \mu(\tau) e^{p(t)} d\tau = \infty$$

QUEUING THEORY

Introduction—Intuitive

Queuing theory is a special study in birth and death processes. These studies are particularly applicable to real life models. Through studies in birth and death processes, mathematicians have developed sets of formulas applicable to a wide spectrum of real world situations. Queuing theory is often called waiting line theory. Businesses are oftentimes concerned with their waiting line of customers. Consider the waiting line at supermarkets where too long a line may deter sales or cause customers to go elsewhere. If the lines are too short, this may indicate to the arriving customer that others are not shopping there because of poor quality, high prices, or other deterring factors. Also consider lines of planes waiting at the airport, waiting lines at the emergency room, and queues of cars on various highway systems. The number of situations involving waiting lines seems boundless as we extend our abstractions to the real world models. Waiting is part of life:[15]

Numerous reasons caused man to colonize—a venture that would have

---

[15] J. A. Panico, *Queuing Theory—A Study of Waiting Lines for Business, Economics, and Science*, Prentice-Hall, Englewood Cliffs, New Jersey, 1969, p. 2.

been unsuccessful if he had not learned tolerance, especially that of waiting for others. As world population grew, so did man's colonies grow into urban communities of various sizes. His life became ordered because he had to rely on the services of others to satisfy his demands. Thus service from others became a critical function of survival. If man had followed a philosophy of "immediate service on demand," the result would have been an uneconomical utilization of his total effort and his problems would have been insurmountable. Waiting, therefore, became part of life.

Let us consider an example: The Ohio River has numerous dams to assure navigation throughout the year. It is less costly to transport materials by boat, but the time from start to destination is much longer. A boat entering the dam's servicing system may get immediate passage through the locks or must wait for others. One boat may be in process and a few others waiting. If you must wait your turn, the products you carry may deteriorate at a loss to the customer. Also consider that your boat is inactive. This causes you, the boat owner, to lose time and your opportunity to service others. This leads to decreased profits. By extending these possibilities, we could hypothesize many other complications causing you or the customer to incur a loss. In the model of our dam, this process compounds if we consider the set of all dams starting at the Gulf of Mexico, up the Mississippi River, and up the Ohio River to the destination at Pittsburgh, Pennsylvania. If we could control the input to our system, called births, or change the output of the system, called deaths, we could conceivably improve the processing time to our advantage.

Queuing theory has its base in the study of birth and death processes where the symbol λ means births and the symbol μ means deaths. In a broader connotation, λ means the average arrivals of elements to the system and μ means average service time. If we use the hospital obstetrical department as an example, λ equals the average number of patients arriving per day and μ equals the average number of days to service each arrival. Once again we must be cognizant of the fact that we are working with average times which signify that the supplying universe of elements form a distribution. This fact, established earlier, accounts for a waiting line forming even when $\lambda/\mu < 1$.

The distributions normally associated with the mathematical formulas of queuing theory are Poisson, exponential, and Erlang. Most formulas are based on Poisson arrivals and exponentional service. Since there is a correspondence between the Poisson, exponential, binomial, and normal distributions, it is also possible to extend the use of the formulas predicated on these distributions. Care should be exercised, however, whenever we use queuing formulas outside the distributions used in the derivation of the formulas.

Using the study of birth and death processes as they apply to queuing theory, we can mathematically predict our individual waiting line problems or predict these problems in tandem with one another. A tandem situation occurs when the output of one queuing system is the input to another. Consider the case of county-wide immunization of children: First you must wait in line to

[374]
BIRTH AND DEATH PROCESSES

register, after registration you must wait in line for your immunization pill, and after that, you must wait in line for cross reference and verification purposes. The arrival rate for the first line is λ, where λ equals the number of patients arriving per hour. The servicing rate is μ. This is the average time required for registration. Once registration is completed you go on to the next station. Thus the output of the first station, μ, is the input λ of the second station.

Queuing theory studies help us determine if more servicing systems will relieve our waiting line. We use this study at banking institutions to determine if more servicing systems, tellers, will relieve our waiting line problem. We can expand, however, only on the basis of economical justification studies coupled with the pure study of the waiting line size and the time each customer must wait.

The mathematical study of waiting lines is restricted to certain distributions and priorities. Change these conditions and the equations lead to complex formulas. This is impractical for those wishing to apply the theory. Also, there is the additional problem of defining the supplying universe or output universe. Furthermore, we may encounter complications in establishing a predictable criterion for either. Some empirical distributions are readily definable and correspond with known distributions. Many others are not.

We surmount these problems by restricting the majority of our equation to Poisson exponential models. Within these criteria the formulas may be used—readily. Also, their use may be extended to other distributions if we establish a correspondence of one distribution to either of our two restricting conditions. In the event we cannot assign known distributions to the empirical data, or in the event the empirical data yields a known distribution that does not correspond to the Poisson exponential model, our process should be examined through techniques of simulation.

Simulation is a technique that actually duplicates real world situations. We assign numbers or symbols to describe an event abstractly. As a comparison, consider the way we determine how many times a shovel handle could be flexed before breaking. We design a machine to exert 50 lb of force on the shovel handle 4 ft from the socket in the blade. The machine would bend the handle 9 in. downward while the shovel blade was held firm in a fixture. This was an attempt to duplicate the real world conditions. This machine operated day and night with men in attendance to record when the shovel broke, the type of wood, and all other pertinent information. We could change the weight to exert 75 lb of force, change the distance from the socket, change the distance flexed, and change many other conditions to gain knowledge about our shovel. We wished to satisfy our customers and provide them a quality product. A whole department of men and considerable space was required for this destructive testing procedure. Over the years, we gathered numerous data pertaining to these experiments. When the computer was introduced to our company, we were able to take the observed historical data, find the parameters governing these tests, assign symbols to the various conditions, change sequences and rhythms, and thereby create the test abstractly. In a few minutes we simulated a whole department's years of work, reduced the labor

BIRTH AND DEATH PROCESSES

force, eliminated machines, and saved the space. Thus we had duplicated abstractly the real world model.

In the study of birth and death models, our accomplishments are greater. Queuing theory, as an extension of birth and death studies, is particularly receptive to these types of analytical studies. Given the supplying distribution (births) and the output distribution (deaths), we may run off years of experiments in a few minutes. One unique feature of queuing theory versus birth and death processes can be found in the fact that we control more of the input–output data than we do in life equations. These equations, life equations, belong to nature; queuing theory equations belong more to man.

Queuing theory simulation techniques are used extensively to design conveyor assembly lines. With this technique we can predict the number of people or machines at each given station and the length of the line. Rather than make mistakes after the fact, we can minimize them before the fact by observing the developments through simulation.

There are many ways to describe the various queuing systems. Mathematicians classify one way, engineers another, and management science another. To simplify our understanding we will classify them intuitively, as

One Line—One Server
One Line—Multiple Server

These two apply both to infinite and finite systems. Another classification is

Multiple Line—Multiple Server

which is best solved through simulation techniques.

One Line—One Server may be described as the single line of cars waiting for service at a car wash.

One Line—Multiple Server is represented by the single line of people waiting their turn for a haircut in a shop of four chairs with no barber perference permitted.

Multiple Line—Multiple Server is represented by three lines of people queue up in front of three separate elevators. Those on the periphery change to different lines as they get smaller.

There are many other queuing systems and we will example a few of them in detail below. The idea we wish to establish, at this point, is that the study of birth and death processes has enabled us to solve problems related to man's everyday problems. Through queuing theory we are able to find the items in Figure 3.

All of these concepts, with respect to line size, time in line, and other soluble factors, are used extensively by business today (Figs. 4 and 5). Here is a theory being put to practical use—everyday. It was derived from the theory of birth and death processes. Thus, what we considered highly theoretical yesterday is applicable today—to the betterment of mankind and to the institutions that service us.

BIRTH AND DEATH PROCESSES

μ = Mean service rate—average number serviced in one unit of time (per channel).
λ = Mean arrival rate—average number arriving in one unit of time.
λ/μ = Clearing ratio (if $\mu > \lambda$, then capacity to serve is greater than demand for service). Often called the traffic intensity ratio.
n = Number of units in the system (waiting or being serviced).
P or Pr = Probability notation.
$P_0(t)$ = Probability of "zero" units in the system at time t. An input will receive immediate service.
$P_3(t)$ = Probability of "three" units in the system at time t. An input must wait for service until these three have been cleared.
$P_n(t)$ = Probability of n units in the system at time t designated as P_n for a finite universe and $P_n(t)$ for an infinite universe.
P_m = Probability of m elements in service or demanding service.
w = Length of waiting line not including those being serviced.
E = Expected value $\sum_{i=0} P_i N_i$
E_w = Expected (average) length of waiting line.
E_0 = Expected number that have not departed a finite universe for service.
E_n = Expected number being serviced plus waiting.
E_s = Expected number being serviced.
E_t = Expected time in line (average time the arriving element must wait before being serviced).
E_e = Expected utilization of s.
E_Ψ = Expected time in system (E_t plus the average time required for service).
m = Total universe supplying input to the system. The universe is either infinite or finite. A finite universe is usually a small countable set of machines, machinists, objects, etc. Each universe has its own distinct formulas. Infinite formulas are used when the arrivals come from an infinite source or a large finite population.
s = Number of servers ... which equals one in single line—single server cases, and more than one in single line—multiple server cases.
$m\lambda$ = Maximum expected arrivals in a unit time when the universe is finite, none having departed for service (usually noted at λ).
$(m - n)\lambda$ = Maximum expected arrivals when n units are either in line or awaiting service. This shows a dependency relationship which is characteristic of a finite set $[(m - n)\lambda = \lambda_n]$.

Fig. 3. Glossary of general terms that can be found by queuing theory. (J. A. Panico, *Queuing Theory—A Study of Waiting Lines for Business, Economics, and Science,* Prentice-Hall, Englewood Cliffs, New Jersey, 1969, pp. 50–51.)

BIRTH AND DEATH PROCESSES

One Line—One Server (Infinite Population)
General Formulas

1. $P_0(t) = 1 - \dfrac{\lambda}{\mu} = Pr \left\{\begin{array}{l}\text{Zero units in the system when the rate of arrival } \lambda \\ \text{and the service } \mu \text{ are given.}\end{array}\right\}$

2. $P_n(t) = \left(\dfrac{\lambda}{\mu}\right)^n P_0(t) = \left(\dfrac{\lambda}{\mu}\right)^n \left(1 - \dfrac{\lambda}{\mu}\right) = Pr \left\{\begin{array}{l}n \text{ units in queue plus being} \\ \text{serviced.}\end{array}\right\}$

3. $E_n = \dfrac{\lambda}{\mu - \lambda} =$ Expected number being serviced plus waiting.

4. $E_w = \dfrac{\lambda^2}{\mu(\mu - \lambda)} = \begin{array}{l}\text{Expected number in queue—(length of waiting line not} \\ \text{including those being serviced).}\end{array}$

5. $E_t = \dfrac{E_w}{\lambda} = \dfrac{\lambda}{\mu(\mu - \lambda)} =$ Expected waiting time in line.

6. $E_\Psi = E_t + \dfrac{1}{\mu} = \dfrac{1}{\mu - \lambda} =$ Expected waiting time in system.

7. $P(N > n) = \left(\dfrac{\lambda}{\mu}\right)^{n+1} = \begin{array}{l}Pr \text{ (The number in the waiting line plus the} \\ \text{number being serviced is greater than } n.)\end{array}$

Restrictions: (a) First Come–First Served Discipline.

(b) $\dfrac{\lambda}{S\mu} < 1$, often called the Traffic Intensity or Clearing Ratio. This restriction must hold, otherwise $P_n(t)$ is not independent of (t).

One Line—One Server (Finite Population)
General Formulas

1. $P_n = \dbinom{m}{n}\left(\dfrac{\lambda}{\mu}\right)^n P_0$ for $0 \leq n \leq S$

2. $P_n = \dfrac{m!}{(m - n)!}\left(\dfrac{\lambda}{\mu}\right)^n P_0$ for $S \leq n \leq m$

3. $\dfrac{P_n}{P_0} = \dfrac{m}{(m - n)!}\left(\dfrac{\lambda}{\mu}\right)^n$

4. $P_0 = \dfrac{1}{\sum\limits_{n=0}^{m} \dfrac{P_n}{P_0}}$

5. $E_w = m - \dfrac{\lambda + \mu}{\lambda}(1 - P_0)$

6. $E_t = \dfrac{1}{\mu(1 - P_0)}(E_w) = \dfrac{1}{\mu}\left(\dfrac{m}{1 - P_0} - \dfrac{\lambda + \mu}{\lambda}\right)$

7. $E_n = E_w + (1 - P_0) = m - \dfrac{\mu}{\lambda}(1 - P_0)$

8. $E_\Psi = E_t + \dfrac{1}{\mu} = \dfrac{1}{\mu}\left(\dfrac{m}{1 - P_0} - \dfrac{\lambda + \mu}{\lambda} + 1\right)$

Restrictions: (a) First Come–First Served Discipline.

(b) $\dfrac{\lambda}{\mu} < 1$.

Fig. 4. One line–one server equations. (J. A. Panico, *Queuing Theory—A Study of Waiting Lines for Business, Economics, and Science,* Prentice-Hall, Englewood Cliffs, New Jersey, 1969, pp. 53–67.)

BIRTH AND DEATH PROCESSES

One Line—Multiple Server (Infinite Population)
General Formulas

1. $P_0(t) = \left[\left\{\sum_{n=0}^{S-1} \frac{1}{n!}\left(\frac{\lambda}{\mu}\right)^n\right\} + \left\{\frac{1}{S!}\left(\frac{\lambda}{\mu}\right)^S\left(\frac{S\mu}{S\mu - \lambda}\right)\right\}\right]^{-1}$

2. $P_n(t) = \frac{1}{n!}\left(\frac{\lambda}{\mu}\right)^n P_0(t)$ for $n < S$

3. $P_n(t) = \frac{1}{S! \cdot S^{n-S}}\left(\frac{\lambda}{\mu}\right)^n P_0(t)$ for $n \geq S$

4. $E_w = \frac{\lambda\mu\left(\frac{\lambda}{\mu}\right)^S}{(S-1)!(S\mu - \lambda)^2} P_0(t)$

5. $E_t = \frac{\mu\left(\frac{\lambda}{\mu}\right)^S}{(S-1)!(S\mu - \lambda)^2} P_0(t) = \frac{E_w}{\lambda}$

6. $E_n = \frac{\lambda\mu\left(\frac{\lambda}{\mu}\right)^S}{(S-1)!(S\mu - \lambda)^2} P_0(t) + \frac{\lambda}{\mu} = E_w + \frac{\lambda}{\mu}$

7. $E_\Psi = \frac{\mu\left(\frac{\lambda}{\mu}\right)^S}{(S-1)!(S\mu - \lambda)^2} P_0(t) + \frac{1}{\mu} = E_t + \frac{1}{\mu}$

Restrictions: (a) First Come–First Served Discipline.
(b) $P = \frac{\lambda}{S\mu} < 1$ or $\frac{\lambda}{\mu} < S$.

One Line—Multiple Server (Finite Population)
General Formulas

1. $P_n = \binom{m}{n}\left(\frac{\lambda}{\mu}\right)^n P_0$ for $0 \leq n \leq S$

2. $P_n = \frac{m!}{(m-n)!S!S^{n-S}}\left(\frac{\lambda}{\mu}\right)^n P_0$ $S \leq n \leq m$

In a multiple server model, $S > 1$, and either formula one or two holds, based on the restrictions imposed. When $S \geq n$, all inputs to the system are receiving service and there will be zero waiting lines.

3. $E_w = \sum_{n=S+1}^{m}(n - S)P_n = P_{S+1} + 2P_{S+2} + 3P_{S+3} + \cdots + (m - S)P_m$

4. $E_n = \sum_{n=0}^{m} nP_n$ where $E_w \subset E_n$

5. The expected machines in operation is given by:

$$E_0 = m - \sum_{n=0}^{m} nP_n = m - E_n$$

(which is simply the total universe minus the expected value of the machines in queue or being serviced).

6. The expected number of operators being utilized equals:

$$E_S = E_n - E_w$$

7. $E_t = \dfrac{E_w}{\mu(E_S)} = \dfrac{1}{\mu(E_S)} \sum_{n=S+1}^{m} (n - S)P_n$

8. $E_\psi = E_t + \dfrac{1}{\mu}$

The fraction or expected percent of a designated unit time that one operator is utilized equals:

$$E_e = \dfrac{1}{S}(E_n - E_w)$$

This fraction may also be shown as:

$$E_e = \sum_{n=S+1}^{m} P_n + \dfrac{1}{S}\sum_{n=0}^{S} nP_n$$

Restriction: (a) First Come–First Served Discipline.
(b) $\dfrac{\lambda}{S\mu} < 1$.

Fig. 5. One line–multiple server equations. (J. A. Panico, *Queuing Theory—A Study of Waiting Lines for Business, Economics, and Science*, Prentice-Hall, Englewood Cliffs, New Jersey, 1969, pp. 53–67.)

Queuing Theory—Mathematical[16]

In the pure birth process we established

$$P_0(t) = e^{-\lambda t}$$

Using queuing theory terms, this means "the probability of zero elements born to the system in time t."

From elementary exponential theory $e^{-\lambda t}e^{\lambda t} = 1$. Substituting $x =$ for $\lambda(t)$, we have $e^{-x}e^x = 1$. The series

$$e^x = \left(1 + x + \dfrac{x^2}{2!} + \dfrac{x^3}{3!} + \cdots + \dfrac{x^n e^{-x}}{n!}\right)$$

Thus

$$e^{-x}\left(1 + x + \dfrac{x^2}{2!} + \dfrac{x^3}{3!} + \cdots + \dfrac{x^n}{n!}\right) = 1$$

and

$$\left(e^{-x} + xe^{-x} + \dfrac{x^2 e^{-x}}{2!} + \dfrac{x^3 e^{-x}}{3!} + \cdots + \dfrac{x^n e^{-x}}{n!}\right) = 1$$

[16] Adapted from J. A. Panico, *Queueing Theory—A Study of Waiting Lines for Business, Economics, and Science*, Prentice-Hall, Englewood Cliffs, New Jersey, 1969, pp. 73–80.

BIRTH AND DEATH PROCESSES

Each term of this distribution describes the probability of a specific event:

$$P_0(t) = e^{-x}$$
$$P_1(t) = xe^{-x}$$

and

$$P_2(t) = \frac{x^2 e^{-x}}{2!}$$

Substituting $x = \lambda t$ back into this original equation, we find that the nth term of our expansion equals

$$P_n(t) = \frac{(\lambda t)^n e^{-\lambda t}}{n!}$$

This expression may be used to find any probability by substituting values into the equation.

One Line–One Server (Infinite Model)—Mathematical[17]

What is the probability of exactly one unit entering the system and requesting service during the interval Δt? The Poisson formula developed earlier will permit us to relate the arrivals to the Poisson in the following manner

$$P_n(\Delta t) = \frac{(\lambda \Delta t)^n e^{-\lambda \Delta t}}{n!} \tag{1}$$

for $n = 1$

$$P_1(\Delta t) = (\lambda \Delta t)(e^{-\lambda \Delta t}) \tag{2}$$

When Δt becomes very small (approaches zero), $e^{-\lambda \Delta t}$ approaches 1, as can be seen from the graph of the function. Therefore

$$P_1(\Delta t) = \lambda \Delta t \tag{3}$$

In order to simplify the derivation, we will make the assumption that the probability of more than one arrival or service requirement during Δt is so small that we can ignore this quantity. With this in mind, we can conclude that the probability of no units entering the system during Δt is $1 - \lambda \Delta t$. Similarly, the probability that no unit requires service during Δt is $1 - \mu \Delta t$.

With this information it is possible to write the probability of n units being in the system at time $t + \Delta t$.

$$P_n(t + \Delta t) = [P_n(t)(1 - \lambda \Delta t)(1 - \mu \Delta t)] + [P_{n+1}(t)(1 - \lambda \Delta t)(\mu \Delta t)] \\ + [P_{n-1}(t)(\lambda \Delta t)(1 - \mu \Delta t)] + [P_n(t)(\lambda \Delta t)(\mu \Delta t)] \tag{4}$$

[17] Adapted from J. A. Panico, *Queuing Theory—A Study of Waiting Lines for Business, Economics, and Science,* Prentice-Hall, Englewood Cliffs, New Jersey, 1969, pp. 73–80.

BIRTH AND DEATH PROCESSES

Since we are assuming the probability of more than one arrival or service during Δt to be zero, these equations describe all possible situations which may occur. The first bracket is the probability of n units in the system at time t, multiplied by the probability of no arrivals during Δt multiplied by the probability of no servicing during Δt. The second is the probability of $n + 1$ units in the system at time t multiplied by the probability of no units entering the system during Δt, multiplied by the probability of one unit being serviced during Δt. The other brackets can be reasoned similarly.

Expanding and reorganizing Eq. (4):

$$P_n(t + \Delta t) = P_n(t)[1 - \lambda \Delta t - \mu \Delta t + 2\mu\lambda(\Delta t)^2] \\ + P_{n+1}(t)]\mu\Delta t - \mu\lambda(\Delta t)^2] + P_{n-1}(t)[\lambda \Delta t - \mu\lambda(\Delta t)^2] \quad (5)$$

If we subtract $P_n(t)$ from both sides and divide by Δt, we obtain

$$\frac{P_n(t + \Delta t) - P_n(t)}{\Delta t} = \mu P_{n+1}(t) - (\lambda + \mu)P_n(t) + \lambda P_{n-1}(t) \\ + \mu\lambda\Delta t[-P_{n+1}(t) + 2P_n(t) - P_{n-1}(t)] \quad (6)$$

As Δt becomes closer and closer to zero, the last term of Eq. (6) approaches zero. Similarly, as Δt approaches zero or becomes smaller and smaller, $P_n(t)$ and $P_n(t + \Delta t)$ will be equal, i.e., the probability of n arrivals in $P_n(t)$ is equal to the probability of n arrivals in $P_n(t + \Delta t)$. Therefore $P_n(t) - P_n(t + \Delta t) = 0$, thus

$$\mu P_{n+1}(t) - (\lambda + \mu)P_n(t) + \lambda P_{n-1}(t) = 0 \quad (7)$$

Let us digress slightly now and find the probability of zero arrivals during $t + \Delta t$, noting that $\lambda P_{-1}(t)$ is dropped because negative arrivals are impossible.

Using Eq. (7) and setting $n = 0$, we obtain

$$\mu P_1(t) - (\lambda + \mu)P_0(t) = 0 \quad (8)$$
$$\mu P_1(t) - \lambda P_0(t) - \mu P_0(t) = 0$$

However, $\mu P_0(t) = 0$ since an item cannot be serviced if there are zero items in service. Therefore

$$\mu P_1(t) - \lambda P_0(t) = 0$$
$$P_1(t) = \left(\frac{\lambda}{\mu}\right)P_0(t) \quad (9)$$

Similarly, setting $n = 1$, we obtain

$$\mu P_2(t) - (\lambda + \mu)P_1(t) + \lambda P_0(t) = 0$$
$$\mu P_2(t) = (\lambda + \mu)\left(\frac{\lambda}{\mu}\right)P_0(t) - \lambda P_0(t)$$
$$P_2(t) = \left[(\lambda + \mu)\left(\frac{\lambda}{\mu}\right)\left(\frac{1}{\mu}\right) - \left(\frac{\lambda}{\mu}\right)\right]P_0(t) \quad (10)$$
$$P_2(t) = \left(\frac{\lambda^2 + \lambda\mu - \lambda\mu}{\mu^2}\right)P_0(t)$$
$$P_2(t) = \left(\frac{\lambda^2}{\mu^2}\right)P_0(t) = \left(\frac{\lambda}{\mu}\right)^2 P_0(t)$$

BIRTH AND DEATH PROCESSES

If we set $n = 2$, we obtain

$$P_3(t) = \left(\frac{\lambda}{\mu}\right)^3 P_0(t) \tag{11}$$

Continuing this procedure and using intuitive logic, we find that

$$P_n(t) = \left(\frac{\lambda}{\mu}\right)^n P_0(t) \tag{12}$$

We know from previous discussion that the sum of all terms in a probability distribution equals 1, i.e.

$$\sum_{n=0}^{\infty} P_n(t) = 1 \tag{13}$$

$$P_0(t) + P_0(t)\left(\frac{\lambda}{\mu}\right) + P_0(t)\left(\frac{\lambda}{\mu}\right)^2 + P_0(t)\left(\frac{\lambda}{\mu}\right)^3 + \cdots + P_0(t)\left(\frac{\lambda}{\mu}\right)^n + \cdots = 1 \tag{14}$$

$$P_0(t)\left[1 + \left(\frac{\lambda}{\mu}\right) + \left(\frac{\lambda}{\mu}\right)^2 + \cdots + \left(\frac{\lambda}{\mu}\right)^n + \cdots\right] = 1$$

This has now taken the form of a geometric progression of the following form:

$$1 + y + y^2 + y^3 + y^4 + \cdots + y^n + \cdots = \frac{1}{1 - y} \tag{15}$$

By letting $y = (\lambda/\mu)$, Eq. (15) can be rewritten as $1/(1 - \lambda/\mu)$. Thus Eq. (14) can also be re-expressed as

$$P_0(t) = \frac{1}{1 - \left(\frac{\lambda}{\mu}\right)} = 1 \tag{16}$$

and by dividing both sides of the equation by $1/(1 - \lambda/\mu)$:

$$P_0(t) = 1 - \frac{\lambda}{\mu} = \frac{\mu - \lambda}{\mu} \tag{17}$$

This will give the probability of no units in the system when given the rate of arrival λ and the rate of service μ.

From Eq. (12) we can compute the probability of $P_n(t)$ in terms of λ and μ by substitution:

$$P_n(t) = \left(\frac{\lambda}{\mu}\right)^n P_0(t) = \left(\frac{\lambda}{\mu}\right)^n \left(1 - \frac{\lambda}{\mu}\right) \tag{18}$$

Expected value is a summations series defined as: (the probability of N_1 occurring) times (the value of N_1) or $[P_r(N_1)][N_1]$, plus (the probability of N_2 occurring) times (the value of N_2), etc. Algebraically, this can be written as

$$E(N) = P_1 N_1 + P_2 N_2 + P_3 N_3 + \cdots = \sum_{i=0}^{\infty} P_i N_i \tag{19}$$

BIRTH AND DEATH PROCESSES

Applying this to our queuing model, we can determine the expected number of units in the system, i.e., the expected number in the waiting line and being serviced.

$$E_{(n)} = \sum_{n=0}^{\infty} P_n(t)(n) = \sum_{n=0}^{\infty} \left(1 - \frac{\lambda}{\mu}\right)\left(\frac{\lambda}{\mu}\right)^n (n)$$

By letting $(\lambda/\mu) = \rho$, the series now becomes

$$E_{(n)} = \sum_{n=0}^{\infty} n(1 - \rho)(\rho)^n = (1 - \rho)(\rho + 2\rho^2 + 3\rho^3 + \cdots)$$

$$E_{(n)} = (1 - \rho)(\rho) \sum_{n=0}^{\infty} n\rho^{n-1}$$

Since

$$\sum_{K=0}^{\infty} K b^{K-1} = \frac{1}{(1 - b)^2}$$

then

$$E_{(n)} = (1 - \rho)(\rho) \frac{1}{(1 - \rho)^2} = \frac{1}{1 - \rho}, \quad \text{for } \rho < 1 \qquad (20)$$

E_n is defined as the expected number in the waiting line and being serviced. E_w is defined as the expected number in the waiting line only. Since only one unit can be in the system for service, $E_n > E_w$.

$$E_n = \sum_{n=0}^{\infty} n P_n(t) \quad \text{and} \quad E_w = \sum_{n=2}^{\infty} (n - 1) P_n(t)$$

By the definition of these two terms,

$$E_w \subset E_n \quad \text{or} \quad E_w \to E_n$$

thus

$$E_n - E_w = [P_1(t) + 2P_2(t) + 3P_3(t) + 4P_4(t) + \cdots] - [P_2(t) + 2P_3(t) + 3P_4(t) + \cdots] = [P_1(t) + P_2(t) + P_3(t) + P_4(t) + \cdots] = [1 - P_0(t)]$$

therefore

$$E_n - E_w = 1 - P_0(t) \quad \text{or} \quad E_w = E_n - (1 - P_0(t))$$

$$E_w = \frac{\lambda}{\mu - \lambda} - (1 - P_0(t)) \qquad (21)$$

$$= \frac{\lambda}{\mu - \lambda} - \left(1 - 1 + \frac{\lambda}{\mu}\right) = \frac{\lambda^2}{\mu(\mu - \lambda)}$$

$(E_n - E_w)$ may also be described as the expected number being serviced, thus $E_s = (1 - P_0(t)) = (\lambda/\mu)$.

BIRTH AND DEATH PROCESSES

If μ represents the average number of services available in on time period, it is reasonable to assume that not all of these available services will be utilized, owing to the restriction that $(\lambda/\mu) < 1$. The average number of services in one time period, therefore, is dictated by λ, the average number of arrivals. So λ equals the average of arrivals per unit of time, but it also equals the average number of services per unit time. The system is limited to service only those which arrive. Unused services cannot be inventoried. If $E_S = [1 - P_0(t)]$ = the expected number being serviced, and μ = the average capacity to serve in a unit time, then $\mu[1 - P_0(t)]$ = the average number serviced in a unit time. Intuitively, the algebraic identity of $\mu[1 - P_0(t)] = \lambda$ is thus proved. From this discussion the expected waiting time in line E_t may be developed.

A new arrival to the system expects to find a fine size of E_w before him; therefore the time he must wait before service is the time required for clearing E_w. Thus

$$\frac{E_w}{\mu}[1 - P_0(t)] = \frac{E_w}{\lambda}$$

is the expected line size divided by the average number serviced in a unit time, which equals E_t, the expected time in the system.

$$E_t = \frac{E_w}{\lambda} = \frac{\lambda^2}{\mu(\mu - \lambda)}\left(\frac{1}{\lambda}\right) = \frac{\lambda}{\mu(\mu - \lambda)} \tag{22}$$

Note that λ and $\mu(1 - P_0(t))$ can be interchanged, but that this applies only to independent arrivals. In the case of finite queues where arrivals are not independent, $(E_w/\mu)(1 - P_0)$ is the proper expression for E_t.

If an element waits E_t before service, then the time in service is $1/\mu$. For example $\mu = 20$ services per hour; the service time for this one element is then $\frac{1}{20}$ hr. From this discussion it follows that the expected time an element spends in the system is $E_w + (1/\mu)$.

Therefore

$$E_\Psi = E_w + \frac{1}{\mu} = \frac{1}{\mu - \lambda} \tag{23}$$

PRACTICAL EXAMPLES

Example 1. Marketing Model.[18] Determination of Brand Share[19]

For an elementary model of births and deaths of customers in a finite model, assume that two products x and y command a finite market. From elementary marketing theory we know that a market saturates because of price, socioeconomic characteristics of customer, geographical limitations of area,

---

[18] See D. W. Miller and M. K. Starr, *Executive Decisions and Operations Research,* Prentice-Hall, Englewood Cliffs, New Jersey, 1963, pp. 171–244, for a more comprehensive discussion of marketing models.

[19] Adapted from J. A. Panico, *Queuing Theory—A Study of Waiting Lines for Business, Economics, and Science,* Prentice-Hall, Englewood Cliffs, New Jersey, 1969, pp. 114–117.

BIRTH AND DEATH PROCESSES

etc. Saturation may refer to two wholesale supply houses which competitively sell a specific item with limited demand.

Consider that farmers within a certain geographical area are serviced by one cooperative that sells two bulk tank cleaners—sanitizing agents. One contains iodine and the other chlorine. The market is limited by the number of dairy farms in the cooperative and the use of the state-approved sanitizers. Any loss of an iodine-user will result in a chlorine-user and vice versa. Thus the market is for most purposes bound.

Assume the market saturates at 16 customers. From this it may be concluded that

x = Iodine-user
B_x = Births of new customers to iodine—death to a chlorine customer
y = Chlorine-user
B_y = Birth of new customers to chlorine—death to an iodine customer
$x \rightarrow y$ = x goes to y = a user of iodine switches brands and is now using chlorine

If a market study shows the switching-characteristics to be $x \rightarrow y = \frac{1}{3}$ (one to three) = for every iodine customer who switches to chlorine, three chlorine customers switch to iodine, it follows that $y \rightarrow x$ = (3 to 1) = for every three who switch to iodine one switches back to chlorine. This relationship holds because the market is finite and farmers must use one of these two state-approved products. This problem may be considered as a finite queuing problem, with respect to chlorine, where the arrivals $\lambda_c = 1$, and $\mu_c = 3$. If this problem had been worked with respect to iodine, then $\lambda_I/\mu_I > 1$, thus

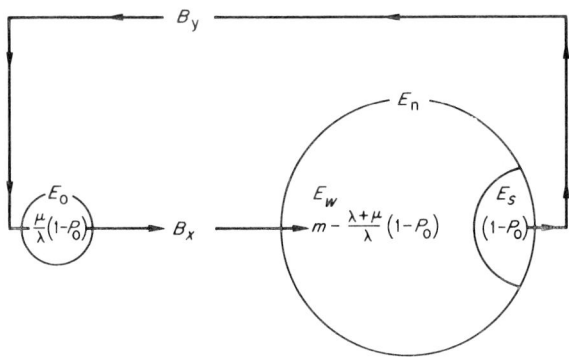

E_0 = Set of chlorine-users, E_n = Set of iodine users
E_w = Customers who have switched to iodine
E_s = Customers about to switch to chlorine but still using iodine

Fig. 6. Steady state of the iodine–chlorine-user model.

BIRTH AND DEATH PROCESSES

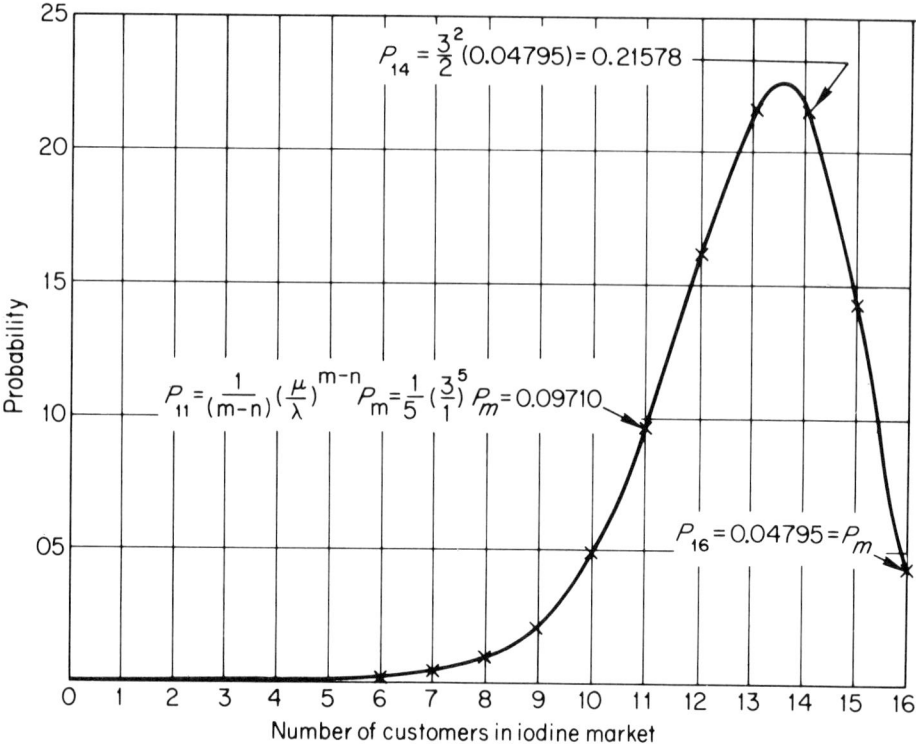

Fig. 7. Iodine market distribution.

violating the restrictions associated with previously given finite queuing formulas. Figure 6 depicts this model after many trials and where the system has reached a steady state.

Notice that E_s is cleared from E_n, the market of iodine, at the rate of $1/[\mu_c(1 - p_0)] = \frac{1}{3}$, while the rate of a departure from E_0, the market size of chlorine, is $\lambda_c = 1$ by definition.

From these data it is possible to determine the market size commanded by each product. It is interesting to note that a market will reach a steady state and will remain split, as shown in Fig. 7, unless a trauma occurs, such as new state laws or allergies to one of the products.

Calculations for E_w and E_n follow by using finite queuing formulas. The first step is to solve for P_m and then for each P_n, given a one line–one server model and first come–first served discipline:

$$\frac{\mu_I}{\lambda_I} = \frac{\lambda_c}{\mu_c} = \frac{1}{3}$$

For every customer buying chlorine, three are departing the set to buy iodine.[20]

$$m = 16$$

Size of universe (number of farms supplied by one cooperative that use either iodine or chlorine sanitizer):

$$P_m = \left[1 + 3 + \frac{(3)^2}{2!} + \frac{(3)^3}{3!} + \cdots + \frac{(3)^{16}}{16!}\right]^{-1} = 20.855365^{-1}$$

$P_m = 0.04795$
$P_{16} = (1)(0.04795) = 0.04795$
$P_{15} = (3)(0.04795) = 0.14385$
$P_{14} = \frac{3^2}{2!}(0.04795) = 0.21578$
$P_1 = \frac{(3)^{15}}{15!}(0.04795) \approx 0$
$P_0 = \frac{(3)^{16}}{16!}(0.04795) = 0.00000009877 \approx 0$

Size of iodine market:

$$E_w = m - \frac{\lambda + \mu}{\lambda}(1 - P_0)$$
$$E_w \approx 16 - 4(1 - 0.0)$$
$$E_w \approx 12$$
$$E_n = E_w + \frac{\lambda}{\mu}$$
$$E_n \approx 12 + \frac{1}{3}$$
$$E_n \approx 12.333$$

Thus, by one interpretation, iodine commands

$$\frac{12.333}{16} \approx 77.1\% \text{ of the market}$$

Another interpretation of the market is shown in Fig. 7 which displays the iodine market size for each P_n. The mode of this graph is approximately 13.5 customers. Remember that the size of the market is 100%, therefore chlorine in this limited model commands the complement to each P_n of iodine. If there were more than two products, other queuing formulas would apply, but the total market would remain equal to 1—provided that it is finite. This model is offered to show that queuing theory may improve the decision-maker's subjective evaluation of his marketing position; it is far from being all-inclusive.

---

[20] This is the same as a finite queuing problem where the rate of arrivals $\lambda = 1$ and the service rate $\mu = 3$. Using these data and solving for E_n will yield the number in the system. This is the expected portion of the market that uses iodine sanitizers.

BIRTH AND DEATH PROCESSES

Example 2. Markovian Queuing Models—Machine Design[21]

Introduction

An interesting queuing problem develops when n is limited although arrivals emanate from an infinite source. Examples of these are:

1. Announcements for laboring jobs at a hand glass company. The foreman limits the size of the line, and the rest are turned away. This still exists in industries today.
2. Lines are limited to the legal seating capacity at athletic events. The rest are turned away.
3. Special sales, offering the first hundred customers discount prices.

These may appear somewhat vague, but an industrial application should strengthen understanding.

Application to Industry

A nailing machine drives four equally spaced nails with one stroke. Each of the four driving heads must have a nail to drive because a missed one must be driven by hand at considerable expense. To minimize such occurrences, each driving head is equipped with a storage tube that holds 10 nails. These tubes are not hand-filled owing to cost. A hopper that holds 10,000 nails is filled at the beginning of the shift and the nails are delivered to the individual tubes by vibrators. If the tube is filled, the nail that is to enter is not admitted and the tube is by-passed. Each tube will have $(10 - 1) = 9$ nails at the conclusion of one successful stroke of four nails and thus may accept one nail from the hopper. Nails feed into the tubes only between strokes, so it is possible that some tubes will begin the next operation with only nine nails in storage because of a missed feed. If this were to continue, an individual tube would be out of nails in 10 strokes, which would result in production delay. The nails cannot haphazardly fall into these tubes, so they must be presented point first. Rather than orient each individual nail, the machine's designers simply introduce an abundance of nails to an orientation slot before the tubes, knowing that the probabilities are high one will be delivered by the vibrators in the proper alignment. Thus, at the conclusion of two strokes, three of the feed slots may have nine nails while one has only eight owing to a missed feed. The object is to have the feed tube long enough so that, given a period of time, enough nails will present themselves to the slot, thereby filling the tube again and virtually guaranteeing that each head will have a nail to drive.

---

[21] Adapted from J. A. Panico, *Queuing Theory—A Study of Witing Lines for Business, Economics, and Science,* Prentice-Hall, Englewood Cliffs, New Jersey, 1969, pp. 121–129.

BIRTH AND DEATH PROCESSES

The length of a tube is very important in the design of the machine. A tube that is too large will result in a larger machine and may prove too cumbersome for production-line work. If shorter tubes are necessary to the design, the probability of correct alignment must be improved. This will increase the nail feed rate, thus allowing each tube to inventory fewer nails.

The nailing machine, when used on a production line, will not be utilized to its full capacity. Randomly-occurring machine breakdowns, a varying work pace, production delays from prior work stations, and other factors contribute to decreased machine efficiency. Thus service time, strokes per hour, are given in average instead of constant units.

From this abbreviated description it may be summarized that:

1. A nail is not admitted to the tube if the tube is full.
2. If the nail is not properly oriented, it will not be admitted.
3. There is a probability that a second, third, ..., tenth stroke may be completed before a nail is presented to the tube due to orientation or jamming problems.[22]
4. Tube length must be held to a minimum because of machine design.
5. The feed tubes are closed during the driving procedure, so a properly oriented nail can only be admitted between strokes.
6. Service, the driving of a nail, occurs randomly as demand for an individual stroke is governed by material flow to the operator and his work pace.
7. A feed tube that inventories nails can be full, partially full, or empty. Thus:
    a. A full feed tube positively rejects since n is limited.
    b. An empty feed tube accepts between strokes provided that the nail is properly oriented.
    c. A partially filled tube may decrease by 1 (machine strokes—the nail is not replaced), increase by 1 (no stroke—1 replaced), stay the same (no stroke—none replaced).

Problem for Solution

An engineer is assigned the problem of redesigning the old machine. He finds that the machine can be substantially reduced in size if the feed tubes are shortened, the orientation device is improved, the hopper reduced, the delivery vibrator improved, etc.[23] He would like to have each head with a feed tube capacity of four.

In the set-up of the problem, the engineer assigns values to his problem so

---

[22] Consider a night club that is ablaze: if the patrons leave in an orderly fashion, all may escape. If they all try to get out simultaneously, there will be a jamming condition and only a few will get out.

[23] When the vibrator's pulsations per minute are altered, the feed rate changes. This feature is especially important when changing nail sizes.

BIRTH AND DEATH PROCESSES

that:

$\lambda = Pr$ (a nail feeds into the tube) = nail's mean arrival rate expressed as a probability

$1 - \lambda = Pr$ (a nail does not feed into tube)

$\mu = Pr$ (machine strokes, and nail departs tube) = nail's mean departure rate expressed as a probability

$1 - \mu = Pr$ (machine does not stroke—zero departures)

$\lambda(1 - \mu)$ = joint probability of: [(arrival)(no stroke)]—line increases by 1

$\mu(1 - \lambda) = Pr$[(stroke)(no arrival)]—line decreases by 1

$1 - [\mu(1 - \lambda) + \lambda(1 - \mu)] = Pr$ (line remains the same)

Figure 8 shows both a transition matrix and transition diagram for the engineer's problem. Suppose that one tube had two nails; locating two on the diagram, it is seen that there are three paths depicting what may occur during the next unit time. One path goes back to one nail, the other loops two and thus remains the same, and the last goes to three, which indicates that the inventory of nails has increased by one. Along these paths are the probabilities for the various events. Thus, going from two to three in one step has a probability of $\lambda(1 - \mu)$. To go from state two to state three in two steps would be

$$P^2_{2,3}[(2 \rightarrow 2 \rightarrow 3) \vee (2 \rightarrow 3 \rightarrow 3)] = \{1 - [\mu(1 - \lambda) + \lambda(1 - \mu)]\}[\lambda(1 - \mu)] + [\lambda(1 - \mu)]\{1 - [\mu(1 - \lambda) + \lambda(1 - \mu)]\}$$

where

$$Pr(2 \rightarrow 2 \rightarrow 3)$$

is the joint probability of the individual events, going from state two to state two, and state two to state three. The probability for $(2 \rightarrow 2 \rightarrow 3)$ is given in the first term of the previous expression. The second term represents the joint probability for the remaining way of going from two to three in two steps. These two terms cannot occur in conjunction, so they are disjointed, mutually exclusive, and their probabilities must be added. Thus the sum of these two terms represents the probability for going from state two to state three in two steps. Finally, notice that this diagram discontinues at four nails because it is impossible to go from four nails back to zero nails in a single step.[24]

The transition matrix of Figure 8 contains the same probabilities as the transition diagram. If a tube contains three nails, the probability of its containing two nails after one stroke of the machine is $P^1_{3,2} = \mu(1 - \lambda)$. This matrix is read by first describing the row and then the column. Thus the intersection of row three, column two, is $\mu(1 - \lambda)$; the row indicates the starting state, and the column indicates the finishing state; notation P^1 represents the values of the intersections after a one-step transition.

[24] J. G. Kemeny, A. Schleifer, Jr., L. L. Snell, and G. L. Thompson, *Finite Mathematics with Business Applications,* Prentice-Hall, Englewood Cliffs, New Jersey, 1964, pp. 229–311, provides an excellent description of finite Markov chains.

BIRTH AND DEATH PROCESSES

TRANSITION MATRIX

$$0' = \begin{array}{c} \\ 0 \\ 1 \\ 2 \\ 3 \\ 4 \end{array} \begin{pmatrix} 0 & 1 & 2 & 3 & 4 \\ 1-\lambda & \lambda & 0 & 0 & 0 \\ \mu(1-\lambda) & 1-[\mu(1-\lambda)+\lambda(1-\mu)] & \lambda(1-\mu) & 0 & 0 \\ 0 & \mu(1-\lambda) & 1-[\mu(1-\lambda)+\lambda(1-\mu)] & \lambda(1-\mu) & 0 \\ 0 & 0 & \mu(1-\lambda) & 1-[\mu(1-\lambda)+\lambda(1-\mu)] & \lambda(1-\mu) \\ 0 & 0 & 0 & \mu & (1-\mu) \end{pmatrix}$$

TRANSITION DIAGRAM

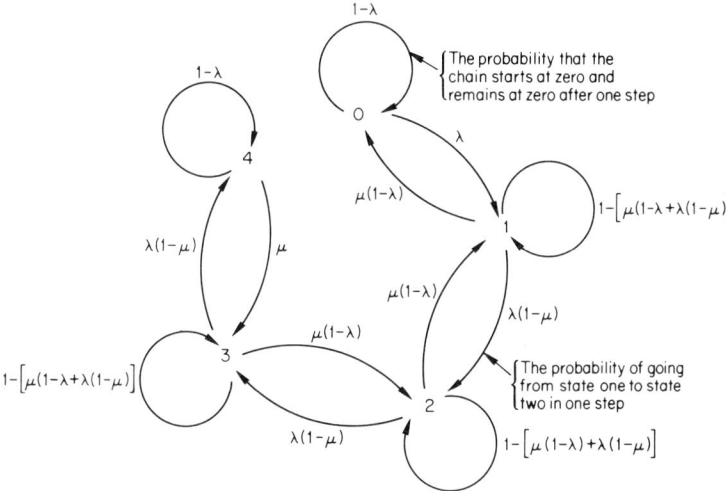

Only unit moves occur.
There is no way of going from state three to state one in one step.
It is a Markov chain of discrete parameters with capped line limits.

- $0 \wedge 0$ Tube empty and nail does not arrive, $0 \to 0$
- $0 \wedge 1$ Tube empty and nail arrives, $0 \to 1$
- $2 \wedge 1$ Tube contains two nails, machine strokes, nail does not enter tube, total nails decrease by one, $2 \to 1$
- $2 \wedge 2$ No stroke, no arrival, total nails in tube remain the same, $2 \to 2$
- $2 \wedge 3$ No stroke, arrival, total nails increase by one, $2 \to 3$
- $4 \wedge 3$ Stroke, nail could not arrive because of previously filled tube, $4 \to 3$
- $4 \wedge 4$ No stroke, no arrival, tube remains filled, $4 \to 4$

Fig. 8. Transition matrix and transition diagram for the nail and tube problem.

$$P^1 = \begin{pmatrix} & 0 & 1 & 2 & 3 & 4 \\ 0 & 0.950 & 0.050 & & & \\ 1 & 0.114 & 0.842 & 0.044 & & \\ 2 & & 0.114 & 0.842 & 0.044 & \\ 3 & & & 0.114 & 0.842 & 0.044 \\ 4 & & & & 0.120 & 0.880 \end{pmatrix}$$

$$P^2 = \begin{pmatrix} 0.908 & 0.090 & 0.002 & & \\ 0.204 & 0.720 & 0.074 & 0.002 & \\ 0.013 & 0.192 & 0.719 & 0.074 & 0.002 \\ & 0.013 & 0.192 & 0.719 & 0.076 \\ & & 0.014 & 0.206 & 0.780 \end{pmatrix}$$

$$P^4 = \begin{pmatrix} 0.843 & 0.146 & 0.010 & & \\ 0.334 & 0.551 & 0.107 & 0.007 & \\ 0.060 & 0.278 & 0.546 & 0.107 & 0.009 \\ 0.005 & 0.056 & 0.278 & 0.547 & 0.114 \\ & 0.005 & 0.060 & 0.311 & 0.624 \end{pmatrix}^a$$

$$P^8 = \begin{pmatrix} 0.760 & 0.206 & 0.030 & 0.002 & 0.001 \\ 0.472 & 0.383 & 0.123 & 0.019 & 0.002 \\ 0.177 & 0.320 & 0.359 & 0.122 & 0.022 \\ 0.042 & 0.140 & 0.317 & 0.365 & 0.136 \\ 0.007 & 0.040 & 0.157 & 0.371 & 0.425 \end{pmatrix}$$

$$P^{16} = \begin{pmatrix} 0.680 & 0.245 & 0.061 & 0.010 & 0.003 \\ 0.562 & .286 & 0.112 & 0.032 & 0.007 \\ 0.354 & 0.292 & 0.216 & 0.103 & 0.035 \\ 0.170 & 0.220 & 0.269 & 0.225 & 0.115 \\ 0.070 & 0.136 & 0.246 & 0.313 & 0.235 \end{pmatrix}$$

$$P^{32} = \begin{pmatrix} 0.624 & 0.257 & 0.086 & 0.024 & 0.008 \\ 0.589 & 0.260 & 0.101 & 0.036 & 0.013 \\ 0.501 & 0.261 & 0.137 & 0.069 & 0.031 \\ 0.382 & 0.248 & 0.182 & 0.123 & 0.064 \\ 0.281 & 0.229 & 0.215 & 0.174 & 0.101 \end{pmatrix}^b$$

$$P^{64} = \begin{pmatrix} 0.595 & 0.257 & 0.098 & 0.036 & 0.013 \\ 0.590 & 0.257 & 0.100 & 0.037 & 0.015 \\ 0.571 & 0.257 & 0.107 & 0.045 & 0.019 \\ 0.541 & 0.256 & 0.119 & 0.057 & 0.026 \\ 0.513 & 0.254 & 0.130 & 0.069 & 0.033 \end{pmatrix}$$

$$P^n = \begin{pmatrix} 0.584 & 0.256 & 0.099 & 0.038 & 0.001 \\ 0.584 & 0.256 & 0.099 & 0.038 & 0.001 \\ 0.584 & 0.256 & 0.099 & 0.038 & 0.001 \\ 0.584 & 0.256 & 0.099 & 0.038 & 0.001 \\ 0.584 & 0.256 & 0.099 & 0.038 & 0.001 \end{pmatrix}^c$$

^{a} These matrices are the squares of their predecessors.

^{b} A matrix is multiplied row vector by column vector. To find the first intersection of P^{64} from P^{32} requires row vector: (0.624, 0.257, 0.086, 0.024, 0.008) multiplies column vector: (0.624, 0.589, 0.501, 0.382, 0.281) = $P^{64}_{0.0}$ = 0.595.

^{c} If P^n is squared, it is the same as multiplying P^n by one; it is thus classified as being a steady state.

Fig. 9. Illustration of how the matrix P^1 approaches a steady state.

To find a two-step transition matrix would require that each intersection be replaced by the probabilities for going from one state to another in two distinct steps. For example, it was previously shown that

$$P^2_{2,3} = 2\{1 - [\mu(1 - \lambda) + \lambda(1 - \mu)]\}[\lambda(1 - \mu)]t$$

Continuing this way, it would be possible to find all values in the two-step transition, but a swifter way would be to multiply the matrix as follows:

$$P^1P^1 = P^2, P^1P^2 = P^3, P^1P^3 = P^4, \ldots, P^1P^{n-1} = P^n$$

After numerous multiplications all rows would have the same values, which would mean that the transition matrix had reached a fixed state. This is called a steady state in queuing theory. Each row of a probability matrix sums to 1, so once a matrix has reached this steady state, additional multiplications will be meaningless. Figure 9 shows that matrix P^1 approaches a steady state at its 64th power, and thus, continuing with these multiplications, the steady-state matrix is developed. These multiplications are at best laborious, but fortunately mathematicians have developed methods through which the values of the rows, in the steady-state matrix, are predictable. These row values will be used in the solution of the engineer's problem.

This problem develops somewhat differently from the previous queuing models in that the line size is capped. Thus, with a line size limitation, there is no restriction covering λ/μ. In any queuing model, as μ grows in relation to λ, the probability of having zero units in the system grows. For a very large μ and a very small λ, say $\lambda/\mu = 3/(4 \times 10^{12})$, then $P_0 \to 1$. In previous discussions it was found that when $\lambda/\mu > 1$, the line increased without limit. This does not hold, however, for the conditions of this example, as the line size is "capped"—limited—to four. Thus as λ/μ grows larger, say $(3 \times 10^{21})/4$, then $P_4 \to 1$ or $P_{nc} \to 1$, where P_{nc} = probability when n is capped.

This problem lends itself to solution through Markovian processes owing to its unit-step characteristics. The restrictions governing this solution are: one line, one server, independent exponential arrivals, no special assumptions other than arrivals are probabalistic, and first come–first served discipline.

Two examples are examined. The first is with a $\lambda/\mu < 1$, while the second is a $\lambda/\mu > 1$. The solution-vector principle, expressed as a formula, is introduced instead of using the successive multiplication techniques as previously given in Figure 9. This formula is readily developed from the transition matrix of Figure 8.

Engineers Solutions

Consider the following two possibilities for one tube.

Example 1

$$\lambda/\mu < 1$$

[394]
BIRTH AND DEATH PROCESSES

Given:

$\lambda = \dfrac{5}{100} = 0.05$ (five of one hundred nails are properly aligned when they approach the feeding device)

$\mu = \dfrac{12}{100} = 0.12$ (the machine has a capacity of 100 strokes per minute but only twelve are used)

$$\begin{pmatrix} & 0 & 1 & 2 & 3 & 4 \\ 0 & 0.950 & 0.050 & & & \\ 1 & 0.114 & 0.842 & 0.044 & & \\ 2 & & 0.114 & 0.842 & 0.044 & \\ 3 & & & 0.114 & 0.842 & 0.044 \\ 4 & & & & 0.120 & 0.880 \end{pmatrix}$$

The solution vector to this matrix, when it reaches a steady state, is found through mathematical analysis to be

$$v \approx \dfrac{(\mu - \lambda)}{\mu(1 - \mu) - \lambda(1 - \lambda)p^4} [1 - \mu, p, p^2, p^3, (1 - \lambda)p^4]$$

where

$$p = \dfrac{P_r \text{ (line increases by 1)}}{P_r \text{ (line decreases by 1)}} = \dfrac{\lambda(1 - \mu)}{\mu(1 - \lambda)}$$

This vector will yield the following values for P:

$$v = (P_0, P_1, P_2, P_3, P_4)$$

Thus by substitution:

$$p = \dfrac{\lambda(1 - \mu)}{\mu(1 - \lambda)} = \dfrac{0.044}{0.114} = 0.38596$$
$$p^2 = 0.14897, \qquad p^3 = 0.05750, \qquad p^4 = 0.00222$$

and the solution vector is:

$$v \approx \dfrac{0.07000}{0.10560 - 0.04750(0.00222)} [0.880, 0.38596, 0.14896, 0.05749, 0.00222(0.950)]$$

Solution vector $\approx (0.58392, 0.25610, 0.09885, 0.03815, 0.00140)$

$P_0 \approx 0.584$ (the tube is empty)
$P_1 \approx 0.256$ (the tube contains one nail)
$P_2 \approx 0.099$ (the tube contains two nails)
$P_3 \approx 0.038$ (the tube contains three nails)
$P_4 \approx 0.001$ (the tube is filled)

BIRTH AND DEATH PROCESSES

Example 2

$$\lambda/\mu > 1$$

This is permissible because the line is capped at four. Given:

$$\lambda = \frac{20}{100} = 0.20$$

$$\mu = \frac{12}{100} = 0.12$$

$$\begin{array}{c} \\ 0 \\ 1 \\ 2 \\ 3 \\ 4 \end{array} \begin{pmatrix} 0 & 1 & 2 & 3 & 4 \\ 0.800 & 0.200 & 0 & 0 & 0 \\ 0.096 & 0.728 & 0.176 & & \\ & 0.096 & 0.728 & 0.176 & \\ & & 0.096 & 0.728 & 0.176 \\ & & & 0.120 & 0.880 \end{pmatrix}$$

$p = 1.8333$, $p^2 = 3.36111$, $p^3 = 6.16204$, $p^4 = 11.29707$

Solution vector:

$$V \approx \frac{0.12 - 0.20}{0.12(0.88) - 0.20(0.80)(11.29707)} [0.88000, 1.83333, 3.36111, 6.16204, 80(11.29707)]$$

$$\approx [0.04137, 0.08618, 0.15799, 0.28965, 0.42482]$$

$P_0 \approx 0.041$ (the tube is empty)
$P_1 \approx 0.086$
$P_2 \approx 0.158$
$P_3 \approx 0.290$
$P_4 \approx 0.425$ (the tube is full)

It follows that for $\lambda/\mu = 0.05/0.12$

$$E_w = \sum_{n=0}^{4} nP_n = 0(0.584) + 1(0.256) + 2(0.099) + 3(0.038) + 4(0.001) = 0.572$$

and for $\lambda/\mu = 0.20/0.12$

$$E_w = \sum_{n=0}^{4} nP_n = 0(0.041) + 1(0.086) + 2(0.158) + 3(0.290) + 4(0.425) = 2.972$$

Thus it appears that a tube that holds four nails will be of sufficient size. This is contingent on the ability to design a feed slot or orientation device that will correctly present 20 of 100 nails.

Only two specific cases were studied, one with $P < 1$, and one with $P > 1$. This was undertaken so that some idea could be gained of where E_w begins insuring against a stock-out. These two E_w's hold only for the values of $\lambda/\mu = 0.05/0.12$ and $\lambda/\mu = 0.20/0.12$, but they serve as indicators of what may be expected for other values of λ/μ.

TABLE 2
Obstetrical.[a,b] Deliveries, Abortions, Others (Actual Data)

Length of stay, days	Patients per month						Poisson predictions with mean = 3.42[d]		Chi-squared testing[c]	
	Actual census					Probability	Expected total	Poisson probability	Calculations	0.05 Level,[e] 7 degrees of freedom
	January	June	September	October	Total					
0[f]	3	2	2	4	11	0.038	10	0.033	$(10 - 11)^2/10 = 0.10$	8 Degrees would be acceptable according to W. G. Cochran[h]
1	8	6	3	7	24	0.083	33	0.114	$(33 - 24)^2/33 = 2.45$	
2	12	10	16	12	50	0.173	56	0.193	$(56 - 50)^2/56 = 0.64$	
3[g]	17	24	25	13	79	0.273	63	0.219	$(63 - 79)^2/63 = 4.06$	
4	15	16	12	13	56	0.194	54	0.186	$(54 - 56)^2/54 = 0.07$	
5	10	10	7	10	37	0.128	36	0.126	$(36 - 37)^2/36 = 0.03$	
6	6	1	3	7	17	0.059	21	0.072	$(21 - 17)^2/21 = 0.76$	
7	3	2	1	2	8	0.028	10	0.035	$(10 - 8)^2/10 = 0.40$	

8	1	1	1	1	4	0.014	0.015	$(4-4)^2/4 = 0$
9	0	1	1	3	2	0.010	0.006	$(2-3)^2/2 = 0.50$
	75	73	71	70	289	100	289	0.999	9.01	14.067

[a] $\dfrac{1}{n}\sum_{i=0}^{9} X_i f_i = \dfrac{1}{289}(0 + 24 + 100 + 237 + 224 + 185 + 102 + 56 + 32 + 27)$.
= patient days/patients = 987/289 = 3.42 average.

[b] Actual data.

[c] From chi-squared charts.

[d] The Poisson prediction and chi-squared values may be found in most handbooks of mathematical tables.

[e] The total calculated value (9.01) is less than the chi-squared value (14.067) for 7 degrees of freedom and a 5% significance level. Theoretically, it may be said with confidence that the Poisson distribution is a good fit. An analyst may ask these questions: Do input data come from a reliable source? What would be the case if $Pr(\text{zero days}) = 0$, or custom provides too much bias? Paraphrasing a national slogan, "The distribution you see may be your own."

[f] There is some error to the category of "Days 0," but it may be utilized for example purposes. Zero patient days is considered an admission for examination but no bed occupancy, which is somewhat vague.

[g] In the chart for "Days 3," length of patient stay is not always determined by condition of patient. Doctor preference, financial situation, custom, demand for beds in the instance of a full house, etc. have a tendency to dictate the bed occupancy period. Fashionable doctors keep patients in hospitals an "acceptable" length of time, which shows that behavioralism influences many individual events that make up the probability distribution. This length of stay, however, is the service time that must be worked with regardless of reasons why.

[h] A. J. Duncan, *Quality Control and Industrial Statistics*, Irwin, Homewood, Illinois, 1956.

BIRTH AND DEATH PROCESSES

Example 3. Administrative Decision Model—Obstetrical Nursing Station[25]

The obstetrical nursing station consists of 22 beds, three nurses, three aides, and one housekeeper, with the staff being reduced slightly during evening shifts. One nurse may be transferred out if demands do not warrant her presence, but she cannot be transferred back during that shift.

State regulation provides that one isolated section of the hospital be allocated for obstetrics. This is an outgrowth of past problems within cross-contamination. Some states have favorably altered this law during recent years.

The maintenance of a completely separate facility with a constant staff presents a difficult problem to the administration of a hospital. In an old hospital to allocate such a facility may result in an over- or underbed situation owing to the physical layout and changing needs. This can result in excessive bed capacity (oversupplying needs) or rejection of obstetrical cases (undersupplying needs)[26]

The problem remains, then, that if a new facility (new hospital or extension of the present one) could be designed, how large should it have to be? Suppose that a mathematical study showed that a smaller facility would guarantee, 95 in 100 trials, that the hospital would have enough capacity. It is doubtful whether the administration would approve a smaller structure, even with these figures, because historical records would show remote instances of heavier demand.

Appalachia Memorial Hospital has a 22 bed Obstetrical Unit. Tables 2 and 3 show utilization records for 1 year. Figure 10 shows that daily demand for beds fluctuates considerably, while Figures 11 and 12 indicate that daily arrivals and length of stay follow a Poisson distribution.

Mathematical Solution to Obstetrical Case

A conflict arises in this case. Here the problem of utility value for money, services, and life all intertwine to emphasize that decision making is not purely

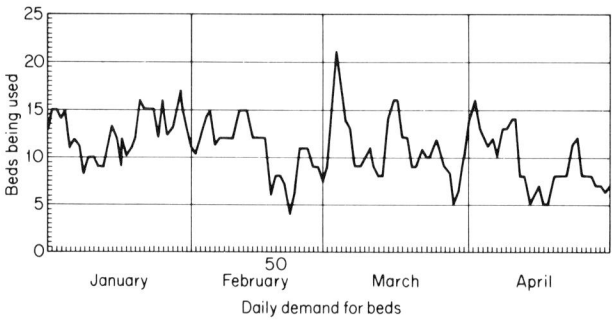

Fig. 10. Daily demand for beds at Appalachia Memorial Hospital.

---

[25] Adapted from J. A. Panico, *Queuing Theory—A Study of Waiting Lines for Business, Economics, and Science*, Prentice-Hall, Englewood Cliffs, New Jersey, 1969, pp. 100–110.
[26] Little condolence is found in either situation, but administrators generally oversupply to placate the patient or ease family emotions.

TABLE 3
Obstetrical Department (Actual Data)

Beds being used	Occurrences, days	Patient days	Actual probability	Poisson probability[b] mean = 9.8
0	0	0	0	0.0001
1	0	0	0	0.0005
2	1	2	0.0027	0.0027
3	1	3	0.0027	0.0087
4	4	16	0.0110	0.0213
5	18[e]	90	0.0493	0.0418
6	28	168	0.0767	0.0682
7	27	189	0.0740	0.0955
8[c]	55	440	0.1507	0.1170
9	51	459	0.1397	0.1274
10	35	350	0.0959	0.1249
11	42	462	0.1151	0.1112
12	37	444[a]	0.1014	0.0908
13	19	247	0.0521	0.0685
14	15	210	0.0411	0.0479
15	18	270	0.0493[e]	0.0313
16	8	128	0.0219	0.0192
17	2	34	0.0055	0.0111
18	2	36	0.0055	0.0060
19	1	19	0.0027	0.0031
20	0	0	0.0000	0.0015
21	1	21	0.0027	0.0007
22	0	0	0.0000	0.0003
23	0	0	0.0000	0.0001
24	0	0	0.0000	0.0001
Total	365	3588[d]	1.00	0.9999

[a] 37 days, 12 beds were occupied which yields a total of (37)(12) = 444 patient days.
[b] From Poisson tables.
[c] 55 days in a total of 365, 8 beds in 24 were being used.
[d] Mean = 3588/365 = 9.83 patients or beds occupied.
[e] 18/365 = 0.0493.

quantitative; but again, few could say after studying the facts of the case that a mathematical approach had not been enlightening.

To solve this problem it became necessary to evaluate what would happen to E_w, E_t, E_n, and E_Ψ for the various values of s. Notice that E_n and E_Ψ approach the means previously found. In a multichannel queuing problem the laborious part involves solving for the P_0 value. This may be reduced, however, by utilizing the series e^x whenever applicable. Consider the problem, given single

BIRTH AND DEATH PROCESSES

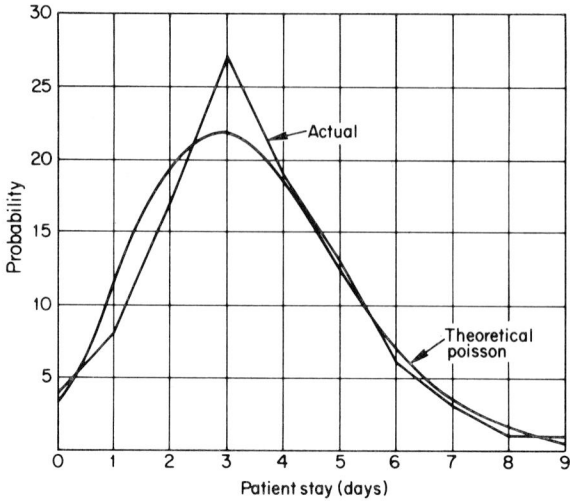

Fig. 11. Daily arrivals at Appalachia Memorial Hospital.

line, multiple server and first come–first served discipline, where:

$\lambda = 2.87$ patients arrive per day

$$\left(\frac{\text{average census}}{\text{average patient stay}} = \frac{9.83}{3.42} = 2.87\right)$$

$\mu = 0.292$ patients served per each bed per day

$$\left(\frac{\text{one bed day}}{\text{average patient stay}} = \frac{1}{3.42} = 0.292\right)$$

$S = 22$ number of beds (stations available)
$\lambda/S\mu < 1 =$ which satisfies the constraints of this problem
$\lambda/\mu = 2.87(3.42) = 9.83$

$$P_0(t) = \left\{\left[\frac{1}{0!}\left(\frac{\lambda}{\mu}\right)^0 + \frac{1}{1!}\left(\frac{\lambda}{\mu}\right)^1 + \frac{1}{2!}\left(\frac{\lambda}{\mu}\right)^2 + \cdots + \frac{1}{21!}\left(\frac{\lambda}{\mu}\right)^{21}\right] \right.$$
$$\left. + \left[\frac{1}{22!}\left(\frac{\lambda}{\mu}\right)^{22}\left(\frac{6.424}{3.554}\right)\right]\right\}^{-1}$$

$$P_0(t) \approx \left[(e^x - + \frac{1}{22!}(9.8)^{22}\left(\frac{6.424}{3.554}\right)\right]$$

From the hospital administrator's viewpoint:

$E_w =$ The number which must be placed in the hall or turned away
$E_t =$ The expected time in the hall
$E_n =$ The expected number in the hall or waiting, plus beds
$E_\psi =$ The expected time in the hall plus beds

BIRTH AND DEATH PROCESSES

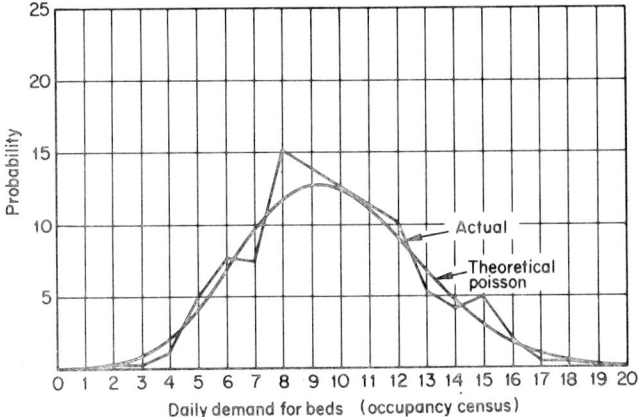

Fig. 12. Length of stay at Appalachia Memorial Hospital.

The objective function of this problem is to minimize E_w and E_t, but the utility for these cannot be measured on cost alone—other factors must be considered. If the administrator wishes to gamble, he may choose a 14-bed department, but if he wishes to be safe he may settle for 16 beds. Optimizing the decision purely through a numerical analysis may be somewhat unreliable, but a decision based solely on intuition is usually worse. If the administrator decides on a 14-bed department, the medical staff may disagree because they vividly remember days of greater demand. (See Fig. 10.)

Choosing the proper-sized facility is extremely important to hospital planners due to rising costs and demands for better service. Any determination of the future size of the obstetrical department would be contingent on the anticipated growth of the population, change in the population's socioeconomic characteristics, and the currently diminishing per capita birth rate.[27]

Table 4 shows the logarithmic calculations for the various number of beds. To solve this problem, S (the number of beds) was altered, and E_w, E_t, E_n, and E_ψ were solved for each corresponding S. When $\lambda/(S\mu) > 1$, the original restrictions are violated. This is why no expected values are shown for S from 0–9. Notice that at $S = 10$, $\lambda/(S\mu)$ approaches 1, which means that arrival rates approach the servicing capacity. This explains why E_w is so large for $S = 10$. Conversely, as the ratio $\lambda/(S\mu)$ approaches zero, E_w similarly gets smaller and also approaches zero. E_t and E_ψ are not reliable measurements for this problem since it is inconceivable that waiting would result in a patient stay of 22.2106 days. This also holds, in part, for E_w and E_n. In this problem, queuing theory is being used to establish S. Thus, if an S of 16 beds were chosen, the administrator might reason that $E_w = (0.0795)$ patients would be in the hall only $E_t = 0.0277$ days, but that this would not increase E_w or E_ψ. The obstetrical

---

[27] A diminishing birth rate will decrease λ, the daily per capita arrivals.

BIRTH AND DEATH PROCESSES

TABLE 4
Solution of Obstetrical Case Through Use of Logarithms

S	$\log\left(\dfrac{\lambda}{\mu}\right)^S$	$\log S!$	$\dfrac{S\mu}{S\mu - \lambda}$	$\dfrac{1}{S!}\left(\dfrac{\lambda}{\mu}\right)^S$	$\sum \dfrac{1}{S!}\left(\dfrac{\lambda}{\mu}\right)^S$
0				1.00	1.00
1	0.9926	0.0000	$\lambda/s\mu > 1$	9.83	10.83
2	1.9852	0.3010	"	48.31	59.14
3	2.9778	0.7782	"	158.50	217.64
4	3.9704	1.3802	"	389.00	606.64
5	4.9630	2.0792	"	765.60	1372.24
6	5.9556	2.8573	"	1253.00	2625.24
7	6.9482	3.7024	"	1762.00	4387.24
8	7.9408	4.6055	"	2163.00	6550.24
9	8.9334	5.5598	"	2365.00	8915.24
10	9.9260	6.5598	58.40	2323.00	11239.24
11	10.9186	7.6012	9.39	2075.00	13314.24
12	11.9112	8.6803	5.53	1702.00	15016.24
13	12.9038	9.7943	4.10	1285.00	16301.24
14	13.8964	10.9404	3.36	903.60	17204.84
15	14.8890	12.1165	2.90	591.60	17796.44
16	15.8816	13.3206	2.59	363.90	18160.34
17	16.8742	14.5511	2.37	210.40	18370.74
18	17.8668	15.8063	2.20	115.10	18485.54
19	18.8594	17.0851	2.07	59.43	18545.27
20	19.8520	18.3861	1.97	29.24	18574.51
21	20.8446	19.7083	1.88	13.68	18588.19
22	21.8372	21.0508	1.81	6.11	18594.30

S	P_0	$(S\mu - \lambda)^2$	E_w	E_t	E_n	E_Ψ
10	$(144579.4)^{-1}$	0.0025	53.9204	18.7859	63.7492	22.2106
11	$(30723.9)^{-1}$	0.1170	5.3294	1.8568	15.1582	5.2815
12	$(22726.3)^{-1}$	0.4020	1.8731	0.6526	11.7019	4.0773
13	$(20284.7)^{-1}$	0.8575	0.8051	0.2805	10.6339	3.7052
14	$(19337.3)^{-1}$	1.4835	0.3695	0.1287	10.1983	3.5534
15	$(18920.5)^{-1}$	2.2801	0.1705	0.0594	9.9993	3.4841
16	$(18738.9)^{-1}$	3.2472	0.0795	0.0277	9.9083	3.4524
17	$(18658.9)^{-1}$	4.3848	0.0364	0.0127	9.8652	3.4374
18	$(18624.0)^{-1}$	5.6930	0.0162	0.0056	9.8450	3.4303
19	$(18608.9)^{-1}$	7.1717	0.0077	0.0027	9.8365	3.4274
20	$(18602.9)^{-1}$	8.8209	0.0029	0.0010	9.8317	3.4257
21	$(18500.2)^{-1}$	10.6406	0.0012	0.0004	9.8300	3.4251
22	$(18599.3)^{-1}$	12.6309	0.0005	0.0002	9.8293	3.4249

department would still only average 9.83 patients per day with a patient stay of 3.42 days because the physician would discharge the patient when she was well enough to go home. Thus E_n and E_Ψ shows that at $S = 16$ the system is approaching its λ/μ and μ values. In fact, these values do not change too drastically for values of $S \geq 13$. The ratio of S_{13} to S_{22} for both E_n and E_Ψ shows a change of only 8.19%. For safety the administrator would have chosen 16 beds but, were he to gamble, he would choose $S = 14$, because E_n and E_Ψ are not *too far* from the actual means, and it *would* be possible to live with an average of 0.3695 patients in the hall for 0.1287 days. If these figures were representative of a diagnostic clinic, E_w (patients waiting for admittance), E_t (days waiting to be admitted), E_n (total number of patients being diagnosed plus waiting for admittance), and E_Ψ (total elapsed time which includes waiting for admittance and time to complete tests) would all have easily detectable meanings.

BIBLIOGRAPHY

Bailey, N. T. J., *The Elements of Stochastic Processes,* Wiley, New York, 1964.
Bartlett, M. S., *An Introduction to Stochastic Processes,* Cambridge University Press, London, 1966.
Baxter, W. E., and C. W. Sloyer, *Calculus with Probability for the Life and Management Sciences,* Addison-Wesley, Reading, Massachusetts, 1973.
Bharucha-Reid, A. T., *Elements of the Theory of Markov Process and Their Application,* McGraw-Hill, New York, 1960.
Bierman, H., Jr., C. F. Bonini, L. E. Fouraker, and R. K. Jaedicke, *Quantitative Analysis for Business Decisions,* Irwin, Homewood, Illinois, 1965.
Billingsley, P., Statistical methods in Markov chains, *Ann. Math. Stat.* **32,** 12–40 (1961).
Bowman, E. H., and R. B. Fetter, *Analysis for Production Management,* Irwin, Homewood, Illinois, 1961.
Chapman, D., A comparative study of several one sided goodness-of-fit tests, *Ann. Math. Stat.* **29,** 655–674 (1958).
Churchman, C. W., R. L. Ackoff, and E. L. Arnoff, *Introduction to Operations Research,* Wiley, New York, 1963.
Clarke, A. B., and R. L. Disney, *Probability and Random Processes for Engineers and Scientists,* Wiley, New York, 1970.
Cooper, R. B., *Introduction to Queuing Theory,* Macmillan, New York, 1972.
diRoccaferrera, G. M. F., *Operations Research Models for Business and Industry,* South-Western Publishing, Cincinnati, Ohio, 1964.
Doob, J. L., *Stochastic Processes,* Wiley, New York, 1953.
Dynkin, E. B., and A. Yushkevich, *Markov Processes Theorems and Problems,* Plenum, New York, 1969.
Feller, W., *An Introduction to Probability Theory and Its Applications,* Wiley, New York, 1965.
Furry, W., On fluction phenomena in the passage of high energy electrons through lead, *Phys. Rev.* **52,** 569 (1937).
Horowitz, I., *An Introduction to Quantitative Business Analysis,* McGraw-Hill, New York, 1965.

BIRTH AND DEATH PROCESSES

Kemeny, J. G., A. Schleifer, Jr., J. L. Snell, G. L. Thompson, *Finite Mathematics with Business Applications,* Prentice-Hall, Englewood Cliffs, New Jersey, 1964.

Kemeny, J. G., and L. Snell, *Finite Markov Chains,* Van Nostrand, New York, 1960.

Kendall, D. G., On the generalized "birth and death" process, *Ann. Math. Stat.* **19,** 1–15 (1948).

Kendall, D. G., and A. N. Kolmogorov, *Foundations of the Theory of Probability,* Chelsea, New York, 1950.

Ledermann, W., and G. E. H. Reuter, Spectral theory for the differential equation of simple birth and death processes, *Phil. Trans. Roy. Soc. London, Ser. A* **246,** 321–369 (1954).

Levine, A., *Theory of Probability,* Addison-Wesley, Reading, Massachusetts, 1971.

Maynard, H. B., *Industrial Engineering Handbook,* McGraw-Hill, New York, 1965.

Miller, D., and M. K. Starr, *Executive Decisions and Operations Research,* Prentice-Hall, Englewood Cliffs, New Jersey, 1964.

Molina, E. C., Telephone trunking problems, *Bell System Tech. J.* **6,** 463 (1927).

Niebel, B. W., *Motion and Time Study,* Irwin, Homewood, Illinois, 1962.

Parzen, E., *Modern Probability Theory and Its Applications,* Wiley, New York, 1960.

Parzen, E., *Stochastic Processes,* Holden-Day, San Francisco, 1962.

Panico, J. A., *Queuing Theory,* Prentice-Hall, Englewood Cliffs, New Jersey, 1969.

Reuter, G. E. H., and W. Ledermann, On the differential equations for the transition probabilities of Markov Processes with enumerably many states, *Proc. Cambridge Philos. Soc.* **49,** 247–262 (1953).

Rosenblatt, M., *Random Processes,* Oxford University Press, Oxford, 1962.

Saaty, T. L., *Elements of Queuing Theory,* McGraw-Hill, New York, 1961.

Sasieni, M., A. Yaspen, and L. Friedman, *Operations Research Methods and Problems,* Wiley, New York, 1958.

Schaifer, R., *Probability and Statistics for Business Decisions,* McGraw-Hill, New York, 1959.

Simmons, G. F., *Differential Equations with Applications and Historical Notes,* McGraw-Hill, New York, 1972.

Yule, G. U., A mathematical theory of evolution, based on the conclusions of Dr. J. G. Willis, F.R.S., *Phil. Trans. Roy. Soc. London, Ser. B* **213,** 21–87 (1924).

Joseph A. Panico

BIVALENT PROGRAMMING BY IMPLICIT ENUMERATION

See Volume 2, page 479

BIVARIATE: THE PROBABILITY DISTRIBUTION OF THE LOGARITHM OF THE SUM OF TWO LOG-NORMALLY DISTRIBUTED RANDOM VARIABLES

INTRODUCTION

Scientists in different fields of endeavor many times transform their experimental or simulated information to a logarithmic scale. Some advantages this type of transformation offer are that it shortens the numerical range of the data, it often normalizes the data, and it stabilizes the variability.

The *log-normal probability distribution,* which plays a major role in our presentation, may in its simplest form be defined as the distribution of a random variable whose logarithm obeys the normal probability distribution. In 1879 McAlister [10] introduced explicitly the theory of the log-normal distribution. He developed expressions for the *mean, median, mode,* and the *second moments* of the probability distribution. McAlister also described a possible application.

In 1903 Kapteyn [7] gave a more precise development of the origin of the distribution and described a mechanism for generating random samples from a log-normal population. Wicksell [17] in 1917 independently gave a similar development of the origin of the distribution and also utilized the method of moments for estimation purposes. In 1919 Nydell [13] calculated the large sample standard errors of the estimators obtained by Wicksell.

There were many scientific discussions and presentations on the subject of the log-normal distribution during the period 1919 to 1931. In 1933 Gaddum [5] and Bliss [2], among others, were developing the probit method for the analysis of biological assays. They became interested in the logarithmic transformation of the data which was effective in normalizing the distribution describing levels of tolerance to the action of drugs in living organisms. During this period many others applied the log-normal distribution very effectively in various bioassay problems.

Cochran [3] suggested in 1939 the use of logarithmic transformations for its stabilizing properties in the statistical analysis of replicated experiments. This suggestion was developed theoretically by Curtiss [4] in 1943.

Here we have given only a very brief historical development of the log-normal probability distribution; for a complete theoretical development the reader is referred to the excellent monograph of Aitchison and Brown [1].

Our primary aim in this presentation is concerned with a modified aspect of the log-normal distribution; namely, the behavior of the logarithm of the sum of two log-normal random variables. The probability distribution of this random variable is important to communication engineers who utilize logarithmic transformation to transfer powers expressed in watts to power levels on a decibel scale. The transformed power levels from individual sources are normally distributed, and the communication engineer seeks the distribution of the transformed power levels of the sum of powers from different sources.

Marlow [9] and Nassel [12] have worked on the power sum of normally distributed random variables and point out some of the theoretical difficulties. Naus [11] derived the moment generating function of the logarithm of the sum of two random variables whose logarithms are independent normal variates with equal variances. From the moment generating function he derives expressions for the expected value and variance of the above random variable. In addition, Naus gave an approximate expression for calculating the expected value.

Hamdan [6] has extended the work of Naus [11] by obtaining the moment generating function of the logarithm of the sum of two variates whose logarithms have a bivariate normal distribution with unequal variances and correlation coefficient ρ. Hamdan also derived expressions for the expected value and variance of the above random variable.

One of the prime tasks in probability theory is to determine the distribution of a random variable which characterizes a given phenomenon, because knowledge of this distribution automatically contributes knowledge of the laws which govern the random variable involved. Recently, Tsokos and Lowrimore [15] have extended the work of Naus [11] by obtaining the probability density function of the logarithm of the sum of two log-normal variates. In addition, they developed the cumulative distribution function, expressions for the expected value, and variance of the above stochastic variable. Furthermore, they obtained estimates of the parameters inherited by the probability distribution of the above variate.

Lowrimore and Tsokos [8] have also generalized the work of Hamdan by deriving the probability density function of the logarithm of the sum of two variates whose logarithms have a bivariate normal distribution. In addition to obtaining the cumulative distribution of the variate, they developed formulas for its expectation and variance. These theoretical findings have been successfully applied to a problem in environmental sciences.

In the following section a brief discussion of some mathematical preliminaries which are needed for the presentation are given. The findings of Naus [11] and Hamdan [6] are summarized in some detail in the section entitled Moment Generating Function of the Logarithm of the Sum of Two Log-Normal Variates. The generalizations of Naus' and Hamdan's works are given in the sections entitled The Probability Distribution of the Logarithm of the Sum of Two Uncorrelated Log-Normal Variates and The Probability Distribution of the Logarithm of the Sum of Two Correlated Log-Normal Variates, respectively. The generalization of the present case to N log-normal random variables is briefly discussed in the final section.

MATHEMATICAL PRELIMINARIES

The *log-normal probability density function* plays a major role in the objectives of the presentation. We shall define this function and discuss some

The Log-Normal Probability Distribution

The log-normal distribution in its simpliest form may be defined as the distribution of a random variable whose logarithm obeys the normal or Gaussian probability density. Let Y be a random variable that is normally distributed with parameters μ_Y and σ_Y. If $Y = \ln X$, or $X = e^Y$, then X is said to have a log-normal probability distribution. This distribution is applicable to many physical problems when the domain of the variate, X, is greater than zero and its histogram is markedly skewed. This skewing occurs when X is affected by random causes that produce small effects that are proportional to the variate X. The outcome of these random causes, each producing a small constant effect, is normally distributed.

The log-normal distribution has been successfully applied in various problems in *anthropometry, life sciences, econometrics, sociology,* and in many *physical and chemical processes.* Aitchison and Brown [1] have written a monograph on the log-normal distribution which gives an extensive development of its theoretical properties and its usefulness in characterizing various problems in the above areas.

Let the random variable Y be *normally distributed:*

$$f(y; \mu_Y, \sigma_Y) = \frac{1}{\sqrt{2\pi}\sigma_Y} \exp\left\{-\frac{1}{2\sigma_Y^2}(Y - \mu_Y)^2\right\}, \quad \begin{array}{l}-\infty < \mu_Y < \infty \\ \sigma_Y > 0 \\ -\infty < y < \infty\end{array}$$

Then the variate $X = e^Y$ is distributed as a log-normal if it has the following function for its probability density:

$$g(x) = \frac{1}{x\sqrt{2\pi}\sigma_Y} \exp\left\{\frac{1}{2\sigma_Y^2}(\ln x - \mu_Y)^2\right\}, \quad x > 0$$

The two parameters which define the probability density completely, μ_Y and σ_Y, play the roles of locating the relative position of the mean and the amount of dispersion of the information with respect to μ_Y, respectively. It can be shown that these parameters are related to the parameters of the random variable X as follows:

$$\mu_Y = \ln\left\{\left(\frac{\mu_X^4}{\mu_X^2 + \sigma_X^2}\right)^{1/2}\right\}$$

and

$$\sigma_Y = \ln\left\{\left(\frac{\mu_X^2 + \sigma_X^2}{\mu_X^2}\right)^{1/2}\right\}$$

BIVARIATE

The *log-normal distribution* possesses a number of interesting properties, most of which are immediate consequences of the normal distribution [1]. The question of when the log-normal distribution is applicable in a given physical problem when a certain amount of information has been obtained can be answered by plotting the cumulative distribution of $\ln X$ on normal probability paper. If the resulting curve is nearly a straight line, then the variate X is lognormally distributed.

The Bivariate Normal Distribution

Finally, we shall state the bivariate normal distribution which will be used extensively in this presentation.

A two-dimensional random variable (X_1, X_2) is said to be distributed as a *bivariate normal* if its point probability density function is

$$f(x_1, x_2; \mu_{X_1}, \mu_{X_2}, \sigma_{X_1}, \sigma_{X_2}, \rho) = K \exp\left\{\frac{1}{2(1-\rho)}\left[\left(\frac{x_1 - \mu_{X_1}}{\sigma_{X_1}}\right)^2 - 2\rho\left(\frac{x_1 - \mu_{X_1}}{\sigma_{X_1}}\right)\left(\frac{x_2 - \mu_{X_2}}{\sigma_{X_2}}\right) + \left(\frac{x_2 - \mu_{X_2}}{\sigma_{X_2}}\right)^2\right]\right\}$$

where

$$K = \frac{1}{2\pi\sigma_{X_1}\sigma_{X_2}\sqrt{1-\rho}}, \quad \begin{array}{l} -\infty < x_1, x_2 < \infty \\ -\infty < \mu_{X_1}, \mu_{X_2} < \infty \\ \sigma_{X_1}, \sigma_{X_2} > 0 \\ -1 < \rho < 1 \end{array}$$

For a complete discussion of the properties and applications of the bivariate normal distribution, see Tsokos [16].

The Mellin Transform

One of the main mathematical tools that we will be employing on the main results of the presentation is the *Mellin transform*. The Mellin transform is defined by the integral

$$f^*(\theta) = \int_0^\infty x^{\theta-1} f(x)\, dx \qquad (1)$$

where θ is complex with

$$\mathrm{Re}(\theta) > \gamma$$

Its inverse is given by the complex integration expressed by

$$f(x) = \frac{1}{2\pi i} \int_{\gamma-i\infty}^{\gamma+i\infty} f^*(\theta) x^{-\theta}\, d\theta$$

The above equations and variation of them will be utilized to obtain the probability density function of the logarithm of the sum of two log-normal random variables.

MOMENT GENERATING FUNCTION OF THE LOGARITHM OF THE SUM OF TWO LOG-NORMAL VARIATES

In this section we shall summarize the initial work on the subject area of Naus [11] and Hamdan [6]. Naus obtained the moment generating function of the logarithm of the sum of two random variables whose logarithms are independent normal variates with equal variances. From this function he obtained expressions for the mean and variance of the above stochastic variable. In addition, approximate estimates are given for the lower moments.

Recently, Hamdan generalized the results of Naus to the case when the logarithms of the random variables have a bivariate normal distribution with unequal variances and correlation coefficient ρ. In addition to the exact estimates of the expectation and variance of the variate, useful estimates of these lower moments are derived.

Moment Generating Function of the Logarithm of the Sum of Two Independent Log-Normal Variates

Naus [11] obtained the moment generating function of the logarithm of the sum of two independent log-normal variates. From this result he developed formulas for the expected value and variance of the desired random variable.

Let X_1 and X_2 be independently and identically distributed normal variates with zero expectation and variance σ^2. Naus has shown that the moment generating function of the random variable Y defined by

$$Y = \ln[\exp(X_1) + \exp(X_2)]$$

is given by

$$M_Y(t) = E(e^Y)$$
$$= 2 \sum_{k=0}^{\infty} \binom{t}{k} \exp[\sigma^2(t^2 - 2kt + 2k^2)/2] F[\sigma(t - 2k)/\sqrt{2}] \quad (3)$$

where $F(\ )$ is the distribution function of the normal distribution with mean zero and variance 1.

To verify the validity of Eq. (3), let

$$\zeta_1 = \frac{X_1 + X_2}{2} \quad \text{and} \quad \zeta_2 = \frac{X_2 - X_1}{2}$$

and note the fact that ζ_1 and ζ_2 are independently and identically normal

BIVARIATE

variates with common zero expectation and variance $\sigma^2/2$. Thus

$$E(e^{Yt}) = E[\exp(X_1) + \exp(X)]^t$$
$$= E[\exp(\zeta_1 t)]E[\exp(-\zeta_2) + \exp(\zeta_1)]^t$$
$$= \frac{\exp(\sigma^2 t^2/4)}{\sqrt{\pi}\sigma} \int_{-\infty}^{\infty} [\exp(-\zeta_2) + \exp(\zeta_1)] \exp(-\zeta_2^2/\sigma^2) d\zeta_2$$
$$= \frac{2\exp(\sigma^2 t^2/4)}{\sqrt{\pi}\sigma} \int_{-\infty}^{0} \exp(-\zeta_2 t)[1 + \exp(2\zeta_2)] \exp(-\zeta_2^2/\sigma^2) d\zeta_2 \quad (4)$$

In Eq. (4) apply the binomial expansion to $[1 + \exp(2\zeta_2)]^t$, change the order of summation and integration, complete the square on the exponent of the integrand, and apply the following transformation:

$$v = \{2\zeta_2 + (t - 2k)\sigma^2\}/\sqrt{2}\sigma$$

to obtain the expression for the moment generating function of the random variable Z given by Eq. (3).

Naus has also shown that the expected value of the random variable Y is given by

$$E(Y) = \frac{\sigma}{\sqrt{\pi}} + 2\sum_{k=1}^{\infty} \frac{(-1)^{k-1}}{k} \exp(k^2\sigma^2) F(-\sqrt{2}k\sigma) \quad (5)$$

Also, he has shown that

$$E(Y^2) = \sigma^2 + \frac{2\sigma}{\sqrt{\pi}} \ln 2 - 4\sigma^2 \exp(\sigma^2) F(-2\sqrt{2}\sigma)$$
$$- 4\sum_{k=2}^{\infty} (-1)^{k-1} \exp(k^2\sigma^2) F(-\sqrt{2}k\sigma) \left\{ \sigma^2 + \frac{1}{k}\left(1 + \frac{1}{2} + \cdots + \frac{1}{k-1}\right)\right\} \quad (6)$$

Using Eqs. (5) and (6), we can obtain the variance

$$\mathrm{Var}(Y) = E(Y^2) - \{E(Y)\}^2$$

To verify Eq. (5), take the derivative of $M_Y(t)$ given by Eq. (3) with respect to t and evaluate it at $t = 0$. Similarly, to derive Eq. (6), we simply take the second derivative of Eq. (3) with respect to t and evaluate it at $t = 0$ to obtain $E(Y^2)$. We should also mention here that in order to be able to perform term by term differentiation in the infinite sums involved, we must be able to show that the derived infinite sum converges uniformly for some range of t. To take the derivative twice in this manner, we need to show that each of the derived sums (i.e., the infinite series of the first and second derivative with respect to t) converges uniformly for $|t| \le c$, where c is some positive constant. Naus [11] has shown that these conditions are satisfied.

It is desirable for various applications of the present results to have approximate estimates of the lower moments. Naus has used an approximate formula of $F(x)$ for large x (18, p. 166) to obtain

$$E(\hat{Y}) = \frac{\sigma}{\sqrt{\pi}} + 2\sum_{k=1}^{m-1} \frac{(-1)^{k-1}}{k} \exp(k^2\sigma^2)F(-\sqrt{2}k\sigma) + \frac{1}{\sigma\sqrt{\pi}}\left\{\frac{\pi^2}{12} - \sum_{k=1}^{m-1} \frac{(-1)^{k-1}}{k^2}\right\} \quad (7)$$

For deriving $E(\hat{Y})$, *apply the approximation*

$$F(-\sqrt{2}k\sigma) \approx \frac{1}{2\sqrt{\pi}k\sigma} \exp(-\sigma^2 k^2), \quad k \geq m$$

in the sum in Eq. (5) and also substitute

$$\sum_{k=1}^{\infty} \frac{(-1)^{k-1}}{k^2} = \frac{\pi^2}{12}$$

to obtain Eq. (7). By choosing m sufficiently large, the right-hand side of Eq. (7) can be made as close to $E(Y)$ as we like.

Moments of the Logarithm of the Sum of Two Log-Normal Variates

Hamdan (6) extended the results of Naus by considering the case when the logarithms of the stochastic variables have a bivariate normal distribution with unequal variances and correlation coefficient ρ.

Let X_1 and X_2 be characterized by the bivariate normal distribution with zero means and variances σ_1^2 and σ_2^2, and correlation coefficient ρ. The moment generating function, $M_Y(t)$, of $Y = \ln[\exp(X_1) + \exp(X_2)]$ is

$$M_Y(t) = E[\exp(X_1) + \exp(X_2)]^t$$
$$= E\{\exp(\zeta_1 t)[\exp(-\zeta_2) + \exp(\zeta_2)]^t\} \quad (8)$$

where

$$\zeta_1 = \frac{X_1 + X_2}{2} \quad \text{and} \quad \zeta_2 = \frac{X_2 - X_1}{2}$$

It is easy to show that (ζ_1, ζ_2) has a bivariate normal distribution with variances σ_1^{*2} and σ_2^{*2} and correlation coefficient ρ^* given by

$$\sigma_1^{*2} = \frac{\sigma_1^2 + 2\rho\sigma_1\sigma_2 + \sigma_2^2}{4}$$

$$\sigma_2^{*2} = \frac{\sigma_1^2 - 2\rho\sigma_1\sigma_2 + \sigma_2^2}{4}$$

and

$$\rho^*\sigma_1^*\sigma_2^* = \frac{\sigma_2^{*2} - \sigma_1^{*2}}{4}$$

BIVARIATE

Hamdan [6] has shown that the moment generating function of the random variable Y is given by

$$M_Y(t) = \sum_{k=0}^{\infty} \binom{t}{k} \exp[b_1^2 + c^2)t^2/2 - 2\sigma_2^{*2}b_1kt + 2\sigma_2^{*2}k^2]F(b_1t - 2\sigma_2^{*2}k)$$

$$+ \sum_{k=0}^{\infty} \binom{t}{k} \exp[b_2^2 + c^2)t^2/2 - 2\sigma_2^{*2}b_2kt + 2\sigma_2^{*2}k^2][1 - F(-b_2t + 2\sigma_2^{*2}k)] \quad (9)$$

where

$$b_1 = \sigma_2^* - \sigma_1^*\rho^*$$
$$b_2 = \sigma_2^* + \sigma_1^*\rho^*$$
$$c^2 = \sigma_1^{*2}(1 - \rho^{*2})$$

and $F(\ )$ is the distribution function of the standard normal.

A brief verification of Eq. (9) is as follows: Calculate the expected value in Eq. (8) by integrating over the bivariate normal distribution of ζ_1 and ζ_2. Begin by completing the square with respect to ζ_1 in the exponent of the bivariate normal density function, and hence integrate with respect to the conditional distribution of ζ_1 given ζ_2. Next, expand $[\exp(-\zeta_2) + \exp(\zeta_2)]^t$ using the binomial theorem and integrate the resulting expression with respect to ζ_2. Note that for the validity of the binomial expansion, $[\exp(-\zeta_2) + \exp(\zeta_2)]^t$ is written as $\exp(-\zeta_2 t)[1 + \exp(2\zeta_2)]^t$ under the integral from $-\infty$ to 0, while it is written as $\exp(+\zeta_2 t)[1 + \exp(-2\zeta_2)]^t$ from 0 to ∞, with respect to ζ_2.

The expected value of the random variable Y is given by

$$E(Y) = \frac{b_1 + b_2}{\sqrt{2\pi}} + 2\sum_{k=1}^{\infty} \frac{(-1)^{k-1}}{k} \exp(2\sigma_2^{*2}k^2)F(-2\sigma_2^*k) \quad (10)$$

Furthermore,

$$E(Y^2) = \frac{1}{2}(b_1^2 + b_2^2 + 2c^2) + \frac{2(b_1 + b_2)}{\sqrt{2\pi}} \ln 2 - 4\sigma_2^*(b_1 + b_2)$$

$$\cdot \exp\{2\sigma_2^{*2}\}F(-2\sigma_2^*) - 4\sum_{k=2}^{\infty} (-1)^{k-1} \exp\{2\sigma_2^{*2}k^2\}F(-2\sigma_2^*k) \quad (11)$$

$$+ \left[\sigma_2^*(b_1 + b_2) + \frac{1}{k}\left(1 + \frac{1}{2} + \cdots + \frac{1}{k-1}\right)\right]$$

Thus, using Formulas (10) and (11) we can obtain the variance of the random variable Y. Furthermore, Hamdan has followed the approach of Naus [11] by using an approximate relation of $F(z)$ for large z to obtain the following estimate of the expected value of Y. This estimate is given by

$$E(\hat{Y}) = \frac{b_1 + b_2}{\sqrt{2\pi}} + 2\sum_{k=1}^{m-1} \frac{(-1)^{k-1}}{k} \exp\{2\sigma_2^{*2}k^2\}$$

$$\cdot F(-2\sigma_2^*k) + \frac{1}{\sigma_2^*\sqrt{2\pi}}\left\{\frac{2}{12} - \sum_{k=1}^{m-1} \frac{(-1)^{k-1}}{k^2}\right\}$$

The above estimate can be made as close to $E(Y)$ as we please by choosing m sufficiently large.

Finally, we should mention that the above results can be generalized to include the case of unequal means of the random variables X_1 and X_2.

THE PROBABILITY DISTRIBUTION OF THE LOGARITHM OF THE SUM OF TWO UNCORRELATED LOG-NORMAL VARIATES

In the previous section it was shown that Naus [11] obtained an expression for the moment generating function of the stochastic variable of the logarithm of the sum of two independently and identically distributed log-normal variates. From this infinite series representation he obtained expressions for the mean and variance of the stochastic variable. Tsokos and Lowrimore [15] have recently generalized Naus' work by obtaining the probability density function which characterizes the behavior of the logarithm of the sum of two identically and independently distributed log-normal variates.

We shall develop the probability density, cumulative distribution of the above variate. In addition we shall estimate the parameters which are inherited in the probability density function and give a numerical comparison with Naus' results.

Formulation of the Probability Distribution

Let X_1 and X_2 be random variables that are independently normally distributed with common mean, μ, and variance, σ^2:

$$f(x_1, x_2; \mu, \sigma^2) = \frac{1}{2\pi\sigma^2} \exp\left\{-\frac{1}{2\sigma^2}[(x_1 - \mu)^2 + (x_2 - \mu)^2]\right\}, \tag{12}$$

$$-\infty < x_1, x_2 < \infty$$
$$-\infty < \mu < \infty$$
$$\sigma > 0$$

The Mellin transform of the stochastic variable Y defined by

$$Y = \exp(X_1) + \exp(X_2)$$

is given by

$$m(\xi) = E(Y^{\xi-1})$$

$$= \frac{1}{2\pi\sigma^2} \int_{-\infty}^{\infty} \int_{-\infty}^{\infty} [\exp(x_1) + \exp(x_2)]^{\xi-1} \tag{13}$$

$$\cdot \exp\left\{-\frac{1}{2\sigma^2}[(x_1 - \mu)^2 + (x_2 - \mu)^2]\right\} dx_1\, dx_2$$

Applying the following transformation to Eq. (13)

$$\zeta_1 = \frac{x_1 - \mu}{\sigma} + \frac{x_2 - \mu}{\sigma} \quad \text{and} \quad \zeta_2 = \frac{x_1 - \mu}{\sigma} - \frac{x_2 - \mu}{\sigma}$$

BIVARIATE

we have

$$m(\xi) = \frac{1}{4\pi} \int_{-\infty}^{\infty} \int_{-\infty}^{\infty} \exp\left\{\left(\frac{\sigma\zeta_1}{2} + \mu\right)(\xi - 1)\right\}$$
$$\left\{2 \cosh\left(\frac{\sigma\zeta_2}{2}\right)\right\}^{\xi-1} \exp\left\{-\frac{\zeta_1^2}{4} - \frac{\zeta_2^2}{4}\right\} d\zeta_1\, d\zeta_2 \quad (14)$$

where

$$\exp\left\{\left(\frac{\sigma\zeta_1}{2} + \mu\right)(\xi - 1)[\exp(\sigma\zeta_2/2) + \exp(-\sigma\zeta_2/2)]^{\xi-1}\right.$$
$$= \exp\left\{\left(\frac{\sigma\zeta_1}{2} + \mu\right)(\xi - 1)\right\}\left[2 \cosh\left(\frac{\sigma\zeta_2}{2}\right)\right]^{\xi-1}$$

Equation (14) can be written as

$$m(\xi) = \frac{1}{2\sqrt{\pi}} \exp\left\{\left[(\xi - 1)\frac{\sigma}{2}\right]^2 + (\xi - 1)\mu\right\} \int_{-\infty}^{\infty} 2\cosh\left(\frac{\sigma\zeta_2}{2}\right)^{\xi-1} \exp\left\{-\frac{\zeta_2^2}{4}\right\} d\zeta_2$$

(15)

Applying the following inversion formula to $m(\xi)$

$$h(y) = \frac{1}{2\pi i} \int_{\gamma+i\infty}^{\gamma-i\infty} x^{-\xi} m(\xi)\, d\xi \quad (16)$$

for $\gamma = 1$ and making the following change of variables

$$\xi = 1 + iv$$

we obtain

$$h(y) = \frac{1}{4\pi^{3/2} y} \int_{-\infty}^{\infty} y^{iv} \exp\left\{\frac{v^2\sigma^2}{4} + ivy\right\} \int_{-\infty}^{\infty} \left(2\cosh\frac{\sigma\zeta_2}{2}\right)^{iv} \exp\left\{-\frac{\zeta_2^2}{4}\right\} d\zeta_2\, dv$$

(17)

Changing the order of integration and completing the square on y in Eq. (17), we have

$$h(y) = \frac{1}{4\pi^{3/2} y} \int_{-\infty}^{\infty} \exp\left\{-\frac{\zeta_2^2}{4}\right\} \int_{-\infty}^{\infty} \exp\left\{-\frac{\sigma^2}{4}\right\}$$
$$\cdot \left\{v - \frac{2i}{2}\left[\mu - \ln y + \ln\left(2\cosh\frac{\sigma\zeta_2}{2}\right)\right]\right\}^2 \quad (18)$$
$$\cdot \exp\left\{-\left[\mu - \ln y + \ln\left(2\cosh\frac{\sigma\zeta_2}{2}\right)\right]^2\right\} dv\, d\zeta_2$$

Integrating out v in Eq. (18), we obtain

$$h(y) = \frac{1}{2\pi\sigma y} \int_{-\infty}^{\infty} \exp\left\{-\left[\mu - \ln y + \ln\left(2\cosh\frac{\sigma\zeta_2}{2}\right)\right]^2 \Big/ \sigma^2\right\} \exp\left\{-\frac{\zeta_2^2}{4}\right\} d\zeta_2 \quad (19)$$

which can be written as

$$h(y) = \frac{\exp[-(\ln y - \mu)^2/\sigma^2]}{2\pi\sigma y} \int_{-\infty}^{\infty} \exp\left\{-\left[\ln\left(2\cosh\frac{\sigma\zeta_2}{2}\right)\right]^2/\sigma^2\right\}$$

$$\cdot \exp\left\{-\left[(\ln y - \mu)\ln\left(2\cosh\frac{\sigma\zeta_2}{2}\right)\right]/\sigma^2\right\} \exp\left\{-\frac{\zeta_2^2}{4}\right\} d\zeta_2 \quad (20)$$

Note that we can write

$$\sum_{n=0}^{\infty} \frac{\left(\frac{\ln y - \mu}{\sigma}\right)^n \left[\frac{\ln(2\cosh \sigma\zeta_2/2)}{\sigma}\right]^2}{n!} = \exp\left\{\frac{(\ln y - \mu)}{\sigma} \ln \frac{(2\cosh \sigma\zeta_2/2)}{\sigma}\right\}$$

Thus Eq. (20) can be written as

$$h(y) = \frac{\exp[-(\ln y - \mu)^2/\sigma]}{2\pi y \sigma} \int_{-\infty}^{\infty} \exp\left\{-\left[\frac{\ln(2\cosh \sigma\zeta_2/2)}{\sigma}\right]^2\right\}$$

$$\cdot \sum_{n=0}^{\infty} \frac{\left(\frac{\ln y - \mu}{\sigma}\right)^2 \left[\frac{\ln(2\cosh \sigma\zeta_2/2)}{\sigma}\right]^2}{n!} \exp\left\{-\frac{\zeta_2^2}{4}\right\} d\zeta_2 \quad (21)$$

Let $Z = \ln Y$, then Eq. (21) becomes

$$g(z) = \frac{\exp[-(z - \mu/\sigma)]^2}{2\pi\sigma} \sum_{n=0}^{\infty} \frac{2^n}{n!} \left(\frac{z - \mu}{\sigma}\right)^n I_n(\sigma) \quad (22)$$

where

$$I_n(\sigma) = \int_{-\infty}^{\infty} \left\{\frac{\ln(2\cosh \sigma\zeta_2/2)}{\sigma}\right\} \exp\left\{-\left[\frac{\ln(2\cosh \sigma\zeta_2/2)}{\sigma}\right]^2\right\} d\zeta_2 \quad (23)$$

Thus Eq. (22) is the probability density function of the logarithm of the sum of two independent log-normal variates with common mean and variance. Since the random variables are independent and identically distributed with common mean and variance, it follows from Eq. (21) that the probability distribution of

$$Y = \exp(X_1) + \exp(X_2)$$

is given by

$$f(y) = \frac{\exp[-(\ln y - \mu)^2/\sigma^2]}{2\pi\sigma y} \sum_{n=0}^{\infty} \frac{2^n}{n!} \left(\frac{\ln y - \mu}{\sigma}\right)^n I_n(\sigma) \quad (24)$$

where $I_n(\sigma)$ is given by Eq. (23).

In what follows we shall show that the cumulative probability distribution of the above variate can be expressed as a linear combination of χ^2 probability functions.

It follows from Eq. (22) that the cumulative distribution function of the variate Z is given by

$$G(z) = \Pr(Z \le z) = \int_{-\infty}^{z} \frac{\exp[-(v - \mu/\sigma)^2]}{2\pi\sigma} \sum_{n=0}^{\infty} \frac{2^n(v - \mu/\sigma)^n}{n!} I_n(\sigma) dv \quad (25)$$

[416]
BIVARIATE

Interchanging the order of summation and integration and making the substitution $t = (v - \mu)/\sigma$ in Eq. (25), we have

$$G(z) = \frac{1}{2\pi} \sum_{n=0}^{\infty} \frac{2^n}{n!} I_n(\sigma) \int_{-\infty}^{(z-\mu/\sigma)} t^n \exp(-t^2) \, dt$$

$$= \frac{1}{2\pi} \sum_{n=0}^{\infty} \frac{2^n}{n!} I_n(\sigma) H_n(z) \qquad (26)$$

where

$$H_n(z) = \int_{-\infty}^{(z-\mu/\sigma)} t^n \exp(-t^2) \, dt \qquad (27)$$

We shall integrate Eq. (27) first for $z < \mu$ and second for $z > \mu$.

The Case Where $z > \mu$

For this case we can write Eq. (27) as

$$H_n(z) = \int_{-\infty}^{0} t^n \exp(-t^2) \, dt + \int_{0}^{(z-\mu/\sigma)} t^n \exp(-t^2) \, dt = I_1 + I_2 \qquad (28)$$

In I_1 of Eq. (28), let $t = -\sqrt{v}$, then we have

$$I_1 = \frac{(-1)^n}{2} \int_{0}^{\infty} v^{(n-1)/2} e^{-v} \, dv$$

$$= \frac{(-1)^n}{2} \Gamma\left(\frac{n+1}{2}\right) \qquad (29)$$

Similarly, let $t = v/\sqrt{2}$ in I_2 of Eq. (28) to obtain

$$I_2 = \frac{1}{2^{(n+1)/2}} \int_{0}^{\sqrt{2}(z-\mu/\sigma)} v^n \exp(-v^2/2) \, dv \qquad (30)$$

We recall that the kth incomplete moment of the normal distribution with $\mu = 0$ and $\sigma^2 = 1$ is given by

$$\mu_k(t) = \frac{1}{\sqrt{2\pi}} \int_{0}^{t} v^k \exp(-v^2/2) \, dv \qquad (31)$$

Thus, using Eq. (31), we can write I_2 as

$$I_2 = \frac{\sqrt{2\pi}}{2^{(n+1)/2}} \mu_n\left\{\sqrt{2}\left(\frac{z-\mu}{\sigma}\right)\right\} \qquad (32)$$

Therefore, for $z > \mu$ we can write

$$H_n(z) = \frac{(-1)^n}{2} \Gamma\left(\frac{n+1}{2}\right) + \frac{\sqrt{2\pi}}{2^{(n+2)/2}} \mu_n\left\{\sqrt{2}\left(\frac{z-\mu}{\sigma}\right)\right\} \qquad (33)$$

The Case Where $z < \mu$

For this case we can write Eq. (27) as

$$H_n(z) = \int_{-\infty}^{0} t^n \exp(-t^2) dt - \int_{(z-\mu/\sigma)}^{0} t^n \exp(-t^2) dt$$

$$= I_1^* + I_2^* \tag{34}$$

The value of the integral I_1^* is the gamma function given by Eq. (29). Using the approach we employed to evaluate I_2, we can write I_2^* as

$$I_2^* = \frac{(-1)^{n+1}\sqrt{2\pi}}{2^{(n+1)/2}} \mu_n\left\{-\sqrt{2}\left(\frac{z-\mu}{\sigma}\right)\right\} \tag{35}$$

Thus for $z < \mu$ we have

$$H_n(z) = \frac{(-1)^n}{2}\Gamma\left(\frac{n+1}{2}\right) + \frac{(-1)^{n+1}\sqrt{2\pi}}{2^{(n+1)/2}} \mu_n\left\{-\sqrt{2}\left(\frac{z-\mu}{\sigma}\right)\right\} \tag{36}$$

Combining Eqs. (33) and (36), we have

$$G(z) = \begin{cases} \dfrac{1}{2\pi}\sum_{n=0}^{\infty}\dfrac{2^n}{n!}I_n(\sigma)\left\{\dfrac{(-1)^n}{2}\Gamma\left(\dfrac{n+1}{2}\right) + \dfrac{\sqrt{2\pi}}{2^{(n+1)/2}}\mu_n\left[\sqrt{2}\left(\dfrac{z-\mu}{\sigma}\right)\right]\right\}, \\ \hfill z < \mu \\ \dfrac{1}{2\pi}\sum_{n=0}^{\infty}\dfrac{2^n}{n!}I_n(\sigma)\left\{\dfrac{(-1)^n}{2}\Gamma\left(\dfrac{n+1}{2}\right) - \dfrac{(-1)^n\sqrt{2\pi}}{2^{(n+1)/2}}\mu_n\left[-\sqrt{2}\left(\dfrac{z-\mu}{\sigma}\right)\right]\right\}, \\ \hfill z > \mu \\ 0, \hfill z = \mu \end{cases} \tag{37}$$

Simplifying Eq. (37), we have

$$G(z) = \frac{1}{2\pi}\sum_{n=0}^{\infty}\frac{(-1)^n}{n!} 2^{n-1} I_n(\sigma)\Gamma\left(\frac{n+1}{2}\right) + L\left[2\left(\frac{z-\mu}{\sigma}\right)\right] \tag{38}$$

where

$$L(t) = \begin{cases} \dfrac{1}{\sqrt{2\pi}}\sum_{n=0}^{\infty}\dfrac{2^{(n-1)/2}}{n!}I_n(\sigma)\mu_n(t), & t > 0 \\ \dfrac{1}{\sqrt{2\pi}}\sum_{n=0}^{\infty}\dfrac{(-1)^{n+1}2^{(n-1)/2}}{n!}I_n(\sigma)\mu_n(-t), & t < 0 \end{cases}$$

Recall that the probability distribution of the χ^2 density function is given by

$$F(\chi_\nu^2) = \frac{1}{2^{(\nu/2)}\Gamma(\nu/2)}\int_0^{\chi^2} t^{(\nu-2)/2}\exp(-t^2/2)dt$$

BIVARIATE

Thus we can write

$$\mu_n(t) = \begin{cases} \dfrac{1}{2}\{(n-1)!\}!F(t_{n+1}^2), & \text{for } n \text{ even} \\[2mm] \dfrac{\{(n-1)!\}!}{\sqrt{2\pi}} F(t_{n+1}^2), & \text{for } n \text{ odd} \end{cases} \quad (39)$$

Substituting Eq. (39) in $L(t)$ given above, we have

$$L(t) = \begin{cases} \dfrac{1}{\sqrt{2}} \sum_{m=0}^{\infty} \dfrac{2^{m-1/2}}{(2m)!} I_{2m}(\sigma)\mu_{2m}(t) \\[2mm] \quad + \dfrac{1}{\sqrt{2\pi}} \sum_{m=0}^{\infty} \dfrac{2^m}{(2m+1)!} I_{2m+1}(\sigma)\mu_{2m+1}(t), \quad t > 0 \\[2mm] \dfrac{-1}{\sqrt{2\pi}} \sum_{m=0}^{\infty} \dfrac{2^{m-1/2}}{(2m)!} I_{2m}(\sigma)\mu_{2m}(-t) \\[2mm] \quad + \dfrac{1}{\sqrt{2\pi}} \sum_{m=0}^{\infty} \dfrac{2^m}{(2m+1)!} I_{2m+1}(\sigma)\mu_{2m+1}(-t), \quad t < 0 \end{cases} \quad (40)$$

Thus

$$L(t) = \begin{cases} \dfrac{1}{\sqrt{2\pi}} \sum_{m=0}^{\infty} \dfrac{2^{m-3/2}}{(2m)!} I_{2m}(\sigma)[(2m-1)!]!F(t_{2m+1}^2) \\[2mm] \quad + \dfrac{1}{2\pi} \sum_{m=0}^{\infty} \dfrac{2^m}{(2m+1)!} I_{2m+1}(\sigma)[(2m)!]!F(t_{2m+2}^2), \quad t > 0 \\[2mm] \dfrac{-1}{\sqrt{2\pi}} \sum_{m=0}^{\infty} \dfrac{2^{m-3/2}}{(2m)!} I_{2m}(\sigma)[2m-1)!]!F(t_{2m+1}^2) \\[2mm] \quad + \sum_{m=0}^{\infty} \dfrac{2^m}{(2m+1)!} I_{2m+1}(\sigma)[(2m)!]!F(t_{2m+2}^2), \quad t < 0 \end{cases} \quad (41)$$

For convenience we write Eq. (41) as

$$L(t) = \begin{cases} M(t) + N(t), & t > 0 \\ M(t) - N(t), & t < 0 \end{cases} \quad (42)$$

where

$$M(t) = \dfrac{1}{2\pi} \sum_{m=0}^{\infty} \dfrac{2^m}{(2m+1)!} I_{2m+1}(\sigma)\{(2m)!\}!F(t_{2m+2}^2) \quad (43)$$

and

$$N(t) = \dfrac{1}{\sqrt{2\pi}} \sum_{m=0}^{\infty} \dfrac{2^{m-3/2}}{(2m)!} I_{2m}(\sigma)\{(2m-1)!\}!F(t_{2m+1}^2) \quad (44)$$

Thus, using Eqs. (42), (43), and (44) in Eq. (38), we obtain

$$G(z) = \frac{1}{2\pi} \sum_{n=0}^{\infty} \frac{(-1)^{n_2 n-1} I_n(\sigma)}{n!} \Gamma\left(\frac{n+1}{2}\right)$$

$$+ M\left\{\sqrt{2}\left(\frac{z-\mu}{\sigma}\right)\right\} + \text{sgn}(z-\mu)N\left\{\sqrt{2}\left(\frac{z-\mu}{\sigma}\right)\right\} \quad (45)$$

Therefore the cumulative distribution of the variate Z is a linear combination of χ^2 probabilities.

A useful variate for applications is the absolute difference of two log-normal random variables. In what follows we shall derive the probability density function of the variate $Y = |\exp(X_1) - \exp(X_2)|$, where X_1 and X_2 are defined as above.

Utilizing the bivariate probability density of the variate (X_1, X_2) and taking the Mellin transform of the stochastic variate Y, we have

$$m_1(\xi) = \frac{1}{2\pi\sigma^2} \int_{-\infty}^{\infty} \int_{-\infty}^{x_2} [\exp(X_2) - \exp(X_1)]^{\xi-1} \exp\left\{-\frac{1}{2\sigma^2}[(x_1-\mu)^2 + (x_2-\mu)^2]\right\} dx_1 \, dx_2 + \frac{1}{2\pi\sigma^2} \int_{-\infty}^{\infty} \int_{x_2}^{\infty} [\exp(X_1) - \exp(X_2)]^{\xi-1}$$

$$\cdot \exp\left\{-\frac{1}{2\sigma^2}[(x_1-\mu)^2 + (x_2-\mu)^2]\right\} dx_1 \, dx_2$$

$$= T_1 + T_2 \quad (46)$$

Let

$$w_1 = x_1 + x_2 \quad \text{and} \quad w_2 = x_2 - x_1$$

Then the integral T_1 of Eq. (46) reduces to

$$T_1 = \frac{1}{4\pi\sigma^2} \int_{-\infty}^{\infty} \exp\left\{\frac{w_1(\xi-1)}{2} - \frac{w_1^2}{4\sigma^2} + \frac{\mu w_1}{\sigma^2} - \frac{\mu^2}{\sigma^2}\right\} dw_1$$

$$\cdot \int_0^{\infty} \{\exp(w_2/2) - \exp(-w_2/2)\}^{\xi-1} \exp(-w_2^2/4\sigma^2) dw_2 \quad (47)$$

Similarly, for

$$w_1 = \frac{x_1 + x_2}{2} \quad \text{and} \quad w_2 = \frac{x_1 - x_2}{2}$$

T_2 of Eq. (46) can be written as

$$T_2 = \frac{1}{4\pi\sigma^2} \int_{-\infty}^{\infty} \exp\left\{\frac{w_1(\xi-1)}{2} - \frac{w_1^2}{4\sigma^2} + \frac{\mu w_2}{\sigma^2} - \frac{\mu^2}{\sigma^2}\right\} dw_1$$

$$\cdot \int_0^{\infty} \{\exp(w_2/2) - \exp(-w_2/2)\}^{\xi-1} \exp(-w_2^2/4\sigma^2) dw_2$$

BIVARIATE

which is identical to Eq. (47). Thus $m_1(\xi)$ can now be written as

$$m_1(\xi) = \frac{1}{2\pi\sigma^2} \exp(-\mu^2/\sigma^2) \int_{-\infty}^{\infty} \exp\left\{-\frac{1}{2\sigma^2}\frac{w_1^2}{2-r}\{(\xi-1)^2 + 2\mu\}\right\} dw_1$$
$$\cdot \int_0^{\infty} \{\exp(w_2/2) - \exp(-w_2/2)\}^{\xi-1} \exp(-w_2^2/4\sigma^2) dw_2 \quad (48)$$

Completing the square on the first integral of Eq. (48) and simplifying, we have

$$m_1(\xi) = \frac{1}{\pi\sigma} \exp\left\{\frac{(\xi-1)^2\sigma^2}{4} + \mu(\xi-1)\right\}$$
$$\cdot \int_0^{\infty} \{\exp(w_2/2) - \exp(w_2/2)\}^{\xi-1} \exp(-w_2^2/4\sigma^2) dw_2 \quad (49)$$

Applying the transformation $w_2 = \sigma\mu$, Eq. (49) becomes

$$m_1(\xi) = \frac{1}{\sqrt{\pi}} \exp\left\{\frac{(\xi-1)^2\sigma^2}{4} + \mu(\xi-1)\right\} \int_0^{\infty} \left(2 \sinh \frac{\sigma u}{2}\right)^{\xi-1} \exp(-u^2/4\sigma^2) du$$

$$(50)$$

Applying the inversion Formula (6) to $m_1(\xi)$ and similar simplifications as employed for the ease of finding the probability density of the sum of two lognormal variates, we have

$$f_1(y) = \begin{cases} \frac{1}{2\pi y\sigma} \exp\left\{-(\ln y - \mu)^2 \frac{1}{\sigma^2}\right\} \sum_{n=0}^{\infty} \frac{2^n N_n(\sigma)}{\sigma^n n!} (\ln y - \mu)^n, & \begin{array}{l} 0 < y < \infty \\ \sigma > 0 \\ -\infty < \mu < 0 \end{array} \\ 0, \quad \text{elsewhere} & (51) \end{cases}$$

where

$$N_n(\sigma) = 2\int_0^{\infty} \left\{\frac{1}{\sigma}\ln\left(2 \sinh \frac{\sigma u}{2}\right)\right\}^n \exp\left\{-\frac{1}{\sigma}\left[\ln\left(2 \sinh \frac{\sigma u}{2}\right)\right]\right\} \exp(-u^2/4) du$$

Thus, for
$$Z = \ln Y = \ln\{|\exp(X_1) - \exp(X_2)|\}$$
Eq. (51) becomes

$$g_1(z) = \frac{1}{2\pi\sigma} \exp\left\{-\left(\frac{z-\mu}{\sigma}\right)^2\right\} \sum_{n=0}^{\infty} \frac{2^n N_n(\sigma)}{n!} \left(\frac{z-\mu}{\sigma}\right)^n, \quad \begin{array}{l} -\infty < \mu \\ z < \infty \\ \sigma > 0 \end{array}$$

with $N_n(\sigma)$ as defined above.

Central Moments of the Probability Distribution of the Variate $Z = \ln Y$

Here we derive the *n*th *central moment* of the logarithm of the sum of two log-normal distributions whose probability density function is given by Eq.

(22). We also give a numerical comparison with the results obtained by Naus [11] for the mean and variance of the stochastic variable Z.

The kth moment with respect to μ is

$$\eta_k = E[Z - \mu]^k$$
$$= \frac{1}{2\pi\sigma} \int_{-\infty}^{\infty} (z-\mu)^k \exp\left[-\left(\frac{z-\mu}{\sigma}\right)^2\right] \sum_{n=0}^{\infty} \frac{2^n I_n(\sigma)}{n!} \left(\frac{z-\mu}{\sigma}\right)^n dz \qquad (52)$$

Interchanging the order of summation and integration and applying the following transformation

$$y = \left(\frac{z-\mu}{\sigma}\right)$$

to Eq. (52) we have

$$\eta_k = \frac{\sigma^k}{2\pi} \sum_{n=0}^{\infty} \frac{2^n I_n(\sigma)}{n!} \int_0^{\infty} y^{[(n+k)/2 - (1/2)]} e^{-y} \, dy \qquad (53)$$

where $n + k$ is even and the integral is 0 for $n + k$ odd. Thus we can write Eq. (53) as

$$\eta_k = \frac{\sigma^k}{2\pi} \sum_{\substack{n=0 \\ n+k \text{ even}}}^{\infty} \frac{2^n}{n!} I_n(\sigma) \Gamma\left(\frac{n+k+1}{2}\right) \qquad (54)$$

and the expected value of the variate Z is given by

$$E(Z) = \mu + \frac{\sigma}{2\pi} \sum_{\substack{n=0 \\ n \text{ odd}}}^{\infty} \frac{2^n}{n!} I_n(\sigma) \Gamma\left(\frac{n+2}{2}\right) \qquad (55)$$

The variance is invariant under translation, so we have

$$\mathrm{Var}(Z) = E[(Z_1 - \mu)^2] - [E(Z - \mu)]^2$$
$$= \frac{\sigma^2}{2\pi} \sum_{\substack{n=0 \\ n \text{ odd}}}^{\infty} \frac{2^n I_n(\sigma)}{n!} \Gamma\left(\frac{n+3}{2}\right) - \left\{\frac{\sigma}{2\pi} \sum_{\substack{n=0 \\ n \text{ odd}}}^{\infty} \frac{2^n}{n!} I_n(\sigma) \Gamma\left(\frac{n+2}{2}\right)\right\}^2 \qquad (56)$$

Table 1 compares the results of Tsokos and Lourimore [15] with those obtained by Naus [11] for the case of $\mu = 0$ and σ varying from 1 to 10. Clearly the present results compare very well with those of Naus. In conclusion we will like to point out that it is easier to compute various moments from the present theoretical derivations.

Estimation of the Parameters of the Probability Distribution of the Variate Z

In this section we derive estimates for the parameters μ and σ of the probability distribution of the stochastic variate Z. We employ two methods to

BIVARIATE

obtain our estimates. First we use the method of *maximum likelihood* and then the *method of moments*.

The logarithm of the likelihood function, $L(\mu, \sigma)$, for a random sample of size r taken from a population which is being characterized by the probability distribution of the variate Z is

$$\ln L(\mu, \sigma) = \sum_{i=1}^{r} \left\{ \left[-\left(\frac{z_i - \mu}{\sigma}\right)^2 + \ln \sum_{n=0}^{\infty} \frac{2^n}{n!} I_n(\sigma) \left(\frac{z_i - \mu}{\sigma}\right)^n \right] \right\} - r \ln(2\pi\sigma) \quad (57)$$

To obtain the maximum likelihood estimates of the true states of nature μ and σ, we equate the partial derivatives with respect to these parameters of Eq. (57) to zero and solve the resulting equations. The partial derivatives of the logarithm of the likelihood function with respect to μ and σ are given by

$$\frac{\partial \ln L(\mu, \sigma)}{\partial \mu} = \sum_{i=1}^{r} \left\{ \frac{2}{\sigma}\left(\frac{z_i - \mu}{\sigma}\right) - \frac{1}{\sigma} \frac{\sum_{n=1}^{\infty} \frac{2^n}{(n-1)!} I_n(\sigma) \left(\frac{z_i - \mu}{\sigma}\right)^{n-1}}{\sum_{n=0}^{\infty} \frac{2^n}{n!} I_n(\sigma) \left(\frac{z_i - \mu}{\sigma}\right)^n} \right\} \quad (58)$$

and

$$\frac{\partial \ln L(\mu, \sigma)}{\partial \sigma}$$

$$= \sum_{i=1}^{r} \left\{ \frac{2}{\sigma}\left(\frac{z_i - \mu}{\sigma}\right)^2 + \frac{\sum_{n=0}^{\infty} \frac{2^n}{n!} \left(\frac{z_i - \mu}{\sigma}\right)^n \left(-\frac{n I_n(\sigma)}{\sigma}\right) + I_n^*(\sigma)}{\sum_{n=0}^{\infty} \frac{2^n}{n!} I_n(\sigma) \left(\frac{z_i - \mu}{\sigma}\right)^n} \right\} - \frac{r}{\sigma} \quad (59)$$

respectively, where

$$I_n^*(\sigma) = \frac{dI_n(\sigma)}{d\sigma} \int_{-\infty}^{\infty} \left\{ \frac{\ln\left(2\cosh\frac{\sigma\zeta_2}{2}\right)}{\sigma} \right\}^{n-1} \left\{ \left[-2\frac{\ln\left(2\cosh\frac{\sigma\zeta_2}{2}\right)}{\sigma} \right]^2 + n \right\}$$

$$\cdot \left\{ \frac{\zeta_2}{2\sigma}\tanh\frac{\sigma\zeta_2}{2} - \frac{\ln\left(2\cosh\frac{\sigma\zeta_2}{2}\right)}{\sigma^2} \right\} \exp\left\{ -\left[\ln\left(\cosh\frac{\sigma\zeta_2}{2}\right)\right]^2/\sigma \right\} \exp(\zeta_2^2/4) d\zeta_2$$

Now we must equate Eqs. (58) and (59) to zero and solve these equations simultaneously for μ and σ. To solve these equations explicitly for μ and σ is not possible; however, we suggest an iterative method for obtaining good estimates of the parameters.

Define the following two matrices

$$A = \begin{bmatrix} a_{11} & a_{12} \\ a_{21} & a_{22} \end{bmatrix} \quad B = \begin{bmatrix} b_{11} & b_{12} \\ d_{21} & b_{22} \end{bmatrix}$$

TABLE 1
Comparison[a] of the Mean and Variance of the Variate Z
for $\mu = 0$ with Those of Naus

σ	Mean	Naus' mean	Variance	Naus' variance
1	3.067	3.067	0.506	0.507
2	3.229	3.230	2.088	2.089
3	3.480	3.480	4.874	4.875
4	3.798	3.798	8.975	8.976
5	4.168	4.168	14.455	14.46
6	4.576	4.576	21.34	21.35
7	5.014	5.014	29.63	29.66
8	5.473	5.474	39.40	39.40
9	5.951	5.951	50.56	50.56
10	6.441	6.442	63.14	63.13

[a] Note that for the purpose of comparing our results with those of Naus [11], we adjusted our calculations to $\log_{10}$ which is consistent with Naus' derivations.

Let

$$\frac{\partial \ln L(\mu, \sigma)}{\partial \mu} = h_1(\mu, \sigma) = 0$$

and

$$\frac{\partial \ln L(\mu, \sigma)}{\partial \sigma} = h_2(\mu, \sigma) = 0$$

The elements of B are computed from the following expressions [14]:

$$b_{11}(k) = \frac{h_1[t_1^{(k)}, \sigma^{(k)}] - h_1[\mu^{(k)}, \sigma^{(k)}]}{t_1^{(k)} - \mu^{(k)}}$$

$$b_{12}(k) = \frac{h_1[\mu^{(k)}, t_2^{(k)}] - h_1[\mu^{(k)}, \sigma^{(k)}]}{t_2^{(k)} - \sigma^{(k)}}$$

$$b_{21}(k) = \frac{h_2[t_1^{(k)}, \sigma^{(k)}] - h_2[\mu^{(k)}, \sigma^{(k)}]}{t_1^{(k)} - \mu^{(k)}}$$

and

$$b_{22}(k) = \frac{h_2[\mu^{(k)}, t_2^{(k)}] - h_2[\mu^{(k)}, \sigma^{(k)}]}{t_2^{(k)} - \sigma^{(k)}}$$

where

$$t_1^{(k)} = \mu^{(k)} + a_{11}^{(k)} h_1[\mu^{(k)}, \sigma^{(k)}] + a_{12}^{(k)} h_2[\mu^{(k)}, \sigma^{(k)}]$$

BIVARIATE

and

$$t_2^{(k)} = \sigma^{(k)} + a_{21}^{(k)} h_1[\mu^{(k)}, \sigma^{(k)}] + a_{22}^{(k)} h_2[\mu^{(k)}, \sigma^{(k)}]$$

Here the superscripts denote the iteration count. For $\mu^{(0)}$ and $\sigma^{(0)}$ sufficiently close to the roots $\hat{\mu}$, $\hat{\sigma}$, and some $\beta^{(0)}$, the sequence of iterations

$$\begin{bmatrix} \mu^{(k+1)} \\ \sigma^{(k+1)} \end{bmatrix} = \begin{bmatrix} \mu^{(k)} \\ \sigma^{(k)} \end{bmatrix} + \begin{bmatrix} b_{11} & b_{12} \\ b_{21} & b_{22} \end{bmatrix}^{-1(k)} \begin{bmatrix} h_1[\mu^{(k)}, \sigma^{(k)}] \\ h_2[\mu^{(k)}, \sigma^{(k)}] \end{bmatrix}$$

will converge to

$$\begin{bmatrix} \hat{\mu} \\ \hat{\sigma} \end{bmatrix}$$

the maximum likelihood estimates of μ and σ. Successive values of $a^{(0)}$ are defined by

$$a^{(k+1)} = -b^{-1(k)}$$

The proper choice of $a^{(0)}$ depends upon the properties of the equation being solved.

We proceed by employing the method of moments to obtain estimates of the unknown parameters.

We have seen that

$$\eta_k = E(Z - \mu)^k = \frac{\sigma^k}{2\pi} \sum_{\substack{n=0 \\ n+k \text{ even}}}^{\infty} \frac{2n}{n!} I_n(\sigma) \Gamma\left(\frac{n+k+1}{2}\right)$$

$$= \psi(\sigma, k) \qquad (60)$$

From Eqs. (55) and (56) and using Eq. (60) we can write

$$E(Z) = \mu + \psi(\sigma, 1)$$

and

$$\text{Var}(Z) = \psi(\sigma, 2) - \psi^2(\sigma, 1)$$

Let $\bar{z}$ and s^2 be the sample estimates of $E(Z)$ and $\text{Var}(Z)$, respectively. Equating the sampled values to the theoretical values we have

$$\mu^* + \psi(\sigma^*, 1) = \bar{z}$$

and

$$\psi(\sigma^*, 2) - \psi^2(\sigma^*, 1) = s^2 \qquad (61)$$

Since the second equation is independent of μ^*, we can solve it for σ^* and insert its value in the first equation to obtain an estimate of μ. Let

$$\phi(\sigma^*) = \psi(\sigma^*, 2) - \psi^2(\sigma^*, 1) - s^2 \qquad (62)$$

and solve $\phi(\sigma^*) = 0$ by the following iterative method:

$$\sigma_{j+1}^* = \sigma_j^* - \frac{\phi(\sigma_j^*)}{Q_j}$$

TABLE 2

j	$\sigma_j{}^*$	$\phi_j(\sigma_j{}^*)$	$\sigma_j{}^* + q_j\phi(\sigma_j{}^*)$	$\phi(\sigma_j{}^* + q_j\phi(\sigma_j{}^*))$	Q_j
0	0.76091	0.07503	0.68588	0.13751	−.83275
1	0.85101	−0.00999	0.83901	0.00197	−.99673
2	0.84098	0.00001	0.84099	0.00000	−.99124
3	0.84099				

where

$$Q_j = \frac{\phi(\sigma_j{}^* + q_j\phi(\sigma_j{}^*)) - \phi(\sigma_j{}^*)}{q_j\phi(\sigma_j{}^*)}$$

and

$$q_j = Q_{j-1}$$

The method requires initial values for σ^* and q.

An Example Using the Method of Moments

An random sample of 10 values from a population which is characterized by the probability distribution of the variate Z with $\mu = 0$ and $\sigma = 1$ revealed the following sampled values:

$$\bar{z} = 0.9134 \quad \text{and} \quad s^2 = 0.3911$$

For starting values we shall assume

$$q_0 = 1 \quad \text{and} \quad \sigma_0{}^* = [\ln(2s^2 + 1)]^{1/2}$$

Table 2 gives the successive iterations from $j = 0$ to $j = 3$.

The method of moments estimates of μ and σ^2 are

$$\sigma^* = 0.84099 \quad \text{and} \quad \mu^* = 0.9134 - \psi(0.84099, 1) = 0.0662$$

An Example Using the Maximum Likelihood Method

A random sample of 100 observations was generated from a population being characterized by Eq. (22) with $\mu = \ln 10$ and $\sigma = 0.8$. We take as estimates of $\mu^{(0)}$ and $\sigma^{(0)}$ the estimates obtained by the method of moments, that is,

$$\mu^{(0)} = 2.2293 \quad \text{and} \quad \sigma^{(0)} = 0.7086$$

Utilizing the iterative method for solving Eqs. (58) and (59), we obtained the estimates of μ and σ given in Table 3.

A Monte Carlo simulation was performed to compare the estimates of μ and σ using the two methods discussed above. From the results obtained in the simulation [8], we can conclude that the method of moments performed about

BIVARIATE

TABLE 3

i	$\hat{\mu}_i$	$\hat{\sigma}_i$
0	2.2282995	0.7085521
1	2.2775508	0.7599893
2	2.3361460	0.75628217
3	2.3466914	0.7703892
4	2.3471334	0.7707610
5	2.3471338	0.7707611

$b_{11}^{(i)}$	$b_{12}^{(i)}$	$b_{13}^{(i)}$	$b_{22}^{(i)}$
0.34847 (−02)	−0.12400 (−02)	−0.12229 (−02)	0.20989 (−02)
0.33355 (−02)	−0.75409 (−03)	−0.73770 (−03)	0.25422 (−02)
0.34424 (−02)	−0.72112 (−03)	−0.72993 (−03)	0.27475 (−02)
0.34444 (−02)	−0.71888 (−03)	−0.72874 (−03)	0.27514 (−02)
0.34444 (−02)	−0.71888 (−03)	−0.72874 (−03)	0.27514 (−02)

as well as the maximum likelihood estimation. Thus, as a result of this finding, one can use the method of moments to obtain estimates of the true states of nature rather than the maximum likelihood method which is more difficult to compute.

Lowrimore and Tsokos [8] have applied the above findings to an environmental problem. This application is concerned with the long-term exposure to low levels of nitrogen dioxide in the ambient atmosphere which has been implicated as a contributing factor in the development of acute respiratory illness.

THE PROBABILITY DISTRIBUTION OF THE LOGARITHM OF THE SUM OF TWO CORRELATED LOG-NORMAL VARIATES

We have shown that Hamdan [6] recently generalized the results of Naus [11] by developing the moment generating function of the probability distribution of the logarithm of the sum of two correlated log-normal random variables with common mean and unequal variances. From this result he obtained the mean and variance of the above stochastic variable.

Lourimore and Tsokos [8] have extended the results of Hamdan by deriving the probability density function of the random variable

$$Z = \ln[\exp(X_1) + \exp(X_2)]$$

where X_1 and X_2 are correlated normal variates. Here we develop this probability distribution and its rth central moments. Finally, we formulate

The Probability Distribution of the Variate Z

Let X_1 and X_2 be characterized by the *bivariate normal distribution*, with common mean, μ, variance, σ^2, and correlation coefficient, ρ. That is,

$$f(x_1, x_2; \mu, \sigma^2, \rho) = \frac{1}{2\pi\sigma^2\sqrt{1-\rho^2}}$$
$$\cdot \exp\left\{-\frac{1}{2\sigma^2(1-\rho^2)}[(x_1-\mu)^2 - 2\rho(x_1-\mu)(x_2-\mu) + (x_2-\mu)^2]\right\}, \quad (63)$$

$$-\infty < x_1, x_2 < \infty$$
$$\sigma > 0$$
$$-\infty < \mu < \infty$$
$$-1 < \rho < 1$$

Upon applying the transformations

$$\zeta_1 = \frac{x_1-\mu}{2} + \frac{x_2-\mu}{2}$$

and

$$\zeta_2 = \frac{x_1-\mu}{2} - \frac{x_2-\mu}{2}$$

the bivariate density function (Eq. 63) becomes

$$f_1(\zeta_1, \zeta_2) = \frac{1}{\pi\sigma^2\sqrt{1-\rho^2}}$$
$$\cdot \exp\left\{-\frac{1}{2\sigma^2(1-\rho^2)}[2(1-\rho)\zeta_1^2 + 2(1+\rho)\zeta_2^2]\right\}, \quad -\infty < \zeta_1, \zeta_2 < \infty \quad (64)$$

The Mellin transform of the variate $Y = \exp(X_1) + \exp(X_2)$ is

$$m(\xi) = \int_{-\infty}^{\infty}\int_{-\infty}^{\infty} [(\exp(x_1) + \exp(x_2)]^{\xi-1} f(x_1, x_2; \mu, \sigma^2, \rho) dx_1 dx_2 \quad (65)$$

and in terms of the variates ζ_1 and ζ_2, Eq. (65) becomes

$$m(\xi) = \frac{\exp[\mu(\xi-1)]}{\pi\sigma^2\sqrt{1-\rho^2}} \int_{-\infty}^{\infty} \exp[\zeta_1(\xi-1)] \exp\left(-\frac{1}{\sigma^2(1+\rho)}\zeta_1^2\right) d\zeta_1$$
$$\cdot \int_{-\infty}^{\infty} [\exp(\zeta_2) + \exp(-\zeta_2)]^{\xi-1} \exp\left(-\frac{\zeta_2^2}{\sigma^2(1-\rho)}\right) d\zeta_2 \quad (66)$$

BIVARIATE

Completing the square on ζ_1 and upon simplifying, Eq. (66) reduces to

$$m(\xi) = \frac{\exp\left(m(\xi - 1) + \frac{\sigma^2(1 + \rho)}{4}(\xi - 1)^2\right)}{\sqrt{\pi}\sqrt{1 - \rho^2}}$$

$$\cdot \int_{-\infty}^{\infty} [\exp(\zeta_2) + \exp(-\zeta_2)]^{\xi-1} \exp\left(-\frac{\zeta_2^2}{\sigma^2(1 - \rho)}\right) d\zeta_2 \quad (67)$$

Applying the inversion Formula (16) to Eq. (67):

$$h(y) = \frac{1}{2\pi i \sqrt{\pi\sigma^2(1 - \rho)}} \int_{1-i\infty}^{1+i\infty} y^{-\xi} \exp\left[\mu(\xi - 1) + \frac{\sigma^2(1 + \rho)(\xi - 1)^2}{4}\right]$$

$$\cdot \int_{-\infty}^{\infty} [\exp(\zeta_2) + \exp(-\zeta_2)]^{(\xi-1)} \exp\left(-\frac{\zeta_2^2}{\sigma^2(1 - \rho)}\right) d\zeta_2 \, d\xi \quad (68)$$

Let $\xi = 1 + iv$ in Eq. (68) and simplifying,

$$h(y) = \frac{1}{2\pi^{3/2}\sigma\sqrt{1 - \rho}y} \int_{-\infty}^{\infty} \exp\left\{-i(\ln y)v + i\mu v - \frac{(1 + \rho)}{4}\sigma^2 v^2\right\}$$

$$\cdot \int_{-\infty}^{\infty} \exp\{[i \ln 2 \cosh \zeta_2]v\} \exp\left(-\frac{\zeta_2^2}{\sigma^2(1 - \rho)}\right) d\zeta_2 \, dv \quad (69)$$

Interchange the order of integration and complete the square in the exponent of the integral in v:

$$h_1(v) = \exp\left\{-\left[\frac{\mu - \ln y + \ln(2 \cosh \zeta_2)}{\sigma^2(1 + \rho)}\right]\right\}$$

$$\cdot \int_{-\infty}^{\infty} \exp\left\{-\left[\frac{\sigma^2(1 + \rho)}{4}\left(v - \frac{2i(\mu - \ln y + \ln(2 \cosh \zeta_2))}{\sigma^2(1 + \rho)}\right)^2\right]\right\} dv \quad (70)$$

Upon evaluating the integral in Eq. (70),

$$h_1(v) = \frac{2\sqrt{\pi}}{\sigma\sqrt{1 + \rho}} \exp\left\{-\frac{[\mu - \ln y + \ln(2 \cos \zeta_2)]^2}{\sigma^2(1 + \rho)}\right\} \quad (71)$$

Substituting Eq. (71) into Eq. (69),

$$h(y) = \frac{1}{\pi\sigma^2\sqrt{1 - \rho^2}y} \exp\left\{-\left[\frac{\ln y - \mu}{\sigma\sqrt{1 + \rho}}\right]^2\right\}$$

$$\cdot \int_{-\infty}^{\infty} \exp\left\{2\left[\frac{\ln y - \mu}{\sigma\sqrt{1 + \rho}} \frac{\ln(2 \cosh \zeta_2)}{\sigma\sqrt{1 + \rho}}\right]\right\} \exp\left\{-\frac{\ln(2 \cosh \zeta_2)}{\sigma\sqrt{1 + \rho}}\right\}^2 \quad (72)$$

$$\cdot \exp\left(\frac{\zeta_2^2}{\sigma^2(1 - \rho)}\right) d\zeta_2$$

Since

$$\exp\left\{2\left[\frac{\ln y - \mu}{\sigma\sqrt{1 + \rho}} \frac{\ln(2 \cosh \zeta_2)}{\sigma\sqrt{1 + \rho}}\right]\right\} = \sum_{n=0}^{\infty} \frac{2^n}{n!} \left\{\frac{\ln(2 \cosh \zeta_2)}{\sigma\sqrt{1 + \rho}}\right\}^n \left\{\frac{\ln y - \mu}{\sigma\sqrt{1 + \rho}}\right\}^n$$

we can write Eq. (72) as

$$h(y) = \frac{\exp\left(-\left\{\frac{\ln y - \mu}{\sigma\sqrt{1+\rho}}\right\}^2\right)}{2\pi\sigma\sqrt{1-\rho^2}\,y} \sum_{n=0}^{\infty} \frac{2^n}{n!} K_n(\sigma, \rho)\left(\frac{\ln y - \mu}{\sigma\sqrt{1+\rho}}\right)^n, \quad \begin{array}{l} -\infty < \mu < \infty \\ \sigma, y > 0 \\ -1 < \rho < 1 \end{array} \quad (73)$$

where

$$K_n(\sigma, \rho) = \frac{2}{\sigma} \int_{-\infty}^{\infty} \left\{\frac{\ln(2\cosh\zeta_2)}{\sigma\sqrt{1+\rho}}\right\}^n \exp\left\{-\left[\frac{\ln(2\cosh\zeta_2)}{\sigma\sqrt{1+\rho}}\right]^2\right\} \exp\left(-\frac{\zeta_2^2}{\sigma^2(1-\rho)}\right) d\zeta_2 \quad (74)$$

Equation (73) is the probability density function of the sum of two correlated log-normal variates with equal mean and variance. Thus the probability distribution of the stochastic variable $Z = \ln Y$ is given by

$$g(z) = \frac{\exp\left(-\left\{\frac{z - \mu}{\sigma\sqrt{1+\rho}}\right\}^2\right)}{2\pi\sigma\sqrt{1-\rho^2}} \sum_{n=0}^{\infty} \frac{2^n}{n!} K_n(\sigma, \rho)\left\{\frac{z - \mu}{\sigma\sqrt{1-\rho}}\right\}^n, \quad \begin{array}{l} -\infty < z, \mu < \infty \\ -1 < \rho < 1 \\ \sigma > 0 \end{array} \quad (75)$$

The cumulative probability distribution of the random variable Z is given by

$$G(z) = \frac{1}{2\pi\sigma\sqrt{1-\rho^2}} \sum_{n=0}^{\infty} \frac{2^n}{n!} K_n(\sigma, \rho) \int_{-\infty}^{z} \left\{\frac{v - \mu}{\sigma\sqrt{1+\rho}}\right\}^n \exp\left(-\left[\frac{v - \mu}{\sigma\sqrt{1+\rho}}\right]^2\right) dv \quad (76)$$

Applying the transformation $t = (v - \mu)/\sigma\sqrt{1+\rho}$ to Eq. (76) and simplifying,

$$G(z) = \frac{1}{2\pi\sqrt{1-\rho}} \sum_{n=0}^{\infty} \frac{2^n}{n!} K_n(\sigma, \rho) H_n^*(z) \quad (77)$$

where

$$H_n^*(z) = \int_{-\infty}^{(z-\mu)/\sigma\sqrt{1+\rho}} t^n \exp(-t^2) dt \quad (78)$$

Using similar arguments as employed in formulating Eqs. (28) to (36):

$$H_n^*(z) = \begin{cases} \frac{(-1)^n}{2} \Gamma\left(\frac{n+1}{2}\right) + \frac{\sqrt{2\pi}}{2^{(n+1)/2}} \mu_n\left\{\sqrt{2}\left[\frac{z-\mu}{\sigma\sqrt{1+\rho}}\right]\right\}, & -\infty < \mu < z \\ \frac{(-1)^n}{2} \Gamma\left(\frac{n+1}{2}\right) + \frac{(-1)^{n+1}\sqrt{2\pi}}{2^{(n+1)/2}} \mu_n\left\{-\sqrt{2}\left[\frac{z-\mu}{\sigma\sqrt{1+\rho}}\right]\right\}, & \mu < z < \infty \end{cases}$$

where $\mu_n(t)$ is given by Eq. (31). Substituting the above expression for $H_n^*(z)$ in Eq. (77) and after simplifying,

$$G(z) = \frac{1}{2\pi\sqrt{1-\rho}} \sum_{n=0}^{\infty} \frac{(-1)^n 2^{n-1}}{n!} K_n(\sigma, \rho) \Gamma\left(\frac{n+1}{2}\right) + L\left\{\sqrt{2}\left[\frac{z-\mu}{\sigma\sqrt{1+\rho}}\right]\right\} \quad (79)$$

BIVARIATE

where

$$L(t) = \begin{cases} \dfrac{1}{\sqrt{2\pi}\sqrt{1-\rho}} \sum_{n=0}^{\infty} \dfrac{2^{(n-1)/2}}{n!} K_n(\sigma, \rho)\mu_n(t), & t \geq 0 \\ \dfrac{1}{\sqrt{2\pi}\sqrt{1-\rho}} \sum_{n=0}^{\infty} \dfrac{(-1)^{n+1}2^{(n-1)/2}}{n!} K_n(\sigma, \rho)\mu_n(-t), & t \leq 0 \end{cases}$$

Using similar arguments as employed at the end of the section entitled Formulation of the Probability Distribution, we can write

$$G(z) = \dfrac{1}{2\pi\sqrt{1-\rho}} \sum_{n=0}^{\infty} \dfrac{(-1)2^{n-1}}{n!} K_n(\sigma, \rho)\Gamma\!\left(\dfrac{n+1}{2}\right) + M_1\!\left[\sqrt{2}\!\left(\dfrac{z-\mu}{\sigma\sqrt{1+\rho}}\right)\right]$$

$$+ \operatorname{sgn}(z-\mu) N_1\!\left[\sqrt{2}\!\left(\dfrac{z-\mu}{\sigma\sqrt{1-\rho}}\right)\right], \qquad -\infty < z < \infty \quad (80)$$

where

$$M_1(t) = \dfrac{1}{2\pi\sqrt{1-\rho}} \sum_{m=0}^{\infty} \dfrac{2^m}{(2m+1)!} K_{2m}(\sigma, \rho)[(2m)!]! F(t^2_{2m+2})$$

and

$$N_1(t) = \dfrac{1}{\sqrt{2\pi}\sqrt{1-\rho}} \sum_{m=0}^{\infty} \dfrac{2^{m-3/2}}{(2m)!} K_{2m}(\sigma, \rho)[(2m-1)!]! F(t^2_{2m+1})$$

The above expression for the cumulative probability distribution of the variate Z can be easily evaluated for specific values of the parameters using electronic computers. To this effect we shall discuss the computational behavior of the expansion $K_n(\rho, \sigma)$.

It is clear from the definition of $K_n(\rho, \sigma)$ by Eq. (74) that it is an even function and can be written as

$$K_n(\sigma, \rho) = \dfrac{4}{\sigma} \int_0^{\infty} \left\{\dfrac{\zeta_2 + \ln[1+\exp(-2\zeta_2)]}{\sigma\sqrt{1+\rho}}\right\}^n$$

$$\cdot \exp\!\left(\dfrac{-2\zeta_2 \ln[1+\exp(2\zeta_2)]}{\sigma^2(1+\rho^2)} - \dfrac{\{\ln[1+\exp(-2\zeta_2)]\}^2}{\sigma^2(1+\rho)}\right) \quad (81)$$

$$\cdot \exp\!\left(-\dfrac{\zeta_2^2}{\sigma^2(1-\rho)} - \dfrac{\zeta_2^2}{\sigma^2(1+\rho)}\right) d\zeta_2$$

where

$$\dfrac{\ln(2\cosh\zeta_2)}{\sigma\sqrt{1+\rho}} = \dfrac{\zeta_2 + \ln[1+\exp(-2\zeta_2)]}{\sigma\sqrt{1+\rho}}$$

Substituting $v = \sqrt{2}\zeta_2/\sigma\sqrt{1-\rho^2}$ in Eq. (81) and simplifying it,

$$K_n(\sigma, \rho) = 2\sqrt{2}\sqrt{1-\rho^2}$$

$$\cdot \int_0^\infty \left\{ \frac{(\sigma\sqrt{1-\rho^2}/2)v + \ln[1 + \exp(-\sqrt{2}\sigma\sqrt{1-\rho^2}v)]}{\sigma\sqrt{1+\rho}} \right\}^n$$

$$\cdot \exp\left\{ \frac{\sqrt{2}\sigma\sqrt{1-\rho^2}v \ln[1 + \exp(-\sqrt{2}\sigma\sqrt{1-\rho^2}v)]}{\sigma^2(1+\rho)} \right. \quad (82)$$

$$\left. - \frac{\{\ln[1 + \exp(-\sqrt{2}\sigma\sqrt{1-\rho^2}v)]\}^2}{\sigma^2(1+\rho)} \right\} \exp(-v^2) dv$$

To control the rapidly varying integrand, we shall scale it so that its maximum value is unity. The necessary scale factor is of the form

$$\left\{ \frac{\ln 2}{\sigma\sqrt{1+\rho}} \right\}^n \exp\left(-\left\{ \frac{\ln 2}{\sigma\sqrt{1+\rho}} \right\}\right)$$

Thus our computational form of $K_n(\sigma, \rho)$ is of the form

$$K_n(\sigma, \rho) = 2\sqrt{2}\sqrt{1-\rho^2}\left\{ \frac{\ln 2}{\sigma\sqrt{1+\rho}} \right\}^n \exp\left\{ -\left[\frac{\ln 2}{\sigma\sqrt{1+\rho}} \right]^2 \right\}$$

$$\cdot \int_0^\infty \left\{ \frac{(\sigma\sqrt{1-\rho^2}v/\sqrt{2}) + \ln[1 + \exp(-\sqrt{2}\sigma\sqrt{1-\rho^2}v)]}{\ln 2} \right\}^n$$

$$\cdot \exp\left\{ -\frac{1}{\sigma^2(1+\rho)} \{v\sigma\sqrt{2}\sqrt{1-\rho^2} \ln[1 + \exp(-v\sigma\sqrt{2}\sqrt{1-\rho^2})] \right.$$

$$\left. + \ln[1 + \exp(-v\sigma\sqrt{2}\sqrt{1-\rho^2})] - (\ln 2)^2 \} \right\} \exp(-v^2) dv$$

which we can write as

$$K_n(\sigma, \rho) = 2\sqrt{2}\sqrt{1-\rho^2}\left\{ \frac{\ln 2}{\sigma\sqrt{1+\rho}} \right\}^n$$

$$\cdot \exp\left(-\left\{ \frac{\ln 2}{\sigma\sqrt{1+\rho}} \right\}^2\right) \int_0^\infty k(\sigma, \rho, v)\exp(-v^2) dv \quad (83)$$

Applying a Gaussian quadrature formula with $2r + 1$ points to Eq. (83):

$$K_n(\sigma, \rho) = 2\sqrt{2}\sqrt{1-\rho^2}\left\{ \frac{\ln 2}{\sigma\sqrt{1+\rho}} \right\}^n \exp\left(-\left\{ \frac{\ln 2}{\sigma\sqrt{1+\rho}} \right\}^2\right) \sum_{j=0}^r \zeta_j k_n(\sigma, \rho, v_j)$$

(84)

where the v_j are the nonnegative roots of the Hermite polynomials of degree $2r$

+ 1. $K_n(\sigma, \rho)$ has been tabulated for specific values of μ and σ:

r	$K_1(0.1, 0)$	$K_1(6, 0)$	$K_{25}(0.1, 0)$	$K_{25}(6, 0)$
24	2.576580032(−20)	1.04238417	4.11355308	1.16943750(05)
31	2.576580032(−20)	1.04245188	4.11355308	1.16943750(05)

and

r	$K_1(0.1, -0.9)$	$K_1(6, -0.9)$	$K_{25}(0.1, -0.9)$	$K_{25}(6, -0.9)$
24	0.0000000000	6.86418695(−01)	0.000000000	1.55518439(08)
31	0.0000000000	6.86418677(−01)	0.000000000	1.55518439(08)

Hence, using electronic computers, one can obtain accurate values of $K_n(\sigma, \rho)$.

Moments of the Random Variable $Z = \ln Y$

The rth central moment of the random variable Z is given by

$$\eta_r = E\{Z - \mu\}^r$$

$$= \frac{1}{2\pi\sigma\sqrt{1-\rho^2}} \int_{-\infty}^{\infty} (z-\mu)^r \exp\left\{-\left[\frac{z-\mu}{\sigma\sqrt{1+\rho}}\right]^2\right\}$$

$$\cdot \sum_{n=0}^{\infty} \frac{2^n}{n!} K_n(\sigma, \rho) \left[\frac{z-\mu}{\sigma\sqrt{1+\rho}}\right]^n dz \quad (85)$$

Applying the transformation $t = (z - \mu)/\sigma\sqrt{1+\rho}$ and interchanging the order of summation and integration,

$$\eta_r = \frac{(\sigma\sqrt{1+\rho})^{r+1}}{2\pi\sigma\sqrt{1-\rho^2}} \sum_{n=0}^{\infty} \frac{2^n}{n!} K_n(\sigma, \rho) \frac{1}{2} \int_{-\infty}^{\infty} t^{n+r} \exp(-t^2) dt \quad (86)$$

The integral in Eq. (86) is 0 for $n + r$ odd, and for $n + r$ even we can write

$$\eta_r = \frac{\sigma^r(1+\rho)^{r/2}}{2\pi\sqrt{1-\rho}} \sum_{\substack{n=0 \\ n+r \text{ even}}}^{\infty} \frac{2^n}{n!} K_n(\sigma, \rho) \Gamma\left(\frac{n+r+1}{2}\right) \quad (87)$$

Thus, in view of Eq. (87),

$$E[Z] = \frac{\sigma\sqrt{1+\rho}}{2\pi\sqrt{1-\rho}} \sum_{\substack{n=0 \\ n \text{ odd}}}^{\infty} \frac{2^n}{n!} K_n(\sigma, \rho) \Gamma\left(\frac{n+2}{2}\right) \quad (88)$$

and the variance of the variate Z is given by

$$\text{Var}(Z) = \frac{\sigma^2(1+\rho)}{2\pi\sqrt{1-\rho}} \sum_{\substack{n=0 \\ n \text{ even}}}^{\infty} \frac{2^n}{n!} K_n(\sigma, \rho) \Gamma\left(\frac{n+3}{2}\right) - \{E(Z)\}^2 \quad (89)$$

Thus, one can utilize the computation techniques discussed in the previous section to calculate the values of the mean and variance of the variate Z. In Ref. 8 we showed numerically that our results compare favorably with those obtained by Hamdan's findings.

Estimates of the Parameters in the Probability Distribution of the Variate Z

We begin by formulating a maximum likelihood estimate for the parameters μ, σ, and ρ of the probability distribution of the variate Z.

The probability density of Z is given by

$$g(z; \mu, \sigma, \rho) = \frac{\exp[-D^2(z; \mu, \sigma, \rho)]}{2\pi\sigma\sqrt{1-\rho^2}} \sum_{n=0}^{\infty} \frac{2^n}{n!} K_n(\sigma, \rho) D^n(z; \mu, \sigma, \rho) \quad (90)$$

where

$$D(z; \mu, \sigma, \rho) = \frac{z - \mu}{\sigma\sqrt{1+\rho}}$$

Taking the natural logarithm of both sides of Eq. (90),

$$\ln g(z; \mu, \sigma, \rho) = -D^2(z; \mu, \sigma, \rho) - \ln 2\pi - \ln \sigma - \frac{1}{2}\ln(1-\rho^2)$$
$$+ \ln\left\{\sum_{n=0}^{\infty} \frac{2^n}{n!} K_n(\sigma, \rho) D^n(z; \mu, \sigma, \rho)\right\} \quad (91)$$

Differentiating first with respect to σ and then with respect to μ and ρ,

$$\frac{\partial \ln}{\partial \sigma} g_i(z; \mu, \sigma, \rho) = \frac{2D^2}{\sigma}(z_i; \mu, \sigma, \rho) - \frac{1}{\sigma}$$
$$+ \frac{\sum_{n=0}^{\infty} \frac{2^n}{n!} D^n(z_i; \mu, \sigma, \rho)\left[-\frac{nK_n(\sigma, \rho)}{\sigma} + \frac{\partial K_n(\sigma, \rho)}{\partial \sigma}\right]}{\sum_{n=0}^{\infty} \frac{2^n}{n!} K_n(\sigma, \rho) D^n(z_i; \mu, \sigma, \rho)} \quad (92)$$

$$\frac{\partial \ln}{\partial \mu} g_i(z_i; \mu, \sigma, \rho) = \frac{2D(z_i; \mu, \sigma, \rho)}{\sigma\sqrt{1+\rho}} - \frac{1}{\sigma\sqrt{1+\rho}}$$
$$+ \frac{\sum_{n=1}^{\infty} \frac{2^n}{(n-1)!} K_n(\sigma, \rho) D^{n-1}(z_i; \mu, \sigma, \rho)}{\sum_{n=0}^{\infty} \frac{2^n}{n!} K_n(\sigma, \rho) D^n(z_i; \mu, \sigma, \rho)} \quad (93)$$

and

$$\frac{\partial \ln}{\partial \rho} g_i(z_i; \mu, \sigma, \rho) = \frac{-D^2(z_i; \mu, \sigma, \rho)}{(1-\rho)} + \frac{\rho}{1+\rho^2}$$

$$+ \frac{\sum_{n=0}^{\infty} \frac{2^n}{n!} D^n(z_i; \mu, \sigma, \rho) \left[\frac{n K_n(\sigma, \rho)}{2(1+\rho)} + \frac{\partial K_n(\sigma, \rho)}{\partial \rho} \right]}{\sum_{n=0}^{\infty} \frac{2^n}{n!} K_n(\sigma, \rho) D^n(z_i; \mu, \sigma, \rho)} \quad (94)$$

The derivatives $\partial K_n(\sigma, \rho)/\partial \sigma$ and $\partial K_n(\sigma, \rho)/\partial \rho$ are given by the expressions

$$\frac{\partial K_n(\sigma, \rho)}{\partial \sigma} = \frac{2}{\sigma} \int_{-\infty}^{\infty} \left\{ \frac{\ln(2 \cosh \zeta_2)}{2\sqrt{1+\rho}} \right\}^n \exp\left\{ -\left[\frac{\ln(2 \cosh \zeta_2)}{\sigma\sqrt{1+\rho}} \right]^2 \right\}$$

$$\cdot \exp\left(-\frac{\zeta_2^2}{\sigma^2(1-\rho)}\right) \left[\frac{2}{\sigma} \left\{ \frac{\ln(2 \cosh \zeta_2)}{\sigma\sqrt{1+\rho}} \right\}^2 + \frac{2\zeta_2^2}{(1-\rho)\sigma^3} - \frac{(n+1)}{\sigma} \right] d\zeta_2 \quad (95)$$

and

$$\frac{\partial K_n(\sigma, \rho)}{\partial \rho} = \frac{2}{\sigma} \int_{-\infty}^{\infty} \left\{ \frac{\ln 2 \cosh \zeta_2}{\sigma\sqrt{1+\rho}} \right\}^n \exp\left\{ -\left[\frac{\ln(2 \cosh \zeta_2)}{\sigma\sqrt{1+\rho}} \right]^2 \right\}$$

$$\cdot \exp\left(-\frac{\zeta_2^2}{\sigma^2(1-\rho)}\right) \left[\frac{(-n)}{2(1+\rho)} + \left\{ \frac{\ln(2 \cosh \zeta_2)}{\sigma\sqrt{1+\rho}} \right\}^2 \right.$$

$$\left. \cdot \frac{1}{1+\rho} - \frac{\zeta_2^2}{\sigma^2(1-\rho)^2} \right] d\zeta_2 \quad (96)$$

respectively. The maximum likelihood estimates for μ, σ, and ρ can be obtained by using the iterative method we discussed in the section entitled Estimation of the Parameters of the Probability Distribution of the Variate Z to solve the following system of equations:

$$\sum_{i=1}^{k} \frac{\partial \ln g}{\partial \sigma}(z_i; \mu, \sigma, \rho) = 0$$

$$\sum_{i=1}^{k} \frac{\partial \ln g}{\partial \mu}(z_i; \mu, \sigma, \rho) = 0$$

$$\sum_{i=1}^{k} \frac{\partial \ln g}{\partial \rho}(z_i; \mu, \sigma, \rho) = 0$$

where k is the random sample size.

To obtain the estimates of the parameters μ and σ, we begin by writing Eq. (88), as

$$E[Z - \mu]^r = \frac{\sigma^r(1+\rho)^{r/2}}{2\pi\sqrt{1-\rho}} \sum_{n=0}^{\infty} \frac{2^n}{n!} K_n(\sigma, \rho) \Gamma\left(\frac{n+r+1}{2}\right)$$

$$= l(\sigma, \rho, r)$$

The first moment with respect to the origin is

$$E[Z] = \mu + l(\sigma, \rho, 1)$$

also

$$E\{Z - E(Z)\} = l(\sigma, \rho, 2) - l^2(\rho, \sigma, 1)$$

and

$$E\{Z - E(Z)\}^3 = l(\sigma, \rho, 3) - 3l(\sigma, \rho, 2)l(\sigma, \rho, 1) + 2l^3(\sigma, \rho, 1)$$

Equating the sample estimates to the theoretical estimates, we obtain the following set of equations:

$$\bar{z} = \mu^* + l(\sigma^*, \rho^*, 1) \qquad (97)$$
$$s^2 = l(\sigma^*, \rho^*, 2) - l^2(\sigma^*, \rho^*, 1) \qquad (98)$$
$$m_3 = l(\sigma^*, \rho^*, 3) - 3l(\sigma^*, \rho^*, 2)l(\sigma^*, \rho^*, 1) + 2l^3(\sigma^*, \rho^*, 1) \qquad (99)$$

where m_3 is the third sample moment with respect to the mean. Equations (98) and (99) are independent of μ^*, thus they can be solved simultaneously for σ^* and ρ^*. Having obtained the estimate for σ and ρ, we can insert them in Eq. (97) to obtain the moment estimate of the parameter μ.

The theoretical developments presented here are important in the study of certain air pollution problems. For example, when the concentration of a particular pollutant results from two sources which do not act independently, the logarithm of the measured pollutant concentration are characterized by the probability density function of the variate Z given by Eq. (75). For additional details concerning this environmental application, see Ref. 8.

GENERALIZATION TO THE CASE OF THE SUM OF THE LOGARITHM OF N LOG-NORMAL VARIATES

In this section we give a brief presentation of extending the results of the section entitled The Probability Distribution of the Logarithm of the Sum of Two Uncorrelated Log-Normal Variates. The results will be generalized to include the case of N log-normal random variables.

We develop the probability density function of the logarithm of the sum of N independent log-normally distributed random variables, indicate the form of the cumulative distribution function, and comment on the approach one should follow in estimating the parameters inherited in the probability distribution.

The Probability Distribution

Let $X_1, X_2, \ldots, X_N$ be a sequence of independent normal random variables with equal mean μ and variance σ^2. Their joint probability density function is

BIVARIATE

given by

$$f(x_1, x_2, \ldots, x_N) = \frac{1}{(2\pi)^{N/2}\sigma^N} \exp\left\{-\frac{1}{2}\sum_{j=1}^{N}\frac{x_j - \mu^2}{\sigma}\right\} \quad (100)$$

The Mellin transform of the variate

$$Y = \sum_{j=1}^{N} \exp(X_j)$$

is

$$m_N(\xi) = E\{Y^{\xi-1}\} = \frac{1}{(2\pi)^{N/2}\sigma^N} \int_{-\infty}^{\infty}\int_{-\infty}^{\infty}\cdots\int_{-\infty}^{\infty} \left\{\sum_{j=1}^{N} \exp(x_j)\right\}^{\xi-1}$$

$$\cdot \exp\left\{-\frac{1}{2}\sum_{j=1}^{N}\left(\frac{x_j - \mu^2}{\sigma}\right)\right\} dx_1, dx, \ldots, dx_N \quad (101)$$

We shall define an orthogonal matrix of the form

$$P_N = \begin{bmatrix} \frac{1}{\sqrt{N}} & p_{12} & p_{13} & \cdots & p_{1N} \\ \frac{1}{\sqrt{N}} & p_{22} & p_{23} & \cdots & p_{2N} \\ \vdots & & & & \\ \frac{1}{\sqrt{N}} & p_{N2} & p_{N3} & \cdots & p_{NN} \end{bmatrix}$$

Applying the following transformation to Eq. (101):

$$\frac{x_1 - \mu}{\sigma} = \frac{1}{\sqrt{N}} y_1 + \sum_{k=2}^{N} p_{1k} y_k$$

$$\frac{x_2 - \mu}{\sigma} = \frac{1}{\sqrt{N}} y_1 + \sum_{k=2}^{N} p_{2k} y_k$$

$$\vdots$$

$$\frac{x_n - \mu}{\sigma} = \frac{1}{\sqrt{N}} y_1 + \sum_{k=2}^{N} p_{nk} y_k$$

we have after integrating y_1,

$$m_N(\xi) = \frac{\exp[\mu(\xi - 1) + \sigma^2(\xi - 1)^2/2N]}{(2\pi)^{(N-1)/2}} \int_{-\infty}^{\infty}\int_{-\infty}^{\infty}\cdots$$

$$\cdot \int_{-\infty}^{\infty}\left\{\sum_{j=1}^{N}\exp\left(\sigma\sum_{k=2}^{N}p_{jk}y_k\right)\right\}^{\xi-1} \exp\left\{-\frac{1}{2}\sum_{j=2}^{N} y_j^2\right\} dy_2\, dy_3 \ldots dy_N \quad (102)$$

Applying the inversion formula to Eq. (102) for $\gamma = 1$, we obtain

$$h_N(y) = \frac{1}{(2\pi)^{(N-1)/2}} \int_{1-i\infty}^{1+i\infty} y^{-\xi} \exp[\mu(\xi - 1) + \sigma^2(\xi - 1)^2/2N] \int_{-\infty}^{\infty} \int_{-\infty}^{\infty} \cdots$$

$$\cdot \int_{-\infty}^{\infty} \left\{ \sum_{j=1}^{N} \exp\left(\sigma \sum_{k=2}^{N} p_{jk} v_k\right) \right\}^{\xi-1} \exp\left\{ -\frac{1}{2} \sum_{j=2}^{N} v_j^2 \right\} dv_2 \, dv_3 \ldots dv_N \, d\xi \quad (103)$$

Applying the transformation $\xi = 1 + it$, and letting

$$\alpha = \sum_{j=1}^{N} \exp\left(\sigma \sum_{k=2}^{N} p_{jk} v_k\right)$$

in Eq. (103),

$$h_N(y) = \frac{1}{(2\pi)^{(N+1)/2}} \int_{-\infty}^{\infty} y^{-it} \exp(it\mu - \sigma^2 t^2/2N) \int_{-\infty}^{\infty} \int_{-\infty}^{\infty} \cdots$$

$$\cdot \int_{-\infty}^{\infty} \alpha^{it} \exp\left\{ -\frac{1}{2} \sum_{n=2}^{N} v_j^2 \right\} dv_2 \, dv_3 \ldots dv_N \, dt \quad (104)$$

Integrating out t in Eq. (104) and simplifying,

$$h_N(y) = \frac{\sqrt{N}}{(2\pi)^{(N/2)\sigma}} \int_{-\infty}^{\infty} \int_{-\infty}^{\infty} \cdots \int_{-\infty}^{\infty} \exp\left(-\frac{N}{2\sigma^2}(\ln \alpha + \mu - \ln y)^2\right)$$

$$\cdot \exp\left\{ -\frac{1}{2} \sum_{j=2}^{N} v_j^2 \right\} dv_2 \, dv_3 \ldots dv_N \quad (105)$$

Completing the square in the first function in the integrand, interchanging the order of summation and integration, and using the fact that

$$\exp[N \ln \alpha (\ln y - \mu)/\sigma] = \sum_{r=0}^{\infty} \frac{N^r (\ln \alpha)^r}{r!} \left(\frac{\ln y - \mu}{\sigma^2}\right)^r$$

we have

$$h_N(y) = \begin{cases} \dfrac{\sqrt{N}}{(2\pi)^{N/2} y \sigma} \exp\left[-\dfrac{N}{2}\left(\dfrac{\ln y - \mu}{\sigma}\right)^2\right] \\ \qquad \cdot \sum_{r=0}^{\infty} \dfrac{N^r}{r!} K_{N,r}(\sigma)\left(\dfrac{\ln y - \mu}{\sigma}\right), \quad -\infty < \mu < \infty \quad (106) \\ 0, \quad \text{elsewhere}, \ 0 < \sigma, y < \infty \end{cases}$$

BIVARIATE

where

$$K_{N,r}(\sigma) = \int_{-\infty}^{\infty} \int_{-\infty}^{\infty} \cdots \int_{-\infty}^{\infty} \ln\left[\sum_{j=1}^{N} \exp\left(\sigma \sum_{k=2}^{N} p_{jk} v_k\right)\right]$$

$$\cdot \exp\left\{-\frac{N}{2}\left[\frac{\ln\left[\sum_{j=1}^{N} \exp\left(\sigma \sum_{k=2}^{N} p_{jk} v_k\right)\right]}{\sigma}\right]^2 - \frac{1}{2}\sum_{j=2}^{N} v_j^2\right\} dv_2\, dv_3 \ldots dv_N \quad (107)$$

Thus the probability density function of the logarithm of the set of N independent log-normal variates, $Z = \ln Y$, is given by

$$g_N(z) = \frac{\sqrt{N}}{(2\pi)^{(N/2)\sigma}} \exp\left[-\frac{N}{2}\left(\frac{z-\mu}{\sigma}\right)^2\right]$$

$$\cdot \sum_{r=0}^{\infty} \frac{N^r}{r!} K_{N,r}(\sigma)\left(\frac{z-\mu}{\sigma}\right)^r, \quad -\infty < z < \infty \quad (108)$$

The cumulative probability distribution function of the random variable Z can be obtained using similar mathematical techniques or those employed in the section entitled The Probability Distribution of the Logarithm of the Sum of the Uncorrelated Log-Normal Variates. The final form of the distribution is given by

$$G_N(z) = \Pr(Z \leq z)$$

$$= \frac{\sqrt{2}}{(2\pi)^{N/2}} \sum_{r=0}^{\infty} \frac{(-1)^r}{2} \frac{(2N)^{r/2}}{r!}$$

$$K_{N,r}(\sigma)\Gamma\left(\frac{r+1}{2}\right) + M\left\{\sqrt{N}\left(\frac{z-\mu}{\sigma}\right)\right\}$$

$$+ \operatorname{sgn}(z-\mu) N\left\{\sqrt{N}\left(\frac{z-\mu}{\sigma}\right)\right\}, \quad -\infty < z < \infty \quad (109)$$

where

$$M(t) = \frac{1}{(2\pi)^{(N-1)/2}} \sum_{m=0}^{\infty} \frac{N^{m+1/2}}{2(2m)!} K_{N,2m}(\sigma)[(2m-1)!]! F(t_{2m+2}^2)$$

$$N(t) = \frac{1}{(2\pi)^{(N-1)/2}} \sum_{m=0}^{\infty} \frac{N^{m+1/2}}{2(2m)!} K_{N,2m}(\sigma)[(2m-1)!]! F(t_{2m+2}^2)$$

and $F(t_{2m+2}^2)$ is as defined in the section entitled Formulation of the Probability Distribution.

Moments of the Variate Z

The kth central moment of the logarithm of the sum of N independent log-normal variates with equal mean and variance is

$$\eta_k = E[Z - \mu]^k = \frac{\sqrt{N}\sigma^{k-1}}{(2\pi)^{N/2}} \int_{-\infty}^{\infty} \exp\left[-\frac{N}{2}\left(\frac{z-\mu}{\sigma}\right)^2\right]$$
$$\cdot \sum_{m=0}^{\infty} \frac{N^j}{j!} K_{N,j}(\sigma) \left(\frac{z-\mu}{\sigma}\right)^{j+k} dz \quad (110)$$

Changing the order of summation and integration and applying the following transformation to Eq. (110),

$$v^2 = \frac{N}{2}\left(\frac{z-\mu}{\sigma}\right)^2$$

we have

$$\eta_k = \frac{2\sqrt{2}\sigma^k}{(2\pi)^{N/2}} \sum_{\substack{j=0 \\ j+k \text{ even}}}^{\infty} \frac{2^{(j+k)/2} N^{(j-k)/2}}{j!} K_{N,j}(\sigma) \Gamma\left(\frac{j+k+1}{2}\right) \quad (111)$$

Thus the expected value of the random variable Z is given by

$$E(Z) = \mu + \frac{2\sqrt{2}\sigma}{(2\pi)^{N/2}} \sum_{\substack{j=0 \\ j \text{ odd}}}^{\infty} \frac{2^{(j+k)/2} N^{(j-k)/2}}{j!} K_{N,j}(\sigma) \Gamma\left(\frac{j+2}{2}\right) \quad (112)$$

and the variance of Z can be obtained from the expression

$$\text{Var}(Z) = \frac{2\sqrt{2}\sigma^2}{(2\pi)^{N/2}} \sum_{\substack{j=0 \\ j \text{ even}}}^{\infty} \frac{2^{(j+k)/2} N^{(j-k)/2}}{j!} K_{N,j}(\sigma) \Gamma\left(\frac{j+3}{2}\right) - \{E(Z)\}^2 \quad (113)$$

The values of the mean and variance of the variate Z are easy to compute once the coefficients of $K_{N,j}(\sigma)$ have been evaluated.

Estimates of the Parameters

Estimates of the parameters of the variate Z whose probability density function is given by Eq. (108) can be obtained using the approach we discussed in the section entitled Estimation of the Parameters of the Probability Distribution of the Variate Z. We next give a brief discussion of the form of the estimates using the method of maximum likelihood and method of moments.

BIVARIATE

Maximum Likelihood Method

The logarithm of the likelihood function of the random variable Z_i, $i = 1, 2, \ldots, m$ is given by

$$\ln g_N(z_i) = -\tfrac{1}{2} N - \frac{N}{2} \ln 2\pi - \ln \sigma$$

$$- \frac{N}{2}\left(\frac{z_i - \mu}{\sigma}\right)^2 + \ln\left\{\sum_{j=0}^{\infty} \frac{N^j}{j!} K_{N,j}(\sigma)\left(\frac{z_i - \mu}{\sigma}\right)^j\right\},$$

$$i = 1, 2, \ldots, n \quad (114)$$

Differentiating Eq. (114) with respect to μ and σ,

$$\frac{\partial \ln g_N(z_i)}{\partial \mu} = \frac{N}{\sigma}\left(\frac{z_i - \mu}{\sigma}\right) - \frac{1}{\sigma} \frac{\displaystyle\sum_{j=1}^{\infty} \frac{N^j}{(j-1)!} K_{N,j}(\sigma)\left(\frac{z_i - \mu}{\sigma}\right)^{j-1}}{\displaystyle\sum_{j=0}^{\infty} \frac{N^j}{j!} K_{N,j}(\sigma)\left(\frac{z_i - \mu}{\sigma}\right)} \quad (115)$$

and

$$\frac{\partial \ln g_N(z_i)}{\partial \sigma}$$

$$= -\frac{1}{\sigma} + \frac{N}{\sigma}\left(\frac{z_i - \mu}{\sigma}\right)^2 + \frac{\displaystyle\sum_{j=0}^{\infty} \frac{N^j}{j!}\left(\frac{z_i - \mu}{\sigma}\right)^j\left\{-\frac{j}{\sigma} K_{N,j}(\sigma) + K'_{N,j}(\sigma)\right\}}{\displaystyle\sum_{j=0}^{\infty} \frac{N^j}{j!} K_{N,j}(\sigma)\left(\frac{z_i - \mu}{\sigma}\right)} \quad (116)$$

where

$$K'_{N,j}(\sigma) = \frac{dK_{N,j}(\sigma)}{d\sigma} = \int_{-\infty}^{\infty}\int_{-\infty}^{\infty}\cdots\int_{-\infty}^{\infty} \left\{\frac{B(\sigma)}{\sigma}\right\}^j \exp\left\{-\frac{N}{2}\left\{\frac{B(\sigma)}{\sigma}\right\}^2\right\}$$

$$\cdot \left\{-\frac{B(\sigma)}{\sigma}\left[\sigma\frac{dB(\sigma)}{d\sigma} - B(\sigma)\right]\right\} + j\left\{\frac{B(\sigma)}{\sigma}\right\}^{j-1}\left\{\sigma\frac{dB(\sigma)}{d\sigma} - B(\sigma)\right\}$$

$$\cdot \exp\left\{-\frac{N}{2}\left(\frac{B(\sigma)}{\sigma}\right)^2\right\} dv_2\, dv_3 \ldots dv_N$$

with

$$B(\sigma) = \ln \sum_{h=1}^{N} \exp\left(\sigma \sum_{k=2}^{N} p_{hk} v_k\right)$$

and

$$\frac{dB(\sigma)}{d\sigma} = \frac{\displaystyle\sum_{h=1}^{N} \exp\left(\sigma \sum_{k=2}^{N} p_{hk} v_k\right) \sum_{k=2}^{N} p_{hk} v_k}{\displaystyle\sum_{h=1}^{N} \exp\left(\sigma \sum_{k=2}^{N} p_{hk} v_k\right)}$$

Thus one can apply similar techniques as in the section entitled Estimation of the Parameters of the Probability Distribution of the Variate Z to obtain the maximum likelihood estimates of μ and σ by solving

$$\sum_{i=1}^{m} \frac{N}{\sigma}\left(\frac{z_i - \mu}{\sigma}\right) - \frac{1}{\sigma}\sum_{i=1}^{m} \frac{\sum_{j=1}^{\infty} \frac{N}{(j-1)!} K_{N,j}(\sigma)\left(\frac{z_i - \mu}{\sigma}\right)^{j-1}}{\sum_{j=0}^{\infty} \frac{N^j}{j!} K_{N,j}(\sigma)\left(\frac{z_i - \mu}{\sigma}\right)^j} = 0$$

and

$$\frac{N}{\sigma}\sum_{i=1}^{m}\left(\frac{z_i - \mu}{\sigma}\right)^2 + \sum_{i=1}^{m} \frac{\sum_{j=0}^{\infty} \frac{N^j}{j!}\left(\frac{z_i - \mu}{\sigma}\right)^j \left\{-\frac{j}{\sigma} K_{N,j}(\sigma) + K'_{N,j}(\sigma)\right\}}{\sum_{j=0}^{\infty} \frac{N^j}{j!} K_{N,j}(\sigma)\left(\frac{z_i - \mu}{\sigma}\right)^j} - \frac{m}{\sigma} = 0$$

Methods of Moments

The approach of estimating the parameters utilizing the method of moments is very similar to the one we employed in the section entitled Estimation of the Parameters of the Probability Distribution of the Variate Z. Thus, we shall not discuss it further.

REFERENCES

1. J. Aitchison and J. Brown, *The Lognormal Distribution*, Cambridge University Press, 1957.
2. C. I. Bliss, The method of probits, *Science* **79**, 38 (1934).
3. W. G. Cochran, Some difficulties in statistical analysis of replicated experiments, *Emp. J. Exp Agric.* **6**, 157 (1938).
4. J. H. Curtiss, On transformation used in the analysis of variance, *Ann. Math. Stat.* **14**, 107 (1943).
5. J. H. Gaddum, Log normal distributions, *Nature* **156**, 463 (1945).
6. M. A. Hamdan, The logarithm of the sum of two correlated lognormal variates, *J. Am. Stat. Assoc.* **66**, 105–106 (1971).
7. J. C. Kapteyn, Skew frequency curves in biology and statistics, in *Astronomical Laboratory*, Noordhoff, Groningen, 1903.
8. G. R. Lowrimore and C. P. Tsokos, Probability distribution of the logarithm of the sum of two variates whose logarithm have a bivariate normal distribution, to appear.
9. N. A. Marlow, A normal limit theorem for power sums of independent random variables, *Bell Syst. Tech. J.* **1967**, 2081–2089.
10. D. McAlister, The law of the geometric mean, *Proc. Roy. Soc.* **29**, 367 (1879).
11. J. I. Naus, The distribution of the logarithm of the sum of two lognormal variates, *J. Am. Stat. Assoc.* **64**, 655–659 (1969).
12. I. E. O. Nasell, Some properties of power sums of truncated normal random variables, *Bell Syst. Tech. J.* **1967**, 2091–2110.

13. S. Nydell, The mean errors of the characteristics in logarithmic normal distribution, *Skand. Aktuar Tidskr.* **2**, 134 (1919).
14. J. F. Traub, *Iterative Methods for the Solution of Equations*, Prentice-Hall, Englewood Cliffs, New Jersey, 1964.
15. C. P. Tsokos and G. R. Lowrimore, The probability distribution of the logarithm of the sum of two log-normal variates, to appear.
16. C. P. Tsokos, *Probability Distributions: An Introduction to Probability Theory with Applications,* Wadsworth, Belmont, California, 1972.
17. S. D. Wicksell, On logarithmic correlation with an application to the distribution of arger at first marriage, *Medd. Lunck Astr., Obs.* **84**, (1917).
18. W. Feller, *An Introduction to Probability Theory and its Applications,* Vol. 1, Wiley, New York, 1957.

Chris P. Tsokos

BLENDING PROBLEM

Blending may be defined as a methodical and systematic process of combining a variety of materials into a homogeneous mass having desired physical or chemical characteristics. The materials to be blended may be classified into two general categories:

A given material, such as iron ore, having the same general composition but widely variable in physical properties and chemical content.
Multiple materials of different physical properties and chemical composition.

The primary objective of the blending process for the first category of materials is to obtain a homogeneous and uniform blend having virtually the identical physical and chemical characteristics as the overall average of the entire input [1]. The primary objective in the blending process for materials in the second category is to obtain a blend having a desired chemical composition.

The basic blending problem formulation consists of some objective which is to be maximized or minimized. For example, a blending problem's objective may be to minimize the error between the required aim blend properties and the actual properties; or, if we have a choice of materials to select from, the objective may be that of selecting the materials meeting the blend requirements and at a minimum cost.

The objectives, therefore, may be explicitly expressed as a mathematical expression containing one or more terms which may be linear, nonlinear, or a combination of both.

The objective function is subject to a series of constraints which state the feasible area of problem solution. For example, a constraint may be that the

BLENDING PROBLEM

sum of the incremental changes in the quantities of the respective input feed materials must be zero in order to maintain a constant production rate. The constraints may also be linear, nonlinear, or a combination of both.

If both the objective function and constraints are linear, the blending problem may be formulated as a linear programming model [2]. If either the constraints or the objective function are nonlinear, the objective function may be expressed as some measure of relative error which is minimized using an iterative procedure [3].

NONLINEAR BLENDING PROBLEM FORMULATION

We shall first discuss the blending problems in which the objective function is expressed as a measure of relative error. The relative error is a measure of the deviation of the actual blend as measured against the desired aim of physical and chemical properties. The relative error may be represented mathematically as a measure of the linear distance between two points in space, namely the desired aim properties and the trial combined analysis. Figure 1 illustrates the basic calculation.

It can be seen that the mathematical model used to evaluate the relative

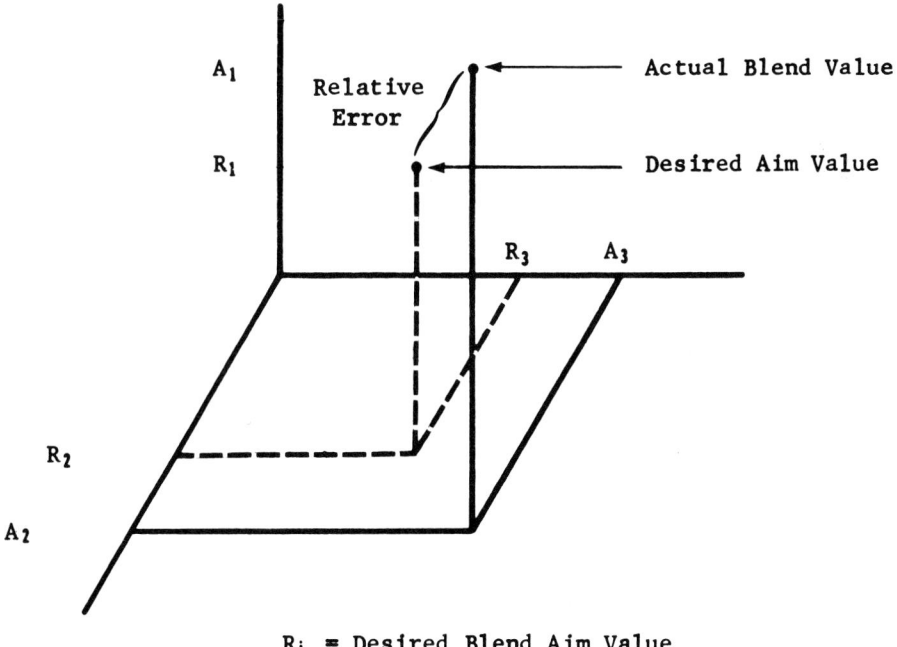

R_i = Desired Blend Aim Value

A_i = Actual Blend Value

Fig. 1. Relative error calculation.

BLENDING PROBLEM

error is not limited to three blend properties but may be extended to n properties. The objective function of the relative error may be expressed mathematically as

$$RE = \sqrt{W_1(A_1 - R_1)^2 + \cdots + W_i(A_i - R_i)^2 + \cdots + W_n(A_n - R_n)^2}$$

where RE = relative error
  A_i = actual blend value of the ith property
  R_i = desired aim value of the ith property
  W_i = relative weighting factor for ith property

The weighting factor, W, is used to determine the relative importance of each variable in the objective function. The method for computing the weighting factor would vary for individual blending problems.

The algorithm used in solving this category of blending problems utilizes the recursive or iterative concept. That is, small incremental changes are made to one or more of the input materials and the change in the relative error evaluated. The iterative process is terminated at such time as the change in the relative error is less than some predetermined value or the error is within acceptable control limits. The recursive, or iterative, algorithm is well suited for use on electronic computers [4].

The format of the constraints which the objective function is subject to may be represented as

$$\begin{bmatrix} \Delta Y_1 \\ \Delta Y_2 \\ \vdots \\ \Delta Y_m \end{bmatrix} = \begin{bmatrix} C_{11} & C_{12} & \cdots & C_{1n} \\ C_{21} & C_{22} & \cdots & C_{2n} \\ \vdots & \vdots & \vdots & \vdots \\ C_{m1} & C_{m2} & & C_{mn} \end{bmatrix} \begin{bmatrix} \Delta X_1 \\ \Delta X_2 \\ \vdots \\ \Delta X_n \end{bmatrix}$$

where: C_{ij} = coefficient of the ith component for the jth input material
  ΔX_j = incremental change in quantity of the jth input material
  ΔY_i = incremental change in the ith component of the blend

The variables in the objective function are computed by

$$A_i = A_{0i} + f(\Delta Y_i)$$

where: A_i = new value of the ith property in the blend
  A_{0i} = original value of the ith property
  $f(\Delta Y_i)$ = incremental change of the ith property

The incremental changes in input materials, ΔX_i, may also be subject to constraints, such as

$$\sum_{i=1}^{N} \Delta X_i = 0$$

in order to maintain a constant production rate.

An example of a blending problem in which the objective function is to minimize the relative error will now be described.

The manufacture of cement requires the intermediate production of a fused mass called "cement clinker" which must meet established specifications for:

Silica ratio, $SR = SiO_2/(Al_2O_3 + Fe_2O_3)$
Tricalcium silicate, C_3S
Tricalcium aluminate, C_3A

The raw materials for producing this clinker are quarried, blended either wet or dry, and charged into a rotary kiln for calcining and burning to clinker.

Various materials which supply CaO, SiO_2, Al_2O_3, and Fe_2O_3 are blended to meet the necessary cement specifications. The raw materials exhibit wide variation in oxide content; consequently, the basic objective of the blending operation is to minimize the deviation of the oxides from the required aim.

The blending process described here is a "wet" system which makes a blended slurry. The blending control strategy is continuous sampling of the input feed slurry, on-line X-ray analysis of the oxide content, and constant adjustment of the feeding ratios of the respective raw materials.

The measurements of the oxide contents are obtained from the on-line X-ray readings taken at 3-minute intervals. The principle of operation of this X-ray analysis is based on the detection and measurement of diffracted X-ray intensities resulting from X-ray excitation of the sample material [5]. The measurements are fed to an on-line computer which then calculates the oxide average that existed in the blended materials over a given interval or compositing period.

The objective of the blending control scheme is to calculate the necessary adjustments in the feed proportions to compensate for the variation in oxides of the input raw materials. The blending control scheme makes adjustments in the feed proportions which minimize the variance in the specification aim for SR, C_3S, and C_3A. Expressed mathematically, the objective function of the blending control scheme is to minimize the relative error:

$$RE = \sqrt{[(SR)_A - (SR)_R]^2 + [(C_3S)_A - (C_3S_R)]^2 + [(C_3A)_A - (C_3A_R)]^2}$$

where
$(SR)_A$ = calculated silica ratio
$(C_3S)_A$ = calculated tricalcium silicate
$(C_3A)_A$ = calculated tricalcium aluminate

The terms in the objective function with the R subscript are desired aim points for the respective blended properties.

The terms in the objective function are recalculated based on the original value and

BLENDING PROBLEM

the incremental changes. For example, the new silica ratio would be calculated as

$$SR_A = \frac{(SiO_2 + \Delta SiO_2)}{(Al_2O_3 + \Delta Al_2O_3) + (Fe_2O_3 + \Delta Fe_2O_3)}$$

The blending control strategy is, in essence, a systematic search for new input feed proportions that will minimize the relative error. The changes resulting from the new feed proportions are calculated as

$$\begin{bmatrix} \Delta CaO \\ \Delta SiO_2 \\ \Delta Al_2O_3 \\ \Delta Fe_2O_3 \end{bmatrix} = [B] \begin{bmatrix} \Delta X_1 \\ \Delta X_2 \\ \vdots \\ \Delta X_n \end{bmatrix}$$

where B is the coefficient matrix for CaO, SiO_2, Al_2O_3, and Fe_2O_3 contents for the respective input feed materials:

$$B = \begin{bmatrix} (CaO)_{11} & (CaO)_{12} & \ldots & (CaO)_{1n} \\ (SiO_2)_{21} & (SiO_2)_{22} & \ldots & (SiO_2)_{2n} \\ (Al_2O_3)_{31} & (Al_2O_3)_{32} & \ldots & (Al_2O_3)_{3n} \\ (Fe_2O_3)_{41} & (Fe_2O_3)_{42} & \ldots & (Fe_2O_3)_{4n} \end{bmatrix}$$

B is constantly being updated based on the chemical analysis of the respective input feed materials:

ΔX_i = incremental changes in quantity of ith input material

The incremental changes in the respective feed materials are subject to

$$\sum_{i=1}^{n} \Delta X_j = 0$$

in order to maintain a constant production rate.

Using the incremental oxide changes and the calculated values from the on-line X-ray analysis, the present system error is calculated. Computation can now be carried out to determine whether another set of feed proportions will give a smaller predicted error. The iterative procedure is continued until a feed proportion is obtained which yields the minimum system error and/or is within the control limits for the silica ratio, tricalcium silicate, and tricalcium aluminate contents.

The terms in the objective function in the "cement clinker" example are related directly to the chemical composition of the blend. The weighting factors, W_i, are all unity.

An example where the terms in the objective function are related directly to the production rate and the weighting factors are not unity is the blending model developed for taconite ore blending [6].

BLENDING PROBLEM

The taconite ore beneficiation process is one which concentrates the iron content into pellets used as blast furnace feed. The basic metallurgical flow is that of:

Crushing the taconite ore as received from the mine such that 95% of the ore is minus ¾ in.
A cyclic processing of the minus ¾ in. ore through ball mill grinding and magnetic separation to obtain a concentrate of 90% minus 270 mesh.
Concentrate sent to agglomerator to produce pellets.

The variables that have a direct impact on the concentrate productivity are:

Grindability index of the taconite ore.
Iron concentrate of finished pellets.
Crude magnetic iron content of the taconite ore.

The weighting factors used to represent these variables are 1.0, 4.8, and 3.2, respectively, for the specific mining operation.

The objective function for the taconite model may be expressed mathematically as

$$RE = \sqrt{(GI_A - GI_R)^2 + 4.8(PC_A - PC_R)^2 + 3.2(MI_A - MI_R)^2}$$

where: GI = grindability index
PC = pellet concentrate
MI = magnetic iron content

The A and R subscripts are the calculated and aim values, respectively.

Blending operations may be single or multiple stage operations, in which each stage contributes to the reduction of the relative error at a given cost. For example, in mining operations various stages can be identified where blending may occur, such as the scheduling of materials from the mine based on drill hole data, yard blending, beneficiation process, and blending after beneficiation of material.

An optimal blending strategy for a multistage blending operation may be generated through the use of dynamic programming. This will require the development of a cost matrix for the reduction of the relative error for the respective blending stages.

Figure 2 shows the effect of blending on chemistry and size variation of blast furnace feed materials [1].

LINEAR PROGRAMMING PROBLEM FORMULATION

The second major type of blending problem is that problem which is solved using linear programming. The basic problem is to purchase or produce input materials having specified characteristics and to blend these input materials to obtain a single resultant material having specific characteristics. The use of

BLENDING PROBLEM

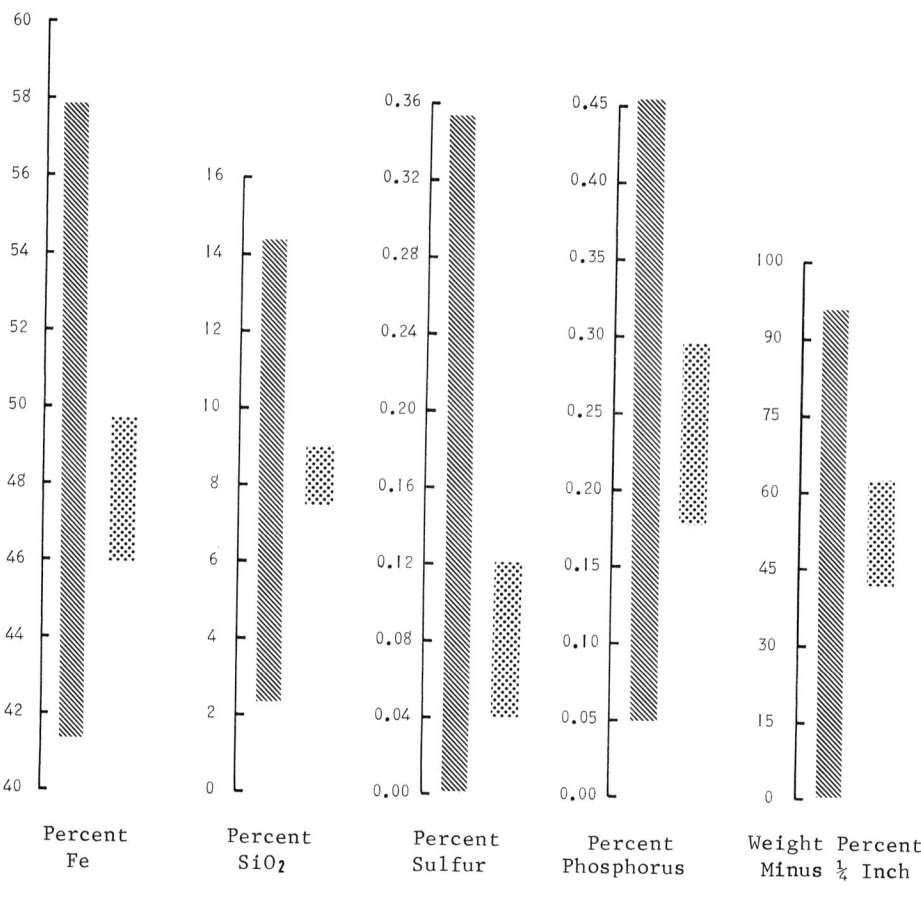

Fig. 2. Effect of blending on chemistry and size variation of blast furnace feed (two α limits).

TABLE 1

	Alloy 1	Alloy 2	Alloy 3	Alloy 4
Cost per unit, $	2.00	1.50	3.00	2.50
Percent of:				
Tin	0	30	40	10
Aluminum	40	30	20	30
Copper	60	40	40	60

BLENDING PROBLEM

linear programming permits the selection of those input materials which will produce the desired output blend at the minimum cost within any operational constraints of the process. The assumption that the blending relationships, production constraints, and costs are linear permits the linear programming technique to obtain this optimal solution. The use of an example will indicate the basic structure of this type of problem.

A producer of special metals desires a final product with a composition of 20% tin, 30% aluminum, and 50% copper. He has four sources of alloys which he may use as input materials to produce this desired blend. The composition of these various alloys is shown in Table 1. The problem is to determine which of these alloys to purchase and in what ratio they should be blended to produce the desired product. Schematically, this can be represented as in Fig. 3.

Any combination of the possible input materials may be chosen. For example, equal ratios of Alloy 1 and Alloy 3 will produce the desired blend at a cost of $2.50 per unit. However, the choice of equal ratios of Alloy 2 and Alloy 4 will also produce the desired product at a cost of only $2.00 per unit. For a real-life problem, the number of alternative possibilities is very large and the linear programming approach selects the best set of input materials and specifies their ratio in producing the desired blend.

For this problem, the variables and model structure would be:

$$A1 = \text{units of Alloy 1 purchased}$$
$$A2 = \text{units of Alloy 2 purchased}$$
$$A3 = \text{units of Alloy 3 purchased}$$
$$A4 = \text{units of Alloy 4 purchased}$$

The objective function is to minimize $z = 2.00\ A1 + 1.50\ A2 + 3.00\ A3 + 2.50\ A4$ subject to:

$$.3\ A2 + .4\ A3 + .1\ A4 = .20 \text{ output required}$$
$$.4\ A1 + .3\ A2 + .2\ A3 + .3\ A4 = .30 \text{ output required}$$
$$.6\ A1 + .4\ A2 + .4\ A3 + .6\ A4 = .50 \text{ output required}$$

The use of equality constraints is not necessary as the desired output may require a certain characteristic to fall within a range, such as the tin content to be between 15 and 25%. Restriction 1 could be replaced by the following inequalities:

$$.3\ A2 + .4\ A3 + .1\ A4 \geq .15 \text{ output required}$$
$$.3\ A2 + .4\ A3 + .1\ A4 \leq .25 \text{ output required}$$

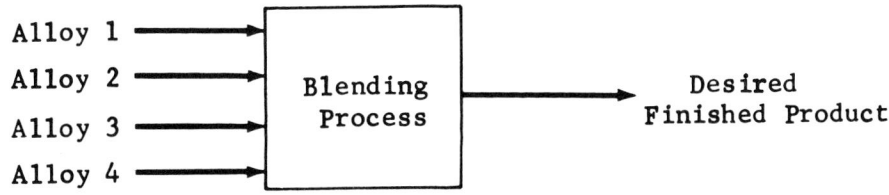

Fig. 3.

BLENDING PROBLEM

While this was an elementary example, it provides the structure of this type of problem. Several extensions have been made to this basic model to make it more useable for specific applications. One extension is the inclusion of production and capacity constraints in addition to the blending constraints. For example, the number of available units of one alloy may be limited due to requirements imposed by the mining facilities.

A second extension is the expansion of the single-product, single-facility model to the multiproduct, multifacility model [8]. This permits the determination of the blend of a number of finished products produced on a number of different facilities from a common set of input materials at the lowest overall total cost. It is important to recognize that the solution may not specify a blend that is optimal for a given product but is optimal from a total cost standpoint of producing all products. The structure of this type of model is shown in Figure 4.

The potential input materials are shown across the top of the matrix. The term $i1j$, for example, indicates the amount of input of material j allocated to facility i to produce a product meeting a given specification. It is apparent that input material j can be used by other facilities to produce different finished blends. While each of the output products may be different, it is possible to produce similar blends from different facilities. This structure permits the model to account for the unique characteristics of individual production facilities in the blending process.

The first application of this type, made in 1945, was to the dietary problem of blending different foods so that adequate levels of nutrition were maintained at a minimum cost [9]. This application, which is still used today at hospitals, schools, and other institutions, provided the impetus to a wide range of different areas.

While each application has made modifications and added specialized constraints to make it more representative of its unique problem, the basic structure, concept, and solution techniques are the same. A few examples of actual applications will illustrate these types of additions and extensions.

Limestone Blending. Limestone is quarried by blasting and is transported to a

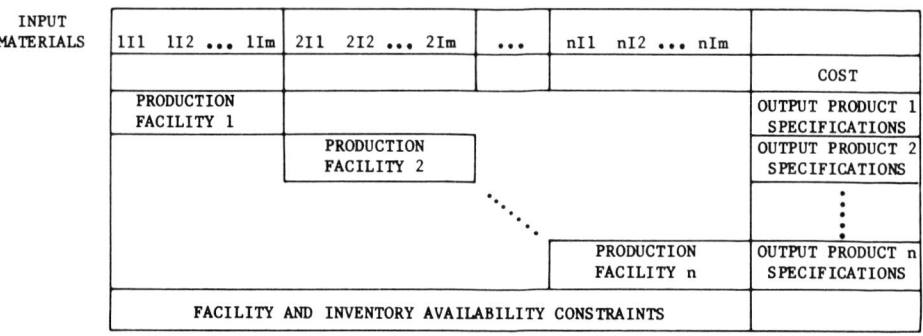

Fig. 4.

BLENDING PROBLEM

screenhouse for further processing. The screenhouse is a multistoried building which contains vibrating metal screens on each floor. The limestone is entered through the top of the screenhouse and passes through the series of screens. The size of the screens becomes progressively smaller as the stone passes downward, and that stone which cannot pass through the open holes in the screen is collected and transferred to stockpiles using conveyor belts. The natural degradation of the stone resulting from the blasting, the angle and speed at which the screens vibrate, and the use of special stone crushers all contribute to the quantities of different stone size produced. The marketable products of this operation consist of different blends of these various size stones. The problem becomes one of not only determining the proper blend, but also of determining the manner in which the production facility should operate so that produced stone sizes can be used to satisfy market demands at the lowest cost.

Petroleum Refinery Operation. An oil refinery consists of a number of process units for separating, changing, or combining crude oil components into a wide range of finished products. Many of these products, such as fuel oil, heating oil, and gasoline, produce several grades, and each grade must have certain ingredients present in prescribed amounts. The refinery also has large volumes of storage for raw materials, intermediate products, and final products. This problem is unique because of two features. First, the output blend is not the result of a single facility but results from a number of operations which feed each other and must be controlled. Second, in addition to a wide range of input components, a number of output products are produced, each using some of these inputs [10].

Blast Furnace Burdening. A blast furnace receives coke, limestone, and iron ore as input materials and as the result of a thermochemical reaction of the input ingredients produces pig iron or hot metal. This hot metal can be cast as a finished product or used as one of the principle ingredients in the production of steel. The problem is to blend these ingredients and operate the furnace in the most economical manner to produce a desired hot metal with specific characteristics. A unique feature of this model is the need to maintain ratio balances between different ores. If two ores can be used only in Proportion a, then

$$X_1/X_2 = a$$

results in the following type of restriction:

$$X_1 - aX_2 = 0$$

A restriction of this type is necessary for each ratio which must be maintained [8].

Another feature of this application is the extension of the general model to include multiperiod planning. This permits the model to determine the quantities and types of materials to use during discrete time periods based on the estimated demand for output and the estimated cost and availability of input materials. The structure of the model within a time period remains the same and is duplicated for each time period. This permits the model to be used as a planning tool in determining production, mining, and purchasing plans.

Electric Arc Furnace. This application is used in producing steel by supplying electrical energy through carbon or graphite electrodes to a mixture of steel scrap and alloying materials. Oxygen, supplied through lances, is blown through the molten bath to oxidize impurities. The composition of the initial charge and the amount and variety of reducing and finishing additives are established using the basic blending model. The unique feature of this approach is the use of a second blending model to control the process. Based on carbometer analysis and spectrograph analysis of the melt, a new linear

BLENDING PROBLEM

program is formulated to determine accurately the quantities of reducing and finishing additives required to achieve the specified steel at the minimum cost [11, 12].

Feed Manufacturing. The feed formulation problem is one of determining the least-cost combination of feedstuff ingredients that can be used to meet predetermined product formulation specifications. Similar to the nutrition problem, this application has used the concept of dual constraints to handle a particular type of nutritional interrelationship which occurs. This interrelationship is one in which the requirement for A will satisfy the requirement also for B, but B cannot satisfy the requirement for A. If the formulation includes only a separate requirement for A and B, the dual role being performed by A is not recognized [13, 14].

With these types of modifications, the basic blending problem has been applied to ice cream blending [15], wool and cotton blending [16], glass production, aluminum alloy production [17], meat blending [18], and investment portfolio makeup. While not exhaustive, this list shows the wide range of activities which are applicable to this approach.

SOLUTION TECHNIQUES

Mathematical techniques, such as linear programming, nonlinear programming, simulation, and heuristic search algorithms, have been employed in the solution of blending problems.

If the blending problem is formulated as a linear programming model, the problem may be solved using existing available computerized linear programming packages. Very large and complex problems, with several thousand restrictions and almost unlimited variables, may be solved using this technique. The selection of which technique is applicable to a specific problem is generally determined by the structure of the problem. If the objective function and constraints can be expressed linearly, the technique of linear programming should probably be used.

The blending problems which may not be formulated as linear programming models—as a consequence of nonlinear objective functions, nonlinear constraints, interaction between dynamic components of the system, etc.—require an in-depth analysis before structuring the model.

The formulated model may be a combination of one or more mathematical techniques, such as heuristic search algorithms and simulation. In general, the size of the problem which can be solved is limited in that computational time may become excessive.

Another area in which the simulation technique has been utilized is in evaluating the blending effect resulting from equipment design [1, 7] and production scheduling [6].

Very little recent work has been done in extending the "state of the art" for the blending problem. The primary emphasis has been on using the technique for specific applications and restructuring the basic model to improve computational efficiencies.

REFERENCES

1. Canadian Institute of Mining and Metallurgy, *Decision-Making in the Mineral Industry,* Special Vol. 12, 1971, Proceedings, 9th International Symposium on Techniques for Decision-Making in the Mineral Industry, Montreal, June 1970, pp. 415–440.
2. A. G. Holzman, H. H. Schaefer, and R. Glaser, *Mathematical Bases for Management Decision Making,* TEMAC, Programmed Learning Material, Encyclopaedia Britannica Press, Chicago, 1962.
3. S. Vajda, *Mathematical Programming,* Addison-Wesley, Reading, Mass., 1961.
4. G. W. Booth and T. I. Peterson, *Non-Linear Estimation,* IBM Share Program, Pa No. 687 WL NLI, 1958.
5. General Electric, *X-Ray Emission Gage XEG-1,* Installation-Operation-Maintenance Direction 12704A.
6. M. L. Kaas, A practical production scheduling model for the taconite industry, in *Proceedings of the Symposium on Computers and Operation Research in Mineral Industry,* Vol. 2, April 1966, Pennsylvania State University.
7. W. A. Laing, A Study of Ore Blending on Bins and Bin Systems by Digital Simulation, Unpublished Master of Science Thesis, University of Cincinnati, Cincinnati, 1967.
8. IBM Manual E20-0160-0, *Linear Programming—Blast Furnace Burdening and Production Planning,* 1965.
9. G. J. Stigler, The cost of subsistence, *J. Farm Econ.* **27**(2), 303–314 (May 1945).
10. W. W. Garvin, H. W. Crandall, J. B. John, and R. A. Spellman, Application of LP in the oil industry, *Manage. Sci.,* **3,** 407–430 (1957).
11. B. T. Bernacchi and E. F. Dudley, Jr., Computerized mathematical analysis for achieving optimum material usage in electric steelmaking, *J. Met.* **18,** 205–209 (February 1966).
12. IBM Manual E20-0147-0, *Linear Programming–Electric Arc Furnace Steelmaking,* April 1965.
13. IBM Manual 020-0148-0, *Linear Programming—Feed Manufacturing,* May 1965.
14. L. W. Swanson and J. G. Woodruff, A sequential approach to the feed-mix problem, *J. Oper. Res. Soc. Amer.* **12**(1), 89–109 (1964).
15. IBM Manual E20-0156-0, *Linear Programming—Ice Cream Blending,* June 1965.
16. IBM Manual E20-0164-0, *Linear Programming—Cotton Blending and Production Allocation,* August 1965.
17. IBM Manual E20-0127-0, *Linear Programming—Aluminum Alloy Blending,* August 1972.
18. IBM Manual E20-0161-0, *Linear Programming—Meat Blending,* April 1966.

B. T. Bernacchi
T. J. Usher

BOLT BERANEK AND NEWMAN INC.

INTRODUCTION

Bolt Beranek and Newman Inc. is a consulting and research and development company based in Cambridge, Massachusetts, with regional offices in six other major United States cities.

Founded in 1948, BBN was initially a partnership of Massachusetts Institute of Technology professors consulting in the areas of acoustics, noise control, and architectural services. Over the years, however, the scope of BBN services has widened and resulted in present capabilities which include computer science and systems, applied physics, oceanology, instrumentation, environmental systems, experimental psychology, and education.

About half of BBN's professional activities are oriented toward computer science and technology, on projects ranging from artificial intelligence to computer network technology to medical computer systems for the research lab and the practitioner's office. Since its entry into the computer field, BBN has focused primarily on the field of man–machine interaction, and in so doing has made major contributions to technological progress in the areas of time-sharing, remote access, computer-assisted instruction, artificial intelligence, and the building of computer networks.

EARLY EFFORTS

BBN's earliest efforts in the computer field grew from the study of problems in man–machine relationships. During the late 1950s BBN embarked on several programs of research intended to make human use of machines more natural and more efficient. The midcentury exponential rise in the number and complexity of machines (and, concomitantly, the degree of man's dependence on technology) dictated close study of man's own capacity to derive those benefits which machines were intended to provide. A machine may operate at peak efficiency, yet its net effect be substantially less efficient if information concerning its function is not available or easily assimilable by its human controller. Thus knowledge of human perceptions and behavior are as essential to the creation of an effective system as are metallurgy and electronics. Given the problem of making humans better controllers of machines, BBN entered the field of control theory, analyzing human perception and reaction factors in control situations and incorporating complementary behavior into machine design.

During this initial period of involvement, BBN intensified its efforts in the field of psychoacoustics (a preexisting offshoot of BBN's major concern with physical acoustics) and began experiments which spanned the entire range of perceptual psychology, which results were fed back both into operator training programs and other machine design. Products of this initial foray included a number of special-purpose computer displays, pilot–vehicle simulators, and analog–digital simulations of a variety of control situations.

MAJOR AREAS OF RESEARCH

Since that time, research into computers at BBN has essentially remained centered on the questions of man–machine interaction. Two generally distinct approaches have been followed, each having slightly differing emphasis on the man–computer problem. One approach attempts to increase both the accessibility of computers and the number of levels of possible human interaction. The second path has involved research into artificial intelligence—the attempt to facilitate human–computer interaction by organizing machine processes to resemble more closely human processes of thought and behavior. This double-flanking movement, combined with ongoing research in behavioral and physical sciences, has yielded enormous benefits for the man–machine partnership in the form of individual devices, new languages, and complete hardware and software systems.

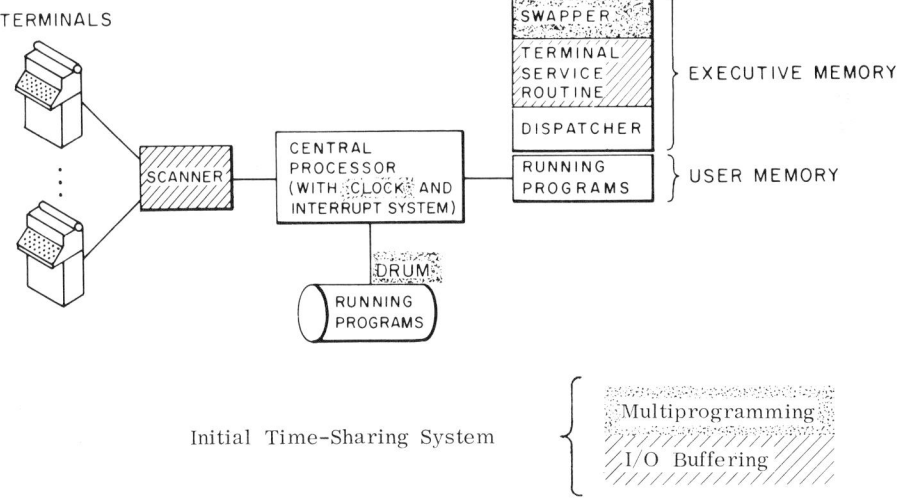

Fig. 1. BBN configured a DEC PDP-1 computer as shown to produce, in September 1962, the first public demonstration of time-sharing. A true time-sharing swapping system, this system permitted three users simultaneously to do machine-language programming and debugging. Over a decade later, the same basic organization is still being used in many time-sharing systems.

BOLT BERANEK AND NEWMAN INC

Accessibility and Interaction

Time Sharing

The pursuit of increased computer accessibility leads to consideration of two types of access: one involves the capability of many users to make use of a single machine; others involve the capability of a single user to call upon the resources of a large number of different machines (for reasons of specialization of function, language, or data base). During the 1960s, BBN developed the means to facilitate both types of access. In 1962 BBN provided the first public demonstration of a time-shared computer system, operating with three terminals on a PDP-1 (Fig. 1).

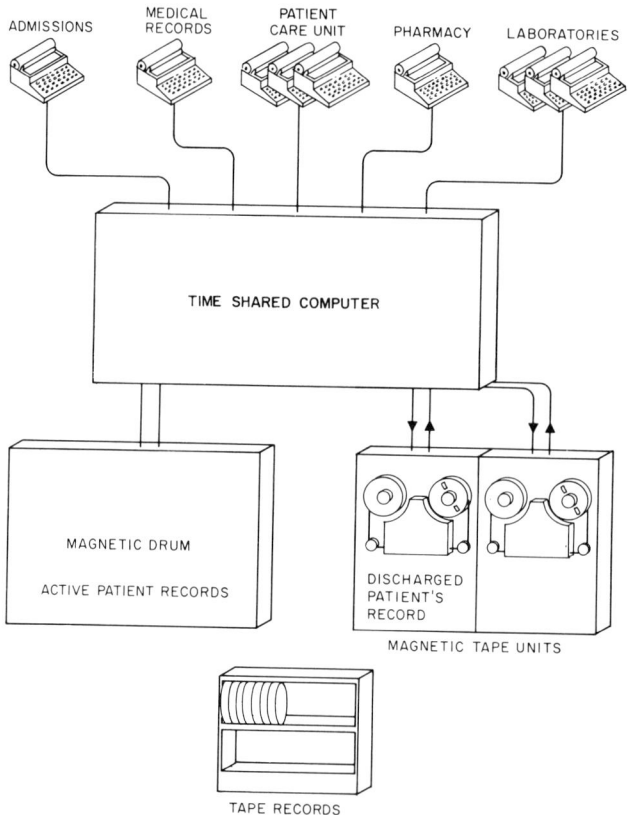

Fig. 2. The computer system shown is a prototype hospital information system developed by BBN and operated on a trial service basis in the Massachusetts General Hospital from 1966 to 1968. The programs stored in the central computer could manipulate medical-record data of any hierarchical level, could perform complex tasks of medication scheduling and charting, and could handle up to 64 terminals simultaneously entering or retrieving clinical information.

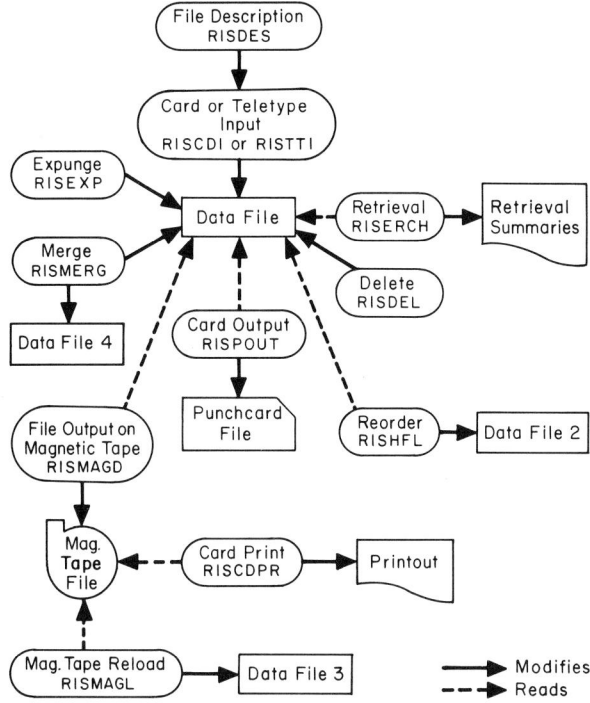

Fig. 3. This is a graphic representation of the interrelationship between the programs and the data of the Information Storage and Retrieval System developed by BBN in the mid-1960s for biomedical researchers at the Massachusetts General Hospital. Unusual features of this data management system include interactive definition of file structures, a user-oriented syntax, description language to specify data formats, compatibility with standard punched-card files, a hierarchical indexing of file-inversion capability, and an ability for the user to generate a variety of retrieval requests simply by answering computer-posed questions.

Concrete application of this major advance followed rapidly as BBN in 1962 undertook to design, develop, and implement a time-shared information system for the Massachusetts General Hospital under the sponsorship of the National Institutes of Health and the American Hospital Association (Figs. 2 and 3). The Hospital Computer Project, as it came to be known, continued for the next 6 years, and culminated in a system which accommodated 64 active terminals and provided storage, processing, and retrieval of patient admission and clinical record files, laboratory results, and medication reporting. Other developments included aids for clinical research, nurse-scheduling, and certain specialized graphics devices.

As previously noted, improvements to the machine component of a man–machine system must be met with an increase in capability of the human element if the system is to be of real value. And so BBN responded to the

[458]
BOLT BERANEK AND NEWMAN INC

Fig. 4. BBN's specially-developed memory pager, for use with the DEC PDP-10, allows users to write programs as if they had over 260,000 words of core memory even though only a small portion of their program need actually be in core. BBN also developed the time-sharing software for this system, which is called TENEX. The system has many special features, such as the ability to run multiple processes that share memory and a pseudointerrupt capability that facilitates interprocess communication. (Courtesy Dan Page.)

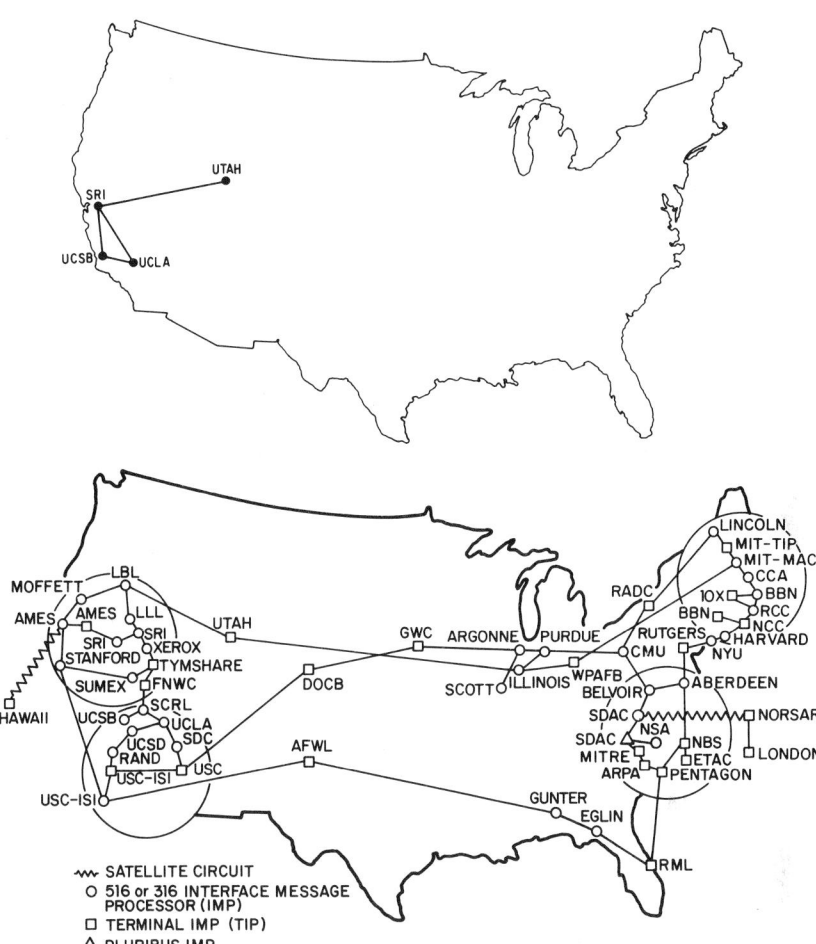

Fig. 5. Top: The initial ARPA Network connected four IMPs, each of which allowed connection into the network of up to four Host computers. Bottom: The October 1975 network interconnects 87 Hosts by means of 34 IMPs, 1 Pluribus IMP, and 25 TIPs. Each TIP allows direct access to the network by up to 63 terminals.

proliferation of time-shared systems (and the yet greater resultant increase in the number of possible users) with the development in 1965 of the special-purpose time-sharing language, TELCOMP. Based upon Rand Corporation's JOSS, TELCOMP permitted users at remote terminals access to a central computer in a simple, English-algebraic language which could be learned by a nonspecialist in a matter of hours. This on-line remote-access system provided

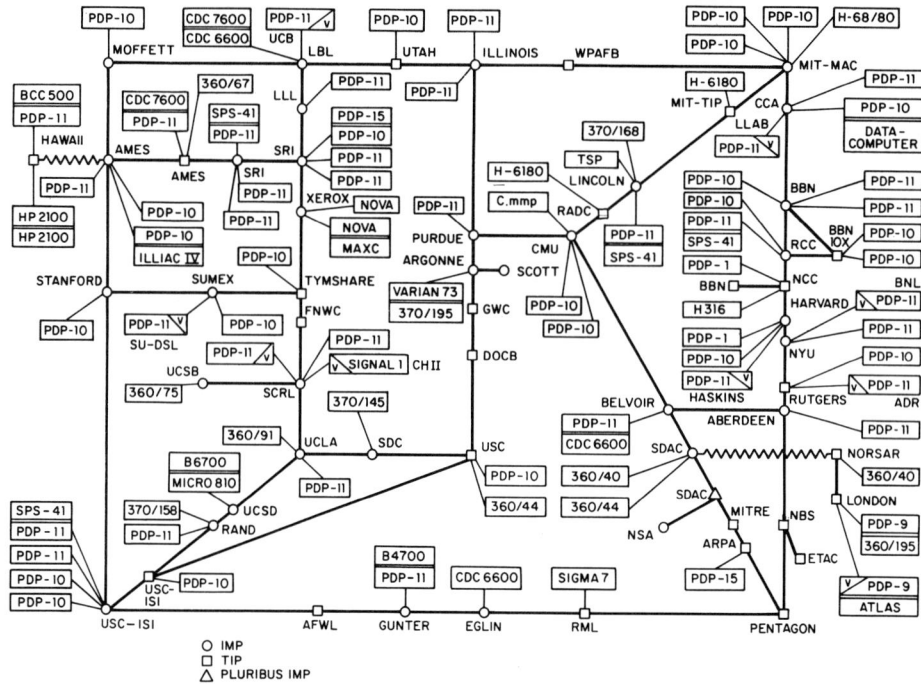

Fig. 6. Resources available to users of the ARPA Network (October 1, 1975) include a wide variety of Host computer types. A user may access any resource on the network from his own computer via IMPs, themselves small computers based on Honeywell models 516 or 316 (the Pluribus IMP is based on the Lockheed SUE), or directly from a terminal through an H316-based TIP. The IMP/TIP subnetwork communicates over leased 50-kbit telephone lines (with the exception of a 230.4-kbit link between the two Ames sites) plus communications satellite links to Hawaii, England, and Norway. BBN is responsible for the design of the IMPs, the TIPs, the network as a whole, and the network's day-to-day operation.

considerable benefits to scientists and engineers who were previously denied access for reasons of distance, finances, or lack of training. Later hardware and software developments gave TELCOMP users the capability for on-line storage and retrieval of information directly in the bulk memory of the central computer.

In 1970 BBN furthered the efficiency of man–computer interaction in the realm of increased multiuser accessibility with the development of TENEX, a paged virtual memory operating system for the time-shared operation of the PDP-10 (Fig. 4). TENEX, providing each user with a 256K-word virtual address space, simplifies the solution of problems requiring programs and data bases larger than the amount of available core memory. Creation and simultaneous operation of hierarchies of interdependent processes, real time response, expanded capabilities for system programming, and direct compatibility with DECSystem-10 code at the object code level are further advantages of the system. The TENEX system has won nationwide popularity, resulting in the existence of about two dozen TENEX systems throughout the United States in mid-1973, with more expected in the future.

The ARPA Network

Just prior to this development, BBN began working on ways to increase computer accessibility in the opposite direction, that is, to grant a single user access to a number of machines. The current product of this work is the ARPA Network, designed and developed under the sponsorship of the Advanced Research Projects Agency of the Defense Department (Figs. 5 and 6). The ARPA Network is a buffered store-and-forward data network that connects a set of geographically separated, heterogeneous, and autonomous computers, designated "Hosts," with the objective of facilitating interactive resource sharing between any set of these Hosts. The Store-and-forward processing is accomplished by a set of identical small computers called Interface Message Processors (IMPs), and users with no Host computer are provided direct terminal access to the network by means of Terminal Interface Message Processors (TIPs) (Fig. 7). The internal operation of the IMP and TIP subnet is self-contained and essentially transparent to persons using the network. An individual may access and use the resources of any of the Host computers as if the remote computer were an extension of the local Host. Developments currently underway include a high-performance modular version of the IMP, known as a Pluribus IMP, and implementation of network links via satellite to Hawaii and Europe.

Interaction via Graphics

With computer accessibility being fostered by two different approaches (i.e., one seeking to increase the number of possible users through time-sharing, the other seeking to make more and different types of computers available), the overall problem of interaction is still only partially addressed. Once widened and simplified access is attained, an efficient interactive relationship depends upon the user's making best use of the accessed machine. Early in the 1960s, BBN began discovering ways to increase the number of levels and types of interaction in the man–machine relationship. Working to extend levels of visual interaction with computers, BBN developed means for facilitating machine presentation of visual information and for direct inputting of graphic information.

Among BBN's first accomplishments in this area was the GRAFACON digital tablet (based upon a development of the Rand Corporation), the first commercial device for direct inputting of graphical position information to a digital computer (Fig. 8). The GRAFACON, with its "writing tablet," offered

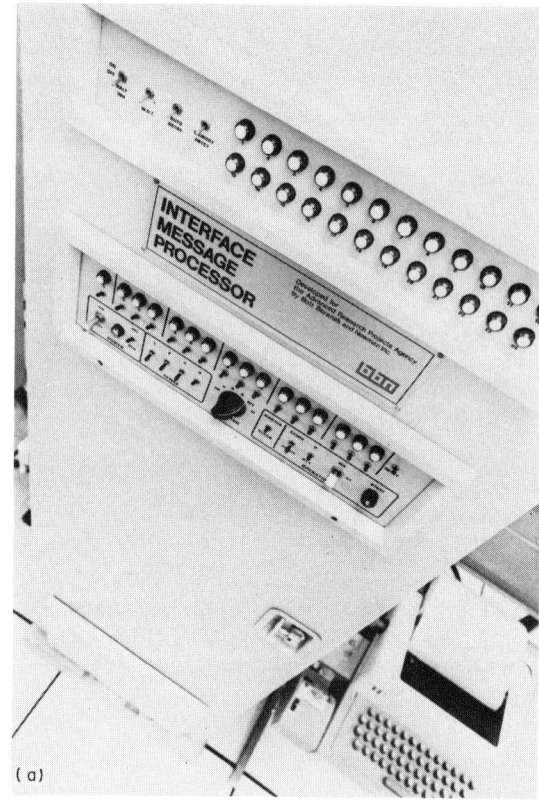

Fig. 7a. The Interface Message Processer (IMP). (Courtesy Dan Page.)

significant improvement in the naturalness of man–machine communication, particularly when used with various BBN-manufactured graphics devices such as the PLOTAMATIC x/y recorder and the TELEPUTER display terminal. Research into the field of interactive computer graphics also found rapid application during this time in the form of complex control-situation simulations. Pilot–vehicle simulators were developed by BBN, drawing on advances in the technology of visual displays, which also included diagnostic instructional monitors in instrument flying and in navigation (Fig. 9).

Later work in the software area has resulted in the design and implementation of general purpose graphics software for the Evans and Sutherland display processor; the design of graphics software which will convey detailed visual information to airtraffic controllers concerning the vectoring of aircraft in landing patterns; and the integration of displays of visual speech correlatives into a CAI system for second-language learning (Fig. 10).

Fig. 7b. The Terminal Interface Message Processor (TIP). (Courtesy Dan Page.)

Interaction via Language

Throughout the history of BBN's involvement with computers, BBN has conducted continuous research at the most basic level of interaction, that of language, in order to make man–machine communication both simpler and more natural.

In the early-1960s BBN developed DECAL, an assembler-compiled hybrid which permitted the intermixing in a program of algebraic statements and explicit machine instructions. Shortly thereafter, BBN personnel began the continuing development of BBN-LISP. An adaptation and extension of LISP 1.5, BBN-LISP was first implemented on the SDS-940 and then on the PDP-10, and is now a major component of the TENEX system.

BBN-LISP facilitates use of TENEX's large memory capability, and possesses many useful interactive system features, such as: sophisticated debugging facilities, a LISP-oriented editor within the system, compatible compiler and interpreter, and the capability for mixing of machine code with LISP expressions via the compiler. One of the more recent additions to BBN-

Fig. 8a. Inputting graphical data via the GRAFACON pen-and-tablet assembly (tablet is a fine wire grid, each line of which is excited with a 10-bit serial pulse train). An intersection is uniquely defined by a signal which the pen picks up capacitively. The digital display device gives decimal indications of pen position coordinates. (Courtesy Nile Beesley.)

Fig. 8b. Operating the GRAFACON pen-and-tablet assembly in conjunction with an IBM 2250 CRT terminal. (Courtesy Nile Beesley.)

Fig. 8c. Digitizing graphical information with the GRAFACON ρ-θ Transducer. The device has two analog voltage outputs proportional to the polar coordinates of the pen position. (Courtesy Photographers III.)

LISP is the "programmer's assistant," a subsystem which enables the user to treat it as an active intermediary, rather than a passive system which merely responds to each input and waits for the next. The "assistant" can remember the user's programming statements and can be instructed to repeat particular operations or sequences of operations, with possible modifications, or to undo effects of operations. Another recent development is a subsystem, CLISP, which permits use of ALGOL-like expressions (e.g., block declarations, infix operators, and if–then statements) within BBN-LISP. The major aim of work with BBN-LISP is to construct a programming environment which "cooperates" with the user in the development of his programs and frees him to concentrate

(b)

(c)

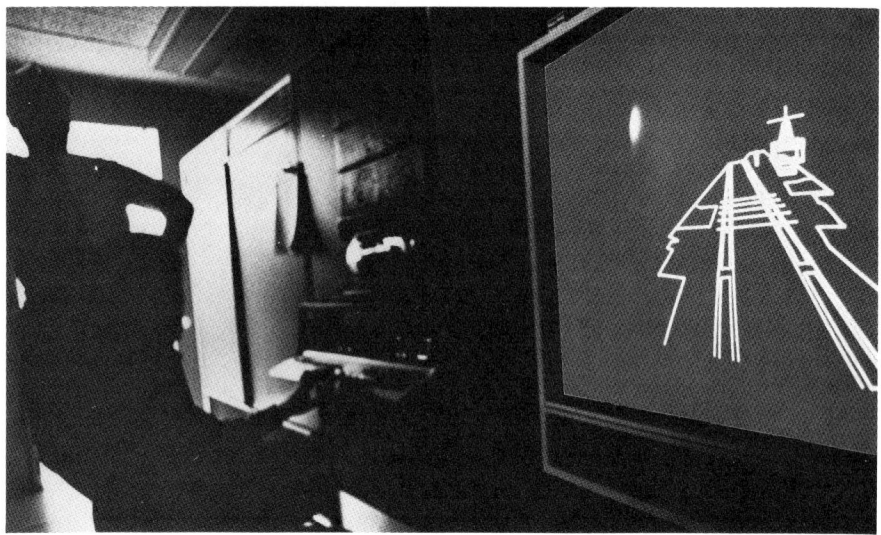

Fig. 9. One BBN endeavor in the area of interactive graphics is the development of graphic software for a system that can display moving pictures in three-dimensional perspective. The hardware for this system includes a special processor for rapidly calculating and presenting each successive frame of the moving picture. The system is being used for flight simulation; each time the pilot moves his controls, the system instantly alters the displayed picture in accordance with the visual change that would have accompanied a similar movement in actual flight. Here the system is being used to simulate landing on an aircraft carrier deck.

more fully on the conceptual difficulties and creative aspects of the problem under consideration.

In addition to the previously described TELCOMP, BBN has developed the related languages STRCOMP and RISCOMP, both JOSS-like conversational languages designed for complex text-manipulation and data-management, respectively. The languages LOGO and MENTOR were developed in the late 1960s for educational purposes, and are described in the following subsection.

BBN's most recent effort in computer language development is PARSEC, designed for use in the PROPHET System (see the section entitled Global Applications). PARSEC is one of the first extensible languages to be used as the implementation language for a large, in-service applications system dealing with real-world problems. It allows the definition of new data types as composites of existing data types, and permits the description of syntax for new commands through transformations which reduce them to combinations of statements which are already defined. PARSEC integrates features drawn from a number of extensible language efforts, combined with the kind of service capabilities which are often omitted in development of new languages: full input/output commands, dynamic overlays, good error recovery, garbage collection, tracing

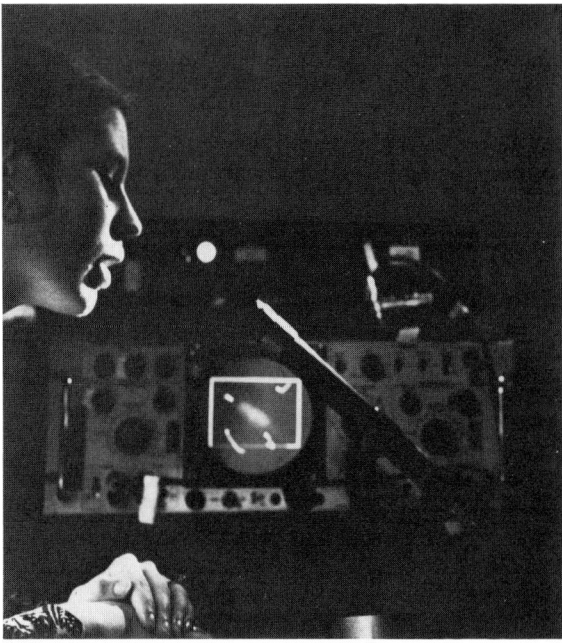

Fig. 10. BBN has explored the use of a computer-based instructional system to help students learn pronunciation of a foreign language. The system lets a student see as well as hear his errors, and for each error indicates the kind and the amount of adjustment he must make to achieve acceptable pronunciation. The computer analyzes certain acoustic properties of the student's utterances, and either represents them directly on a display scope or infers from them some anatomical concomitant, for example, the position and movement of the student's tongue.

and debugging aids, and a broad set of numeric and string manipulation system functions.

Artificial Intelligence and CAI

Natural communication with computers is a point of intersection with the other major line of research undertaken by BBN—artificial intelligence. Here BBN has attempted to facilitate human–computer interaction by organizing machine processes to resemble more closely human processes of thought and behavior. Expanding from its first ventures in psychoacoustics and control theory, the BBN Behavioral Sciences Division has conducted research into several areas of human behavior, the findings of which have been applied to machine strategies. Studies of the structure of language in man have had their results applied to the design of more natural (i.e., human-like) language-

PHYSICAL EXAM?

Fine. What in particular would you like to know?

CHEST EXAM?

It is common practice in the medical profession to begin an examination by checking the patient's general appearance.

GENERAL APPEARANCE?

Acutely prostrated, lying in bed on his right side. Looks acutely ill, sweaty, apprehensive, but alert. Paroxysmal cough, bringing up a little rusty streaked sputum. Breathing with difficulty.

EENT EXAM?

Check all the vital signs first!

PULLS?

Do you mean pulse?

YES.

100 a minute. Occasional extra systole.

LABORATORY REPORTS?

Fine. Which lab tests would you like to have done?

RBC?

A red count will be done. Results will be sent to you as soon as possible.

. . .

Some of the first series of lab reports have just come in. Urine exam: insufficient fluid for analysis.
RBC: 5 million.
WBC: 15500.
Differential: Shift to left.
When the other reports are in you'll be notified. Before proceeding with the reexamination it might be instructive to pause and consider the diagnostic implications of the information at hand. Perhaps you think it too early to arrive at any definitive conclusion. On the other hand, you may be prepared to make the diagnosis now. Are you?

NO.

Fine. Nevertheless, we've got a fair amount of information—at least enough to raise some, perhaps several, diagnostic possibilities. Have you any in mind?

YES.

Name one.

PULMONARY INFARCTION.

Fine. Pleural pain, dyspnea, fever and the physical exam signs and symptoms are certainly consistent with pulmonary infarction. Do you think shaking chills and the presence of rusty sputum further support this diagnosis?

NO.

Right. Though the white count is consistent, isn't it?

NO.

Wrong. The white count *is* consistent. This should further support your diagnosis. We've considered one possibility. Do you have another diagnosis in mind?

NO.

In that case I'd like to talk about viral pneumonia. The tachycardia, high WBC, elevated respiratory rate, shaking chills, bloody sputum and severe pleural pain all lend weight to that diagnosis—right?

APPENDICITIS.

Sounds good! But what about the history of cough and the chest signs? What evidence would help you establish this diagnosis?

EVIDENCE FROM ABDOMINAL EXAM.

Right! Go to it!

ABDOMINAL EXAM?

The heart exam should be done before this.

HEART EXAM?

Unchanged, except systolic murmer more prominent.

ABDOMINAL EXAM?

Pain localizing in lower right quadrant with continuing diffuse abdominal tenderness.

APPENDICITIS.

Appendicitis? Nonsense. By this time you should have your attention focused on a different part of the patient's anatomy.

. . .

PNEUMOCCAL PNEUMONIA.

Are you absolutely sure?

YES.

You can't be until you have irrefutable evidence. What would help you nail down the diagnosis?

EVIDENCE FROM SPUTUM SMEAR AND CULTURE.

Good. Anything else?

NO.

I think you might also want evidence from x-ray findings. Go ahead and we'll see what happens.

Fig. 11. A socratic system protocol. This is a series of excerpts taken from a transcript of inputs and outputs obtained on a socratic system interaction in a medical diagnosis run. Ellipses indicate omissions. The student inputs are expressed in catital letters. The computer outputs are expressed in lower case letters.

processing schemes in machines. Similarly, inquiries into the nature of human control behavior, pattern recognition, and speech comprehension have yielded new strategic knowledge which found rapid application to problems of machine sensor–information integration, automatic pattern recognition, and verbal command strategies for computers.

By integrating various human-modeled machine processes, BBN has been able to produce computer systems which perform complex human-type decision-making and monitoring functions, among them automated biology and psychology laboratories and computerized air-traffic control systems. An early development was a software system which allowed the machine to edit and simplify its own programs.

A particularly vivid example of this sort of adaptive research at BBN is in the area of semantic net theory. Curious as to the associative nature of the structure of meanings in the human mind, BBN researchers embarked on a series of experiments intended, in effect, to map human semantic organization. Taking differential response times of subjects adjudging the truth or falsity of conceptually related statements to be an indicator of the relative "semantic distance" between the implicit concepts, BBN researchers constructed an explanatory model of the apparent interlinked hierarchical semantic structure. Software configurations modeled along the selfsame lines as these perceived "semantic nets," and incorporating the appropriate syntactical strategies, produced programs capable of generating whole discourses of sentences from component morphemes, rather than regurgitating entire, prefabricated, specifically programmed responses.

Of particular significance in this area is the application of principles of artificial intelligence to computer-assisted instruction. In 1964, BBN developed a "socratic dialog" program for CAI which enabled the machine "instructor" by inferential and deductive rules to pose questions to a student and to supply answers and clarifications (Fig. 11). The following year a new language, MENTOR, was developed, for use by educators in creating socratic-type CAI programs for their students.

Another striking advance in the use of computers for teaching purposes came with BBN's development of SCHOLAR (Figs. 12 and 13) a CAI program based on the formulation of semantic net theory noted above. SCHOLAR is capable of engaging the student in mixed-initiative dialog, wherein the student may take the initiative in querying the computer or turn the initiative over to the machine, in which event the machine may opt to lecture or query the student. Based on cues from the student's response times and actual responses (and, of course, from his questions), the computer stages reviews and formulates quizzes, generating its "utterances" from scratch, i.e., basic morphemic constituents.

LOGO is an educational language devised by BBN researchers to teach school children techniques of problem solving. In learning to use LOGO, a procedure-oriented extensible language, young students learn not only the basics of programming, but the basics of problem-directed thinking. A most popular application of LOGO is in the programming of Irving, a turtle-like robot,

```
*SCHOLAR)
++++++++++++++++++++++++++++++++++++++++++++++++++++

    HELLO, MY NAME IS SCHOLAR. I WILL HELP YOU IN REVIEWING
    THE GEOGRAPHY OF SOUTH AMERICA. THIS IS ABC REGIONAL
    HIGH SCHOOL. TODAY IS 04/29/70.
    WHEN YOU ARE READY TO START, TYPE READY --- REMEMBER
    TO TERMINATE WITH AN ASTERISK * FOLLOWED BY A CARRIAGE
    RETURN.

*READY*
    PLEASE TYPE YOUR NAME --- MR., MISS, OR MRS. FOLLOWED
    BY FIRST NAME, MIDDLE NAME OR MIDDLE INITIAL, AND LAST
    NAME.

*MR. JAMES R. JONES*S*ES*
    NAME OF YOUR INSTRUCTOR, PLEASE:

*MR. BROWN*
    LET'S BEGIN OUR DISCUSSION NOW, MR. JONES.
++++++++++++++++++++++++++++++++++++++++++++++++++++
    SELECT AN ALTERNATIVE FROM THE LIST:
    214000.
    800300.
    49883.
    63690.
    FOR THE QUESTION:
        APPROX WHAT IS THE AREA OF CHILE?

*800300*
    YOUR ANSWER IS INCORRECT.
    THE CORRECT ANSWER IS: 214000.

    USE ONE OF THE FOLLOWING:
    SUCRE
    FRENCH
    ARGENTINA
    SPANISH
    TO ANSWER THE QUESTION:
        WHAT IS THE LANGUAGE IN CHILE?
*
    YOU ARE TAKING TOO MUCH TIME...
*SPANICH*
    YOU SHOULD HAVE WRITTEN "SPANISH".
    VERY GOOD.

    PLEASE INDICATE IF THE FOLLOWING STATEMENT IS CORRECT
                OR INCORRECT:
    THE AREA OF PARAGUAY IS APPROX 47432 SQUARE MILES.

*WHAT IS THE AREA OF BRAZIL?*

        THE AREA OF BRAZIL IS APPROX 3600000. SQUARE MILES.
    NOW ANSWER THE QUESTION YOU DIDN'T ANSWER BEFORE.

*FALSE*
    REPHRASE YOUR STATEMENT. I CAN'T UNDERSTAND IT.
*INCORRECT*
    VERY GOOD.
    THE AREA OF PARAGUAY IS APPROX 157000 SQUARE MILES.

    APPROX WHAT IS THE POPULATION IN BRAZIL?
*60000000.*
    APPROXIMATELY TRUE, BUT A MORE EXACT VALUE IS 70000000.
*TELL ME SOMETHING ABOUT PERU.*

    WAIT A MINUTE. I'M CHECKING MY FILES.
    LET'S PROCEED NOW.

        PERU IS A COUNTRY.
        IT IS IN SOUTH AMERICA.
        THE POPULATION IS APPROX 7000000. PEOPLE.
        THE CAPITAL IS LIMA.

*Q/A*
    DO YOU WANT TO CHANGE THE GENERAL MODE OF THE INTERACTION
                TO Q/A?
    PLEASE ANSWER Y OR N.

*Y*
    OK, MR. JONES. LET'S GO AHEAD.

*PLEASE, TELL ME MORE ABOUT PERU.*
        THE AREA OF PERU IS APPROX 480000. SQUARE MILES.
        THE LANGUAGE IS SPANISH.
*HOW MANY SQUARE MILES ARE THERE IN BRAZIL?*
        THE AREA IS APPROX 3600000. SQUARE MILES.
*WHAT IS THE PRINCIPAL RELIGION IN URUGUAY?*
        THE PRINCIPAL RELIGION IN URUGUAY IS CATHOLICISM.
*
    WELL, HAVE YOU MADE UP YOUR MIND?
*COULD YOU PLEASE INDICATE THE PRINCIPAL RIVERS IN
    ARGENTINA?*
    I DON'T UNDERSTAND YOUR WORD "INDICATE". I'LL GIVE
            YOU ANOTHER CHANCE.
*THE PRINCIPAL RIVERS IN ARGENTINA ARE ----.*
        THE PRINCIPAL RIVERS IN ARGENTINA ARE THE RIO DE LA PLATA,
        THE PARANA, THE URUGUAY RIVER, THE SALADO, THE
        PARAGUAY RIVER, AND THE PILCOMAYO.

*MIXINIT*
    DO YOU WANT TO CHANGE THE GENERAL MODE OF THE INTERACTION
                TO MIXINIT?
    PLEASE ANSWER Y OR N.

*Y**
    OK, MR. JONES. LET'S GO AHEAD.
    WHERE IS BRAZIL?

    PLEASE HURRY UP. I'M WAITING FOR YOUR STATEMENT.
*IN SOUTHAMÉRICA*
    I BELIEVE YOU MEANT TO TYPE "SOUTH AMERICA".
    THAT'S RIGHT.
    IS IT CORRECT TO SAY THAT THE CITIES IN BRAZIL ARE
        SAO PAULO, RIO DE JANEIRO, BRAZILIA, PORTO ALEGRE,
        BAHIA, RECIFE, SANTOS, MANAOS, AND BELEM?
*YES*
    THAT'S FINE.
    THE CITIES IN BOLIVIA ARE ----.
*LA PAZ, SUCRE, BOGOTA, AND ACONCAGUA*
    AT LAST! ANYWAY, LET US SEE WHAT YOU HAVE JUST WRITTEN.
    HAVEN'T YOU INCORRECTLY USED "BOGOTA" AND "ACONCAGUA"?
    ON THE OTHER HAND "LA PAZ" AND "SUCRE" IS CORRECT.
    THE COMPLETE ANSWER ALSO INCLUDES POTOSI, COCHABAMBA,
                    AND SANTA CRUZ.

*WHAT IS CORDOBA?*
        CORDOBA IS A CITY.
        IT IS LOCATED IN ARGENTINA.
        THE POPULATION IS 700000. PEOPLE.
        . . . .
```

Fig. 12. Here is an excerpt of a mixed-initiative CAI protocol using SCHOLAR; the subject matter in this case is South American geography. Not only does the computer have the capability to pose several types of questions (e.g., true–false, multiple-choice, WH-type, completion), but it can also answer these sorts of questions when the student takes the initiative.

[472]
BOLT BERANEK AND NEWMAN INC

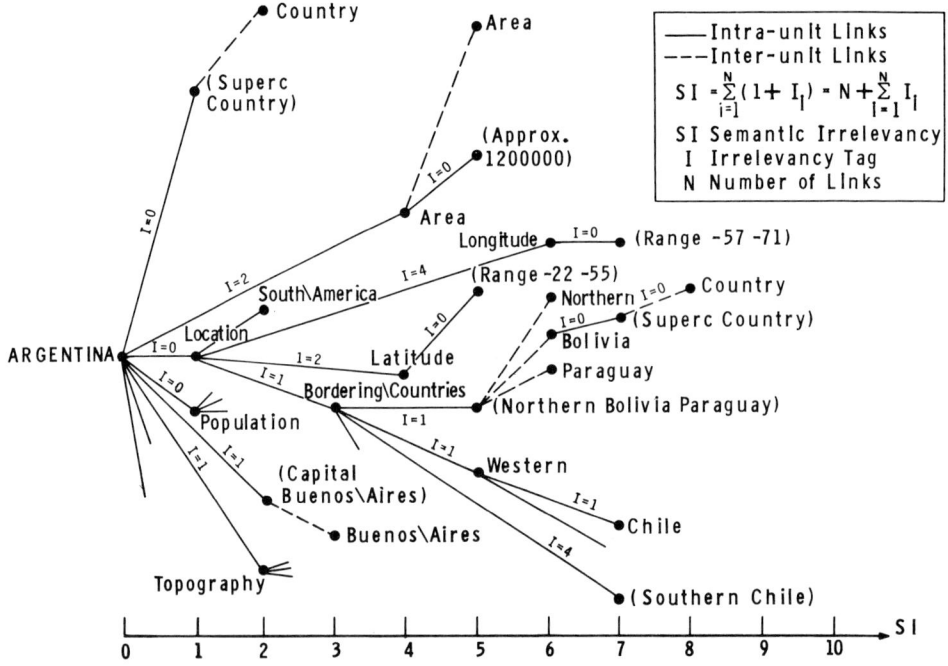

Fig. 13. SCHOLAR is information-structure-oriented, utilizing a data base of a complex but well-defined information structure in the form of a network of facts, concepts, and procedures. It is a semantic network in that its elements are units of information defining words and elements in the form of multilevel tree lists; the elements of those lists point in turn to their respective units, and so on. Pictured is a diagram of the semantic structure for the network node "Argentina."

to run mazes, search for articles, and otherwise be an object of fascination (Fig. 14).

Other ventures in the use of computers as teaching machines include programs for speech aids to the deaf and for second-language learning, both of which involve, in part, rather ingenious matching tasks with CRT-displayed visual correlatives of speech patterns (Fig. 15).

GLOBAL APPLICATIONS

BBN researchers have integrated advances made in both accessibility and compatibility of communication, developing systems for lifting man–machine interaction out of the rather limited domain of specialists, thereby making such interaction more global in its applications and concerns.

In 1962 BBN began to explore the "library" concept in great detail and projected a theoretical and structural basis for a computer-oriented, worldwide

Fig. 14. Irving the Electronic Turtle with his young programmers. Using the BBN-developed LOGO programming language, children at a teletype terminal remotely control Irving. In setting up a program to solve a relatively complex problem—such as getting Irving through a maze—the child works out a sequence of elementary procedures; he can readily see the effect of errors in his procedures and try to fix them. An experimental approach to problem solving is thereby fostered; the child learns to describe and control processes while seeing them realized in a concrete fashion.

information system, termed "The Library of the Twenty-First Century." It was proposed that, in the library of the future, the two primary functions of a library (viz., as an information dispensary and as a storage center for the documents which contain that information) should be fully separated, the efficiency of the dynamic function—that of information dispensing—being enhanced by external restructuring of the information from books and other documents. The study discussed the possibility of, and limits appertaining to, machine storage of the total of the world's knowledge, and as regards retrieval, the possibility of the library's resources reaching into every institution and household, library terminals being as ubiquitous as telephones. Numerous projections of the means by which the requisite despecialization of man–computer communications might be accomplished were presented in the study, along with methods for utilizing the enormous capabilities of machines for searching and correlating to allow the "library" itself to perform the bulk of all informational research.

Many of the potentialities envisioned in the automated library study, as regards global access and ease of human–computer communication, have

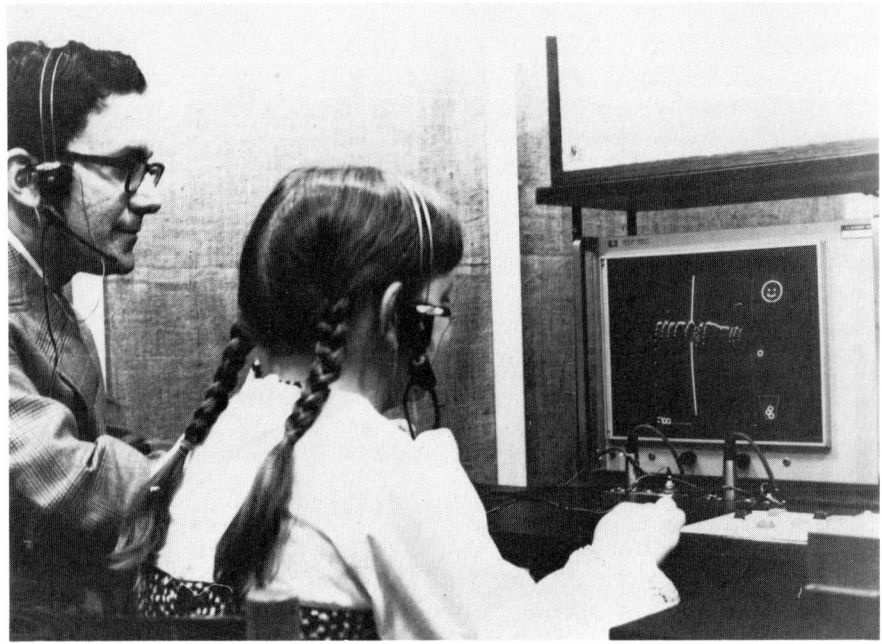

Fig. 15. BBN is currently working to provide computerized speech aids for the deaf. With the device pictured here, a deaf child can receive visual feedbacks of speech efforts. By using the correct pitch and volume, the child can put the ball through the gate and score a basket. (Courtesy Dan Page.)

already begun to be realized at BBN. The goal of pervasive access has been, in kind, accomplished with the development of the ARPA Network, previously described. Despecialization of man–machine interaction has proceeded apace, as embodied in the teaching machines and educational systems discussed in the foregoing section.

Two BBN-developed systems, developed in the 1970s, most aptly illustrate the integration of BBN's dual approaches into an optimum man–machine system. Both products of BBN's Medical Systems activity, these systems, designated PROPHET and CAPO, are dynamic applications of human–computer interaction in the present state of the art.

PROPHET, developed under the sponsorship of the National Institutes of Health, is a computer system for research pharmacologists which fulfills both a "lab-notebook" function, with fully-automated real-time storage, classification, and calculation of experimental data, and a "library" function, designed to provide a large shared data base and potential immediate access by the user to new experimental data as it is entered by other researchers (Fig. 16). The PROPHET system makes fullest use of developments in graphics and natural language communication; numerical and textual data may be entered both from the terminal keyboard and a pen-and-tablet assembly, the latter of which also allows entry of graphical data, such as molecule drawings. This arrangement admits of several types of interaction, and the system is thoroughly user-oriented, its high-level command language based on an extensible procedural language with most of the complexities absorbed into the lower-level software. The system does not require the researcher who is employing it to be a computer specialist; it communicates clearly and simply, and liberally prompts the user. PROPHET performs a wide variety of complex searching and organizing tasks—constructing tables, plotting graphs, creating Dreiding-model molecular representations, presenting such conformations in various aspects of rotation, and transforming of data across these modes. In addition, PROPHET

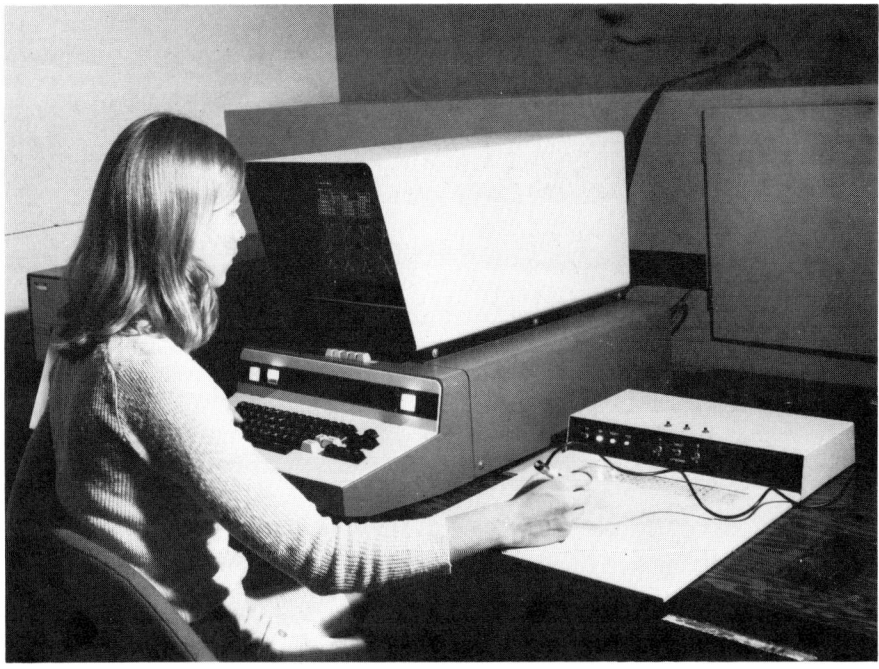

Fig. 16. This PROPHET system terminal is one of several located at pharmacological research centers and connected over high-speed telephone lines to an information-handling system that BBN helped develop. Displayed in the upper portion of the screen is a table of summary data on the action of the enzyme glutamine synthetase. The four molecules shown in the lower portion are the Dreiding-model correspondents of the molecules listed in column four of the table (substrate analogs and inhibitors of the enzyme). The molecular drawings were first entered into the system through the connected tablet and can henceforth be called for display and manipulation by indication of the chemical formula (which may originally be computed from the sketch itself). (Courtesy Hutchins Photo.)

Fig. 17. Using a terminal like the one shown, patients can give their medical history in response to computer-generated questions. After the patient/computer interview, the computer prints a concise summary for the physician, starring any important positive finding for the physician to follow up. BBN has implemented and evaluated several such programs in physicians' offices and has found that in many cases 10 to 15 min of physician time can be saved during each new patient visit. (Courtesy Hutchins Photo.)

permits access to these data to be restricted to a particular user or shared among members of a research group or with the system at large.

In terms of man–machine systems, PROPHET is a significant development, integrating multiuser accessibility with ease and depth of interaction; and global implementation of PROPHET (and like systems for other sciences) is, because of BBN's advances in network technology, a realizable goal.

The CAPO (Computer Aids in the Physician's Office) Project, is another BBN endeavor (sponsored by HEW's Health Services and Mental Health Administration), with great potentiality for widespread man–machine interaction (Fig. 17). CAPO adapts computer aids for physicians, featuring in-office remote time-sharing terminals; it combines PROPHET's ease of use with a wider variety of applications, allowing even greater opportunity for interaction. The system, wherein each installation consists of a CRT terminal and printer linked to a central computer, is designed for use by the physician, nurses, paramedics, and the patient himself. Presently implemented and deployed are the following capabilities: automated medical history-taking, in which the patient is presented a self-branching, multiple choice history questionnaire which he completes by typing in his answers at the terminal (thus freeing medical staff for more directly medically related tasks); automated third-party billing, in which the system itself calculates and prints the bill; and automated patient scheduling (relieving medical personnel of routine administrative tasks).

Software developments include patient education (in matters of diet, chronic illness self-care, and self-administration of medicines); nurse and paramedic education, training, and monitoring; automated filing system (with the potentiality of integrating billing, scheduling, and history-taking functions); and automated preliminary and supplementary patient diagnoses. There is also a projected capability for the system to serve as a storehouse of general medical and diagnostic information and as a source for continuing physician education.

The PROPHET and CAPO systems exemplify what must be the desired goal of research into the problem of natural, efficient man–machine interaction. These systems allow the nonspecialist (in the case of CAPO, the complete layman) to interact effectively with a computer; they free human endeavor from a variety of routine tasks, tasks which are eminently the province of the machine; and lastly, the systems fulfill a vital and necessary social function in the form of improved health care.

SELECTED BIBLIOGRAPHY

Barnett, G. O., and P. A. Castleman, A time-sharing computer system for patient-care activities, *Comput. Biomed. Res.* **1**(1), 41–51 (March 1967).

Bobrow, D. G., J. D. Burchfiel, D. L. Murphy, and R. S. Tomlinson, TENEX: A paged time-sharing system for the PDP-10, *Commun. ACM* **15**(3), 135–143 (March 1972).

Feurzeig, W., and G. Lukas, A programmable robot for teaching, in *Preprints of the Proceedings of the World Congress of Cybernetics and Systems, Oxford, England, September 1972.*

Heart, F. E., R. E., Kahn, S. M. Ornstein, W. R. Crowther, and D. C. Walden, The Interface Message Processor for the ARPA computer network, in *Proceedings of the AFIPS Spring Joint Computer Conference,* Vol. 36, 1970, pp. 551–567.

McCarthy, J., S. Boilen, E. Fredkin, and J. C. R. Licklider, A time-sharing debugging system for a small computer, in *Proceedings of the AFIPS Spring Joint Computer Conference,* Vol. 23, 1963, pp. 51–57.

Murphy, D. L., and D. G. Bobrow, Structure of a LISP system using two-level storage, *Commun. ACM* **15**(3), 155–159 (March 1967).

Phil Bertoni
Paul A. Castleman

[478]

BOLZANO SEARCH

INTRODUCTION

The basic idea of the Bolzano method is to employ a repeated bisection to locate the position of an unknown object. To imitate a well-known whimsical exposition, let us consider the problem of capturing a lion in the Sahara Desert, given that the desert has area 2^{16} square units, that it is surrounded by a fence, and that it contains exactly one lion.

First, we build a fence exactly across the middle of the desert, and thus obtain two fields, each of area 2^{15}. The lion must be in one of these fields; let us restrict consideration to the field containing the lion. Now build a second fence to bisect the lion field; we get two more fields, each of area 2^{14}. Pick the field containing the lion.

By continuing this process, we obtain a sequence of fields of smaller and smaller areas (2^{16}, 2^{15}, 2^{14}, . . . , 2^8, 2^7, . . .). When we have finally fenced off a field that encloses the lion snugly enough, we can claim to have captured the lion.

When we translate this idea into mathematical terms, we start out with an interval $[a, b]$ containing a single root of the equation $f(x) = 0$ such that $f(a)$ and $f(b)$ have opposite signs. Thus the root is tied down as lying in an interval of length $b - a$.

Now bisect the interval at $(b + a)/2$. Then $f((b + a)/2)$ will differ in sign from either $f(a)$ or $f(b)$, and the required root will lie in one of the new intervals that is, in either $[a, (b + a)/2]$ or in $[(b + a)/2, b]$. Pick that interval containing the root, and we now have established that the root lies in an interval of length $(b - a)/2$.

After n repetitions of this process, the root will have been specified as lying in a very narrow interval of length $(b - a)/2^n$.

A MORE FORMAL DESCRIPTION OF BOLZANO SEARCH

The process of Bolzano search may be described more formally in the following manner.

We are given two values $x_1 = a$ and $x_2 = b$ with corresponding ordinates $f(x_1)$ and $f(x_2)$ such that $f(x_1)f(x_2) < 0$ and $a < b$. The problem is then to determine a value x such that $f(x) = 0$ and $x_1 < x < x_2$. In practice, since only a finite number of figures will be carried in calculation of values $f(x)$, it will be considered satisfactory if a value $\bar{x}$ is determined such that $|f(\bar{x})| \leq \epsilon$, where $\epsilon > 0$ represents some preassigned accuracy condition.

The first step of the method is to form $x_3 = (x_1 + x_2)/2$ and to evaluate $f(x_3)$. Now from the set $Q = \{x_1, x_2, x_3\}$, two points x_1' and x_2' are selected such that

$$[x_1' \leq x_2'] \wedge [f(x_1')f(x_2') \leq 0] \wedge [|f(x_1')f(x_2')| = \min_{x_i, x_j \in Q} |f(x_i)f(x_j)|]$$

The process is then repeated with x_1' and x_2' replacing the original x_1 and x_2.

After k steps, it is apparent that the zero x of $f(x)$ has been determined as lying in an interval of length $|b - a|2^{-k}$; if it is required to determine an approximation $\bar{x}$ of x to an accuracy requirement ϵ, then the total number of steps required is $\{\log_2((b - a)/\epsilon)\}$, where $\{y\}$, as usual, denotes the least integer $\geq y$.

The above method is, of course, noniterative, but is only comparable in accuracy with a first-order iterative process (at any stage, the correction provided by the bisection procedure can, in general, only add one correct binary decimal to the binary expression for the root).

IMPROVED METHODS OF BOLZANO SEARCH

The slow place-by-place determination involved in repeated bisection of the interval containing the required zero is irksome, and many variants of the basic method have been devised. Notable among these are those of Van Wijngaarden, Zonnevald, Dijkstra, and Dekker [8], and of Brent [1], which use combinations of Bolzano search with linear and quadratic interpolation to accelerate convergence. However, both methods do resort to unmodified Bolzano search if the function $f(x)$ is of a pathological form. Brief descriptions of these two algorithms follow.

The process described by Dekker et al. is not the most common form of their algorithm, and a slight variant of their procedure due to Peters and Wilkinson [6] is described instead.

The algorithm is entered with two values $\bar{x}_1$ and $\bar{x}_2$ such that $f(\bar{x}_1)f(\bar{x}_2) \leq 0$. The set $P = \{x_1, x_2, x_3\}$ is formed by renaming $\bar{x}_1$ and $\bar{x}_2$ so that $|f(x_1)| \geq |f(x_2)|$ and $x_3 \leftarrow x_1$. Now the quantities $\alpha = (x_1 + x_2)/2$ and $\beta = (x_2 f(x_3) - x_3 f(x_2))/(f(x_3) - f(x_2))$ are calculated; if β lies between x_2 and α, then $x_4 \leftarrow \beta$; otherwise $x_4 \leftarrow \alpha$. The set Q is taken as $\{P, x_4\} = \{x_1, x_2, x_3, x_4\}$. From Q, the subset $P' = \{x_1', x_2', x_3'\}$ is selected such that

$$\{f(x_2')f(x_1') \leq 0\} \wedge \{|f(x_2')| \leq |f(x_1')|\} \wedge \{|f(x_2')f(x_1')| = \min_{x_i, x_j \in Q} |f(x_i)f(x_j)|\}$$

then $x_3' \leftarrow x_1'$ if $x_2' = x_2$; otherwise, $x_3' \leftarrow x_2$. With the set P', a new set Q is defined as above, and the process is repeated.

A stopping criterion for this algorithm is essential since, although the required zero of $f(x)$ always lies between x_1 and x_2, it is no longer safe to assume that $|x_1^{(k)} - x_2^{(k)}| \to 0$ as the process is repeated. It may easily happen that no bisection step is performed, and that repeated linear interpolation produces the sequence shown in Figure 1.

In Figure 1, the relative positions of the points x_1, x_2, and x_3 are illustrated at some stage in the process for which $x_1 < x < x_2 < x_3$. It is seen that, when x_4 is calculated using linear interpolation with x_2, x_3, $f(x_2)$, and $f(x_3)$, then x_4 lies

BOLZANO SEARCH

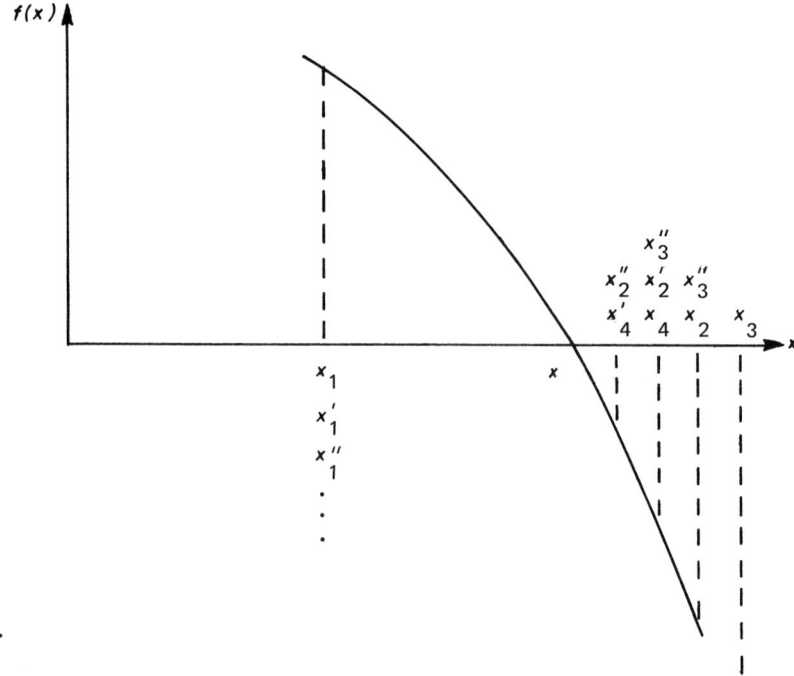

Fig. 1.

between x and x_2. Then we define $x_2' = x_4$; x_1 remains unchanged in value; and we define x_3' to be the old value of x_2. The relative situation is unchanged; so the type of geometric configuration is repeated, and $|x_1^{(k)} - x_2^{(k)}|$ approaches the finite limit, namely, $|x_1^{(k)} - x|$, as $k \to \infty$ (not zero as might be expected). Note that $x_1 = x_1' = x_1'' = \ldots = x_1^{(k)} = \ldots$.

The most obvious method of overcoming this disadvantage is to arrange that, if at some stage k the set Q is such that

$$|x_4^{(k)} - x_2^{(k)}| < \epsilon$$

then $x_4^{(k)}$ is replaced by $x_2^{(k)} + \epsilon |x_1^{(k)} - x_2^{(k)}|/(x_1^{(k)} - x_2^{(k)})$. This ensures ultimately that a value of $x_2^{(k+1)}$ is obtained such that

$$f(x_2^{(k+1)})f(x_1^{(k)}) \geq 0$$

Since

$$|f(x_2^{(k+1)})| \leq |f(x_2^{(k)})|$$

and

$$f(x_2^{(k+1)})f(x_2^{(k)}) \leq 0$$

it follows that

$$f(x_1^{(k+1)})f(x_1^{(k)}) \leq 0$$

This establishes that $|x_1^{(k)} - x_2^{(k)}| \to 0$, as required.

The most usual choice for ϵ is of the form

$$\epsilon = \alpha|x_2^{(k)}| + u$$

where $\alpha|x_2^{(k)}|$ represents a relative error condition involving the precision with which the arithmetic is performed, and u is some general accuracy level required in the estimate of the zero.

A disadvantage of the above method is that functions can be constructed (cf. Brent [2]) for which this variant of the algorithm of Dekker et al. takes a step of ϵ every time, and thus the total number of steps needed to obtain the final estimate of the zero may be of the order of $|x_1 - x_2|/\epsilon$. The modifications due to Brent [1] ensure that convergence to the zero only takes, in the worst possible case, a total of $\log_2^2(|x_1 - x_2|/\epsilon)$ steps. In general, however, convergence with this improved method will take far fewer function evaluations than use of either pure Bolzano search or the algorithm of Dekker, because, where possible, inverse quadratic interpolation or linear interpolation is used.

In detail the algorithm is as follows: the procedure is entered with the values $\tilde{x}_1, \tilde{x}_2 \ni f(\tilde{x}_1)f(\tilde{x}_2) \leq 0$; then the set $P = \{x_1, x_2, x_3\}$ is defined by renaming $\tilde{x}_1, \tilde{x}_2$ $\ni |f(x_2)| \leq |f(x_1)|$ and assigning to x_3 the value x_1. The values p and q, where p/q is either a linearly interpolated value or a value obtained by inverse quadratic interpolation, are computed using, in the latter case, the fact that the parabola interpolating to $(x_1, f(x_1))$, $(x_2, f(x_2))$, and $(x_3, f(x_3))$ can be written as

$$x = \frac{(y - f(x_1))(y - f(x_2))x_3}{(f(x_3) - f(x_1))(f(x_3) - f(x_2))}$$
$$+ \frac{(y - f(x_2))(y - f(x_3))x_1}{(f(x_1) - f(x_2))(f(x_1) - f(x_3))}$$
$$+ \frac{(y - f(x_1))(y - f(x_3))x_2}{(f(x_2) - f(x_1))(f(x_2) - f(x_3))}$$

The zero x^* of this parabola occurs when $y = 0$; thus

$$x^* = \frac{f(x_1)f(x_2)x_3}{(f(x_3) - f(x_1))(f(x_3) - f(x_2))}$$
$$+ \frac{f(x_2)f(x_3)x_1}{(f(x_1) - f(x_2))(f(x_1) - f(x_3))}$$
$$+ \frac{f(x_1)f(x_3)x_2}{(f(x_2) - f(x_1))(f(x_2) - f(x_3))}$$

If the abbreviations $r_1 = f(x_3)/f(x_1)$, $r_2 = f(x_2)/f(x_1)$, and $r_3 = f(x_2)/f(x_3)$ are made, then

$$x^* = x_2 - \frac{p}{q}$$

where

$$p = \pm r_3[(x_1 - x_2)r_1(r_1 - r_2) - (x_2 - x_3)(r_2 - 1)]$$

and

$$q = \pm(r_1 - 1)(r_2 - 1)(r_3 - 1)$$

Now it is assumed that $f(x)$ is a single-valued function, and Figure 2 illustrates

BOLZANO SEARCH

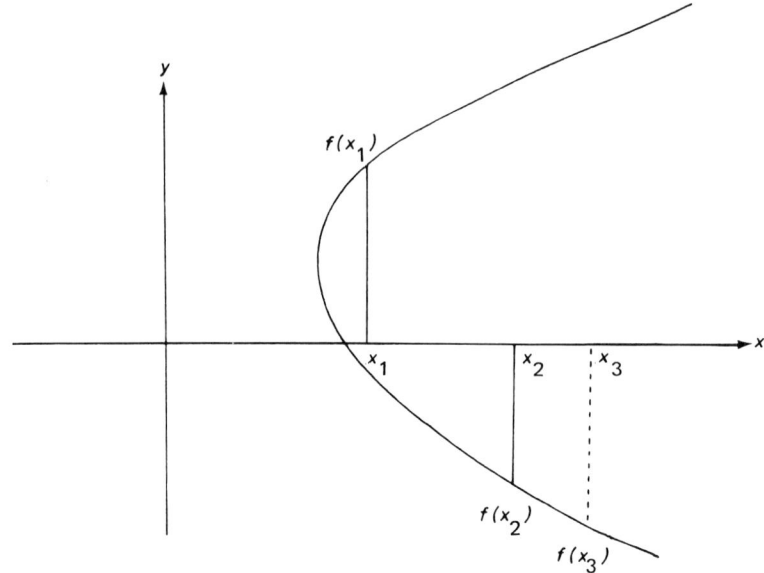

Fig. 2.

the case which can occur when the vertex of the parabola

$$(x - u) = a(y - v)^2$$

lies to the left of the line $x = x_1$. Clearly, in this case, we are unlikely to obtain a good approximation to a single-valued function $f(x)$ over the range $[x_1, x_2]$, and it appears to be good strategy to restrict the use of inverse quadratic interpolation to use of that set of parabolas which are single-valued along the arc joining the points $(x_1, f(x_1))$ and $(x_2, f(x_2))$.

The limiting case for such a set of curves is furnished by the quadratic in y in which the vertical tangent is actually at the point $(x_1, f(x_1))$. In this case, we consider the value x_2 for which $f(x_2) = -f(x_1)$, and verify that the quadratic equation is

$$x - x_1 = \frac{(x_2 - x_1)}{4[f(x_1)]^2}(y - f(x_1))^2$$

which has the zero

$$x = x_1 + \frac{(x_2 - x_1)}{4}$$

Thus it is acceptable to let $x_4 \leftarrow x_2 - p/q$ if p/q is up to ¾ of the distance from x_2 to x_1. Otherwise a step of Bolzano search will be forced, and $x_4 \leftarrow (x_1 + x_2)/2$.

The set Q is again defined as $\{P, x_4\}$, and the three elements of the new set $P' = \{x_1', x_2', x_3'\}$ are determined from Q, subject to the conditions previously detailed for the Peters and Wilkinson [6] method. The process is repeated with the new set P'. To avoid the case when a step of ϵ is repeatedly forced and convergence becomes slow, the following strategy is adopted.

If the current stage of the process is k, if $p^{(k)}/q^{(k)}$ is the predicted step in $x_2^{(k)}$, and if $p^{(k-2)}$ was the step at the stage $k - 2$, then if the logical expression

$$\{|p^{(k-2)}/q^{(k-2)}| < \epsilon\} \vee \{|p^{(k)}/q^{(k)}| \geq \tfrac{1}{2}|p^{(k-2)}/q^{(k-2)}|\}$$

is true, then a step of Bolzano search will be done instead of interpolation. Of course,

$$p^{(k)}/q^{(k)} \leftarrow \tfrac{1}{2}(x_1^{(k)} - x_2^{(k)})$$

An error analysis of the floating point arithmetic involved indicates (see Wilkinson [9] and Brent [1]) that the quantities α and u involved in defining ϵ should be

$$\alpha = 6\beta^{1-\tau}$$

for τ-digit truncated floating point arithmetic with base β or

$$\alpha = 3\beta^{1-\tau}$$

for τ-digit rounded arithmetic; $u > 0$ is some absolute user-specified tolerance.

THE BRACKETING TECHNIQUE OF COX

This is also a hybrid method, which uses prediction and/or bisection. If, at any stage k, it should happen that a predicted change in the estimate of the zero is such as to make the approximation at stage $k + 1$ lie outside the kth interval, then the predicted increment is discarded, and a Bolzano bisection is performed instead.

The algorithm is more than a slight modification of the method of Peters and Wilkinson [6], because derivatives as well as function values straddling the zero are used. Complete details and discussion of convergence appear in Cox [3] and in the ensuing correspondence [4, 5, 7].

In essence, the procedure is most simply stated as follows. The set

$$Q: \{x_k, x_{k+1}, f(x_k), f(x_{k+1}), f'(x_k), f'(x_{k+1})\}$$

is given such that

$$(x_k < x_{k+1}) \wedge (f(x_k)f(x_{k+1}) \leq 0)$$

is true. The elements of Q are, of course, such as to define uniquely each of the three functions

$$u(x) = a_{k+2} + b_{k+2}x + c_{k+2}x^2 + d_{k+2}x^3$$

$$v(x) = \frac{a_{k+2} + b_{k+2}x + c_{k+2}x^2}{d_{k+2} + x}$$

BOLZANO SEARCH

and

$$y(x) = \frac{x - a_{k+2}}{b_{k+2} + c_{k+2}x + d_{k+2}x^2}$$

but the latter function possesses the advantage of having a single easily identifiable root. Thus, when a_{k+2}, b_{k+2}, c_{k+2}, and d_{k+2} are determined so that, when $y(x)$ is used as an interpolator to produce the set

$$R: \{f(x_k), f(x_{k+1}), f'(x_k), f'(x_{k+1})\}$$

then the estimate $x_{k+2} = a_{k+2}$ is given by

$$x_{k+2} = a_{k+2} = \frac{(x_k + x_{k+1})f_k f_{k+1}(f_{k+1} - f_k) - (x_{k+1} - x_k)(x_k f_{k+1}^2 f_k' + x_{k+1} f_k^2 f_{k+1}')}{2f_k f_{k+1}(f_{k+1} - f_k) - (x_{k+1} - x_k)(f_{k+1}^2 f_k' + f_k^2 f_{k+1}')}$$

or, in a computationally more useful form,

$$x_{k+2} = x_k + \frac{(x_{k+1} - x_k)f_k f_{k+1}(f_{k+1} - f_k) - (x_{k+1} - x_k)^2 f_k^2 f_{k+1}'}{2f_k f_{k+1}(f_{k+1} - f_k) - (x_{k+1} - x_k)(f_{k+1}^2 f_k' + f_k^2 f_{k+1}')} \quad (1)$$

or

$$x_{k+2} = x_{k+1} + \frac{(x_k - x_{k+1})f_k f_{k+1}(f_k - f_{k+1}) - (x_{k+1} - x_k)^2 f_{k+1}^2 f_k'}{2f_k f_{k+1}(f_k - f_{k+1}) - (x_k - x_{k+1})(f_k^2 f_{k+1}' + f_{k+1}^2 f_k')} \quad (2)$$

The question of whether $x_{k+2} \in [x_k, x_{k+1}]$ depends, since $f_k f_{k+1} \leq 0$, on whether

$$(x_{k+2} - x_k)(x_{k+2} - x_{k+1}) \leq 0$$

Thus

$$(x_{k+1} - x_k)f_k f_{k+1}[f_{k+1}(f_{k+1} - f_k)$$
$$- (x_{k+1} - x_k)f_k f_{k+1}'][f_k(f_{k+1} - f_k) - (x_{k+1} - x_k)f_{k+1}f_k'] \geq 0$$

Since $f_k f_{k+1} \leq 0$, it follows that

$$[f_{k+1}(f_{k+1} - f_k) - (x_{k+1} - x_k)f_k f_{k+1}'] \cdot [f_k(f_{k+1} - f_k) - (x_{k+1} - x_k)f_{k+1}f_k'] \leq 0$$

is a necessary and sufficient condition for $x_{k+2} \in [x_k, x_{k+1}]$.

In summary, the algorithm executes these sequential steps:

(a) Q is the set

$$\{x_k, x_{k+1}, f_k, f_{k+1}, f_k', f_{k+1}'\} \ni (x_k < x_{k+1}) \wedge (f_k f_{k+1} \leq 0)$$

(b) The denominator of the expressions (1) and (2) for x_{k+2} is evaluated; if it is zero, a step in Bolzano search is made, that is, step (e).

(c) If the last improvement to the approximate value of the zero was made using Eq. (1), then it is used to *complete* the calculation of x_{k+2}; otherwise, Eq. (2) is employed.

(d) If $x_{k+2} \notin [x_k, x_{k+1}]$, execute step (e). Otherwise, define P as the augmented set $\{Q, x_{k+2}, f(x_{k+2}), f'(x_{k+2})\}$; then do step (f).

(e) Make a step of Bolzano search, and define $x_{k+2} = (x_k + x_{k+1})/2$. Then P is the set $\{Q, x_{k+2}, f(x_{k+2}), f'(x_{k+2})\}$.

(f) From P, determine the subset

$$Q': \{x'_k, x'_{k+1}, f(x'_k), f(x'_{k+1}), f'(x'_k), f'(x'_{k+1})\}$$

such that the logical expression

$$(x'_k < x'_{k+1}) \wedge (f(x'_k)f(x'_{k+1}) \leq 0) \wedge (|f(x'_k)f(x'_{k+1})| = \min_{u,v \in I} |f(u)f(v)|)$$

where $I = \{x_k, x_{k+1}, x_{k+2}\}$ is true.

(g) If $f(x_{k+2}) = 0$, then the estimate of the approximate root is taken to be x_{k+2}, and the process finishes. If, in the set Q', $|x'_{k+1} - x'_k|$ is less than some prescribed error tolerance ϵ, then the estimate is x_{k+2}, and again the process terminates. Otherwise, the process is repeated from step (a), using the new set Q' to replace Q.

OBSERVATIONS

(1) As x_{k+1} tends to the exact value of the root with x_k fixed, the algorithm tends to the Newton iteration

$$x_{k+2} = x_{k+1} - \frac{f(x_{k+1})}{f'(x_{k+1})}$$

(2) Although the Newton method may fail when $f'(x_k) = 0$, the above method does not, but uses full Bolzano search instead.

REFERENCES

1. R. P. Brent, An algorithm with guaranteed convergence for finding a zero of a function, *Comput. J.* **14**, 422–425 (1971).
2. R. P. Brent, *Algorithms for Minimization without Derivatives*, Prentice-Hall, Englewood Cliffs, New Jersey, 1971.
3. M. G. Cox, A bracketing technique for computing a zero of a function, *Comput. J.* **13**, 101–102 (1970).
4. M. G. Cox, Communication to the editor, *Comput. J.* **14**, 72 (1971).
5. M. G. Cox, Communication to the editor, *Comput. J.* **14**, 326 (1971).
6. G. Peters and J. H. Wilkinson, Eigenvalues of $Ax = \lambda Bx$ with band symmetric A and B, *Comput. J.* **12**, 398–404 (1969).
7. W. Squire, Communication to the editor, *Comput. J.* **14**, 72 (1971).
8. A. Wijngaarden, J. A. Zonnevald, and E. W. Dijkstra, in *Programs AP200 and AP230 De Serie AP200* (T. J. Dekker, ed.), Mathematical Centre, Amsterdam, 1963.
9. J. H. Wilkinson, *Rounding Errors in Algebraic Processes*, H.M.S.O., London, 1963.

R. G. Stanton
W. D. Hoskins

BOOLEAN ALGEBRA
See Abstract Algebra

BOREL FIELD (BOREL SET)

Borel field (Borel set) is a class of sets first introduced by the French mathematician E. Borel in his *Leçons sur la théorie des fonctions* (1898). In it, Borel extended the concept of measure on intervals on the real line to a more general class of sets which can be generated by repeatable countable unions and intersections of intervals. The class of sets obtained in this way has come to be known as Borel field on the real line, and parallel ideas have been used to construct Borel fields in more abstract spaces.

Let Ω be any abstract space. A class of subsets of Ω is said to be a σ-algebra if it satisfies the following conditions: (1) the null set is a member of the class; (2) the class is closed under complementation and countable unions. By using De Morgan's law, it is easy to see that a σ-algebra is closed under countable intersections as well. The largest σ-algebra of subsets of Ω is the class of all subsets of Ω while the smallest σ-algebra consists of the null set and Ω. If $\mathscr{C}$ is any class of subsets of Ω, then the smallest σ-algebra which contains $\mathscr{C}$ is called the minimal σ-algebra generated by $\mathscr{C}$ and is the intersection of all σ-algebras which contain $\mathscr{C}$. (Since the class of all subsets of Ω is a σ-algebra and contains $\mathscr{C}$, the minimal σ-algebra containing $\mathscr{C}$ always exists.) In an arbitrary topological space, the minimal σ-algebra which contains the class of open sets (equivalently, closed sets) is known as the Borel field and the sets belonging to the Borel field are called Borel sets. If the topology admits a countable base, then the Borel field coincides with the minimal σ-algebra generated by the countable base. Thus, on the real line, the Borel field may be generated by open intervals with rational end points. Moreover, since closed, open, or half-open intervals with arbitrary end points can be generated by countable unions and intersections of open intervals with rational end points, the Borel field on the real line coincides with the smallest σ-algebra generated by such intervals.

The notion of forming a product Borel field by combining a number of Borel fields is important and interesting. Let Ω_i ($i = 1, 2, \ldots, n$) be n arbitrary topological spaces and let $\mathscr{B}_i$ be the Borel field in Ω_i ($i = 1, 2, \ldots, n$). Then the product Borel field $\mathscr{B}_1 \otimes \mathscr{B}_2 \otimes \cdots \otimes \mathscr{B}_n$ is defined to be the smallest σ-algebra which contains all "rectangles" $A_1 \times A_2 \times \cdots \times A_n$, where $A_i \in \mathscr{B}_i$. $\mathscr{B}_1 \otimes \mathscr{B}_2 \otimes \cdots \otimes \mathscr{B}_n$ will be, in general, contained in the larger Borel field in $\Omega_1 \times \Omega_2 \times \cdots \times \Omega_n$ with its usual product topology. But if the topology of each Ω_i has a countable base, then the two Borel fields become identical. And, in that case, it is possible to generate the Borel field with "rectangles" whose

BOREL FIELD (BOREL SET)

sides belong to the countable bases of the respective topologies. Thus in R^n the Borel field is the smallest σ-algebra which contains all n dimensional open rectangles with rational corner points.

In the space $\Pi_{t \in T} R_t = R^T$, where T is any index set (uncountable or countable) and R_t is a copy of the real line with its associated Borel field $\mathcal{B}_t$, the smallest σ-algebra which contains all "rectangles" of the form $\Pi_{t \in T} A_t$, where $A_t \in \mathcal{B}_t$ for $t \in T$ and $A_t = R_t$ for all but a finite number of t is called the product Borel field in R^T. Similarly, product Borel fields for infinite (countable or uncountable) products of arbitrary topological spaces have been defined.

The proof of the existence of Borel fields for topological spaces is not a constructive one and offers little insight into the structure of Borel sets. However, for metric spaces, Borel fields can be represented as the transfinite union (the first uncountable ordinal type) of classes of sets $G_0, G_1, G_2, \ldots, G_\eta, \ldots$, where G_0 is the class of open sets, and for odd η the sets in G_η are countable intersections of sets belonging to G_ξ with $\xi < \eta$, while for even η they are countable unions of sets belonging to G_ξ with $\xi < \eta$. It is understood that the limit ordinals are even. It is also possible to represent the Borel field as the transfinite union of classes of sets $F_0, F_1, F_2, \ldots, F_\eta, \ldots$, where F_0 is the class of closed sets. And for odd η the sets in F_η are countable unions of sets belonging to F_ξ with $\xi < \eta$, while for even η they are countable intersections of sets belonging to F_ξ with $\xi < \eta$. It is obvious that for each ordinal ξ, $F_\xi \subset F_{\xi+1}$ and $G_\xi \subset G_{\xi+1}$, but it is also true that $F_\xi \subset G_{\xi+1}$ and $G_\xi \subset F_{\xi+1}$. The sets belonging to F_ξ and G_ξ are known as Borel sets of order ξ. In metric spaces the two methods generate the same Borel field, but in an arbitrary topological space, these methods may not generate the same class of sets. In general, if C_0 is the class of open sets in any topological space, the Borel field can be represented as the transfinite union of classes of sets $C_0, C_1, \ldots C_\xi, \ldots$, where the sets in C_ξ are complements and countable unions of sets in $\cup C_\eta$ for all $\eta < \xi$.

Borel introduced Borel sets on the real line in connection with the problem of extension of measure. Later on, Lebesgue was able to extend the concept of measure to a wider class of sets which contains the Borel field as a subclass. Members of the extended class of sets are called Lebesgue measurable sets. Thus not only are there sets on the real line which are not Borel sets, but there are even Lebesgue measurable sets which are not Borel sets. However, every Lebesgue measurable set is a Borel set up to a subset of a Borel set of Lebesgue measure 0.

Borel sets can be quite complicated in structure, but given any Borel set on the real line with finite Lebesgue measure, it is possible to find a finite number of disjoint intervals such that the symmetric difference of the Borel set and the union of these intervals will have Lebesgue measure as small as one wants to make. Thus, following Littlewood, we can roughly say that Borel sets on the real line with finite Lebesgue measure are nearly a finite union of intervals.

The utility of the Borel field lies in the fact that it is a sufficiently large class of sets such that standard operations of analysis (lim sup, lim inf, etc.) can be performed while staying within the class. Moreover, given a σ-finite measure

[488]
BOREL FIELD (BOREL SET)

on an algebra of subsets which generates the Borel field, it can be extended uniquely to a measure on the Borel field. Because of these reasons, Borel field constitutes a convenient analytical framework for many areas of mathematics and it has been especially useful in probability theory and statistics.

BIBLIOGRAPHY

Halmos, P. R., *Measure Theory*, Van Nostrand, Princeton, New Jersey, 1961.
Hausdorff, F., *Set Theory* (translated by John R. Aumann *et al.*), Chelsea, New York, 1962.
Kuratowski, K., *Topology*, Vol. 1 (translated by J. Jaworowski), Academic, New York, (1966).
Littlewood, J. E., *Lectures on the Theory of Functions*, Oxford University Press, Oxford, 1944.
Loéve, M., *Probability Theory*, Van Nostrand, Princeton, New Jersey, 1963.
Sierpinski, W., *General Topology* (translated by C. C. Krieger), University of Toronto Press, Toronto, 1952.

B. B. Bhattacharyya

BOX-JENKINS APPROACH TO TIME SERIES ANALYSIS AND FORECASTING

INTRODUCTION

The expression "time series" can be used to refer to any process that follows a consistent ordering. Traditionally the expression has been applied most often to time-dependent phenomena but it may also be used to describe space-dependent variables in fields such as astronomy and geological exploration. A time series may be a continuous record or a discrete set of observations.

In this article a time series will be a sequence of values at discrete and equally spaced intervals. For simplicity each interval is assumed to have unit length. The measured value of the series at time t will be denoted by y_t so that the entire series can be written as

$$\ldots, y_{t-1}, y_t, y_{t+1}, \ldots$$

or as $\{y\}$. Conceptually, such a series may be imagined to extend indefinitely into the past and into the future although, of course, in practice only a sample of finite length is available for analysis.

SMOOTHING AND FORECASTING

Like other types of data, time-dependent data can be analyzed in a variety of ways, depending upon the final objective of the analysis. Two common operations are *smoothing* and *forecasting*. Unfortunately, in classical analysis of time series considerable confusion has arisen because the distinction between these two operations has not always been stated precisely. Smoothing generally implies some form of empirical representation of the local behavior of a time series about a point within the available data record, the objective being to estimate the mean level or trend at that point. Forecasting is the estimation of future series values beyond the available data record.

Traditional approaches to time series analysis have usually considered a series to consist of three components: trend, oscillatory behavior, and random fluctuation. These terms are necessarily vague, it never being possible to decide in practice where one component ends and another begins. However, speaking generally, these terms have been given the following interpretations.

"Trend" refers to a steady change in overall level of a time-dependent variable. Its definition in any particular case depends upon the scale of reference. What may seem like a steady increase in level over an interval of a few months may be only part of a slow oscillation whose period is perhaps many years. Circumstances normally dictate the time span during which information is required so that seldom does this become a serious problem. A trend is by nature smooth in behavior, and this has led customarily to its representation by a polynomial of appropriate degree.

Some writers have subdivided "oscillatory fluctuations" about the trend into cyclical and noncyclical components. They imply by "cyclical" a strictly periodic occurrence such as the rotation of the earth about the sun. Consequently the term "oscillatory" refers to any performance pattern beyond the trend, this pattern possibly changing its characteristics as time elapses.

The "random" component is that part of the behavior of a time series which is unpredictable from past series performance. The random element at time t is usually assumed to be drawn from a continuous probability distribution whose mean is zero and whose variance is constant. Random elements at time t and $t + l$ are assumed to be independent.

Early methods for obtaining smoothed values of the level and trend at a particular position in a time series that did not exhibit periodic behavior involved a "sliding polynomial" of low degree applied at the position of interest. Several moving average formulas resulting from this approach have been proposed to achieve a form of local representation of the series behavior [17, 19]. Periodic series were dealt with by "removal" of cyclic components using some form of harmonic function or another form of moving average prior to calculating smoothed values of the level and trend.

The arbitrary nature of these types of smoothing operations often creates significant difficulties in interpretation of the behavior of the original time series under study [6, 13, 18]. The smoothed series will exhibit certain characteristics which the original series does not, such characteristics having been induced by the smoothing operation. Consequently, one cannot consider either the smoothed series or alternatively the deviations from the smoothed series as if the operation had never been performed.

Although some degree of arbitrariness is to be expected in the choice of smoothing procedure, any procedure for forecasting future values of a time series should depend upon the deterministic and stochastic nature of the available series record. It is unreasonable to expect a smoothing function, designed to describe local behavior of a series, to serve equally well as a forecasting function. A mathematical model fitted to the entire available data record should be used as a basis for forecasting. Such a model should include both the deterministic and stochastic components of the series fluctuations. The deterministic component is necessarily peculiar to the particular phenomenon under study. Significant contributions to the early development of linear models for the stochastic behavior of time series were made by Yule [22], Wold [21], and Bartlett [1]. Wold's suggestions of systematic approaches to the identification and fitting of linear models to time-dependent data have served as a basis for many more recent developments in this field. In particular, the Box-Jenkins approach [4] to time series analysis and forecasting is clearly in the spirit of Wold's proposals.

Modeling methods described in this article will be restricted to the stochastic portion of the series behavior. That is, it will be assumed that the series being forecast is the original time series *minus* any deterministic function values. In many situations it may not be feasible to formulate a deterministic model. In such cases the following procedures would then provide forecasts of future values of the original series.

SPECTRAL ANALYSIS

Although spectral analysis methods are not discussed in this article, they occupy an important place in the general field of time series analysis [12]. The spectrum of a time series is a characterization of the frequency components in that series. If questions pertaining to series behavior at particular frequencies arise, then spectral methods form a natural approach to arriving at appropriate answers. The models discussed in this article are not expressed in the frequency domain but rather in the time domain and are intended to provide information about series behavior at particular points in time.

THE BOX-JENKINS APPROACH TO TIME SERIES ANALYSIS

An important guideline in selecting an appropriate model to represent a particular time series is to locate a model form which involves as few parameters as possible. Box and Jenkins [2–4] have proposed an iterative three-stage procedure to accomplish this objective in an efficient manner. The three stages are:

1. Identification
2. Estimation
3. Diagnostic checking

In the identification stage, sample statistics calculated from the series data record are used to suggest a tentative model form. Then the unknown parameters in this model form are estimated by fitting the model form to the data record. The third stage involves subjecting the fitted model to rigorous diagnostic tests to determine its adequacy as a representation of the data record. If inadequacies are detected, the model form is modified in a suitable manner and stages 1 through 3 are repeated. Only a confirmed adequate fitted model is used to forecast future values of the time series.

The model forms used by Box and Jenkins are members of a general class of linear stochastic models which includes traditional autoregressive and moving average forms. Box and Jenkins have extended this class to accommodate seasonal and nonstationary forms of series behavior. Considerable success has been achieved using models from this extended class to represent the stochastic behavior of a number of time series from a broad variety of fields of application.

A GENERAL CLASS OF LINEAR STOCHASTIC MODELS

In selecting a general model form to represent univariate time series it is reasonable in many cases to express the current observed series value y_t as a linear function of previous observed series values, $y_{t-1}, y_{t-2}, \ldots$, and current and previous random errors, a_t and $a_{t-1}, a_{t-2}, \ldots$. One such form that is particularly parsimonious in its use of parameters is

$$y_t = \phi_{11}y_{t-1} + \phi_{12}y_{t-2} + \cdots + \phi_{1p_1}y_{t-p_1} + a_t - \theta_{11}a_{t-1} - \theta_{12}a_{t-2} - \cdots - \theta_{1q_1}a_{t-q_1} \tag{1}$$

where, for all t,
$$E(a_t) = 0$$
and
$$E(a_t a_{t-j}) = \begin{cases} \sigma_a^2, & \text{for } j = 0 \\ 0, & \text{for } j \neq 0 \end{cases} \tag{2}$$

The general class of models (1) is referred to as the ARMA (autoregressive-moving average) class since the terms

$$\phi_{11}y_{t-1} + \phi_{12}y_{t-2} + \cdots + \phi_{1p_1}y_{t-p_1}$$

are indeed autoregressive terms and the terms

$$-\theta_{11}a_{t-1} - \theta_{12}a_{t-2} - \cdots - \theta_{1q_1}a_{t-q_1}$$

BOX-JENKINS APPROACH

constitute the moving average portion of the model. More explicitly, model (1) is referred to as an ARMA (p_1, q_1) model to denote an autoregressive component of order p_1 and a moving average component of order q_1.

By using the backward shift operator B, where

$$B^j y_t = y_{t-j} \qquad (3)$$

model (1) can be written more compactly as

$$\phi_1(B) y_t = \theta_1(B) a_t \qquad (4)$$

where

$$\phi_1(B) = (1 - \phi_{11} B - \phi_{12} B^2 - \cdots - \phi_{1p_1} B^{p_1}) \qquad (5)$$

is an *autoregressive operator* in B and

$$\theta_1(B) = (1 - \theta_{11} B - \theta_{12} B^2 - \cdots - \theta_{1q_1} B^{q_1}) \qquad (6)$$

is a *moving average operator* in B.

A process $\{y\}$ whose joint probability distribution remains unchanged through time is called a *stationary* process. Model (4) can be written as

$$y_t = \phi_1^{-1}(B) \theta_1(B) a_t \qquad (7)$$

so that the current observed series value is a linear function of only current and past random errors. The expression on the right-hand side of Eq. (7) will have a finite variance only if all of the roots of the polynomial $\phi_1(B)$ lie outside the unit circle. Consequently the stochastic process represented by model (4) will be stationary only if all of the roots of $\phi_1(B)$ lie outside the unit circle.

Box and Jenkins have imposed an analogous but independent constraint on the moving average parameters in model (4) to ensure *invertibility*. An invertible process is one that can be expressed in the form

$$\phi_1(B) \theta_1^{-1}(B) y_t = a_t \qquad (8)$$

so that the current observed series value is a linear function of past observed series values plus a current random error and the dependence of y_t on $y_{t-1}, y_{t-2}, \ldots$ decreases for more and more distant prior series values. Decreasing dependence is ensured if all of the roots of the polynomial $\theta_1(B)$ lie outside the unit circle.

NONSTATIONARY TIME SERIES

A large number of time series encountered in practice are nonstationary. Some tend to be explosive in nature, arising from roots of $\phi_1(B)$ lying well inside the unit circle. For many others, however, nonstationarity exists because one or more of the roots of $\phi_1(B)$ are equal to 1 but no roots lie inside the unit circle. Box and Jenkins refer to such processes as *homogeneously nonstationary* processes. A time series $\{y\}$ that behaves in this fashion can be transformed into a stationary series {**w**} by differencing it a number of times equal to the number of roots d_1 lying on the unit circle. Model (4) can then be extended to accommodate both stationary and homogeneously nonstationary behavior using the more general form

$$\phi_1(B)(1-B)^{d_1}y_t = \theta_1(B)a_t \tag{9}$$

or, equivalently,

$$\phi_1(B)w_t = \theta_1(B)a_t \tag{10}$$

where

$$w_t = (1-B)^{d_1}y_t \tag{11}$$

Box and Jenkins have named models of the form (9) ARIMA (autoregressive-integrated moving average) models and have used the label (p_1, d_1, q_1) to refer to individual model forms in this class.

For example, the (0, 1, 1) ARIMA model

$$(1-B)y_t = (1-\theta_{11}B)a_t \tag{12}$$

is a commonly occurring special case of the general form (9). As shown by Muth [15], minimum variance forecasts derived from this model are exactly the first-order exponential smoothing estimates proposed by Holt [11], Brown and Meyer [8], and others.

SEASONAL MODEL FORMS

Time series exhibiting periodic behavior, hereafter referred to as *seasonal* time series, can be accommodated within the general class of ARIMA models (9) by a further extension [5]. For example, if a periodicity of s_1 intervals exists within a series, then the model

$$\phi_1(B)\Phi_1(B)(1-B)^{d_1}(1-B^{s_1})^{D_1}y_t = \theta_1(B)\Theta_1(B)a_t \tag{13}$$

would be appropriate where

$$\Phi_1(B) = (1 - \Phi_{11}B^{s_1} - \Phi_{12}B^{2s_1} - \cdots - \Phi_{1P_1}B^{P_1 s_1}) \tag{14}$$
$$\Theta_1(B) = (1 - \Theta_{11}B^{s_1} - \Theta_{12}B^{2s_1} - \cdots - \Theta_{1Q_1}B^{Q_1 s_1}) \tag{15}$$

and D_1 is the degree of differencing by period s_1 that is required in combination with differencing d_1 times by period 1, to reduce the series {**y**} to a stationary series. Model (13) is referred to as a (p_1, d_1, q_1) $(P_1, D_1, Q_1)_{s_1}$ ARIMA model.

The manner in which appropriate values of d_1 and D_1 are determined for a particular time series is part of the identification stage and is discussed in the following section.

It is not uncommon to encounter time series in which more than one periodicity occurs. For example, traffic densities in large urban centers would

BOX-JENKINS APPROACH

be expected to reveal strong periodicities of 1 day, 7 days, and 12 months. A linear stochastic model that accommodates three types of seasonal behavior is

$$\phi_1(B)\Phi_1(B)\Phi_2(B)\Phi_3(B)(1-B)^{d_1}(1-B^{s_1})^{D_1}(1-B^{s_2})^{D_2}(1-B^{s_3})^{D_3}y_t$$
$$= \theta_1(B)\Theta_1(B)\Theta_2(B)\Theta_3(B)a_t \quad (16)$$

where $\Phi_2(B)$, $\Phi_3(B)$, $\Theta_2(B)$, $\Theta_3(B)$, D_2, and D_3 are defined in analogous fashion to $\Phi_1(B)$, $\Theta_1(B)$, and D_1, respectively. Model (16) can be extended in an obvious fashion to deal with more than three periodicities. Formidable as the model form (16) may appear, it should be recognized that by suitable multiplication of the operators this model can be reduced to the simpler general form

$$d(B)\phi(B)y_t = \theta(B)a_t \quad (17)$$

where

$$d(B) = (1-B)^{d_1}(1-B^{s_1})^{D_1}(1-B^{s_2})^{D_2}(1-B^{s_3})^{D_3} \quad (18)$$
$$\phi(B) = \phi_1(B)\Phi_1(B)\Phi_2(B)\Phi_3(B) = (1 - \phi_1 B - \phi_2 B^2 - \cdots - \phi_p B^p) \quad (19)$$
$$\theta(B) = \theta_1(B)\Theta_1(B)\Theta_2(B)\Theta_3(B) = (1 - \theta_1 B - \theta_2 B^2 - \cdots - \theta_q B^q) \quad (20)$$

IDENTIFICATION

Selection of a model form to represent tentatively a given time series is carried out by locating the particular form from the general class (17) whose autocorrelation function (acf) and partial autocorrelation function (pacf) most closely resemble the estimated acf and pacf of the data record. A useful summary of acf behavior for several commonly occurring nonseasonal and seasonal ARMA models is given by Box and Jenkins along with pacf patterns for selected low order nonseasonal ARMA models. MacCormick [14] has discussed acf and pacf behavior for higher order nonseasonal models, and Hamilton [10] has recently described a useful technique for characterizing pacf behavior for seasonal models.

The kth lag autocorrelation ρ_k can be estimated by

$$r_k = \frac{\sum_{t=1}^{N-k}(y_t - \bar{y})(y_{t+k} - \bar{y})}{\sum_{t=1}^{N}(y_t - \bar{y})^2}, \quad k = 0, \pm 1, \pm 2, \ldots \quad (21)$$

where N is the number of observations in the data record and

$$\bar{y} = \frac{1}{N}\sum_{t=1}^{N} y_t \quad (22)$$

An approximate expression derived by Bartlett [1] for the variance of r_k for lags $k > q$ is

$$\operatorname{var}(r_k) \approx \frac{1}{N}\left[1 + 2\sum_{j=1}^{q} \rho_j^2\right] \tag{23}$$

where q is the lag beyond which the theoretical acf may be safely assumed to be zero. To use Eq. (23) the estimates $r_1, r_2, \ldots, r_q$ would be used in place of the true but unknown values $\rho_1, \rho_2, \ldots, \rho_q$. Bartlett also demonstrated the potentially high degree of correlation that can exist between autocorrelation estimates at neighboring lags.

The kth lag partial autocorrelation π_k can be estimated by $\hat{\pi}_k$, the estimate of the parameter ϕ_k obtained by fitting a kth order autoregressive model to the data record. Quenouille [16] showed that for a purely autoregressive series of order p the standard error of $\hat{\pi}_j$ is approximately $1/\sqrt{N}$ for all lags $j > p$ and that the estimates $\hat{\pi}_j$ ($j > p$) are essentially independently distributed.

For stationary series the acf is effectively equal to zero for sufficiently large lags. As explained by Box and Jenkins, the manner in which the acf approaches zero depends upon the nature of the autoregressive and moving average components in the model. Consequently, if the estimated acf for a data record shows no tendency to approach zero for increasing lag, it can be concluded that the series is nonstationary. In an attempt to eliminate the nonstationarity, the original series is differenced once and the estimated acf of the series $\{(1 - B)\mathbf{y}\}$ is examined. It too may exhibit nonstationarity, leading to an investigation of the series $\{(1 - B)^2\mathbf{y}\}$. This differencing procedure continues until the smallest value d_1 is found for which the series $\{(1 - B)^{d_1}\mathbf{y}\}$ is stationary.

For seasonal series it may also be necessary to difference the original data record with respect to each period. Thus, for example, the resulting stationary series produced from an original data record $\{\mathbf{y}\}$ with two periodicities of s_1 and s_2 intervals could be $\{(1 - B)^{d_1}(1 - B^{s_1})^{D_1}(1 - B^{s_2})^{D_2}\mathbf{y}\}$. The degrees of differencing d_1, D_1, and D_2 would be the smallest necessary to yield a stationary series.

In difficult situations the tentative model form selected at this stage by matching the estimated acf and pacf of the stationary series derived from the original data record with an appropriate member of the ARMA class may not be a correct model form. Although experience has shown that it is usually possible to make a reasonable first guess, it should be emphasized again that this is only the first stage of an iterative procedure. The proposed model form will be fitted to the data record and an examination of the residuals from this fit will indicate whether additional terms are required or existing terms are expendable. This leads to a second iteration and so on.

Crude estimates of the unknown parameters in the proposed model form can be obtained by equating a sufficient number of numerical values of the estimated acf to the corresponding theoretical acf expressions for the model. These crude estimates serve as useful starting values for those cases in which more efficient estimation procedures must be carried out in an iterative fashion.

BOX-JENKINS APPROACH

ESTIMATION

The general ARIMA model (17) can be written as

$$w_t = \phi_1 w_{t-1} + \phi_2 w_{t-2} + \cdots + \phi_p w_{t-p} + a_t - \theta_1 a_{t-1} - \theta_2 a_{t-2} - \cdots - \theta_q a_{t-q} \tag{24}$$

where

$$w_t = d(B)y_t. \tag{25}$$

If in addition to the assumptions (2) the error terms $\{a\}$ are assumed to be normally distributed, then maximum likelihood estimates of the $p + q$ parameters in model (24) are those parameter values that minimize the sum of squares

$$S(\boldsymbol{\phi}, \boldsymbol{\theta}) = \sum_{t=1}^{n} a_t^2 \tag{26}$$

where n is the number of observations in that stationary differenced series. However, from (24)

$$a_t = w_t - \phi_1 w_{t-1} - \phi_2 w_{t-2} - \cdots - \phi_p w_{t-p} + \theta_1 a_{t-1} + \theta_2 a_{t-2} + \cdots + \theta_q a_{t-q} \tag{27}$$

and consequently evaluation of $a_1, a_2, \ldots, a_p$ would require knowledge of the differenced series values $w_0, w_{-1}, \ldots, w_{1-p}$ which occurred prior to the data record and also previous random errors $a_0, a_{-1}, \ldots, a_{1-q}$. The expected value of zero can be used for each of the previous random errors but an alternative scheme is necessary to obtain acceptable estimates of previous values of the differenced series.

If p is small relative to n, the length of the differenced data record, one satisfactory parameter estimation procedure is to minimize the reduced sum of squares

$$\sum_{t=p+1}^{n} a_t^2$$

using the value zero for all a's prior to $t = p + 1$. For nonseasonal series this solution is often quite acceptable. However, for many seasonal series the loss of information using this approach would be unacceptable. In the case of monthly data, for example, it would not be unusual to require 12 or 24 or 36 "starting values." For such situations the following more precise estimation procedure has been proposed by Box and Jenkins.

Any time series $\{w\}$ that can be described by the general model (24)

$$\phi(B)w_t = \theta(B)a_t \tag{28}$$

can also be described by the *reverse model*

$$\phi(B^{-1})w_t = \theta(B^{-1})\epsilon_t \tag{29}$$

where ϵ_t is also a random error term for which

$$E(\epsilon_t) = 0 \tag{30}$$

and

$$E(\epsilon_t \epsilon_{t-j}) = \begin{cases} \sigma_\epsilon^2, & \text{for } j = 0 \\ 0, & \text{for } j = 0 \end{cases} \quad \text{for all } t \tag{31}$$

and $B^{-1} w_t = w_{t+1}$.

Derivations of the relationships between the sequences $\{a\}$ and $\{\epsilon\}$ have been shown by Box and Jenkins. Using forecast procedures which are described in the section entitled Forecasting, the p "prior" series values, w_0, $w_{-1}, \ldots, w_{1-p}$ can be estimated by forecasting *backwards* in the data record, one step at a time, beginning with the backward forecast of w_{n-p} from $t = n - p + 1$ so that all necessary starting values are available. The initial backward forecast errors $\hat{\epsilon}_n, \hat{\epsilon}_{n-1}, \ldots, \hat{\epsilon}_{n-p+1}$ are assumed to be zero. Then the one step backward forecast of w_{n-p-1} from $t = n - p$ is calculated, then the one step backward forecast of w_{n-p-2} from $t = n - p - 1$, and so on. The backward forecasting procedure terminates when one-step backward forecasts of $w_0, w_{-1}, \ldots, w_{1-p}$ have been made. The estimates $\hat{w}_1, \hat{w}_{-1}, \ldots, \hat{w}_{1-p}$ obtained in this manner will be maximum likelihood estimates given the choice of model form and the parameter values. The unconditional expected value of zero is used for each of the random errors $a_0, a_{-1}, \ldots, a_{1-q}$. Now calculation of $a_1, a_2, \ldots, a_n$ can proceed and maximum likelihood estimates of the parameters in the proposed model form can be found.

It is of interest to note that for purely autoregressive models, parameter estimates may be obtained by linear least squares estimation, whereas for models with moving average terms, nonlinear least squares methods are required.

Care must be exercised in interpreting the estimated results. The estimates of the autoregressive parameters in model (24) must be such that each of the individual autoregressive operators in Eq. (19), $\phi_1(B)$, $\Phi_1(B)$, etc., ensures stationary performance. Similarly, the estimates of the moving average parameters in model (24) must be such that each of the individual moving average operators in Eq. (20), $\theta_1(B)$, $\Theta_1(B)$, etc., ensures invertible performance. These restrictions could be incorporated within the estimation procedure by the imposition of suitable constraints in the least squares calculations. In the interest of parsimony, checks should also be made at this stage to determine whether any of the parameters in the fitted model might be deleted without serious effect upon the fit to the data record.

DIAGNOSTIC CHECKING

If the fitted model of form (24) is an adequate representation of the true stochastic behavior of the data record, then the residuals

$$\hat{a}_t = w_t - \hat{\phi}_1 w_{t-1} - \hat{\phi}_2 w_{t-2} - \cdots - \hat{\phi}_p w_{t-p} + \hat{\theta}_1 \hat{a}_{t-1} + \hat{\theta}_2 \hat{a}_{t-2} + \cdots + \hat{\theta}_q \hat{a}_{t-q} \tag{32}$$

should closely resemble white noise. That is, the properties of the series $\{\hat{a}\}$

will be approximately those of the series {a} described in Eqs. (2) and an estimate of σ_a^2 will be provided by

$$s_a^2 = \frac{\sum_{t=1}^{n} \hat{a}_t^2}{n - p - q} \qquad (33)$$

The values of the estimated autocorrelation function of $\{\hat{a}\}$, $r_1(\hat{a})$, $r_2(\hat{a})$, ..., should therefore be approximately normally distributed about a mean of zero with variance $1/n$. Actually, $1/n$ is a suitable value for the variance of all estimated autocorrelations except those at low lags but should be regarded only as an upper bound for the variance of estimated autocorrelations at low lags [9, 7]. Significantly large values of the estimated autocorrelation function of $\{\hat{a}\}$ indicate some doubt about the adequacy of the fitted model and in fact can be used to suggest appropriate modifications to the model form.

A useful simultaneous test of all estimated autocorrelations for lags 1 to K, where K is a large value such as 20 or 30, has been suggested by Box and Pierce [7]. They have demonstrated that if $\{\hat{a}\}$ is approximately white noise, then $n \sum_{k=1}^{K} r_k^2(\hat{a})$ is approximately distributed as a χ^2 variable with $K - p - q$ degrees of freedom. A significantly large value of this statistic would also suggest some form of model inadequacy, and the values $r_k(\hat{a})$ at individual lags would then have to be examined to determine the particular nature of the inadequacy.

Another diagnostic tool of value for revealing undetected periodicities in the residuals is the cumulative periodogram. For a discrete white noise series, a_1, a_2, ..., a_n, as defined by Eqs. (2), the periodogram component for frequency $f_i = i/n$ can be defined as

$$I(f_i) = \frac{2}{n} \left[\left(\sum_{t=1}^{n} a_t \cos 2\pi f_i t \right)^2 + \left(\sum_{t=1}^{n} a_t \sin 2\pi f_i t \right)^2 \right], \qquad i = 1, 2, \ldots, n/2 \qquad (34)$$

The normalized cumulative periodogram

$$C(f_j) = \frac{\sum_{i=1}^{j} I(f_i)}{\sigma_a^2}, \qquad j = 1, 2, \ldots, n/2 \qquad (35)$$

plotted against j is a straight line with slope 2 and intercept 0. Consequently, if the fitted model is adequate, the estimates $\hat{C}(f_j)$ produced from Eq. (35) by substituting the residuals $\{\hat{a}\}$ for the random errors $\{a\}$, and s_a^2 from Eq. (33) for σ_a^2, should be scattered about this straight line. Approximate Kolmogorov-Smirnov probability limits can be used to detect significant departures from the line. Any periodicity f_m in the residual series would produce a cluster of neighboring $\hat{C}(f_j)$ values well removed from the straight line about the abscissa m.

If, as a result of either the autocorrelation or the cumulative periodogram tests, or for some other reason, a *particular form* of model inadequacy is suspected, a modified model form incorporating appropriate additional terms can be fitted to the data and the fit of this more elaborate model can then be compared directly to that of the original model. This procedure is referred to as overfitting.

There remains a need for additional diagnostic tests for other particular forms of model inadequacy, such as a sudden change in the nature of the stochastic behavior of a series or a gradual shift from one periodicity to another.

FORECASTING

When a fitted model has been found to perform satisfactorily when subjected to the diagnostic tests, it may be used to calculate forecasts of series values beyond the data record. In using the model in this way it is implicitly assumed that the series will continue to behave in the same manner as the data record.

In the following development of forecasts it is assumed that an adequate form of stochastic model is being employed and that the values of the coefficients in this model are known. Box and Jenkins have shown that the effect of the latter assumption is to increase the variance of a forecast by a factor of the order of $(1 + 1/n)$, where n is the number of values in the available data record used to fit the stochastic model.

Using the general ARIMA model form (17), a forecast made at time t of the series value at time $t + l$ can be developed as follows. It will be convenient to express model (17) in the equivalent form

$$\phi^*(B)y_t = \theta(B)a_t \qquad (36)$$

where $\theta(B)$ is defined in Eq. (20), and

$$\phi^*(B) = d(B)\phi(B)$$
$$= (1 - \phi_1^*B - \phi_2^*B^2 - \cdots - \phi_v^*B^v) \qquad (37)$$

where $d(B)$ and $\phi(B)$ are defined in Eqs. (18) and (19), respectively, so that

$$v = p + d_1 + D_1 + D_2 + D_3 + \cdots \qquad (38)$$

It has been shown by Whittle [20] and others that at time t the minimum mean square error forecast (which is also the minimum variance forecast under the above assumptions) of y_{t+l} is $E_t(y_{t+l})$, where E_t denotes the conditional expectation given all information up to and including time t. Now from model (36)

$$y_{t+l} = \phi_1^* y_{t+l-1} + \phi_2^* y_{t+l-2} + \cdots + \phi_v^* y_{t+l-v}$$
$$+ a_{t+l} - \theta_1 a_{t+l-1} - \theta_2 a_{t+l-2} - \cdots - \theta_q a_{t+l-q} \qquad (39)$$

Then $E_t(y_{t+l})$, which will also be denoted by $\hat{y}_t(l)$ for $l > 0$, can be expressed as

$$E_t(y_{t+l}) = \phi_1^* E_t(y_{t+l-1}) + \phi_2^* E_t(y_{t+l-2}) + \cdots + \phi_v^* E_t(y_{t+l-v})$$
$$+ E_t(a_{t+l}) - \theta_1 E_t(a_{t+l-1}) - \theta_2 E_t(a_{t+l-2}) - \cdots - \theta_q E_t(a_{t+l-q}) \qquad (40)$$

where

$$E_t(y_{t+j}) = \begin{cases} y_{t+j}, & \text{for } j \leq 0 \\ \hat{y}_t(j), & \text{for } j > 0 \end{cases} \quad (41)$$

and

$$E_t(a_{t+j}) = \begin{cases} a_{t+j}, & \text{for } j \leq 0 \\ 0, & \text{for } j > 0 \end{cases} \quad (42)$$

Furthermore, it can be seen that the one step ahead forecast error is

$$y_{t+1} - \hat{y}_t(1) = a_{t+1} \quad (43)$$

This approach, using expression (40), provides an easy method for obtaining minimum variance forecasts. It incorporates a natural adaptive feature in that forecasts made at any time are always based on the most current information. A forecast made at time t uses observed y's up to time t and conditional expected values of y's beyond time t as well as known one step ahead forecast errors $a_1, a_2, \ldots, a_t$ up to time t and zeros (their expected values) for a's beyond time t.

For a data record of N observations, for example, forecasts would usually be desired for future series values at $t = N + 1$, $t = N + 2$, etc. The sensible base point for these forecasts would be $t = N$, the time of the last recorded value in the data record. Then, from Eq. (40) the minimum mean square error forecast of y_{N+1} would be

$$E_N(y_{N+1}) = \hat{y}_N(1) = \phi_1^* y_N + \phi_2^* y_{N-1} + \cdots + \phi_v^* y_{N+1-v}$$
$$- \theta_1 a_N - \theta_2 a_{N-1} - \cdots - \theta_q a_{N+1-q} \quad (44)$$

The values of $a_N, a_{N-1}, \ldots, a_{N+1-q}$, the one step ahead forecast errors of y_N, $y_{N-1}, \ldots, y_{N+1-q}$, respectively, will already have been calculated during the estimation stage using the accepted adequate model form (and using the assumption stated at the beginning of this section that the residuals $\{\hat{a}\}$ are being used as the true random errors $\{a\}$).

From the same base point, $t = N$, the minimum mean square error forecast of y_{N+2} could now be calculated from Eq. (40) as

$$E_N(y_{N+2}) = \hat{y}_N(2) = \phi_1^* \hat{y}_N(1) + \phi_2^* y_N + \cdots + \phi_v^* y_{N+2-v}$$
$$- \theta_2 a_N - \theta_3 a_{N-1} - \cdots - \theta_q a_{N+2-q} \quad (45)$$

Continuing this way it is a straightforward operation to compute several forecasts from a given base point t, beginning with lead time $l = 1$ and continuing with lead times $l = 2$, $l = 3$, and so on as far as desired. It will be noted that the method is of a "bootstrap" nature in that $\hat{y}_t(l)$, the forecast at base point t for lead time l, uses all of the "prior" forecasts from that base point, $\hat{y}_t(l - 1), \hat{y}_t(l - 2), \ldots, \hat{y}_t(1)$.

Although, as just demonstrated, forecasts can be calculated very simply using the difference equation (40) directly, Box and Jenkins have also derived equivalent forecast functions which are explicit solutions of particular difference equations of form (40). These alternative forms, which may involve polynomials, exponentials, and sines and cosines, are adaptive expressions in that the values of their coefficients change for each different forecast.

Many traditional approaches to time series forecasting begin with guessing the form of an explicit forecast function from a visual examination of the data record and fitting it to the data record by arbitrary methods. This unreliable approach, although still in use, has led to serious forecast errors in many cases. The only reliable basis for forecasting the stochastic behavior of a time series is by using an adequate stochastic model developed from the data record. The Box and Jenkins three-stage iterative procedure provides a systematic route to such a model.

To evaluate the variance of a forecast, it is helpful to express model (36) in the form

$$y_t = \pi_t y_0 + \pi_{t+1} y_{-1} + \cdots + \pi_{t+p-1} y_{1-v} \\ + a_t - \psi_1 a_{t-1} - \psi_2 a_{t-2} - \cdots - \psi_{t+q-1} a_{1-q} \quad (46)$$

where the π weights and the ψ weights can be determined by successive substitution for $y_{t-1}, y_{t-2}, \ldots, y_1$ in terms of prior y's and a's. Now for $l > 0$,

$$y_{t+l} = \pi_{t+l} y_0 + \pi_{t+l+1} y_{-1} + \cdots + \pi_{t+l+v-1} y_{1-v} \\ + a_{t+l} - \psi_1 a_{t+l-1} - \cdots - \psi_{t+l+q-1} a_{1-q} \quad (47)$$

so that

$$E_t(y_{t+l}) = \hat{y}_t(l) = \pi_{t+l} y_0 + \pi_{t+l+1} y_{-1} + \cdots + \pi_{t+l+v-1} y_{1-v} \\ - \psi_l a_t - \psi_{l+1} a_{t-1} - \cdots - \psi_{t+l+q-1} a_{1-q} \quad (48)$$

The variance of the forecast $\hat{y}_t(l)$ is then

$$V(l) = \{[y_{t+l} - \hat{y}_t(l)]^2\} \\ = E_t([a_{t+l} - \psi_1 a_{t+l-1} - \cdots - \psi_{l-1} a_{t+1}]^2) \\ = \left(1 + \sum_{j=1}^{l-1} \psi_j^2\right) \sigma_a^2 \quad (49)$$

It will be recalled that a fitted stochastic model is used to calculate forecasts only if it provides an adequate representation of the series data record. Consequently, σ_a^2 can be estimated by s_a^2, defined in Eq. (33). If the random errors $\{a\}$ can be assumed to follow a normal distribution, then approximate 95% probability error limits for $\hat{y}_t(l)$ are given by

$$\hat{y}_t(l) \pm 1.96[V(l)]^{1/2} \quad (50)$$

As indicated by Eq. (49), these limits become more widely spaced as the lead time l increases.

Box and Jenkins have also described methods of updating forecasts as additional series observations become available. The new information can be used to calculate one step ahead forecast errors, i.e., the $\hat{a}$'s. Through careful monitoring of the $\hat{a}$'s, the adequacy of the fitted stochastic model, and the

BOX-JENKINS APPROACH

resulting forecast model, can be checked continuously. Changes may occur either in the values of the parameters in the model or in the form of the model itself. A need exists for efficient methods of detecting such changes and adapting the model in an appropriate manner.

SUMMARY

As the sophistication of technology in the world increases, the need for reliable forecasting procedures becomes more critical. Population growth, resource inventories, and aerospace guidance systems all require accurate and precise forecasts of future performance. Traditional forecasting procedures using arbitrary functional forms selected from visual examination of past data are not acceptable for such applications. Forecasts using an adequate stochastic model form do provide dependable estimates of future stochastic behavior of a time series based upon the available data record. Box and Jenkins have proposed a systematic procedure for developing an adequate stochastic model using the data at hand. A tentatively selected model form is subjected to successive stages of parameter estimation, diagnostic checking, and model modification in an iterative manner until no evidence of model inadequacy remains. Only then is the fitted model used to forecast future series performance. Forecasts can be calculated in simple bootstrap fashion directly from the fitted model, and probability error limits for these forecasts can also be evaluated.

REFERENCES

1. M. S. Bartlett, On the theoretical specification and sampling properties of autocorrelated time-series, *J. R. Stat. Soc. (Suppl.)* **8**, 27–41 (1946).
2. G. E. P. Box and G. M. Jenkins, Some statistical aspects of adaptive optimization and control, *J. R. Stat. Soc. (B)* **24**, 297–343 (1962).
3. G. E. P. Box and G. M. Jenkins, Further contributions to adaptive quality control: Simultaneous estimation of dynamics: Nonzero costs, *Bull. Int. Stat. Inst.* **34**, 943 (1963).
4. G. E. P. Box and G. M. Jenkins, *Time Series Analysis, Forecasting and Control*, Holden-Day, San Francisco, 1970.
5. G. E. P. Box, G. M. Jenkins, and D. W. Bacon, Models for forecasting seasonal and non-seasonal time series, in *Advanced Seminar on Spectral Analysis of Time Series* (B. Harris, ed.), Wiley, New York, 1967, pp. 271–311.
6. G. E. P. Box and P. Newbold, Some comments on a paper of Coen, Gomme and Kendall, *J. R. Stat. Soc. (A)* **134**, 229–240 (1971).
7. G. E. P. Box and D. A. Pierce, Distribution of residual autocorrelations in autoregressive-integrated moving average time series models, *J. Am. Stat. Assoc.* **65**, 1509–1526 (1970).
8. R. G. Brown and R. F. Meyer, The fundamental theorem of exponential smoothing, *Oper. Res.* **9**, 673–685 (1961).

9. J. Durbin, Testing for serial correlation in least-squares regression when some of the regressors are lagged dependent variables, *Econometrica* **38**, 410–421 (1970).
10. D. C. Hamilton, Identification of Multiplicative Models for Seasonal Time Series, M.A. Thesis, Queen's University, Kingston, Ontario, 1973.
11. C. C. Holt, *Forecasting Trends and Seasonals by Exponentially Weighted Moving Averages (O.N.R. Memorandum, No. 52)*, Carnegie Institute of Technology, Pittsburgh, Pennsylvania, 1957.
12. G. M. Jenkins and D. G. Watts, *Spectral Analysis and Its Applications*, Holden-Day, San Francisco, 1968.
13. M. G. Kendall, The effect of the elimination of trend on oscillations in time-series, *J. R. Stat. Soc.* **104**, 43-52 (1941).
14. A. J. A. MacCormick, Investigation of the Behavior of Autocorrelation and Partial Autocorrelation Functions with Application to Identification of Autoregressive Moving Average Models in Time Series Analysis, Ph.D. Thesis, University of Wisconsin, Madison, Wisconsin, 1970.
15. J. F. Muth, Optimal properties of exponentially weighted forecasts of time series with permanent and transitory components, *J. Am. Stat. Assoc.* **55**, 299–306 (1960).
16. M. H. Quenouille, Approximate tests of correlation in time series, *J. R. Stat. Soc. (B)* **11**, 68–84 (1949).
17. M. Sasuly, *Trend Analysis of Statistics*, Brookings Institution, Washington, D.C., 1934.
18. E. Slutzky, The summation of random causes as the source of cyclic processes, *Econometrica* **5**, 105–146 (1937).
19. E. T. Whittaker and G. Robinson, *The Calculus of Observations*, 4th ed., Blackie, London, 1944.
20. P. Whittle, *Prediction and Regulation by Linear Least-Squares Methods*, English Universities Press, London, 1963.
21. H. O. Wold, *A Study in the Analysis of Stationary Time Series*, Almquist and Wicksell, Uppsala, 1938.
22. G. U. Yule, On the time correlation problem, *J. R. Stat. Soc.* **84**, 497–537 (1921).

D. W. Bacon

Ref
QA
76.15
E5
v.3

APR 5 1977